# RISK ASSESSMENT

## STATISTICS IN PRACTICE

*Advisory Editor*

**Wolfgang Jank**
University of Maryland, USA

*Founding Editor*

**Vic Barnett**
Nottingham Trent University, UK

---

The texts in the series provide detailed coverage of statistical concepts, methods, and worked case studies in specific fields of investigation and study.

With sound motivation and many worked practical examples, the books show in down-to-earth terms how to select and use an appropriate range of statistical techniques in a particular practical field. Readers are assumed to have a basic understanding of introductory statistics, enabling the authors to concentrate on those techniques of most importance in the discipline under discussion.

The books meet the need for statistical support required by professionals and research workers across a range of employment fields and research environments. Subject areas covered include medicine and pharmaceutics; industry, finance, and commerce; public services; the earth and environmental sciences.

A complete list of titles in this series appears at the end of the volume.

# RISK ASSESSMENT
## Theory, Methods, and Applications

**MARVIN RAUSAND**
Norwegian University of Science and Technology

 **WILEY**

**A JOHN WILEY & SONS, INC., PUBLICATION**

*Library of Congress Cataloging-in-Publication Data:*

Rausand, Marvin.
  Risk assessment : theory, methods, and applications / Marvin Rausand.
       p. cm. — (Statistics in practice)
Includes index.
  ISBN 978-0-470-63764-7 (hardback)
1 Technology—Risk assessment. 2. Risk assessment. I. Title.
  T174.5.R37 2011
    363.1'02—dc22                                    2011010971

10 9 8 7 6 5 4 3 2 1

*To Hella,*
*Guro, and Idunn*

# CONTENTS

## PART III   APPENDICES

# PREFACE

This book gives a comprehensive introduction to risk analysis and risk assessment, and the main methods for such analyses. It deals with accidents that may occur in technical or sociotechnical systems with focus on sudden, major accidents. Day-to-day occupational accidents and negative health effects due to long-term exposure are therefore outside the scope of the book.

In 1991, the Norwegian standard NS 5814, *Requirements to Risk Analysis*, was issued and I wrote a small book in Norwegian called *Risk Analysis: Guidance to NS 5814* (Rausand, 1991). The book was very basic but filled a purpose and was used extensively. I began to write the current book in 1995 after the first edition of the book *System Reliability Theory* was published. After awhile I realized that writing a book on risk assessment was much more difficult than writing a book on system reliability. This was due mainly to the confusing terminology, the multidisciplinary character of the topics, and the overwhelming number of reports and guidelines that had been written.

In 2008, the second edition of NS 5814 was issued and the guideline had to be updated and extended. This resulted in the book *Risk Analysis: Theory and Methods* (Rausand and Utne, 2009b), which is written in Norwegian and coauthored by Ingrid Bouwer Utne. The book was strongly influenced by the manuscript of the current book, has a similar structure, but is more basic and straightforward.

The current book is divided into two main parts. Part I introduces risk analysis and defines and discusses the main concepts used. Our understanding of how accidents occur will always influence our approach to risk assessments, so a chapter describing accident models and accident causation is therefore included. Input data requirements and data quality are also presented in a separate chapter. The various steps of a risk assessment are explained and arranged in a structure.

Part II deals with the main methods of risk analysis, such as preliminary hazard analysis, HAZOP, fault tree analysis, and event tree analysis. Special problem areas such as common-cause failures and human errors are also discussed. Part II ends with a brief survey of the development and application of risk assessment in some main application areas.

Part III of the book contains appendices. Some main results from probability and statistics are given in Appendix A. Readers who have not taken a basic course in probability and statistics should consider reading this appendix first. Other readers may find it useful to check formulas in the appendix. Part III also contains a list of acronyms and a glossary of main terms used in risk assessment.

The book gives several references to laws, regulations, and standards. When using these references, you should always check to see if new versions have been made available.

Several organizations have issued a number of technical reports and guidelines related to risk assessment. Many of these are of very high quality but often use conflicting terminology, and they present a multitude of methods with more or less the same purpose. Very few textbooks on risk assessment are on the market, however.

To contribute to a more standardized terminology in risk assessment, I have put considerable effort into using a stringent terminology and giving clear definitions. The main definitions are written as separate paragraphs preceded by the symbol ☞.

When writing this book, I have read guidelines from many different organizations and tried to extract the main messages from these guidelines. Such guidelines seem to be issued faster than I am able to read, so I cannot claim that I cover all of them. There are certainly several important organizations that I have missed while searching for guidelines. Among these are obviously guidelines that are written in languages that I am not able to understand.

I have selected methods that are commonly applied and that I find useful. Whether or not this is a good selection is up to you to judge. The book may perhaps be accused of being old-fashioned because I have included mainly proven methods instead of brand-new suggestions.

Within some areas of risk assessment, such as human reliability analysis, there are a vast number of approaches, and it seems to be a strategy that every person working with human reliability should develop her/his own method.

Suggestions for further reading are provided at the end of each chapter. I do not claim that the references listed are the most relevant that can be found. Rather, these are the references I have found most useful and that are most in line with the views presented in this book.

The book is written mainly as a textbook for university courses in risk analysis and risk assessment. For this reason, a set of problems have been developed and are available on the book's homepage, http://www.ntnu.edu/ross/books/risk.

The book is also intended to be a guide for practical risk assessments. The various methods are therefore described sufficiently that you should be able to use the method after having read the description. Each method is described according to the same structure, and the various steps of the methods are listed and often also illustrated in workflow diagrams. The descriptions of the methods are, as far as possible, self-contained, and it should therefore not be necessary to read the entire book to have enough background to use the individual methods.

The descriptions and examples given in the book are largely from Europe, especially from Norway. I trust, however, that most of the book is also relevant in other parts of the world.

The book is written in a style similar to that used in my book on system reliability theory (Rausand and Høyland, 2004). Some methods are treated in both books, but from different standpoints. Several issues are described in more detail in Rausand and Høyland (2004), and I therefore recommend that you have both books available, even if it is not strictly required.

I hope that you will enjoy reading this book and that you will find it useful. If you have questions or comments, you will find my email address on the book's homepage (see below).

M. RAUSAND

*Trondheim, Norway*
*March 15, 2011*

# ACKNOWLEDGMENTS

It is a pleasure to acknowledge and thank several friends and colleagues whose ideas and suggestions have contributed greatly to the book. I mention them in alphabetical order.

- Stein Haugen is a professor in risk analysis at NTNU and has extensive experience using risk analyses in industry projects. He has read several chapters and given many helpful comments that have improved the book.

- Per Hokstad of SINTEF coauthored an earlier version of Chapter 15 on common-cause failures and has strongly influenced the content of that chapter.

- Inger Lise Johansen is a Ph.D. student at NTNU. I have the pleasure of being the supervisor of her master's thesis and currently of her Ph.D. project. Her master's thesis was written in parallel with Chapters 2 and 4 of this book, and she has made significant contributions to these chapters. She has also read several other chapters, reformulated some of my clumsy expressions, added content, and made valuable comments as to both language and content.

- Ondřej Nývlt of the Czech Technical University in Prague spent six months at NTNU as an exchange Ph.D. student. I had the pleasure of being his local supervisor, and he helped me to write the section on Petri nets in Chapter 10.

- Ingrid Bouwer Utne coauthored the Norwegian book *Risk Analysis; Theory and Methods* (Rausand and Utne, 2009a) while she was a postdoc at NTNU. Our discussions and her ideas have also clearly influenced the current book.

- Knut Øien of SINTEF is also an adjunct professor in risk assessment at NTNU. He coauthored an early draft of Chapter 13 on human reliability analysis and has read and commented on the final version. Chapter 17, describing the development and application of risk assessment, is based on a note in Norwegian that Knut Øien and I wrote some years ago.

I also acknowledge the editing and production staff at John Wiley & Sons for their careful, effective, and professional work.

I thank the International Electrotechnical Commission (IEC) for permission to reproduce information from the standards IEC 60300-3-9 ed.1.0 (1995), IEC 60300-3-4 ed.2.0 (2007), IEC 60050-191 ed.1.0 (1990), IEC 61508-0 ed. 1.0 (2005), IEC 61508-4 ed.2.0 (2010), IEC 61508-1 ed.2.0 (2010), IEC 61508-6 ed.2.0 (2010). All such extracts are copyright of IEC, Geneva, Switzerland. ©All rights reserved. Further information on the IEC is available from http://www.iec.ch. IEC has no responsibility for the placement and context in which the extracts and contents are reproduced by the author, nor is IEC in any way responsible for the other content or accuracy herein.

Point 2.13 from NS-ISO 31000:2009 Risk management - Principles and guidelines, as well as definitions in 2.1.1, 2.1.5, 2.1.13, 2.1.20 and Table A.1 from NS-EN ISO 17776:2002 are reproduced in this book under license from Standard Online AS 03/2011. ©All rights reserved. Standard Online makes no guarantees or warranties as to the correctness of the reproduction.

Several references are given to publications by the UK Health and Safety Executive (HSE). This is public sector information published by the HSE and licensed under the Open Government Licence v.1.0.

The book was completed during my sabbatical year at ParisTech, Ecole Nationale Supérieure d'Arts et Métiers (ENSAM) in Aix en Provence, France. I am very grateful to Professor Lionel Roucoules and his colleagues, who helped me and made this stay a positive experience.

During the writing of the book, I have read many books, scientific articles, standards, technical reports, guidelines, and notes related to risk assessment. I have tried to process, combine, and reformulate the information obtained and I have tried to give proper references. If I unconsciously copied sentences without giving proper reference, it has not been my intention, and I apologize if that has happened.

In the preface of the book *The Importance of Living* (William Morrow, New York, 1937), Lin Yutang writes: "I must therefore conclude by saying as usual that the merits of this book, if any, are largely due to the helpful suggestions of my collaborators, while for the inaccuracies, deficiencies and immaturities of judgment, I alone am responsible." If the word *collaborators* is replaced by *colleagues and references*, this statement applies equally well for the current book.

M.R.

**PART I**

# INTRODUCTION
# TO RISK ASSESSMENT

# CHAPTER 1

# INTRODUCTION

> Risk is a curious and complex concept. In a sense it is unreal in that it is always concerned
> with the future, with possibilities, with what has not yet happened.
>
> —Elms (1992)

## 1.1 Introduction

If you ask ten people what they mean by the word *risk*, you will most likely get
ten different answers. The same inconsistency also prevails in newspapers and other
media. A brief search for the word *risk* in some Internet newspapers gave the results
in Table 1.1. In some of the statements, the word *risk* can be replaced with *chance*,
*likelihood*, or *possibility*. In other cases, it may be synonymous with *hazard*, *threat*,
or *danger*. The situation is not much better in the scientific community, where the
interpretation is almost as varying as among the general public. A brief search in risk
assessment textbooks, journal articles, standards, and guidelines will easily prove
that this applies also for the specialists in risk assessment.

In 1996, the prominent risk researcher Stan Kaplan received the Distinguished
Award from the Society of Risk Analysis. To express his gratitude, Kaplan gave a

*Risk Assessment: Theory, Methods, and Applications,* First Edition.
By Marvin Rausand. Copyright © 2011 John Wiley & Sons, Inc.

Table 1.1    The word *risk* as used in some Internet newspapers (in May 2010).

| |
|---|
| ...the government would risk a humiliating defeat... |
| ...people judged to be at high risk of having a fall... |
| ...there's no simple equation for predicting divorce risk... |
| ...investors are willing to take on a high risk... |
| ...encouraged financiers to seek out greater profits by taking risks in areas beyond regulatory purview... |
| ...the flight from risk has hit the stock markets... |
| ...investments that had put their capital at risk... |
| ...we could put at risk our food and water supplies... |
| ...she was considered at risk because of her work... |
| ...because of the risk of theft... |
| ...the number of homes exposed to flood risk could increase... |
| ...a more environmentally risky mode of getting our energy... |
| ...risk appetite for equities and corporate bonds... |
| ...by reducing the risk of collisions with vehicles... |
| ...bicycle helmets have been shown to reduce the risk of head injuries by up to 88 percent... |
| ...a high-risk attempt to plug the leaking oil well... |
| ...carries an accident risk of "Chernobyl proportions"... |
| ...that created the illusion that risk was being responsibly managed... |

talk to the plenary session at the society's annual meeting. In the introduction to this talk, he said: [1]

> The words of risk analysis have been, and continue to be a problem. Many of you remember that when our Society for Risk Analysis was brand new, one of the first things it did was to establish a committee to define the word "risk." This committee labored for 4 years and then gave up, saying in its final report, that maybe it's better not to define risk. Let each author define it in his own way, only please each should explain clearly what way that is (Kaplan, 1997).

### 1.1.1  Three Main Questions

Risk (as used in this book) is always related to what can happen in the future. In contrast to our ancestors, who believed that the future was determined solely by the acts of God (e.g., see Bernstein, 1996), we have the conviction that we can analyze and manage risk in a rational way. Our tool is *risk analysis*, and the goal is to inform decision-making concerning our future welfare.

[1]Reprinted from Risk Analysis, Vol. 17, Kaplan, S. "The words of risk analysis", Copyright (1997), with permission from Wiley-Blackwell.

The possibility of harmful events is an inherent part of life. Such events can be caused by natural forces, such as flooding, earthquake, or lightning; technical failures; or human actions. Some harmful events can be foreseen and readily addressed, while others come unexpectedly because they appear unforeseeable or have only a very remote likelihood of occurrence. In many systems, various safeguards are installed to prevent harmful events or to mitigate the consequences should such events occur. Risk analysis is used to identify the causes of harmful events, to determine the possible consequences of harmful events, to identify and prioritize barriers, and to form a basis for deciding whether or not the risk related to a system is *tolerable*.

A risk analysis is carried out to provide answers to the following three main questions (Kaplan and Garrick, 1981):

Q1. *What can go wrong?*
    To answer this question, we must identify the possible *hazardous events*[2] that may lead to *harm* to some *assets* that we want to keep and protect. These assets may be people, animals, the environment, buildings, technical installations, infrastructure, cultural heritage, our reputation, information, data, and many more.

Q2. *What is the likelihood of that happening?*
    The answer can be given as a qualitative statement or as probabilities or frequencies. We consider the hazardous events that were identified in Q1, one by one. To determine their likelihood, we often have to carry out a causal analysis to identify the basic causes (*hazards* or *threats*) that may lead to the hazardous event.

Q3. *What are the consequences?*
    For each hazardous event, we must identify the potential harm or adverse *consequences* to the assets mentioned in Q1. Most systems have *barriers* that are installed to prevent or mitigate harm. The harm to the assets is dependent on whether or not these barriers function when the hazardous event takes place.

For now, we suffice by defining risk as the answer to these three questions.

## 1.1.2  A Conceptual Model

For each hazardous event that is identified by answering Q1, the analytical process used to answer Q2 and Q3 may be illustrated by Figure 1.1. The figure illustrates that various hazards and/or threats may lead to a hazardous event, and that the hazardous event may in turn lead to many different consequences. Various barriers are often available between the hazards/threats and the hazardous event, and also between the hazardous event and the consequences. The model in Figure 1.1 is called a *bow-tie model* because it resembles the bow-tie that men sometimes use in place of a necktie with a formal suit.

[2]Kaplan and Garrick (1981) use the term *scenario* instead of *hazardous event*.

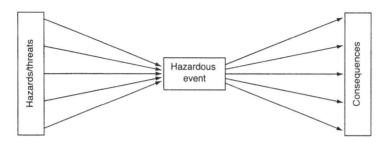

**Figure 1.1** A simplified bow-tie model.

The bow-tie model is useful for illustrating both the conception and analysis of risk. The terms needed to answer the three related questions of Kaplan and Garrick (1981) have, however, been interpreted differently by various sources and practitioners, as have the methods in which they are used. Today, numerous laws and regulations require that risk analyses or risk assessments be carried out, but there is still no unified terminology or standard framework for carrying out these assessments.

### 1.1.3 Objective of the Book

The main objective of this book is to give a comprehensive introduction to risk assessment and present the essential theory and the main methods that can be used to perform a risk assessment of a technical or sociotechnical system.

More specific objectives are:

(a) To present and discuss the terminology used in risk assessment of technical and sociotechnical systems. A vague hope is that this may contribute to a more harmonized terminology in risk assessment.

(b) To define and discuss how risk can be quantified and how these metrics may be used to evaluate the tolerability of risk.

(c) To present the main methods for risk assessment and discuss the applicability, advantages, and limitations of each method.

(d) To present and discuss some main problem areas related to risk assessment (e.g., human errors, dependent failures).

(e) To describe how a risk assessment may be carried out in practice and illustrate some important application areas.

### 1.1.4 Focus of the Book

This book is mainly concerned with risk related to:

- a technical or sociotechnical *system* in which

- *events* may occur in the *future* and that

- have *unwanted consequences*

- to *assets* that we want to protect.

The systems to be considered may be any type of engineered system, ranging from small machines up to complex process plants or transportation networks. This book does not cover all aspects of risk, but is limited to *accidents* where an abrupt event may give negative outcomes (some kind of loss or damage). Adverse effects caused by continuous and long-term exposure to a hazardous environment or dangerous materials (e.g., asbestos) are thus not covered unless the exposure is caused by a specific event (e.g., an explosion). Neither is an objective of this book to present and discuss detailed physical consequence models, such as fire and explosion models.

In the financial world, investments are often made and risk is taken to obtain some benefit. The outcome may be either positive or negative, and risk is then a statement about the *uncertainty* regarding the outcome of the investment. This interpretation of the word *risk* is not relevant for this book, which is concerned exclusively with adverse outcomes.

The main focus of the book is risk assessment *per se*, not how the results from the assessment may be used or misused. Some issues related to risk *management* are, however, discussed briefly in Chapter 5.

The objective of this introductory chapter is to introduce the main concepts used in risk assessment and to place risk assessment into a decision-making context.

## 1.2   Risk Analysis, Assessment, and Management

### 1.2.1   Risk Analysis

So far, we have mentioned risk analysis several times, but not given any clear definition. A commonly used definition is:

☞ **Risk analysis**: Systematic use of available information to identify hazards and to estimate the risk to individuals, property, and the environment (IEC 60300-3-9, 1995).

A risk analysis is always a *proactive* approach in the sense that it deals exclusively with potential accidents. This is opposed to accident investigation, which is a *reactive* approach that seeks to determine the causes and circumstances of accidents that have already happened.

***Three Main Steps.***   As indicated in Section 1.1, a risk analysis is carried out in three main steps by providing answers to the three questions in Section 1.1.1:

1. *Hazard identification.* In this step, the hazards and threats related to the system are identified together with the potential hazardous events. As part of this process, assets that may be harmed are also identified.

2. *Frequency analysis*. This step will usually involve a deductive analysis to identify the causes of each hazardous event and to estimate the frequency of the hazardous event based on experience data and/or expert judgments.

3. *Consequence analysis*. Here, an inductive analysis is carried out to identify all potential sequences of events that can emerge from the hazardous event. The objective of the inductive analysis is usually to identify all potential end consequences and also their probability of occurrence.

***Qualitative vs. Quantitative Analysis.*** The risk analysis may be qualitative or quantitative, depending on the objective of the analysis.

☞ **Qualitative risk analysis**: A risk analysis where probabilities and consequences are determined purely qualitatively.

☞ **Quantitative risk analysis (QRA)**: A risk analysis that provides numerical estimates for probabilities and/or consequences—sometimes along with associated uncertainties.

A QRA is best suited for quantifying risk associated with low-probability and high-consequence events, and may range from specialized probabilistic assessment to large-scale analysis. The term *semiquantitative risk analysis* is sometimes used to denote risk analyses that quantify probabilities and consequences approximately within ranges.

***Remark***: Some industries use other names for the QRA. In the U.S. nuclear industry and in the space industry, the QRA is called *probabilistic risk analysis* (PRA). In the European nuclear industry, QRA is referred to as *probabilistic safety analysis* (PSA), whereas the maritime industry uses the term *formal safety assessment* (FSA). The term *total risk analysis* (TRA) sometimes appears in the Norwegian offshore industry. ⊕

***Types of Risk Analyses.*** Risk analyses can be classified in many different ways. One attempt of classification can be made on the basis of Figure 1.2, which displays three categories of hazards and and three categories of assets in a $3 \times 3$ matrix.

This book is concerned mainly with the last column of Figure 1.2, where the hazard source is a technical system or some dangerous materials. The other types of risk analyses are, however, also discussed briefly.

### 1.2.2  Risk Evaluation

We distinguish between risk analysis and *risk evaluation*, which may be defined as:

☞ **Risk evaluation**: Process in which judgments are made on the tolerability of the risk on the basis of a risk analysis and taking into account factors such as socioeco-

| Assets | Hazard source | | |
|---|---|---|---|
| | Humans | The environment | Technology / materials |
| Humans | 1 | 2 | 3 |
| The environment | 4 | 5 | 6 |
| Material / financial | 7 | 8 | 9 |

**Figure 1.2**    Different types of risk analyses.

nomic and environmental aspects (IEC 60300-3-9, 1995).

The risk evaluation will sometimes include a comparison of the results from the risk analysis with some *risk acceptance criteria*. Risk acceptance criteria are discussed further in Chapter 4.

Too often, it happens that the management does the risk evaluation without any involvement from those who have produced the risk analysis. This may create communication problems and lead to erroneous inferences, and it is therefore strongly recommended that the risk analysts also be involved in the evaluation.

## 1.2.3 Risk Assessment

When risk analysis and risk evaluation are carried out in a joint process, we say that we do a *risk assessment*.

☞ **Risk assessment**: Overall process of risk analysis and risk evaluation (IEC 60300-3-9, 1995).

**EXAMPLE 1.1    Five steps to risk assessment**

The UK HSE has published a simple and informative introduction to risk assessment called *Five steps to risk assessment* (HSE, 2006). The five steps are:

1. Identify the hazards.

2. Decide who might be harmed and how.

3. Evaluate the risks and decide on precautions.

4. Record your findings and implement them.

5. Review your assessment and update if necessary.                    ⊕

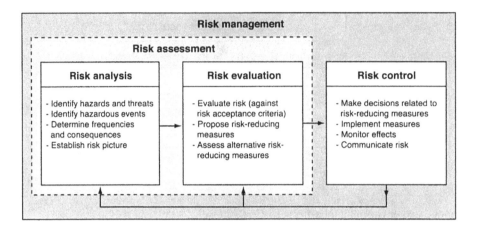

**Figure 1.3**    Risk analysis, evaluation, assessment, and management (see also IEC 60300-3-9, 1995).

*Remark*: Some books and guidelines do not distinguish between risk analysis and risk assessment and tend to use the term *risk assessment* also when risk evaluation is not part of the job. Other guidelines define risk assessment as an add-on to risk evaluation. An example here is the U.S. Federal Aviation Administration, which defines risk assessment as "the process by which the results of risk analysis are used to make decisions" (US FAA, 2000, App. A).                                    ⊕

### 1.2.4  Risk Management

If we, in addition, identify and (if necessary) implement risk-reducing actions and survey how the risk changes over time, we conduct *risk management*.

☞ **Risk management**: A continuous management process with the objective to identify, analyze, and assess potential hazards in a system or related to an activity, and to identify and introduce risk control measures to eliminate or reduce potential harms to people, the environment, or other assets.

Slightly different definitions of risk management may be found in guidelines and textbooks. Some of these stress that risk management is a proactive and systematic approach to setting the best course of action under uncertainty, and that it also involves communicating the risk to the various stakeholders (e.g., see Treasury Board, 2001).

Although this book is focused primarily on risk analysis, we also present some views on risk evaluation and risk management. The elements of risk management are illustrated in Figure 1.3 and are discussed further in Chapter 5.

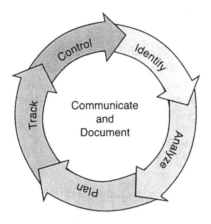

**Figure 1.4**    Continuous risk management process (based on NASA, 2008).

***Continuous Risk Management.***    Risk management is a continuous management process, which often contains the following six elements as illustrated in Figure 1.4 (e.g., see NASA, 2008) [3]:

*Identify.*  Before the risk can be managed, the hazards and the potential hazardous events must be identified. The identification process may reveal problems before they come to the surface. The problems should be stated, describing what, when, where, how, and why the hazardous event might happen.

*Analyze.*  Analysis means in this regard to convert data related to risk into decision-relevant information. The data may be related to the likelihood of a hazardous event and the severity of harm if the event should happen. The analysis provides the basis from which the company can prioritize the most critical risk elements.

*Plan.*  Here, the risk information is turned into decisions and actions. Planning involves developing actions to address individual hazards, prioritizing risk-reducing actions, and creating an integrated risk management plan. The key to risk action planning is to consider the future consequences of a decision made today.

*Track.*  Tracking consists of monitoring the risk level and the actions taken to reduce the risk. Appropriate risk metrics are identified and monitored to enable the evaluation of the status of risk.

*Control.*  Here, proposed risk-reducing actions are executed and controlled. The step is integrated into general management and relies on management processes to

---

[3] A similar figure may also be found in the following: Strategy Unit (2002, p. 44) and Treasury Board (2001, p. 26).

control risk action plans, correct deviations from plans, respond to events, and improve risk management processes.

*Communicate and Document.* The activities described above should be documented and communicated. Risk communication is placed at the center of the model to emphasize both its pervasiveness and its criticality. Without effective communication, no risk management approach can be viable. A system for documentation and tracking of risk decisions must be implemented.

## 1.3 The Study Object

In this book, the object of analysis is a technical or sociotechnical system. We refer to this as the *study object* or the *system*. A system may be defined as:

☞ **System**: Composite entity, at any level of complexity, of personnel, procedures, materials, tools, equipment, facilities, and software. The elements of this composite entity are used together in the intended operational or support environment to perform a given task to achieve a specific objective (IEC 60300-3-9, 1995).

When analyzing a study object, it is always wise to remember the influential risk researcher Jens Rasmussen's statement that "a system is more than the sum of its elements" (Rasmussen, 1997).

### 1.3.1 The Sociotechnical System

If people have important roles or relations to and within a system, we often refer to the study object as a *sociotechnical system*. A sociotechnical system will contain several types of elements, such as:

- *Hardware* (H). Any physical and nonhuman element of the study object, such as workspace, buildings, machines, equipment, and signs.

- *Software* (S). Nonmaterial elements of the study object: for example, computer software, work procedures, norms, checklists, and practices.

- *Liveware* (L). Personnel, such as operators, maintenance staff, service personnel, visitors and third parties. Liveware also includes such elements as teamwork and leadership.

- *Management/organization* (M). Management, policies, strategies, training, and so on.

- *Environment* (E). The internal and external environment in which the study object operates.

The various elements of the study object are illustrated in Figure 1.5. In a risk analysis, it is important to consider all these elements and the interfaces between them.

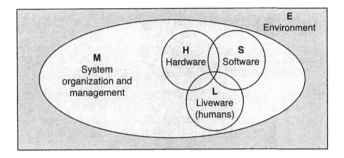

**Figure 1.5**   The elements of a study object (see also IEC 60300-3-4, 2007).

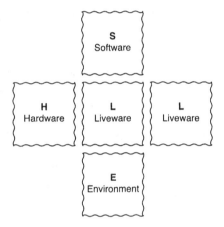

**Figure 1.6**   SHEL model.

Most study objects will also have interfaces with other objects that have to be considered in the risk analysis. To make sure that all relevant interfaces are considered, the aviation industry advocates the SHEL model.

### 1.3.2   The SHEL Model

The SHEL model was developed within the aviation industry through the 1970s and early 1980s. The name of the model is derived from the initial letters of its four elements: software (S), hardware (H), environment (E), and liveware (L).

The SHEL model is illustrated in Figure 1.6, where the boxes are drawn with rugged lines to emphasize the often complicated interfaces between the elements. In a risk analysis, all possible interfaces should be studied. Important interfaces are (e.g., see ICAO, 2009):

(a) *Liveware-Hardware (L-H)*. This interface between the human and the hardware is often called the *man-machine interface*.

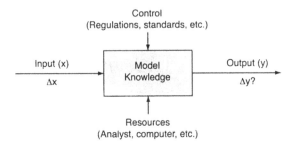

**Figure 1.7**  System inputs and outputs.

(b) *Liveware-Software (L-S)*. This interface describes the relationship between the personnel and the computer software, checklists, and so on. It depends on the presentation format, clarity, and the use of symbols.

(c) *Liveware-Liveware (L-L)*. This interface covers the relationship between the individual and other persons in the workplace. It depends on leadership, cooperation, teamwork, and personal interactions.

(d) *Liveware-Environment (L-E)*. This interface concerns the relationship between the individual and her/his internal and external environments. The internal environment involves factors such as temperature, light, noise, vibration, and air quality. The external environment includes such things as weather conditions and external systems that may influence the working conditions.

### 1.3.3  Complexity and Coupling

When analyzing the relationships between the elements in a sociotechnical system, risk assessment is riddled by two main challenges: complexity and coupling. These concepts were actualized in Charles Perrow's seminal book *Normal Accidents: Living with High-Risk Technologies* (Perrow, 1984) and are discussed further in Chapter 6.

*Complexity.*  The input and output of a system or a system element are illustrated in Figure 1.7. The input $x$ (which may be a vector) will produce an output $y$ (which may also be a vector). If a change $\Delta x$ is made to the input, knowledge and models may be used to predict the change $\Delta y$ of the output. The complexity of the system is characterized by our ability to predict the change $\Delta y$ of the output caused by a specified change $\Delta x$ of the input. If we, without any uncertainty, can predict the change $\Delta y$, the system is said to be *linear*. In the opposite case, the system is said to be *complex*. The degree of complexity increases with the uncertainty about the value of $\Delta y$. The extreme case is when we do not have any clue about what will happen to $y$ when we change the input $x$.

Complexity leads to several challenges in a risk analysis, as pinpointed by Leveson (1995):

**Table 1.2**    Characteristics of tight and loose coupling systems.

| Tight coupling | Loose coupling |
| --- | --- |
| Delays in processing not possible | Processing delays are possible |
| Order of sequences cannot be changed | Order of sequence can be changed |
| Only one method is applicable to achieve the goal | Alternative methods are available |
| Little slack possible in supplies, equipment, personnel | Slack in resources possible |
| Buffers and redundancies may be available, but are deliberately designed-in, and there is no flexibility | Buffers and redundancies fortuitously available |
| Substitutions of supplies, equipment, and personnel may be available, but are limited and designed-in | Substitutions are fortuitously available |

*Source*: Adapted from Perrow (1984), also cited by Stewart and Melchers (1997).

Many of the new hazards are related to increased complexity (both product and process) in the systems we are building. Not only are new hazards created by the complexity, but the complexity makes identifying them more difficult.

The ever-increasing integration of information and communication technology in systems and the expanding digital infrastructure are important contributors to system complexity. This problem is discussed further by Grøtan et al. (2011).

***Coupling.***    The other important concept discussed by Perrow (1984) is *coupling*, which may be defined as a measure of the strength of the interconnectedness between system components. Perrow (1984) is concerned mainly with *tight coupling*:

The sub-components of a tightly coupled system have prompt and major impacts on each other. If what happens in one part has little impact on another part, or if everything happens slowly (in particular, slowly on the scale of human thinking times), the system is not described as *tightly coupled*. Tight coupling also raises the odds that operator intervention will make things worse, since the true nature of the problem may well not be understood correctly.

Some of the main characteristics of tight and loose coupling are listed in Table 1.2.

## 1.4  Accident Categories

When analyzing risk, the most suitable approach will vary with the type of accidents we are faced with. Different types of accidents may be distinguished by their frequency, origin, and/or impact.

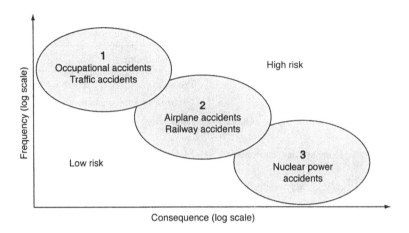

**Figure 1.8**   Three main categories of accidents (adapted from Rasmussen, 1997).

### 1.4.1   Jens Rasmussen's Categories

Accidents can, according to Rasmussen (1997), be classified into three main categories, as illustrated in Figure 1.8.

***Accidents of Category 1.***   Some accidents, such as road traffic accidents and minor occupational accidents, occur so often and so "regularly" that we may predict the number of similar accidents in the near future based on past observations. Accidents of this category are characterized by a relatively high frequency and a correspondingly low consequence.

***Accidents of Category 2.***   Accidents of category 2 in Figure 1.8 occur rather seldom and have more severe consequences than the accidents in category 1. Examples of such accidents are major industrial accidents, air accidents, railway accidents, and maritime accidents. In the aftermath of such accidents, detailed accident investigations are usually carried out to identify the possible causes of the accident and what could have been done to prevent it from occurring. To determine the risk related to such accidents, it is not sufficient to base the assessment on the number of accidents observed in the past. Rather, we should carry out a detailed risk analysis to identify all the possible hazards and accident scenarios that have yet to occur. Each part of the system is then analyzed and the total risk is determined based on the risk related to the various parts.

***Accidents of Category 3.***   Accidents of category 3 in Figure 1.8 occur very seldom, but when they do, they have catastrophic and wide-ranging consequences. An example of an accident in this category is the Chernobyl nuclear power accident in 1986. For such accidents, it has no meaning whatsoever to try to determine the risk based on historical data. It is therefore necessary to carry out detailed risk analyses of the various parts of the system.

The risk analyses that are covered in this book are mainly relevant for systems that produce accidents in categories 2 and 3.

### 1.4.2 James Reason's Categories

The prominent risk researcher James Reason (Reason, 1997) classifies accidents into two main types. The first type is *individual accidents*, which are accidents that are caused and suffered by single individuals. These types of accidents are relatively common, as can be illustrated by the relatively high number of both road traffic accidents and falls in their homes by elderly people. The second type Reason calls *organizational accidents*. These are fortunately relatively rare, but may have a large-scale impact on populations. Organizational accidents are generally characterized by multiple causes and numerous interactions between different system elements. It is this type of accident that is of main interest in this book. Reason's categories of accidents are also discussed in Section 2.7.2.

Table 1.3 outlines some of the most severe accidents we have witnessed in the last few decades, which all classify as organizational accidents according to Reason's categorization.

## 1.5   Risk in Our Modern Society

### 1.5.1   Increasing Risk

Most safety researchers agree that the risk in our society has been increasing steadily throughout the last two to three decades. Reasons for this trend may include (e.g., see Rasmussen, 1997; Leveson, 2004):

- The very fast pace of technological change and the more and more complex relationships between humans and automation.

- The steadily increasing scale of industrial installations, which increases the potential for large-scale accidents.

- The rapid development of information and communication technology, which leads to a high degree of integration and coupling of systems. This is claimed to improve flexibility, but may also increase the likelihood of accidents.

- The aggressive and competitive environment that companies have to operate in, which encourages higher speed of operation, harder use and less maintenance of equipment, and few buffers.

- The steady demand for higher speed (faster cars, trains, ships, airplanes).

- The increased likelihood of sabotage and terrorism.

- The increasing use of multicultural work forces (often motivated by cost reduction), which may introduce cultural barriers and language problems.

**Table 1.3**   Some major accidents.

| Location of accident | Year | Consequences |
|---|---|---|
| Flixborough, UK | 1974 | Explosion and fire, 27 killed, more than 100 injured. |
| Seveso, Italy | 1976 | Dioxin release, 2 000 poisoned, contamination of environment, mass evacuation. |
| North Sea, Norway | 1977 | Oil/gas blowout on *Bravo* platform, pollution of sea. |
| Three Mile Island, USA | 1979 | Complex accident. Had potential for a major release of radiation. |
| Newfoundland, Canada | 1982 | Platform *Ocean Ranger* lost, 84 killed. |
| Bhopal, India | 1984 | Release of toxic methyl isocyanate, 3 800 killed, 20 000 injured, 200 000 evacuated. |
| Mexico City, Mexico | 1984 | Explosion and fire at LPG storage and distribution depot at San Juan Ixhautepec. Around 500 killed. |
| USA | 1986 | Explosion of *Challenger* space shuttle. 7 killed. |
| Chernobyl, Ukraine | 1986 | Explosion and atomic fallout at nuclear power station. |
| Basel, Switzerland | 1986 | Fire at Sandoz warehouse. Rhine River contaminated, severe environmental damage. |
| Zeebrügge, Belgium | 1987 | The car and passenger ferry *Herald of Free Enterprise* capsized. 193 killed. |
| North Sea, UK | 1988 | Explosion and fire on the *Piper Alpha* platform. Platform lost, 167 killed. |
| Pasadena, USA | 1989 | Explosion and fire, 23 killed, 100 injured. |
| Alaska, USA | 1989 | Oil spill from tanker *Exxon Valdez*. Severe environmental damage. |
| Amsterdam, The Netherlands | 1992 | Boeing 747 cargo plane crashed near Schipol airport. 43 killed. |
| Baltic Sea | 1994 | The car and passenger ferry *Estonia* capsized, claiming 852 lives. |
| Eschede, Germany | 1998 | High-speed train derailed. 101 killed, 88 injured. |
| Longford Australia | 1998 | Explosion and fire, 2 killed, Melbourne without gas for 19 days. |
| Bretagne, France | 1999 | Loss of tanker *Erika*. Major oil spill. |
| Enschede, The Netherlands | 2000 | Explosion in fireworks plant. 22 killed, 1 000 injured, more than 300 homes destroyed. |
| Toulouse, France | 2001 | Explosion and fire in fertilizer plant. 30 killed, 2 000 injured, 600 homes destroyed. |
| Galicia, Spain | 2002 | Loss of tanker *Prestige*, major oil spill. |
| Texas City, USA | 2005 | Explosion and fire, 15 killed, 180 injured. |
| Hertfordshire, UK | 2005 | Explosion and fire at Buncefield Depot. |
| Gulf of Mexico | 2010 | Blowout and explosion on the drilling rig *Deepwater Horizon*. 11 killed, 17 injured, rig lost, major oil spill. |

– The emerging climate changes and instability of weather conditions, leading to more frequent and more severe flooding, storms, and so on.

## 1.5.2   Experience of Major Accidents

During the last three to four decades, a number of major accidents have made the public increasingly aware of the risks posed by certain technical systems and activities. Several accidents have also changed the authorities' attitudes toward such systems. The industry itself is also concerned, since the consequences of such accidents not only incur enormous costs, but may even force a company out of business and seriously damage the image of an entire industry. Examples of accidents with far-reaching effects on the attitudes of regulatory and legislative bodies are listed in Table 1.3.

These accidents are representative of a large number of accidents that have served to remind us that safety can never be taken for granted. Macza (2008) discusses several of these accidents and the society's response to each accident with respect to legislation changes and other actions.

## 1.6   Safety Legislation

Many laws and regulations have emerged or been changed after major accidents, which have called for an increasingly structured approach to safety legislation. Safety legislation has a long history. As early as 1780 B.C., Hammurabi's code of laws in ancient Mesopotamia contained punishments based on a peculiar "harm analogy." Law 229 of this code states:

> If a builder builds a house for someone, and does not construct it properly, and the house that he built falls in and kills its owner, then that builder shall be put to death.

Safety legislation has traditionally been based on a *prescriptive* regulating regime, in which detailed requirements for the design and operation of a plant are specified by the authorities. The trend in many countries is now a move away from such prescriptive requirements toward a *performance-based* regime, which holds the management responsible for ensuring that appropriate safety systems are in place. Hammurabi's law may be the earliest example of a performance-based standard (Macza, 2008). Goal orientation and risk characterization are two major components of modern performance-based regimes, which have been endorsed enthusiastically by international organizations and various industries (Aven and Renn, 2009b).

## 1.6.1   Safety Case

Several countries have introduced a *safety case* regime. A safety case is a risk management system that requires the operator of a facility to produce a document which:

(a) Identifies the hazards and potential hazardous events.

(b) Describes how the hazardous events are controlled.

(c) Describes the safety management system in place to ensure that the controls are effective and applied consistently.

The detailed content and the application of a safety case vary from country to country, but the following elements are usually important[4]:

- The safety case must identify the safety critical aspects of the facility, both technical and managerial.

- Appropriate performance standards must be defined for the operation of the safety critical aspects.

- The workforce must be involved.

- The safety case is produced in the knowledge that a competent and independent regulator will scrutinize it.

### 1.6.2   Risk Assessment in Safety Legislation

In Europe, a number of EU directives and regulations have been issued that make it mandatory to carry out various types of risk assessment of a wide range of potentially hazardous systems and activities. This is also the case in other parts of the world. Some main laws are introduced briefly below to illustrate the wide span of application:

- The EU Directive on the control of major accident hazards involving dangerous substances (82/501/EEC) is often referred to as the *Seveso directive* since it was issued in response to the Seveso accident in 1977. The Seveso directive was amended in 1986 and 1988 to take into account the lessons learned from the Bhopal disaster and the Sandoz fire. A more significant revision of the directive was issued in 1996 as a consequence of the Piper Alpha disaster, and is called the *Seveso II directive* (EU, 1996).[5]

  The application of the Seveso II directive depends on the quantities of dangerous substances present (or likely to be present) at an establishment. Two levels ("tiers") of duty are specified in the directive, corresponding to two different quantities (or thresholds) of dangerous substances. Sites exceeding the higher, "upper tier" threshold are subject to more onerous requirements than those that qualify as "lower tier."

  Similar legislation is also implemented in several other countries: for example, as 29 CFR 1910.119, "Process safety management of highly hazardous chemicals," in the United States. This law requires that process hazard analyses (PrHAs) be carried out.

---

[4]Based on http//www.nopsa.gov.au.
[5]In the UK, the Seveso II directive is implemented as the *control of major accident hazard* (COMAH) regulation.

- The EU machinery directive (89/392/EEC) covering safety aspects of a wide range of machines was introduced in 1989. This directive requires that risk analyses are carried out for some dangerous machines, and a specific risk analysis standard, ISO 12100 (2010), has been developed for this purpose. Similar legislation has been implemented in several countries.

- The Health and Safety at Work etc. Act of 1974 (HSWA) is the principal health and safety law in the UK. It places general duties on employers to ensure the health, safety, and welfare of their employees at work, and also to conduct their undertaking in such a manner that persons outside their employment are not exposed to risks. Employers must carry out various risk assessments to ensure that these duties are met "so far as is reasonably practicable" (SFAIRP).

- The Offshore Installations (Safety Case) Regulations 1992, issued by the UK Health and Safety Executive (HSE), require that specific risk assessments be carried out and that a safety case be developed and kept "alive" (i.e., updated).

- The U.S. Maritime Transportation Security Act (2004). This act is designed to protect U.S. ports and waterways from a terrorist attack. It requires vessels and port facilities to conduct risk and vulnerability assessments.

- In Norway, regulations concerning the implementation and use of risk analyses in petroleum activities have been issued by the Petroleum Safety Authority Norway and the Norwegian Ministry of the Environment. A special standard, NORSOK Z-013 (2010), has been developed to support the required risk assessments.

### 1.6.3   Risk Analysis Standards and Guidelines

A wide range of standards and guidelines for risk analysis have been issued. Some of these are listed in Table 1.4. The list is provided as an illustration and is far from being complete.

## 1.7   Risk and Decision-Making

Even though numerous laws and regulations require that risk assessments be carried out, it is important to understand that a risk assessment should never be performed simply to satisfy some regulatory requirement. Rather, it should be performed with the intention of providing information for decision-making about risk.

The objective of almost any risk assessment is to support some form of decision-making where risk is an important decision criterion. Decisions may relate to the following questions (e.g., see HSE, 2001a; Holmgren and Thedén, 2009):

(a) Should the activity be permitted?

(b) Are additional barriers or other system improvements necessary to reduce the risk?

**Table 1.4**   Standards and guidelines for risk analysis (some examples).

*International standards*

(a) IEC 60300-3-9: *Dependability Management—Application Guide: Risk Analysis of Technological Systems.*

(b) ISO 12100: *Safety of Machinery—General Principles for Design: Risk Assessment and Risk Reduction.*

(c) ISO 31000: *Risk Management: Principles and Guidelines.*

(d) ISO 31010: *Risk Management: Risk Assessment Techniques.*

(e) ISO 17776: *Petroleum and Natural Gas Industries—Offshore Production Installations: Guidelines on Tools and Techniques for Hazard Identification and Risk Assessment.*

(f) ISO 14971: *Medical Devices: Application of Risk Management to Medical Devices.*

*National general standards and guidelines*

(a) NS 5814: *Requirements to Risk Assessments*, Norwegian standard.

(b) CAN/CSA-Q634-91: *Risk Analysis Requirements and Guidelines*, Canadian standard.

(c) CAN/CSA-Q850: *Risk Management: Guideline for Decision-Makers*, Canadian standard.

*Process industry standards and guidelines*

(a) CCPS: *Guidelines for Hazard Evaluation Procedures.*

(b) CCPS: *Guidelines for Chemical Process Quantitative Risk Analysis.*

(c) DOE-HDBK-1100-96: *Chemical Process Hazards Analysis.*

*Oil/gas industry standards and guidelines*

(a) NORSOK Z-013: *Risk and Emergency Preparedness Analysis.*

*Nuclear industry standards and guidelines*

(a) NUREG/CR-2300: *PRA Procedures Guide: A Guide to the Performance of Probabilistic Risk Assessment for Nuclear Power Plants.*

*Space industry standards and guidelines*

(a) NASA: *Probabilistic risk assessment procedures guide for NASA managers and practitioners.*

(b) ESA: *Space Product Assurance; Hazard Analysis.*

*Railway standards and guidelines*

(a) EN 50126: *Railway Applications: The Specification and Demonstration of Reliability, Availability, Maintainability, and Safety (RAMS).*

(b) RSSB: *Engineering Safety Management (The Yellow Book).*

*Maritime standards and guidelines*

(a) IMO: *Guide for Formal Safety Assessment (FSA) for Use in the IMO Rule-Making Process.*

(b) ABS: *Guide for Risk Evaluations for the Classification of Marine-Related Facilities.*

*Electronics industry guidelines*

(a) SEMATECH: *Hazard analysis guide: A reference manual for analyzing safety hazards on semiconductor manufacturing equipment.*

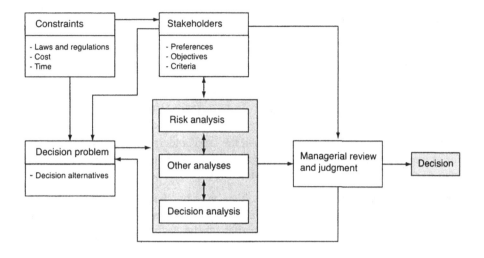

**Figure 1.9**    Decision framework (adapted from Aven, 2003).

(c) Which of various options, involving different combinations of safety and expenditure, should be preferred?

(d) How much should be invested to improve the safety of the system?

To answer questions like these, the decision-maker must decide if, or when, the system or the activity is *safe enough*. By that we mean that the risk is considered so low that further barriers and other improvements are not required.

### 1.7.1  Model for Decision-Making

It is important to remember that risk is always only one dimension of a decision problem. Operational, economic, social, political, and environmental considerations may also be important decision criteria. A decision is never made in a vacuum. There are always constraints, such as laws and regulations, time and cost limits, and so on, that need to be adhered to, and there are usually a set of *stakeholders* who have interests in the decision and who will seek to influence the decision-making in different ways. A simple model for decision-making involving risk is illustrated in Figure 1.9, which is an expanded version of a similar figure in Aven (2003, p. 98).

The results from a risk assessment can be used as:

– Direct input to decisions (see Figure 1.9)

– Indirect input to decisions: for example, by influencing stakeholders

The actual decision must be taken by the management and is not part of the risk assessment process as described in this book.

### 1.7.2   Stakeholders

As illustrated in Figure 1.9, the decision process may be influenced by stakeholders, who may be defined as:

☞ **Stakeholder**: Person or organization that can affect, be affected by, or perceive themselves to be affected by a decision or activity (ISO 31000, 2009).

This definition covers many more than the stakeholders indicated in Figure 1.9: for example, people who are affected by the consequences of a possible accident but who do not have the ability or power to influence the decision.

***Categories of Stakeholders.*** Stakeholders may be classified in many different ways. One such classification is based on the stakeholders' (i) power, (ii) urgency, and (iii) legitimacy. Stakeholders may alternatively be classified as (Yosie and Herbst, 1998):

(a) People who are affected directly by a decision to take action on any issue or project.

(b) People who are interested in a project or activity, want to become involved in the process, and seek an opportunity to provide input.

(c) People who are more generally interested in the process and may seek information.

(d) People who are affected by the outcome of a decision but are unaware of it or do not participate in the stakeholder process.

Some stakeholders may have several roles in relation to the system. The consequences of an accident will be different for various stakeholders, depending on their relation to the assets that are harmed. If a worker is killed in an accident, her husband and children will, for example, get consequences other than those that would be received by her employer.

### 1.7.3   Deterministic Decision-making

Deterministic decision-making means that decisions are made without any consideration of the likelihood of the possible outcomes. Scenarios are predicted based on a deterministic view of the future, assuming that a bounding set of fault conditions will lead to one undesired end event. To prevent this end event from occurring, the decision-maker relies on traditional engineering principles, such as redundancy, diversity, and safety margins.

### 1.7.4   Risk-Based Decision-making

Risk-based decision-making (RBDM) is a decision-making process that is based almost solely on the results of a risk assessment. The U.S. Department of Energy defines RBDM as:

☞ **Risk-based decision-making (RBDM)**: A process that uses quantification of risks, costs, and benefits to evaluate and compare decision options competing for limited resources (adapted from US DOE, 1998).

The U.S. Coast Guard gives a detailed description of the RBDM process in the four volumes of USCG (2008). The process can be split into four steps:

1. Establish the decision structure (identify the possible decision options and the factors influencing these).

2. Perform the risk assessment (e.g., as described in this book).

3. Apply the results to risk management decision-making (i.e., assess the possible risk management options and use the information from step 2 in the decision-making).

4. Monitor effectiveness through impact assessment (track the effectiveness of the actions taken to manage the risk and verify that the organization is getting the results expected from the risk management decisions).

USCG (2008) may be consulted for details about the various steps.

### 1.7.5  Risk-Informed Decision-making

The RBDM approach has been criticized for putting too much focus on probabilistic risk estimates and paying too little attention to deterministic requirements and design principles. To compensate for this weakness, the risk-informed decision-making approach has emerged. This approach may be defined as:

☞ **Risk-informed decision-making (RIDM)**: An approach to decision-making representing a philosophy whereby risk insights are considered together with other factors to establish requirements that better focus the attention on design and operational issues commensurate with their importance to health and safety (adapted from NUREG-1855, 2009).

A slightly different definition is given in NASA (2007). The RIDM process can, according to NUREG-1855 (2009), be carried out in five steps:

1. Define the decision under consideration (including context and boundary conditions).

2. Identify and assess the applicable requirements (laws, regulations, requirements, accepted design principles).

3. Perform risk-informed analysis, consisting of:

    (a) Deterministic analysis (based on engineering principles and experience and prior knowledge).

(b) Probabilistic analysis (i.e., a risk assessment including an uncertainty assessment).

4. Define the implementation and monitoring program. An important part of the decision-making process is to understand the implications of a decision and to guard against any unanticipated adverse effects.

5. Integrated decision. Here the results of steps 1 through 4 are integrated and the decision is made. This requires that the insights obtained from all the other steps of the RIDM process be weighed and combined to reach a conclusion. An essential aspect of the integration is consideration of uncertainties.

The main difference between RBDM and RIDM is that with RBDM, the decisions are based almost solely on the results of the probabilistic risk assessment, whereas following RIDM, the decisions are made on the basis of information from the probabilistic risk assessment as well as from deterministic analyses and technical considerations.

### 1.7.6  The Validity of Risk Assessment

All risk analyses require a wide range of data and assumptions that may be more or less uncertain. Whenever possible, the data and the assumptions should reflect reality as closely as possible. This is not always feasible, and some decision-makers therefore question the validity of the results from risk analysis. A pertinent answer to this type of question is given by Garrick (2008):

> [...] there is seldom enough data about future events to be absolutely certain about when and where they will occur and what the consequences might be. But "certainty" is seldom necessary to greatly improve the chances of making good decisions.

Whenever possible, assumptions should, however, be made to err on the side of conservatism. Such assumptions, known as "conservative best estimates," are to ensure that the assumptions do not result in underestimation of risk and, ultimately, unsafe decisions (NSW, 2003). Uncertainty in risk assessment is discussed further in Chapter 16.

### 1.7.7  Closure

It is important to be aware that it is never possible for a system to operate with zero risk. Even if a company may be able to operate without a serious incident ever occurring, the potential will always exist. This is why it is so important for operators to understand the risk they face and to fully appreciate the implications of any changes they make to their operations.

Before we dive further into the realm of risk terminology and assessment methodologies, it should be stressed that a risk assessment is of limited value if it is not going to be used, that is, as a basis for decision-making. A general recommendation is therefore:

If you do not have a specified decision problem, do not carry out any risk assessment!

## 1.8    Structure of the Book

This book has two main parts and one appendix part.

### 1.8.1    Part I: Introduction to Risk Assessment

The first part has seven chapters, which introduce risk analysis and risk assessment. This introductory chapter has presented the main concepts of the book and placed risk assessment into a decision-making context. The remaining chapters are organized as follows: The main concepts are defined and discussed in Chapter 2 and several examples are given. Various types of hazards and threats related to a system are presented and discussed in Chapter 3. Problems related to quantifying risk are discussed in Chapter 4, and several risk metrics are defined. Several approaches to deciding whether a risk level is acceptable or not are presented. In Chapter 5, risk analysis and risk assessment are set into a risk management framework. The various steps in a risk analysis are presented and discussed briefly, and the competence of the study team and the quality requirements are highlighted. A risk assessment is always influenced by the study team's perception of the potential accidents and accident causation, and accident models are therefore presented and discussed in Chapter 6. Part I is concluded by Chapter 7, which lists and describes the input data that are required for a risk assessment.

### 1.8.2    Part II: Risk Assessment Methods and Applications

Part II presents the main methods for risk analysis according to a structure that follows the main steps of a risk analysis. Chapter 8 discusses the main features of the various methods, especially how the analysis should be planned, prepared, and reported. Chapter 9 presents a number of methods for hazard identification: among them preliminary hazard analysis (PHA) and HAZOP. Chapter 10 presents methods for cause and frequency analysis, such as fault tree analysis and Bayesian networks, while Chapter 11 presents methods for development of accident scenarios, where event tree analysis is the most common method. Safety barriers are discussed in Chapter 12, and a number of methods for barrier analysis are presented and discussed. Human errors and human reliability are discussed in Chapter 13 together with several models for human reliability assessment. Job safety analysis (JSA) is covered in Chapter 14. This deviates slightly from the main structure of Part II, since JSA is a separate method for analyzing the risk related to a specific job/task. Dependent failures and common-cause failures (CCFs) are discussed in Chapter 15, and several CCF models are presented. The uncertainties related to the results from a risk analysis are often of concern, and this is treated in Chapter 16. Part II is concluded in Chapter 17 by a historical account and status of the development of risk assessment in some selected application areas.

The various analytical methods are, as far as possible, presented according to a common structure. The description of each method is designed to be self-contained such that you should be able to carry out the analysis without having to read the entire book or search other sources. A consequence of this strategy is that the same information may be found in the description of several methods.

### 1.8.3   Part III: Appendices

Appendix A presents some main elements of probability theory. An introduction to probability theory is given together with some elements from system reliability and Bayesian methods. If you are not familiar with probability theory, you may find it useful to read this appendix in parallel with the chapters that use probability arguments.

Part III also contains a list of abbreviations and acronyms used in the book and a glossary of the main risk concepts. Many of the terms in the glossary are defined throughout the book. In cases where conflicting definitions are used in the literature, several definitions are listed in the glossary.

Additional material related to the book is available on the web site:

`http://www.ntnu.edu/ross/books/risk`

### 1.9   Additional Reading

The following titles are recommended for further study related to Chapter 1.

– *Five steps to risk assessment* (HSE, 2006) gives a very brief but well-structured introduction to risk assessment.

– *Probabilistic risk assessment procedures guide for NASA managers and practitioners* (Stamatelatos et al., 2002a) is developed for space applications but also provides valuable information for other application areas.

– *Risk Analysis in Engineering: Techniques, Tools, and Trends* (Modarres, 2006) is a textbook providing a thorough introduction to risk analysis that can be considered a competitor to the current book. The form and structure of the two books are, however, different.

– *Probabilistic Risk Analysis: Foundations and Methods* (Bedford and Cooke, 2001) is a textbook on risk analysis with a strong focus on probabilistic aspects.

– *Risk Analysis: Assessing Uncertainties Beyond Expected Values and Probabilities* (Aven, 2008) is a monograph that discusses specific conceptual issues related to risk analysis.

# CHAPTER 2

# THE WORDS OF RISK ANALYSIS

...the defining of risk is essentially a political act.

—Roger E. Kasperson

## 2.1 Introduction

This chapter has the same title as Stan Kaplan's talk to the Annual Meeting of the Society of Risk Analysis in 1996 when he received the Society's Distinguished Award. The talk was later published in the journal *Risk Analysis* and has become one of the most influential articles on risk concepts (Kaplan, 1997).

The risk concept was introduced briefly in Chapter 1. When we ask "What is the risk?", we really ask three questions: (i) What can go wrong? (ii) What is the likelihood of that happening? and (iii) What are the consequences?

**Inger Lise Johansen**, NTNU, has made important contributions to this chapter.

*Risk Assessment: Theory, Methods, and Applications,* First Edition.
By Marvin Rausand. Copyright © 2011 John Wiley & Sons, Inc.

To be able to answer these questions, we first need to clearly define what we mean by the words used in the questions, and we also need to define several other, associated terms.

## 2.2   Events and Scenarios

To be able to answer the first question, we need to specify what we mean by "What can go wrong?" The answer must be one or more *events*, or sequences of events. An event is defined as:

☞ **Event**: Incident or situation which occurs in a particular place during a particular interval of time (AS/NZS 4360, 1995).

In this book, the term *event* is used to denote a future occurrence. The duration of the event may range from very short (e.g., an instantaneous shock) to a rather long period.

We distinguish between two types of events that can go wrong: (i) *hazardous events*, and (ii) *initiating events*. When the answer to the question "What can go wrong?" is a sequence of events, we call this sequence of events an *accident scenario*, or simply a scenario.

The terms *hazardous event*, *initiating event*, and *accident scenario* are defined and discussed later in this chapter. For a more thorough discussion, see Johansen (2010b).

### 2.2.1   Hazardous Event

A hazardous event is defined as:

☞ **Hazardous event**: The first event in a sequence of events that, if not controlled, will lead to undesired consequences (harm) to some assets.

A hazardous event may alternatively be defined as "the point at which control of the hazard is lost." This is the point from which further barriers (safeguards) can only mitigate the consequences of the event.

The term *hazard* is defined and discussed in Chapter 3. At this stage it is sufficient to say that a hazard is often linked to energy of some type and that a hazardous event occurs when the energy is released. In the process industry, two main categories of hazardous events are "loss of containment" and "loss of physical integrity."

Several alternative terms for *hazardous event* are used in the literature. Among these are *accident initiator, accident initiating event* (e.g., used by Stamatelatos et al., 2002a), *accidental event, critical event, undesired event, initiating event,* TOP *event, process deviation, potential major incident,* and *process demand*. We have chosen the term *hazardous event* since it is used in the important standards ISO 12100 (2010) and IEC 60300-3-9 (1995).

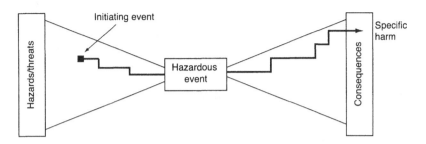

**Figure 2.1**    Accident scenario illustrated in a bow-tie diagram.

### 2.2.2   Initiating Event

Some of the methods for risk analysis (see Part II) need a more flexible concept than that permitted by our definition of hazardous event. We will therefore also use the term *initiating event* or *initiator*, which is defined as:

☞ **Initiating event** (or **initiator**): An identified event that upsets the normal operations of the system and may require a response to avoid undesirable outcomes (adapted from IAEA, 2002).

In contrast to a hazardous event, an initiating event may be defined anywhere in the event sequence from the first deviation until harm takes place. The initiating event may even represent the hazardous event. This is because an initiating event is an analytical concept, which is entirely up to the analyst to choose, depending on the hazard and barriers under study. In all cases, the initiating event will require some actions from the system safety functions.

### 2.2.3   Accident Scenario

An accident scenario is defined as:

☞ **Accident scenario**: A specific sequence of events from an initiating event to an undesired consequence (or harm) (adapted from IMO, 2002).

The concept of accident scenario is illustrated principally as a particular path in the bow-tie diagram in Figure 2.1. The sequence of events is considered to start when the initiating event occurs and is terminated at a uniquely defined end event. The end event may be an undesired consequence, situation, or event. In Figure 2.1, the initiating event develops into a hazardous event where the energy is released.

The path in an accident scenario is diverted as barriers are activated. An accident scenario will usually involve a sequence of events and several barriers, but may also be a single event. The latter case happens if an initiating event gives harm to an asset directly without the involvement of barriers. The concept of accident scenario is discussed further by Khan and Abbasi (2002) and is also a central element in the ARAMIS methodology (ARAMIS, 2004).

**▉ EXAMPLE 2.1   Accident scenario in a process plant**

A possible accident scenario which starts with a gas leak in a petroleum process plant might proceed as follows:

1. A gas leak from flange A occurs (i.e., the hazardous event).

2. The gas is detected and the alarm goes off.

3. The process shutdown system fails to shut off the gas flow to the flange.

4. The gas is ignited and a fire occurs.

5. The firefighting system functions as intended and the fire is extinguished within approximately 1 hour.

6. No persons are injured, but the accident leads to significant material damage and a 20-days production stoppage (i.e., the end event).          ⊕

Note that defining a hazardous event or an accident scenario is not to say that it will indeed occur. For the purpose of describing an accident that has already occurred, *accident course* is considered a more appropriate term.

***Special Categories of Accident Scenarios.***   In many risk analyses, it will require too much time and too many resources to study all the possible accident scenarios. A set of representative scenarios are therefore selected for detailed analysis. These are often called *reference scenarios*.

☞ **Reference accident scenario**: An accident scenario that is considered to be representative of a set of accident scenarios that are identified in a risk analysis, where the scenarios in the set are considered to be likely to occur.

In some applications, it may be relevant to consider the worst possible scenarios:

☞ **Worst-case accident scenario**: The accident scenario with the highest consequence that is physically possible regardless of likelihood (Kim et al., 2006).

A worst-case release scenario may, for example, involve the release of the maximum quantity of some dangerous material during "worst-case" weather conditions. Worst-case scenarios are often used in establishing emergency plans, but should not be used in, for example, land use planning (see Chapter 4).

Since a worst-case accident scenario will often have a remote probability of occurrence, a more credible accident scenario may be more relevant.

☞ **Worst credible accident scenario**: The highest-consequence accident scenario identified that is considered plausible or reasonably believable (Kim et al., 2006).

## 2.3  Probability and Frequency

> Probability is the most important concept in modern science, especially as nobody has the slightest notion of what it means.
>
> —Bertrand Russell

To answer the second question in the triplet definition of risk, "What is the likelihood of that happening?", we need to use concepts from probability theory.

A brief introduction to probability theory is given in Appendix A. Essentially, the probability of an event $E$ is a number between 0 and 1 (i.e., between 0% and 100%) that expresses the likelihood that the event will occur in a specific situation, and is written as $\Pr(E)$. If $\Pr(E) = 1$, we know with certainty that event $E$ will occur, while for $\Pr(E) = 0$ we are certain that event $E$ will not occur.

### 2.3.1  Probability

Probability is a complex concept about whose meaning many books and scientific articles have been written. There are three main approaches to probability: (i) the classical approach, (ii) the frequentist approach, and (iii) the Bayesian or subjective approach.

> People have argued about the meaning of the word "probability" for at least hundreds of years, maybe thousands. So bitter, and fervent, have the battles been between the contending schools of thought, that they've often been likened to religious wars. And this situation continues to the present time (Kaplan, 1997).

*Classical Approach.*    The classical approach to probability is applicable in only a limited set of situations where we consider experiments with a finite number $n$ of possible outcomes, and where each outcome has the same likelihood of occurring. This is appropriate for many simple games of chance, such as tossing coins, rolling dice, dealing cards, and spinning a roulette wheel.

We use the following terminology: An *outcome* is the result of a single experiment, and a *sample space* $S$ is the set of all the possible outcomes. An *event* $E$ is a set of (one or more) outcomes in $S$ that have some common properties. When an outcome that is a member of $E$ occurs, we say that the event $E$ occurs. These and many other terms are defined in Appendix A.

Since all $n$ possible outcomes have the same likelihood of occurring, we can find the likelihood that event $E$ will occur as the number $n_E$ of outcomes that belong to $E$ divided by the number $n$ of possible outcomes. The outcomes that belong to $E$ are sometimes called the *favorable* outcomes for $E$. The likelihood of getting an outcome from the experiment that belongs to $E$ is called the *probability* of $E$:

$$\Pr(E) = \frac{\text{no. of favorable outcomes}}{\text{total no. of possible outcomes}} = \frac{n_E}{n} \qquad (2.1)$$

The event $E$ can also be a single outcome. The likelihood of getting a particular outcome is then called the probability of the outcome and is given by $1/n$.

When—as in this case—all the outcomes in $S$ have the same probability of occurrence, we say that we have a *uniform* model.

**■ EXAMPLE 2.2   Flipping a coin**

Consider an experiment where you flip a coin. The experiment has $n = 2$ possible outcomes and the sample space of the experiment is $S = \{H, T\}$, where $H$ means that the outcome is a head, and $T$ that it is a tail. We assume that the coin is *fair* in the sense that both outcomes have the same probability of occurring. We want to find the probability of getting the event $E = \{H\}$. Only one of the $n = 2$ outcomes is favorable for this event (i.e., $n_E = 1$), and the probability of $E$ is therefore

$$\Pr(E) = \frac{n_E}{n} = \frac{1}{2}$$

$\oplus$

**■ EXAMPLE 2.3   Rolling two dice**

Consider an experiment where you roll two dice, one red and one blue. In this case, there are $n = 36$ possible outcomes and the sample space is

$$S = \begin{cases} (1,1) & (1.2) & (1,3) & (1,4) & (1.5) & (1,6) \\ (2,1) & (2,2) & (2,3) & (2,4) & (2,5) & (2,6) \\ (3,1) & (3,2) & (3,3) & (3,4) & (3,5) & (3,6) \\ (4,1) & (4,2) & (4,3) & (4,4) & (4,5) & (4,6) \\ (5,1) & (5,2) & (5,3) & (5,4) & (5,5) & (5,6) \\ (6,1) & (6,2) & (6,3) & (6,4) & (6,5) & (6,6) \end{cases}$$

where the first number is the outcome of the red die and the second of the blue die.

We assume that the dice are fair such that all outcomes in $S$ have the same probability of occurring. The event $E_1 =$ "same number of eyes on both dice" has $n_{E_1} = 6$ favorable outcomes and the probability of $E_1$ is

$$\Pr(E_1) = \frac{n_{E_1}}{n} = \frac{6}{36} = \frac{1}{6}$$

For the event $E_2 =$ "the sum of the eyes is 9," we have $n_{E_2} = 4$ and the probability of $E_2$ is

$$\Pr(E_2) = \frac{n_{E_2}}{n} = \frac{4}{36} = \frac{1}{9}$$

*Frequentist Approach.* The frequentist approach restricts our attention to phenomena that are inherently repeatable under essentially the same conditions. We call each repetition an *experiment*, and assume that each experiment may or may not give the event $E$. The experiment is repeated $n$ times as we count the number $n_E$ of the $n$ experiments that end up in the event $E$. The *relative frequency* of $E$ is defined as

$$f_n(E) = \frac{n_E}{n}$$

Since the conditions are the same for all experiments, the relative frequency will approach a limit when $n \to \infty$. This limit is called the *probability* of $E$ and is denoted by $\Pr(E)$

$$\Pr(E) = \lim_{n \to \infty} \frac{n_E}{n} \tag{2.2}$$

If we do a single experiment, we say that the probability of getting the outcome $E$ is $\Pr(E)$ and consider this probability a property of the experiment.

### EXAMPLE 2.4   Repeated experiments

Reconsider the experiment in Example 2.2. If you repeat the experiment several times and after each experiment calculate the relative frequency of heads ($E = \{H\}$), you will note that the relative frequency $f_n(E)$ fluctuates significantly for small values of $n$. When $n$ increases, $f_n(E)$ will come closer and closer to $1/2$. The probability of getting the event $E$ (head) is therefore

$$\Pr(E) = \lim_{n \to \infty} \frac{n_E}{n} = \frac{1}{2}$$

If we flip the coin once, we say that the probability of getting a head ($E$) is $\Pr(E) = 1/2$. We note that this probability is the same as the one we got by using the classical interpretation in Example 2.2.  ⊕

Notice that if the coin is *not* fair, we cannot use the classical approach, but the frequentist approach is still appropriate.

### EXAMPLE 2.5   Flipping a thumbtack

Consider an experiment where you flip a classical thumbtack (drawing pin). The experiment has two possible outcomes and the sample space is $S = \{U, D\}$, where $U$ means that the thumbtack will land point up and $D$ that it will land point down. In this case there is no symmetry between the two outcomes. We can therefore not use the classical approach to determine $\Pr(U)$, but have to carry out a large number of experiments to find $\Pr(U)$. The probability that we find may be considered a property of this particular thumbtack. If we choose another type of thumbtack, we will most likely get another probability.  ⊕

***Bayesian Approach.*** In a risk analysis, we almost never have a finite sample space of outcomes that will occur with the same probability. The classical approach to probability is therefore not appropriate. Furthermore, to apply the frequentist approach, we must at least be able to imagine that experiments can be repeated a large number of times under nearly identical conditions. Since this is rarely possible, we are therefore left with a final option, the Bayesian approach. In this approach, the probability is considered to be subjective and is defined as:

☞ **Subjective probability**: A numerical value in the interval $[0, 1]$ representing an individual's *degree of belief* about whether or not an event will occur.

In the Bayesian approach, it is not necessary to delimit probability to outcomes of experiments that are repeatable under the same conditions. It is fully acceptable to give the probability of an event that can only happen once. It is also acceptable to talk about the probability of events that are not the outcomes of experiments, but rather are statements or propositions. This can be a statement about the value of a nonobservable parameter, often referred to as a *state of nature*. To avoid a too-complicated terminology, we will also use the word *event* for statements, saying that an event occurs when a statement is true.

The degree of belief about an event $E$ is not arbitrary but is the analyst's best guess based on her available knowledge $\mathcal{K}$ about the event. The analyst's (subjective) probability of the event $E$, given that her knowledge is $\mathcal{K}$, should therefore be expressed as

$$\Pr(E \mid \mathcal{K}) \tag{2.3}$$

The knowledge $\mathcal{K}$ may come from knowledge about the physical properties of the event, earlier experience with the same type of event, expert judgment, and many other information sources. For simplicity, we often suppress $\mathcal{K}$ and simply write $\Pr(E)$. We should, however, never forget that this is a conditional probability depending on $\mathcal{K}$.

In a risk analysis, the word *subjective* may have a negative connotation. For this reason, some analysts prefer to use the word *personal probability*, since the probability is a personal judgment of an event that is based on the analyst's best knowledge and all the information she has available. The word *judgmental probability* is also sometimes used. To stress that the probability in the Bayesian approach is subjective (or personal or judgmental), we refer to the *analyst's* or *her/his/your/my* probability instead of *the* probability.

🖥 **EXAMPLE 2.6    Your subjective probability**

Assume that you are going to do a job tomorrow at 10:00 o'clock and that it is very important that it not be raining when you do this job. You want to find your (subjective) probability of the event $E$: "rain tomorrow between 10:00 and 10:15." This has no meaning in the frequentist (or classical) approach, because the "experiment" cannot be repeated. In the Bayesian approach, your probability

$\Pr(E)$ is a measure of your belief about the weather between 10:00 and 10:15. When you quantify this belief and, for example, say that $\Pr(E) = 0.08$, this is a measure of your belief about $E$. To come up with this probability, you may have studied historical weather reports for this area, checked the weather forecasts, looked at the sky, and so on. Based on all the information you can get hold of, you believe that there is an 8% chance that event $E$ occurs and that it will be raining between 10:00 and 10:15 tomorrow.                                              $\oplus$

The Bayesian approach can also be used when we have repeatable experiments. If we flip a coin and we know that the coin is symmetric, we believe that the probability of getting a head is $1/2$. The frequentist and the Bayesian approach will in this case give the same result.

An attractive feature of the Bayesian approach is the ability to update the subjective probability when more *evidence* becomes available. Assume that an analyst considers an event $E$ and that her initial or *prior* belief about this event is given by her prior probability $\Pr(E)$:

☞ **Prior probability**: An individual's belief in the occurrence of an event $E$ prior to any additional collection of evidence related to $E$.

Later, the analyst gets access to the data $D_1$, which contains information about event $E$. She can now use *Bayes formula* to state her updated belief, in light of the evidence $D_1$, expressed by the conditional probability

$$\Pr(E \mid D_1) = \Pr(E) \cdot \frac{\Pr(D_1 \mid E)}{\Pr(D_1)} \tag{2.4}$$

which is a simple consequence of the multiplication rule for probabilities

$$\Pr(E \cap D_1) = \Pr(E \mid D_1) \cdot \Pr(D_1) = \Pr(D_1 \mid E) \cdot \Pr(E)$$

The analyst's updated belief about $E$, after she has access to the evidence $D_1$, is called the *posterior probability* $\Pr(E \mid D_1)$.

☞ **Posterior probability**: An individual's belief in the occurrence of the event $E$ based on her prior belief *and* some additional evidence $D_1$.

Initially, the analyst's belief about the event $E$ is given by her prior probability $\Pr(E)$. After having obtained the evidence $D_1$, her probability of $E$ is, from (2.4), seen to change by a factor of $\Pr(D_1 \mid E) / \Pr(D_1)$.

Bayes formula (2.4) can be used repetitively. Having obtained the evidence $D_1$ and her posterior probability $\Pr(E \mid D_1)$, the analyst may consider this as her *current* prior probability. When additional evidence $D_2$ becomes available, she may update her current belief in the same way as above, and obtain her new posterior probability:

$$\Pr(E \mid D_1 \cap D_2) = \Pr(E) \cdot \frac{\Pr(D_1 \mid E)}{\Pr(D_1)} \cdot \frac{\Pr(D_2 \mid E)}{\Pr(D_2)} \tag{2.5}$$

Further updating of her belief about $E$ can be done sequentially as she obtains more and more evidence.

*Remark*: *Thomas Bayes* (1702–1761) was a British Presbyterian minister who has become famous for formulating the formula that bears his name—Bayes' formula (often written as Bayes formula). His derivation was published (posthumously) in 1763 in the paper *An essay towards solving a problem in the doctrine of chances* (Bayes, 1763). The general form of the formula was formulated in 1774 by the French mathematician *Pierre-Simon Laplace* (1749–1825). ⊕

*Likelihood.* By the posterior probability $\Pr(E \mid D_1)$ in (2.4), the analyst expresses her belief about the unknown state of nature $E$ when the evidence $D_1$ is given and known. The interpretation of $\Pr(D_1 \mid E)$ in (2.4) may therefore be a bit confusing since $D_1$ is known. Instead, we should interpret $\Pr(D_1 \mid E)$ as the *likelihood* that the (unknown) state of nature is $E$, when we know that we have got the evidence $D_1$.

In our daily language, *likelihood* is often used with the same meaning as *probability*. There is, however, a clear distinction between the two concepts in statistical usage. In statistics, likelihood is a distinctive concept that is used, for example, when we estimate parameters (maximum likelihood principle) and for testing hypotheses (likelihood ratio test).

*Remark*: In Chapter 1 and the first part of Chapter 2, we have used the word *likelihood* as a synonym for probability, as we often do in our daily parlance. The reason for this rather imprecise use of the word *likelihood* is that we wanted to avoid using the word *probability* until it was properly introduced—and also because we wanted to present the main definitions of risk concepts with the same wording that is used in standards and guidelines. ⊕

### 2.3.2 Controversy

The debate between the frequentists and the Bayesians, or subjectivists, has been going on for more than 200 years. The subjectivist position is aptly summarized by de Finetti (1974):

> My thesis, paradoxically, and a little provocating, but nevertheless genuinely, is simply this
>
> PROBABILITY DOES NOT EXIST.
>
> The abandonment of superstitious beliefs about the existence of Phlogiston, the Cosmic Ether, Absolute Space and Time, ... or Fairies and Witches, was an essential step along the road to scientific thinking. Probability, too, if regarded as something endowed with some kind of objective existence, is no less a misleading misconception, an illusory attempt to exteriorize or materialize our true probabilistic beliefs.

In risk analysis, it is not realistic to assume that the events are repeatable under essentially the same conditions. We cannot, for example, have the same explosion over and over again under the same conditions. This means that we need to use the Bayesian approach. Although most risk analysts agree on this view, there is an ongoing controversy about the interpretation of the subjective probability. There are two main schools:

1. The first school claims that the subjective probability is *subjective* in a strict sense. Two individuals will generally come up with two different numerical values of the subjective probability of an event, even if they have exactly the same knowledge. This view is, for example, advocated by Lindley (2007), who claims that individuals will have different preferences and hence judge information in different ways.

2. The second school claims that the subjective probability is dependent only on *knowledge*. Two individuals with exactly the same knowledge $\mathcal{K}$ will always give the same numerical value of the subjective probability of an event. This view is, for example, advocated by Jaynes (2003), who states:

   > A probability assignment is "subjective" in the sense that it describes a state of knowledge rather than any property of the "real" world, but is "objective" in the sense that it is independent of the personality of the user. Two rational human beings faced with the same total background of knowledge must assign the same probabilities [also quoted and supported by Garrick (2008)].

The quotation from Jaynes (2003) also touches on another controversy: that is, whether the probability of an event $E$ is a *property* of the event $E$, the experiment producing $E$, *or* a subjective probability that exists only in the individual's mind.

### ▟ EXAMPLE 2.7   Constant failure rate

A specific valve is claimed to have a constant failure rate $\lambda$ (see Appendix A). The failure rate is a parameter of the time to failure distribution of the valve and it is not possible to *observe* the value of $\lambda$. The value of $\lambda$ can sometimes be *estimated* based on recorded times-to-failure of several valves of the same type. We may consider a statement (event) $E = \{\lambda > \lambda_0\}$, where $\lambda_0$ is some specified value. In this case, the controversy concerns whether the probability $\Pr(E)$ is a property of the valve or just a value that exists in the analyst's mind.          $\oplus$

### ▟ EXAMPLE 2.8   Ignition of a gas leak

Consider a gas leak in a process plant. Let $p$ denote the probability that the gas leak will ignite. If the ignition probability $p$ is considered to be a *property* of this situation, the analyst's job is to try to reveal the true value of $p$. After gathering all the information she can get hold of, she may specify her degree of belief about this ignition probability by the estimate $\hat{p}$. In this case, it gives meaning to a discussion of whether or not $\hat{p}$ is an accurate estimate of $p$, and she may try to assess the uncertainty of $\hat{p}$. This is discussed further in Chapter 16.

If, however, we believe that the ignition probability exists only in our minds, it would be meaningless to try to determine the accuracy of her estimate $\hat{p}$, since a "true" value of $p$ does not exist. She may obviously discuss the uncertainty related to the knowledge, data, and information she has used to come up with her estimate, but not the accuracy of the value as such.                                    ⊕

The mathematical rules for manipulating probabilities are well understood and are not controversial. A nice feature of probability theory is that we can use the same symbols and formulas whether we choose the frequentist or the Bayesian approach, and whether or not we consider probability as a property of the situation. The interpretation of the results will, however, be different.

***Remark***: Some researchers claim that the frequentist approach is *objective* and therefore the only feasible approach in many important areas: for example, when testing the effects of new drugs. According to their view, such a test cannot be based on subjective beliefs. This view is probably flawed since the frequentist approach also applies models that are based on a range of assumptions, most of which are subjective.                                    ⊕

### 2.3.3  Frequency

When an event $E$ occurs more or less frequently, we often talk about the frequency of $E$ rather than the probability of $E$. We may ask, for example: "How frequently does event $E$ occur?"

Fatal traffic accidents occur several times per year, and we may record the number $n_E(t)$ of such accidents during a period of length $t$. A fatal traffic accident is understood as an accident where one or more persons are killed. The frequency of fatal traffic accidents in the time interval $(0, t)$ is given by

$$f_t(E) = \frac{n_E(t)}{t} \tag{2.6}$$

The "time" $t$ may be given as calendar time, accumulated operational time (e.g., the accumulated number of hours that cars are on the road), accumulated number of kilometers driven, and so on.

In some cases, we may assume that the situation is kept unchanged and that the frequency will approach a constant limit when $t \to \infty$. We call this limit the *rate* of the event $E$ and denote it by $\lambda_E$:

$$\lambda_E = \lim_{t \to \infty} \frac{n_E(t)}{t} \tag{2.7}$$

**Table 2.1**   Some types of assets.

| | |
|---|---|
| – Humans (first, second, third, fourth party) | – Historical monuments, national heritage objects |
| – Community | – Financial assets |
| – The environment (animals, birds, fish, air, water, soil, landscape, natural preserve areas, built environment) | – Intangibles (e.g., reputation, goodwill, quality of life) |
| | – Timing or schedule of activities (project or mission risk) |
| – Performance (e.g., availability of a production system, punctuality of a railway service) | – Organizational behavior |
| – Material assets (e.g., buildings, equipment, infrastructure) | |

In the frequentist interpretation of probability, parameters like $\lambda_E$ have a true, albeit unknown value. The parameters are estimated based on observed values, and confidence intervals are used to quantify the variability in the parameter estimators.

Models and formulas for the analysis may be found in Appendix A.

## 2.4  Assets and Consequences

To answer the third question in the triplet definition of risk "What are the consequences?", we first have to identify who—or what—might be harmed. In this book, these "objects" are called *assets*.

☞ **Asset**: Something we value and want to preserve.

*Assets* are also called *targets, vulnerable targets, victims, recipients, receptors*, and *risk-absorbing items*. Examples of assets are listed in Table 2.1. Note that the sequence of the assets in Table 2.1 does not imply any priority or ranking.

### 2.4.1  Categories of Human Victims

In a risk analysis, humans are usually considered to be the most important assets. The possible victims of an accident are sometimes classified according to their proximity to and influence on the hazard (Perrow, 1984):

1. *First-party victims*. These are people directly involved in the operation of the system.

2. *Second-party victims*. These are people who are associated with the system as suppliers or users, but exert no influence over it. Even though such exposure

may not be entirely voluntary, these people are not innocent bystanders, because they are aware of (or could be informed about) their exposure. Passengers on airplanes, ships, and railways, for example, are considered to be second-party victims.

3. *Third-party victims*. These are innocent bystanders who have no involvement in the system: for example, people living in the neighborhood of a plant.

4. *Fourth-party victims*. These are victims of yet-unborn generations. The category includes fetuses that are carried while their parents are exposed to radiation or toxic materials, and all those people who will be contaminated in the future by residual substances, including substances that become concentrated as they move up the food chain.

---

**▣  EXAMPLE 2.9   Victims of railway accidents**

The railway industry sometimes classifies human assets in five categories:

(a) Passengers

(b) Employees

(c) People on the road or footpath crossings of the line

(d) Trespassers (who are close to the line without permission)

(e) Other persons                                                                              ⊕

---

### 2.4.2  Consequences and Harm

A *consequence* involves specific damage to one or more assets and is also called *adverse effect, impact, impairment*, or *loss*. The term *harm* is used in several important standards, including IEC 60300-3-9 and ISO 12100.

☞ **Harm**: Physical injury or damage to health, property, or the environment
(IEC 60300-3-9, 1995).

*Consequence Categories.*   The adverse effects of an accident may be classified into several categories related to the assets, such as:

  – Loss of human life

  – Personal injury

  – Reduction in life expectancy

  – Damage to the environment (fauna, flora, soil, water, air, climate, landscape)

- Damage to material assets

- Investigation and cleanup costs

- Business-interruption losses

- Loss of staff productivity

- Loss of information

- Loss of reputation (public relations)

- Insurance deductible costs

- Fines and citations

- Legal action and damage claims

- Business-sustainability consequences

- Societal disturbances

- Consequences related to so-called "soft values," such as reduction of human well-being and loss of freedom.

*Remark*: The consequences we consider here are mainly unwanted (negative) consequences that represent some kind of loss. It is, however, possible that a hazardous event may also lead to wanted or positive consequences. Such positive consequences are not considered in this book. ⊕

For harm to people, it is common to distinguish between:

- *Temporary harm.* In this case the person is harmed but will be totally restored and able to work within a period after the accident.

- *Permanent disability.* In this case the person will get permanent illness or disability. The degree of disability is sometimes given as a percentage.

- *Fatality.* The person will die from the harm, either immediately or because of complications. The fatality may sometimes occur a long time after the accident: for example, due to cancer caused by radiation after a nuclear accident.

### 2.4.3 Severity

It is often useful to classify the possible consequences of a hazardous event according to their *severity*:

☞ **Severity**: Seriousness of the consequences of an event expressed either as a financial value or as a category.

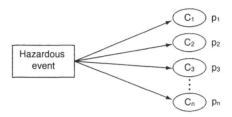

**Figure 2.2**     Consequence spectrum for a hazardous event.

It is most common to express the severity as categories: for example, as *catastrophic*, *severe loss*, *major damage*, *damage*, or *minor damage*. Each category has to be described. This is discussed further in Section 4.4.

### 2.4.4  Consequence Spectrum

A hazardous event may lead to a number of potential consequences $C_1$, $C_2$, ..., $C_n$. The probability $p_i$ that consequence $C_i$ will occur depends on the physical situation and whether or not the barriers are functioning. The possible consequences and the associated probabilities resulting from the hazardous event are illustrated in Figure 2.2.

The diagram in Figure 2.2 is called a *consequence spectrum*, a *risk picture*, or a *risk profile* related to the hazardous event. The consequence spectrum may also be written as a vector:

$$C = [C_1, C_2, \ldots, C_n]_{[p_1, p_2, \ldots, p_n]} \tag{2.8}$$

In Figure 2.2 and in the vector (2.8), we have tacitly assumed that the consequences can be classified into a finite number ($n$) of discrete consequences.

An activity may lead to several potential hazardous events. It may therefore be relevant to set up the consequence for an activity rather than for a single hazardous event. Each hazardous event will then have a consequence spectrum, as illustrated in Figure 2.2. If we combine all the relevant hazardous events, we can establish a consequence spectrum for the activity that is similar to that of a hazardous event. The consequence spectrum may also be presented in a table, as shown in Table 2.2.

In some cases, it may be possible to measure the consequences in a common unit (e.g., in U.S. dollars). Let $\ell(C_i)$ denote the *loss* in dollars if consequence $C_i$ occurs, for $i = 1, 2, \ldots, n$. The loss spectrum for the hazardous event can then be pictured as in Figure 2.3.

In this case, it may also be meaningful to talk about the mean consequence or *mean loss* if the hazardous event should occur:

$$E[\ell(C)] = \sum_{i=1}^{n} \ell(C_i) \cdot p_i \tag{2.9}$$

Note that (2.9) is the *conditional* mean loss given that the specified hazardous event has occurred.

**Table 2.2**   Consequence spectrum for an activity (example).

| $i$ | Consequence ($C_i$) | Probability ($p_i$) |
|---|---|---|
| 1 | Operator is killed | 0.001 |
| 2 | Operator is permanently disabled | 0.004 |
| 3 | Operator is temporarily injured | 0.008 |
| ⋮ | ⋮ | ⋮ |
| n | Minor material damage | 0.450 |

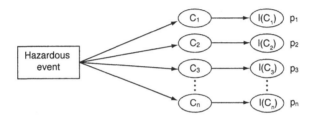

**Figure 2.3**   Loss spectrum for a hazardous event.

### 2.4.5   Time of Recording Consequences

Some of the consequences of an accident may occur immediately, while others may not materialize until years after the accident. People are, for example, still dying of cancer in 2011 as a consequence of the Chernobyl disaster in 1986. A large quantity of nuclear fallout was released and spread as far as northern Norway. During the accident, only a few persons were harmed physically, but several years after the accident, a number of people developed cancer and died from the fallout. The same applies for other accidents involving dangerous materials. When we assess the consequences of an accident, it is therefore important not only to consider the immediate consequences, but also to consider the delayed effects.

### 2.5   Risk

According to Timmerman (1986), the word *risk* entered the English language in the 1660s from the Italian word *riscare*, which means to navigate among dangerous rocks. As pointed out in Chapter 1, we will use the term *risk* only in relation to future events that may, or may not happen. We never use the term *risk* when we talk about our more or less dangerous past. The term is also restricted to "negative" consequences—even if risk refers to both gains and losses in economic theory.

**Table 2.3**    Risk related to a system (example).

| $i$ | Event $i$ | Frequency ($f_i$) | Consequence ($C_i$) |
|---|---|---|---|
| 1 | Gas leak in area 1 | 0.01 | Consequence spectrum 1 |
| 2 | Falling load from crane 2 | 0.03 | Consequence spectrum 2 |
| ⋮ | ⋮ | ⋮ | ⋮ |

*Remark*: One should, however, note that the labeling of a consequence as positive or negative represents social judgments and cannot be derived from the nature of the hazardous events (Klinke and Renn, 2002). ⊕

As indicated in Chapter 1, there is no universally accepted definition of risk. In this book, we define risk as the answer to the three questions of Kaplan and Garrick (1981):

☞ **Risk**: The combined answer to three questions: (1) What can go wrong? (2) What is the likelihood of that happening? and (3) What are the consequences?

The answers to the three questions may be presented as in Table 2.3, where the column "Event $i$" denotes an initiating event, a hazardous event, or an accident scenario. For most applications, we recommend that the events be defined as hazardous events. The frequency $f_i$ is the frequency of event $i$. Instead of frequency, it may sometimes be relevant to use probability. The consequence spectrum $C_i$ describes the consequences that may occur if event $i$ has occurred. The probabilities will depend on the capability and reliability of the reactive barriers that are available in the system.

The risk related to a specified event may be illustrated by a bow-tie diagram such as the one in Figure 1.1. If we move the event to the left in the diagram, the number of possible event sequences will increase. In most cases, the frequency analysis will then be simpler and the consequence analysis will be more complex. On the other hand, if we move the event to the right in the bow-tie diagram, the frequency analysis will be more complicated and the consequence analysis will be simpler. To define the event as a complete accident scenario will be the extreme point in this respect, for which the consequence spectrum will be reduced to the consequences of a single end event. Which of these approaches gives the best and most complete result will depend on the system.

In the following, we assume that the event is a hazardous event and denote the various events by $s_1, s_2, \ldots, s_n$. Kaplan and Garrick (1981) express the risk $R$ related to the system by the set of triplets

$$R = \left\{ \langle s_i, f_i, C_i \rangle \right\}_{i=1}^{n}$$

If all relevant hazardous events are included, the set of triplets can be considered to be complete and hence to represent the risk. The consequence spectrum $C_i$ is a multidimensional vector which includes damage to people, property, the environment, and so on. $C_i$ may also be timedependent if the magnitude of damage varies with time. A nuclear meltdown, for example, will have different consequences depending on at which point in time one stops to "measure" the damage.

The probability $p$ associated with each consequence lies between 0 and 1, where $p = 0$ means that the event is impossible and $p = 1$ signals that it is always true. Both extremities correspond to a fatalistic world view in which the future is conceived of as independent of human activities. According to Rosa (1998), the term *risk* would be of no use in such a world of predetermined outcomes. At the heart of the concept of risk is thus the idea that the consequences admit to some degree of uncertainty.

### 2.5.1  Alternative Definitions of Risk

Several alternative definitions of risk have been suggested in the literature. Among these are:

(a) *Combination of the frequency, or probability, of occurrence and the consequences of a specified hazardous event* (IEC 60300-3-9, 1995).

In this definition, risk is linked to one specific hazardous event. We may, for example, talk about the risk related to a specific gas leak or related to falling loads from a crane. This is different from the definition we are using, where the risk is related to a system or an activity for which several hazardous events may occur.

(b) *The possibility that human actions or events lead to consequences that harm aspects of things that human beings value* (Klinke and Renn, 2002).

(c) *Situation or event where something of human value (including humans themselves) has been put at stake and where the outcome is uncertain* (Rosa, 1998).

(d) *Uncertainty about and severity of the consequences (or outcomes) of an activity with respect to something that humans value* (Aven and Renn, 2009a).

(e) *The probability that a particular adverse event occurs during a stated period of time, or results from a particular challenge* (Royal Society, 1992, p. 22).

(f) *Risk refers to the uncertainty that surrounds future events and outcomes. It is the expression of the likelihood and impact of an event with the potential to influence the achievement of an organization's objectives* (Treasury Board, 2001).

Thorough discussions of the various definitions and aspects of risk are given, for example, by Lupton (1999) and Johansen (2010b).

### 2.5.2 Safety Performance

In this book we use the word *risk* to describe our uncertainty about adverse events that may occur in the *future*. Sometimes, decision-makers may be wondering "whether the estimated risk in the coming period (e.g., five years) is higher or lower than the risk was in the past period." With our definition of risk, speaking of risk in the past has no meaning. This is because when a period is over, there is no uncertainty related to what happened in that period. We therefore need another term that can be used to describe what happened in a past period—and will use the term *safety performance*.

☞ **Safety performance**: An account of all accidents that occurred in a specified (past) time period, together with frequencies and consequences observed for each type of accident.

The frequencies can be given by many different "time" concepts: for example, per calendar time, per hour in operation, per kilometer driven, and so on. In this way, the estimated risk in the coming period can be compared to the safety performance in the past period.

We should remember that the occurrence of hazardous events and accidents is—at least partly—a random process. If the risk in the coming period is estimated to be rather high, and by the end of that period we find that the safety performance in the period showed no accidents, this does not mean that the risk analysis was wrong.

▉ **EXAMPLE 2.10   Helicopter transport risk**

SINTEF, a Norwegian research organization, has for more than 20 years carried out a sequence of safety studies of helicopter transport to and from Norwegian offshore oil and gas installations. This transport has resulted in several accidents, and the main objectives of the studies have been to identify the main contributors to the high risk and to propose risk-reducing measures.

Data from accidents have been collected and the safety performance has been analyzed to identify causal factors and trends. During these 20 years, there have been a lot of changes related to helicopter design, equipment, and maintenance, to the air traffic control, to heliports and helidecks, and so on.

A goal of the Norwegian petroleum authorities is to reduce the helicopter transport risk and they therefore ask: "What is the risk in the coming period compared to the risk in the previous period?" Risk analyses have been carried out to estimate the risk in the coming period (e.g., five years), and the risk estimates have been compared with the safety performance in previous periods.
⊕

### 2.5.3 Risk-Influencing Factors

Hokstad et al. (2001) define a risk-influencing factor as:

☞ **Risk influencing factor (RIF)**: A relatively stable condition that influences the risk.

A RIF is not an isolated event but an enduring condition that influences the occurrence of hazardous events and the performance of the barriers. RIFs may therefore be categorized as either frequency-influencing factors or consequence-influencing factors. The RIFs represent average conditions that can be improved by certain actions and hence are under the influence of risk managers.

▨ **EXAMPLE 2.11    Risk-influencing factors in helicopter transport**

As part of the helicopter safety studies (see Example 2.10), SINTEF has identified a set of RIFs that influence the risk of helicopter transport. The RIFs are classified into three main categories:

(a) *Operational RIFs*, which relate to the activities that are necessary to ensure that helicopter transport is safe and efficient on a day-to-day basis: for example, operations, procedures, and maintenance.

(b) *Organizational RIFs*, which comprise the organizational basis, support, and control of helicopter activities concerning helicopter manufacturers, operators, and so on.

(c) *Regulatory and customer-related RIFs*, which concern requirements and controlling activities from national and international aviation authorities and customers.                                                                                    ⊕

RIFs play a central role in the risk assessment methodology BORA (barrier and operational risk analysis), which models the effect of operational and organizational factors on risk in offshore activities (Sklet, 2006b). Following this methodology, the performance of safety barriers is assessed by use of *risk influence diagrams* and weighting of relevant RIFs. BORA is discussed further in Chapter 12.

### 2.5.4  Desired Risk

Within the field of risk analysis, risk is usually considered to be an unwanted side effect of technological activities. However, in our modern society, risk is sometimes deliberately sought and desired. Machilis and Rosa (1990) refer to this as desired risk:

☞ **Desired risk**: Risk that is sought, not avoided, because of the thrill and intrinsic enjoyment it brings.

Gambling, high-speed driving, drug use, and recreational activities such as hanggliding, skydiving, and mountain climbing are high-risk activities that people engage in for reasons of sensationseeking, social reward, and mastery. Common to all is that risk is attractive and essential to the experience. In the eye of the performer, it is therefore not a principal aim to minimize desired risk, but rather, to seek it out.

### 2.5.5 Risk Homeostasis

Wilde (1982) claims that every person has her or his own fixed level of acceptable risk. If the perception of danger increases, people behave more cautiously. On the other hand, people tend to behave less cautiously in situations where they feel safer or more protected. This theory is called *risk homeostasis*. Wilde (1982) argues that the same is also true for larger human systems: for example, a population of car drivers. When the technical safety of cars increases, the drivers will tend to drive less cautiously.

### 2.5.6 Residual Risk

Risk analysis provides an estimate of the risk associated with a particular set of hazardous events. After the analysis has been completed, it must be determined whether the risk is acceptable or if risk-reducing measures are necessary. The risk that remains after introducing such measures is the residual risk:

☞ **Residual risk**: The risk that remains after engineering, administrative, and work practice controls have been implemented (SEMATECH, 1999).

Residual risk is closely related to risk acceptance. If acceptable risk is defined according to the ALARP principle (see Chapter 4), then residual risk means the risk that is evaluated to be as low as reasonably practicable. By reference to deterministic risk acceptance criteria, the residual risk is, instead, acceptable at the cutoff limit and no further evaluation is required. Note that this also holds for unmitigated consequences that are considered acceptable without implementation of risk-reducing measures.

### 2.5.7 Perceived Risk

When people without professional expertise make intuitive judgments about risk, it is not called risk assessment, but *risk perception*.

☞ **Risk perception**: Subjective judgment about the characteristics and severity of risk.

Risk perception consists basically of our attitudes and mental images of the severity of risks. It is influenced by a broad set of phenomena that go beyond the mere technical conception of risk as a combination of accident scenarios, probabilities, and adverse outcomes. Central to risk perception are factors such as voluntariness, novelty, controllability, and dread (Slovic, 1987).

Several theories have been proposed to explain why different people make different judgments of risks. Psychology approaches are concerned with cognitive biases (called *heuristics*) and negative affect, while anthropologists explain risk perception as a product of cultural belonging and institutional mistrust. Interdisciplinary approaches, such as the framework *social amplification of risk* (Kasperson et al., 1988), focus on information processes, institutional structures, and social responses.

Studying risk perception is important because it explains how people behave in hazardous situations and make decisions in face of risk. Carefully designed risk management programs, such as antismoking campaigns, are of little value if people perceive the risk as low and do not see the need to comply. On the other hand, the public resistance toward nuclear power plants in the United States and Europe in the 1970s demonstrated that risk perceptions may cause a riot even though risk assessments conclude that the risk is low.

◨ **EXAMPLE 2.12   Aversion to major accidents**

> For most people, a major accident with 100 fatalities occurring once per 100 years will be more significant than 100 annual accidents with one fatality per accident, even though the average fatality rate per year is the same. This reflects our aversion to major accidents or dread consequences.            ⊕

Factors that affect our perception of risk are described differently in the literature, but the following factors are often included:

- Familiarity (a new risk may be treated with greater caution than an old one).

- Voluntariness (people are more tolerant of risks when they can control their exposure to the hazard).

- Degree of control (tolerance of risk is higher if the probability of risk can be influenced).

- Potential for catastrophe (there is a lower tolerance for risks that could result in a catastrophe).

- Dread (some risks induce more fear than others).

- How well known the risk is to science.

### 2.5.8  Controversy

The old controversy on probability has evolved into conflicts over the interpretation of quantitative risk analysis and its results.

***Classical Approach.***   In the classical approach to risk analysis, risk is considered to be a *property of the world*, and the objective of the risk analysis is to describe and characterize this risk as accurately as possible. The result of the quantitative risk analysis, the risk picture, is considered to be a description and estimate of the *true* risk, which exists, but is not known to us.

Some authors consider this risk as an objective property of an event, a system, or an activity. They talk about *objective risk* or *real risk* and quantify the risk as a listing of consequences with associated probabilities. Hansson (2010) claims that we have objective risk when:

☞ **Objective risk**: An accurate and reasonably complete characterization of a risk can be made by stating (only) objective facts about the physical world.

**Bayesian Approach.** In the Bayesian or subjective approach to risk assessment, risk is considered to be a *mental construction* without any counterpart in the real world. According to Slovic (1992):

> Human beings have invented the concept of "risk" [ ... ] there is no such thing as "real risk" or "objective risk."

If risk does not exist as a "property of the world," it exists only as a perception in our minds and Shrader-Frechette (1991) claims that:

> In sum, there is no distinction between perceived and actual risks because there are no risks except perceived risks. If there were hazards that were not perceived, then we would not know them.

Hansson (2010) uses the term *subjective risk* when:

☞ **Subjective risk**: An accurate and reasonably complete characterization of a risk does not refer to any objective facts about the physical world.

Klinke and Renn (2002) argue that a purely subjective risk interpretation may have limitations and state that "If risk assessments are nothing but social constructions, they have no more normative validity for guiding regulatory action than stakeholder estimates or public perceptions." Although the analysis is based on subjective interpretations of a socially constructed concept, this does not diminish the value of risk assessment, according to Bayesian followers. We can still gain useful knowledge about the factors that influence risk and provide reasonable measures for our degree of belief through judgment and deliberation. Note that now the uncertainty of the results is not related to whether the probability is close to some *true* measure, but rather to the range of subjective beliefs.

**Dual View.** Some authors take a pragmatic view and consider risk to be a property of the world when this seems relevant and to be a mental construction when they have problems with the first view. Hansson (2010) states that these authors have a dual view on risk:

☞ **Dual view on risk**: An accurate and reasonably complete characterization of a risk must refer to objective facts about the physical world and to (value) statements that do not refer to objective facts about the physical world.

We will not pursue this discussion further here, but refer the reader to the vast literature in this field. A good starting point may be Rosa (1998) and Aven (2003).

***Positivistic versus Constructivistic Paradigm.*** Risk research is predominated by two contending paradigms for understanding risk; positivistic science and constructivism. The paradigms are rooted in philosophy and the notion of *ontology*, which relates to states of the world and their nature of existence (Rosa, 1998).

The positivistic way of thinking is based on the ontology of *realism*. Here, the world is believed to exist independent of human observation and existence. There is only one world, which is a world that is real and made of objective states. This is the very basis of science, which presupposes that the world is amenable to systematic inquiry. Since any risk analysis is based on science, ontological realism is also the bedrock of risk analysis. Risk is in this interpretation an objective state of the world that exists whether or not we know about it.

In contrast is the constructivistic paradigm, which denies that risk is anywhere but in our minds. The world cannot be separated from our interpretation of it, and there is no existence beyond our perception. It therefore becomes meaningless to distinguish between "risk" and "perceived risk," since *all* risks are perceived (Shrader-Frechette, 1991). At the constructivist extreme, the *cultural theory* of Douglas and Wildavsky (1983) defines risk as a social construction that is devoid of objective reality. Risk is hence not a physical but a cultural phenomenon, which comes into existence first when we have defined it as such.

The problem with extreme accounts of both positivism and constructivism is that they take a reductionistic view of risk as a mere scientific or sociological concept. Risk is independent of neither context nor the physical world:

> Whatever our perceptions, right or wrong, some risks are undeniably real—not merely our cultural judgment about them (Rosa, 1998, p. 32).

We will all die someday, but it is not death itself that is the risk; it is its cause and timing. It is therefore useful to distinguish between the realism (ontology) and our knowledge of risk, which need not necessarily coincide (Rosa, 1998).

The following example may be too simplistic, but it illustrates that the risk may be real—at least in some cases.

### ▉ EXAMPLE 2.13 Russian roulette

Consider a game of Russian roulette, where a person places a single round in a revolver with six chambers, spins the cylinder, points the muzzle against her head (temple) and pulls the trigger. The risk may be characterized by three elements:

1. Hazardous event: The round is discharged.

2. Probability: One out of six outcomes will cause the hazardous event to occur. To obtain symmetry, the other five "rounds" may be dummies with the same weight as the real round. If we assume that the cylinder is spun properly, and that a high-quality revolver and high-quality ammunition are used, the probability of the hazardous event is close to $1/6$.

3. Consequence: If the revolver is held properly, the person will die immediately if the hazardous event occurs. ⊕

**Table 2.4**   Categories of barriers.

| *Physical barriers*: | *Administrative barriers*: |
|---|---|
| – Equipment and engineering design | – Hazard identification and analyses |
| – Personal protective equipment (e.g., clothes, hard hats, glasses) | – Line management oversight |
| | – Supervision |
| – Fire walls, shields | – Inspection and testing |
| – Safety devices (e.g., relief valves, emergency shutdown systems, fire extinguishers) | – Work planning |
| | – Work procedures |
| – Warning devices (e.g., fire and gas alarms) | *Management barriers*: |
| | – Training |
| | – Knowledge and skills |
| | – Rules and regulations |

## 2.6   Barriers

As mentioned in Chapter 1, most well-designed systems have *barriers* that can prevent or reduce the probability of hazardous events, or stop or mitigate their consequences.

☞ **Barrier**: Physical or engineered system or human action (based on specific procedures or administrative controls) that is implemented to prevent, control, or impede energy released from reaching the assets and causing harm.

Barriers are also called *safeguards, protection layers, defenses*, or *countermeasures*. Barriers are discussed in more detail in Chapter 12. Some categories of barriers are listed in Table 2.4.

### 2.6.1   Classification of Barriers

Johnson (1980) classifies barriers as:

1. Barriers that surround and confine the energy source (the hazard).

2. Barriers that protect the asset.

3. Barriers that separate the hazard and the asset physically, in time or space.

Barriers may be classified further as:

*Proactive barriers.* These barriers are also called prevention and control barriers. Proactive barriers are installed to prevent hazardous events from occurring.

*Reactive barriers.* These barriers are also called *mitigation barriers.* Reactive barriers are activated after a hazardous event has taken place to stop or mitigate one or more of the event sequences that may follow after the hazardous event.

▇ **EXAMPLE 2.14    Barriers related to gas leaks in petroleum process plants**

Barriers that are installed to stop or mitigate the consequences of a gas leak in a petroleum process plant may comprise:

– Gas detection system and alarm

– Process shutdown system

– Isolation of ignition sources

– Firefighting systems

– Fire walls

– Evacuation systems                                                           ⊕

### 2.6.2  Mitigation

The word *mitigation* is often used in association with barriers. In most dictionaries, mitigation is defined as:

☞ **Mitigation**: Action to reduce the severity, seriousness, or painfulness of something.

In risk management, the word *mitigation* is used primarily in relation to reactive barriers that are implemented to avoid, minimize, or rectify consequences to assets after a hazardous event has occurred.

### 2.6.3  Defense-in-Depth

The defense-in-depth strategy was introduced in the nuclear industry and is the practice of having multiple, redundant, and independent barriers related to a single hazardous event. The goal is to create and maintain multiple barriers that will compensate for potential human errors and mechanical failures, so that no single layer, no matter how robust, is relied upon exclusively. Defense-in-depth is usually a deterministic strategy in the sense that it is not based on the results of a risk analysis.

## 2.7  Accidents

Johnson (1980) defines an accident as:

☞ **Accident (1)**: An unwanted transfer of energy, because of lack of barriers and/or controls, producing injury to persons, property, or process, preceded by sequences of planning and operational errors, which failed to adjust to changes in physical or human factors and produced unsafe conditions and/or unsafe acts, arising out of the risk in an activity, and interrupting or degrading the activity.

An alternative and more brief definition of an accident is:

☞ **Accident (2)**: A sudden, unwanted, and unplanned event or event sequence that leads to harm to people, the environment, or other assets.

Definition (2) implies that an accident is not predictable with respect to whether and when it will occur. The definition also emphasizes that an accident is a distinct event and not a long-term exposure to some dangerous material or energy. Suchman (1961) argues that an event can be classified as an accident only if it is unexpected, unavoidable, and unintended.

Accidents and accident models are discussed in more detail in Chapter 6.

### ▣  EXAMPLE 2.15   Helicopter accidents

In the helicopter studies of SINTEF, helicopter accidents are classified into eight categories:

1. Accident during takeoff or landing on a heliport

2. Accident during takeoff or landing on a helideck (i.e., on an offshore platform)

3. Accident caused by critical aircraft failure during flight

4. Midair collision with another aircraft

5. Collision with terrain, sea, or a building structure

6. Personnel accident inside a helicopter (i.e., caused by toxic gases due to fire or cargo)

7. Personnel accident outside a helicopter (i.e., hit by tail rotor)

8. Other accident

The studies are limited to accidents involving helicopter crew and passengers. Accidents involving other persons and other assets are not included.          ⊕

### 2.7.1 Incidents and Near Accidents

The term *incident* may be defined as:

☞ **Incident**: An unplanned and unforeseen event that may or may not result in harm to one or more assets.

According to this definition, an accident is a special case of incident: that is, an incident that results in harm to assets. Incidents are sometimes referred to as *mishaps*.

*Remark*: It is not always easy to distinguish between the concepts of hazardous event and incident. A hazardous event is a single event that initiates a release of energy and a sequence of events that may ultimately damage an asset. An incident may be a single event or a sequence of events that may or may not harm an asset. $\oplus$

The term *near accident* may be defined as:

☞ **Near accident**: An unplanned and unforeseen event that could reasonably have been expected to result in harm to one or more assets, but actually did not.

With this terminology, a near accident is an incident that is not an accident. A near accident is also called a *near miss*.

Near accidents are sometimes referred to as *precursors*, as they typically comprise hazardous events where the protecting barriers have functioned properly. A precursor may also be a protection system that was out of service, such that if a hazardous event had occurred, a release of energy would have taken place (e.g., see US DOE, 1996b).

### 2.7.2 Special Types of Accidents

Accident causation and accident models are discussed in more detail in Chapter 6. The development of accident theory has been strongly influenced by the views of Charles Perrow and James Reason, who have introduced new notions for major accidents.

Reason (1997) introduced the concept of organizational accident, which may be defined as:

☞ **Organizational accident**: A comparatively rare, but often catastrophic, event that occurs within complex modern technologies (e.g., nuclear power plants, commercial aviation, the petrochemical industry, chemical process plants, marine and rail transport, banks, and stadiums) and has multiple causes involving many people operating at different levels of their respective companies. Organizational accidents will often have devastating effects on uninvolved populations, assets, and the environment.

Reason (1997) calls accidents that cannot be classified as organizational accidents, individual accidents:

☞ **Individual accident**: An accident in which a specific person or group is often both the agent and the victim of the accident. The consequences to the people concerned may be great, but their spread is limited.

In his pioneering book *Normal Accidents: Living with High-Risk Technologies*, Perrow (1984) introduces the concepts of *system accident* and *normal accident*. We return to the normal accident theory in Chapter 6, so here we just define his concept of system accident:

☞ **System accident**: An accident that arises in the interactions among components (electromechanical, digital, and human) rather than in the failure of individual components (Perrow, 1984).

In analogy with the terminology of Reason (1997), an accident that cannot be classified as a system accident is sometimes called a component failure accident:

☞ **Component failure accident**: An accident arising from component failures, including the possibility of multiple and cascading failures (e.g., see Leveson, 2004)

## 2.8  Uncertainty

*Uncertainty* is a term with several meanings. In a general sense, it covers anything that is not known certainly or exactly. Within the risk assessment community, uncertainty has been used both as a synonym for risk and as an expression of the confidence we have in the results of risk assessment. Since the term *risk* has no meaning for outcomes that are certain, uncertainty is closely related to risk. It is, all the same, a wider concept that should be delimited to prevent miscommunication. In this book we accept the fact that uncertainty is a central element of risk as a general expression of lacking certainty, but reserve the term for the following interpretation:

☞ **Uncertainty**: A measure of the confidence we have in the results of risk assessment.

This definition captures the many manifestations of uncertainty that affect the robustness of risk assessment. We are uncertain about the scenarios to expect and what outcomes to consider, the assigned probabilities, our preferences, our values, and our very capabilities for evaluating these (Hansson, 1996).

***Types of Uncertainty.***   Uncertainty can be categorized into two main types:

1. *Aleatory uncertainty.* This is uncertainty due to natural variation and intrinsic randomness. Examples are wind speed, precipitation, and product quality.

Aleatory uncertainty is also called *random* or *irreducible uncertainty*, because it cannot be reduced by acquiring more knowledge.

2. *Epistemic uncertainty.* This type of uncertainty comes from lack of knowledge. Examples concern the health effects of nanoparticles and the effect of $CO_2$ discharges on global warming. Epistemic uncertainty can be reduced by knowledge acquisition and is therefore referred to as *reducible uncertainty*. In contrast to aleatory uncertainty, epistemic uncertainty depends on knowledge of the assessor and hence is also called *subjective uncertainty*.

Although aleatory uncertainty is principally irreducible, it is interesting to note that phenomena that at first were regarded as aleatory have become epistemic with the progress of time and science. Keeping the distinction between aleatory and epistemic uncertainty is nonetheless valuable, as it pinpoints which uncertainties are prone to reduction in the short term.

Epistemic uncertainty is related to ignorance, which may or may not be conscious. Conscious ignorance means that we are aware of our lacking awareness and take it into account when we perform and document our analysis. Unconscious ignorance means that we do not know that we do not know, which is more serious, as it gives a false sense of confidence in the results of risk assessment.

**Contributors to Uncertainty.** There are three main contributors to uncertainty in risk assessment:

(a) *Completeness uncertainty* relates to aspects that are not considered in the analysis. Unidentified hazardous events, for example, will not be included in the analysis and hence lead to underestimation of risk.

(b) *Model uncertainty* derives from the inadequacy of models to represent real-world phenomena. Mathematical and logic models are always simplifications of reality and therefore introduce uncertainty.

(c) *Parameter uncertainty* concerns the accuracy and applicability of input data to, for example, failure rates, and human error probabilities.

Other sources of uncertainty are lacking knowledge about possible consequences (*consequence uncertainty*), nonconservative approximations and errors made in calculations (*calculation uncertainty*), poor skills in risk analysis (*competence uncertainty*), and analytical constraints with respect to time and cost (*resource uncertainty*).

The different types of uncertainty and various methods of treatment are covered in more detail in Chapter 16.

## 2.9  Vulnerability and Resilience

### 2.9.1  Vulnerability

NS 5814 (2008) defines vulnerability as:

☞ **Vulnerability**: The inability of an object to resist the impacts of an hazardous event and to restore it to its original state or function following the event.

Vulnerability is a system property that influences the consequences should a hazardous event occur. Reducing the vulnerability will therefore reduce the risk related to a hazardous event, whereas the opposite is not necessarily true. The attributes of vulnerability are *sensitivity* (to a certain type of stress) and *adaptive capacity* for accommodating change.

Vulnerability is influenced by factors both internal and external to a system:

*Internal factors:*

- System attributes (e.g., complexity of interactions and tightness of couplings)
- Technical failures and hazards
- Human and organizational factors
- Maintenance factors
- Staff factors (e.g., safety culture and availability of skilled personnel)

*External factors:*

- Environmental factors
- Societal factors
- Infrastructure factors
- Legal factors
- Financial factors
- Market factors

### 2.9.2 Resilience

Resilience is in many respects the opposite of vulnerability. Foster (1993) defines resilience as:

☞ **Resilience**: The ability to accommodate change without catastrophic failure, or the capacity to absorb shocks gracefully.

The word *resilience* conveys the ability to recover and to be brought back into shape or position after being stressed. *Resilience* is a broader term than *robustness*, which is a static concept that is basically synonymous with damage tolerance. In addition to the ability to withstand damage, resilience also has a dynamic component, that is, adaptation to a new situation. Resilience is therefore a pervasive property that influences a system's response to a wide range of stressors and threats (e.g., see Rosness et al., 2004; Hollnagel et al., 2006).

## 2.10  Safety and Security

In risk analysis, it is important to identify all the relevant hazardous events. The hazardous events may be random, such as technical failures and natural events (e.g., lightning, flooding), or due to deliberate actions, such as computer hacking and arson. The term *safety* is often used when we talk about random events, while *security* is used in relation to deliberate actions. The term *total safety* is sometimes used to cover both safety and security.

### 2.10.1  Safety

Safety is a problematic concept that is used with many different meanings. Many standards and guidelines related to risk assessment use the word *safety* but avoid defining the concept. An exception is MIL-STD-882D (2000), which gives the following definition:

☞ **Safety** (1): Freedom from those conditions that can cause death, injury, occupational illness, damage to or loss of equipment or property, or damage to the environment.

According to this definition, safety implies that all hazards are removed and that no assets will be harmed. For most practical systems, safety is therefore not attainable, and may be considered a Utopia.

Many risk analysts feel that the definition of safety in MIL-STD-882D is not of any practical use and that we need a definition such that safety is an attainable state. The following definition is therefore proposed:

☞ **Safety** (2): A state where the risk has been reduced to a level that is as low as reasonably practicable (ALARP) and where the remaining risk is generally accepted.

This definition implies that a system or an activity is considered to be *safe* if the risk related to the system/activity is considered to be acceptable. Safety is therefore a relative condition which is based on a judgment of the acceptability of risk. What is meant by acceptable risk and ALARP is discussed further in Chapter 4.

### 2.10.2  Security

Security is, like safety, a relative concept which is closely related to risk acceptability. The principal difference between safety and security is *intentionality*; security is characterized by adversary intent to do harm. Assessing security risk therefore changes the first question of Kaplan and Garrick (1981) into how someone can *make* something happen. This complicates risk assessment, as the range of possible events is restricted only by the assessor's imagination and ability to put herself in the situation of a potential enemy or criminal.

Central to an understanding of the concept of security are the terms *threat*, *threat agent*, and *vulnerability*:

**Threat.**   The term *threat* refers to the source and means of a particular type of attack.

☞ **Threat**: Anything that might exploit a vulnerability.

Any potential cause of an incident can be considered a threat. A fire, for example, is a threat that could exploit vulnerability due to flammable materials. The concept is closely related to, but differs from, the concept of hazard (see Chapter 3), which is not directed to exploit a vulnerability. A threat is therefore a hazard, but a hazard need not be a threat.

**Threat Agent.**   The term *threat agent* is used to indicate an individual or group that can manifest a threat. When analyzing security risk, it is fundamental to identify *who* could want to exploit the vulnerabilities of a system, and *how* they might use them against the system.

☞ **Threat agent**: A person or a thing that acts, or has the power to act, to cause, carry, transmit, or support a threat.

To cause harm, a threat agent must have the *intention*, *capacity*, and *opportunity* to cause harm. *Intention* means the determination or desire to achieve an objective. *Capacity* refers to the ability to accomplish the objective, including the availability of tools and techniques as well as the ability to use these correctly. *Opportunity* to cause harm implies that the asset must be vulnerable to attack.

### 2.10.3   Vulnerability

Within the terminology of security, vulnerability may be defined specifically as:

☞ **Vulnerability**: A *weakness* of an asset or group of assets that can be exploited by one or more threat agents, for example, to gain access to the asset and subsequent destruction, modification, theft, and so on, of the asset or parts of the asset.

Vulnerability refers in this respect to the security flaws in a system that allow an attack to be successful. These weaknesses may be categorized as physical, technical, operational, and organizational.

### 2.10.4   IT Security

Although security is still a somewhat immature issue in the community of risk assessment, it has become a well-matured discipline within the field of information technology (IT). The main attributes of IT security are *availability*, *confidentiality*, and *integrity*.

(a) *Availability.* This is a security principle that concerns the ability of an IT system or service to perform its intended function(s) when required.

For an information system to fulfill its purpose, the information must be available when needed. Many IT systems aim to remain available at all times, which requires that service disruptions due to power outages, hardware failures, and system upgrades be prevented.

(b) *Integrity.* This is a security principle which requires that data and system configurations be modified only by authorized personnel and activities.

Data integrity means that data cannot be modified without authorization. This comprises all possible causes of modification, including software and hardware failure, environmental events, and human intervention. Integrity is violated when, for example, an employee accidentally deletes important data files or an unauthorized user vandalizes a web site.

(c) *Confidentiality.* This is a security principle which states that data should be accessed only by authorized people.

Confidentiality concerns disclosure of information to unauthorized individuals or systems. The principle is enforced by encrypting data during transmission, limiting the places where it might appear (in log files, backups, and so on), and restricting access to databases.

## 2.11  Additional Reading

The following titles are recommended for further study related to Chapter 2.

- *The words of risk analysis* (Kaplan, 1997) is a basic reference and should be mandatory reading for all people working with risk analysis.

- *Foundations of risk assessment* (Johansen, 2010b) was written in parallel with this chapter and gives a more thorough discussion of some of the main risk concepts.

- *Metatheoretical foundations for post-normal risk* (Rosa, 1998) provides a thorough discussion of the risk concept—whether risk is a "state of the world" or just a "social construction" that exits in our minds. The article is well written, but in a language that may be difficult for engineers.

- *Foundations of Risk Analysis: A Knowledge and Decision-Oriented Perspective* (Aven, 2003) discusses many of the basic concepts of risk analysis.

- *Understanding Uncertainty* (Lindley, 2007) gives a detailed introduction to the logic of uncertainty and to subjective (personal) probability. The book is easy to read and does not require detailed knowledge of mathematics and probability theory.

# CHAPTER 3

# HAZARDS AND THREATS

It is impossible to win the great prizes of life without running risks.

—Theodore Roosevelt

## 3.1 Introduction

Any risk analysis has to be based on a careful consideration of the hazards and threats that are relevant for the study object in its operating context. This chapter defines, explains, and gives examples of typical hazards and threats. Hazards are most often linked to some type of energy, and energy sources are therefore highlighted. Generic lists of hazards, threats, and energy sources are valuable tools for the identification of potential hazardous events. Examples of such lists are provided in this chapter. The possibility of technical failures is a special category of hazards, and the concepts *failure* and *failure modes* are therefore defined and briefly discussed.

*Risk Assessment: Theory, Methods, and Applications,* First Edition.
By Marvin Rausand. Copyright © 2011 John Wiley & Sons, Inc.

## 3.2 Hazards

A hazard is defined as:

☞ **Hazard**: A source of danger that may cause harm to an asset.

A "source of danger" is a property, a situation, or a state. It is not an event but a prerequisite for the occurrence of a hazardous event that may lead to harm to an asset. A hazard is often, but not always, related to energy of some kind.

Some examples of hazards are:

- Ice on a sidewalk is a hazard, because you could slip, fall, and hurt yourself.

- Drunk driving is a hazard, because you have a reduced alertness and may harm yourself and others.

- Exposure to asbestos is a hazard, because it can lead to several serious diseases.

A hazard may be considered to be a *dormant potential for harm* which is present in one form or another in the system or its environment. Some authors use the term *risk factor* instead of *hazard*.

*Remark*: The Seveso II directive (EU, 1996) on "the control of major-accident hazards involving dangerous substances" is focused on dangerous substances and defines the term *hazard* as "the intrinsic property of a dangerous substance or physical situation, with a potential for creating damage to human health and/or the environment." Although this definition is more specific, it is seen to be fully in line with our definition of a hazard. $\oplus$

### 3.2.1 Generic List of Hazards

A generic list of hazards is often a useful tool in a risk analysis. An example of such a list is given in Table 3.1. More comprehensive lists of hazards may be found in the literature. Hazards relevant for machinery systems are, for example, listed in ISO 12100. The various hazards in Table 3.1 are listed without explanation and may therefore be misinterpreted. When we say, for example, that "earthquake" is a hazard, we mean the latent potential for an earthquake, not the event when an earthquake occurs. The same applies for other hazards.

It is sometimes claimed that a hazard has more remote causes that represent the "true hazards." This is, for example, the case when we study the risk of explosion from the storage of a flammable substance. The main hazard in this case is often assumed to be the amount of the flammable substance, but it is also possible to say that the hazard comprises the intrinsic properties of the substance that is stored. For the purpose of the risk analysis, it is usually most beneficial to define the hazard as the storage of the flammable substance (e.g., see HSE, 2001b).

**Table 3.1**   Generic hazard list (not exhaustive).

**Mechanical hazard**

- Kinetic energy
- Acceleration or retardation
- Sharp edges or points
- Potential energy
- High pressure
- Vacuum
- Moving parts
- Rotating equipment
- Reciprocating equipment
- Stability/toppling problems
- Degradation of materials (corrosion, wear, fatigue, etc.)

**Dangerous materials**

- Explosive
- Oxidizing
- Flammable
- Toxic
- Corrosive
- Carcinogenic

**Electrical hazards**

- Electromagnetic hazard
- Electrostatic hazard
- Short circuit
- Overload
- Thermal radiation

**Termic hazards**

- Flame
- Explosion
- Surfaces with high or low temperature
- Heat radiation

**Radiation hazards**

- Ionizing
- Nonionizing

**Noise hazards**

- External
- From internal machines

**Hazards generated by neglecting ergonomic principles**

- Unhealthy postures or excessive effort
- Inadequate local lightning
- Mental overload or underload, stress
- Human error, human behavior
- Inadequate design or location of visual display units

**Environmental hazards**

- Flooding
- Landslide
- Earthquake
- Lightning
- Storm
- Fog

**Organizational hazards**

- Safety culture
- Maintenance (less than adequate)
- Competence (less than adequate)
- Crowd control

**Sabotage/terrorism**

- Cyber threat
- Arson
- Theft
- Sabotage
- Terrorism

**Interaction hazards**

- Material incompatibilities
- Electromagnetic interference and incompatibility
- Hardware and software controls

### 3.2.2 Triggering Event

Some hazards require a *triggering event* to lead to a hazardous event, while other hazards may gradually develop into a hazardous event. An example of the latter category is inner corrosion in a gas pipeline. Corrosion is a hazard and may develop over time until a gas leak (i.e., a hazardous event) suddenly occurs. Triggering events are often, but not always, technical failures or human errors. The triggering event may be said to *release* a hazard.

☞ **Triggering event**: An event or condition that is required for a hazard to give rise to an accident.

■ **EXAMPLE 3.1    Climbing a ladder**

If you climb a ladder, for example to paint your house, you will gain potential energy and you may fall down. In this case, the potential energy is a hazard. While you work, standing on the ladder, you are exposed to the hazard. The potential energy is an *intrinsic hazard* of using a ladder. If you tread wrong or there is a weak step in the ladder, the hazard may be released and you will fall down. The hazardous event in this case is when you start to fall down.    ⊕

■ **EXAMPLE 3.2    Icy road**

A hazard when driving a car is "ice on the road." The triggering event "rapid change of direction" can, combined with the hazard, lead to the hazardous event "loss of control" and potentially to the consequence "death of driver."    ⊕

In some cases, several hazards can be present and combined can lead to an accident. In Example 3.2 the following hazards may, for example, be present: "ice on the road," "high speed" (i.e., high kinetic energy) and "driver using her non-hands-free mobile phone," Each of these hazards might lead to the hazardous event "loss of control", but in combination, the probability of the hazardous event would be much higher.

■ **EXAMPLE 3.3    Crane operation**

A crane is used to lift heavy elements on a construction site. The lifting operation has several hazards. One of these hazards is the potential energy of a lifted element. This hazard is an intrinsic hazard of the lifting operation, since it is not possible to lift anything without creating potential energy. The potential energy can be released, for example, if the triggering event "chain breaks" occurs. This triggering event will lead to the hazardous event "uncontrolled fall of the element." The consequence of the fall depends on where the element falls

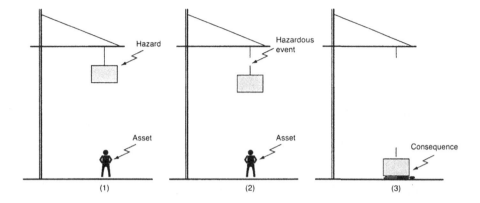

**Figure 3.1**    Hazard, hazardous event, and consequence (Example 3.3).

down—if there are people or important equipment (i.e., assets) in the area. The concepts used in this example are illustrated in Figure 3.1.                     ⊕

### 3.2.3  Safety Issue

The European Aviation Safety Agency (EASA) has introduced the concept *safety issue*:

☞ **Safety issue**: The manifestation of a hazard or combination of several hazards in a specific context.

Many hazards are intrinsic properties of the system operation. It is, for example, not possible to fly an airplane without kinetic and potential energy, so it does not help us simply to identify these hazards. A safety issue is, according to EASA, a combination of one or more hazards and a triggering event. If we are able to identify all relevant safety issues, this may be a good starting point for risk reduction.

### 3.2.4  Active Failures and Latent Conditions

Reason (1997) distinguishes between *active failures* and *latent conditions*. Active failures are events that trigger unwanted events. Examples of active failures are violations and errors by field operators, pilots, and control room operators.[1] These are the people in the operation—what Reason calls the *sharp end* of the system. Latent conditions do not trigger an accident immediately, but they lie dormant in the system and may contribute to a future accident. Examples of latent conditions

---

[1] Human errors are discussed further in Chapter 13.

are poor design, maintenance failures, poor and impossible procedures, and so on. Latent conditions can increase the probability of active failures.

Latent conditions are seen to be similar to hazards, and active failures are similar to triggering events.

## 3.3   Classification of Hazards

Hazards can be classified in many different ways. So far, no universally accepted classification system has emerged. A few classifications are listed in the following:

*Based on the main contributor to an accident scenario:*

(a) *Technological hazards* (e.g., related to equipment, software, structures, transport)

(b) *Natural (or environmental) hazards* (e.g., flooding, earthquake, lightning, storm, high/low temperatures)

(c) *Organizational hazards* (e.g., long working hours, inadequate competence, inadequate procedures, inadequate maintenance, inadequate safety culture)

(d) *Behavioral hazards* (e.g., drugs/alcohol, lack of concentration)

(e) *Social hazards* (e.g., hacking, theft, arson, sabotage, terrorism, war)

*Based on the origin of a technological hazard:*

(a) Mechanical hazards

(b) Electrical hazards

(c) Radiation hazards

   ...and so on

*Based on the nature of the potential harm:*

(a) Cancer hazards

(b) Suffocation hazards

(c) Pollution hazards

   ...and so on

*Based on the boundaries of the study object/system:*

(a) *Endogenous hazards* (i.e., hazards that are internal in the system being analyzed)

(b) *Exogenous hazards* (i.e., hazards that are external to the system being analyzed)

**Table 3.2**    Hazards for a ship (Example 3.4).

| Exogenous hazards | Endogenous hazards |
|---|---|
| Hazards external to a ship are, for example: | Hazards onboard a ship: |
| – Storms, lightning, tsunami | – In accommodation areas: combustible furnishings, cleaning material in stores, oil/fat in galley equipment, etc. |
| – Poor visibility | |
| – Submerged objects, other ships | – In deck areas: cargo, crane operations, slippery deck, electrical connections, etc. |
| – War, sabotage | |
| …and many more | – In machinery spaces: cabling, fuel and diesel oil, fuel oil piping and valves, refrigerants, etc. |
| | – Sources of ignition: naked flame, electrical appliances, hot surface, sparks from hot work, deck and engine room machinery |
| | – Operational hazards to personnel: long working hours, working on deck at sea, cargo operation, tank surveys, onboard repairs, etc. |

◼  **EXAMPLE 3.4    Hazards for a ship**

Some typical hazards for a ship are classified as exogenous and endogenous hazard and are listed in Table 3.2. The list is not complete.                    ⊕

## 3.4  Threats

The terms *threat* and *threat agent* were defined and discussed briefly in Section 2.10. Examples of threats are: arson, theft, cyberattacks, sabotage, and terrorism. A specific realization of a threat is a hazardous event. Consider a specific theft. A possible threat that can lead to this event is that drug addicts must steal to buy drugs.

A threat agent is often a person who exploits a threat and commits an action that may lead to a hazardous event. The threat agent does not need to be a single person but can be a group of people, an organization, and even a nation. Threat agents may be internal (e.g., own employees) or external people.

To commit an evil action, the threat agent must have *intention* and *capacity* to carry out the action. Intentions may change fast, and therefore the threats may, unlike hazards, change fast.

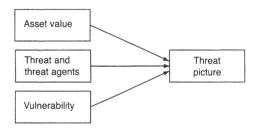

**Figure 3.2**    The elements of a threat picture.

*Remark*: In our daily language, the term *threat* is also used for hazards with a high potential of harm even when a threat agent is not involved. We may, for example, say that a big dam is a threat to people living downstream from the dam and that storage of a hazardous substance is a threat to the surrounding environment.    ⊕

### 3.4.1  Threat Picture

A listing of all potential threats together with an associated evaluation of the threats is often called a *threat picture*. As illustrated in Figure 3.2, the threat picture is determined by three elements:

1. *Asset value.* The value of the asset determined by its importance to the system or the operation. It is sometimes difficult to quantify the value since it cannot always be assigned a monetary value.

2. *Threat and threat agents.* This is represented by the external or internal persons who have the intention and capacity of harming, compromising, or stealing the asset specified.

3. *Vulnerability.* This consists of the technical, organizational, human, or routine failures and deficiencies that threat agents may exploit.

▉ **EXAMPLE 3.5    Threats to information systems**

Some special threats to a computerized information system are listed in Table 3.3. Several generic hazards listed in Table 3.1 may also be relevant.    ⊕

### 3.5  Energy Sources

Many hazards are rooted in some type of energy. To identify hazards, it is often helpful to start with a list of relevant energy sources. Some main energy sources are

**Table 3.3**    Threats to a computerized information system and its operation (Example 3.5).

| Disclosure threats | Human threats |
| --- | --- |
| – Accessibility by unauthorized individuals | – Theft |
| – Printout of internal storage | – Fraud |
| – Reading outside assigned storage area | – Riot |
| – Disclosure during technical services | – Sabotage |
| – Output to wrong recipient | – Vandalism |
| – Improper output | – Procedural errors |
| | – Processing errors |
| | – Accidental alteration |
| | – Accidental destruction |
| | – Deliberate alteration |
| | – Deliberate destruction |

**Table 3.4**    Energy sources.

| | |
| --- | --- |
| – Acoustic | – Kinetic (rotational) |
| – Atmospheric | – Magnetic |
| – Chemical | – Mechanical |
| – Corrosive | – Nuclear |
| – Electrical | – Pathogenic |
| – Electromagnetic | – Pneumatic |
| – Explosive, pyrophoric | – Potential |
| – Flammable | – Pressure |
| – Gravitational (mass, height) | – Thermal |
| – Hydraulic | – Toxic |
| – Kinetic (linear) | |

listed in Table 3.4. For more details and subcategories, see, for example, Johnson (1980, p. 37).

## 3.6 Technical Failures

Failures and malfunctions of technical items may be relevant as both hazards and triggering events. A failure is defined as:

☞ **Failure**: The termination of a required function.

A failure is always linked to a function of the item and occurs when the item is no longer able to perform a function according to the performance standard specified.

A failure may also be that a component performs its function when not required or performs its function as required, but does not stop operating when the required function is completed. Therefore, the term *failure* also covers functioning when not required, as well as not functioning when required (e.g., see NUREG/CR-4780, 1989).

▣ **EXAMPLE 3.6  Pump failure**

Consider a pump that is installed to supply water to a process. To function as required, the pump must supply between 60 and 65 liters of water per minute. If the output from the pump deviates from this interval, the required function is terminated and a failure occurs. ⊕

A failure is an event that occurs at a specific time, which may, or may not, be possible to observe. When a failure has occurred and persists, the item has a *fault*. A fault is hence a state of the item and not an event. The term *fault* is also used for a system where one or more components are not able to perform their functions as required. A failure may lead to many different faults, which are often referred to as *failure modes* (i.e., states).[2]

☞ **Failure mode**: The effect by which a failure is observed on a failed item
(IEC 60050-191, 1990).

Generally, a failure mode describes the way in which the failure happens and its impacts on the item's operation.

▣ **EXAMPLE 3.7  Pump failure (cont'd.)**

Reconsider the pump in Example 3.6. The following failure modes may occur:

– No output (the pump does not supply any water)

– Too low output (i.e., the output is less than 60 liters per minute)

---

[2]Such a state should be called a *fault mode*, but the term *failure mode* is used so commonly that it is difficult to change.

- Too high output (i.e., the output is more than 65 liters per minute)

- Pump does not start when required

- Pump does not stop when required

- Pump starts when not required

  ...more failure modes depending on other functional requirements: for example, related to power consumption or noise                                   ⊕

Some of the possible causes of a failure are classified as *failure mechanisms* and are defined as:

☞ **Failure mechanism**: A physical, chemical, or other process that leads to failure.

The pump in Example 3.6 may, for example, fail due to the failure mechanisms corrosion, erosion, and/or fatigue. Failure may also occur due to causes that are not failure mechanisms. Among such causes are operational errors, inadequate maintenance, overloading, and so on.

### 3.6.1  Failure Classification

***According to the Cause of the Failure.***    In some applications, it may be beneficial to classify failures as:

(a) *Primary failure.* A failure caused by natural aging of an item that occurs under conditions within the design envelope of the item. Repair is necessary to return the item to a functioning state.

(b) *Secondary failure.* A failure caused by excessive stresses outside the design envelope of the item. Such stresses can be shocks from thermal, mechanical, electrical, chemical, magnetic, or radioactive energy sources. The stresses may be caused by neighboring items, the environment, or by system operators/plant personnel. A repair action is necessary to return the item to a functioning state.

(c) *Command fault.* A failure caused by an improper control signal or noise. A repair is usually not required to return the item to a functioning state. Command faults are sometimes referred to as *transient failures*.

***According to the Degree of the Failure.***    Failure modes may also be classified according to the the *degree* of the failures. The failure modes in the OREDA database (see Chapter 7) are, for example, classified as:

(a) *Critical.* A failure that causes immediate and complete loss of a system's capability of providing its output.

(b) *Degraded.* A failure that is not critical but that prevents the system from providing its output within specifications. Such a failure would usually, but not necessarily, be gradual or partial, and may develop into a critical failure in time.

(c) *Incipient.* A failure that does not immediately cause loss of a system's capability of providing its output, but which, if not attended to, could result in a critical or degraded failure in the near future.

For more details about failures and failure classification, see Rausand and Høyland (2004, Chap. 3).

## 3.7 Human and Organizational Factors

Human errors and organizational deficiencies are very often found to be among the causes of accidents and incidents. Human errors are further discussed in Chapter 13. Organizational factors are not treated further in this book.

## 3.8 Additional Reading

The following titles are recommended for further study related to Chapter 3.

– *What Went Wrong? Case Histories of Process Plant Disasters* (Kletz, 1998) presents and discusses a number of process accidents that give insight into why and how accidents may occur.

– *System Reliability Theory; Models, Statistical Methods, and Applications* (Rausand and Høyland, 2004) gives a thorough introduction to the main concepts of failures and failure classification and how these concepts are used in reliability analyses.

– *The basic concepts of failure analysis* (Rausand and Øien, 1996) discusses the main concepts of failure analysis and the relation between these concepts.

# CHAPTER 4

# HOW TO MEASURE AND EVALUATE RISK

You cannot solve a problem until you can measure it.

—Daniel Patrick Moynihan

## 4.1 Introduction

Risk assessments are usually performed to provide input to a decision. The decision may, for example, concern modification of equipment, allocation of risk reduction expenditures, or siting of a hazardous plant. Common to all is the need to specify what to measure and how to evaluate what has been measured. How we measure risk will ultimately determine what information we can get from a risk analysis and the validity of our conclusions.

In this chapter we consider how to quantify and evaluate risk to humans. We first introduce various indicators for expressing quantities of risk, before discussing qualitative and quantitative principles for evaluating whether the risk is acceptable.

**Inger Lise Johansen**, NTNU, has made important contributions to this chapter.

*Risk Assessment: Theory, Methods, and Applications,* First Edition.
By Marvin Rausand. Copyright © 2011 John Wiley & Sons, Inc.

Acceptable risk is a compound expression that has been disputed since the late 1960s, when societal debates incited the general public on issues of facility siting and technology development. Fischhoff et al. (1981) concluded that no risk is acceptable in isolation:

> Strictly speaking, one does not accept risks. One accepts options that entail some level of risk among their consequences.

## 4.2   Risk Indicators

A quantitative assessment of the risk related to a system or activity has to be based on one or more indicators. An *indicator* is, in this context, a quantity that provides information about the level of risk (Øien, 2001). There are two main types of indicators: one, called a *risk indicator*, that is used to predict what will happen in the future, the other, to address what has happened in the past.

☞ **Risk indicator**: A parameter that is estimated based on risk analysis models and by using generic and other available data. A risk indicator presents our knowledge and belief about a specific aspect of the risk of a *future* activity or a *future* system operation.

The "risk level" in the past, was called safety performance in Section 2.5.2 and an indicator of this performance is therefore called a *safety performance indicator*.

☞ **Safety performance indicator**: A parameter that is estimated based on experience data from a specific installation or an activity. A safety performance indicator therefore tells us what has happened.

Risk indicators are used to assess (prospective) risk, whereas safety performance indicators are used mainly for monitoring purposes, that is, to check whether the safety performance has been constant, increasing, or decreasing, and to compare the safety performance of one activity with that of other activities.

⬛ **EXAMPLE 4.1   Risk indicator for deep-diving operations**

A company is about to launch a new type of equipment for deep-diving operations. Let $\theta$ denote the probability that the diver will be killed during a specific diving operation when using the new equipment. The probability $\theta$ may be considered as a parameter that can be estimated based on risk analysis of the new equipment and the diving operation, combined with generic data from similar equipment and similar diving operations. The estimate is based on available knowledge and data, and gives an indication of what risk the diver will face by using the new equipment. The value of $\theta$ is therefore a risk indicator. Note that $\theta$ only provides partial information about the risk the diver is facing, since it is concerned only with the fatality risk, not with the probability of being injured.

When the new equipment has been used for some time, we may estimate the parameter $\theta$ from the recorded data by standard statistical techniques. We denote this estimate by $\theta^*$ to distinguish it from the (prospective) risk indicator. The estimate $\theta^*$ is a safety performance indicator that tells us what has been experienced.                                                          $\oplus$

Let $\theta$ be a parameter that provides information about the risk of a system or an activity. In the following, we use the same symbol, $\theta$, to denote the risk indicator, that is, the prospective estimate that is deduced from risk models and generic data. We use $\theta^*$ to denote the safety performance indicator that is estimated based on experience data.

It is important to note that a single risk indicator does not give a complete picture of the risk but, rather, is an indication of one dimension of the risk (e.g., personnel risk).

## 4.3  Risk to People

A single death is a tragedy, a million deaths is a statistic.

—Josef Stalin

Most people would agree that there is a difference between exposing few and many people to a hazard, even though this may not matter very much to a specific person being exposed.

Risk to humans can be classified into two distinct groups:

(a) *Individual risk* is the risk that an individual person is exposed to during a specific time period (usually, one year). Individual risk is usually addressed in terms of a *hypothetical* or *statistical person*, who is an individual with some defined, fixed relationship to the hazard. This may be the most exposed person, for example a train driver, or a person with some assumed pattern of life. The analyst has to define a number of hypothetical persons to ensure that the entire exposed population is addressed. Individual risk does not depend on the number of people who are exposed to the hazard.

☞ **Individual risk**: The frequency with which an individual may be expected to sustain a given level of harm from the realization of specified hazards (IChemE, 1992).

(b) *Group risk* is the risk experienced by a group of people. When common citizens are exposed, the group risk is often called *societal risk*. In this book we prefer the term *group risk* both when the group members are employees in a specific company and when they are common citizens. The group risk is a combination of individual risk levels and the number of people at risk, that is, the population being exposed.

The following definition by the UK Institution of Chemical Engineers is often cited:

☞ **Societal risk**: The relationship between frequency and the number of people suffering from a specified level of harm in a given population from the realization of specific hazards (IChemE, 1992).

An example of group (or societal) risk is air travel. Major airplane disasters cause grief and shock throughout a country, followed by detailed inquiries into their causes and demands of general action to reduce this sort of risk. It is such reactions that distinguish group risks from the more mundane risks that do not have disaster potentials, such as motoring, even though the latter may result in many more fatalities per year.

Several measures for individual and group (societal) risk are presented in the following sections.

### 4.3.1 Individual Risk per Annum

Consider an individual who is exposed to a specified set of hazards, $a$. The hazards may be due to a special activity or a special situation: for example, driving a motorcycle or living near a hazardous plant. A relevant risk indicator may be the probability that the individual will be killed due to the specified hazards $a$ during a period of one year. The resulting risk indicator is called the *individual risk per annum* ($IRPA_a$), with respect to the hazards $a$, and is defined as

$$IRPA_a = Pr(\text{individual is killed due to hazards } a \text{ during one year's exposure}) \quad (4.1)$$

$IRPA_a$ may be estimated based on the number of fatalities observed in a specified time period for a specific group of individuals who have been exposed to the same hazards $a$, by

$$IRPA_a^* = \frac{\text{observed no. of fatalities due to hazards } a}{\text{total no. of person-years exposed}} \quad (4.2)$$

The $IRPA_a^*$ is now a safety performance indicator that gives us an indication of the individual risk in the specific group of individuals in the specified (earlier) time period.

🖵 **EXAMPLE 4.2 Individual accident risk in Norway**

In 2009, 1 989 persons were killed in accidents in Norway out of a total population of about 4 900 000 people. For a person chosen at random from this population, the probability of being killed in 2009 was

$$IRPA^* = \frac{1\,989}{4\,900\,000} \approx 4 \cdot 10^{-4} \quad (4.3)$$

This means that in a group of 10 000 persons chosen at random, on the average four got killed in an accident in 2009. The expression (4.3) is an estimate of the total individual risk per annum (IRPA) of a person chosen at random among all inhabitants in Norway.

A detailed analysis of the mortality data shows that the total IRPA* is strongly dependent on age and gender. A high percentage of the fatalities are elderly people who fall in their homes. The lowest total IRPA* is observed for children in the age range from 5 to 15 years. In this age range, the total IRPA* is about $2 \cdot 10^{-5}$. This means that in a randomly chosen group of 100 000 children between 5 and 15 years old, approximately two children die per year. The average IRPA* for this group of children has been rather stable over many years in Norway, and approximately the same value is also found in most countries in Western Europe. ⊕

### ▣ EXAMPLE 4.3   Individual risk for air travel

Consider a person who is traveling by air between two cities $n$ times a year. The frequency of accidents on this stretch has been estimated to be $\lambda$. The $IRPA_a$ for this activity is then

$$IRPA_a = \lambda \cdot \Pr(\text{the person is on board the flight})$$
$$\cdot \Pr(\text{the person is killed} \mid \text{the person is on board})$$

⊕

### ▣ EXAMPLE 4.4   Individual risk on cargo ships

Consider the individual risk for crew members on cargo ships. Some hazards are relevant only during ordinary working hours, whereas other hazards are relevant 24 hours a day. The type of accident under consideration will therefore determine whether the exposure time should be measured as working hours or as total time spent onboard. Assume that we have data from an accumulated number of $\tau_s = 29\,500$ cargo ship-years (one ship-year is of one ship during one year). Each ship has an average number of crew members (persons on board, POB) = 25, and each crew member spends on average $a = 50\%$ of the year onboard. Further assume that $n = 490$ crew members have been killed during this exposure time. The safety performance during this period is hence

$$IRPA^* = \frac{n}{\tau_s \cdot POB} \cdot a = \frac{490}{29\,500 \cdot 25} \cdot 0.5 \approx 3.3 \cdot 10^{-4}$$

Note that by using this safety performance indicator, we do not distinguish between single fatalities and multiple fatalities in major accidents. ⊕

## 4.3.2   Potential Equivalent Fatality

In many cases the risk to people is not adequately described by the fatality risk, and injuries should also be taken into account. This is sometimes done by comparing injuries and disabilities with fatalities and trying to calculate a *potential equivalent fatality*.

☞ **Potential equivalent fatality (PEF)**: A convention for aggregating harm to people by regarding major and minor injuries as being equivalent to a certain fraction of a fatality (RSSB, 2007).

**▣ EXAMPLE 4.5 London Underground QRA**

In a QRA of London Underground Limited[1] potential injuries were classified into minor and major injuries. Major injuries were given the weight 0.1, such that ten major injuries were considered to be "equivalent" to one fatality (i.e., $10 \times 0.1 = 1$). Minor injuries were given the weight 0.01, such that a hundred minor injuries were considered "equivalent" to one fatality.  $\oplus$

### 4.3.3 Localized Individual Risk

The *localized individual risk* (LIRA) is defined as:

☞ **Localized individual risk (LIRA)**: The probability that an average unprotected person, permanently present at a specified location, is killed in a period of one year due to an accident at a hazardous installation (e.g., see Jonkman et al., 2003).

LIRA is also called *location-specific individual risk* (LSIR) and *Individual risk index*, and is used mainly for *land-use planning*.

***LIRA Is a Property of the Location.*** In the definition of LIRA, it is assumed that the person is always present at a given location. Since LIRA remains unchanged irrespective of whether a person is at the spot when an accident occurs, it can rightfully be claimed that LIRA is a geographic rather than an individual risk measure. Due to its location-specific properties, LIRA is used almost exclusively for *land-use planning* related to hazardous installations (e.g., see Laheij et al., 2000). Requirements for land-use planning are included as Article 12 in the EU Seveso II directive (EU, 1996) and a guideline related to these requirements has been developed (EU-JRC, 2006).

***LIRA for Different Types of Accidents.*** Consider a hazardous installation that may produce $m$ independent types of accidents $A_1, A_2, \ldots, A_m$. Let $\lambda_i$ denote the frequency of the occurrence of accidents of type $A_i$, for $i = 1, 2, \ldots, m$. Assume that an average unprotected person is permanently present at a location with coordinates $(x, y)$ on a map. Based on an analysis of the stresses and doses of toxic gases to

---

[1]http://www.yellowbook-rail.org.uk/resources/models/
yellowbookR1.pdf.

which the person will be exposed during an accident of type $\mathcal{A}_i$, we may estimate the probability that she or he will be killed,

Pr(unprotected person located at $(x, y)$ is killed | accident $\mathcal{A}_i$ has occurred)

Let us for brevity denote this probability by Pr(fatality at $(x, y)$ | $\mathcal{A}_i$). The LIRA at location $(x, y)$ due to accident of type $\mathcal{A}_i$ is now

$$\text{LIRA}_i(x, y) = \lambda_i \cdot \text{Pr(fatality at } (x, y) \mid \mathcal{A}_i) \quad \text{for } i = 1, 2, \ldots, m$$

The total LIRA at location $(x, y)$ due to the hazardous installation is

$$\text{LIRA}(x, y) = \sum_{i=1}^{m} \lambda_i \cdot \text{Pr(fatality at } (x, y) \mid \mathcal{A}_i)$$

The definition of LIRA$(x, y)$ may be modified to take into account the proportion of time $a$ the individual is actually present at location $(x, y)$. In this case, the risk may be written as

$$\text{LIRA}(x, y) = \sum_{i=1}^{m} \lambda_i \cdot \text{Pr(fatality at } (x, y) \mid \mathcal{A}_i) \cdot a$$

The vulnerability of the individual with respect to the effects of the accident may be incorporated into the model in the same way as the presence of the individual.

### ▉ EXAMPLE 4.6    LIRA with reduced exposure

Consider an office building that is located at the coordinates $(x, y)$ near a hazardous installation. At this location, the localized risk LIRA$(x, y)$ has been determined. An individual will be present in the office building for approximately 1 500 hours per year. The probability that she or he is present in the office building at a random point in time is hence $1\,500/8\,760 \approx 17\%$. The building serves as a protection layer and the individual will therefore have a lower risk while she or he is inside the building. Let $p(x, y)$ denote the probability that the individual will be killed by a fatal dose at location $(x, y)$. If we assume that both $p(x, y)$ and the accident probability remain constant over the day, the individual risk of the person due to the hazardous installation is approximately IRPA $\approx \text{LIRA}(x, y) \cdot p(x, y) \cdot 0.17$. If the probability of the accident varies over the day, and is higher during normal working hours, we have to do a more thorough analysis.                                                                                    ⊕

## 4.3.4    Risk Contour Plots

The geographical feature of LIRA may be used to illustrate the risk in the vicinity of a hazardous installation—by an *individual risk contour plot*, as shown in Figure 4.1.

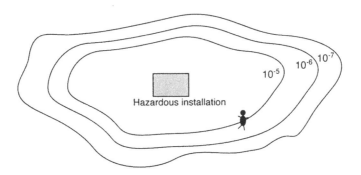

**Figure 4.1**   Risk contour plot example.

The contours show how LIRA varies in an area around a hazardous installation, and hence the risk to which an unprotected individual would be exposed if she was present continuously at a given location.

The risk contour is drawn on a map of the area around the hazardous installation. The geographical area must usually be divided into smaller areas to make the calculation manageable. The LIRA must then be calculated for each area, by adding up the hazards that may affect this area. The LIRA is usually split into levels, such as $10^{-5}$, $10^{-6}$, $10^{-7}$, and so on. A $10^{-5}$ *iso-risk contour* is then drawn around the areas with an LIRA of $\geq 10^{-5}$. Thereafter, a similar $10^{-6}$ contour is drawn around the areas with LIRA $\geq 10^{-6}$; and so on. If an average unprotected individual is permanently present at a $10^{-5}$ iso-risk contour, she or he will have a probability of being killed that equals $10^{-5}$ per year. The distance from the hazardous installation to an iso-risk contour will depend on the type of hazards, the topography, the dominant wind direction, and so on. Since risk contours may be tedious to calculate by hand, a number of computer programs have been developed for this purpose.

Risk contours do not take into account any actions that people might take to escape from an event, or the actual time that people are present. Also note that the number of people who are exposed to the risk is not a consideration. The risk contour is simply an indication of how hazardous the area is. It is typically used in layout and siting reviews of industrial plants. Risk contours may also be established for areas around airports and roads where hazardous goods are transported.

### ▉ EXAMPLE 4.7   Iso-risk contours in the Netherlands

In the Netherlands, no new dwellings or vulnerable installations, such as kindergartens or hospitals, are allowed within the $10^{-6}$ (per annum) iso-risk contour. Less vulnerable installations, such as offices, are allowed in the zone between the $10^{-5}$ and the $10^{-6}$ (per annum) iso-risk contours (Laheij et al., 2000).   ⊕

**Table 4.1**    Individual risk criteria for various installations.

| Exposure type | Risk level |
|---|---|
| Hospitals, schools, child-care facilities, nursing homes | Less than $5 \cdot 10^{-7}$ |
| Residential developments and places of continuous occupation (hotels/resorts) | Less than $1 \cdot 10^{-6}$ |
| Commercial developments, including offices, retail centers, warehouses with showrooms, restaurants and entertainment centers. | Less than $5 \cdot 10^{-6}$ |
| Sporting complexes and active open space areas | Less than $1 \cdot 10^{-5}$ |
| Industrial sites | Less than $5 \cdot 10^{-5}$ |

*Source*: Data from various Australian authorities.

Several countries have defined maximum LIRA values for different types of installations. The data in Table 4.1 are compiled from various Australian authorities and are used for land-use planning.

### 4.3.5  Reduction in Life Expectancy

Death and disability due to a specific hazard need not occur during the course of the hazardous activity, but may also be delayed for several years. An employee's risk of immediate death due to an accident at work might, for example, be less than the risk of developing a fatal cancer due to an accidental release of a carcinogenic material. However, in the first case, she might die as a young woman, whereas the latter may allow her to work for 20–30 years before any cancer is developed.

The risk indicators that have been introduced so far do not distinguish between fatalities of young and old people. To cater to the age of the victim, the *reduction in life expectancy*, RLE, has been suggested as a risk indicator. If a person dies at age $t$ due to an accident, the $\mathrm{RLE}_t$ is defined as

$$\mathrm{RLE}_t = t_0 - t$$

where $t_0$ denotes the mean life length of a randomly chosen person of the same age as the person killed, who has survived up to age $t$. The $\mathrm{RLE}_t$ is seen to be equal to the *mean residual life* of the individual who is killed at age $t$. The RLE puts increased value on young lives, since the reduction in life expectancy depends on the age at death.

To calculate the *average* reduction in life expectancy $\mathrm{RLE}_{av}$ of a specified group of persons exposed to a certain hazard, we have to compare the observed life expectancy with the estimated life expectancy of the same group in the absence of the hazard. The life expectancy of the group may sometimes differ significantly from that of the general population of the country.

A table of the estimated average reduction in life expectancy $\mathrm{RLE}_{av}^*$ due to some selected causes is presented by Fischhoff et al. (1981). A brief extract of their data is presented in Table 4.2.

**Table 4.2**   Estimated average reduction in life expectancy due to various causes.

| Cause | Days |
|-------|------|
| Heart disease | 2 100 |
| Cancer | 980 |
| Stroke | 520 |
| Motor vehicle accidents | 207 |
| Accidents in home | 95 |
| Average job, accidents | 74 |
| Drowning | 41 |
| Accidents to pedestrians | 37 |

*Source*: Fischhoff et al. (1981).

### 4.3.6   Lost-Time Injuries

A *lost-time injury* (LTI) is an injury that prevents an employee from returning to work for at least one full shift. The frequency of LTIs is often used as a safety performance indicator and is defined as

$$\text{LTIF}^* = \frac{\text{no. of lost-time injuries (LTIs)}}{\text{no. of hours worked}} \cdot 2 \cdot 10^5 \qquad (4.4)$$

The LTIF* is usually calculated per annum (or per month).

### ▣  EXAMPLE 4.8   Calculating LTIF

An average employee works around 2 000 hours per year.[2] A total of $2 \cdot 10^5 =$ 200 000 hours is therefore approximately 100 employee-years. If a company has an LTIF* $= 10$ LTIs per 200 000 hours of exposure, this means that on average one out of ten employees will experience an LTI during one year.         ⊕

Some companies/organizations may use another time scale and, for example, define the LTIF* as the number of LTIs per million ($10^6$) hours worked. The following safety performance indicators are also sometimes used:

- The (average) time between LTIs in a specified population

- The time since the previous LTI in a specified population

- The frequency of injuries requiring medical treatment

**Lost Workdays Frequency.**   The LTIF* does not weight the seriousness of the injury, so a fatal accident has the same effect on the LTIF* as does a broken finger.

---

[2]In many countries, normal work-hours are less than 2 000 per year, and closer to 1 750.

The seriousness of an LTI may be measured by the number of workdays lost due to the LTI, and the *lost workdays frequency*, LWF*, may alternatively be used as a safety performance indicator. The LWF* is defined as

$$LWF^* = \frac{\text{no. of lost workdays due to LTIs}}{\text{no. of hours worked}} \cdot 2 \cdot 10^5$$

- Some companies and organizations use another time scale and define the LWF* as the number of lost workdays due to LTIs per million ($10^6$) hours of exposure.

- The average number of workdays lost per LTI is found from LWF*/LTIF*.

- The LWF* is sometimes called the S-rate (severity rate).

- Fatalities and 100% permanent disability are sometimes decided to account for 7 500 workdays (Kjellén, 2000).

### ▉ EXAMPLE 4.9   Calculating LWF

Consider a company with a total of 150 000 employee-hours per year, which corresponds to approximately 75 employees working full time (2 000 hours per year). Assume that the company has had 8 LTIs during one year, which corresponds to LTIF* = 10.7 LTIs per 200 000 hours of exposure. Assume that the company has lost 107 workdays due to LTIs. This corresponds to LWF* ≈ 144 lost workdays per 200 000 hours of exposure. Note that the LWF* does not tell us anything about the seriousness of each LTI and whether the lost workdays are equally distributed: for example, if seven LTIs caused only one day lost while the eighth caused 100 lost workdays.                                          ⊕

### 4.3.7   Relation Between the Frequencies of Fatalities and Injuries

Several studies have been carried out to establish the relationship between the frequencies of serious and minor accidents and other dangerous events. At the basis of this research is the assertion of a general relationship between higher event frequencies and lower severity classes, as illustrated in Figure 4.2.

The results from the various studies are difficult to compare, because they use different definitions of severe and minor accidents, near misses, and so on. A certain pattern may, however, be observed.

*Heinrich's Triangle.*   Heinrich (1931) studied railway accidents and found the following relationship:

| | |
|---|---|
| 1 | major accident |
| 29 | minor accidents |
| 300 | near-miss incidents |

When this distribution is depicted in a triangle similar to Figure 4.2, it is often referred to as *Heinrich's triangle, Heinrich's pyramid*, or *Heinrich's iceberg*. The

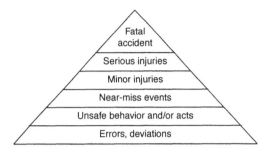

**Figure 4.2**   Accident ratio triangle.

iceberg metaphor is used to remind us that in the same way as that about 90% of an iceberg is submerged under water and is hence invisible, major/fatal accidents are only the visible tip of the iceberg. The "submerged" section is divided into layers, where the bottom layer consists of the nonreportable and "invisible" incidents.

In 1974–1975, Tye and Pearson analyzed almost 1 000 000 accidents in British industry and found the following distribution:

| | |
|---|---|
| 1 | fatal or serious injury |
| 3 | minor injuries—when the victim would be absent from work for up to 3 days |
| 50 | injuries requiring first-aid treatment |
| 80 | property damage accidents |
| 400 | non-injury/damage accidents or near misses |

Another distribution is reported by Bird and Germain (1986):

| | |
|---|---|
| 1 | serious or disabling injury |
| 10 | minor injuries |
| 30 | property damage accidents (all types) |
| 600 | incidents with no reported injury or damage (near misses) |

Heinrich's iceberg theory is still very popular and has been used actively in safety management. Many safety practitioners believe that a reduction in nonreportable incidents (events at the bottom of the triangle) should lead to a reduction in the number of events at the exposed top of the iceberg. The popular understanding is that major accidents, minor accidents, and no-injury accidents arise from the same causal factors, such that risk-reducing measures directed at these causal factors will influence major accidents, minor accidents, and no-injury accidents to the same degree. An implication of this interpretation is that a low LTIF can be taken as a trustworthy indicator of a low risk of major accidents. This is a dangerous philosophy that is not supported in the original paper of Heinrich (1931). It is the firm belief of the author of this book that this view is wrong and that the causes of minor incidents will usually be different from those of major accidents. A low LTIF is hence not an indication of a low major accident risk (see also Rosness et al., 2004).

**Figure 4.3**    Risk contour plot where several people are exposed to the risk.

### 4.3.8  Potential Loss of Life

The *potential loss of life* (PLL) is one of the most commonly used measures of group risk, and is defined as:

☞ **Potential loss of life (PLL)**: The PLL is the expected number of fatalities within a specified population (or within a specified area $A$) per annum.

The PLL is one of the most simple risk indicators for group (societal) risk. It does not distinguish between one accident that causes 100 deaths and 100 accidents each of which causes one death over the same period of time. As such, the PLL fails to reflect the contrast between society's strong reaction to rare but major accidents and its quiet tolerance of the many small accidents that occur frequently (Hirst, 1998). The PLL is also known as the *annual fatality rate* (AFR).

*PLL Within an Area.*    Reconsider the hazardous installation illustrated in Figure 4.1, but assume that several people are exposed to the risk, as illustrated in Figure 4.3 Let IRPA$(x, y)$ denote the individual risk per annum of an individual who is located at the coordinates $(x, y)$ on a map, and let $m(x, y)$ denote the population density as a function of the coordinates $(x, y)$. We assume that the presence of the persons at the location and their vulnerability to the risk have been incorporated into the estimate of IRPA$(x, y)$. The expected number of fatalities per year, the PLL, within a specified area $A$ can then be determined by

$$\text{PLL}_A = \iint_A \text{IRPA}(x, y)\, m(x, y)\, dx\, dy \qquad (4.5)$$

*PLL for a Specified Population.*    Assume that all the members of a population have the same individual risk per annum, IRPA. Let $n$ denote the number of members of the population. The PLL is then determined by

$$\text{PLL} = n \cdot \text{IRPA} \qquad (4.6)$$

In some situations it may be easier to consider various types of accidents one by one. Assume that $m$ distinct types of accidents have been identified, and let $\lambda_i$ [year$^{-1}$]

**Table 4.3**   PLL* for some selected types of occupations in Norway, based on the average number of fatalities in 2004–2008.

| Type of occupation | PLL* |
| --- | --- |
| Agriculture | 9.4 |
| Transport and communication | 7.2 |
| Construction | 6.4 |
| Health and social services | 1.6 |

*Source*: The Norwegian Labour Inspection Authority (2009).

denote the frequency of accidents of type $i$ for $i = 1, 2, \ldots, m$. Let $n_i$ denote the number of persons who are affected by an accident of type $i$, and let $p_i$ denote the probability that an average person will be killed if an accident of type $i$ should occur. The PLL relative to accidents of type $i$ is therefore

$$\text{PLL}_i = n_i \cdot \lambda_i \cdot p_i \tag{4.7}$$

The total PLL for all types of accidents is thus

$$\text{PLL} = \sum_{i=1}^{m} \text{PLL}_i \tag{4.8}$$

The PLL may also be used as a safety performance indicator, PLL*, where PLL* is the number of fatalities observed within a specified population (or within a specified area $A$) per annum. The PLL* may be plotted as a function of the year and used to check whether or not there is a trend in the risk level. Note that PLL* is often a very unstable estimate for the PLL because it is strongly influenced by major accidents.

■ **EXAMPLE 4.10   PLL for selected types of occupations in Norway**

The Norwegian Labour Inspection Authority collects data related to all occupational accidents in Norway and classifies the data into different categories. The PLL* for the various occupations can then be calculated for each year. Table 4.3 provides the average PLL* for the period 2004–2008 for some selected types of occupations.                                                                    ⊕

### 4.3.9   Fatal Accident Rate

The *fatal accident rate* (FAR) was introduced by ICI as a risk indicator for occupational risk within the chemical industry in the UK. The FAR is now the most common risk indicator for occupational risk in Europe. FAR is defined as:

**Table 4.4** Experienced FAR* values for the Nordic countries for the period 1980–1989.

| Industry | FAR* (Fatalities per $10^8$ working hours) |
| --- | --- |
| Agriculture, forestry, fishing, and hunting | 6.1 |
| Raw material extraction | 10.5 |
| Industry, manufacturing | 2.0 |
| Electric, gas, and water supply | 5.0 |
| Building and construction | 5.0 |
| Trade, restaurant, and hotel | 1.1 |
| Transport, post, and telecommunication | 3.5 |
| Banking and insurance | 0.7 |
| Private and public services, defense, etc. | 0.6 |
| Total | 2.0 |

*Source*: Data from the Danish Working Environment Service (1993).

☞ **Fatal accident rate (FAR)**: The expected number of fatalities in a defined population per 100 million hours of exposure.

$$\text{FAR} = \frac{\text{expected no. of fatalities}}{\text{no. of hours exposed to risk}} \cdot 10^8 \qquad (4.9)$$

The FAR value may be given the following interpretation: If 1 000 persons work 2 000 hours per year during 50 years, their cumulative exposure time will be $10^8$ hours. FAR is then the estimated number of these 1 000 persons who will die in a fatal accident during their working lives.

The FAR value is considered to be useful for comparing the average risk in different occupations and activities. It is, however, not always easy to establish the time spent at risk, especially for part-time activities or subpopulations at risk.

In industrial risk analyses, the number of exposure hours is normally defined as the number of working hours. For offshore oil and gas risk analyses, the FAR value is sometimes calculated based on the actual working hours, and sometimes on the total hours the personnel are on the installation.

The corresponding safety performance indicator, FAR*, may be defined as

$$\text{FAR}^* = \frac{\text{observed no. of fatalities}}{\text{no. of hours exposed to risk}} \cdot 10^8 \qquad (4.10)$$

In 1993, a report concerning fatal accidents in the Nordic countries (Denmark, Finland, Norway, and Sweden) was published by the Danish Working Environment Service. The FAR* values presented in Table 4.4 are based on this report.

Similar data from the UK are presented in Table 4.5. Note that the data in Tables 4.4 and 4.5 are difficult to compare since the industry or activity groups are not defined in the same way.

**Table 4.5** Experienced FAR* values for the UK.

| Activity/industry | FAR* (Fatalities per $10^8$ hours of exposure) |
| --- | --- |
| Factory work (average) | 4 |
| Construction (average) | 5 |
| Construction, high-rise erectors | 70 |
| Manufacturing industry (all) | 1 |
| Oil and gas extraction | 15 |
| Travel by car | 30 |
| Travel by air (fixed wing) | 40 |
| Travel by helicopter | 500 |
| Rock climbing while on rock face | 4 000 |

*Source*: Data from Hambly (1992).

**Table 4.6** Experienced FAR values for offshore workers in the UK and Norwegian sector of the North Sea for the period 1 January 1980–1 January 1994.

| Area | Condition for calculation | FAR* (Fatalities per $10^8$ working hours) |
| --- | --- | --- |
| UK | Total FAR* | 36.5 |
| | Excl. Piper Alpha accident | 14.2 |
| Norway | Total FAR* | 47.3 |
| | Excl. Alexander Kielland accident | 8.5 |

*Source*: Data from Holand (1996).

FAR* is an unbiased but rather nonrobust estimate of the FAR value, due to its strong dependency on major accidents. If we calculate FAR* over an interval $(0, t)$, where $t$ is increasing, FAR* may have a low value until the first major accident occurs. Then the estimate takes a leap before it starts to decrease until the next major accident occurs. This is illustrated clearly in Table 4.6, which presents the estimated FAR* values for offshore workers in the UK and Norwegian sectors of the North Sea for the period 1 January 1980–1 January 1994. Two major accidents occurred in this period; the Alexander Kielland platform capsized in the Norwegian sector of the North Sea on 27 March 1980 with the loss of 123 lives, and the Piper Alpha platform exploded and caught fire in the British sector of the North Sea on 6 July 1988 with the loss of 167 lives. It is clear that the total experienced FAR* value is dominated by these two accidents.

The FAR value is generally considered to be a very useful overall risk indicator. It may, however, be a very coarse measure. This is because the FAR value (and FAR*) applies for all members of a specified group, without considering that various members of the group may be exposed to significantly different levels of risk. In Table 4.6, for example, all offshore workers are considered to be members of the same group. The FAR values thus represent an average for all offshore workers, even though it is obvious that the production crew, the drilling crew, and the catering crew are exposed to different levels of risk. They are exposed to some common job-specific hazards (such as collapse of the entire installation), but many significant hazards are clearly job-specific. Hence, although the FAR for all workers may be considered acceptable for a given situation, it could happen that, for example, the drilling crew had a very high FAR.

The FAR values are therefore sometimes split over various activities or risk factors.

***Accident Rates in Transport.*** The transport sector sometimes uses exposure measures other than hours. In aviation, it is common to use:

- No. of flight hours

- No. of person flight hours

- No. of aircraft departures

The aviation $FAR_a$ is often defined as

$$FAR_a = \frac{\text{no. of accident-related fatalities}}{\text{no. of flight hours}} \cdot 10^5$$

The $FAR_a$ therefore expresses the number of fatalities per 100 000 hours flown.

An alternative to $FAR_a$ is related to the number of departures:

$$FAR_d = \frac{\text{no. of accident-related fatalities}}{\text{no. of aircraft departures}} \cdot 10^5$$

In the railway and road transport sectors, the following exposure measures are sometimes used:

- No. of kilometers driven

- No. of person kilometers

- No. of person travel hours

Relevant risk measures are therefore:

- No. of fatalities per 100 million person kilometers

- No. of fatalities per 100 million vehicle kilometers

### 4.3.10  Deaths per Million

The *number of deaths per million* (DPM) people belonging to a specified group is sometimes used as a safety performance indicator. Figure 4.4 presents the fatality

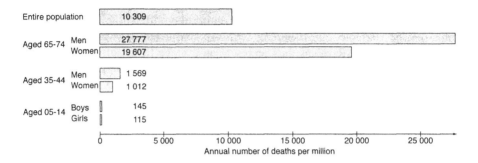

**Figure 4.4** Annual number of deaths for various age groups in the UK based on deaths in 1999 (Source: HSE, 2001a).

risk as a function of age for some age groups in the UK. The data cover both accident fatalities and fatalities due to illness.

If we pick a person in the UK at random, without regard to age and gender, the figures in Figure 4.4 indicate that she or he will die during the next year with a probability approximately equal to $10\,309/10^6 \approx 1.03\%$. Note that we have to be very careful when using this type of historical data for predictions because the health situation in a country may change over time and the distribution between the various age groups may vary.

Individual safety performance statistics are published annually for most countries. These statistics are usually split into various categories, and can, for example, be used to estimate:

– The annual probability that an average woman between 50 and 60 years old will die due to cancer.

– The annual probability that an average employee in the construction industry will be killed in an occupational accident.

Individual risk usually varies greatly from activity to activity and from industry to industry. Some overall figures are presented in Table 4.7.

When presenting risk figures, it should always be specified to whom or to what group of people the figures apply. It would, for example, be meaningless to say that the national average risk of being killed while hanggliding is one in 20 million. What we are really interested in is the risk to the people who actually practice hanggliding.

***Remark***: By counting the number of fatalities as we do in Table 4.7, we do not distinguish between the deaths of young and old people. We also treat as equivalent deaths that come immediately after the accident and deaths that follow painful and debilitating disease.                                                                        ⊕

**Table 4.7** Annual risk of death from industrial accidents to employees for various industry sectors.

| Industry sector | Annual risk | Annual risk |
|---|---|---|
| Fatalities to employees | 1 in 125 000 | $8 \cdot 10^{-6}$ |
| Fatalities to self-employed | 1 in 50 000 | $20 \cdot 10^{-6}$ |
| Mining and quarrying of energy producing materials | 1 in 9 200 | $109 \cdot 10^{-6}$ |
| Construction | 1 in 17 000 | $59 \cdot 10^{-6}$ |
| Extractive and utility supply industries | 1 in 20 000 | $50 \cdot 10^{-6}$ |
| Agriculture, hunting, forestry, and fishing (not sea fishing) | 1 in 17 200 | $58 \cdot 10^{-6}$ |
| Manufacture of basic metals and fabricated metal products | 1 in 34 000 | $29 \cdot 10^{-6}$ |
| Manufacturing industry | 1 in 77 000 | $13 \cdot 10^{-6}$ |
| Manufacture of electrical and optical equipment | 1 in 500 000 | $2 \cdot 10^{-6}$ |
| Service industry | 1 in 333 000 | $3 \cdot 10^{-6}$ |

*Source*: Adapted from HSE (2001b).

### 4.3.11 FN Curves

The possible consequences of an accident may in many cases vary over a wide range. It has therefore been found useful to present the consequences versus their frequencies in a graph. To make the graph more "stable," it has become common to plot the cumulative frequency $f(c)$ of a consequence $C \geq c$. This type of plotting is attributed to Farmer (1967), who plotted cumulative frequencies of various releases of I-131 from thermal nuclear reactors. Curves of this type are therefore sometimes called *Farmer curves*.

When the relevant consequences are the number of fatalities, $N$, the curve is usually called an *FN curve*. The FN curve is a descriptive risk indicator that provides information on how a risk is distributed over small and large accidents. An example of an FN curve is shown in Figure 4.5, where the frequency $F$ on the ordinate axis is the frequency of "exceedance," meaning that $F(n)$ denotes the frequency of accidents where the consequence is $n$ or more fatalities.

Assume that fatal accidents in a specified system or within a specified area occur according to a homogeneous Poisson process with frequency $\lambda$ (per annum). By *fatal accident* we mean an accident with at least one fatality. Let $N$ denote the number of fatalities of a future fatal accident. Since all accidents under consideration are fatal accidents, we know that $\Pr(N \geq 1) = 1$. The frequency of fatal accidents with $n$ or

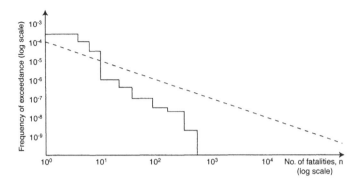

**Figure 4.5**  FN curve example.

more fatalities is therefore

$$F(n) = \lambda_{[N \geq n]} = \lambda \cdot \Pr(N \geq n) \tag{4.11}$$

and the FN curve is obtained by plotting $F(n)$ as a function of $n$, for $n = 1, 2, \ldots,$ as shown in Figure 4.5. The frequency of accidents with exactly $n$ fatalities is therefore

$$f(n) = F(n) - F(n + 1) \tag{4.12}$$

Since $f(n) \geq 0$ for all $n$, the FN curve must be either flat or falling.

The probability that a future accident will have exactly $n$ fatalities is

$$\Pr(N = n) = \Pr(N \geq n) - \Pr(N \geq n + 1) = \frac{F(n) - F(n + 1)}{\lambda} \tag{4.13}$$

The mean number of fatalities in a single, future accident is

$$E(N) = \sum_{n=1}^{\infty} n \cdot \Pr(N = n) = \sum_{n=1}^{\infty} \Pr(N \geq n) \tag{4.14}$$

The mean number of fatal accidents per annum is $\lambda$ (since we use years as the time unit), and the mean total number of fatalities per annum is therefore

$$E(N_{\text{Tot}}) = \lambda \cdot E(N) = \sum_{n=1}^{\infty} \lambda \cdot \Pr(N \geq n) = \sum_{n=1}^{\infty} F(n) \tag{4.15}$$

which can be represented by the "area" under the FN curve in Figure 4.5. FN curves for some types of transport systems are illustrated in Figure 4.6.

The FN curve may be used for at least three purposes:

– To show the historical record of accidents

– To depict the results of quantitative risk assessments

– To display criteria for judging the tolerability or acceptability of outputs from quantitative risk assessments

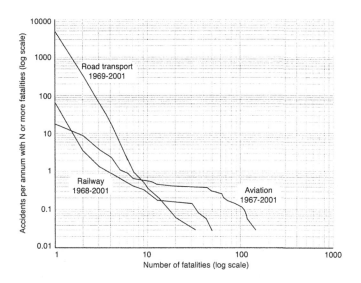

**Figure 4.6**    FN curve example (adapted from HSE, 2003b).

***FN Criterion Lines.***    By introducing criterion lines in the FN diagram as shown in Figure 4.7, the outputs from quantitative risk assessment can be judged against a predefined level of acceptable risk. An FN-criterion line is determined by two parameters (Ball and Floyd, 1998):

1. An anchor point, $(n, F(n))$, which is a fixed pair of consequence and frequency.

2. A risk aversion factor, $\alpha$, which determines the slope of the criterion line.

Given an anchor point and a risk aversion factor $\alpha$, the criterion line is constructed from the equation:[3]

$$F(n) \cdot n^\alpha = k_1 \qquad (4.16)$$

where $k_1$ is a constant. By taking logarithms, the equation becomes

$$\log F(n) + \alpha \log n = k \qquad (4.17)$$

where $k = \log k_1$. If plotted in a coordinate system with logarithmic scale, like in Figure 4.7, this function will produce a straight line with slope $-\alpha$.

As illustrated in Figure 4.7, two different lines are usually drawn, thus splitting the area in three regions: an unacceptable region, a tolerable ALARP region, and a broadly acceptable region. The ALARP principle is described further in Section 4.5.3.

The anchor points and the slopes have to be deduced from risk acceptance criteria. With the values chosen in Figure 4.7, the upper FN criterion line indicates that it

---

[3]This equation is often written as $F \cdot N^\alpha = k_1$.

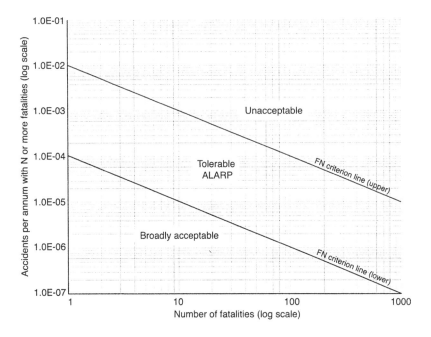

**Figure 4.7**   FN criterion lines (example).

is considered to be unacceptable to have fatal accidents with a higher frequency than $10^{-2}$ per year. Similarly, the lower FN criterion line indicates that a situation where fatal accidents occur with a frequency of less than $10^{-4}$ per year is broadly acceptable. The region between the two lines is often called the ALARP region. In this region the risk is considered to be tolerable if the ALARP principle is followed.

The slope in Figure 4.7 is based on $\alpha = 1$. A higher value of $\alpha$ will give a steeper line, indicating *risk aversion* to accidents with a high number of fatalities. *Risk aversion* means being more than proportionally concerned with the number of fatalities per accident. A risk-averse person regards an accident that kills several persons as being less acceptable than several accidents that collectively take the same number of lives. Accounting for risk aversion in policy-making is a controversial issue, and there are therefore different opinions regarding what value of $\alpha$ to employ. In the UK, HSE prescribes a so-called "risk neutral" factor of $\alpha = 1$, which means that the frequency of an accident that kills 100 people (or more) should be approximately 10 times lower than one that kills 10 people (or more). The Dutch government, on the other hand, promotes a risk aversion factor of $\alpha = 2$. An accident that kills 100 people (or more) is then required to have approximately 100 times lower frequency than an accident that kills 10 people (or more). For a thorough discussion on this issue, the reader is referred to Skjong et al. (2007) and Ball and Floyd (1998). Note that both settle for an aversion factor of $\alpha = 1$ to avoid implicit judgments of risk acceptability.

***Some Comments.***    To investigate the properties of the FN criterion line, we assume that accidents occur according to the assumptions of a specified line with aversion factor $\alpha = 1$ and formula $F(n) \cdot n = k_1$.

For $n = 1$, we get $F(1) = k_1$. The constant $k_1$ is therefore equal to the total frequency of fatal accidents. The frequency of fatal accidents with a single fatality is $f(1) = F(1) - F(2) = k_1 - k_1/2 = k_1/2$. The assumptions behind the criterion line therefore imply that exactly half of the fatal accidents have a single fatality.

In general (when $\alpha = 1$), the frequency of an accident with exactly $n$ fatalities is

$$f(n) = F(n) - F(n+1) = \frac{k_1}{n(n+1)} \tag{4.18}$$

which implies that all numbers $n$ of fatalities occur with a certain regularity.

If risk is calculated as the expected annual consequence, the risk contribution from accidents with $n$ fatalities is $\Delta R_n = n \cdot f(n) = k_1/(n+1)$ and decreases with the number of fatalities.

The FN criterion line is sometimes claimed to be an *iso-risk* line, usually without any clear definition of what is meant by the term *iso-risk*. In light of the value of $\Delta R_n$, the iso-risk assertion might be discussed.

With the same assumptions, the expected number of annual fatalities would be

$$E(N_{\text{Tot}}) = \sum_{n=1}^{\infty} n \cdot f(n) = k_1 \cdot \sum_{n=1}^{\infty} \frac{1}{n+1} = \infty$$

In most cases, however, the number of persons exposed is limited to some value $n_{\max}$ and the expected number of annual fatalities is therefore

$$E(N_{\text{Tot}}) = k_1 \cdot \sum_{n=1}^{n_{\max}} \frac{1}{n+1} \tag{4.19}$$

FN criterion lines are widely used to evaluate the group (societal) risk of an activity or system. Their use is, however, contested. Among the critics are Evans and Verlander (1997), who claim that FN criterion lines provide illogical recommendations if, for example, the line is exceeded in one area but is otherwise lower. Albeit the FN criterion lines are usually considered to provide valuable guidance to decisions on risk acceptability, the user should therefore be aware of the limitations of this approach.

## 4.4  Risk Matrices

A *risk matrix* is a tabular illustration of the frequency and severity of hazardous events or accident scenarios. The risk matrix may be used to rank hazardous events according to their significance, to screen out insignificant events, or to evaluate the need for risk reduction for each event (e.g., see HSE, 2001a).

**Table 4.8** Frequency classes.

| Category | Frequency (per year) | Description |
|---|---|---|
| 5. Fairly normal | $10-1$ | Event that is expected to occur frequently |
| 4. Occasional | $1-0.1$ | Event that happens now and then and will normally be experienced by the personnel |
| 3. Possible | $10^{-1}-10^{-3}$ | Rare event, but will possibly be experienced by the personnel |
| 2. Remote | $10^{-3}-10^{-5}$ | Very rare event that will not necessarily be experienced in any similar plant |
| 1. Improbable | $0-10^{-5}$ | Extremely rare event |

There are no accepted standards related to the size of the matrix, the labeling of the axes, and so on. In most risk matrices, the frequency and the severity are divided into three to six categories, with the frequency on the horizontal axis and the severity on the vertical axis. In the risk matrix illustrated in Figure 4.8, five categories are used for both the frequency and the severity. Each cell in the matrix corresponds to a specific combination of frequency and severity, which can be assigned a priority number or some other risk descriptor. The categories can be either quantitatively or qualitatively expressed, and may include consequences to people, the environment, assets, and/or reputation. The classifications of frequencies and severities are discussed below.

### 4.4.1 Classification of Frequencies

In most applications it is sufficient to group the frequencies (both when it is a risk indicator and a safety performance indicator) in rather broad classes, for example, by using the categories in Table 4.8. Although these categories are commonly used, several other classifications may be found in standards and guidelines. When defining frequency categories, it is common to let the frequency in one category be about 10 times higher than in the preceding category. By this approach, the category numbers will be approximately on a logarithmic scale.

### 4.4.2 Classification of Consequences

The consequences of an accident may be classified into different levels according to their *severity*. An example of such a classification is given in Table 4.9.

Table 4.9 represents typical categories. When a risk assessment of a specific system is carried out, it is often beneficial to adapt the categories to the situation at hand. The severity categories are usually defined such that the severity of a category is approximately ten times higher than the severity of the preceding category. By this approach, the severity numbers will also be on a logarithmic scale.

| Probability/ Consequence | 1 Improbable | 2 Remote | 3 Possible | 4 Occasional | 5 Fairly normal |
|---|---|---|---|---|---|
| 5 Catastrophic | 6 | 7 | 8 | 9 | 10 |
| 4 Severe loss | 5 | 6 | 7 | 8 | 9 |
| 3 Major damage | 4 | 5 | 6 | 7 | 8 |
| 2 Damage | 3 | 4 | 5 | 6 | 7 |
| 1 Minor damage | 2 | 3 | 4 | 5 | 6 |

Acceptable - only ALARP actions considered

Acceptable - use the ALARP principle and consider further analysis

Not acceptable - risk reduction required

**Figure 4.8** Risk matrix.

**Table 4.9** Classification of consequences according to their severity.

| Category | Consequence types | | |
|---|---|---|---|
| | People | Environment | Property |
| 5. Catastrophic | Several fatalities | Time for restitution of ecological resources ≥ 5 years | Total loss of system and major damage outside system area |
| 4. Severe loss | One fatality | Time for restitution of ecological resources =2–5 years | Loss of main part of system; production interrupted for months |
| 3. Major damage | Permanent disability, prolonged hospital treatment | Time for restitution of ecological resources ≤ 2 years | Considerable system damage; production interrupted for weeks |
| 2. Damage | Medical treatment and lost-time injury | Local environmental damage of short duration (≤ 1 month) | Minor system damage; minor production influence |
| 1. Minor damage | Minor injury, annoyance, disturbance | Minor environmental damage | Minor property damage |

**Table 4.10** Severity classification in MIL-STD-882D (2000).

| Category | Description |
|---|---|
| Catastrophic | Any failure that could result in deaths or injuries or prevent performance of the intended mission |
| Critical | Any failure that will degrade the system beyond acceptable limits and create a safety hazard (could cause death or injury if corrective action is not taken immediately) |
| Major | Any failure that will degrade the system beyond acceptable limits but can be counteracted or controlled adequately by alternative means |
| Minor | Any failure that does not degrade the overall performance beyond acceptable limits—one of the nuisance variety |

Another commonly used classification is given in Table 4.10.

### 4.4.3 Risk Index

The risk $R$ associated with a hazardous event may, as we described in Section 2.2, be "calculated" by multiplying the probability (or frequency) of the event by the consequences $C$ of the event, so that $R = C \cdot p$. If we take the logarithm of this expression, we get

$$\log R = \log C + \log p \qquad (4.20)$$

As mentioned above, it is common to set up frequency and consequence categories on a logarithmic scale, so that the frequency/consequence of a class is 10 times higher than in the preceding class. It is therefore common to use logarithms with base 10.

If we choose the unit of measure such that the consequence $C_1$ in consequence class 1 gives $\log C_1 = 1$, the consequence of class 2 will be approximately $C_2 = 10 \cdot C_1$, and the logarithm is $\log C_2 = \log(10 \cdot C_1) = 2$. In the same way $\log C_3 = 3$, and so on. The same applies for the frequency classes.

The *risk index* of a hazardous event is defined as the logarithm of the risk associated with the event and is found by adding the frequency class of the event with the severity class of the event.

### ▣ EXAMPLE 4.11    Fire in a subway train

Consider hazardous event $A$: fire with smoke in a subway train in a tunnel.

- The consequence is assessed based on Table 4.9. We assume 3–10 fatalities and get consequence class 5.

- The probability is assessed based on Table 4.8. We assume that hazardous event $A$ occurs once every 10–100 years and get probability class 3.

The risk index for hazardous event (accident scenario) $A$ is then $5 + 3 = 8$. The numbers in this example are not based on a thorough analysis and are included only as an illustration.                                                                    ⊕

The risk index is also called the *risk priority number* (RPN) of the hazardous event. In the risk matrix in Figure 4.8, the risk indices for the various combinations are calculated as shown in the matrix. Since this matrix is a $5 \times 5$ matrix, the risk indices will range from 2 to 10.

Following the approach described above, it is implied that events with the same risk index will have approximately the same risk. It is sometimes relevant to group hazardous events that have risk indices in a certain range and treat them similarly. In Figure 4.8, three different ranges/areas are distinguished as defined by the UK Civil Aviation Authority (UK CAA, 2008, p.12):

(a) *Acceptable.* The consequence is unlikely or not severe enough to be of concern; the risk is tolerable. However, consideration should be given to reducing the risk further to as low a level as reasonably practicable (ALARP), to further minimize the risk of an accident or incident.[4]

(b) *Review.* The consequence and/or probability is of concern; measures to mitigate the risk to as low as reasonably practicable (ALARP) should be sought. Where

---

[4]The ALARP principle is discussed further in Section 4.5.3.

the risk is still in the review category after this action, the risk may be accepted provided that the risk is understood and has the endorsement of the person who is ultimately accountable for safety in the organization.

(c) *Unacceptable.* The probability and/or severity of the consequence is intolerable. Major mitigation will be necessary to reduce the probability and severity of the consequences associated with the hazard.

In the risk matrix in Figure 4.8, the acceptable region is in the lower left corner of the matrix and covers the events with risk index 2–5. The unacceptable region is in the upper right corner and covers events with risk indices 8–10, while the review region is in the midregion of the matrix, covering events with risk indices 6 and 7.

### 4.4.4   An Alternative Risk Matrix

ISO 17776 (2002) uses a more comprehensive risk matrix with four consequence categories: people, assets, environment, and reputation. Each category has six severity levels, as illustrated in Figure 4.9. By including asset and reputation risk, the risk matrix addresses important aspects of strategic decision-making in companies.

Notice that this risk matrix uses a more factual probability terminology (e.g., has occurred in operating company) instead of more general statements (e.g., remote— likely to occur sometime). This approach may make the risk matrix easier to apply in systems with a long operating history, but somewhat difficult in new systems with limited experience.

### 4.4.5   Advantages and Limitations

*Advantages.*   The main advantages are that risk matrices are:

- easy to use and do not require extensive training;
- easy for decision-makers to understand;
- a common tool in risk assessment, with a long track record;
- a good basis for risk discussions;
- suitable for relative ranking of risks, prioritizing risk reduction measures, and when examining the need for more detailed analyses.

*Limitations.*   The main limitations are that risk matrices:

- do not follow any standard terminology or layout, so it may be difficult to compare results from different studies;
- look at the hazardous events one by one rather than in accumulation, whereas risk decisions should really be based on the total risk of an activity;
- can be used only for hazardous events identified (the risk matrix does not identify any additional hazardous events).

| Severity ranking | Consequences | | | | Increasing probability | | | |
|---|---|---|---|---|---|---|---|---|
| | People | Assets | Environment | Reputation | A | B | C | D |
| | | | | | Has occurred in industry | Has occurred in operating company | Occurred several times a year in operating company | Occurred several times a year in location |
| 0 | Zero injury | Zero damage | Zero effect | Zero impact | Manage for continued improvement | | | |
| 1 | Slight injury | Slight damage | Slight effect | Slight impact | | | | |
| 2 | Minor injury | Minor damage | Minor effect | Limited impact | | | | |
| 3 | Major injury | Local damage | Local effect | Considerable impact | | | | |
| 4 | Single fatality | Major damage | Major effect | Major national impact | Incorporate risk-reducing measures | | Failed to meet screening criteria | |
| 5 | Multiple fatalities | Extensive damage | Massive effect | Major international impact | | | | |

**Figure 4.9** Risk matrix (reproduced from ISO 17776, 2002, with permission from Standard Online AS).

For further discussion, see, for example, NASA (2007, p. 145). Because of the analyst's freedom in choosing consequence categories, risk matrices can capture both individual and group (societal) risk. A combination may even be possible, by expressing the most serious consequences by multiple fatalities and the lower end of the scale by IRPA (Johansen, 2010a).

## 4.5 Risk Acceptance Criteria

The standard NS 5814 (2008) states that "the results of risk analysis must be compared with the criteria for acceptable risk" and requires that *risk acceptance criteria* be established before conducting a risk analysis.

Risk acceptance criteria are defined by NS 5814 (2008) as:

☞ **Risk acceptance criteria**: Criteria used as a basis for decisions about acceptable risk.

Risk acceptance criteria may be quantitative or qualitative (NS 5814, 2008). According to NSW (2008b), it is essential that certain qualitative principles be adopted, irrespective of the numerical value of quantitative acceptance criteria. Common qualitative criteria are:

- All avoidable risks should be avoided.
- Risks should be reduced wherever practicable.
- The effects of events should be contained within the site boundary.
- Further development should not pose any incremental risk.

Risk acceptance criteria may be based on requirements from authorities, standards, experience, theoretical knowledge, and norms. The level of risk that is considered "acceptable" in a given context depends on several factors, among others the benefit we have from the activities that cause the risk and whether or not the risk is voluntary. NS 5814 (2008) defines acceptable risk as:

☞ **Acceptable risk**: Risk that is accepted in a given context based on the current values of society and in the enterprise.

Fischhoff et al. (1981) have been influential in stating that no risk is acceptable in isolation or in a universal sense. It is therefore somewhat misleading to talk about acceptable *risk*, they claim: rather one should speak in terms of acceptable *options*. The acceptability of an option represents a trade-off among the full set of associated risks, costs, and benefits of an option. In turn, the desirability of these factors depends on the other options, values, and facts examined in the decision-making process. Owing to this fact, the most acceptable option in an acceptable-risk problem may not be the option with the least risk. According to Fischhoff et al. (1981):

> Acceptable risk problems are decision problems, that is, they require a choice among alternatives. That choice is dependent on values, beliefs and other factors.

Therefore, there can be no single, all-purpose number that expresses the acceptable risk for a society ....

■ **EXAMPLE 4.12    Risk acceptance criteria for nuclear power plants**

Much effort has been devoted to establishing quantitative risk acceptance criteria in the nuclear power industry. The following items have, for example, been proposed as candidates for setting quantitative criteria (e.g., see Cameron and Willers, 2001; CNCS, 2009):

(a) The overall risk to the public.

(b) The risk to an individual.

(c) The sum of frequencies of all event sequences that can lead to a release of radioactive material that may require temporary evacuation of the local population (called *small release frequency*—SRF).

(d) The sum of frequencies of all event sequences that can lead to a release of radioactive material that may require long-term relocation of the local population (called *large release frequency*—LRF).

(e) The conditional probability of containment failure (given core damage).

(f) The sum of frequencies of all event sequences that lead to significant core degradation (called *core damage frequency*—CDF).

(g) The probability of a particular accident sequence.

(h) The reliability of individual safety systems.

Quantitative criteria for new nuclear power plants could, for example, be formulated as (CNCS, 2009):

$CDF \leq 10^{-5}$ per reactor year

$SRF \leq 10^{-5}$ per reactor year

$LRF \leq 10^{-6}$ per reactor year

There is, however, still no general agreement on the values to be used for these limits.                                                                      ⊕

### 4.5.1    Acceptable and Tolerable Risk

Risk acceptance is basically a question of the benefits you hope to receive from accepting a risk. Some people seem to accept a very high risk voluntarily if the benefit they receive is very high to them. An industrial worker may, for example, accept the risk from the plant that employs her because this activity provides her income. Her neighbor, on the other hand, may find that the group (societal) risk from the same plant is totally unacceptable, as she receives no direct benefit from its operations. Who, then is the legitimate decision-maker? A manager accepting a risk that she herself will not be exposed to, may have very little trouble doing so. The worker or neighbors who face the risk with their own lives may be of another opinion.

To capture the complexity of acceptable risk problems, HSE (1992) distinguishes between *tolerable* and *acceptable* risk:

According to HSE (1992):

> [Tolerability] refers to the willingness to live with a risk so as to secure some certain benefits and in the confidence that it will be properly controlled. [...] To *tolerate* a risk means that we do not regard it as negligible or something we might ignore, but rather as something we need to keep under review and reduce still further if and as we can. For a risk to be *acceptable* on the other hand means that for purposes of life or work, we are prepared to take it pretty well as it is.

Based on this distinction, the UK legislation operates with three categories of risk: acceptable, tolerable, and broadly acceptable (HSE, 2001b):

– Activities with an *unacceptable level of risk* are regarded as unacceptable except in extraordinary circumstances (such as wartime), whatever their benefits. Activities causing such risk would be prohibited, or would have to reduce the risk whatever the cost.

– Activities with a *tolerable level of risk* are tolerated in order to secure certain benefits. In this region, the risk is kept as low as reasonably practicable (ALARP), by adopting reduction measures unless their burden (in terms of cost, effort, or time) is grossly disproportionate to the reduction of risk they offer.

– A *broadly acceptable level of risk* implies that the risk level is generally regarded as insignificant. Further actions to reduce the risk are not normally required.

The Royal Society (1992) describes a similar conceptual framework for risk to members of the public. Above a certain level, which is proposed to be 1 in 10 000 per year, the risk should be considered intolerable and call for immediate action to reduce them irrespective of the cost—even when the person exposed judges that she or he has some commensurable benefit. A risk of 1 in 1 000 000 is suggested as being broadly acceptable to the public. Between these two levels the risk is considered tolerable but not negligible, and there is a need to reduce it further "as far as is reasonable practicable." Below the broadly acceptable level the risk is considered to be negligible and an employer should not be required to seek further improvement. It is notable that the intolerable level is of the same order of magnitude as the current risk level for traffic accidents.

### 4.5.2 Value of Life

To determine the value of a human life is a very controversial task, and many people find such a task distasteful. To be able to compare potential harm to people with benefits, risk reduction costs, and other types of risk, we are, however, sometimes forced to quantify the loss of a human life or an injury in monetary units.

***Value of a Statistical Life.***   All people take risks, some of which could be avoided at the expense of either time or money. When we spend money to reduce risk, we are, whether we like it or not, implicitly making a trade-off between the cost of the risk-reducing measure and a benefit (i.e., a reduced probability of death). The ratio of the cost we are willing to accept in exchange for a small change in the probability of a fatality is expressed in units of "dollars per death," or the monetary value of a fatality (Ashenfelter, 2005).

The term *statistical life* is used since the cost-benefit evaluation concerns the *probability* of saving a life, but also because we want to consider the life of a "general" person, that is, a person chosen at random from a population. This is because for most people, the value of life will be quite different depending on whose life we consider. Generally, the value of our own life and the lives of our family will be considerably higher than the value of the life of someone we do not know.

Consider a decision-maker who is considering implementing a specified risk-reducing measure that will increase the cost of an investment by $\Delta c$. A risk analysis shows that this measure will reduce the probability of a fatality by $\Delta p$. If the decision-maker evaluates and decides which $\Delta c$ she is willing to invest in order to obtain the reduction $\Delta p$, the cost-benefit factor $v = \Delta c / \Delta p$ can be used to derive her value of a statistical life (VSL). VSL is obviously not a constant but will depend on the probability $p$ of a fatality, the total value of the investment, the consequences of a fatality for the company's reputation, and so on.

There has been considerable research into the value of a statistical life, and different VSL values have been used in specific studies. The VSL values typically range from 1 to 15 million U.S. dollars.

Note that the VSL is not a "value (or price) of life" in the sense of a sum that any given individual would accept in compensation for the certainty of his or her own death. Rather, it is derived from studies of what a company or the public would be willing to pay for a reduction in already low levels of residual risk. A VSL is hence a measure of a company's or society's values.

*Alternative Concepts*   Several similar concepts are sometimes used. Among these are:

(a) *Societal willingness to pay.* The principle is described in more detail by Pandey and Nathwani (2004), who also propose to include a life quality index in the assessment of our willingness to pay.

(b) *Value of averting (or preventing) a fatality* (VAF). This is an aggregate willingness to pay for typically very small reductions in the individual probability of death.

(c) *Implied cost of averting a fatality* (ICAF). The International Maritime Organization (IMO) uses the ICAF as part of its decision rules:

$$ICAF = \frac{\text{net annual cost of measure}}{\text{reduction in annual fatality rate}} \qquad (4.21)$$

(d) *Net cost of averting a fatality* (NCAF). This measure accounts for the economic benefits of risk-reducing measures. Economic benefits (or risk reduction) may also include the economic value of reduced pollution.

$$NCAF = \frac{\Delta\text{cost} - \Delta\text{economic benefits}}{\Delta\text{risk}}$$

### 4.5.3  Approaches to Risk Acceptance

A number of different approaches have been developed for determining whether or not the risk related to a system or an activity is acceptable. Some of the most commonly used approaches are described briefly below.

***The ALARP Principle.***    ALARP is an acronym for "as low as reasonably practicable" and is the UK principle for risk acceptability. ALARP has two main components:

(a) It provides a framework for analyzing risk (i.e., identifying risks and risk reducing measures). This requires explicit description and analysis of risk tolerability.

(b) It involves a method of determining if the cost of a risk-reducing measure is disproportionate to the benefits it will provide, and hence if the measure should be implemented.

When using the ALARP principle, the risk is divided into three levels, as illustrated in Figure 4.10 (HSE, 2001b):

1. An *unacceptable region*, where risks are intolerable except in extraordinary circumstances, and risk reduction measures are mandatory.

2. A middle band, or *ALARP region*, where risk reduction measures are desirable but may not be implemented if their cost is *grossly disproportionate* to the benefit gained.

3. A *broadly acceptable region*, where no further risk reduction measures are needed. In this region, further risk reduction is uneconomical and resources could be spent better elsewhere to reduce the total risk.

We thus have to state two risk limits: an *upper limit* (i.e., between the unacceptable region and the ALARP region) over which the risk cannot be justified on any grounds, and a *lower limit* (i.e., between the ALARP region and the broadly acceptable region) under which the risk is considered generally acceptable.

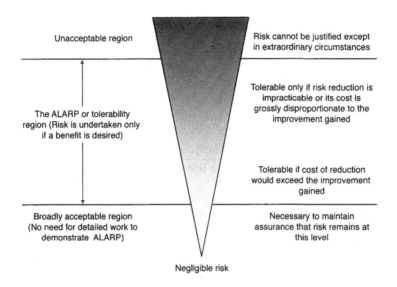

**Figure 4.10**    The ALARP principle.

**Table 4.11**    ALARP limits in the UK.

| Limit | Probability per year | | For whom |
|-------|----------------------|--------|----------|
| Upper | 1 in 1 000 | $10^{-3}$ | the workforce |
| | 1 in 10 000 | $10^{-4}$ | the public (for existing industrial plants) |
| | 1 in 100 000 | $10^{-5}$ | the public (for new industrial plants) |
| Lower | 1 in 1000 000 | $10^{-6}$ | the public |

The ALARP principle was introduced in the TOR framework on tolerability of risk from UK nuclear stations (HSE, 1992), and has subsequently been adapted for general applications in HSE (2001b).

The ALARP principle is relevant primarily for risk to humans. The vertical axis in Figure 4.10 (not shown) is thus a measure of individual risk, for example IRPA. The UK HSE has defined the upper and lower limits for IRPA in Table 4.11.

The risk is usually in the ALARP region, which is the region where the risk must be reduced to an ALARP level. In determining what is "reasonably practicable," the following four items must be considered:

1. The severity of the hazardous event in question.

2. The state of knowledge about the hazardous event, and the ways of preventing or mitigating its effects.

3. The availability and suitability of ways to prevent the hazardous event or to mitigate its effects.

4. The cost of preventing the hazardous events or mitigating its effects.

*Cost-Benefit Assessment*    ALARP implies that a cost-benefit approach must be adopted to decide what constitutes a "reasonable" level. In the ALARP region, the notion "grossly disproportionate" is central. It requires that a risk-reducing measure be implemented if the cost of the measure is not *grossly disproportionate* to the benefit gained. A disproportion factor $d$ may be calculated as

$$d = \frac{\text{cost of the risk-reducing measure}}{\text{benefit of the risk reduction}} \tag{4.22}$$

The cost of the risk-reducing measure is an estimate of the total cost, which covers purchase, installation, and training, but also cost implications related to the operation of the system, for example: reduced productivity. [If reduced productivity has a strong influence on a decision not to implement, the company should show that phasing or scheduling the work to coincide with planned downtimes (e.g., for maintenance) would not change the balance].

The benefit of implementing a risk-reducing measure is an estimate of the "cost" reduction implied by fewer injuries and fatalities, and also of possibly reduced input resources and/or improved system productivity.

The evaluation of disproportionality is carried out by first defining a disproportionality limit $d_0$. If the actual factor $d$ as calculated by (4.22) is less than $d_0$, the risk-reducing measure should be implemented, and if $d > d_0$, it should not be implemented. A disproportionality limit of, for example, $d_0 = 3$ means that for a measure to be rejected, the costs should be more than three times larger than the benefits. There are no strict authoritative requirements on what limit to employ, but it may seem reasonable to use a higher value of $d_0$ for high risks (i.e., close to the upper limit) than to lower risks.

A challenge with the cost-benefit approach is that it raises the problem of expressing not only the costs, but also the risk-reducing benefits in monetary terms. This is a particularly sensitive issue when it comes to putting a value on human life. To guide decision-making, some companies use internal criteria for the value of human life. An alternative to such explicit valuation of human life is simply to calculate the cost-benefit ratio for any risk-reducing measure, and to look out for any clearly unreasonable situations. If the value of life is not quantified, then resources, which also have value, cannot be allocated rationally to develop and implement countermeasures to protect life.

In essence, the ALARP principle states that money must be spent to reduce risks until they are reasonably low, and must continue to be spent for as long as it is cost-effective to do so and the risk is not negligible. If a "tolerable" level of risk can be reduced further at a reasonable cost and with little effort, it should be. At the same time, the ALARP principle recognizes that not all risk can be eliminated. Since it may not be practicable to take further action to reduce the risk or to identify the accidents that pose the risk, there will always be some residual risk of accidents.

*Remark*: In the UK Health and Safety at Work Act and in other regulations, the term *SFAIRP* is often used instead of *ALARP*. The two concepts are, however, similar and can usually be interchanged. SFAIRP is an acronym for "so far as is reasonably practicable."                                                                                                  ⊕

*The ALARA Principle.* ALARA is an acronym for "as low as reasonably achievable", which is the risk acceptability framework in the Netherlands. The ALARA principle is conceptually similar to ALARP, but does not include any region of broad acceptability. Until 1993, the region of negligible risk was part of the Dutch policy. Subsequently, it has been abandoned on the grounds that all risks should be reduced as long as it is reasonable (Bottelberghs, 2000). ALARA has, however, gained a somewhat different interpretation in practice. According to Ale (2005), it is common practice in the Netherlands to focus on complying with the upper limit rather than evaluating the reasonable practicality of further action. The unacceptable region in ALARA is, on the other hand, generally stricter than the one in ALARP, and the risk levels usually end up in the same range.

*The GAMAB Principle.* GAMAB is an acronym of the French expression *globalement au moins aussi bon*, which means "globally at least as good." The principle assumes that an acceptable solution already exists and that any new development should be at least as good as the existing solutions. The expression *globalement* (in total) is important here, because it provides room for trade-offs. An individual aspect may therefore be worsened if it is overcompensated by an improvement elsewhere.

The GAMAB principle has been used in decision-making related to transportation systems in France, where new systems are required to offer a total risk level that is globally as low as that of any existing equivalent system. The principle is also included in the railway RAMS standard EN 50126 (1999). A recent variant of GAMAB is GAME, which rephrases the requirement to at least *equivalent*.

GAMAB is a technology-based criterion, which means that it uses existing technology as the point of reference. By applying this principle, the decision-maker is exempted from the task of formulating a risk acceptance criterion, since it is already given by the present level of risk (e.g., see Johansen, 2010a).

*The MEM Principle.* MEM is an acronym for *minimum endogenous mortality*, which is a German principle that uses the probability of dying of natural causes as a reference level for risk acceptability. The principle requires that new or modified technological systems must not cause a significant increase in the IRPA of any person (Schäbe, 2001). MEM is based on the fact that death rates vary with age and the assumption that a portion of each death rate is caused by technological systems (Nordland, 2001).

Endogenous mortality means death due to internal causes, such as illness or disease. In contrast, exogenous mortality is caused by the external influences of accidents. The endogenous mortality rate is the rate of deaths due to internal causes of a given population at a given time. As shown in Section 4.5.3, children between 5 and 15 have the minimum endogenous mortality rate, which in Western countries is about $2 \cdot 10^{-4}$ per year, per person on average (EN 50126, 1999). This means that, on average, one in a group of 5 000 children will die each year. The MEM principle requires any technological system not to impose a significant increase in risk compared to this level of reference.

According to the railway standard EN 50126 (1999), such a "significant increase" is equal to 5% of MEM. This is deduced mathematically from the assumption that people are exposed to roughly 20 types of technological systems. Among these are technologies of transport, energy production, chemical industries, and leisure activities. Assuming that a total technological risk in the size of the minimum endogenous mortality is acceptable, the contribution from each system is confined to

$$\Delta IRPA \leq MEM \cdot 5\% = 10^{-5} \tag{4.23}$$

A single technological system thus poses an unacceptable risk if it increases IRPA by more than 5% of MEM. It should be emphasized that this criterion concerns the risk to any individual, not only the age group that provides the reference value. Unlike ALARP and GAMAB, MEM offers a universal quantitative risk acceptance criterion that is derived from the minimum endogenous mortality rate.

**Societal Risk Criteria.**   In 2001, the UK HSE published the report *Reducing Risks, Protecting People* (HSE, 2001b), which includes a proposed societal risk criterion which says that for any single industrial installation, "the risk of an accident causing the death of 50 or more people in a single event should be regarded as intolerable if the frequency is estimated to be more than one in five thousand per annum." This was the first time there had been a widely consulted and published criterion of this type.

**The Precautionary Principle.**   The precautionary principle differs from the other approaches described in this chapter. Common for these approaches is that they are *risk-based*, which means that risk management is to rely on the numerical assessment of probabilities and potential harms (Klinke and Renn, 2002). The precautionary principle is, in contrast, a *precaution-based* strategy for handling uncertain or highly vulnerable situations. The precaution-based approach does not provide any quantitative criterion to which the assessed risk level can be compared. Risk acceptability is instead a matter of proportionality between the severity of potential consequences and the measures that are taken in precaution.

The original definition of the precautionary principle is given in principle 15 of the UN declaration from Rio in 1992 (UN, 1992):

☞ **Precautionary principle**: Where there are threats of serious or irreversible damage, lack of full scientific certainty shall not be used as a reason for postponing cost-effective measures to prevent environmental degradation.

The precautionary principle is invoked where

- There is good reason to believe that harmful effects may occur to human, animal, or plant health, or the environment.

– The level of scientific uncertainty about the consequences or frequencies is such that risk cannot be assessed with sufficient confidence to inform decision-making.

Invocation of the precautionary principle may be appropriate with respect to, for example, genetically modified plants where there is good reason to believe that the modifications could lead to harmful effects on existing habitats, and there is a lack of knowledge about the relationship between the hazard and the consequences. A contrary example is that of the offshore industries, for which the hazards and consequences are generally well understood and conventional assessment techniques can be used to evaluate the risks by following a cautionary approach. Invocation of the precautionary principle is therefore extremely unlikely to be appropriate offshore.

## 4.6 Closure

There has been an ongoing discussion in the scientific community regarding the adequacy of risk acceptance criteria for making decisions about risk. Among the critics is Terje Aven (e.g., see Aven, 2007; Aven and Vinnem, 2005), who has questioned the use of risk acceptance criteria from a decision theoretical and ethical perspective. Risk acceptability evaluations must be based on ALARP-considerations, he claims, and not static criteria that fail to address the relationships among risks, benefits, and improvement.

Johansen (2010a) takes a more pragmatic perspective by suggesting that risk acceptance criteria should be evaluated according to their feasibility to the decision-maker and the extent to which they promote sound decisions. The first issue is primarily a matter of what risk indicators to apply (e.g., FN-criterion lines versus IRPA), and their ability to rank alternatives and provide precise recommendations with little uncertainty. The second is a matter of how the criteria are derived (e.g., MEM versus ALARP) and the extent to which they encourage improvement or preservation of status quo and allow for balancing risks with other considerations. Although useful for evaluating risk, it is recommended that practitioners interpret risk acceptance criteria as guiding benchmarks rather than rigid limits of acceptability.

## 4.7 Additional Reading

The following titles are recommended for further study related to Chapter 4.

– *Societal risks* (Ball and Floyd, 1998) discusses societal risk and different regulatory practices for establishing FN criterion lines.

– *Acceptable Risk* (Fischhoff et al., 1981) is a pioneering book on risk acceptability, which evaluates three principal approaches to acceptable risk problems: expert judgment, bootstrapping (accepting what has been accepted in the past), and formal analysis.

- *Reducing Risks, Protecting People: HSE's Decision-Making Process* (HSE, 2001b) presents the ALARP framework in the decision-making context of the UK HSE.

- *The Tolerability of Risk from Nuclear Power Stations* (HSE, 1992) explains the principal thinking behind HSE's approach to risk acceptability.

- *Foundations and fallacies of risk acceptance criteria* (Johansen, 2010a) was written in parallel with this book and offers more principal discussions on the use of risk acceptance criteria.

- *Risk and emergency preparedness analysis* (NORSOK Z-013, 2010) provides a nice overview of the pros and cons of various risk indicators.

- *Risk evaluation criteria* (Skjong et al., 2007) presents a comprehensive review of risk indicators and evaluation criteria in the marine industry.

- *Offshore Risk Assessment: Principles, Modeling and Application of QRA Studies* (Vinnem, 2007) discusses trends and risk indicators for harm to people and the environment in offshore industries.

# CHAPTER 5

# RISK MANAGEMENT

## 5.1 Introduction

This chapter gives a survey of the various steps in a risk analysis and describes the role of risk analysis and risk assessment in the risk management process. The application of bow-tie diagrams and bow-tie analysis in a risk management process is outlined briefly. Different types of risk analyses are discussed together with quality requirements and the competence of the study team. Risk management is mentioned briefly, but management aspects are outside the scope of this book. The most common analytical methods for risk analysis are discussed in Chapters 9–11.

## 5.2 Risk Management

In Chapter 1, risk management was defined as a continuous management process with the objective of revealing, analyzing, and assessing potential hazardous events in a system, and identifying and introducing efficient risk control measures to eliminate or reduce possible harm to people, the environment, or other assets. Risk man-

*Risk Assessment: Theory, Methods, and Applications,* First Edition.
By Marvin Rausand. Copyright © 2011 John Wiley & Sons, Inc.

agement is an integrated part of all good management and has, in our context, three main elements:

1. *Risk analysis*
   The objectives of risk analysis are to:

   (a) Identify hazards and threats related to the study object (system).

   (b) Identify potential hazardous events that may occur related to the study object.

   (c) Find the causes of each hazardous event.

   (d) Identify barriers and safeguards that can prevent or reduce the probability of hazardous events and/or the consequences of these events, and assess the reliability of these barriers.

   (e) Identify accident scenarios related to each hazardous event and determine the consequences and frequencies of these (i.e., establish the risk picture).

2. *Risk evaluation*
   The objectives of risk evaluation are to:

   (a) Assess the risk picture that was established in item 1(e), and, as far as possible, compare the risk with established risk acceptance criteria.

   (b) Consider alternative system and/or operational solutions.

   (c) Describe the risk that is related to the study object.

   (d) Propose risk-reducing measures and assess the effect of the risk reduction provided by each of them in relation to the cost of the measures.

   (e) Provide input to decision-making related to risk.

3. *Risk control and risk reduction*
   Relevant tasks within this activity are to:

   (a) Make decisions regarding the introduction of new risk-reducing measures or the modification of existing measures.

   (b) Implement risk-reducing measures.

   (c) Monitor the risk and propose and evaluate changes when appropriate.

   (d) Communicate risk issues to relevant stakeholders and the general public.

   (e) Make other decisions related to risk, for example:

       – Is it acceptable to continue a particular activity at the current risk level?
       – Will it be appropriate to implement a proposed risk-reducing measure?
       – Which of several proposed measures will it be best to implement?
       – How much must be invested to reduce the risk?

The related activities of the risk management process are illustrated in Figure 5.1.

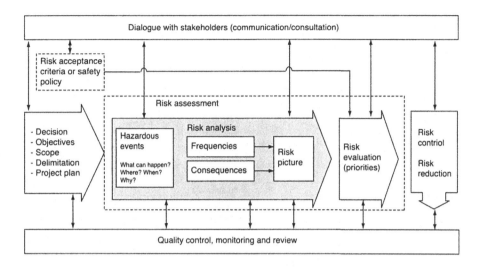

**Figure 5.1**    The elements of risk management (adapted with permission from AusAID, 2005).

## 5.3  Bow-Tie Analysis

Bow-tie diagrams have been mentioned several times in this book. A bow-tie diagram depicts the relationships between an identified hazardous event, its causes and consequences, and the barriers that have been implemented to reduce the probability of the hazardous event and to mitigate its consequences (e.g., see Cockshott, 2005).

The origin of the method is not quite clear, but since the early 1990s the oil company Shell has made a significant contribution to enhancing use of the method. Bow-tie diagrams have been used actively in safety reports for the petrochemical industry in the UK and were later adopted by, for example, the U.S. FAA. Bow-tie diagrams are also a central element in the ARAMIS method (Salvi and Debray, 2006) that was developed to support the risk analyses required by the Seveso II directive (EU, 1996).

Bow-tie diagrams have also proved to be an effective tool for training operators to recognize the risks and to take appropriate action to prevent accidents (Cardwell, 2008).

A typical bow-tie diagram is shown in Figure 5.2. Note that a separate bow-tie diagram has to be established for each hazardous event. The bow-tie diagram links the hazards and the consequences through a series of event lines and illustrates the "routes" to accidents. The barriers that have been, or are planned to be, implemented are linked to the event lines to which they are relevant.

In some applications, it may be pertinent to illustrate the influences from engineering, maintenance, and operation activities on the various hazards and safeguards, as indicated in Figure 5.2. The bow-tie diagram will then be even more suitable for risk management, since it provides a diagrammatic representation of the relationship be-

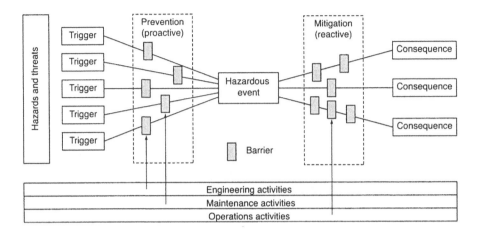

**Figure 5.2** Bow-tie diagram.

tween the actions in engineering, maintenance, and operation and the hazards being managed. Proposed changes in actions and management systems can then be linked directly to the various hazards, barriers, and risk.

The bow-tie diagram is not designed to identify hazardous events but, rather, to illustrate the physical and procedural controls that are in place to manage these events.

### 5.3.1 Analysis Procedure

The starting point for a bow-tie analysis is that one or more hazardous events have been identified. A bow-tie analysis for a single hazardous event involves the following steps:

1. Specify the hazardous event (what it is, where it occurs, and when it occurs).

2. Identify hazards, threats, and triggering events associated with the hazardous event and link them to the hazardous event—singly or in combination.

3. List existing and feasible proactive barriers related to the hazardous event and the hazards identified and enter them into the diagram.

4. Identify possible event sequences that may follow the hazardous event.

5. List existing and feasible reactive barriers/safeguards that may stop the event sequence or reduce the consequences, and enter them into the diagram.

6. List all potential undesirable consequences of the hazardous event.

7. Identify influences from engineering, maintenance, and operational activities on the various barriers and illustrate the influences on the bow-tie diagram.

## 5.4    Risk Analysis

As outlined in Chapter 1, a risk analysis is carried out to answer three questions:

1. What can go wrong? (i.e., hazard identification)

2. What is the likelihood of that happening? (i.e., frequency analysis)

3. What are the consequences? (i.e., consequence analysis)

The main objective of performing a risk analysis is to support a specific decision-making process, and a risk analysis should never be initiated without a clear reference to a relevant decision problem and the input needed to reach a decision. If the decision is an accept/reject decision, it should be emphasized that a clear definition of the acceptance criteria has to be established before the risk analysis is started. Participation from top management in defining the risk analysis objectives is important. The result of a risk analysis is not only an answer to the question "What is the risk?" but, more important, a framework for intelligent and visible risk management.

### 5.4.1    Types of Risk Analysis

Risk analyses and risk assessments may be classified in many different ways: for example, as qualitative versus quantitative, as illustrated in Figure 5.3. A similar figure is also presented by Arendt (1990).

***Qualitative Risk Analysis.***    A qualitative risk analysis uses words and/or descriptive scales to describe the frequency of the hazardous events identified and the severity of the potential consequences that may result from these events. The scales may be adapted or adjusted to suit the circumstances, and different descriptions may be used for different categories of the risk.

Qualitative risk analysis may be used:

- As an initial screening activity to identify accident scenarios that require more detailed analysis

- When the level of risk does not justify the time and effort required for a more detailed analysis

- When the data available are inadequate for a quantitative analysis

***Semiquantitative Risk Analysis.***    In a semiquantitative risk analysis, the qualitative scales are given values. The numbers allocated to each description do not have to have any accurate relationship to the actual magnitude of the frequency or the severity. The numbers can be combined in different ways to present a risk picture. The objective is to produce a more detailed prioritization than may be achieved in a qualitative analysis, not to suggest any realistic values for the risk, as is attempted in a quantitative analysis. An example of such a semiquantitative combination is the risk priority number (RPN) discussed in Section 4.4.3.

*Quantitative Risk Analysis.* A quantitative risk analysis uses numerical values for frequencies, consequences, and severities. The numerical values may come from many different sources (see Chapter 7). Several different names are used for quantitative risk analysis. Among these are:

*Quantitative risk analysis/assessment (QRA).* This term is used for many different types of risk analyses in several different application areas.

*Probabilistic risk analysis/assessment (PRA).* This expression was introduced in the U.S. nuclear power industry and was later adopted by NASA.

*Probabilistic safety analysis/assessment (PSA).* This is the same type of analysis as a PRA, but the term PSA is used mainly in Europe.

*Process hazard analysis (PrHA).* This term is used in the United States for a specific risk analysis mandated by OSHA in its process safety management regulation for processes that handle highly hazardous chemicals.

*Formal safety analysis/assessment (FSA).* The International Maritime Organization (IMO) introduced this term for risk analyses in the maritime industry. The same term is also used by the petroleum industry in Australia.

*Total risk analysis/assessment (TRA).* Some operators in the offshore oil and gas industry use this term.

The first comprehensive PRA was the *Reactor Safety Study* (NUREG-75/014), carried out from 1970 to 1975 by a team headed by Norman Rasmussen for the U.S. Nuclear Regulatory Commission (U.S. NRC), originally the Atomic Energy Commission. Several of the methods that are currently used in quantitative risk analyses were developed as part of this study.

The approach taken in a QRA (or a similar analysis) is to decompose the system into subsystems and components (e.g., valves, pumps), stopping the decomposition at a point where substantial amounts of data are available for most of the components of the resulting model.

Even if few actual system accidents have been observed, we can expect to find significant data on the frequencies of pump and valve failures, revealed both during operation and during routine testing. Using such data to estimate component failure rates, one can then aggregate the resulting failure rate estimates according to the QRA model to derive an estimate of the overall frequency of accidents for the system in question (e.g., see Bier, 1999).

### 5.4.2 Risk Acceptance Criteria

Risk acceptance criteria are criteria that are used to express a risk level that is considered to be tolerable for the system or activity in question (e.g., see NORSOK Z-013, 2010). Risk acceptance criteria are discussed in Section 4.5.

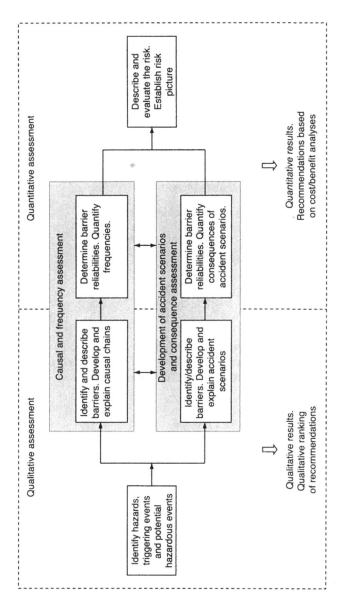

**Figure 5.3**    The risk assessment process – qualitative versus quantitative risk assessment.

### 5.4.3   The Steps in a Risk Analysis

A risk analysis may be carried out as a number of steps. The steps required depend on the scope of the analysis and the complexity of the study object. The eleven steps presented below are often included in quantitative risk analyses.

1. Plan and prepare the risk analysis.

2. Define and delimit the system and the scope of the analysis.

3. Identify hazards and potential hazardous events.

4. Determine causes and frequency of each hazardous event.

5. Identify accident scenarios (i.e., event sequences) that may be initiated by each hazardous event.

6. Select relevant and typical accident scenarios.

7. Determine the consequences of each accident scenario.

8. Determine the frequency of each accident scenario.

9. Assess the uncertainty.

10. Establish and describe the risk picture.

11. Report the analysis.

For each step, some main issues and questions to be answered are listed below. The steps are listed in a logical sequence, but some of the steps may change place in the actual performance of the risk analysis. The steps and the connections between them are illustrated in Figure 5.4.

**Step 1:** *Plan and Prepare the Risk Analysis.*   A risk analysis has to be thoroughly planned and prepared. This is important for the quality and applicability of the results from the analysis. Some questions that must be considered carefully are:

1.1 *Establish the objectives and the boundary conditions for the risk analysis*

(a) What is the background for the risk analysis? Why is the risk analysis carried out?

(b) To what decision(s) should the risk analysis give input?

(c) What information must the risk analysis provide (type and format)?

(d) Which requirements of the risk analysis are given in laws, regulations, and standards?

(e) When must the results from the risk analysis be available? It is important that the risk analysis be started up and managed such that the results are available and can be used when the decision has to be made.

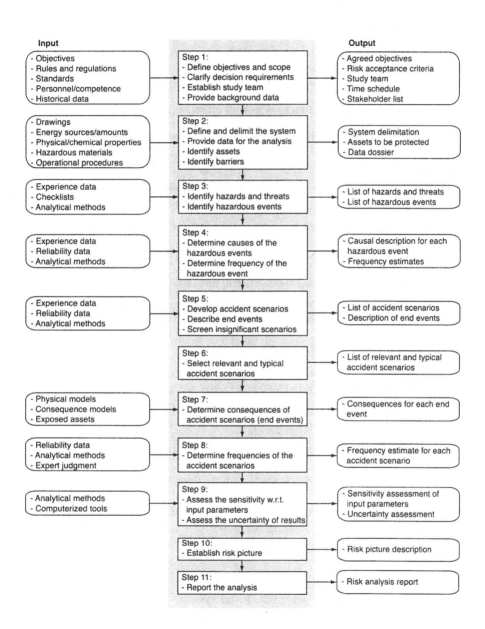

**Figure 5.4**    The steps in a risk analysis.

(f) Who are the stakeholders for the analysis? Who should be informed about and/or involved in the risk analysis? (The involvement is especially relevant for the risk evaluation—whether or not the risk is acceptable.)

(g) To what degree have the stakeholders been involved in the design or operation of the study object?

(h) Have any risk acceptance criteria been established?

(i) Has the company defined any overall safety objectives?

1.2 *Establish study team, ensure quality and involvement*

(a) Should existing personnel be used or external consultants?

(b) Which competence areas are required to carry out the analysis?

(c) How should the quality of the work be controlled?

(d) How should stakeholders be informed/involved?

1.3 *Select analytical approach*

(a) What approach is most appropriate to meet the objectives?

(b) Will this approach be responsive to the nature of the potential hazards, the data available, and the decision needs?

1.4 *Provide background information*

(a) What has earlier taken place related to the study object (e.g., protests and complaints from stakeholders, court trials, and media coverage)?

(b) Which hazardous events or accidents have occurred related to the study object or similar objects?

(c) What is generally considered to be acceptable risk for this type of system?

**Step 2: Define and Delimit the System and the Scope.** To carry out a risk analysis, it is necessary to fully understand the functions of the system, both in normal operation and during different deviations from normal operation. When external consultants carry out the risk analysis, it is important that personnel who are familiar with the system and/or activity cooperate with the external team.

2.1 *System function*

(a) Which functions are performed by the system?

(b) Which inputs are required for each function? (e.g., electric power, water)

(c) Which parts of the system should be covered by the risk analysis?

(d) Which life-cycle phases should be covered by the analysis?

(e) Which operational phases should be covered by the analysis? (e.g., normal operation, maintenance, startup)

(f) What is the political or societal importance of the system?

2.2 *Assets and consequences*

(a) Which assets may be harmed by an accident—within and outside the system boundaries?

(b) Which consequences should be considered?

(c) Which hazards should be considered? (e.g., technological hazards, natural hazards, deliberate actions)

(d) What types of accidents should have priority in the analysis? (e.g., fires, toxic release, accidents that may harm a third party)

2.3 *Safety barriers and emergency provisions*

(a) Which safety barriers (proactive and reactive) are available in the system? (e.g., alarms, emergency stop, firefighting system)

(b) Which external emergency functions are available (e.g., fire brigade, first aid, ambulances, search and rescue services), and how available and reliable are these?

(c) How much time will these rescue services need to arrive at the accident location?

2.4 *Detailedness of the analysis*

(a) How detailed should the risk analysis be?

(b) What types of events may be disregarded?

(c) Is the detailedness chosen commensurate with the importance of the decision to be made and the boundary conditions of the analysis?

2.5 *Data dossier*

(a) For which parameters and other quantities do we need to find input data?

(b) Where can we find such data?

(c) To what degree can we trust the quality of each data source?

**Step 3: Identify Hazards and Potential Hazardous Events.** This is one of the most important steps in the risk analysis process. If a hazard or a hazardous event is not identified, it will not be included in the risk analysis.

3.1 *Identify hazards and threats*

(a) Which hazards can lead to hazardous events related to the system?

(b) Where are these hazards located?

(c) To what types of threats can the system be exposed?

(d) Which threat agents are relevant?

    (e) Where are these threat agents?

    (f) Which assets are they likely to attack?

3.2 *Identify hazardous events*

    (a) Which hazardous events can potentially occur?

    (b) Where in the system can each hazardous event take place?

    (c) Are there any actions that we should take at this stage to avoid the hazardous event or reduce the risk related to this event?

This part of the analysis will sometimes include a *risk screening* of the hazardous events to determine if and to what detail each hazardous event should be subject to further analysis.

**Step 4: Determine the Causes and Frequency of Each Hazardous Event.** A causal analysis is carried out for each of the hazardous events that were identified and found to be significant in step 3. The most commonly used method for this step is fault tree analysis, which is presented in Section 10.3.

4.1 *Causal analysis*

    (a) What are the causes of the hazardous event? (Both immediate and root causes should preferably be identified.)

    (b) Which proactive barriers are installed to prevent or reduce the probability of the hazardous event?

    (c) How effective and reliable are these barriers?

    (d) Which combinations of events will potentially lead to the hazardous event?

4.2 *Frequency analysis*

    (a) Do we have data that can be used to determine the frequency of the hazardous event?

    (b) How often will the hazardous event occur? (Alternatively: What is the probability that the hazardous event will occur in a given situation?)

    (c) Which causes/events are most important for whether or not the hazardous event will occur?

**Step 5: Identify Accident Scenarios.** Each hazardous event will be the initiator of one or more event sequences that ultimately will harm assets. The possible event sequences are usually identified and described by an event tree analysis (see Section 11.2). Each path through the event tree represents an accident scenario. The endpoint of the path, called the *end event*, represents the point where one or more assets are harmed.

5.1 *Development of accident scenarios*

  (a) Which reactive barriers are installed to stop or mitigate the effects of accident scenarios starting from the hazardous event?
  (b) How effective and reliable are these barriers?
  (c) Which external events and conditions may influence the event sequences?
  (d) Which event sequences are significant?

5.2 *Description of end events*

  (a) What is the end event of each accident scenario (event sequence)?
  (b) What are the characteristics of each end event?
  (c) Which assets are harmed?
  (d) How are the assets harmed?

Accident scenarios with end events that do not lead to any significant harm to assets may be disregarded in the further analysis.

**Step 6:    Select Relevant and Typical Accident Scenarios.**    Step 5 will usually identify a large number of accident scenarios. In some cases, this number is so high that it is not realistic to analyze all the scenarios. Some will be similar and have the same or almost the same consequences. It is therefore necessary to reduce the number of events and study only some representative accident scenarios in detail.

6.1 *Select representative accident scenarios*

  (a) Which accident scenarios can give worst-case consequences?
  (b) Which accident scenarios can lead to the worst-credible-case consequences?
  (c) Which accident scenarios are representative for larger groups of scenarios?

6.2 *Define representative accident scenarios*
  Each of the representative accident scenarios must be defined and delimited.

  (a) What characterizes the scenario?
  (b) Where can the hazardous event take place?
  (c) When (in what phase) can the hazardous event occur?

**Step 7: Determine the Consequences of the Accident Scenario.**    In this step, the consequences of the end events of the representative accident scenarios are identified and quantified.

  (a) Which assets are exposed to the end event?

  (b) What are the accident loads to each asset?

  (c) Which barriers and safety functions are installed to stop or mitigate the effect of the end event? (e.g., personal protection equipment, fire protection)

  (d) Which resources (internal and external) can contribute to reducing the consequences for the assets? (e.g., fire brigade, ambulance)

***Step 8: Determine the Frequency of Each Accident Scenario.*** In this step, the accident scenarios from step 6 are studied, one by one. The frequency of the associated hazardous event was determined in step 4 and the conditional probability of the accident scenario (given this hazardous event) can be determined from the event tree analysis in step 5 if relevant input data are available. The formulas required for this quantification are given in Section 11.2.

***Remark***: Step 7 can be carried out before or after step 8. By taking step 7 first, the possible consequences of each accident scenario are determined and the frequency analysis of scenarios with insignificant consequences may be skipped or made rather roughly. On the other hand, if step 8 is done first, the frequency of each accident scenario is determined and the consequence analysis of scenarios with a very low frequency and a low consequence potential may be skipped or made rather roughly.

***Step 9: Assess the Uncertainty.*** The results of a risk analysis will often be subject to many types of uncertainty. The uncertainty may have many different origins. Uncertainty is discussed further in Chapter 16. It may also be relevant to carry out a sensitivity analysis associated with the uncertainty analysis. A sensitivity analysis is defined as:

☞ **Sensitivity analysis**: Analysis that examines how the results of a calculation or model vary as individual assumptions are changed (AS/NZS 4360, 1995).

9.1 *Sensitivity analysis*

(a) Will a quantitative analysis of the sensitivity improve the risk assessment (i.e., will it be worthwhile)?

(b) Which input quantities are most important? (This importance can often be found by using various types of importance measures.)

(c) What is the effect on the risk if we vary the value of these quantities? (e.g., by doubling, halving)

9.2 *Uncertainty analysis*

(a) Will a quantitative uncertainty analysis improve the risk assessment (i.e., will it be worthwhile)?

(b) What are the major sources of uncertainty?

(c) Are time and resources available to carry out a complex analysis?

(d) Will a quantitative estimate of uncertainty improve the decision? How will the decision be affected by this uncertainty analysis?

(e) How will the uncertainty be communicated to the decision-makers?

(f) What is the uncertainty of the results of the analysis caused by:

　　　－ The methods and models we have chosen
　　　－ The data we have used
　　　－ The calculations we have made
　（g）What is the uncertainty caused by:
　　　－ Sloppy/lacking formulation of the objectives of the analysis and/or
　　　　the boundary conditions for the analysis
　　　－ Time pressure
　　　－ Inadequate quality control of the work
　　　－ Inadequate access to modern computer tools
　　　－ Inadequate competence of the study team

**Remark**: It is obvious that it will not be possible to fully quantify this uncertainty, but the study team should be aware of the various contributors to uncertainty and express how they have tried to reduce the uncertainty.　　　　　　　　　　　　⊕

**Step 10:    Establish the Risk Picture.**    The most important result from the risk analysis is a description of the *risk picture*. This is a listing of the accident scenarios together with the associated frequencies and consequences. The consequences are sometimes transferred into severities. The risk picture is also called a *consequence spectrum*. Sometimes, it may also be relevant to establish bow-tie diagrams (see Figure 5.2) for each hazardous event. The main issues in this step are:

1. Which hazardous events have been identified and selected for further analysis?

2. Which accident scenarios have been identified and selected for further analysis?

3. What is the frequency of each of these accident scenarios?

4. Which consequences can arise from each accident scenario?

5. Is it relevant to present the risk picture as a set of bow-tie diagrams?

6. What level of risk is posed by the accident scenarios identified, individually and in total?

7. Is the risk level plausible and in accordance with the risk acceptance criteria?

　The risk picture can be presented in many different ways, for example:

(a) A listing of all relevant hazardous events (from step 3) together with the frequency of the event (from step 4) and the combined consequences and frequencies of all the accident scenarios arising from the hazardous event (from steps 7 and 8)

(b) A listing of all the relevant accident scenarios (from steps 5 and 6), together with frequencies and consequences (from steps 7 and 8)

If only some representative accident scenarios have been analyzed (step 6), it is important to remember that these scenarios represent a group that may contain several scenarios. To present a complete risk picture, all the scenarios should be covered.

*Step 11: Report the Analysis.*    The risk analysis must be reported such that it can fulfill its intended purpose.

1. What are the requirements in reporting the analysis?

2. Who is going to read the report?

3. Will the report or parts of the report be available to the public?

4. How comprehensive should the report be?

5. How should the report be presented? (e.g., to the media, in public meetings, to authorities, on the Internet)

6. Should parts of the analysis be presented in other ways than in a report? (e.g., brochures, video)

## 5.5  Risk Evaluation

Risk evaluation was defined in Chapter 1 as the process where the risk picture for the study object is evaluated and compared with risk acceptance criteria and/or safety policies. In addition, identification and documentation of additional risk-reducing measures are important in the risk evaluation process.

The main steps in the risk evaluation process are to:

1. *Evaluate the risk against risk acceptance criteria*

   (a) Is the risk determined by the risk analysis acceptable in relation to the risk acceptance criteria? (if such criteria are established)

   (b) Is the risk acceptable compared to the risk in similar systems and activities?

2. *Suggest and evaluate potential risk-reducing measures*

   (a) What risk-reducing measures are relevant?

   (b) What is the potential risk reduction for each of these measures?

## 5.6  Risk Control and Risk Reduction

There are two main types of risk-reducing measures:

1. *Preventive measures* intended to reduce the frequency of one or more hazardous event. Such measures are also called *proactive* or *frequency-reducing measures*.

2. *Mitigating measures* intended to avoid or reduce the consequences of a potentially hazardous event. Such measures are also called *reactive* or *consequence-reducing measures*.

In general, frequency-reducing measures should have higher priority than consequence-reducing measures, whenever this is possible.

Haddon's ten strategies, which are discussed in Section 6.4.2, may be used as an effective guide when proposing risk-reducing measures. More detailed approaches are outlined in NASA (2007), NSW (2003), and IMO (2002).

Haddon's ten strategies may be combined into four categories:

(a) *Eliminate, substitute, and/or minimize.* This strategy will result in an *inherently safer design*, and may, for example, be achieved by (i) avoiding using a hazardous substance, by (ii) substituting the hazardous substance with a less hazardous substance, and/or by (iii) minimizing the amount of the substance used and stored in the system.

(b) *Prevent.* This strategy involves reducing the probability or frequency of one or more hazardous events . This can be accomplished by design changes or by implementing proactive barriers (for more on barriers, see Chapter 12).

(c) *Detect and warn.* This implies transmitting information about the hazardous event to control systems and operators such that preventive intervention is possible.

(d) *Mitigate.* This is accomplished by (i) introducing reactive barriers that can stop or reduce the rate of energy that is released by the hazardous event, by (ii) separating the assets from the energy (e.g., fences, fire walls), by (iii) making the assets less vulnerable to impacts (e.g., hard hats, protective clothing), and by (iv) improving first aid and rehabilitating systems (e.g., ambulances, hospitals).

The resulting proposals for risk-reducing measures have to be evaluated and compared with respect to the probable risk reduction and the cost of implementing the measures (single or in combination). This is discussed further, for example, by Aven and Renn (2009b).

### 5.6.1 Control of Human Error

Prevention of accidents requires a reduction in the number of human errors or making the system more error tolerant.

Three main strategies are used to control and avoid human errors:

(a) *Error reduction.* This involves designing the systems to help the user avoid errors or correct errors that have just been made (e.g., see RSSB, 2007).

(b) *Error capturing.* The intent of this strategy is to "capture" the error before any adverse consequences of the error are felt. An example of an error-capturing strategy is supervision and third-party checking of the task.

(c) *Error tolerance.* This refers to the ability of a system to accept an error without serious consequences.

## 5.7   Competence Requirements

To which degree the risk analysis will meet the objectives depends on the competence of the study team. Necessary elements of competence which are often required include:

- Knowledge/understanding of the study object

- Probability theory and statistics

- Chemical, mechanical, electrical, structural, or nuclear competence

- Health competence, including toxicology

- Social science, including economy, psychology, and sociology

- Human factors and human reliability

- Organization and management and the impact on safety

## 5.8   Quality Requirements

The main quality characteristics of any sound scientific investigation are:

(a) Consistency in internal logic

(b) Empirical support

(c) Predictability of outcomes under similar conditions

### 5.8.1   Specific Requirements

Some specific requirements related to the quality of the risk assessment process include:

1. A clear objective for the analysis must be defined, one that reflects the information the decision-maker needs as input to her decision-making.

2. The extent and content of the risk analysis must be decided such that it can provide answers that can meet the objectives in point 1.

3. The resources allocated to the risk analysis must be comparable with the importance of the decision to be made.

4. The analysis must be objective, systematic, structured, and—as far as possible—evidence-based.

5. All assumptions made during the analysis must be documented and be included in the report from the analysis.

6. All results from the risk analysis should be traceable back to the various inputs that produce the result.

7. All calculations should be self-checked by the individual analyst and/or other study team members.

8. The risk analysis should be verified as a whole by an independent person. The following issues should be checked as a minimum:

   (a) Is the scope of the analysis appropriate for the stated objectives?

   (b) Are all critical assumptions credible?

   (c) Have appropriate methods, models, and data been used?

   (d) Are the analysis repeatable by personnel other than the original analyst (i.e., is the analysis properly documented and transparent)?

   (e) Are the results insensitive to the way the data and the results are formatted?

9. The risk must always be described qualitatively and, as far as possible, quantitatively.

10. The uncertainties of the results and the main causes of uncertainty should be described.

11. The risk analysis should be transparent and understandable by all stakeholders to whom the report will be presented.

12. Public participation should be encouraged, especially as it relates to evaluation of the risk.

13. The risk analysis must be easy to update—to take future changes into account.

### 5.8.2   Outsourcing of Risk Assessment

A risk analysis will always influence the mindset of the people who carry out the analysis. This is perhaps one of the most important results of the analysis. It is therefore important that people from management participate actively in the risk analysis, and that the company not outsource the analysis without participating in it.

## 5.9   Additional Reading

The following titles are recommended for further study related to Chapter 5.

- *Dependability Management—Application Guide: Risk Analysis of Technological Systems* (IEC 60300-3-9, 1995) provides an overview of the various steps of a risk assessment and gives guidance to the choice of methods—and should be mandatory reading for all risk analysts.

- *Hazard identification, risk assessment, and risk control* (NSW, 2003) is well written and gives a good overview of the various phases and steps of a risk assessment.

- *Probabilistic risk assessment (PRA) procedures for NASA programs and projects* (NASA, 2010) is a comprehensive guide to quantitative (probabilistic) risk assessment in the space industry, but is also valuable in other application areas.

- *Guide for formal safety assessment (FSA) for use in the IMO rule-making process* (IMO, 2002) is written for maritime applications, but gives valuable advice on other types of risk assessments.

- *Offshore Risk Assessment: Principles, Modeling, and Application of QRA Studies* (Vinnem, 2007) is written for offshore oil and gas applications, but is also a valuable guide for other application areas.

# CHAPTER 6

# ACCIDENT MODELS

> Accident models form the basis for all hazard analysis and risk assessment techniques.
> —Leveson (2004)

## 6.1 Introduction

To understand the mechanisms of accidents and to develop accident prevention and control strategies, it is essential to know about and learn from past accidents (Khan and Abbasi, 1999). Accident data are therefore collected and stored in various databases (see Chapter 7), and accident models have been developed to support accident investigations.

Although accident investigation is outside the scope of this book, it forms the basis for much of the material presented. This is because accident models influence our perception of potential accidents and our approach to risk assessment.

The first accident models were very simple and attributed accidents primarily to single technical failures. A bit later, human factors and human errors were included in the models. Current accident researchers realize that systems also consist of societal, organizational, and environmental elements in addition to technology and individuals, which should all be integrated into the accident model (e.g., see Leveson, 2004; Qureshi, 2008).

Many accident models are focused primarily on occupational accidents and are, as such, outside the scope of this book. Brief descriptions of some of these models are included for historical reasons, mainly because we can learn from them and because they have formed the basis for more complex models of major accidents.

### 6.1.1 Accident Classification

Accidents may be classified in many different ways, one of which is related to the context in which the accident occurs. We may therefore distinguish among:

- Nuclear accidents
- Process plant accidents
- Aviation accidents
- Railway accidents
- Ship accidents
- Road traffic accidents
- Occupational accidents
- Home accidents

...and so on

Each category can be divided further into several subcategories, as shown in Example 6.1 with respect to aviation accidents.

**EXAMPLE 6.1 Aviation accidents**

Aviation accidents can, according to ICAO (2009), be classified as:

- Accident during takeoff or landing
- Technical failure during flight
- Controlled flight into terrain, power line, etc.
- Midair collision
- Harm to people in or outside the aircraft
- Other accidents (e.g., lightning strike, icing, extreme turbulence) ⊕

Accidents may also be classified according to the asset that is harmed: for example, personnel accident or environmental accident. Another way of classifying accidents is according to severity: for example, as a minor accident, fatal accident, major accident, and catastrophe/disaster.

A *major accident* in aviation is, for example, defined by the U.S. National Transportation Safety Board as:

☞ **Major accident** (in aviation): An accident in which any of three conditions is met:

- The airplane was destroyed; or
- There were multiple fatalities; or
- There was one fatality and the airplane was damaged substantially.

### 6.1.2  Accident Investigation

There are two main objectives of an accident investigation: (i) to assign blame for the accident, and (ii) to understand why the accident happened so that similar future accidents may be prevented. The second objective is of most interest for this book (e.g., see Leveson, 2004).

An accident investigation is always based on some underlying model of accident causation. If, for example, investigators consider an accident to be a sequence of events, they will start to describe the accident as such a sequence and perhaps forget to consider other possibilities. As for all types of investigations, we have the general problem that "what-you-look-for-is-what-you-find" (e.g., see Lundberg et al., 2009).

A survey of methods for accident investigations is given by Sklet (2004), and a more thorough introduction to accident investigation is given in the DOE Workbook *Conducting Accident Investigations* (US DOE, 1999).

### 6.2  Accident Causation

Effective prevention of accidents requires proper understanding of their causes. Several approaches to accident causation have been used throughout history, some of which are mentioned in this chapter.

### 6.2.1  Acts of God

Accidents that are outside human control are sometimes claimed to be *acts of God*. Examples of such accidents are natural disasters caused by earthquakes, hurricanes, flooding, lightning, and so on. In earlier times, many accidents were considered acts of God, meaning that nobody could be held responsible for the accident and that there was no possibility of preventing the accident.

This view has few supporters today. Many of the accidents that earlier were considered acts of God can now be prevented or at least forecast, and their consequences can be mitigated by many different means.

## 6.2.2 Accident Proneness

Studies of accidents in the 1920s suggested that accidents were caused by individuals who were more disposed than others to being injured. It was claimed that these individuals had inherent characteristics that predisposed them to a higher probability of being involved in accidents. This theory, called the *accident proneness theory*, is very controversial, but is still influential in, for example, accident investigations by police. Some accident studies support the theory by showing that injuries are not distributed randomly. Other studies have shown that there is no scientific basis for the accident proneness theory.

Today's researchers tend to view accident proneness as associated with the propensity of individuals to take risks or to take chances. This provides a more positive view of safety, as behavior can be changed even if the propensity to take risk cannot.

## 6.2.3 Classification of Accident Causes

Several taxonomies of factors contributing to accidents have been developed. The taxonomies use such classifications as natural or man-made, active or passive, obvious or hidden, and initiating or permitting. On a general level, the causes and contributing factors are often classified as follows:

– *Direct causes* are the causes that lead immediately to accident effects. Direct causes are also called *immediate causes* or *proximate causes*, as they usually result from other, lower-level causes.

– *Root causes* are the most basic causes of an accident. The process used to identify and evaluate root causes is called *root cause analysis*.

– *Risk-influencing factors* (RIFs) are background factors that influence the causes and/or the development of an accident.

▋ **EXAMPLE 6.2   Direct causes of airplane accidents**

A study by the aircraft manufacturer Boeing determined the direct causes of airplane accidents in the interval 1992–2001:

| Percent | Cause |
|---|---|
| 66 | Flight crew error |
| 14 | Aircraft error (mechanical, electrical, electronic) |
| 10 | Weather |
| 5 | Air traffic control |
| 3 | Maintenance |
| 3 | Other (e.g., bombs, hijackings, shoot-downs) |

*Source*: Statistical Summary of Commercial Jet Airplane Accidents
Worldwide Operations 1959–2001, Boeing, Airplane Safety.

### ▉ EXAMPLE 6.3   Automobile accident causes

The majority of automobile accidents can be attributed to one or more of the following causal factors[1]:

– Equipment failure

  - Brakes
  - Tires
  - Steering and suspension

– Road design

  - Visibility
  - Surface
  - Traffic control devices
  - Behavioral control devices
  - Traffic flow

– Road maintenance

  - Surface condition (e.g., potholes)
  - Salting and sanding
  - Maintenance activities
  - Construction activities

– Weather conditions

  - Snow/ice
  - Rain
  - Wind
  - Fog

– Driver behavior

  - Speeding
  - Violation of rules
    . . . and many more                                              ⊕


## 6.3   Accident Models

Accident models are simplified representations of accidents that have already oc-curred or might occur in real life. Each accident model has its own characteristics based on what types of causal factors it highlights (Kjellén, 2000).

---

[1]More details may be found at http://www.smartmororist.com.

### 6.3.1   Objectives of Accident Models

Accident models may be used for many different purposes. Among these are:

1. Accident investigation

   (a) To assign blame for an accident.

   (b) To understand why the accident happened so that similar accidents may be prevented in the future.

2. Prediction and prevention

   (a) To identify potential deviations and failures that may lead to accidents in new or existing technical and sociotechnical systems.

   (b) To propose changes to existing or new technical and sociotechnical systems to prevent deviations and failures that may lead to accidents.

3. Quantification

   (a) To estimate probabilities of deviations and failures that may lead to accidents.

   (b) To provide input to quantitative risk assessments.

### 6.3.2   Classification of Accident Models

The available accident models may be classified in many different ways. Any attempt at classification is, however, problematic, since several methods may either fall outside the classification or fit into several categories. A simple classification of the models and methods that are presented in this chapter is outlined below. Some models are described in other chapters of the book, for example, as modules of more comprehensive approaches. The respective chapters are then indicated in the classification scheme.

1. *Energy and barrier models.* These models are based primarily on the simple hazard-barrier-target model of Gibson (1961), illustrated in Figure 6.1.

   (a) Barrier analysis (Chapter 12)

   (b) Energy flow and barrier analysis (Section 12.8)

2. *Event sequence models.* These models explain an accident as a sequence of discrete events that occur in a particular temporal order. Event sequence models are attractive because they are easy to understand and can be represented graphically, but may in many cases be too simple.

   (a) Heinrich's domino model

   (b) Loss causation model

   (c) Event tree analysis (Section 11.2)

Hazard  Barrier  Asset

**Figure 6.1** The hazard-barrier-asset model.

(d) Layer of protection analysis (LOPA) (Section 12.9)

3. *Event causation and sequencing models*

(a) Root cause analysis

(b) Fault tree analysis (Section 10.3)

(c) Man-technology-organization (MTO)

(d) Management oversight and risk tree (MORT)

(e) Tripod-Delta

4. *Epidemiological accident models.* These models regard the onset of accidents as analogous to the spreading of a disease, that is, as the outcome of a combination of factors, some manifest and some latent, which happen to exist together in space and time.

(a) Reason's Swiss cheese model

5. *Systemic accident models.* These models attempt to describe the characteristic performance on the level of the system as a whole, rather than that of specific cause-effect "mechanisms" or even epidemiological factors (Hollnagel, 2004).

(a) Hierarchical sociotechnical framework

(b) Systems-theoretic accident model and processes (STAMP)

(c) Normal accident theory

6. *Accident reconstruction methods.* These methods are used primarily in accident investigations to describe what really happened.

(a) Sequentially timed events plotting (STEP)

(b) Man-technology-organization (MTO)

(c) Tripod-Beta

(d) AcciMap

Note that some accident models appear in more than one category. For a more thorough classification of accident models, see, for example, Qureshi (2008) and Hollnagel (2004). A comprehensive review of occupational accident models is given by Attwood et al. (2006).

## 6.4   Energy and Barrier Models

Energy and barrier models are based on the idea that accidents can be understood and prevented by focusing on dangerous energies and the means by which such energies can reliably be separated from vulnerable targets (Gibson, 1961; Haddon, 1970, 1980). These models have had a great impact on practical safety management.

The basic elements of an energy and barrier model are:

1. *Energy source.* Most systems have a range of energy sources. Energy sources are discussed in Chapter 3.

2. *Barriers.* As described in Chapter 12, there can be many different types of barriers. One way of classifying barriers is (Hollnagel, 2004):

    (a) *Physical.* Obstructions, hindrances, guards, walls, fences, etc

    (b) *Functional.* Mechanical (interlocks), logical, spatial, passwords

    (c) *Symbolic.* Signs and signals, procedures

    (d) *Immaterial.* Rules, laws, religious beliefs, cultural norms

3. *Energy pathways.* These are the pathways from the energy source to the vulnerable assets, which may go through air, pipe, wire, and so on.

4. *Assets.* The assets that are exposed to the energy may be people, property, the environment, and so on. Assets are discussed further in Chapter 2.

### 6.4.1   Barrier Analysis

A barrier analysis is performed to identify administrative, management, and physical barriers that can prevent or minimize the probability and severity of an accident. Barriers and barrier analysis are discussed further in Chapter 12, where several barrier analysis methods are described. Among these are:

– Energy flow and barrier analysis (EFBA)

– Layer of protection analysis (LOPA)

– Barrier and operational risk analysis (BORA)

### 6.4.2   Haddon's Models

William Haddon was both a physician and an engineer who was engaged in designing safer roads in the United States in the late 1950s. He developed a framework for analyzing injuries based on three attributes:

(a) *Human.* This refers to the person at risk of injury.

(b) *Equipment.* This is energy (e.g., mechanical, thermal, electrical) that is transmitted to the human through an object or a path (another person, animal).

(c) *Environment.* This includes all the characteristics of the environment in which the accident takes place (e.g., road, building, sports arena) and the social and legal norms and practices in the culture and society at the time (e.g., norms about discipline, alcohol consumption, drugs).

Haddon further considered these three attributes in three phases:

(a) *Pre-injury phase.* This is about stopping the injury event from occurring by acting on its causes (e.g., pool fences, divided highways, and good road or house design).

(b) *Injury phase.* This is to prevent an injury or reduce the seriousness of an injury when an event actually occurs by designing and implementing protective mechanisms (e.g., wearing mouth guard, seat belt, or helmet).

(c) *Post-injury phase.* This is to reduce the seriousness of an injury or disability immediately after an event has occurred by providing adequate care (e.g., the application of immediate medical treatment such as first aid), as well as in the longer term working to stabilize, repair, and restore the highest level of physical and mental function possible for the injured person.

Haddon's accident prevention approach has three main components:

1. A causal sequence of events

2. Haddon's matrix

3. Haddon's ten countermeasure strategies

**Causal Sequence of Events.** To find which factors to include in the Haddon matrix, thinking in terms of a "causal sequence of events" that leads to injuries is recommended. See Chapters 11 and 13 for more about sequence-of-events models.

**Haddon's Matrix.** The Haddon matrix (Haddon, 1970) is used to identify injury prevention measures according to the three phases (pre-injury, injury, and post-injury) and the three attributes (human, equipment, and environment), as illustrated in Figure 6.2. The environment is sometimes divided into two subattributes: the physical and the social environments.

**Haddon's Ten Countermeasure Strategies.** Haddon's basic idea is that accidents occur when assets are affected by harmful energy in the absence of effective barriers between the energy source and the object. He systematized known principles of accident prevention into 10 different strategies for loss reduction. These are related to different points of intervention according to Figure 6.2.

*Pre-injury phase*

1. Eliminate energy concentration (e.g., avoid driving, use a nondangerous substance).

| | | Factors | | |
|---|---|---|---|---|
| | | Human | Equipment | Environment |
| **Phases** | Pre-injury | Training Alertness | Maintenance ESP system | Road quality Weather |
| | Injury | Reaction Robustness | Airbag Headrest | Midroad barrier |
| | Post-injury | First aid Ambulance | Possibility to open doors; fuel leakage | Equipment to open wreck |

**Figure 6.2**    Haddon's matrix (example for a traffic accident).

2. Limit the amount of energy (e.g., reduce storage of fuels, reduce speed).

3. Prevent uncontrolled release of energy (e.g., use interlocks, strengthen the containment).

*Injury phase*

4. Reduce rate or spatial distribution of energy released (e.g., slow down speed, reduce burning rate).

5. Separate the victims and the energy released in space and/or time (e.g., remotely controlled systems, electric lines out of reach).

6. Separate the victims from the energy by physical barriers (e.g., fire walls, dampers, and doors).

7. Modify the qualities of the energy, such as its contact surface, subsurface, or basic structure (e.g., padded contact areas, airbags in cars).

8. Make the vulnerable target more resistant to damage from the energy flow (e.g., conditioning and weight training programs, earthquake-proof structures).

*Post-injury phase*

9. Limit the development of damage (e.g., fire suppression systems, emergency medical procedures).

10. Take action to ameliorate damage (e.g., intermediate- and long-term medical procedures).

Strategies 1, 2, 3, 4, and 7 aim to eliminate or modify the hazard, whereas strategies 5 and 6 endeavor to limit the hazardous exposure of potential victims or assets. Strategies 8, 9, and 10 are related to protection and rehabilitation of the victims or assets. Higher-level loss control strategies may be formulated with reference to the ten basic strategies.

Implementation of risk-reducing measures should, according to ISO 12100 (2010), be done with the following priorities:

1. *Safe design.* Eliminate the hazard and/or reduce the risk through design measures.

2. *Barriers.* Reduce the risk through the use of barriers (i.e., safety devices—see Chapter 12).

3. *Warning.* Reduce the risk through the use of warning devices (e.g., red lights, alarms).

4. *Training.* Reduce the risk through special safety training (e.g., requirements for certificates) and/or safety procedures.

Haddon noted that each of the ten strategies could be turned into its opposite, that is, into a strategy to increase damage. In principle, the list may thus be used to identify the strategies a threat agent actor may choose to impose damage intentionally (e.g., see Rosness et al., 2004).

**Haddon's 4Es.** Haddon classified injury prevention (i.e., risk reduction) efforts into four categories, which are often referred to as Haddon's 4Es:

$E_1$: *Engineering.* Controlling the hazards through design changes, process changes, and maintenance.

$E_2$: *Environment.* Making the physical and social environment safer.

$E_3$: *Education.* Training workers and operators related to all facets of safety, providing the required information to individuals, and convincing management that attention to safety pays off.

$E_4$: *Enforcement.* Ensuring that workers as well as management follow internal and external rules, regulations, and standard operating procedures.

## 6.5 Sequential Accident Models

Sequential accident models explain accidents as the result of a sequence of discrete events that occur in a particular order.

### 6.5.1 Heinrich's Domino Model

Heinrich's domino model is one of the earliest sequential accident models (Heinrich, 1931). The model identifies five causal factors and events that are present in most accidents:

1. *Social environment and ancestry* related to where and how a person was raised, and undesirable character traits which may be inherited: for example, recklessness and stubbornness.

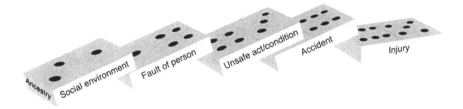

**Figure 6.3**   The domino model.

2. *Fault of the person* or carelessness that is created by the social environment or acquired by ancestry.

3. *Unsafe act or condition* that is caused by careless persons or poorly designed or improperly maintained equipment.

4. *Accident* that is caused by an unsafe act or an unsafe condition in the workplace.

5. *Injury* from the accident.

Heinrich (1931) arranges the five factors in a domino fashion, such that the fall of the first domino results in the fall of the entire row. The corresponding model is therefore called the *domino model* and is illustrated in Figure 6.3.

Strictly speaking, the domino model is not an accident causation model, but rather a conceptual representation of how injuries occur. It focuses on people, not on technical equipment, as the main contributors to accidents. The sequence of events illustrates that there is not a single cause, but many causes of an accident.

The domino model is sometimes called the *sequence of multiple events model*, because it implies a linear one-to-one progression of events leading to an accident. It is deterministic, in the sense that the outcome is seen as a necessary consequence of one specific event. Just as when playing domino, the removal of one factor will stop the sequence and prevent the injury. The domino model therefore implies that accidents can be prevented through control, improvement, or removal of unsafe acts or physical hazards.

When the domino model was proposed, it represented a redirection in the search to understand an accidents as being the result of a sequence of discrete events. The domino theory was later criticized because it describes accidents in far too simple a manner. It has also been criticized because it models only single sequences of events, and because it does not try to explain why unsafe acts are taken, or why hazards arise.

### 6.5.2   Loss Causation Model

The loss causation model, a modified version of the original domino model, was developed by Bird and Germain (1986) on behalf of the International Loss Control

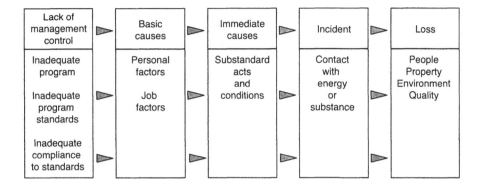

**Figure 6.4**    The main elements of the loss causation model.

Institute. The model, which is often referred to as the ILCI model, considers an accident as a sequence of events involving:

1. Lack of management control

2. Basic causes (personal factors or job factors)

3. Immediate causes (substandard acts and conditions)

4. Incident (contact with energy, substance, and/or people)

5. Loss (people, property, environment, and material)

The main elements of the loss causation model are illustrated in Figure 6.4. The three last elements of the loss causation model are similar to those of the domino model, except that the term *injury* has been replaced by the more general term *loss*, and the term *accident* has been replaced by *incident*. The change from *accident* to *incident* may indicate that the model is also suitable for analyzing undesired events that do not necessarily lead to significant loss. The first two elements represent the root causes, focusing on management factors such as, inadequate program, inadequate standards, job factors, and personal factors. Note that these factors are similar to those found in quality assurance programs.

The five main elements of the loss causation model may be described briefly as follows (e.g., see Sklet, 2002):

*Lack of management control* may indicate a lack of internal standards concerning elimination or reduction of risk, which may be related to:

  – Hazard identification and risk reduction

  – Performance appraisal

  – Communication between employees and management

It may also be that internal standards are in place but are outdated or inadequate. Another and often interrelated case may be that management and/or employees do not follow the established internal standards.

*Basic causes* are divided into two main groups, personal factors and job factors. The personal factors may be related to:

- Physical capacity/stress
- Mental capacity/stress
- Knowledge
- Skill
- Motivation

The job factors may be related to inadequate:

- Supervision
- Engineering
- Purchasing
- Maintenance
- Tools and equipment
- Work standards
- Quality/reliability of tools and equipment

*Immediate causes* are acts and conditions that may be related to:

- Inadequate barriers (including personal protective equipment)
- Inadequate alarms/warning systems
- Poor housekeeping
- Influence of alcohol/drugs
  . . . and so on

*Incident* describes the contact between the energy source and one or more assets (e.g., people, property, the environment) and is the event that precedes the loss. The immediate causes of an incident are the circumstances that immediately precede the contact. These circumstances can usually be sensed and are often called *unsafe acts* or *unsafe conditions*. In the loss causation model, the terms *Substandard acts* (or practices) and *substandard conditions* are used.

*Loss* is the potential result of an incident in relation to one or more assets.

Checklists play a major role when investigating accidents based on this model. A special chart has been developed for accident investigation, which acts as a checklist and reference to ensure that the investigation covers all facets of an accident.

The International Safety Rating System (ISRS),[2] which is operated by Det Norske Veritas, is based on the loss causation model.

---

[2]ISRS is a registered trademark of Det Norske Veritas, Høvik, Norway.

**Figure 6.5**    Rasmussen and Svedung's accident model.

### 6.5.3  Rasmussen and Svedung's Model

Rasmussen and Svedung (2000) describe an accident as a linear sequence of causes and events, as illustrated in Figure 6.5. The model has a structure similar to that of an accident scenario in a bow-tie diagram, but its interpretation is different.

The main elements in Rasmussen and Svedung's model are:

(a) *Root cause.* According to the terminology used in this book, this represents a hazard or a threat, or a combination of several hazards/threats. Actions to prevent accidents of similar types are to eliminate or reduce these hazards and threats.

(b) *Causal sequences.* Proactive barriers are installed in most systems to prevent hazardous events. For a hazardous event to occur, the causal sequences must have found a loophole in these barriers, or the barriers must have been too weak to withstand the loads from the hazards. Actions to prevent the accident are then to install new barriers or to improve existing ones.

(c) *Hazardous event.* A hazardous event will, as discussed in Chapter 2, inevitably lead to harm to people, the environment, or other assets if the event is not "contained". In some cases it may be difficult to decide which event in an event sequence should be defined as the hazardous event.

(d) *Event sequences.* As for the causal sequences, most well-designed systems will have barriers intended for stopping or reducing the development of consequence sequences following a hazardous event. These barriers are often called *reactive barriers.* To create harm, there must be "holes" in these barriers. Actions to prevent the accident are then to install new barriers or to improve existing ones.

(e) *Persons, assets.* These are the assets that are harmed during an accident. To reduce the harm in similar future accidents, it will be necessary to reduce the exposure, strengthen the defenses, establish better first-aid systems, and/or implement other mitigating actions.

Rasmussen and Svedung's model as presented in Figure 6.5 is a small part of a much more comprehensive accident model framework; see Rasmussen and Svedung (2000) for more details.

### 6.5.4  STEP

The sequentially timed events plotting (STEP) method was developed by Hendrick and Benner (1987). STEP is principally an accident investigation tool whose main

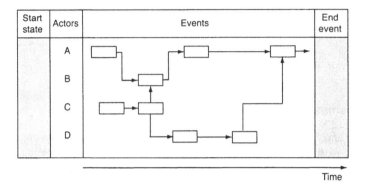

**Figure 6.6** STEP diagram (main elements).

purpose is to reconstruct an accident by plotting the sequence of contributing events and actions into a STEP diagram. The accident is viewed as a process that starts with an undesired change in the system and ends in an end event where some assets are harmed. The structure of a STEP diagram is shown in Figure 6.6.

The main elements of a STEP diagram are:

(a) The *start state* describes the normal state of the system.

(b) The *initial event* is the event that disturbed the system and initiated the accident process. The initial event is an unplanned change done by an actor.

(c) The *actors* that changed the system or intervened to control the system. An actor does not need to be a person. Technical equipment and substances can also be actors. The actors are listed in the column "Actors" in the STEP diagram.

(d) The elementary *events*. An event is an action committed by a single actor. Events are used to develop the accident process and are drawn as rectangles in the STEP diagram. A brief description of each event is given in the rectangles.

(e) The events are assumed to flow logically in the accident process. *Arrows* are used to illustrate the flow.

(f) A *timeline* is used as the horizontal axis in the STEP diagram for recording when the events started and ended. The timeline does not need to be drawn on a linear scale, as the main point is to keep the events in order, that is, to define their temporal relation.

(g) The *end event* of the STEP diagram is the point where an asset is harmed and the point that defines the end of the diagram.

The actors can be involved in two types of events: they can introduce a change (deviation), or they can correct a deviation. The action can be physical and observable, or mental if the actor is a person (e.g., see Sklet, 2002).

The analysis starts with definitions of the initial event and the end event of the accident sequence. Then the analysts identify the main actors and the events (actions) that contributed to the accident, and position the events in the STEP diagram. The following information should be recorded:

– The time at which the event started

– The duration of the event

– The actor that caused the event

– The description of the event

– A reference to where/how the information was provided

All events should have incoming and outgoing arrows to indicate "preceded by" and "following after" relationships between events. Special attention should be given to the interactions between the actors. Note that the focus should be on actions rather than their reasons.

When developing the STEP diagram, the analysts should repeatedly ask: "Which actors must do what to produce the next event?" If an earlier event is necessary for a later event to occur, an arrow should be drawn from the preceding event to the resulting event. For each event in the diagram, the analysts should ask: "Are the preceding events sufficient to initiate this event or were other events necessary?"

The accuracy of the event representation may be checked by using the *back-STEP technique*, which reasons backwards in order to determine how each event could be made to occur. Reasoning backwards helps the analysts to identify other ways in which the accident process could have occurred and measures that could have prevented the accident. In this way, STEP can also be used to identify safety problems and to make recommendations for safety improvements (Kontogiannis et al., 2000).

## 6.6   Epidemiological Accident Models

Epidemiological accident models consider the events leading to an accident as analogous to the spreading of a disease. An accident is in this view conceived as the outcome of a combination of factors, some manifest and some latent, that happen to coexist in time and space. A good account of this work has been provided by Reason (1990, 1997).

### 6.6.1   Reason's Swiss Cheese Model

The Swiss cheese model was developed by James Reason, who uses slices of Swiss cheese as an analogy to barriers. Figure 6.7 illustrates the principal idea behind the model, namely that barriers may, like cheese slices, have holes of different sizes and at different places. The holes are referred to as *latent failures* or *latent conditions*. The Swiss cheese model shows the development of an accident from these

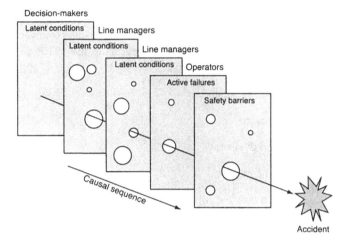

**Figure 6.7**   Reason's Swiss cheese model.

latent conditions to active failures which both penetrate a series of safety barriers and eventually lead to accidents. This is illustrated by an arrow passing through the holes of several slices of cheese in Figure 6.7.

The main elements of the Swiss cheese model are:

(a) *Decision-makers.* This typically includes corporate management and regulatory authorities, who are responsible for the strategic management of available resources in order to achieve and balance two distinct goals: the goal of safety, and the goal of time and cost. This balancing act often results in *fallible decisions*.

(b) *Line managers.* These are the people who are responsible for implementing the decisions made by the decision-makers. They adopt and implement the everyday activities of the operations.

(c) *Preconditions.* The decisions made by the decision-makers and the actions implemented by line management create many of the preconditions in which the workforce attempts to carry out their responsibilities safely and effectively.

(d) *Unsafe acts.* These are unsafe acts carried out by the workers/operators.

(e) *Last barriers.* These are the defenses or safeguards that are in place to prevent injury, damage, or costly interruptions in the event of an unsafe act.

Several versions of the Swiss cheese model have been presented, and the model has been improved and changed over the years.

■ **EXAMPLE 6.4   Herald of Free Enterprise**

The roll-on roll-off car and passenger ferry *Herald of Free Enterprise* capsized on 6 March 1987, just after having left the Belgian port of Zeebrugge. A total of

193 passengers and crew were killed in the accident, which has been analyzed in detail using many different methods. In relation to the Swiss cheese model, the main contributing factors to the accident are seen to be:

*Decision-makers*

- Inherently unsafe "top-heavy" ferry design
- Failure to install bow door indicator

*Line managers*

- Negative reporting culture
- Poor rostering

*Preconditions*

- Fatigue
- Choppy sea
- Pressure to depart early
- "Not my job" culture

*Unsafe acts*

- Assistant bosuns fail to shut bow doors
- Captain leaves port with bow doors open                          $\oplus$

## 6.6.2  Tripod

Tripod[3] is a safety management approach that was developed in a joint project by the University of Leiden (The Netherlands) and the University of Manchester (UK) for use in the oil and gas industry. The project was initiated in 1988 on commission by the oil company Shell (Reason, 1997).

The Tripod safety management system is now called Tripod-Delta in order to distinguish it from its close relative, Tripod-Beta:

*Tripod-Delta* is a safety management system and a proactive method for accident prevention.

*Tripod-Beta* is a method for accident investigation and analysis. As such, it is a reactive approach that is used mainly after an accident has taken place in order to prevent recurrence.

To prevent the recurrence of an accident, it is not sufficient to understand what happened, it is even more important to understand why it happened. Accident investigation is therefore a necessary part of any safety management system.

---

[3] Tripod is a registered trademark of AdviSafe Risk Management BV, Den Helder, The Netherlands.

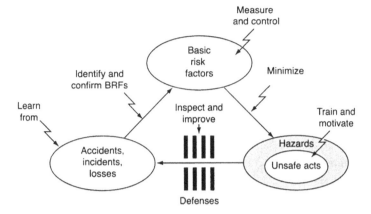

**Figure 6.8**   The three feet of Tripod-Delta: general failure types, unsafe acts, and negative outcomes.

***Tripod-Delta.***   Tripod-Delta got its name from the three-part structure in Figure 6.8, consisting of:[4]

1. Basic risk factors

2. Hazards and unsafe acts

3. Accidents, incidents, and losses

Tripod-Delta focuses on all levels of the organization, not only on the immediate causes of an accident. Accidents occur because protective barriers fail, and these may fail when people make mistakes or commit active failures. Active failures are more likely under certain *preconditions*, which are made possible by latent failures, which again are caused by some *basic risk factors*. The basic risk factors are in turn caused by fallible management decisions. This sequence of causes constitutes the Tripod accident causation model, which is illustrated in Figure 6.9. Wagenaar et al. (1990) call this a *general accident scenario*, as it shows the general pattern of factors leading to accidents.

> Accidents are the end-results of long chains of events that start with decisions at management level (Wagenaar et al., 1990).

***Basic Risk Factors.***   Tripod-Delta emphasizes that the immediate causes of an accident (e.g., technical failures, unsafe acts, human errors) do not occur in isolation but are influenced by one or more *basic risk factors*.[5] The basic risk factors are *latent* and *hidden* in the organization, but may contribute to accidents indirectly. They

[4]The figures and the table in this section are reproduced with permission from AdviSafe Risk Management BV.
[5]The basic risk factors were earlier called *general failure types*.

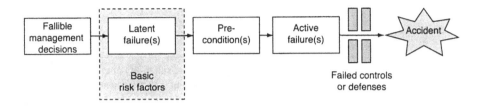

**Figure 6.9**    The Tripod accident causation model (adapted from Wagenaar et al., 1990).

have been compared to diseases—you cannot see them directly, only through their symptoms.

☞ **Basic risk factors (BFRs)**: "... those features of an operation that are wrong and have been so for a long time, but remain hidden because their influences do not surface without a local trigger" (Wagenaar et al., 1990).

Tripod-Delta defines 11 basic risk factors that cover human, organizational, and technical problems, as listed in Table 6.1 (see Tripod Solutions, 2007). The basic risk factors have been identified based on brainstorming, accident analyses, studies of audit reports, and theoretical studies (Groeneweg, 2002).

Ten of the basic risk factors lead up to hazardous events and are therefore sometimes called *preventive factors* to reflect that it is possible to prevent accidents by improving these factors. The eleventh basic risk factor is aimed at controlling the consequences after an accident has occurred, and is sometimes called the *mitigating factor*. Of the ten preventive basic risk factors, there are five *generic* factors (6–10 in Table 6.1) and five *specific* factors (1–5 in Table 6.1).

Most of the basic factors are determined by decisions or actions taken by planners, designers, or managers who are far away from the scene of a potential accident. The basic risk factors will, by their nature, have a broad impact. Identifying and controlling these factors will therefore have a wider benefit than influencing the immediate cause of a specific accident.

The *preconditions* in Figure 6.9 are the environmental, situational, or psychological system states, or even states of mind, that promote, or directly cause, active failures. Preconditions form the link between active and latent failures and may be viewed as the sources of human error (see Chapter 13).

The original accident causation model in Figure 6.9 has been updated to better fit the current version of Tripod-Delta. The updated model is shown in Figure 6.10.

**The Tripod-Delta Survey.**    Tripod-Delta contains a tool for assessing the soundness of an organization in terms of safety. This tool, the Tripod-Delta survey, is based on a database with around 2 000 questions.

The survey is carried out using questionnaires, either on paper or by use of a computer. All employees of the organization should, preferably, take part in the survey and answer it anonymously. A questionnaire contains 275 questions (25 for

Table 6.1 Basic risk factors.

| No. | Basic risk factor | Definition |
|---|---|---|
| 1. | Hardware | Poor quality, condition, suitability or availability of materials, tools, equipment, or components. |
| 2. | Design | Ergonomically poor design of tools or equipment (not user friendly). |
| 3. | Maintenance management | No or inadequate performance of maintenance tasks and repairs. |
| 4. | Housekeeping | No or insufficient attention given to keeping the work floor clean or tidied up. |
| 5. | Error-enforcing conditions | Unsuitable physical performance of maintenance tasks and repairs. |
| 6. | Procedures | Insufficient quality or availability of procedures, guidelines, instructions, and manuals (specifications, "paperwork," use in practice). |
| 7. | Incompatible goals | The situation in which employees must choose between optimal working methods according to the established rules on the one hand, and the pursuit of production, financial, political, social, or individual goals on the other. |
| 8. | Communication | No or ineffective communication between the various sites, departments, or employees of a company or with the official bodies. |
| 9. | Organization | Shortcomings in the organization's structure, the organization's philosophy, organizational processes, or management strategies, resulting in inadequate or ineffective management of the company. |
| 10. | Training | No or insufficient competence or experience among employees (not sufficiently suited/inadequately trained). |
| 11. | Defenses | No or insufficient protection of people, material, and environment against the consequences of the operational disturbances. |

*Source*: Adapted from Tripod Solutions (2007).

each basic risk factor) from the pool of 2 000 questions. For some industries, a "preferred selection" of questions is available. This means that these questions have been used and validated in this type of industry.

Examples of questions are:

- In the area in which you work, is it always clear who is responsible for what?

- During the past four weeks, did you have to work with procedures that included conflicting information?

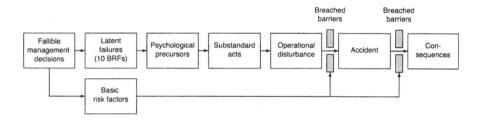

**Figure 6.10**    Updated Tripod-Delta accident causation model.

– Has this year's budget been reduced because of underspending from the preceding year's budget?

The results of the Tripod-Delta survey are analyzed by a set of proprietary statistical tools to identify the strengths and weaknesses of the safety of the organization in relation to the eleven basic risk factors. Based on the strengths and weaknesses identified, *risk profiles* for the basic risk factors are generated. This profile is presented as a bar chart giving a "cause for concern" rating to each of the basic risk factors.

Tripod-Delta contains additional tools for evaluating the safety management system performance and the management's policy and commitment. Also, these tools are based on pre-made questions that are answered by a simple "yes," "no," or "N.A." (not applicable) reply. More details may be found, for example, in Reason (1997, pp.131–138) or by visiting `http://www.advisafe.com`.

***Tripod-Beta.***    Tripod-Beta is a method used to perform accident analysis in parallel with accident investigation. Feedbacks from the analyses give investigators the opportunity to validate findings, confirm the relevance of risk management measures, and identify new investigation possibilities. As for Tripod-Delta, Tripod-Beta can be used for both accidents and operational disturbances.

Tripod-Beta merges two different models, the *hazard and effects management process (HEMP) model* and the Tripod-Delta theory of accident causation. The HEMP model is used to illustrate the actors and the barriers that contributed to a particular accident, as illustrated in Figure 6.11. Two main elements are required for an accident to occur: (i) a hazard and (ii) a target (or asset).[6] The hazard is usually controlled by one or more barriers and the target is normally protected by defenses or mitigating barriers. When the hazard controls and the defenses fail at the same time as illustrated in Figure 6.11, an accident occurs.

Figure 6.10 presents the accident causation model that is used in Tripod-Beta for identifying the causes of the breached controls and defenses as illustrated in the HEMP model. Tripod-Beta is different from conventional approaches to accident investigation, since no research is done to identify all the contributing substandard

---

[6]In recent versions of Tripod-Beta, *agent* or *agent of change* has replaced the term *hazard* and *object* has replaced the term *target*.

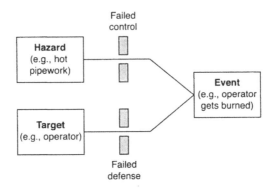

**Figure 6.11** The basic HEMP model as part of Tripod-Beta.

acts or clusters of substandard acts. Rather, the aim of investigation is to find out whether any of the basic risk factors are acting. When the basic risk factors have been identified, their impact can be reduced or even eliminated. Thus, the real source of problems is tackled instead of the symptoms.

Tripod-Beta is supported by a software tool that provides the user with a tree-like overview of the accident that is being investigated. It is a menu-driven tool that guides the investigator through the investigation process.

## 6.7 Event Causation and Sequencing Models

### 6.7.1 MTO-Analysis

The basis for the MTO method is that humans, technology, and the organization are equally important when analyzing accidents (Sklet, 2002).

M. (Man): This category comprises the workers at the sharp end. Attributes to be considered can be classified as:

- Generic
- Specific (gender, race, age, education)
- Personality (values, beliefs, thrust)

T. (Technology): This category include equipment, hardware, software, and design. The attributes may be classified as:

- Function level
- System level
- Human-machine interaction (interface details)
- Automation level
- Transparency

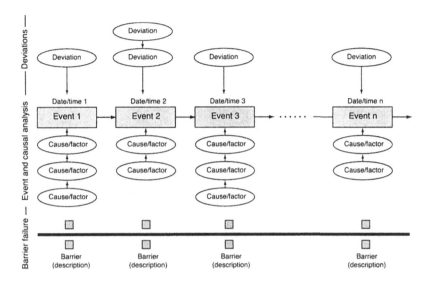

**Figure 6.12**    MTO diagram (main elements).

O. (Organization): This category comprises management, owners, and authorities. The attributes may be classified as (e.g., see Rasmussen, 1997):

- National /government
- Regional
- Company (culture and environment)
- Risk management

MTO-analysis of an accident is based on three main elements (e.g., see Sklet, 2002):

1. A structured analysis by use of an *event and cause diagram* as shown in Figure 6.12, to describe the accident event sequence. Possible technical and human causes of each event are identified and positioned vertically in relation to the events in the diagram.

2. A *change analysis* describing how events have deviated from earlier events or common practice. Normal situations and deviations are also illustrated in the diagram.

3. A *barrier analysis* identifying technical, human, and administrative barriers that have failed or are missing. Missing or failed barriers are represented below the events in the diagram. (Barrier analysis is discussed further in Chapter 12.)

The main elements of the resulting diagram, called an *MTO-diagram*, are shown in Figure 6.12.

The basic questions in the analysis are:

(a)  What could have prevented continuation of the accident sequence?

(b)  What could the organization have done in the past to prevent the accident?

The last important step in the MTO-analysis is to identify and present recommendations. The recommendations might be technical, human, and/or organizational, and should be as realistic and specific as possible.

A checklist for identification of failure causes is also part of the MTO-analysis (Sklet, 2002). The checklist contains the following factors:

1. Organization

2. Work organization

3. Work practice

4. Management of work

5. Change procedures

6. Ergonomic/deficiencies in the technology

7. Communication

8. Instructions/procedures

9. Education/competence

10. Work environment

For each of these failure cause factors, there is a detailed checklist of basic or fundamental causes. Examples of basic causes for the failure cause "work practice" are:

- Deviation from work instruction

- Poor planning or preparation

- Lack of self-inspection

- Use of wrong equipment

- Wrong use of equipment

MTO-analyses have been widely used in the Swedish nuclear industry and in the Norwegian offshore oil and gas industry (IFE, 2009). The MTO approach has emerged in several variants, which differ according to their main focus. Acronyms such as OMT and TMO are also seen (see also Niwa, 2009).

### 6.7.2 MORT

The management oversight and risk tree (MORT) approach was developed by W. G. Johnson for the U.S. nuclear industry in the early 1970s. MORT is described thoroughly in several user's manuals and textbooks (e.g., see San 821-2, 1973; Johnson, 1980; Vincoli, 2006; NRI, 2009).

MORT is based on energy and barrier concepts, and is used primarily for three main purposes:

1. Accident investigation

2. Support for safety audits

3. Evaluation of safety programs

MORT is a deductive technique that applies a pre-designed generic tree diagram, called a MORT chart, which has gate symbols similar to those of a fault tree (see Section 10.3). The MORT chart contains approximately 100 problem areas and 1 500 possible accident causes, which are derived from historic case studies and various research projects.

The TOP structure of the MORT chart is shown in Figure 6.13.[7] The tree structure is quite complex and is intended to be used as both a reference and a checklist. To perform a MORT analysis, you need to have the complete MORT chart available. This can be downloaded from http://www.nri.eu.com.

The TOP event of the MORT chart represents the accident (experienced or potential) to be analyzed. Once the extent of the accident has been established, the analyst arrives at the first logic gate, which is an OR-gate. The inputs to an OR-gate are the two main branches, which are denoted SM and R in Figure 6.13. The SM-branch is again split into the two main branches denoted S and M, which are connected through an AND-gate to indicate that both have to be considered in combination. The three main branches address different topics that each influence the TOP event accident:

*S-branch.* This branch contains factors representing specific oversights and omissions associated with the accident.

*M-branch.* This branch presents general characteristics of the management system that contributed to the accident.

*R-branch.* This branch contains assumed risks—risk aspects that are known, but for some reasons are not controlled.

**S-branch.** The S-branch focuses on the events and conditions of the accident, the potential harmful energy flows (hazards) or environmental conditions, the people or objects of value (i.e., the assets) that are vulnerable to an unwanted energy flow, and the controls and barriers that should protect these assets from harmful consequences.

---

[7]This TOP structure has been slightly reorganized to fit into one page.

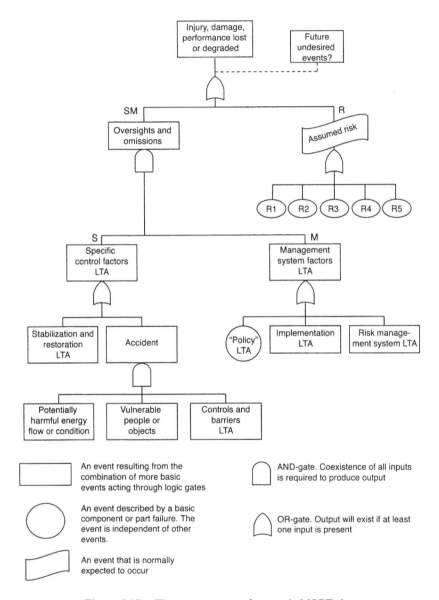

**Figure 6.13** The TOP structure of a generic MORT chart.

Haddon's ten strategies (Haddon, 1980) for accident prevention are key elements in this branch.

Three basic types of barriers are considered in MORT:

1. Barriers that surround and confine the energy source (i.e., the hazard)

2. Barriers that protect the asset

3. Barriers that separate the hazard and the asset physically in time or space

The time is not explicitly included, but the MORT chart is designed such that the time develops from left to right, and the sequence of causes develops from bottom to top.

Factors that relate to the different life-cycle phases of the system are recognized at the next level of the S-branch (not shown in Figure 6.13). The phases are the project phase (design and plan), startup (operational readiness) and operation (supervision and maintenance). The idea here is to link barrier failures to their first occurrence in the life cycle.

**M-branch.** The M-branch is used to evaluate why the inadequacies revealed in the S-branch have been allowed to occur. Events and conditions of the S-branch will therefore have their counterparts in the M-branch. At the M-branch, the analyst's thinking is expanded to the total management system. Thus, any recommendations will affect many other possible accident scenarios as well. The most important safety management functions are represented in the M-branch:

– Policy, goals, requirements, and so on

– Implementation

– Follow-up (including risk assessment)

These are the same basic elements that we find in the quality assurance principles of the ISO quality management standards (ISO 9000, 2005).

**R-branch.** The R-branch consists of assumed risks, that is, events and conditions that are known to the management and have been evaluated and accepted at the proper management level prior to the MORT analysis. Other events and conditions that are revealed through the evaluations following the S- and M-branches are denoted "less than adequate" (LTA).

The MORT user's manual contains a collection of questions related to whether specific events and conditions are "adequate" or LTA. Comments on best practices in the safety literature and criteria to assist the analyst in this judgment can also be found in the user's manual. Although the judgments made by the analyst are partly subjective, Johnson (1980) claims that MORT considerably enhances the capability of the analyst to identify underlying causes in the accident analysis.

The MORT approach has received international recognition, and it has been applied to a wide range of projects, from investigation of occupational accidents to hazard identification. The interest in MORT has increased recently thanks to the activities of the Noordwijk Risk Initiative Foundation, which has issued a new and updated MORT manual (NRI, 2009) and made additional resources available on its Internet page, http://www.nri.eu.com.

### Advantages and Limitations

*Advantages*   The main advantages are that MORT:

- is a systematic and well-proven approach;

- has a good user's manual that has been updated (NRI, 2009);

- systematically examines all possible causal factors;

- is ideal when there is a shortage of expertise to ask the right questions;

- evaluates multiple causes of accidents;

- works well for complex accidents involving multiple systems;

- looks beyond immediate causes to include management/program factors, root causes, and contributory causes.

*Limitations*   The main limitations are that MORT:

- is time-consuming and tedious to use;

- requires extensive training;

- is inappropriate for relatively simple accidents;

- may focus more on management than on the particular accident event;

- may lead to recommendations that are too broad (e.g., more training, more supervision);

- does not cater to temporal relationships between events.

## 6.8   Systemic Accident Models

The systemic accident models posit that an accident occurs when several causal factors (e.g., human, technical, and environmental) exist coincidentally in a specific time and space (Hollnagel, 2004).

### 6.8.1  Rasmussen's Sociotechnical Framework

Chapter 1 indicated some causes for the increasing risk in modern sociotechnical systems. The main causes have been studied by Rasmussen (1997), who claims that the accident models that have been described so far in this chapter are inadequate for studying accidents in such modern sociotechnical systems. Rasmussen advocates a system-oriented approach based on control theory concepts, proposing a framework for modeling the organizational, management, and operational structures that create the preconditions for accidents.

This section is based on Rasmussen (1997), Rasmussen and Svedung (2000), and the comparative studies by Qureshi (2008).

***Structural Hierarchy.***    Rasmussen (1997) views risk management as a *control problem* in the sociotechnical system, where unwanted consequences are seen to occur due to loss of control of physical processes. Safety depends on our ability to control these processes and thereby to avoid accidental side effects that cause harm to assets.

The sociotechnical system involved in risk management is described by Rasmussen in several hierarchical levels, ranging from legislators to organization and operation management, to system operators. Figure 6.14 illustrates a hierarchy with six levels, but the number of levels and their labels may vary across industries (Qureshi, 2008).

The six levels in Figure 6.14 are (e.g., see Rasmussen, 1997; Qureshi, 2008):

1. *Government.* This level describes the activities of the government, which controls safety in the society through policy, legislation, and budgeting.

2. *Regulators and associations.* This level describes the activities of regulators, industrial associations, and unions, which are responsible for implementing the legislation in their respective sectors.

3. *Company.* This level concerns the activities of the particular company.

4. *Management.* This level concerns management in the particular company and their policies and activities to manage and control the work of their staff.

5. *Staff.* This level describes the activities of the individual staff members who are interacting directly with the technology and/or the processes being controlled, such as control room operators, machine operators, maintenance personnel, and so on.

6. *Work.* This level describes the application of the engineering disciplines involved in the design of potentially hazardous equipment and operating procedures for process control in, for example, nuclear power generation and aviation.

The type of knowledge required to evaluate the various levels in Figure 6.14 are listed to the left of each level in the figure, and the environmental stressors that are influencing the levels are listed on the right-hand side. Traditionally, each level is

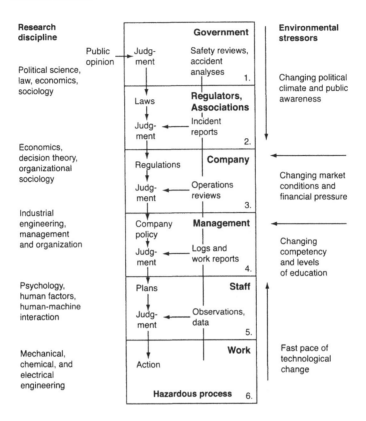

**Figure 6.14**    Hierarchical model of sociotechnical system involved in risk management (Reproduced from Rasmussen and Svedung (2000) with permission from the Swedish Civil Contingencies Agency).

studied separately by a particular academic discipline without detailed consideration of the processes at the lower levels. The framework in Figure 6.14 points to a critical factor that is overlooked by the horizontal research efforts: the additional need for "vertical" alignment across the levels. The organizational and management decisions made at higher levels should transmit down the hierarchy, whereas information about processes at lower levels should propagate up the hierarchy. This vertical flow of information forms a closed-loop feedback system, which plays an essential role in the safety of the overall sociotechnical system. Accidents are hence caused by decisions and actions by decision-makers at all levels, not just by workers at the process control level (see Qureshi, 2008).

***System Dynamics.***    It is not possible to establish procedures for every possible condition in complex and dynamic sociotechnical systems. In particular, this concerns emergency, high-risk, and unanticipated situations (Rasmussen, 1997).

Decision-making and human activities are required to remain between the bounds of the workspace, which are defined by administrative, functional, and safety con-

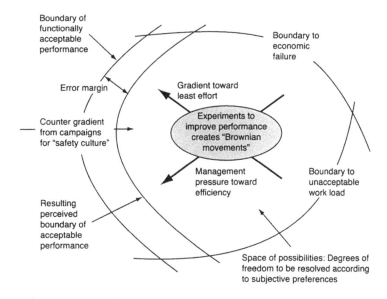

**Figure 6.15**   Boundaries of safe operation (Reproduced from Rasmussen (1997) with permission from Elsevier).

straints. Rasmussen (1997) argues that in order to analyze the safety in a work domain, it is important to identify the boundaries of safe operations and the dynamic forces that may cause the sociotechnical system to migrate towards or cross these boundaries. Figure 6.15 shows the dynamic forces that can cause a complex sociotechnical system to modify its structure and behavior over time.

The space of safe performance in which actors can navigate freely is confined within three boundaries, which relate to:

(a)  Individual unacceptable workload

(b)  Economic failure

(c)  Functionally acceptable performance (e.g., safety regulations and procedures)

Due to the combined effect of management pressure for increased efficiency and a trend toward least effort, Rasmussen (1997) argues that behavior is likely to migrate toward the boundary of acceptable risk. The exact boundary between acceptable and unacceptable risk is not always obvious to the actors, especially in complex systems where different actors attempt to optimize their own performance without complete knowledge as to how their decisions may interact with decisions made by other actors. At each level in the sociotechnical hierarchy, people are working hard to respond to pressures of cost-effectiveness, but they do not see how their decisions interact with those made by other actors at different levels in the system. Rasmussen claims that these uncoordinated attempts of adaptation are slowly but surely "preparing the stage for an accident." He therefore argues that efforts to improve

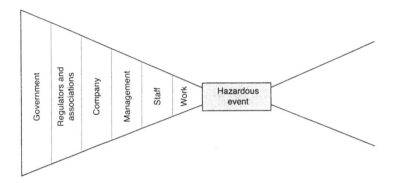

**Figure 6.16**  The causal part of a bow-tie diagram explained by Rasmussen's sociotechnical system model.

safety-critical decision-making should focus on making the boundaries towards un-acceptable risk visible and known, such that the actors are given the opportunity to control their behavior at the boundaries. Traditional strategies for ensuring safe handling of conflicting goals rarely meet these objectives (Qureshi, 2008; Størseth et al., 2010).

***An Alternative Presentation.***   Rasmussen's model of a sociotechnical system in Figure 6.14 can also be used together with a bow-tie diagram (e.g., see Figure 5.2) to further explain the causes of a hazardous event. The left-hand causal part of the bow-tie diagram may then be illustrated as in Figure 6.16. Niwa (2009) applies this approach when analyzing a major railway accident that occurred in April 2005 in Japan.

### 6.8.2  AcciMap

AcciMap is an accident analysis diagram proposed by Rasmussen (1997). AcciMap illustrates the interrelationships between causal factors at all six levels in Figure 6.14, thereby highlighting the problem areas that should be addressed to prevent similar accidents from occurring in the future.

The analysis is carried out by asking why an accident happened, that is, by identifying the factors that caused it or failed to prevent its occurrence. This is repeated for each of the causal factors, so as to gain an understanding of the context in which the sequence of events took place. An AcciMap should not only include events and acts in the direct flow of events, it should also serve to identify decisions at the higher level in the sociotechnical system which have influenced the conditions leading to the accident through their normal work activities, and how conditions and events interacted with each another to produce the accident (Svedung and Rasmussen, 2002). The development of an AcciMap is therefore useful to highlight the organizational and systemic inadequacies that contributed to the accident, thereby ensuring that at-

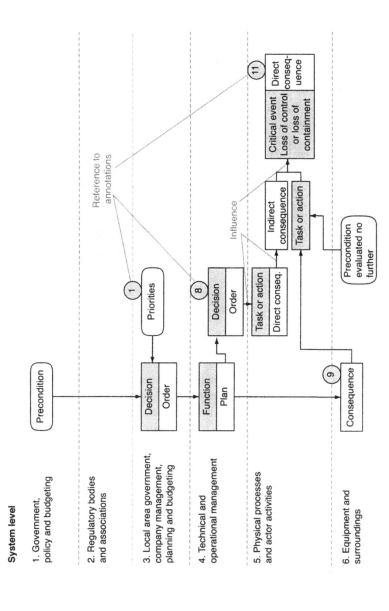

**Figure 6.17** AcciMap structure and symbols (Reproduced from Rasmussen and Svedung (2000) with permission from the Swedish Civil Contingencies Agency).

tention is not directed solely toward the events, technical failures, and human errors that led directly to the accident.

The main structure and the symbols used in an AcciMap are illustrated in Figure 6.17.

The stepwise construction of an AcciMap is described in detail by Rasmussen and Svedung (2000), who also provide several examples. An illustrative example is also provided by Qureshi (2008).

The objective of AcciMap is to identify potential improvements, not to allocate responsibility for an accident. The diagram is therefore not established as a representation of facts, but rather as an identification of factors that should be improved to avoid future accidents. AcciMap is for this reason not a pure accident investigation tool, but also a methodology for proactive risk management in a dynamic society (Rasmussen, 1997).

Svedung and Rasmussen (2002) designed a *generic* AcciMap to show the factors, especially the decisions, which may generate a typical scenario (i.e., a scenario that is representative of several accidents) in a particular domain of application. They have also constructed an ActorMap, which lists the actors involved in the generic AcciMap, from the company management level to the highest level (e.g., government). Further, an InfoMap has been introduced to deal with the interaction between actors in terms of the form and content of communications between the various decision-makers.

### 6.8.3 Normal Accidents

The normal accident theory was developed by Charles Perrow in 1979 when he was advising a Presidential commission investigating the nuclear accident at Three Mile Island, Harrisburg, PA. Perrow (1984) claims that some sociotechnical systems have properties that will naturally lead to accidents. He identifies two important system characteristics that make complex sociotechnical systems especially prone to major accidents: *interactive complexity* and *tight coupling*. His claim is that accidents such as the Three Mile Island accident must be considered as "normal" consequences of interactive complexity and the tight coupling in sociotechnical systems. His theory was therefore called *normal accident theory*.

☞ **Normal accident**: Multiple failure accident in which there are unforeseen interactions that make them very difficult or impossible (with our current understanding of the system) to diagnose.

Normal accidents are also called *system accidents*. Even if the normal accident theory asserts that the occurrence of accidents is inevitable, it does not mean that we should not, or cannot, do anything about them. In fact, the normal accident theory proposes a shift of focus within accident prevention. Accident analysis should "focus on the properties of systems themselves, rather than on the errors that owners, designers, and operators make in running them" (Perrow, 1984). The conclusion of

Perrow is that in accident analysis, "what is needed is an explanation based upon system characteristics" (Huang, 2007).

***Complexity and Coupling.***    The concepts of complexity and coupling were introduced briefly in Chapter 1. Perrow (1984) claims that some sociotechnical systems, such as major nuclear power plants, are characterized by high interactive complexity. These systems are difficult to control, not only because they consist of many components, but because the interactions among components are complex.

*Interactive Complexity*    Perrow uses *linear systems* as a contrast to *complex systems* (Figure 6.18). A system is *linear* when we are able to "understand" the system and can predict what will happen to the output of the system when we change the input. The terms *input* and output are interpreted here in a general way. Input changes may, for example, be a component failure, a human error, and a wrong set-point for a pressure switch. Linear interactions between the system components lead to predictable and comprehensible event sequences.

Interactions are said to be *nonlinear* when we are not able to predict the effect on the system output when we change the input. Nonlinear interactions will therefore lead to unexpected event sequences.

Nonlinear interactions are often related to feedback loops, which means that a change in one component may escalate due to a positive feedback or be suppressed by a negative feedback. Feedback loops are sometimes introduced to increase efficiency in the work process. However, interactive complexity makes abnormal states difficult to diagnose, because the conditions that cause them may be hidden by feedback controls that are introduced to keep the system stable under normal operation. Moreover, the effects of possible control actions are difficult to predict, since positive or negative feedback loops may propagate, attenuate, or even reverse the effect in an unforeseeable manner (e.g., see Rosness et al., 2004).

Interactive complexity may be defined as:

☞ **Interactive complexity**: Failures of two or more components interact in an unexpected way—due to a multitude of connections and interrelationships.

Some attributes of interactive complexity are listed in Table 6.2. The complexity can be technological or organizational—and sometimes a bit of both.

*Tight Coupling*    Another system characteristic that makes control difficult is *tight coupling*. Tightly coupled systems are characterized by the absence of "natural" buffers and will therefore have little or no slack. They respond to and propagate perturbations rapidly, such that operators do not have the time or ability to determine what is wrong. As a result, human intervention is both unlikely and improper (Sammarco, 2005).

Tight couplings are sometimes accepted as the price to be paid for increased efficiency. An example is just-in-time production, which is a production philosophy that allows companies to cut inventory costs but makes them more vulnerable if a link in

**Table 6.2**    Attributes of interactive complexity.

| Complex system attributes | Comments |
|---|---|
| Proximity | Close proximity of physical components or process steps, very little underutilized space. |
| Common-cause connections | Many common-cause connections. |
| Interconnected subsystems | Many interconnections—failures can "jump" across subsystem boundaries. |
| Substitutions | Limited possibilities for substitution of people, hardware, or software. Strict requirements for each element. |
| Feedback loops | Unfamiliar and unintended feedback loops. |
| Control parameters | Multiple and interacting control parameters. |
| Information quality | Indirect, inferential, or incomplete information. |
| Understanding of system structure and behavior | Limited, incomplete, or incorrect understanding of the system and its structure. |

*Source*: Adapted from Sammarco (2003).

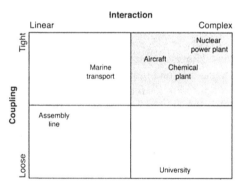

**Figure 6.18**    Interactions and coupling.

the production chain breaks down. In other cases, tight couplings may be the consequence of restrictions on space and weight. On an offshore oil and gas platform, for example, the technical systems have to be packed tightly, which makes it more challenging to keep fires and explosions from propagating or escalating (Rosness et al., 2004). Tight coupling may be defined as:

☞ **Tight coupling**: Processes that are part of a system happen quickly and cannot be turned off or isolated—due to direct and immediate connections and interactions between components.

Some attributes of tight coupling are listed in Table 6.3.

**Table 6.3** Attributes of tight coupling.

| Tight coupling attributes | Comments |
|---|---|
| Time dependency | Delays in processing are not tolerated. |
| Sequences | Processes are rigidly ordered and cannot be changed (A must follow B, etc.). |
| Flexibility | The is only one path to a successful outcome or to implement a function. |
| Slack | Little or no slack is permissible in supplies, equipment, personnel, and in system structure or behavior—precise quantities of specific resources are required for a successful outcome. |
| Substitutions | Substitutions of supplies, equipment, and personnel may be available, but are limited and designed-in. |

*Source*: Adapted from Sammarco (2003).

*Remark*: The normal accident theory has provoked a lot of controversy, mainly because Perrow concludes that some technologies should be abandoned in their current form because they cannot be adequately controlled by any conceivable organization. Some analysts have criticized the normal accident theory because it does not include any criteria for measuring complexity and coupling. Complexity measures are discussed further by Sammarco (2003, 2005). $\qquad\qquad\oplus$

### 6.8.4  High-Reliability Organizations

The theory of high-reliability organizations (HROs) was developed partly as a reaction to the challenges posed by the normal accident theory (La Porte and Consolini, 1991; Weick and Sutcliffe, 2007). Another background for HRO theory was the observation that a number of complex, high-risk organizations (e.g., aircraft carriers, nuclear submarines, air traffic control systems) had been able to operate for decades without any accidents. This implied that the normal accident theory could not be fully correct, and that it should be possible prevent serious accidents by properly managed organizational processes and practices.

The HRO perspective focuses on being proactive and on predicting and preventing potential dangers as early as possible. A central risk reduction strategy is to build *organizational redundancy*. This strategy requires that a sufficient number of competent personnel be available so that overlap in competence, responsibilities, and possibilities for observation can be achieved. Workplace design should allow, and even encourage, counsel seeking, observation of other people's work, and intervention in case of erroneous actions. Moreover, it is necessary to build a culture that encourages questioning and intervention. Another strategy is to build organizations with a capacity for spontaneous, adaptive reconfiguration (Rosness et al., 2004).

## 6.8.5 STAMP

Another systemic accident model, called the *systems-theoretic accident model and processes* (STAMP), was proposed by Leveson (2004). In STAMP, the most basic concept is not an event but a *constraint*, and the main causes of an accident are viewed as inappropriate or inadequate control or enforcement of safety-related constraints on the development, design, and operation of the system. Control is also imposed by the management functions in an organization and by the social and political system within which the organization exists. The role of all of these factors must be considered in accident analysis.

A STAMP accident analysis can be conducted in two stages (Qureshi, 2008):

1. Development of the hierarchical control structure, which includes identification of the interactions between the system components and identification of the safety requirements and constraints.

2. Classification and analysis of flawed control (constraint failures), which includes the classification of causal factors followed by the reasons for flawed control and dysfunctional interactions.

STAMP has been used to analyze several major accidents: for example, a major railway accident in China (Ouyang et al., 2010).

## 6.9 Additional Reading

The following titles are recommended for further study related to Chapter 6.

- *Risk management in a dynamic society: A modeling problem* (Rasmussen, 1997) is one of the most important articles that has been written on risk management— a must for all risk analysts!

- *Managing the Risks of Organizational Accidents* (Reason, 1997) is referred to in several chapters of this book and is a valuable source of information for all who are working with accident analysis and risk assessment.

- *Prevention of Accidents Through Experience Feedback* (Kjellén, 2000) presents and discusses accident models and provides valuable information related to the relationship between accident models and risk analysis.

- *Organizational accidents and resilient organizations: Five perspectives* (Rosness et al., 2004) presents and compares five different perspectives on accident causation and analysis.

- *A review of accident modeling approaches for complex critical sociotechnical systems* (Qureshi, 2008) reviews and compares several accident modeling approaches. Many of the models in this book are also covered in this report. The report is well written and easy to read.

# CHAPTER 7

# DATA FOR RISK ANALYSIS

> To understand the mechanisms of accidents and to develop accident prevention and control
> strategies, it is essential to know about and learn from past accidents.
>
> —Khan and Abbasi (1999)

## 7.1 Introduction

A quantitative risk analysis requires access to a wide range of data. This chapter
gives an overview of important types of data and where some of these can be found.
In some industries, it is mandatory to collect, analyze, and store data relating to
accidents and incidents. A few examples are given to illustrate the requirements:

- *Nuclear power industry.* In this industry, the data collection is rooted in the international convention on nuclear safety. According to this convention, each con-
  tracting party commits to taking the appropriate steps to ensure that:

  > ...incidents significant to safety are reported in a timely manner by the holder of
  > the relevant license to the regulatory body; [and that] programs to collect and ana
  > lyze operating experience are established, the results obtained and the conclusions

*Risk Assessment: Theory, Methods, and Applications,* First Edition.
By Marvin Rausand. Copyright © 2011 John Wiley & Sons, Inc.

drawn are acted upon and that existing mechanisms are used to share important experience with international bodies and with other operating organizations and regulatory bodies (IAEA, 1994a).

- *Aviation.* According to EU directive 2003/42/EC on "Occurrence reporting in civil aviation" (EU, 2003), data related to all civil aviation incidents and accidents must be collected, reported, and analyzed. The organization ECCAIRS has been established to "assist national and European transport entities in collecting, sharing and analyzing their safety information in order to improve public transport safety."

- *Industry covered by the EU Seveso II directive.* Companies in Europe that have to comply with the Seveso II directive (EU, 1996) are obliged to collect and report data in a specified format to the national authorities and to the eMARS database.[1]

In the United States, the Reliability Information Analysis Center (RIAC) has been established to "improve the productivity of researchers, engineers, and program managers in the research, development and acquisition communities by collecting, analyzing, applying, and disseminating worldwide scientific and technical information". RIAC is a U.S. Department of Defense (DoD) information analysis center and maintains several databases providing reliability data.

In Europe, the European Safety, Reliability and Data Association (ESReDA) was established in 1992 as a forum for the exchange of information, data, and results from research in safety and reliability. ESReDA has published several handbooks related to safety and reliability data.

In this book, the term *database* is used to denote any type of data source, from a brief data handbook to a comprehensive computerized database. A listing of databases is provided on the book's web site. Please consult this website for updated Internet addresses and references to various data sources.

## 7.2  Types of Data

The main types of data that are needed as input to a risk analysis are:

*Technical data.* A variety of technical data is needed in order to understand all the functions of a technical system and to establish system models such as fault trees and event trees.

For a process plant, the study team should, for example, have access to P&I diagrams; which devices are, or will be, installed; which dangerous substances are present in the system; and where these substances are stored and used. Technical data are usually obtained from the system owner, equipment manufacturers, technical manuals, and so on.

*Operational data.* To understand how components and subsystems are operating and to establish flow and system models, a wide range of operational data are required.

---

[1]See http://emars.jrc.ec.europa.eu/.

Procedures for normal operation, startup, and shutdown of the system are examples of this type of data. Procedures for handling abnormal situations are another category.

*Accident data.* The study team should have knowledge of previous accidents and near accidents in the same type of, or similar systems. Many databases containing descriptions of past accidents have been established (see Section 7.3).

*Hazard data.* There are two main types of hazard data: (i) checklists of relevant hazards and (ii) information (e.g., fact sheets) about dangerous substances and dosages that will harm human beings and the environment.

Lists of relevant hazards have been developed for several application areas. An example of such a list for machinery systems may be found in ISO 12100 (2010). Several organizations maintain databases with information about dangerous substances and can sometimes supply relevant and updated information to study teams performing risk analyses. More knowledge is needed regarding the dangers related to mixtures of substances.

Previous experience related to dangerous situations and dangerous substances in the plant being analyzed will also be important information.

*Reliability data.* This is information related to how and how often the components and subsystems in a system may fail. Several reliability databases have been established: both generic and company-specific databases. A generic database provides average data for a rather wide application area, while a company-specific database is based on reported failures and other events from the actual application of the equipment (see Section 7.4). Some application areas have also established joint databases for several companies, such as the Offshore Reliability Database (OREDA) for the offshore oil and gas industry (OREDA, 2009).

Some reliability databases provide failure rates for each relevant failure mode of the equipment, while other databases give only the total failure rates. In some cases, multiple components could fail because of common-cause failures (see Chapter 15). In such cases it is also necessary to obtain estimates of how often such failures will occur. Such estimates are found in very few databases, but in most cases, the estimates must be determined by using checklists (for details see Chapter 15). In sociotechnical systems, it is also necessary to estimate the probability of human errors. This is discussed further in Chapter 13.

*Maintenance data.* These are data that tell us how the technical components and subsystems will be, or are planned to be, maintained, and how long the repair or downtime will be. Safety equipment, such as fire and gas detection systems and emergency shutdown systems, is often part of passive systems that must be tested to determine whether or not it is functioning. In such cases it is necessary to know how the systems are tested, the time between tests, and the proportion of failures that can be revealed by a test.

*Meteorological data.* Weather conditions can affect both the probability of hazardous events and the consequences of such events. The dominant wind direction can, for example, determine in which direction a cloud of hazardous gas is likely to move.

*Data on natural events.* For some systems, natural events such as floods, landslides, storms, earthquakes, and lightning strikes are important causes of accidents. In such cases it will be important to have access to estimates of the magnitude and frequency of such events.

*Exposure data.* To determine the consequences of a hazardous event, it is necessary to have information about where people reside and how often and how long they stay at the various locations. For workers in the system, it will also be relevant to know what personal protective equipment is used.

*Environmental data.* The environmental consequences of a potential accident depends on how fragile the environment is, what plants and animal species are exposed to impact, and so on.

*External safety functions.* In many cases, external safety functions such as fire engines, ambulances, and hospitals are important to limit the consequences of an accident. Data relating to the capacity and availability of such systems are then important input data to the risk analysis.

*Stakeholder data.* Usually, there are several stakeholders to a risk assessment. The stakeholders may, among other things, affect how the analysis should be carried out and how it should be reported. It is important to recognize who are, or who may be, important stakeholders and to know their requirements regarding the risk analysis process and reporting of the analysis.

These categories of data are far from being sufficient in all risk assessments. To discuss all the types of data that might be needed, would be excessive for this book. A survey of data that are often included in risk analysis are also found in the Norwegian risk assessment standard NS 5814 (2008).

## 7.3  Accident Data

Several databases with information about accidents and incidents have been established. Some of these are official databases that are established by the authorities and have good quality assurance. Others are established by consulting companies, interest groups, or even individuals. The quality of this type of databases varies greatly. Some databases are very detailed, whereas others provide only a brief description of the accident/incident and provide no information about the causes of the accident/incident. Some databases cover only major accidents, whereas others focus on occupational accidents or accidents in which, generally, only one person is affected in each accident.

### 7.3.1 Purpose of Accident and Incident Databases

Data from accidents may, according to Kvaløy and Aven (2005), be used to:

- Monitor the risk and safety level

- Give input to risk analyses

- Identify hazards

- Analyze accident causes

- Evaluate the effect of risk-reducing measures

- Compare alternative areas of efforts and measures

### 7.3.2 Some Accident and Incident Databases

Some of the databases providing accident and incident data are listed below. The list is far from exhaustive.

The *Major Accident Reporting System (eMARS)* was established to support the EU Seveso directive (EU, 1996) and is operated by the Major Accident Hazards Bureau (MAHB) of the Joint Research Centre in Ispra, Italy, on behalf of the EU. Seveso II plants in Europe have to report all accidents and incidents to the eMARS database using a rather detailed format. The online database covers all industrial accidents and near accidents involving hazardous materials within the EU, and currently (2011) contains information from more than 790 events since 1986. The information contained in eMARS is available to all public except the restricted data which is only for the EU Member States.

The data in eMARS comprise, among several other items:

- Type of accident/incident
- Industry where accident/incident occurred
- Activity being carried out
- Components directly involved
- Causative factors (immediate and underlying)
- Ecological systems affected
- Emergency measures taken

Several EU countries have established national accident and incident databases that complement and extend the eMARS database. Among these are:

- The *Failure and Accident Technical Information System (Facts)* is a database operated by the Dutch research organization TNO. The database contains information about more than 23 900 industrial accidents and incidents from

1900 until the present. The information in the Facts database is collected from symposium proceedings and periodic journals with a focus on industrial safety, risk management, and loss prevention. Other important sources are companies, authorities, rescue services, and so on.

- *Analysis, Research, and Information on Accidents (ARIA)* is a database operated by the French Ministry of Ecology and Sustainable Development. ARIA covers accidents and incidents that have, or might have, caused damage to health or public safety, agriculture, nature, or the environment. The events are caused mainly by industrial or agricultural facilities, but transportation of hazardous materials is also covered. The database contains (per 2010) more than 37 000 accidents and incidents, most of which have occurred in France.

The *Process Safety Incident Database (PSID)* provides information about accidents and incidents involving hazardous materials. The database is operated by the Center for Chemical Process Safety of the American Institute of Chemical Engineers (AIChE). Currently, the database contains around 650 incidents.

The *Incident Reporting System (IRS)* is a database of accidents and incidents in nuclear power plants. The database is operated by IAEA, Department of Nuclear Safety, Vienna, Austria. Almost all countries with a nuclear power program participate in IRS.

The *Aviation Accident Database* is one of several databases providing data for aviation accidents and incidents. The Aviation Accident Database is operated by the U.S. National Transport Safety Board, Office of Aviation Safety. In Europe, *EC-CAIRS*, a center for coordination of accidents and incidents has been established to support EU directive 2003/42/EC on occurrence reporting in civil aviation (EU, 2003) and to "assist national and European transport authorities and accident investigation bodies in collecting, sharing and analyzing their safety information in order to improve public transport safety." See also ATSB (2006).

The *International Road Traffic and Accident Database (IRTAD)* was established in 1988 as part of the OECD Road Transport Research Program. Data are supplied from a large number of countries in a common format and analyzed by the IRTAD group. All IRTAD members have full access to the database.

The *World Offshore Accident Database (WOAD)* provides information about accidents in the offshore industry since 1975. The database is operated by Det Norske Veritas (DNV) and access to the database is subject to paying an annual fee. DNV publishes an annual report with summaries of individual accidents and accident trends. WOAD is based largely on publicly available data that are processed by DNV.

The *SINTEF Offshore Blowout Database* contains data on offshore blowouts and is operated by SINTEF, the Norwegian research organization. The data are based largely on public sources. Access to data requires membership in the project.

Other databases are listed on the book's homepage.

### 7.3.3 Accident Investigation Reports

An independent party usually investigates major accidents, and the investigation reports are often made public. Investigation reports of U.S. chemical accidents may, for example, be found on the homepage of the U.S. Chemical Safety Board (http://www.csb.gov). Many of these reports are very detailed, and some are accompanied by videos.

An example of a far-reaching accident investigation is Lord Cullen's inquiry into the Piper Alpha disaster in the North Sea in 1988.[2] His report led to new legislation, new operational procedures, and new ways of conducting risk assessments. Many people working with risk assessments might learn a lot from reading the report.

In Norway, the government commissions the accident investigations of major accidents, and the reports are published as official NOU-reports. These reports are often a basis for proposed changes in laws and regulations that are presented to the parliament.

## 7.4 Component Reliability Data

There are two main types of component reliability data: (i) descriptions of single failure events and (ii) estimates of failure frequencies/rates.

### 7.4.1 Component Failure Event Data

Many companies maintain a component failure event database as part of their computerized maintenance recording system. Failures and maintenance actions are recorded related to the various components. The data are used in maintenance planning and as a basis for system modifications. In some cases, companies exchange information recorded in their component failure report databases. An example is the U.S. Government Industry Data Exchange Program (GIDEP).

Some industries have implemented a failure reporting analysis and corrective action system (FRACAS), as described in MIL-STD-2155 (1985). By using FRACAS or similar approaches, failures are formally analyzed and classified before the reports are stored in the failure report database.

### 7.4.2 Component Failure Rates

A wide range of component failure rate databases is available. A component failure rate database provides estimates of failure rates for single components. Some databases may also give failure mode distributions and repair times. Databases with information about manufacturer/make of the various components are usually confidential to people outside a specific company or group of companies. An exam-

---

[2]For more information on the Piper Alpha accident, see, for example, http://en.wikipedia.org/wiki/Piper_Alpha.

ple is the Offshore Reliability Database (OREDA) where the detailed computerized database is available only to the companies participating in OREDA.

The failure rate estimates may be based on:

1. Recorded failure events

2. Expert judgment

3. Laboratory testing

or a combination of these.

It is usually assumed that the components have constant failure rate $\lambda$ and hence that failures occur as a homogeneous Poisson process (HPP) with intensity $\lambda$. Let $N(t)$ denote the number of failures during an accumulated time in service $t$. The HPP assumption implies that

$$\Pr(N(t) = n) = \frac{(\lambda t)^n}{n!} e^{-\lambda t} \quad \text{for } n = 0, 1, 2, \ldots \tag{7.1}$$

The mean number of failures during an accumulated time in service $t$ is then

$$E(N(t)) = \lambda \cdot t \tag{7.2}$$

The meaning of the parameter $\lambda$ is then

$$\lambda = \frac{E(N(t))}{t} \tag{7.3}$$

such that $\lambda$ is the mean number of failures per unit time in operation.

An obvious estimator for $\lambda$ is then

$$\hat{\lambda} = \frac{N(t)}{t} = \frac{\text{observed number of failures}}{\text{accumulated time in service}} \tag{7.4}$$

This estimator is seen to be unbiased, and a 90% confidence interval for $\lambda$ when $n$ failures is observed during the time in operation $t$ is found to be

$$\left( \frac{1}{2t} z_{0.95,2n}, \frac{1}{2t} z_{0.05,2(n+1)} \right) \tag{7.5}$$

where $z_{\alpha,m}$ is the upper $(1-\alpha)$ percentile of a chi-square distribution with $m$ degrees of freedom.

### 7.4.3   Generic Reliability Databases

A wide range of generic reliability databases is listed on the book's web page. Several databases have similar formats and give the same type of information. Most of the commercially available reliability data sources are based on an assumption of constant failure rates. Some sources distinguish between different failure modes and present failure rate estimates for each failure mode, whereas other sources present only a total failure rate covering all failure modes. Some few sources also give estimates of the repair times associated with various failure modes.

Most reliability data sources maintain their own web pages, presenting information about their data sources. In this section, the main data sources are mentioned briefly. More information may be obtained by following the links on the book's homepage.

The *Process Equipment Reliability Database (PERD)* is operated by the Center for Chemical Process Safety of AIChE, and contains reliability data for process equipment. Data are only available to members of the PERD project.

*Electronic Parts Reliability Data (EPRD)* is available from the Reliability Information Analysis Center (RIAC). This handbook of more than 2 000 pages contains failure rate estimates for integrated circuits, discrete semiconductors (diodes, transistors, optoelectronic devices), resistors, capacitors, and inductors/transformers—obtained from field usage of electronic components.

*Nonelectronic Parts Reliability Data (NPRD)* is available from the Reliability Information Analysis Center (RIAC). This handbook of about 1 000 pages provides failure rates for a wide variety of component types, including mechanical, electromechanical, and discrete electronic parts and assemblies.

*MIL-HDBK-217F, Reliability Prediction of Electronic Equipment*, contains failure rate estimates for the various part types used in electronic systems, such as integrated circuits, transistors, diodes, resistors, capacitors, relays, switches, and connectors. The estimates are based mainly on laboratory testing with controlled environmental stresses, so the failure rates in MIL-HDBK-217F (1991) are therefore related only to component-specific (primary) failures. The basic failure rate of a component found for normal stress levels in the laboratory is denoted $\lambda_B$. The effects of influencing factors such as quality level, temperature, and humidity are given in tables in MIL-HDBK-217F that are used to find the failure rate $\lambda_P$ for the relevant application and environment, as

$$\lambda_P = \lambda_B \cdot \pi_Q \cdot \pi_E \cdot \pi_A \cdots \tag{7.6}$$

where the influencing $\pi$-factors are given in MIL-HDBK-217F. Failures due to external stresses and common-cause failures are not included. The data are not related to specific failure modes.

MIL-HDBK-217F remains an active U.S. Department of Defense (DoD) handbook, but is no longer being actively maintained or updated. RIAC, who maintained the handbook on behalf of DoD, is instead promoting a computerized system called 217Plus.

The French FIDES initiative is a promising extension of the MIL-HDBK-217F approach, see http://www.fides-reliability.org/.

*Offshore Reliability Data (OREDA)* contains data from a wide range of components and systems used in offshore oil and gas installations, collected from installations in several geographic areas. The computerized database is available only to

OREDA participants, but several OREDA handbooks have been published presenting generic data. The data are classified under the following main headings (i) machinery, (ii) electric equipment, (iii) mechanical equipment, (iv) control and safety equipment, and (v) subsea equipment.

*MechRel* is an open reliability data source developed for mechanical equipment by the Naval Surface Warfare Center. It contains a "Handbook of Reliability Prediction Procedures for Mechanical Equipment" and a "Mechanical Reliability Prediction Software Package" that can be downloaded from their web page.

The *Reliability Data for Control and Safety Systems* data handbook has been developed to support reliability assessments of safety instrumented systems that should comply with IEC 61508 (2010). The handbook is based partly on data from OREDA and is developed by SINTEF, the Norwegian research organization.

The *Safety Equipment Reliability Handbook (SERH)* is a handbook in three volumes covering reliability data for safety instrumented systems. The handbook has been developed by exida.com and the three volumes cover (1) sensors, (2) logic solvers and interface modules, and (3) final elements.

*IEEE Std. 500* is a handbook providing failure rate estimates for various electrical, electronic, sensing, and mechanical components (IEEE Std. 500, 1984). A Delphi method (see Section 7.7) combined with field data is used to produce component failure rate estimates. The data come from nuclear power plants, but similar applications are also considered as part of the Delphi method process. The data in the handbook are now rather old.

*International Common Cause Data Exchange (ICDE)* is a database operated by the Nuclear Energy Agency (NEA) on behalf of nuclear industry authorities in several countries. Various summary reports are also available on the Internet for non-members.

The *Common-Cause Failure Data Base (CCFDB)* is a data collection and analysis system operated by the U.S. Nuclear Regulatory Commission (NRC). CCFDB includes a method for identifying common-cause failure (CCF) events, coding and classifying those events for use in CCF studies, and a computer system for storing and analyzing the data. CCFDB is described thoroughly by NUREG/CR-6268 (2007).

*European Industry Reliability Data (EIReDA)* gives failure rate estimates for components in nuclear power plants operated by EDF in France. EIReDA PC is a computer version of the EIReDA data bank. Data relate to the electrical, mechanical, and electromechanical equipment of nuclear plants.

The *Reliability and Availability Data System (RADS)* was developed by the U.S. Nuclear Regulatory Commission (NRC)[3] to provide reliability and availability data

---

[3]See: https://nrcoe.inel.gov/secure/rads/

needed to perform generic and plant-specific assessments and to support PRA and risk-informed regulatory applications. Data are available for the major components in the most risk important systems in both boiling water reactors and pressurized water reactors. Some generic data from RADS are publicly available on `http://nrcoe.inl.gov/resultsdb/RADS/`.

### 7.4.4   Failure Modes and Mechanisms Distributions

Some of the failure rate databases listed above include failure rates estimated for various failure modes. These estimates can then be used to determine the relative probabilities of the various component failure modes. A specific handbook has been developed for this purpose:

*Failure mode/mechanism distributions (FMD-97)* is a handbook published by RIAC that provides the relative probabilities of occurrence of the various failure modes and failure mechanisms of a wide range of electrical, electronic, mechanical, and electromechanical parts and assemblies. The handbook may be used to support reliability analyses such as FMECA.

### 7.4.5   Data Analysis and Data Quality

For more than 30 years, significant effort has been devoted to the collection and processing of reliability data. Despite this great effort, the quality of the data available is still not good enough.

**Data Analysis.**   The quality of the data presented in the databases obviously depends on the way the data are collected and analyzed. Several guidelines and standards have been issued to obtain high quality in data collection and analysis. Among these are:

1. *Handbook on quality of reliability data* (ESReDA, 1999)

2. *Guidelines for Improving Plant Reliability Through Data Collection and Analysis* (CCPS, 1998)

3. ISO 14224 *Petroleum, Petrochemical, and Natural Gas Industries: Collection and Exchange of Reliability and Maintenance Data for Equipment* (ISO 14224, 2006)

4. *Handbook of Parameter Estimation of Probabilistic Risk Assessment* (NUREG/CR-6823, 2003)

**Data Quality.**   There are several quality requirements for a good reliability data source. Among these are:

*Accessibility.* The database must be easily accessible such that resources are not wasted on searching for the data.

*User-friendliness.* The database must be user-friendly, with sufficient help for the user such that she does not misinterpret the estimates in the database.

*System/component boundaries.* The physical and operational boundaries for the systems and components in the database must be specified such that the user can know which failures are covered by the estimate.

*Traceable sources.* The sources of the raw data must be specified such that the user can check whether her application of the systems and components is compatible with the application for which the data were collected.

*Failure rate function.* Almost all commercially available reliability databases provide only constant failure rates, even for mechanical equipment that degrades due to such mechanisms as erosion, corrosion, and fatigue. When the failure rate function is assumed to be constant, this should, as far as possible, be justified in the database: for example, by trend testing.

*Homogeneity.* If the raw data come from different samples (e.g., different installations), the database should, as far as possible, verify that the samples are homogeneous.

*Updating.* The database must be updated regularly, such that the failure rate estimates, as far as possible, are applicable for the current technology.

Any risk analysis will be based on historical event frequencies and failure rates. In areas with rapid technological development, the technology to be used in a new plant may be rather different from the ones that were used in previous plants and from which our estimates originate. When such historical data are used, a clear argument should be presented that the data are compatible with the technology being used in the study object.

### 7.4.6 Plant-Specific Reliability Data

The approach in MIL-HDBK-217F outlined in equation (7.6) is a simple example of a *proportional hazards model* where the actual failure rate $\lambda_P$ for a specific operational and environmental context is determined by multiplying the basic failure rate $\lambda_B$ by a number of influencing coefficients. These coefficients are also called *covariates* and *concomitant variables*.

The MIL-HDBK-217F approach may seem simple, but a lot of research has been carried out to determine the various coefficients. If the temperature in the given context, for example, is 90°C, the influencing coefficient given in MIL-HDBK-217F covers both the effect of the increased temperature and the importance of the temperature as an influencing factor. Similar influencing coefficients have not been developed for mechanical, electro-mechanical, and more complex equipment.

The general expression of the proportional hazards model when it is assumed that the basic failure rate is constant (i.e., with no wear-out effects) is

$$\lambda_P = \lambda_B \cdot h(\pi_1, \pi_2, \ldots, \pi_m) \tag{7.7}$$

**Table 7.1** Examples of influencing factors.

| Group | Influencing factor |
|---|---|
| Design | System type |
| | Working principle |
| | Dimensions (size, length, volume, weight) |
| | Materials |
| | Component quality (quality requirements, controls) |
| | Special characteristics |
| Manufacture | Manufacturer |
| | Manufacturing process (procedures, controls) |
| Installation | Location (access facilities) |
| | Assembly/activation (procedures, control) |
| Operation | Type of loading (cyclic, random) |
| | Frequency of use |
| | Loading charge/activation threshold |
| | Electrical loading (voltage, intensity) |
| | Mechanical constraints (vibration, friction, shocks) |
| | Temperature |
| | Corrosion/humidity |
| | Pollution |
| | Other stresses (electromagnetic, climate) |
| | Performance requirements |
| | Failure modes (recorded failures) |
| Maintenance | Frequency of preventive maintenance |
| | Quality of preventive maintenance |
| | Quality of corrective maintenance |

*Source*: Adapted from Brissaud et al. (2010).

where $\pi_1, \pi_2, \ldots, \pi_m$ are the influencing coefficients. In some cases, one or more of these coefficients may vary with time.

In general, a large number of factors may influence the failure rate. Some examples of influencing factors are given in Table 7.1.

A possible approach to estimating a plant-specific failure rate $\lambda_P$ for a given component is the following:

1. Estimate the failure rate $\lambda_B$ in a normal (basic) operating context. This estimate can sometimes be found from generic reliability databases. If not, $\lambda_B$ has to be estimated based on observed data or expert judgments. The estimate of $\lambda_B$ is

assumed to reflect the average operating and environmental conditions in the relevant industry.

2. Identify the factors (e.g., from Table 7.1) that are considered to have the highest influence on the component's failure rate. The various factors should be studied carefully to avoid dependencies, for example, that (i) the influence of a factor takes place only through another factor and that (ii) it is the combined effect of two factors that is important and not the single factors.

### ■ EXAMPLE 7.1 Shutdown valve in an oil pipeline

Consider a shutdown valve in an oil pipeline. The essential function of the valve is to stop the flow of oil in the pipeline if a hazardous event occurs on the downstream side of the valve. The ability to close tightly is dependent on the wear of the valve seat and seals, and the failure rate of the failure mode "leakage through the valve in closed position" is found to be influenced by the flow rate through the valve and the content of sand particles in the fluid. A careful analysis shows that the main influencing factor is the combination of these two factors: high flow rate in combination with a high sand content in the fluid. When this combined factor is taken into account, the two single factors have a negligible influence. ⊕

For the purpose of the remaining analyses, the number of influencing factors should be kept as small as possible. Let the $k$ remaining influencing factors be denoted by $y_1, y_2, \ldots, y_k$, and let $y_{0,1}, y_{0,2}, \ldots, y_{0,k}$ denote the normal (i.e., industry average) level of the influencing factors.

A Bayesian network diagram (see Section 10.4) may, for example, be used to illustrate the influences.

3. Weigh the influencing factors according to their importance for the failure rate. This has to be done by several experts based on physical and engineering knowledge. Let $\omega_i$ denote the weight of influencing factor $y_i$, for $i = 1, 2, \ldots, k$. The weights are allocated such that $\sum_{i=1}^{k} \omega_i = 1$.

4. Record the current (i.e., plant-specific) level of the influencing factors and denote these by $y_{c,1}, y_{c,2}, \ldots, y_{c,k}$. Determine a *score* $\sigma_{c,i}$ for the current level of influencing factor $y_i$, for $i = 1, 2, \ldots, k$, such that

$$\sigma_{c,i} = 1, \text{ when } y_{c,i} \approx y_{0,i}$$
$$\sigma_{c,i} < 1, \text{ when } y_{c,i} \text{ is considered to be more } benign \text{ than } y_{0,i}$$
$$\sigma_{c,i} > 1, \text{ when } y_{c,i} \text{ is considered to be more } hostile \text{ than } y_{0,i}$$

This means that when all the influencing factors are similar to the industry average, $\sigma_{c,i} = 1$ for all $i$, and $\lambda_P = \lambda_B$, meaning that the basic (i.e., industry average) failure rate $\lambda_B$ can be used as plant-specific failure rate.

5. The plant-specific failure rate $\lambda_P$ is then determined by

$$\lambda_P = \lambda_B \cdot \prod_{i=1}^{k} \omega_i \cdot \sigma_{c,i} = \lambda_B \cdot \prod_{i=1}^{k} \pi_i \qquad (7.8)$$

where $\pi_i = \omega_i \cdot \sigma_{c,i}$ denotes the influencing coefficient for factor $y_i$.

This five-step approach is similar to the MIL-HDBK-217F approach and is also the basis for the recent approaches in Haugen et al. (2007) and Brissaud et al. (2010). The BORA approach (Haugen et al., 2007) is presented in detail in Chapter 12. A slightly different approach is presented by Øien (2001).

How to determine the scores when $y_{c,i} \neq y_{0,i}$ is not obvious, and several different approaches have been proposed by Øien (2001); Haugen et al. (2007); Brissaud et al. (2010). Most of these approaches start by defining a worst and a best level that can be found in the industry for each influencing factor and thereafter adjusting the resulting failure rate. Interested readers should consult these sources, or read Chapter 12 carefully.

## 7.5  Human Error Data

### 7.5.1  Introduction

Human errors and human reliability are discussed in Chapter 13. Several databases that provide data related to human errors are available. As for technical failures, the data can be divided into two types: (i) descriptions of human errors and (ii) probabilities of typical human errors in a specified context. The second type is often presented as *human error probabilities* (HEPs).

### 7.5.2  Human Error Databases

A human error database gives a description of the various errors that have occurred within a particular system, along with their associated causal factors and consequences. Most safety-critical systems have an error database of some type.

The *Computerized Operator Reliability and Error Database (CORE-DATA)* was established by the University of Birmingham in England (HSE, 1999). CORE-DATA is a database of human or operator errors that have occurred within the nuclear, chemical, and offshore oil domains. CORE-DATA uses the following data sources as its input:

- Incident and accident report data
- Simulator data from training and experimental simulations
- Experimental data
- Expert judgment data

The information in the CORE-DATA database is analyzed and contain the following information elements (adapted from Basra and Kirwan, 1998).

1. *Task description*, where a general description is given of the task being performed and the operating conditions.

2. *Human error mode*. This is similar to a component failure mode and is a description of the observable manifestation of the error: for example, action too late, action too early, incorrect sequence, and so on.

3. *Psychological error mechanisms*. This element provides a description of the operator's internal failure modes, such as attention failure, cognitive overload, misdiagnosis, and so on.

4. *Performance shaping factors*, where a description of the performance shaping factors that contributed to the error mode are described: for example, ergonomic design, task complexity, and so on.

5. *Error opportunities* that quantify how many times a task was completed and the number of times the operator failed to achieve the desired outcome: for example, 1 error in 50.

6. *Nominal HEP*. This is the mean HEP of a given task, calculated as the number of errors observed divided by the number of opportunities for error.

    ... and several more.

### 7.5.3  Human Error Probabilities

Several data sources for human errors are available. Among these are:

The *Human Performance Evaluation System (HPES),* established by the Institute for Nuclear Power Operations in Atlanta, Georgia, requires a membership fee for access to data but annual summary reports are published. HPES provides data for human errors in the nuclear power industry and gives HEP estimates and information as to root causes of the errors.

*Handbook of human reliability analysis with emphasis on nuclear power plant applications* (Swain and Guttmann, 1983) presents 27 tables of probabilities for human error, together with so-called *performance shaping factors* (PSFs) that can be used to adapt the HEPs to a specific situation/application. The data are most relevant for nuclear industry applications.

*Human Error Assessment and Reduction Technique (HEART)* contains a table with generic HEPs, together with performance-shaping factors and a procedure for adapting the HEPs to specific applications. The HEART calculation procedure is more simple than the one proposed by Swain and Guttmann (1983) (see above).

*A Guide to Practical Human Reliability Assessment* (Kirwan, 1994) has an appendix (II) with HEPs from generic sources, operational plants, ergonomic experiments, and simulators.

*Human Reliability&Safety Analysis Data Handbook* (Gertman and Blackman, 1994) gives a thorough discussion of challenges and problems related to human reliability data and also presents some data.

The *Computerized Operator Reliability and Error Database (CORE-DATA),* described in Section 7.5.2, provides quantitative data, and thus is also a data source for HEP estimates.

There are many more data sources for human error. Interested readers can, for example, search for these on the Internet. A good starting point is http://en.wikipedia.org/wiki/Human_error.

## 7.6  Software Failure Data

More and more systems have embedded software, and this software is sometimes an important contributor to system failures. Software failures are different from component failures and human errors since they generally do not occur at random. Software failures are caused by inherent faults/defects in the programs that will result in a failure when specific inputs to the program are present. These inputs may, or may not, occur randomly. When a software fault is revealed and corrected (debugged), the failure possibility is removed and the failure can never occur again.

The probabilities of software failures are difficult to estimate and are therefore often left out of the quantitative analysis. This is, for example, the case for safety instrumented systems (see Chapter 12). The main standard for such systems, IEC 61508, gives strict requirements for the calculation of failure probabilities for hardware failures, but recommends that software failures not be quantified but, rather, are subject to a careful quality assurance of the software development process (see part 3 of IEC 61508). As far as is known by the author, no databases for software failures are available.

## 7.7  Expert Judgment

As mentioned earlier in this chapter, the use of expert judgment becomes necessary when data from real applications are scarce or nonexisting. Expert judgment elicitation is a process for obtaining data directly from experts in response to a specified problem. This may be related to the structure of the models and to the parameters and variables used in the models. The expert judgment process may be formal or informal, and may involve only one expert or a group of individuals with various types of expert knowledge. Several structured processes for eliciting information from experts have been suggested in the literature and have been proven useful in practical risk analyses.

It is not an objective of this book to give a thorough introduction to expert judgment elicitation. Interested readers may consult, for example, Cooke (1991) and Ayyub (2001).

*Remark*: As mentioned in Section 7.4, the failure rate estimates in IEEE Std. 500 (1984) were produced by a Delphi method. A *Delphi method* is a special procedure for expert judgment elicitation where the individual experts answer questionnaires in two or more rounds. After each round, a facilitator provides an anonymous summary of the experts' forecasts from the previous round as well as the reasons they provided for their judgments. In this way, the experts are encouraged to revise their earlier answers in light of the replies of other members of their panel. During this process, it is believed that the answers will converge toward the "correct" answer. The process is terminated when a predefined stop criterion is met (e.g., number of rounds, stability of results) and the mean or median scores of the final rounds determine the results. For more information about the Delphi method, see http://en.wikipedia.org/wiki/Delphi_method.                                                                    ⊕

## 7.8   Data Dossier

When the report from a risk analysis is presented, what data the risk analysis is based on is sometimes questioned. It is important that the choice of input data is thoroughly documented, especially the choice of reliability data. It is therefore recommended that a *data dossier* be set up that presents and justifies the choice of data for each component or input event in the risk analysis. An example of such a data dossier is shown in Figure 7.1. In many applications, a simpler data dossier may be used.

## 7.9   Additional Reading

The following titles are recommended for further study related to Chapter 7.

- *System Reliability Theory: Models, Statistical Methods, and Applications* (Rausand and Høyland, 2004). Chapter 14 of this book gives a survey of data sources and problems related to data collection and databases.

- *The Reliability Data Handbook* (Moss, 2005) gives a thorough description of the use of data in reliability analysis, including data collection, data analysis, and evaluation of the goodness of the data.

- *Reliability and Risk Assessment* (Andrews and Moss, 2002) describes methods for reliability and risk analysis. Chapter 12 deals with data collection and analysis of reliability data. The book also includes three case studies.

- *A Guide to Practical Human Reliability Assessment* (Kirwan, 1994) gives a good introduction to human reliability assessment and data needed for such analyses.

- *Elicitation of Expert Opinions for Uncertainty and Risks* (Ayyub, 2001) gives a thorough introduction to expert judgment elicitation.

| Data dossier | |
|---|---|
| **Component:** Hydraulically operated gate valve | **System:** Pipeline into pressure vessel A1 |

**Description:** The valve is a 5-inch gate valve with a hydraulic "fail safe" actuator. The fail safe-function is achieved by a steel spring that is compressed by hydraulic pressure. The valve is normally in the open position and is only activated when the pressure in the vessel exceeds 150 bar. The valve is function-tested once a year. After a function test, the valve is considered to be "as good as new." The valve is located in a sheltered area and is not exposed to frost/icing.

| Failure mode: | Failure rate (per hour): | Source: |
|---|---|---|
| - Does not close on command | $3.3 \times 10^{-6}$ <br> $1.2 \times 10^{-6}$ | Source A <br> Source B |
| - Leakage through the valve in closed position | $2.7 \times 10^{-6}$ | Source A |
| - External leakage from valve | $4.2 \times 10^{-7}$ | Source A |
| - Closes spuriously | $3.8 \times 10^{-6}$ <br> $7.8 \times 10^{-6}$ | Source A <br> Source B |
| - Cannot be opened after closure | 1/300 | Expert judgment |

**Assessment:**

The failure rates are based on sources A and B. The failure rate for the failure mode "cannot be opened after closure" is based on the judgments from three persons with extensive experience from using the same type of valves and is estimated to one such failure per 300 valve openings. Source B is considered to be more relevant than source A, but source B gives data for only two failure modes. Source B is therefore used for the failure modes "does not close on command" and "closes spuriously", while source A is used for the remaining failure modes.

**Testing and maintenance:**

The valve is function-tested after installation and thereafter once per year. The function test is assumed to be a realistic test, and possible failures detected during the test are repaired immediately such that the valve can be considered "as good as new" after the test. There are no options for diagnostic testing of the valve.

**Comments:**

The valve is a standard gate valve that has been used in comparable systems for a long time. The data used therefore have good validity and are relevant for the specified application.

**Figure 7.1**    Example of a reliability data dossier

**PART II**

---

# RISK ASSESSMENT METHODS AND APPLICATIONS

---

# CHAPTER 8

# RISK ASSESSMENT PROCESS

We never analyze a system—we analyze only a conceptual model of a system.

—P. L. Clemens

## 8.1 Introduction

Part II of the book presents a number of methods that can be used as part of a risk analysis. The part is divided into nine chapters and each method is presented in the chapter where it is most relevant. Some methods are very specialized, while others have a wider scope and therefore span several aspects of a risk analysis. This makes it difficult to get a stringent classification, and some methods could therefore have been presented in more than one chapter.

The order of Chapters 9–11 is according to the main structure of a risk analysis as illustrated in Figure 8.1. Barriers are important in all risk analyses and the barrier concept is therefore discussed thoroughly in Chapter 12, and several methods for barrier analysis are presented. Human errors are claimed to be a major factor in many major accidents. Human errors and human reliability are therefore discussed

*Risk Assessment: Theory, Methods, and Applications,* First Edition.
By Marvin Rausand. Copyright © 2011 John Wiley & Sons, Inc.

in Chapter 13 and several methods for human reliability assessment are presented. Another important factor in many accidents is common-cause failure. Such failures are discussed in Chapter 15. The uncertainty of risk analysis results and the sensitivity of input parameters are discussed in Chapter 16. The two remaining chapters in Part II deviate a bit from the main structure. Chapter 14 presents job safety analysis and contains elements from several of the other chapters. Chapter 17 gives a survey of how, and to what degree, risk analyses and risk assessments are used in some important application areas.

### 8.1.1   Structure of Method Presentations

The objective of this part is to describe each method so thoroughly that you are able to use it after having read the relevant section. All methods are described according to the same structure:

1. Introduction
   The method is introduced briefly together with its background.

2. Objectives and applications
   The objectives of the method are given as an itemized list and the most common application areas are outlined.

3. Method description
   The theoretical background for the method is described briefly. For simple methods, this step is sometimes skipped or integrated in the next item.

4. Analytic procedure
   A procedure recommended for use of the method is described in a number of steps. In most cases, this procedure is also illustrated in a workflow diagram.

5. Resources and skills required
   The resources and the skills required to carry out the analysis are described briefly. This part also includes computer programs, standards, and guidelines where applicable.

6. Advantages and limitations
   The main advantages and limitations of the method are presented as itemized lists.

The method descriptions included in this part do not cover all details about each method. Recommendations for further study are therefore included at the end of each chapter.

Chapter 5 describes briefly the main steps in the risk assessment process. Some of these steps are independent of the methods we decide to use and are therefore similar for all risk assessments. This applies, for example, to

(a) the planning and preparation of the study, which comprises system description, formation of a study team, establishment of a project plan, and familiarization with the study object, and to

(b) the reporting of the study.

To avoid repeating these issues for each method, a common description is given in Sections 8.2 and 8.3, respectively.

To plan and prepare a risk assessment, you should start by carefully reading Section 5.3 and answering all the questions posed in that section. The present chapter does not make Section 5.3 redundant, but rather, comments on and extends that section.

## 8.2 Plan and Prepare

For a risk assessment to provide the required results, it is important that the assessment process be carefully planned and prepared. One can easily be impatient in this part of the study, aching to get on with the "real work" as soon as possible. In most cases, however, it is beneficial to allocate sufficient time and resources to the preparation of the study.

The step "plan and prepare" is covered by steps 1 and 2 in Section 5.4, and involves:

1. Defining the objectives of the risk assessment

2. Appointing a study team and organizing the work

3. Establishing a project plan (including time and resources)

4. Describing and delimiting the study object (physically, operationally, and with respect to the hazards covered)

5. Becoming familiar with the study object

6. Providing background information (laws, regulations, previous incidents, etc.)

7. Choosing the risk assessment approach

The activities will not necessarily be carried out in this sequence. Sometimes we must run several activities in parallel and also jump from one activity to another. The choice of approach may, for example, imply that the competence in the study team must be supplemented with an additional specialist, and delimitation of the study object may require that the project plan be revised.

### 8.2.1 Objectives

The reason for performing a risk assessment may vary, but common to all risk assessments is that they should provide input to some decision-making. It is therefore important that the study team understand the requirements of this input and gives clear and specific answers to the questions that are listed in step 1 in Section 5.4. If

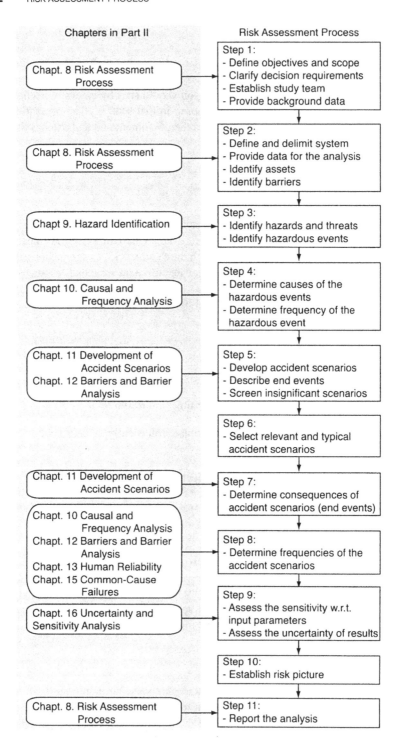

**Figure 8.1** The structure of Part II of the book, related to the risk assessment process.

the objective of the risk assessment is not clear from the beginning, it is not likely that the assessment will answer the questions that need to be answered.

If the plant management has defined the risk acceptance criteria to be used in risk evaluation, these must be known to the study team such that the results from the risk assessment are given in a comparable format (see Chapter 4).

Defining the scope of the risk assessment should involve the following steps (see IEC 60300-3-9, 1995, Para. 5.2):

– Describe the reasons for performing the risk assessment. This will involve:

  - Formulation of the objectives of the risk assessment based on the main concerns identified.

  - Defining the criteria for success/failure of the system. The main concern may be some undesirable outcome (e.g., system failure, release of toxic material) or a potentially harmful condition.

– Specify the system to be assessed. This should include a description and delimitation of:

  - The system

  - The boundaries and interfaces with related systems, both physical and functional

  - The environmental conditions

  - The energy, materials, and information flowing across boundaries

  - The operating conditions to be covered by the risk assessment and any relevant limitations.

– Identify information sources that provide details of the technical, environmental, legal, organizational, and human circumstances that are relevant to the activity and the problem being assessed. In particular, any circumstances related to safety should be described.

– State the assumptions and constraints governing the risk assessment.

– Identify the decisions that have to be made, the required output from the study and the decision-makers.

## 8.2.2 Study Team

The risk assessment is carried out by a study team that is led by a team leader. The study team must comprise persons with necessary knowledge of the study object and how the safety is managed/maintained. The team should have competence from different sectors, and the team members should come from different levels of the organization. Depending on the competence of the study team, it may be relevant to include external experts.

The study team must have competence in risk assessment methods and relevant consequence modeling, as well as relevant system and operational competence. The latter may, for example, include competence within fabrication and installation activities (see also IEC 60300-3-9, 1995, para 5.1.1). The number of persons taking part in the study will vary depending on the scope of the risk assessment and the complexity of the study object.

In some cases, it may be relevant to contract a consulting company to carry out the risk assessment. If the risk assessment is done by external consultants, it is important that in-house personnel carefully follow the assessment process to ensure that the company accepts ownership of the results.

The competence and experience of each member of the study team should be documented, along with their respective roles in the team.

In cases where external stakeholders are exposed to risk, it should be considered if, and to what degree, these should be involved in the risk assessment.

### 8.2.3 Project Planning

When the results from the risk assessment are to be used as the basis for a decision, it is of paramount importance that the assessment process be planned such that the results are available in due time. The study team should, in cooperation with the management, decide on a time schedule and estimate the resources that are required to do the risk assessment. The extent of the assessment will depend on the complexity of the study object, the severity of the risk, the competence of the study team, how important the decision is considered to be, the time available for the study, access to data, and so on.

When the decision is related to authority requirements, and/or relevant guidelines and standards are available, it must first be checked to see if these impose any constraints on how the risk assessment should be executed.

In many risk assessments, it is difficult to delimit the study object and to decide which assumptions and conditions should apply. What should be covered in the risk assessment, and what can be disregarded? In the first steps of a risk assessment, the objective should be to establish a picture of the most important risk issues related to the study object. Later on, the risk assessment may be extended to cover specific parts of the study object under special conditions.

### 8.2.4 System Description

The study object must be divided into reasonable parts for analysis. Depending on the complexity of the study object, these parts may be subsystems, assemblies, subassemblies, and components. A numerical coding system corresponding to the system breakdown should be established, such that each part is given a unique number. In the offshore oil and gas industry, this hierarchy is usually referred to as the *tag number system*.

Several methods are available for the system breakdown. It is most common to use some sort of hierarchical structure. In some cases, it is most relevant to focus on functions, while in others, the focus is on the physical elements.

To describe the system and its elements, several issues must be addressed. All technical, organizational, and human attributes that are relevant for the study should be described in the detail necessary. Attributes that are relevant for the safety of the system, especially, must be listed. The interface with the rest of the "world" and relevant political, social, and economic issues should also be mentioned. In this context, it is important to cover possible external assistance in case of an accident.

When describing the system, the study team should ask:

- What *inputs* to the system/element are required?

- What *functions* are performed by the system/element?

- What are the *outputs* from the system/element?

Answering these questions will provide the necessary insight into the system and its surroundings.

## 8.2.5 Familiarization

When the study team has been established, it is important that the team members become familiar with the study object and its operational and environmental conditions. It is important that the study team have access to all relevant information and documentation. Information sources of interest typically include (e.g., see IAEA, 2002):

- System layout drawings, including the relation to other systems and assets

- System flow, logic, and control diagrams

- Descriptions of normal and possible abnormal operations of the system

- Inventories of hazardous materials

- Operation procedures and operator training material

- Testing and maintenance procedures

- Emergency procedures

- Previous risk assessments of the same or similar systems

- Descriptions of engineered safety systems (barriers) and safety support systems, including reliability assessments

- Description of previous hazardous events and accidents in the system

- Feedback from experiences at similar systems

- Environmental impact assessments (if relevant)

### 8.2.6   Document Control System

The number of documents required to support a risk assessment can be substantial. A document control system should therefore be established to manage the various documents and other information sources. This system must control the updating, revision, issue, or removal of reports in accordance with the quality assurance program to ensure that the information is always up to date.

### 8.2.7   Laws and Regulation

Most study objects have to comply with a number of laws and regulations. Many of these set requirements for health and safety, and some of them also require that risk assessments be performed. It is important that the study team be familiar with these laws and regulations, such that the requirements are covered in the risk assessment.

Specific risk assessment standards and/or guidelines have been developed for some types of study objects or application areas. The study team must be familiar with these standards and guidelines.

### 8.2.8   Input Data

A number of data sources are required for a risk assessment. The various types of data and data sources are discussed in Chapter 7.

### 8.2.9   Selection of Method

Several approaches have been developed for risk assessment. Which to chose depends on the objectives of the study, the type and complexity of the study object, the resources available, access to input data, and so on. An overview of the most relevant methods is given in Table 8.1, together with an indication of the phase(s) of a system's life in which they are suitable.

When the system is analyzed in the early design phase, we may start with rather coarse methods, such as preliminary hazard analysis (see Section 9.4), since at this stage we do not have access to the details of the system. As the development project progresses and we know more details, we may carry out more detailed analyses.

### 8.3   Reporting

To be useful as a decision basis, the decision-makers must be able to understand the conclusions and recommendations made by the study team. The information from the risk assessment must therefore be presented as clearly and concisely as possible.

The risk assessment is usually presented in a report, but may also be accompanied by brochures, slide presentations, and videos. Reporting is a key aspect of the risk assessment and should be initiated as early as possible in the assessment process.

The decisions to be made are often important and far-reaching. It is therefore important that the decision-makers can have confidence in all the findings made by

**Table 8.1** Applicability of analysis methods in the various stages of a risk assessment.

| Method (Chapter) | Early design | Design | Operation | Modification |
|---|---|---|---|---|
| Checklists (9) | M | M | G | M |
| Preliminary hazard analysis (9) | G | B | B | M |
| HAZOP (9) | M | G | M | G |
| SWIFT (9) | G | M | M | G |
| FMECA (9) | B | G | M | G |
| Fault tree analysis (10) | B | G | G | G |
| Bayesian networks (10) | M | G | G | G |
| Petri nets (10) | B | G | G | G |
| Event tree analysis (11) | B | G | G | G |
| Human reliability analysis (13) | B | G | G | G |
| Safety audits (5) | B | B | G | B |

G = good/suitable, M = medium/could be used, B = bad/not suitable.

the study team. The risk assessment reports must be well founded and trustworthy, and it must be possible to review and verify all the results. All conclusions and recommendations must be traceable to documents describing the background, models, input data, calculations, and so on.

The complexity of a risk assessment, and probabilistic methods in particular, may pose a significant barrier to an understanding of the report. It is therefore important that the main results be described clearly and documented in a language that decision-makers and other stakeholders understand.

The level of detail in the report(s) should correspond to the risk level. A system with a low level of risk will normally require a less extensive report than that for a system with a very high level of risk.

How the report is written and the level of detail also depend on the objectives of the study and for whom the report is intended:

(a) The report will only be used as a decision basis for the line management, and no external parties are expected to get access to the report.

(b) The report will be used by the company management to establish good risk management practices. Thus, the results of the risk assessment can be used to help define the requirements for various elements of the facility safety program, including maintenance, training, operating procedures, safety inspections and audits, and management of change.

(c) The report will be presented to the board of directors as a background for strategic discussions.

(d) The report will be made public. This is, for example, required for companies that have to fulfill the requirements of the EU Seveso II directive (EU, 1996).

(e) The results and the report will be presented at public meetings with stakeholders.

Some laws and regulations have special requirements to the format of the risk assessment report. This applies, for example, to the Seveso II directive.

### 8.3.1  Contents of the Report

A possible structure of a risk assessment report is presented below. It is recommended that too much narrative text be avoided and that important points be enumerated for referential purposes.

***Title Page.***   In cases where the risk assessment has to be updated regularly, the initial and all subsequent revision numbers should be recorded on the report's title page and in the table of contents. The title page should show the date of the latest revision, the revision number, and be signed (e.g., see US DOE, 2004).

***Disclaimer***

***Executive Summary.***   The main results should be listed, together with recommendations for risk-reducing measures and further actions. When the report is updated, the revision number and who has performed the assessment should be noted.

(a) Introduction (including why the risk assessment is executed)

(b) Objectives and limitations

(c) Analysis approach

(d) Main conclusions and recommendations (each conclusion or recommendation should be briefly justified)

The summary report should provide an overview of the background, assumptions, objectives, scope, results, and conclusions at a level that is useful to a wide audience of safety specialists and at the same time is adequate for high-level review.

***Document References.***   All the documents and other information sources used in the risk assessment should be listed, together with proper references.

***Acronyms and Glossary.***   Special terms or concepts that are used in the study should be listed and defined and/or explained.

***Study Team.***   The name, position, competence, and role of each member of the study team should be listed.

*Introduction.* The introduction should describe the background for the study, the objectives, and the assumptions, together with a clear and concise tabulation of all known limitations and constraints associated with the risk assessment. Incidents and accidents that have taken place in similar systems should be listed.

The time interval during which the risk assessment was performed should also be recorded.

*System Description.* The study object is described briefly together with its main functions. References to more detailed descriptions should be given. Conditions and limitations for operation of the study object should also be mentioned: for example, owners, responsibilities, location, staffing level and important stakeholders (e.g., customers, passengers).

The description should contain sufficient information to verify that the system is consistent with the assumptions made in the risk assessment.

*Analysis Approach.* This part of the report should give an overview of the analytical methods that have been used: for example, FMECA and HAZOP. In general, arguments for choosing these particular methods should also be given.

*Risk Acceptance Criteria.* Acceptance criteria are important for evaluating the risk and should therefore be listed in the report. If risk matrices are used, the frequency and severity classification should be defined.

*Hazards and Hazardous Events.* Hazards, threats, and hazardous events that have been identified should be listed in this part: for example, in the format of a table. In some cases, it may be relevant to give a more detailed description of the most important hazardous events.

*Models.* The models, methods, and tools that are used in the risk assessment should be described, together with possible limitations of these in relation to the assessment.

*Data and Data Sources.* It is important to list and describe the information that is used such that the risk assessment can be verified by a third party. The data used should, as far as possible, be documented in a data dossier (see Chapter 7). A review of previous accidents and near-accidents in similar applications should be part of this chapter.

*Frequency and Consequence Analysis.* This chapter presents the frequency and the consequences of each hazardous event. These should be combined to present the risk picture. Depending on the analytical approach selected, the results may often be presented in tables.

*Sensitivity and Uncertainty Assessments.* The results from the risk assessment are subject to a wide range of uncertainties, depending on the input data, the models and methods used, and the knowledge of the study team (see Chapter 16). To give a realistic picture of the risk, the uncertainty of the input data should be discussed. In some cases, it may be relevant to run sensitivity analyses to show how the uncertainty in the input data influences the end result. The report should address any analytical limitations that are expected to affect the main results of the risk assessment.

*Identification and Assessment of Risk-Reducing Measures.*  Based on the results from the risk assessment, it should be considered whether any risk-reducing measures should be implemented. Possible safeguards that have been identified in the assessment should be described in this chapter.

*Discussions of Results.*  It is important to discuss the results from the risk assessment and to check that they are compatible with the objectives of the study. Have we addressed the questions we were asked to answer? We must check whether the analyses are sufficient, or if it is necessary to do more detailed analyses. All this should be mentioned in the report.

*Conclusions and Recommendations.*  Finally, all the conclusions that may be drawn from the risk assessment should be listed, along with possible proposals for further work. It is important to check that all recommended changes to the system or its operation have properly been listed as *action items*.

*Appendices.*  In most cases several documents, drawings, detailed worksheets, and so on, have been used in the risk assessment. These are often too voluminous to be included in the main report and should therefore either be included as appendices to the report or be mentioned in the document references.

The amount of information in the appendices should be limited. If in doubt about the benefit of including material as an appendix, it should probably be omitted.

A slightly different report structure is described in Chapter 5 of US DOE (2004), and some valuable advice on writing an efficient report based on a risk assessment is given by IAEA (1994b).

The report must always be written such that it can be reviewed, verified, and updated. After completion, the risk assessment report should be reviewed and factually validated by the company. It may also be beneficial to have a third-party review before the results are used.

The risk assessment will sometimes cover deliberate actions and the system's vulnerability relative to these threats. It is then important to realize that notes, worksheets, and other documentation from the risk assessment will be sensitive data that should be kept confidential. This documentation must therefore be graded and kept confidential. Nothing makes a company more vulnerable than a vulnerability study that has gone astray!

## 8.4  Updating

All systems will change with time. Although the results from the risk assessment constitute important information for maintaining the safety of a system, this information will soon be outdated if the risk assessment is done once and for all. To ensure that the information remains up to date, it is important that the company have a clear policy on how and when the risk assessment must be updated. A possibility is to carry out a risk assessment at regular intervals (e.g., every five years) or when important modifications are made to the system. For some types of systems, authorities require that the risk assessment be updated after all major modifications and once every five years.

Keeping the risk assessment documentation updated makes it possible to assess the risk associated with any proposed changes to the facility.

## 8.5  Additional Reading

The folllowing titles are recommended for further study related to Chapter 8.

- *Systems Engineering and Analysis* (Blanchard and Fabrycky, 1998) is not a book on risk assessment, but presents methods for describing systems as technical and functional hierarchies. In addition, the book is a good source for general system analysis.

- *Dependability Management—Application Guide: Risk Analysis of Technological Systems* (IEC 60300-3-9, 1995) is the main general standard for risk analysis of technological systems.

- *Application of probabilistic safety assessment (PSA) for nuclear power plants* (IAEA, 2001) and *Procedures for conducting probabilistic safety assessment of non-reactor nuclear facilities* (IAEA, 2002), issued by the International Atomic Energy Agency, give clear advice to the nuclear industry on the execution of quantitative risk assessment. Many of the views also apply in other application areas.

- *Probabilistic risk assessment (PRA) procedures for NASA programs and projects* (NASA, 2010) is a detailed guideline for risk assessment in the space industry, but is also a valuable source in other application areas.

# CHAPTER 9

# HAZARD IDENTIFICATION

One should expect that the expected can be prevented, but the unexpected should have been expected.

—Norman Ralph Augustine

## 9.1 Introduction

This chapter deals with the first question in the triplet definition of risk: What can go wrong? Answering this question implies identifying all the hazards and threats and all the hazardous events that can cause harm to one or more assets. Several methods have been developed for these purposes and these methods are usually referred to as *hazard identification methods*.

☞ **Hazard identification**: The process of identifying and describing all the signif-icant hazards, threats, and hazardous events associated with a system (DEF-STAN 00-56, 2007).

*Risk Assessment: Theory, Methods, and Applications,* First Edition.
By Marvin Rausand. Copyright © 2011 John Wiley & Sons, Inc.

### 9.1.1 Objectives of Hazard Identification

The objectives of the hazard identification process are to:

(a) Identify all the hazards and hazardous events that are relevant during all intended use and foreseeable misuse of the system, and during all interactions with the system.

(b) Describe the characteristics, and the form and quantity, of each hazard.

(c) Describe when and where in the system the hazard is present.

(d) Identify possible triggering events related to each hazard.

(e) Identify under what conditions the hazard could lead to a hazardous event and which pathways the hazard may follow.

(f) Identify potential hazardous events that could be caused by the hazard (or in combination with other hazards).

(g) Make operators and system owners aware of hazards and potential hazardous events.

### 9.1.2 Hazard Identification Methods

The hazard identification methods that are described in this chapter are:

*Hazard Log*
   This is not a hazard identification *method*, but rather a useful tool for recording information about hazards and hazardous events, and for keeping this information updated.

*Checklist and Brainstorming*
   In many cases, it is useful to start with a list of generic hazards and/or generic hazardous events and to decide if, where, and how these events may occur for the system being analyzed. Such a list of generic events is, for example, given in HSE (2001a) for risk analysis of offshore oil and gas installations. A small part of the list is presented in Table 9.1 for illustration. Teamwork and brainstorming sessions may be used to come up with details about the events.

*Preliminary Hazard Analysis (PHA)*
   PHA is a rather simple method and is commonly used to identify hazards in the design phase of a system. The analysis is called "preliminary" because its results are often updated as more thorough risk analyses are carried out. PHA may also be used in later phases of the system's life cycle, and can, for relatively simple systems, be a complete and sufficient risk analysis. A simplified PHA is sometimes called a HAZID.

**Table 9.1**   List of generic hazardous events on offshore oil and gas installations.

| *Blowouts* | *Nonprocess spills* |
|---|---|
| – Blowout in drilling | – Chemical spills |
| – Blowout in completion | – Methanol/diesel/aviation fuel spills |
| – Blowout in production | – Bottled gas spills |
| – Blowout in workover | – Radioactive material releases |
| – etc. | – etc. |
| *Process leaks*—leaks of gas or oil from: | *Marine collisions* |
| – Wellhead equipment | – Supply vessels |
| – Separators and other process equipment | – Standby vessels |
| – Compressors and other gas treatment equipment | – Passing merchant vessels |
| – Process pipes, flanges, valves, pumps | – Fishing vessels |
| – etc. | – Drilling rigs |
|  | – etc. |
| *Nonprocess fires* | *And several more categories* |
| – Fuel gas fires |  |
| – Electrical fires |  |
| – Accommodation fires |  |
| – Methanol/diesel/aviation fuel fires |  |
| – etc. |  |

*Source*: Extract adapted from HSE (2001a).

### Change Analysis

Change analysis is used to identify hazards and threats related to planned modifications of a system. The analysis is carried out by comparing the properties of the modified system with a basic (known) system. Change analysis may also be used to evaluate modifications to operating procedures.

### Failure Modes, Effects, and Criticality Analysis (FMECA)

FMECA (or FMEA) was one of first methods for system reliability analysis, and the first guideline was issued in 1949. The objective of FMECA of a technical system is to identify all the potential failure modes of the system components, identify the causes of these failure modes, and assess the effects that each failure mode may have on the entire system.

### Hazard and Operability (HAZOP) Study

The HAZOP approach was developed to identify deviations and dangerous situations in a process plant. The method is based on teamwork and brainstorming that is structured based on guidewords. The method has been used with great success and is today a standard method for risk assessment in the design of process plants. HAZOP is also used in later phases of a system's life cycle, especially related to modifications of the system. A variant of HAZOP can be used to identify hazards in complex work procedures.

*Structured What-If Technique (SWIFT)*

SWIFT is carried out by a group of experts in a brainstorming session where a set of what-if questions are asked—and answered. The work is structured using a special checklist. The method was earlier called a "what-if/checklist" method. SWIFT can be used as a simplified HAZOP and can be applied to the same type of system.

*Master Logic Diagram (MLD)*

MLD may be used to identify hazards in complex systems that are exposed to a wide range of hazards and failure modes. The method resembles fault tree analysis (see Section 10.3), but is clearly distinguishable from this with several specific features. MLD is mentioned only briefly in this chapter, and interested readers are advised to consult the literature (e.g., see Modarres, 2006).

Several methods containing modules for hazard identification are discussed elsewhere in the book, for example in Chapter 12 related to barrier analysis and in Chapter 13 related to human errors. No method can identify all the hazardous events that can potentially occur in a system, and it is always possible that unidentified hazardous events will occur. A hazardous event that is not identified will not be controlled and will therefore always lead to a higher risk than assessed.

The effectiveness of any hazard identification analysis depends entirely on the experience and creative imagination of the study team. The methods applied only impose a disciplined structure on the work.

**Remark**: Hazard identification methods are sometimes classified as *brainstorming methods* or *functional methods* (e.g., see de Jong, 2007). The brainstorming methods are employed mainly by a group of experts and carried out in specific meetings. Examples of brainstorming methods are HAZOP and SWIFT. The functional methods are based on a detailed analysis of system structures and functions. An example of a functional method is FMECA. Most of the methods have elements of both types and we therefore do not use this categorization in this chapter.  ⊕

## 9.2 Hazard Log

It is often beneficial to enter the results of the hazard identification process into a *hazard log*. The hazard log is also called a *hazard register* or a *risk register*. A hazard log may be defined as (see also CASU, 2002):

☞ **Hazard log**: A log of hazards of all kinds that threaten a system's success in achieving its safety objectives. It is a dynamic and living document, which is populated through the organization's risk assessment process. The log provides a structure for collating information about risk that can be used in risk analyses and in risk management of the system.

The hazard log should be established early in the design phase of a system or at the beginning of a project and be kept up to date as a *living document* throughout the lifecycle of the system or project. The hazard log should be updated when new hazards are discovered, when there are changes to identified hazards, or when new accident data become available.

The hazard log is usually established as a computerized database, but can also be a document. The format of the hazard log varies a lot depending on the objectives of the log and the complexity and risk level of the system, and may range from a simple table, listing the main hazards that are related to the system, to an extensive database with several sub-databases. Elements often included in a (comprehensive) hazard log are:

1. *Hazards*

   (a) A unique reference to the hazard (number or name)

   (b) Description of the hazard (e.g., high pressure)

   (c) Where is the hazard present? (e.g., in the laboratory building)

   (d) Where can more information about the hazard be found? (e.g., toxicity data in book A)

   (e) What is the quantity/amount of the hazard? (e.g., 200 m$^3$ of diesel oil, 500 psi pressure)

   (f) When is the hazard present? (e.g., while hoisting a craneload)

   (g) Which triggering events can release the hazard? (e.g., operator error)

   (h) Which risk-reducing measures can be implemented related to the hazard? (e.g., replace a fluid with a less toxic fluid)

2. *Hazardous events*

   (a) A unique reference to the hazardous event (number or name)

   (b) Description of the hazardous event (e.g., gas leakage from pipeline A at location B)

   (c) Which hazards and triggering events can lead to the hazardous event? (e.g., a craneload falls on a pressurized gas pipeline). A link should be made to the relevant hazards in the hazard sub-log.

   (d) In which operational phases can the hazardous event occur? (e.g., during maintenance)

   (e) How often will the hazardous event occur? (e.g., frequency class 2)

   (f) What is the worst credible consequence of the hazardous event? (e.g., a major fire)

   (g) How serious is the worst credible consequence of the hazardous event? (e.g., consequence class 4)

   (h) Which proactive safeguards can be implemented to reduce the frequency of the hazardous event? (e.g., improved inspection program)

(i) Which reactive or mitigating safeguards can be implemented? (e.g., improved firefighting system)

(j) How much would the proposed safeguards reduce the risk? (e.g., RPN reduced from 6 to 4)

All hazardous events that can conceivably happen should be included, not only those that have already been experienced.

A log of experienced or potential incidents (or accident scenarios) may also be included in the hazard log. The contents of this log may be:

3. *Incidents (or accident scenarios)*

   (a) A unique reference to the incident (number or name)

   (b) Description of the incident (event sequence or accident scenario)

   (c) Has the incident occurred in this system or in any similar systems? If "yes," provide reference to the incident investigation report, if such a report exists.

   (d) How often will the incident occur?

   (e) What is/was the consequence of the incident? (Use the worst credible consequence for accident scenarios)

   (f) Which reactive or mitigating safeguards can be implemented?

   (g) Refer to the treatment of the accident scenario in the quantitative risk assessment if such an assessment has been carried out.

**Remark**: A number of databases contain information about previous accidents and near accidents (see Chapter 7). These provide valuable information on how accidents can actually arise. The relevant information in these sources should be reflected in the hazard log, in addition to the information from the operator's own site or company. However, historical data alone cannot be relied on, since accidents that have already occurred may not represent the entire range of possible accidents, particularly when dealing with major accidents (see also NSW, 2003).                                      ⊕

The hazard log can sometimes include a sublog of deliberate and hostile actions: for example:

4. *Threats and vulnerabilities*

   (a) A unique reference to the threat (number or name)

   (b) Description of the threat (e.g., arson, vandalism, computer hacking)

   (c) Where is the threat relevant? (e.g., computer network)

   (d) What are our main vulnerabilities? (e.g., no entrance control)

   (e) Who are the relevant threat agents? (e.g., visitors)

   (f) What unwanted events may take place? (e.g., loss of confidential information)

System: Process plant X  Name: Marvin Rausand
Reference:  Date created: 2010-12-20

| Hazard / threat | Where? | Amount | Safeguard | Comments |
|---|---|---|---|---|
| Trichlorethylene | Storage 2 | 1 barrel | Locked room | |
| Pressurized gas | Pressure vessel 3 | 10 m$^3$ (5 bar) | Fenced | |
| Gasoline | Beneath pump | 3000 L | Under earth | |
| | | | | |

**Figure 9.1**  Simple hazard log (example).

(g) How often will this event occur?

(h) How serious is the event? (Use the worst credible consequence)

(i) Which safeguards can be implemented?

It may further be beneficial to maintain a journal as a historical record of the hazard log. This journal may, for example, contain:

5. *Journal*

(a) The date the hazard log was started

(b) References to relevant laws, regulations, and company objectives related to the risk of the system

(c) For each entry entered into the log: date and cause

(d) For each entry that has been modified: date and cause

(e) References between the hazard log and more detailed risk analyses

(f) References to safety reviews and project decisions

More information may be added to the hazard log as desired.

A hazard log is especially valuable in the design phase, but accidents and near accidents that occur in the operational phase should also be compared with the hazard log, and the log should be updated accordingly.

An example of a very simple hazard log is shown in Figure 9.1, and a slightly more complex hazard log structure is shown in Figure 9.2. These logs are not based on a thorough analysis and are included only as an illustration. For a more detailed hazard log structure with explanations of the various entries, see UK CAA (2006, App. F).

System: Process plant X

Reference:

Date created: 2010-05-17

Date modified: 2010-12-20

Name: Marvin Rausand

| No. | Hazard description | Hazard presence | | Hazard quantity/amount | Possible hazardous event | Consequence (Harm to what?) | Risk | | | Risk-reducing measures | Residual risk | Planned date | Responsible |
|---|---|---|---|---|---|---|---|---|---|---|---|---|---|
| | | Where | When | | | | Freq. | Sev. | RPN | | | | |
| 1 | Sulfuric acid tank A1 | Production hall 2 | Always | 10 m³ | Tank rupture (due to falling load) | Direct impact - skin burns (5 operators) | 1 | 4 | 5 | Restricted area | | | |
| | | | | | | Sulfur fumes - eyes, respiratory tract (approx. 25 operators) | | | | | | | |
| | | | | | | Production stop (>2 days) | | | | | | | |
| 2 | | | | | Outlet pipe rupture | Direct impact - skin burns (2 operators) | 2 | 2 | 4 | Automatic shut-down valve close to tank | | | |
| | | | | | | Sulfur fumes - eyes, respiratory tract (5 operators) | | | | | | | |
| | | | | | | Production stop (1 day) | | | | Procedures for crane operations | | | |

**Figure 9.2**    Hazard log (example).

## 9.3  Checklist Methods

### 9.3.1  Introduction

A hazard checklist is a written list of hazards or hazardous events that have been derived from past experience. The entries of the list are often formulated as *questions* that are intended to help the study team consider all aspects of safety related to a study object. A checklist analysis for hazard identification is also called a *process review*.

Checklists may be based on previous hazard logs and should be made specifically for a process or an operation. Checklists should be regarded as living documents that need to be audited and updated regularly.

Generic hazard checklists consist of standard lists of hazards or hazard categories. A generic checklist for major accident hazards on an offshore installation is, for example, given in HSE (2001a).

### 9.3.2  Objectives and Applications

The objectives of a checklist analysis are to:

(a)  Identify all the hazards that are relevant during all intended use and foreseeable misuse of the system, and during all interactions with the system.

(b)  Identify required controls and safeguards.

(c)  Check that available controls and safeguards conform to the requirements specified.

Checklist approaches are used in a wide range of application areas and for many different purposes. The main focus has, however, been on early design phases and on the establishment of work procedures (e.g., see HSE, 2001a). Checklists have been used further to ensure that organizations are complying with standard practices. Hazard checklists may be useful further as part of other and more detailed hazard identification methods.

### 9.3.3  Analysis Procedure

A checklist analysis does not normally follow any strict procedure. An important task is to prepare a suitable checklist. A checklist is usually a list of questions related to potential hazardous event categories, and is developed based on a system analysis, its operating history, and experience from past accidents and near accidents.

. In some cases, process reviews are carried out without using a written checklist, and the study team must employ a "mental checklist." This approach is, of course, much more liable to omission of potential hazardous events. Table 9.2 is an example of a portion of a checklist.

**Table 9.2**   Process/system checklist for the design phase.

**Materials**. Review the characteristics of all process materials: raw materials, catalysts, intermediate products, and final products. Obtain detailed data on these materials, such as:

*Flammability*

- What is the autoignition temperature?
- What is the flash point?
- How can a fire be extinguished?

*Explosivity*

- What are the upper and lower explosive limits?
- Does the material decompose explosively?

*Toxicity*

- What are the breathing exposure limits (e.g., threshold limit values, immediate dangerous to life and health)?
- What personal protective equipment is needed?

*Corrosivity and compatibility*

- Is the material strongly acidic or basic?
- Are special materials required to contain it?
- What personal protective equipment is needed?

*Waste disposal*

- Can gases be released directly to the atmosphere?
- Can liquids be released directly to water?
- Is a supply of inert gas available for purging equipment?
- How would a leak be detected?

*Storage*

- Will any spill be contained?
- Is this material stable in storage?

*Static electricity*

- Is bonding or grounding of equipment needed?
- What is the conductivity of the materials, and how likely are they to accumulate static?

*Reactivity*

- Critical temperature for autoreaction?
- Reactivity with other components including intermediated?
- Effect of impurities?

*Source*: Adapted from CCPS (2008).

### 9.3.4   Resources and Skills Required

No specific skills are required, but the study team must maintain strict attention to details and perseverance in obtaining information. The information required varies depending on the checklist chosen.

### 9.3.5   Advantages and Limitations

*Advantages.*   The main advantages are that the checklist approach:

- can be used by non-system experts;

- makes use of experience from previous risk assessments;

- ensures that common and more obvious problems are not overlooked;

- is valuable in the design process for revealing hazards otherwise overlooked;

- requires minimal information about the installation, and so is suitable for concept design.

*Limitations.*  The main limitations are that the checklist approach:

- is limited to previous experience, and thus may not anticipate hazards in novel designs or novel accidents from existing designs;

- can miss hazards that have not been seen previously;

- does not encourage intuitive/brainstorming thinking, and gives limited insight into the nature of the hazards related to the study object.

Overall, a generic hazard checklist is useful for most risk assessments, but should not be the only hazard identification method, except for standard installations whose hazards have been studied in more detail elsewhere.

## 9.4  Preliminary Hazard Analysis

### 9.4.1  Introduction

*Preliminary hazard analysis* (PHA) is used to identify hazards and potential accidents in the early stages of system design, and is basically a review of where energy or hazardous materials can be released in an uncontrolled manner. The PHA technique was developed by the U.S. Army (MIL-STD-882D), and has been used with success both for safety analysis within the defense and for safety analysis of machinery and process plants. A PHA is called "preliminary" because it is usually refined through additional and more thorough studies. Many variants of PHA have been developed and they appear under different names, such as *hazard identification* (HAZID) and *rapid risk ranking* (RRR).

### 9.4.2  Objectives and Applications

The overall objective of a PHA is to reveal potential hazards, threats, and hazardous events early in the system development process, such that they can be removed, reduced, or controlled in the further development of the project.
    More specific objectives of a PHA are to:

(a) Identify the assets that need to be protected.

(b) Identify the hazardous events that can potentially occur.

(c) Determine the main causes of each hazardous event.

(d) Determine how often each hazardous event may occur.

(e) Determine the severity of each hazardous event.

(f) Identify relevant safeguards for each hazardous event.

(g) Assess the risk related to each hazardous event.

(h) Determine the most important contributors to the risk (and rank the contributors).

PHA is best applied in the early design phases of a system, but can also be used in later phases. PHA can be a stand-alone analysis or a part of a more detailed analysis. When the PHA is part of a more comprehensive risk assessment, the results of the analysis are used to screen events for further study.

### 9.4.3   Analysis Procedure

The PHA can be carried out in seven steps. Steps 1 and 7 are described in Chapter 8 and the details of these steps are therefore not repeated here. We first list the seven steps and then give a more thorough description of steps 2–6.

1. Plan and prepare.

2. Identify hazards and hazardous events.

3. Determine the frequency of hazardous events.

4. Determine the consequences of hazardous events.

5. Suggest risk-reducing measures.

6. Assess the risk.

7. Report the analysis.

The analysis procedure is illustrated in Figure 9.3.

#### *Step 2: Identify Hazards and Hazardous Events*

*2.1 Identify hazards and threats*   The aim of this activity is to get an overview of the hazards and treats that are, or might be, present in the study object. It is often helpful to use experience from similar systems and hazard checklists, such as the one in Table 3.1. In many cases, it may be beneficial to establish a hazard log for the study object. In this activity, personnel from all parts of the company (study object) should take part. For each hazard/threat that is identified, the study team records *what* the hazard/threat consists of, *where* it is found, and the *amount* of the hazard.

PHA is basically a brainstorming technique, but an organized approach may help starting the process, for example, by asking such questions as:

– Are there any hardware hazards?

**Input**

**Output**

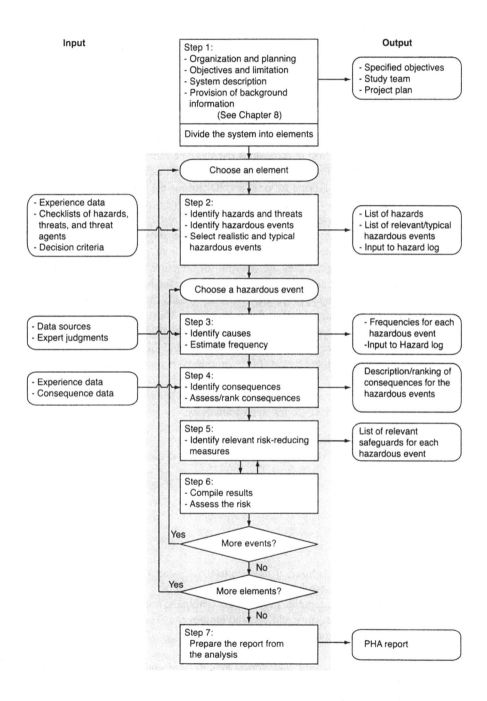

Step 1:
- Organization and planning
- Objectives and limitation
- System description
- Provision of background
  information
        (See Chapter 8)

Divide the system into elements

- Specified objectives
- Study team
- Project plan

Choose an element

- Experience data
- Checklists of hazards,
  threats, and threat
  agents
- Decision criteria

Step 2:
- Identify hazards and threats
- Identify hazardous events
- Select realistic and typical
  hazardous events

- List of hazards
- List of relevant/typical
  hazardous events
- Input to hazard log

Choose a hazardous event

- Data sources
- Expert judgments

Step 3:
- Identify causes
- Estimate frequency

- Frequencies for each
  hazardous event
-Input to Hazard log

- Experience data
- Consequence data

Step 4:
- Identify consequences
- Assess/rank consequences

Description/ranking of
consequences for the
hazardous events

Step 5:
- Identify relevant risk-reducing
  measures

List of relevant
safeguards for each
hazardous event

Step 6:
- Compile results
- Assess the risk

Yes

More events?

No

Yes

More elements?

No

Step 7:
Prepare the report from
the analysis

PHA report

**Figure 9.3**  Analysis workflow for PHA

– Are there any software hazards?

– Are there any human-induced hazards?

– Are there any procedure-related hazards?

– Are there any obvious interface hazards between software, hardware, and humans?

*2.2 Identify potential hazardous events* Personnel from all parts of the system should participate in identifying hazardous events. The meeting may preferably be arranged as a brainstorming session. The hazards and threats that were identified in activity 2.1 are discussed one by one, and hazardous events that may be caused by these hazards/threats – or in combination with other hazards/threats—are listed. This list may be rather long, but we should not be too restrictive at this stage of the analysis with respect to what is entered into the list. The study team can later sort the list and filter out nonrelevant events. All events that are suggested should be listed, irrespective of whether or not they are relevant for the current hazard/threat. If new hazards or threats are revealed, they should be added to the hazard log.

In many cases it may be appropriate to identify events in specific categories: for example, (i) random events and (ii) deliberate actions. These categories can be split into subcategories, and thus make it easier to identify relevant events. As new events are identified, new subcategories are often identified—and this process goes in a loop until the study team considers the list of hazardous events to be sufficient related to the objectives of the study.

During this session, the study team tries to identify what may happen in the future. In this work, it may be helpful to use such sources as:

– Reports from previous accidents and incidents

– Accident statistics

– Expert judgments

– Operational data

– Existing emergency plans

To identify deliberate actions, it may be useful to start by identifying potential threat agents. To group these into categories may be of help in order to identify potential actions. Possible categories may be data criminals, normal criminals, visitors, external staff, competitors, drug addicts, and employees. The description of actions should include a description of the mode of action.

*2.3 Select realistic and typical hazardous events* Depending on the study objectives and the time and resources available, it may be necessary to reduce the number of hazardous events. The study team should first refine the list and remove events that have no, or very low, significance for the risk. These may be events with a very low probability of occurrence or have a very low consequence if they occur. Events that

| Hazard / threat\n\nLocation | Fire | Crushing | Explosion | Falling person | Falingl load | Theft | | | | |
|---|---|---|---|---|---|---|---|---|---|---|
| Laboratory | X | | X | | | | | | | |
| Chemical storage | X | | X | | | X | | | | |
| Workshop | X | X | X | X | | X | | | | |
| Garage | X | X | | X | X | X | | | | |
| Data server | X | | | | | | | | | |
| Admin. building | X | | | X | | X | | | | |
| | | | | | | | | | | |
| | | | | | | | | | | |

**Figure 9.4**    Hazards and threats in various locations of the study object.

are removed from the list should be documented by a brief note describing why they have been left out. Each of the remaining events should be clearly defined, especially related to *what* is happening, *why* it is happening, and *where* it is happening.

To get an overview of all the hazardous events, it may be appropriate to enter them into a matrix such as the one illustrated in Figure 9.4. When a hazardous event is considered to be relevant for a specific location, a cross is entered into the matrix to indicate that this event must be treated in the further analysis.

To aid the further analysis, a PHA worksheet such as the one in Figure 9.5 may be used. It is usually most efficient to complete the evaluation of one event (both frequency and consequence) before studying the next event.

***Step 3: Determine the Frequency of Hazardous Events.***    In this step, the study team identifies and discusses the causes, and estimates the frequency of each of the hazardous events that were found in step 2.3. The causal analysis is usually rather brief and coarse, and only the obvious causes of each event are recorded. The frequencies are usually estimated as frequency classes: for example, as proposed in Table 4.8.

The frequency estimation is usually based on historical data (e.g., has a similar event occurred earlier?), expert judgments, and assumptions about the future. The historic data may comprise statistics and reports from near accidents and special events from the company (or plant), from other industry, from organizations, and from authorities.

In addition to the causes, the safeguards that have already been implemented to prevent the hazardous event should be assessed. For more details about safeguards (barriers), see Chapter 12.

Study object: LNG transport with tank truck
Reference:

Date: 2010-12-20
Name: Marvin Rausand

| System element or activity | Hazard / threat | No. | Hazardous event (what, where, when) | Cause (triggering event) | Consequence (harm to what?) | Freq. | Cons. | RPN | Risk-reducing measure | Respons-ible | Comment |
|---|---|---|---|---|---|---|---|---|---|---|---|
| Flexible pipe | Human error | 1 | Driver leaves the LNG terminal without disconnecting the filling tube from the tank | - Lack of attention<br>- Disturbed in her work | - LNG leakage (not ignited) | 3 | 2 | 5 | Install barrier in front of truck that only can be opened when the flexible pipe is disconnected | | |
| | | | | | - Fire/ explosion | 1 | 5 | 6 | Install alarm in truck when flexible pipe is connected | | |
| Tank truck | Driving route | 2 | Tank truck backs into concrete pillar when arriving at the customer's LNG tank | Narrow lane and poor visibility require the tank truck to back into the LNG reception area | - Damage to tank truck, no leakage of LNG | 2 | 2 | 4 | New design of access to the area | | |
| | | | | | - Hole in tank, both inner and outer tank | | | | | | |
| | | | | | -a. Not ignited | 2 | 3 | 5 | | | |
| | | | | | -b. Fire/-explosion | 1 | 5 | 6 | | | |

**Figure 9.5**    Sample PHA worksheet.

***Step 4: Determine the Consequences of Hazardous Events.*** In this step, the possible consequences following each of the hazardous events in step 2.3 are identified and assessed. The assessment should consider both immediate consequences and consequences that will emerge after some time. Several approaches are used. Among these are to assess:

(a) The most probable case

(b) The worst conceivable case

(c) The worst credible case (i.e., the worst case that may reasonably occur)

Which approach to select will depend on the objectives of the PHA, and whether or not the PHA is a first step in a more comprehensive risk analysis.

In many cases it may be appropriate to assess the consequences for the various categories of assets: for example, related to people (employees, third party), the environment, facilities, equipment, reputation, and so on. Assets that may be harmed are discussed further in Section 2.4.

When the consequences of a hazardous event have been assessed, each consequence should be classified into one of a small number of groups: for example, as in Table 4.9. When assessing the consequences, the safeguards that have been introduced to mitigate the consequences should also be taken into account.

***Remark***: Hammer (1993) claims that the benefit from this consequence ranking is rather limited. He recommends using the available time to eliminate or reduce the consequences instead of ranking them. On the other hand, MIL-STD-882 requires that such a column for consequence ranking be part of the PHA worksheet.     ⊕

***Step 5: Suggest Risk-Reducing Measures.*** When the study team considers the safeguards already in place, suggestions for new or improved safeguards and other risk-reducing measures will often emerge. All these suggestions should be noted as they emerge. The focus on identifying new or improved safeguards will depend on the objectives of the analysis. The study team should focus primarily on identifying hazards, threats, and hazardous events and on describing the level of risk for the object of the study. To develop a comprehensive list of new risk-reducing measures is generally not an important objective of the PHA.

The list of proposed risk-reducing measures should be screened and systemized to reveal if any of the proposals will have an effect on more than one hazardous event. Finally, the study team should make a brief cost/benefit assessment of each proposal. Safeguards (barriers) are discussed further in Chapter 12.

***Step 6: Assess the Risk.*** In this step, the risk related to the study object is described as a listing of all the potential hazardous events, together with their associated frequencies and consequences. A risk priority number (RPN) is sometimes calculated for each hazardous event.

The hazardous events may further be entered into a risk matrix to illustrate the risk and to indicate the most serious events. This may be helpful when improvements are to be evaluated and/or ranked. Risk matrices are discussed further in Section 4.4.

***Step 7: Report the Analysis.***   The results and the lessons learned from the PHA must be reported to the management, safety personnel, and other stakeholders, such that the results from the analysis can be used for safety management. The results from a PHA are usually presented in a specific PHA worksheet, as illustrated in Figure 9.5.

### ◼ EXAMPLE 9.1   LNG transport system

A tank truck is used to transport liquefied natural gas (LNG) from an LNG terminal to a customer. The object of our study comprises uploading of LNG to the tank truck, transport to the customer, unloading of the LNG, and transport (empty) back to the LNG terminal. Uploading and unloading of the LNG is carried out by the truck driver through a flexible pipe equipped with a quick coupling. The truck is driving on a public road with normal traffic.

The potential hazardous events can be classified into two main groups:

1. Events that do not result in release of LNG, comprising

   – Normal traffic accidents

   – Harm to the driver during uploading or unloading of LNG

2. Events that result in release of LNG, comprising

   – Rupture of the flexible pipe

   – Cracks or holes in the LNG tank

   – Release from the safety valve

   – Release of LNG during coupling or uncoupling of the flexible pipe

Some hazards related to the LNG transport system are shown in the PHA worksheet in Figure 9.5. The worksheet is only an illustration and not the result of a thorough study of the LNG transport system.                                    ⊕

*Remark*: Some guidelines for PHA recommend using a worksheet with two separate columns for *Risk* (including frequency, consequence, and RPN), one for the current design, and one when proposed safeguards have been implemented. In this way, it is possible to study the effect of the safeguards proposed. This is not done in Figure 9.5, but such a column can easily be added.                                    ⊕

*HAZID.* In some applications, it may be relevant to use a simplified worksheet, as shown in Figure 9.6. The analysis based on such a simplified worksheet is sometimes called a simplified PHA, or a HAZID. The application of the HAZID worksheet in Figure 9.6 is illustrated by some hazards that are relevant for Example 9.1. The objective of a HAZID is to reveal the hazardous events that should be subject to further study in a more detailed risk analysis.

As seen from both worksheets, it is often problematic to estimate the frequencies and the consequences. The same hazardous event may give many different consequences. A possible approach is to reveal the most relevant consequences, classify these into consequence classes and then estimate the related frequencies. This is done in the PHA worksheet shown in Figure 9.5. In the HAZID worksheet shown in Figure 9.6, only an average consequence is presented. This will not give sufficient information about the risk, but since the analysis is performed to reveal events that should be subject to further analysis, this approach may be sufficient.

### 9.4.4 Resources and Skills Required

The analysis may be carried out by one or two experienced engineers, preferably those who have a background as safety engineers. The PHA requires experience and understanding of the system.

Since the PHA is carried out in an early stage of the project, a limited amount of information about the system will normally be available. For a process plant, the process concept has to be settled before the analysis is initiated. At that point in time, the most important chemicals and reactions are known, together with the main elements of the process equipment (e.g., vessels, pumps).

The PHA must be based on all the safety-related information about the system, such as design criteria, equipment specifications, specifications of materials and chemicals, previous accidents, and previous hazard studies of similar systems that are available at the time when the analysis is performed (e.g., see MIL-STD-882D, 2000).

Computerized tools and a variety of hazard checklists are available and may assist the study team in performing the PHA.

### 9.4.5 Standards and Guidelines

No specific international standard for PHA has been developed, but the method is described in MIL-STD-882D (2000) *Standard Practice for System Safety*. PHA is also described thoroughly in *Guideline for Hazard Evaluation Procedures* (CCPS, 2008) and in several textbooks on risk assessment and safety engineering.

### 9.4.6 Advantages and Limitations

*Advantages.* The main advantages are that PHA:

- is simple to use and requires limited training;

- is a necessary first step in most risk analyses and has been used extensively in defense and process applications;

- identifies and provides a log of hazards and their corresponding risks;

- can be used in early project phases, that is, early enough to allow design changes;

- is a versatile method that can cover a range of problems.

*Limitations.* The main limitations are that PHA:

- is difficult to use to represent events with widely varying consequences;

- fails to assess risks of combined hazards or coexisting system failure modes;

- may be difficult to use to illustrate the effect of safeguards and to provide a basis for prioritizing safeguards.

## 9.5 Change Analysis

### 9.5.1 Introduction

*Change analysis* is used to determine the potential effects of some proposed modifications to a system or a process. The analysis is carried out by comparing the new (changed) system with a basic (known) system or process.

A change is often the source of deviation in the system operation and may lead to process disturbances and accidents. It is therefore important that the possible effects of changes be identified and that necessary precautions be taken. In the following, the term *key difference* is used to denote a difference between the new and the basic system that can lead to a hazardous event or can influence the risk related to the system. The *system* can be a sociotechnical system, a process, or a procedure.

### 9.5.2 Objectives and Applications

The main objectives of a change analysis are to:

(a) Identify the key differences between the new (changed) system and a basic (known) system.

(b) Determine the effects of each of these differences.

(c) Identify the main system vulnerabilities caused by each difference.

(d) Determine the risk impact of each difference.

(e) Identify which new safeguards and/or other precautions are necessary to control the risk impacts.

Study object: LNG transport with tank truck

Date: 2010-12-20

Reference:

Name: Marvin Rausand

| No. | Hazardous event (what, where, when) | Justification of frequency class | Freq. class | Justification of consequence class | Cons. class | RPN color code |
|---|---|---|---|---|---|---|
| 1 | Tank truck collides with another vehicle | The road has poor visibility and several crossing roads. The traffic is dense and the road is sometimes slippery. | 4 | The most common damage is limited to the body of the truck. The tank is assumed to be punctured in one out of 50 collisions (both the inner and the outer tank). In two out of five of these cases, the gas is assumed to be ignited. | 2 | 6 (yellow) |
| 2 | Leakage of gas through the safety valve | The safety valve is tested and maintained at regular intervals (every third month). The transport company has extensive experience data for this type of valves. | 3 | The most common damage is that gas leaks out without being ignited. The gas is assumed to be ignited in 1 out of 100 such cases. This is most relevant during filling and emptying when the gas concentration becomes highest because the truck is standing idle and the area is sheltered. | 2 | 5 (yellow) |

**Figure 9.6**   Sample HAZID worksheet.

Change analysis can be applied to all types of systems, ranging from simple to complex. This includes situations in which system configurations are altered, operating practices or policies are changed, new or different activities will be performed, and so on.

### 9.5.3 Analysis Procedure

A change analysis can be carried out in six steps. Steps 1 and 6 are described in Chapter 8 and are therefore not treated further here.

1. Plan and prepare.

2. Identify the key differences (between the new system and the basic system).

3. Evaluate the possible effects of the differences (positive and/or negative related to the risk).

4. Determine the risk impacts of the differences.

5. Examine important issues in more detail.

6. Report the analysis.

The analysis workflow is illustrated in Figure 9.7.

***Step 2: Identify the Key Differences.*** This step is based on a detailed description of both the basic (known) system and the new (changed) system. Differences between the two systems are identified by comparison and brainstorming. Various checklists may also be useful. At this point, all differences, regardless of how subtle, should be identified and listed.

***Step 3: Evaluate the Possible Effects of the Differences.*** In this step, the various differences identified in step 2 are evaluated, one by one. For each difference, the study team decides whether or not it can lead to harm to any assets. Both positive and negative effects on the risk impact should be recorded. The differences that can lead to, or influence harm, are listed as key differences, ordered into similar groups, and given unique reference numbers. This process often generates recommendations to design changes and better control in relation to the key differences.

***Step 4: Determine the Risk Impacts of the Differences.*** Here, the study team evaluates the risk impact of each key difference. A risk evaluation approach such as a risk matrix may be used to indicate how the differences affect the risk to the various assets. As part of this process, additional safeguards and possible changes to existing safeguards are proposed when required.

***Step 5: Examine Important Issues in More Detail.*** During the change analysis process, important issues may be revealed that will need further analysis. The study team describes these issues and gives recommendations for further analysis by other risk assessment tools. In some cases, such analyses may be carried out by the study team as part of the change analysis.

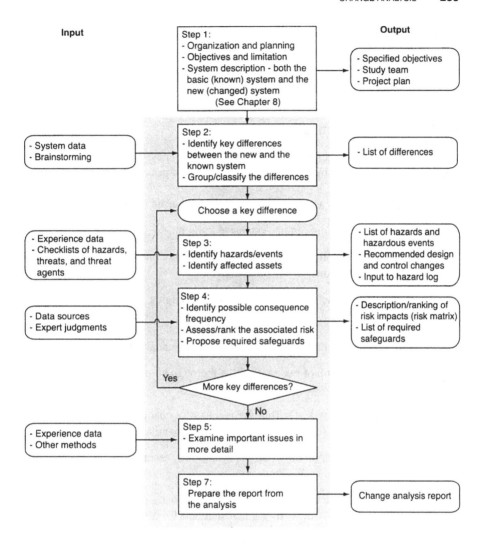

**Figure 9.7**    Analysis workflow for change analysis.

### 9.5.4    Resources and Skills Required

A change analysis may be carried out by two or more experienced engineers. The analysis requires a thorough knowledge of the system and the risk issues of the basic system. At least one of the study team members should have a background as a safety engineer.

### 9.5.5 Standards and Guidelines

No specific standards or guidelines have been developed. The method is described in some textbooks on safety engineering, but usually not in more detail than in this book.

### 9.5.6 Advantages and Limitations

Change analysis can be applied meaningfully only to a system for which baseline risk has been established by experience or as a result of prior risk analyses.

*Advantages.* The main advantages are that the change analysis:

- is efficient and does not require extensive training;

- systematically explores all the differences that may introduce significant risks or may have contributed to an actual incident;

- is effective for proactive risk assessment in changing situations and environments.

*Limitations.* The main limitations are that the change analysis:

- relies on a comparison of two systems. A thorough knowledge of the risk issues related to the basic system is therefore crucial;

- does not quantify risk levels (but the results of a change analysis can be used with other risk assessment methods to produce quantitative risk estimates);

- is strongly dependent on the expertise of the study team.

*Remark*: Other use of the term *change analysis*: The basic premise of change analysis is that if a system performs to a given standard for a period of time and then suddenly fails, the failure will be due to a change or changes in the system. By identifying these changes, it should then be possible to discover the factors that led to the failure arising. $\oplus$

## 9.6 FMECA

### 9.6.1 Introduction

*Failure modes and effects analysis* (FMEA) was one of the first systematic techniques for failure analysis of technical systems. The technique was developed by reliability analysts in the late 1940s to identify problems in military systems. The traditional FMEA is carried out for each component in a technical system to identify and describe the possible failure modes, failure causes, and failure effects. When we, in addition, describe or rank the severity of the various failure modes, the technique is called *failure modes, effects, and criticality analysis* (FMECA). The border-line between FMEA and FMECA is vague and thus there is no reason to distinguish between them. In the following, we use the term *FMECA*.

### 9.6.2 Objectives and Applications

The objectives of an FMECA are to:

(a) Identify how each of the system components can conceivably fail (i.e., what are the failure modes?)

(b) Determine the causes of these failure modes.

(c) Identify the effects that each failure mode can have on the rest of the system.

(d) Describe how the failure modes can be detected.

(e) Determine how often each failure mode will occur.

(f) Determine how serious the various failure modes are.

(g) Assess the risk related to each failure mode.

(h) Identify risk-reducing actions/measures that may be relevant.

FMECA is used mainly in the design phase of a technical system to identify and analyze potential failures. The analysis is qualitative, but may have some quantitative elements, including specifying the failure rate of the failure modes and a ranking of the severity of the failure effects.

FMECA can also be used in later phases of a system's life cycle. The objective is then to identify parts of the system that should be improved to meet certain requirements regarding safety or reliability, or as input to maintenance planning.

Many industries require that an FMECA be integrated in the design process of technical systems, and that FMECA worksheets be part of the system documentation. This is, for example, a common practice for suppliers to the defense, aerospace, and automobile industries. The same requirements are also becoming common in the offshore oil and gas industry.

### 9.6.3 Method Description

FMECA is a simple technique and does not build on any particular algorithm. The analysis is carried out by reviewing as many components, assemblies, and subsystems as possible to identify failure modes, causes, and effects of such failures. For each component, the failure modes and their resulting effects on the rest of the system are entered into a specific FMECA worksheet.

FMECA is mainly an effective technique for reliability engineering, but it is also often used in risk analyses. There are several types of FMECAs. In the context of risk analysis, the most relevant type is the *product* or *hardware FMECA*, which is also called a *bottom-up FMECA*, and this section is restricted to this type. Since FMECA was developed as a reliability technique, it will also cover failure modes that have little or no relevance for the system risk. When the objective of the FMECA is to provide input to a risk analysis, these failure modes may be skipped in the FMECA.

When performing an FMECA, it is important to keep the definition of a *failure mode* in mind. As explained in Chapter 3, a failure mode may be regarded as a deviation from the performance criteria for the component/item.

### 9.6.4  Analysis Procedure

The FMECA may be carried out in seven steps:

1. Plan and prepare.

2. Carry out system breakdown and functional analyses.

3. Identify failure modes and causes.

4. Determine the consequences of the failure modes.

5. Assess the risk.

6. Suggest improvements.

7. Report the analysis.

Steps 1 and 7 are described thoroughly in Chapter 8, so are not repeated here. A few comments on step 7 are given, however. The analysis workflow is illustrated in Figure 9.8.

A dedicated FMECA worksheet is used when performing the analysis. A typical FMECA worksheet is illustrated in Figure 9.10. Steps 3–6 are described by referring to the relevant columns in this worksheet.

***Step 2: Carry Out System Breakdown and Functional Analyses.***    The main tasks of this step are to:

(a) Define the main functions (missions) of the system and specify the function performance criteria.

(b) Describe the operational modes of the system.

(c) Break down the system into subsystems that can be handled effectively. This can be done: for example, by establishing a hierarchical structure, as illustrated in Figure 9.9.

(d) Review the system functional diagrams and drawings to determine interrelationships between the various subsystems. These interrelations may be illustrated

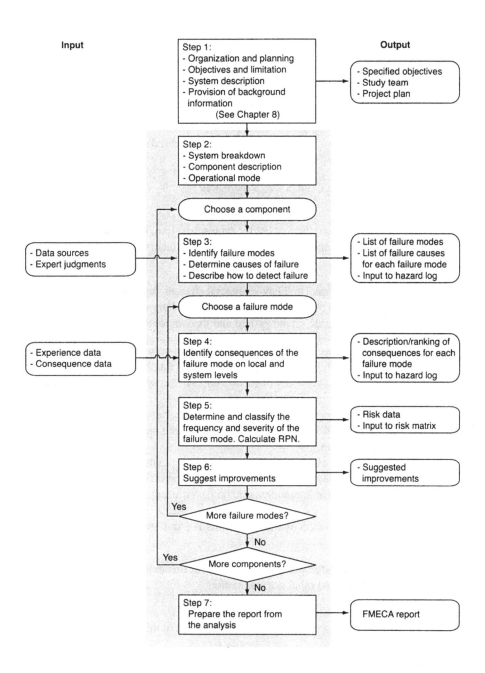

**Figure 9.8** Analysis workflow for FMECA.

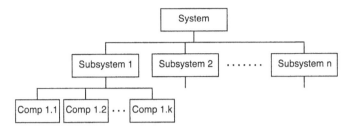

**Figure 9.9**    System described by a hierarchical structure.

by drawing functional block diagrams where each block corresponds to a subsystem.

(e) Prepare a complete component list for each subsystem. Each component should be given a unique identification number. These numbers are sometimes referred to as *tag numbers*.

(f) Describe the operational and environmental stresses that may affect the system and its operation. These should be reviewed to determine the adverse effects that they could generate on the system and its components.

Items at the lowest level of the hierarchical system are called *components* here. The structure in Figure 9.9 has only three levels. The number of levels that should be used depends on the complexity of the system. All subsystems do not have to be broken down to the same number of levels.

The functions and their performance requirements for each component should be discussed and understood by the study team. The same applies to all subsystems, sub-subsystems, and so on.

The FMECA is most often applied to the components on the lowest level in the system hierarchy, but may also be applied to other levels: for example, the sub-subsystem level. The term components is, however, used in the description of the worksheet.

The results of step 2 are entered into columns 1–3 in Figure 9.10.

*Reference (col. 1)*
   A unique reference to the component is given in this column. The reference can be to a drawing or some other documentation.

*Function (col. 2)*
   The function(s) of the component is (are) described in this column.

*Operational mode (col. 3)*
   The component may have various operational modes: for example, running or standby. Operational modes for an airplane may, for example, include taxi, take-off, climb, cruise, descent, approach, flare-out, and roll.

Study object:  Process-system east

Reference:  Process diagram 14.3-2010

Date:  2010-12-20

Name:  Marvin Rausand

| Description of unit | | | Description of failure | | | Effect of failure | | Risk | | | | Risk reducing measure | Respons-ible | Comment |
|---|---|---|---|---|---|---|---|---|---|---|---|---|---|---|
| Ref. no. | Function | Operational mode | Failure mode | Failure cause | Detection of failure | On the sub-system | On the sys-tem function | Freq-uency | Seve-rity | Detect-ability | RPN | | | |
| (1) | (2) | (3) | (4) | (5) | (6) | (7) | (8) | (9) | (10) | (11) | (12) | (13) | (14) | (15) |
| 4.1 | Close gas flow | Normal operation | Valve fails to close on demand | Spring broken / Hydrates in valve / Too high friction in actuator | Periodic function test | Shutdown function failed | Production must be stopped | 2 | 4 | 4 | 10 | Periodic control of spring / Periodic operation of valve | | |
| | | | Leakage through the valve | Erosion in valve seat / Sand between valve seat and gate | Periodic function test | Shutdown function degraded | System must be repaired within one month | 2 | 3 | 5 | 10 | Improved startup control to prevent sand production | | |
| 4.2 | Open gas flow | Closed | Valve cannot be opened on command | Leakage in hydraulic system / Too high friction in actuator | Immediately detected | Cannot start production | System cannot produce | | | | | | | |

**Figure 9.10**  Example of an FMECA worksheet.

***Step 3: Identify Failure Modes and Causes.*** For each component, the relevant failure modes and failure causes are identified. Experience data and generic failure mode checklists may provide useful help. The results of step 3 are entered into columns 4–6 in Figure 9.10.

*Failure mode (col. 4)*

For each function and operational mode, the related failure modes are identified and recorded, one by one. When identifying failure modes, it is important to relate these to the functions and the performance criteria for the component.

*Failure cause (col. 5)*

For each failure mode in column 4, the possible failure causes and failure mechanisms are recorded. Relevant failure causes are corrosion, erosion, fatigue, overstress, maintenance errors, operator errors, and so on.

*Detection of failure (col. 6)*

The possible ways of detecting the identified failure modes are then recorded. These may involve condition monitoring, diagnostic testing, functional testing, human perception, and so on. One failure mode is that of *evident failures*. Evident failures are detected instantly when they occur. The failure mode "spurious stop" of a pump with the operational mode "running" is an example of an evident failure. Another type of failure is the *hidden failure*. A hidden failure is normally detected only during testing of the component. The failure mode "fail to start" of a fire pump with the operational mode "standby" is an example of a hidden failure. When FMECA is used in the design phase, this column will record the designer's recommendations for condition monitoring, functional testing, and so on.

***Step 4: Determine the Consequences of the Failure Modes.*** For each failure mode, the credible consequences are entered into columns 7 and 8 in the FMECA worksheet in Figure 9.10.

*Local effects of failure (col. 7)*

Here, the consequences that the failure mode will have on the next higher level in the hierarchy are recorded.

*System effects of failure (col. 8)*

All the main effects of the failure mode on the primary function of the system are now recorded. The resulting operational status of the system after the failure may also be recorded, that is, whether the system is functioning, or has to be switched over to another operational mode.

***Step 5: Assess the Risk.*** In this step, the frequency and severity of the consequences of each failure mode are estimated and recorded in classes. In some cases it is also relevant to record the detectability of the failure mode. An RPN is sometimes also calculated. The results are entered into columns 9–12 in the FMECA worksheet in Figure 9.10.

*Failure rate (col. 9)*

Failure rates for each failure mode are then recorded. In many cases it is more suitable to classify the failure rate in rather broad classes (see Table 4.8). Note that the failure rate with respect to a failure mode might be different for the various operational modes. The failure mode "Leakage to the environment" for a valve may, for example, be more likely when the valve is closed and pressurized than when the valve is open.

*Severity (col. 10)*

The severity of a failure mode is usually interpreted as the worst *credible* consequence of the failure, determined by the degree of injury, environmental damage, or system damage that could ultimately occur (see Table 4.9).

*Detectability (col. 11)*

The consequences of a failure mode are sometimes dependent on how fast the failure mode can be detected. We classify the detectability in five groups, where group 1 means that the failure is detected immediately and group 5 means that the failure mode will normally not be detected. In the example in Figure 9.10, the failure mode "Valve fails to close on command" is assessed as group 4, since the failure mode cannot be revealed until a functional test is performed: for example once per six months.

*RPN (col. 12)*

The risk priority number (RPN) was defined in Chapter 4 and is here a combination of the three preceding columns. RPN of a failure mode is computed by summing the class numbers for frequency, severity, and detectability for that failure mode.

**Remark**: In the other methods described in this chapter, the RPN is computed by summing the frequency class and the severity class for the events. For FMECA, it may also be relevant to include a class number related to how easy it is to detect the failure. This is not always relevant, but in many cases it may be.

Some guidelines for FMECA recommend that each of the three categories (frequency, severity, and detectability) is divided into 10 classes and that the RPN is computed by *multiplying* the three class numbers. It is very difficult to see any good theoretical justification for this approach, especially when using a logarithmic scale for each class. We therefore disregard this approach.          ⊕

### Step 6: Suggest Improvements

*Risk-reducing measures (col. 13)*

Possible actions to correct the failure and restore the function or prevent serious consequences are then recorded. Actions that are likely to reduce the frequency of the failure modes should also be recorded.

*Responsible (col. 14)*

Here, the name of the person who should be responsible for the follow-up of the failure mode and/or the risk-reducing measures that have been identified is recorded.

*Comments (col. 15)*

This column may be used to record pertinent information not included in the other columns.

***Step 7: Report the Analysis.*** A wide range of results are likely to be produced as a result of the FMECA process, and it is important to summarize both the process and the results in an FMECA report. When analyzing a large or complex system, several FMECA processes may have been running at the same time. The FMECA report is a place to bring together the results of these analyses. The hazards identified by the FMECA process should be entered in the hazard log and be maintained as part of this log. As mentioned earlier in this section, there are several variants of the FMECA worksheet. The main columns are, however, covered in the worksheet in Figure 9.10. In the same way as for the PHA, the various failure modes may be entered into a risk matrix (see Section 4.4).

## 9.6.5 Resources and Skills Required

An FMECA can be carried out by a single person or by a study team, depending on the complexity of the system. FMECA does not require any deep analytical skills, but requires a thorough understanding of the study object, its application, and operational and environmental conditions.

Although the FMECA process itself is simple, it can be time-consuming and the quantity of data assessed and recorded can make it appear complicated. A structured and disciplined approach is essential if the full benefit of the FMECA is to be delivered.

Several computer programs have been developed for FMECA. A suitable program can significantly reduce the workload of an FMECA and make it easier to update the analysis.

***Remark***: An FMECA of a complex system may be a tedious and boring job—and is therefore sometimes left to junior personnel. Some companies have realized that this practice often results in mediocre quality of the FMECA and have therefore started using another approach that is similar to HAZOP (see Section 9.7). In this approach, a group of experts carry out the FMECA as a top-down analysis. When the significant failures have been identified and prioritized, junior personnel may fill in the necessary gaps. ⊕

***Standards and Guidelines.*** Several standards have been issued for FMECA. Among these are:

- IEC 60812: *Procedure for Failure Modes and Effects Analysis (FMEA)* (IEC 60812, 2006)

- SAE ARP 5580: *Recommended Failure Modes and Effects Analysis (FMEA) Practices for Non-automobile Applications* (SAE ARP 5580, 2001)

- SEMATECH: *Failure Modes and Effects Analysis (FMEA): A Guide for Continuous Improvement for the Semiconductor Equipment Industry* (SEMATECH, 1992)

### 9.6.6 Advantages and Limitations

*Advantages.* The main advantages are that FMECA:

- is widely used and easy to understood and interpret;

- provides a comprehensive hardware review;

- is suitable for complex systems;

- is flexible such that the level of detail can be adapted to the objectives of the analysis;

- is systematic and comprehensive, and should be able to identify all failure modes with an electrical or mechanical basis;

- is supported by efficient computer software tools.

*Limitations.* The main limitations of FMECA are that:

- its benefits depend on the experience of the analyst(s);

- it requires a hierarchical system drawing as the basis for the analysis, which the analysts usually have to develop before the analysis can start;

- it considers hazards arising from single-point failures and will normally fail to identify hazards caused by combinations of failures;

- it can be time-consuming and expensive.

Another drawback is that all component failures are examined and documented, including those that do not have any significant consequences. For large systems, especially systems with a high degree of redundancy, the amount of unnecessary documentation work is a major disadvantage.

## 9.7 HAZOP

### 9.7.1 Introduction

A *hazard and operability* (HAZOP) study is a systematic hazard identification process that is carried out by a group of experts (a HAZOP team) to explore how the system or a plant may deviate from the design intent and create hazards and operability problems. The analysis is done in a series of meetings as a guided brainstorming based on a set of *guidewords*. The HAZOP approach was developed by ICI Ltd. in 1963 for the chemical industry (Kletz, 1999).

### 9.7.2 Objectives and Applications

The objectives of a HAZOP study are to:

(a) Identify all deviations from the way the system is intended to function: their causes, and all the hazards and operability problems associated with these deviations.

(b) Decide whether actions are required to control the hazards and/or the operability problems, and if so, to identify the ways in which the problems can be solved.

(c) Identify cases where a decision cannot be made immediately, and to decide on what information or actions are required.

(d) Ensure that actions decided are followed up.

(e) Make operators aware of hazards and operability problems.

HAZOP studies have been used with great success in the chemical and petroleum industries, for reviewing the process design in order to obtain safer, more efficient, and more reliable plants. HAZOP has become a standard activity in the design of the process systems on offshore oil and gas platforms in the North Sea. Today, HAZOP is used for hazard identification in many different application areas.

The HAZOP approach was developed initially to be used during the design phase, but can also be applied to systems in operation. Several variants of the original HAZOP approach have been developed. Among the available approaches are:

*Process HAZOP*
This is the original HAZOP approach that was developed to assess process plants and systems. This approach is described in the rest of this section.

*Human HAZOP*
This is a "family" of more specialized HAZOPs focusing on human errors rather than on technical failures (see Chapter 13).

*Procedure HAZOP*
This HAZOP approach is used to review procedures or operational sequences

(sometimes denoted SAFOP—*safe operation study*). A procedure HAZOP may also be seen as an extension of a job safety analysis as described in Chapter 14.

*Software HAZOP*
This variant of HAZOP is used to identify possible errors in the development of software.

A *drillers' HAZOP* was developed by Comer et al. (1986) and is a method for performing HAZOP-like studies of oil and gas drilling systems and procedures. The drillers' HAZOP uses the same basic approach as the traditional process HAZOP, but with other guidewords. The driller's HAZOP is applied to sequences of operations or work tasks, and the same technique was later adapted to other offshore operations, such as diving operations, subsea tie-in operations, and well workovers.

### 9.7.3  Method Description

The HAZOP analysis is performed in a series of meetings that are arranged as brainstorming sessions supported by guidewords, process parameters, and various checklists.

The system or plant is divided into a number of *study nodes* that are examined one by one. For each study node, the *design intent* and the normal state are defined. Then *guidewords* and *process parameters* are used in brainstorming sessions to give rise to proposals for possible *deviations* in the system.

**Guidewords.**  The guidewords and process parameters are supposed to stimulate individual thought and induce group discussions. Some typical guidewords are listed in Table 9.3. Several slightly different lists of guidewords may be found in the literature. The guidewords and process parameters should be combined in such a way that they lead to meaningful process deviations. All the guidewords cannot be applied to all process parameters.

**Process Parameters.**  Typical process parameters for a chemical process are:

- Flow

- Pressure

- Temperature

- Level

- Composition

### EXAMPLE 9.2  HAZOP questions

During the sessions, the HAZOP leader (i.e., the chairperson of the HAZOP team) will usually stimulate the discussion by asking such questions as:

**Table 9.3**   Generic HAZOP guidewords.

| guideword | Deviation |
| --- | --- |
| NO/NONE | No part of the design intention is achieved (e.g., no flow, no pressure, when there should be). |
| MORE OF | An increase above the design intention is present, more of a physical property than there should be (e.g., higher flow, higher pressure, higher temperature). |
| LESS OF | A decrease below the design intention is present, less of a relevant physical property than there should be (e.g., lower flow, lower pressure, lower temperature). |
| AS WELL AS | The design intent is achieved, but something else is present. |
| PART OF | Only some of the design intention is achieved, wrong composition of process fluid. A component may be missing or of too low/ high ratio. |
| REVERSE | The design intention is the opposite of what happens. |
| OTHER THAN | The design intention is substituted by something different. |
| EARLY | Something happens earlier in time than expected. |
| LATE | Something happens later in time than expected. |
| BEFORE | Relating to the sequence of order, something happens before it is expected. |
| AFTER | Relating to a sequence of order, something happens after it is expected. |

1. Could there be "no flow"?

2. If so, how could it arise?

3. What are the consequences of "no flow"?

4. Are the consequences hazardous, or do they prevent efficient operation?

5. Can "no flow" be prevented by changing the design or operational procedures?

6. Can the consequences of "no flow" be prevented by changing the design or operational procedures?

7. Does the severity of the hazard or problem justify the extra expense?   ⊕

### 9.7.4 Analysis Procedure

The most common HAZOP study is carried out during the detailed engineering phase, and involves eight steps:

1. Plan and prepare.

2. Identify possible deviations.

3. Determine causes of deviations.

4. Determine consequences of deviation.

5. Identify existing barriers/safeguards.

6. Assess risk.

7. Propose improvements.

8. Report the analysis.

Steps 1 and 8 are described in Chapter 8, and only some elements of these steps are discussed here. The HAZOP workflow is illustrated in Figure 9.11.

A slightly different description of the HAZOP procedure is given by UK CAA (2006).

**HAZOP Worksheet.** The results from the HAZOP study are usually documented in a specific worksheet. An example of a HAZOP worksheet is shown in Figure 9.12. The columns in this worksheet are numbered from 1 to 13, and these are referred to when describing the HAZOP procedure. There is no standard worksheet, and several variants are used. Some worksheets do not include columns for risk ranking.

**Step 1: Plan and Prepare.** The main elements of this step are discussed in Chapter 8, but a few issues need some additional comments:

*1.1 Establish the HAZOP team* The composition and the knowledge of the HAZOP team are very important for the success of the analysis. The HAZOP team should be a multidisciplinary team of experts, typically 5–8 persons who have extensive knowledge of the design, operation, and maintenance of the plant, and thus should be able to evaluate all the likely effects of deviations from the design intent.

A HAZOP team assigned to consider a new chemical plant may, for example, comprise the following (e.g., see NSW, 2008a):

– *HAZOP leader.* The HAZOP leader must be familiar with the HAZOP technique. The HAZOP leader has the responsibility for ensuring that all the tasks involved in planning, running, recording, and implementing the study are carried out. Her

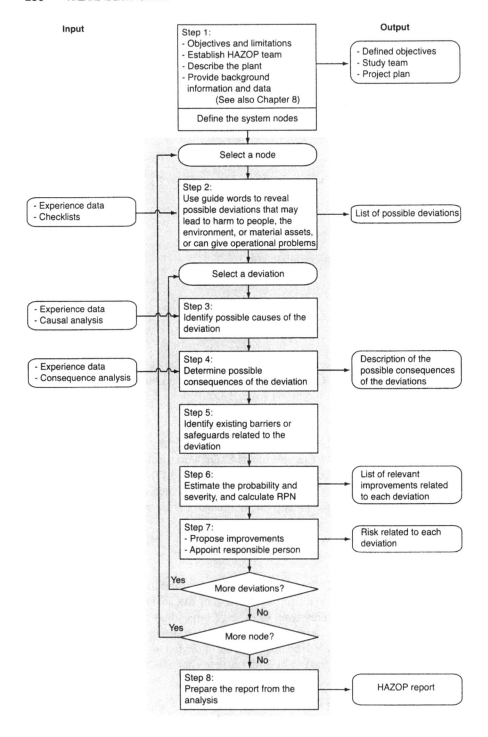

**Figure 9.11** Analysis workflow for HAZOP.

main task during the meetings is to ensure that the team works together to a common goal. The HAZOP leader should be independent of the project but be familiar with the design representations (e.g., P&IDs, block diagrams) and the technical and operational aspects of the system. It is essential that the HAZOP leader is experienced.

– *Design engineer.* A project design engineer who has been involved in the design and who is concerned with the project costs.

– *Process engineer.* This is usually a chemical engineer who is responsible for the process flow diagram and development of the P&IDs.

– *Electrical engineer.* This is usually an engineer who was responsible for the design of the electrical systems in the plant.

– *Instrument engineer.* The instrument engineer who designed and selected the control systems for the plant.

– *Operations manager.* This is preferably the person who will be in charge of the plant when it moves to the commissioning and operating stages.

– *HAZOP secretary.* The HAZOP secretary should take notes during meetings and assist the HAZOP leader with the administration of the HAZOP study.

At least one member of the HAZOP team must have sufficient authority to make decisions affecting the design or operation of the system.

*1.2 Provide required information*  Before the first HAZOP meeting, the required information should be provided [e.g., process flowsheets, piping and instrumentation diagrams (P&IDs), equipment, piping and instrumentation specifications, control system logic diagrams, layout drawings, operation and intervention procedures, emergency procedures, codes of practice]. For systems in operation, one has to check that the system is identical to the as-built drawings (which is not always the case).

*1.3 Divide the system into sections and study nodes*  The system and/or activity should be divided into major elements for analysis, and the design intent and normal operating conditions for the section should be established.

The analysis of a process system is normally based on process elements, such as vessels, pumps, compressors, and the like. Process streams leading into, or out of an element are analyzed one by one. These process streams are often called *study nodes*.

**Step 2: Identify Possible Deviations.**  The HAZOP team starts the examination of a study node by agreeing on the purpose and the normal state of the node. The HAZOP leader then suggests combinations of guidewords and process parameters to guide the team into identifying process deviations and the causes of the deviations.

The results of step 2 are entered into columns 1–4 in Figure 9.12.

*No. (col. 1)*

A unique reference to the deviation is given in this column. The default reference is a number.

*Study node (col. 2)*

The name (or identification) of the study node, possibly together with a process parameter, is entered into column 2. If necessary, the study node may be accompanied by a reference to a drawing (e.g., a P&ID).

*Guideword (col. 3)*

The guideword used is listed in column 3.

*Deviation (col. 4)*

The deviation generated by applying the guideword to the study node (and the process parameter) is described briefly in column 4. A more detailed description may be supplied in a separate file.

**Step 3: Identify Causes of Deviations.** To identify the possible causes of a deviation is an important part of the HAZOP study. The identified causes are entered into column 5.

*Possible causes (col. 5)*

For each deviation in column 4, the possible causes are recorded.

**Step 4: Determine Consequences of Deviation.** For each deviation, the *credible* consequences are entered into column 6 in the HAZOP worksheet in Figure 9.12.

*Possible consequences (col. 6)*

All the main consequences of the identified deviation are now recorded. Both safety-related consequences and possible operability problems are recorded.

**Step 5: Identify Existing Barriers (Safeguards).** To be able to come up with relevant proposals for improvement, the HAZOP team must be familiar with the existing barriers (safeguards) that have already been incorporated in the system.

*Existing barriers (col. 7)*

The existing barriers related to the deviation are recorded.

**Step 6: Assess Risk.** In this step, the risk related to each deviation is evaluated. The step is not part of all HAZOP studies.

*Frequency (col. 8)*

The frequency of occurrence of each deviation is briefly estimated as broad frequency classes (see Table 4.8).

*Severity (col. 9)*

The severity of a deviation is usually taken to be for the worst credible consequence of the deviation, determined by the degree of injury, environmental damage, material damage, or system/production disturbance that can ultimately occur (see Table 4.9).

*RPN (col. 10)*

The risk priority number (RPN) of a deviation is computed by summing the class numbers for the frequency and severity of the deviation.

*Risk matrix*   The frequency (col. 8) and the severity (col. 9) of each deviation can be entered into a risk matrix as outlined in Section 4.4 and hence can be used to compare the risk of a deviation with some acceptance criteria, if this is relevant. The risk matrix can also be used to evaluate recommendations for improvements (i.e., risk reduction).

**Step 7: Propose Improvements.**   Proposed improvements are recorded in column 11 of the HAZOP worksheet in Figure 9.12.

*Proposed improvements (col. 11)*

Possible actions to prevent the deviation or to mitigate the consequences are recorded.

*Responsible (col. 12)*

The name of the person who should be responsible for the follow-up of the deviation and/or the proposed improvement is recorded.

*Comments*   Possible comments related to the 12 first columns are entered into column 13.

**Step 8: Report the Analysis.**   The HAZOP study may be very time-consuming, and reporting is often done only by reporting potential problems, to avoid much repetition. This may, however, later cause people to wonder whether a deviation has been missed or has been dismissed as insignificant.

It is often recommended that a table summarizing the responses to the deviations be prepared, and highlight those deviations that are considered hazardous and credible. In addition, a comment should added on how to detect and/or prevent the deviation.

The remaining hazards should be entered into the *hazard log*, if such a log is maintained for the system in question.

🔲 **EXAMPLE 9.3   Filling a bucket**

Consider the "process" of filling a bucket with water through a bathroom sink faucet (tap). The water in the bucket should have a medium temperature (approx. 50 degrees Celsius). A simple HAZOP analysis of this process is (partly) documented in the HAZOP worksheet in Figure 9.12.                                  ⊕

## 9.7.5   Resources and Skills Required

A HAZOP study is carried out as a number of brainstorming sessions by a team of 5–8 experts working together under the guidance of a HAZOP leader with thorough

Study object: Filling a bucket with water
Reference:

Date: 2010-12-20
Name: Marvin Rausand

| No. | Study node | Guide word | Deviation | Possible causes | Possible consequences | Existing barriers | Risk Freq. | Risk Sev. | RPN | Proposed improvements | Responsible | Comments |
|-----|-----------|-----------|-----------|-----------------|----------------------|-------------------|-----------|-----------|-----|----------------------|-------------|----------|
| (1) | (2) | (3) | (4) | (5) | (6) | (7) | (8) | (9) | (10) | (11) | (12) | (13) |
| 1 | Faucet (flow) | No | No flow | Faucet is closed | No water in bucket | No | 1 | 2 | 2 | | | |
| 2 | | More | More flow | Faucet is opened too much or too fast | The bucket fills up too fast. Risk of splashing around the bucket | Visual inspection | 2 | 2 | 4 | More attention when filling the bucket | | |
| 3 | | Less | Less flow | Faucet is not sufficiently open | The bucket is filled too slowly | Visual inspection | 2 | 1 | 3 | | | |
| 4 | | Part of | Part of flow | Failure in faucet such that cold or hot water is prevented from flowing | Water in the bucket is either too cold or too hot | Periodic control maintenance | 3 | 2 | 5 | Check with finger (carefully) | | |
| 5 | | Other than | Other than flow | Air in water produces pressure shocks | Splashing around the bucket, slow filling | No | 1 | 3 | 4 | | | |
| 6 | Faucet (temperature) | More | High temperature | Faucet is adjusted to too high a temperature | Too hot water in the bucket; burning risk | No | 2 | 3 | 5 | Check with finger (carefully) | | |
| 7 | | Less | Low temperature | Faucet is adjusted to too low a temperature | Too cold water in the bucket | No | 2 | 1 | 3 | Check with finger (carefully) | | |

**Figure 9.12**  HAZOP worksheet for "filling a bucket with water".

experience in the HAZOP study technique. A HAZOP secretary is responsible for producing the record of the team's discussions and decisions.

Each meeting should not last more than approximately three hours, because most people's attention decreases after three hours at a stretch. To give the team members time to attend to their other duties, there should be no more than 2–3 meetings per week. Most HAZOP studies can be completed in 5–10 meetings, but for large projects, it may take several months even with 2–3 teams working in parallel on different sections of the plant (RSC, 2007).

Several computer programs have been developed to support the HAZOP study. Some expert systems for HAZOP have also been developed to support the HAZOP leader and the study process.

***Standards and Guidelines.***    Two recommended sources for further information about HAZOP are:

- IEC 61882: *Hazard and Operability Studies (HAZOP Studies): Application Guide* (?)

- Section 5.3 of the book *Guidelines for Hazard Evaluation Procedures* (CCPS, 2008)

### 9.7.6  Advantages and Limitations

***Advantages.***    The main advantages are that the HAZOP study:

- is widely used and its advantages and limitations are well understood;

- uses the experience of operating personnel as part of the team;

- is systematic and comprehensive, and should identify all hazardous process deviations;

- is effective for both technical faults and human errors;

- recognizes existing safeguards and develops recommendations for additional ones;

- is suitable for systems requiring interaction of several disciplines or organizations.

***Limitations.***    The main limitations are that a HAZOP study:

- is strongly dependent on the facilitation of the leader and the knowledge of the team;

- is optimized for process hazards, and needs modification to cover other types of hazards;

- requires development of procedural descriptions which are often not available in appropriate detail. However, the existence of these documents benefits the operation;

- produces a lengthy documentation (for complete recording).

HAZOP analyzes a system or process using a "section by section" approach. As such it may not identify hazards related to interactions between different nodes.

## 9.8  SWIFT

### 9.8.1  Introduction

A *structured what-if technique* (SWIFT) is a systematic brainstorming session where a group of experts with detailed knowledge about the study object raise *what-if* questions to identify possible hazardous events, their causes, consequences, and existing barriers, and then suggests alternatives for risk reduction. Estimation of the frequency and severity of the various hazardous events may, or may not, be part of the SWIFT analysis.

### 9.8.2  Objectives and Applications

The objectives of a SWIFT analysis are similar to the objectives of a HAZOP study, but usually with less focus on operability problems:

(a) To identify all hazardous events, with their causes and consequences.

(b) Evaluate whether or not the safeguards that have been introduced are adequate.

(c) To decide whether actions are required to control the hazardous events and, if necessary, to propose risk-reducing measures.

A SWIFT analysis is suitable for mainly the same applications as a HAZOP study. Whether a SWIFT analysis or a HAZOP study should be conducted is dependent primarily on how detailed the analysis must be. SWIFT may, like HAZOP, be applied to work procedures, and is then usually based on a task analysis (see Chapter 13).

A SWIFT analysis is most often carried out after a preliminary hazard analysis.

### 9.8.3  Method Description

What-if analyses have long been used in simple risk analyses (CCPS, 2008). The main difference between a SWIFT analysis and a traditional what-if analysis is that the questions in SWIFT are structured based on a checklist. The SWIFT approach was earlier called a "what-if/checklist" analysis (CCPS, 2008). The borderline between SWIFT and a traditional what-if analysis is, however, rather vague.

SWIFT has several similarities to a HAZOP study. The main differences are that SWIFT considers larger modules and that checklists and what-if questions are used instead of guidewords and process parameters. A SWIFT analysis is therefore not so detailed and thorough as a HAZOP study, and is easier and faster to conduct.

A study team meeting typically starts by discussing in detail the system, function, or operation under consideration. Drawings and technical descriptions are used, and the team members may need to clarify to each other how the details of the system functions and may fail.

The next phase of the meeting is a brainstorming session, where the team leader guides the discussion by asking questions starting with "What if?" The questions are based on checklists and covers such topics as operation errors, measurement errors, equipment malfunction, maintenance, utility failure, loss of containment, emergency operation, and external stresses. When the ideas are exhausted, previous accident experience may be used to check for completeness.

▇ **EXAMPLE 9.4    Examples of what-if? questions**

What-if ...

  – the wrong chemical is supplied?

  – the water pump fails?

  – the operator forgets to switch off the electric power?

  – the valve cannot be opened?

  – a fire occurs?

  – the operator is not present when a specified event occurs?               ⊕

It may also be relevant to use such questions as "How could ...?" and "Is it possible that ...?" In some cases, it may be appropriate to pose all the questions in a brainstorming manner before trying to answer them.

### 9.8.4   Analysis Procedure

A SWIFT analysis may be carried out in eight steps:

1. Plan and prepare.

2. Identify possible hazardous events.

3. Determine causes of hazardous event.

4. Determine the consequences of hazardous events.

5. Identify existing barriers.

6. Assess risk.

7. Propose improvements.

8. Report the analysis.

Steps 1 and 8 are described in Chapter 8 and are not discussed further here. The other steps are similar to the corresponding steps in a HAZOP study. The analysis process is illustrated in Figure9.13.

**SWIFT Worksheet.** The results from the SWIFT analysis are usually documented in a specific worksheet. An example of a SWIFT worksheet is shown in Figure 9.14. The columns in this worksheet are numbered from 1 to 11, and these are referred to when describing the SWIFT procedure. There is no standard worksheet, and several variants are used. Some worksheets do not include columns for risk ranking.

**Step 2: Identify Possible Hazardous Events.** These problems may have been revealed earlier by a PHA. Develop a response to the initial what-if questions. Generate additional questions and respond to these.

*No. (col. 1)*
A unique reference to the what-if question is given in this column. The default reference is a number.

*Study node (col. 2)*
The what-if question is entered into column 2.

**Step 3: Determine Causes of Hazardous Events.** The identified causes of the hazardous event (i.e., the answer to the what-if question in column 2) are entered into column 3.

*Possible causes (col. 3)*
For each what-if question in column 2, the possible causes are recorded.

**Step 4: Determine the Consequences of Hazardous Events.** For each what-if question, the *credible* consequences are entered into column 4 in the SWIFT worksheet in Figure 9.14.

*Possible consequences (col. 4)*
All the main consequences of the hazardous event resulting from the answer to the what-if question are now recorded.

**Step 5: Identify Existing Barriers.** To be able to come up with relevant proposals for improvement, the study team must be familiar with the existing barriers (safeguards) that have already been incorporated in the system.

*Existing barriers (col. 5)*
The existing barriers related to the hazardous event are recorded.

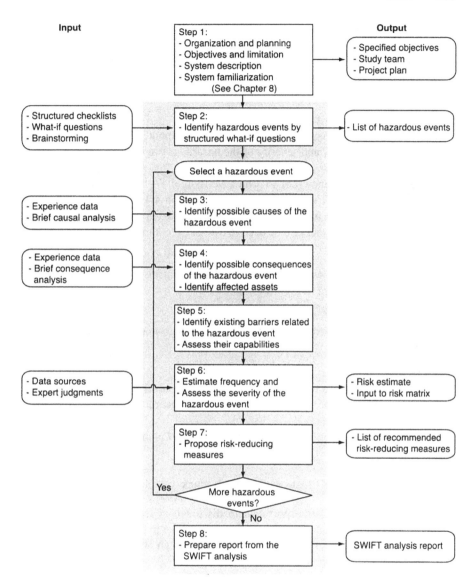

**Figure 9.13**    Analysis workflow for SWIFT.

***Step 6: Assess Risk.***    In this step, the risk related to each hazardous event is evaluated. The step is not part of all SWIFT analyses.

*Frequency (col. 6)*

The frequency of occurrence of each hazardous event is estimated briefly as broad frequency classes (see Table 4.8).

*Severity (col. 7)*

The severity of a hazardous event is usually taken to be for the worst credible consequence of the event, determined by the degree of injury, environmental damage, material damage, or system/production disturbance that can ultimately occur (see Table 4.9).

*RPN (col. 8)*

The risk priority number (RPN) of a deviation is computed by summing the class numbers for frequency and severity of the hazardous event.

*Risk matrix* The frequency (col. 6) and severity (col. 7) of each hazardous event can be entered into a risk matrix as outlined in Section 4.4 and hence can be used to compare the risk of a hazardous event with some acceptance criteria, if this is relevant. The risk matrix can also be used to evaluate recommendations for improvements (i.e., risk reduction).

**Step 7: Propose Improvements.** Proposed improvements are recorded in column 9 of the SWIFT worksheet in Figure 9.14.

*Proposed improvements (col. 9)*

Possible actions to prevent the hazardous event or to mitigate the consequences are recorded.

*Responsible (col. 10)*

The name of the person who should be responsible for the follow-up of the hazardous event and/or the proposed improvement is recorded.

*Comments* Possible comments related to the 10 first columns are entered into column 11.

■ **EXAMPLE 9.5** **LNG transport by tank truck**

Reconsider the LNG transport system discussed in Example 9.1. Some few what-if questions related to this system are analyzed in the SWIFT worksheet in Figure 9.14. The result are not based on a thorough analysis and are included only as an illustration. ⊕

### 9.8.5 Resources and Skills Required

The what-if analysis relies on a team of experts brainstorming to generate a comprehensive review. The relevance and completeness of the analysis are therefore dependent on the competence and experience of the team members. At least one of the team members should be familiar with the analysis process and should be able to come up with a list of initial what-if questions. The number of team members required will depend on the complexity of the system or process. For rather simple systems/processes, 3–5 team members will be sufficient.

Study object:    LNG transport system

Date: 2010-12-20

Reference:

Name: Marvin Rausand

| No. | What if? | Possible causes | Possible consequences | Existing barriers | Risk | | | Proposed improvements | Respon-sible | Comment |
|-----|----------|-----------------|----------------------|-------------------|------|------|------|----------------------|-------------|---------|
| | | | | | Freq. | Sev. | RPN | | | |
| (1) | (2) | (3) | (4) | (5) | (6) | (7) | (8) | (9) | (10) | (11) |
| 1 | The driver leaves without disconnect-ing the flexible hose? | - Time pressure<br>- Driver distraction | - The hose breaks<br>- Gas is released<br>- Fire/explosion likely | Procedure | 3 | 3 | 6 | Install barrier in front of truck that can be opened only when the flexible pipe is disconnected | | |
| 2 | The quick-release coupling of the hose is released during filling? | - Not properly connected<br>- Technical failure in coupling | - Driver is hit<br>- Gas is released<br>- Fire/explosion likely | Preventive maintenance of coupling | 3 | 2 | 5 | - New/better coupling<br>- Improved maintenance<br>- Improved driver training | | |
| 3 | The tank truck runs off the road on "Main Street" | - Slippery (icy) road<br>- Heavy traffic<br>- Many children are crossing the road<br>- Technical failure<br>- Interaction with other vehicle | - Puncture of tank (inner/outer)<br>- Fire/explosion likely<br>- High number of victims | - Driver training<br>- Traffic control | 2 | 4 | 6 | - Improved driver training<br>- Alternative route | | |

**Figure 9.14**    Example of a SWIFT worksheet for Example 9.5.

***Standards and Guidelines*** SWIFT and what-if analysis are described in several guidelines, textbooks, and research reports. The most authoritative source may be:

– *Guideline for Hazard Evaluation Procedures* (CCPS, 2008)

### 9.8.6 Advantages and Limitations

The what-if analysis is suitable primarily for relatively simple systems. The analysis will usually not reveal problems with multiple failures or synergistic effects. The what-if analysis is applicable to almost any type of applications especially those dominated by relatively simple failure scenarios.

***Advantages.*** The main advantages of using SWIFT are that it (HSE, 2001a):

– is very flexible, and applicable to any type of installation, operation, or process, at any stage of the life cycle;

– creates a detailed and auditable record of the hazard identification process;

– uses experience of operating personnel as part of the team;

– is quick, because it avoids repetitive considerations of deviations;

– is less time-consuming than other systematic techniques, such as HAZOP.

***Limitations.*** The main limitations of SWIFT are that it:

– is not inherently thorough and foolproof;

– works at the system level, such that lower-level hazards may be omitted;

– is difficult to audit;

– is highly dependent on checklists prepared in advance;

– is heavily dependent on the experience of the leader and the knowledge of the team.

## 9.9 Master Logic Diagram

A *master logic diagram* (MLD) is a graphical technique that can be used to identify hazards and hazard pathways that can lead to a specified TOP event (i.e., an accident) in the system. The hazards and pathways are traced down to a level of detail at which all important safety functions and barriers are taken into account. When this is accomplished, the causal events that can threaten a safety barrier or function can be listed. An MLD resembles a fault tree (see Section 10.3), but differs in that the initiators defined in the MLD are not necessarily failures or basic events.

MLDs are not pursued further in this book. Interested readers may consult Modarres (2006) and Papazoglou and Aneziris (2003). A case study illustrating how MLD can be used to identify failure modes of an intelligent detector is presented by Brissaud et al. (2011).

## 9.10 Additional Reading

The following titles are recommended for further study related to Chapter 9.

- *Guidelines for Hazard Evaluation Procedures* (CCPS, 2008) is an excellent source for more information about hazard identification methods.

- *Hazard Analysis Techniques for System Safety* (Ericson, 2005) presents many of the same methods as presented in this chapter.

- *Guidance on the conduct of hazard identification, risk assessment and the production of safety cases* (UK CAA, 2006) by the UK Civil Aviation Authority is a well-written and clear guide to hazard identification and risk assessment for aviation applications, but may also be a valuable source in other application areas.

- *Basic Guide to System Safety* (Vincoli, 2006) introduces several hazard identification approaches and provides examples.

- *Procedure for Failure Modes and Effects Analysis (FMEA)* (IEC 60812, 2006) is the main international standard for FMECA.

- *Hazop and Hazan* (Kletz, 1999) gives a thorough introduction to HAZOP.

- *HAZOP guidelines: Hazardous Industry Planning Advisory Paper No. 8* (NSW, 2008a) gives a thorough introduction to the HAZOP process. A worked example of a HAZOP study is included as Appendix 2.

- *Hazard and operability studies (HAZOP)* (RSC, 2007), published by the UK Royal Society of Chemistry, gives a brief but very clear introduction to the HAZOP process.

# CHAPTER 10

# CAUSAL AND FREQUENCY ANALYSIS

## 10.1 Introduction

This chapter deals with the second question in the triplet definition of risk: How often will the hazardous event occur? To answer this question, it is often necessary to identify and analyze the possible causes of the hazardous event. The potential hazardous event must be identified and defined prior to the causal analysis, for example, by using the hazard identification methods described in Chapter 9.

### 10.1.1 Objectives of the Causal and Frequency Analysis

The objectives of the causal and frequency analysis are to:

(a) Determine the causes of the defined hazardous event. How far the causal sequences should be pursued depends on the objective of the analysis and the data available.

(b) Establish the relationship between the hazardous event and the basic causes.

(c) Determine the frequency of the hazardous event based on a careful examination of the basic causes and the causal sequences.

*Risk Assessment: Theory, Methods, and Applications,* First Edition.
By Marvin Rausand. Copyright © 2011 John Wiley & Sons, Inc.

(d) Determine how important each cause is in relation to the frequency of the hazardous event.

(e) Identify existing and potential proactive barriers and evaluate the effectiveness of each barrier and the barriers in combination.

### 10.1.2   Methods for Causal and Frequency Analysis

Five different methods of causal and frequency analysis are described in this chapter:

*Cause and effect diagrams*
Cause and effect diagrams have their origin in quality engineering, and can be used to identify causes of a hazardous event. The method is easy to use and does not require extensive training. It can be used only for causal analysis and does not provide quantitative answers.

*Fault tree analysis*
Fault tree analysis is the most commonly used method for causal analysis of hazardous events. The method is well documented and has been used in a wide range of application areas. Fault tree analysis is suitable for both qualitative and quantitative analysis of complex systems, but is not well suited to handle dynamic systems and systems with complex maintenance. The method is also sometimes too rigid in its requirements regarding binary states and Boolean logic.

*Bayesian networks*
Bayesian networks are getting increasing popular and are in many cases a good alternative to fault tree analysis. A Bayesian network can totally replace any fault tree and is much more flexible. A main drawback of Bayesian networks is related to its complex and time-consuming quantification.

*Markov methods*
Markov methods are used mainly to analyze small but complex systems with dynamic effects. As such, Markov methods can be combined with, and compensate for some of the weaknesses of fault tree analysis. Markov methods are well documented and can give analysts deep insight into system properties and operation. Markov methods are not suitable for the identification of causes of the hazardous event.

*Petri nets*
Petri nets can replace Markov methods and can also be used for quantitative analysis of any fault tree. Petri nets are very flexible and can be used to model any type of system. As for Markov methods, Petri nets are not suitable for identifying the causes of a hazardous event.

For causal analysis, one of the first three methods should be selected. In most cases, the most suitable methods will be either a fault tree analysis or an analysis based on Bayesian networks. Which of these to choose depends on the knowledge and experience of the study team and on the availability of efficient computer programs.

To model the causal sequences and to determine the frequency of the hazardous event, all of the last four methods can be used. Which of these to choose, depends on the system and the complexity of the causal sequences. In most cases, it is sufficient to use fault tree analysis or Bayesian networks, but if the system is complex with dynamic features, Markov methods or Petri nets may be a better choice. If the study team is familiar with Petri nets, this will often be the best choice.

The three latter methods are general methods that can used for many different purposes, and it is outside the scope of this book to present all the features of the methods. A brief introduction to each method is given and its application in the causal analysis of risk analysis is highlighted. Readers who are interested in a more thorough treatment are advised to consult the sources listed as additional reading at the end of the chapter.

The causal analysis can be applied to any event in the system. To indicate this flexibility, we use the term *critical event* instead of *hazardous event* in the rest of this chapter.

## 10.2 Cause and Effect Diagram Analysis

### 10.2.1 Introduction

Analysis using a *cause and effect diagram* (also called an Ishikawa diagram[1] or fishbone diagram) may be used to identify, sort, and describe the causes of a specified event.

### 10.2.2 Objectives and Applications

The main objectives of a cause and effect diagram analysis are:

(a) To identify the causes of a defined critical event in a system.

(b) To classify the causes into groups.

(c) To acquire and structure the relevant knowledge and experience of the study team.

The cause and effect diagram analysis is done by a study team as a brainstorming session. Cause and effect diagrams are commonly used in product design, but can also be used for simple causal analyses of critical events as part of a risk analysis of rather simple systems. For complex systems, fault tree analysis would be a better method. A cause and effect diagram has some similarities with a fault tree, but is purely qualitative, less structured, and cannot be used as a basis for quantitative analysis.

---

[1] Named after Japanese professor Kaoro Ishikawa (1915–1989), who developed the diagrams.

### 10.2.3  Method Description

A cause and effect diagram analysis is not based on any extensive theoretical basis, and is merely a graphical representation and structuring of the knowledge and ideas generated by the study team during brainstorming sessions. Causes are arranged according to their level of importance or detail, resulting in a tree structure that resembles the skeleton of a fish with the main causal categories drawn as bones attached to the spine of the fish. The diagram is therefore also called a fishbone diagram.

### 10.2.4  Analysis Procedure

A cause and effect diagram analysis is normally carried out in four steps:

1. Plan and prepare.

2. Construct the cause and effect diagram.

3. Analyze the diagram qualitatively.

4. Report the analysis.

Steps 1 and 4 are discussed in Chapter 8 and not treated further here.

***Step 2:  Construct the Cause and Effect Diagram.***    To construct a cause and effect diagram, the study team starts with a specified critical event. The critical event is briefly described in a box at the right end of the diagram, which constitutes the "head of the fish." The central spine from the left is drawn as a thick line pointing to this box, and the major categories of potential causes (see Table 10.2) are drawn as bones to the spine, as illustrated in Figure 10.1. When analyzing technical systems, the following six (6M) categories are frequently used:

1. Man (i.e., people)

2. Methods (e.g., work procedures, rules, regulations)

3. Materials (e.g., raw materials, parts)

4. Machinery (e.g., technical equipment, computers)

5. Milieu (e.g., internal/external environment, location, time, safety culture)

6. Maintenance

The categories should, however, be selected to fit the actual application. It is usually recommended not to use more than seven major categories.

Brainstorming is used to identify the factors (or issues) that may affect the critical event within each M-category. The team may, for example, ask: "What are the machine issues affecting/causing...?" This is repeated for each M-category and factors/issues are identified and entered into the diagram as arrows pointing to the relevant M-category.

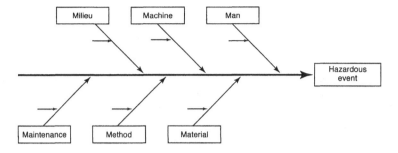

**Figure 10.1**   The main elements of a cause and effect diagram.

**Table 10.1**   Some basic causes of failure.

| Man | Machinery |
|---|---|
| – Operator error | – Poor design |
| – Lack of knowledge | – Poor equipment or tool placement |
| – Lack of skill | – Defective equipment or tool |
| – Stress | – Incorrect tool selection |
| – Inadequate capability | *Milieu (i.e., environment)* |
| – Improper motivation | – Untidy workplace |
| *Methods* | – Inadequate job design or layout of work |
| – Lack of procedures | – Surfaces poorly maintained |
| – Inadequate procedures | – Too high physical demands of the task |
| – Practices are not the same as written procedures | – Forces of nature |
| – Poor communication | *Maintenance* |
| *Materials* | – Poor maintenance program |
| – Lack of raw material | – Poor maintainability |
| – Low-quality material | – Poor maintenance performance |
| – Wrong type for job | – Lack of maintenance procedure |

Each factor is then analyzed in the same way to produce subfactors that are represented as arrows pointing to the relevant factor. Asking why this is happening for each factor/issue carries the analysis forward. Additional levels may be included under each subfactor, if required. The analysis is continued until we no longer get useful information from asking: "Why can this happen?" The main elements of a cause and effect diagram are shown in Figure 10.1.

A main value of cause and effect diagram analysis lies in the very process of producing the diagrams. This process often leads to ideas and insights that you might not otherwise have come up with.

*Step 3: Analyze the Diagram Qualitatively.*   When the team members agree that an adequate amount of detail has been provided under each major category, the diagram is analyzed by grouping the causes. One should look especially for causes that appear in more than one category. For those items identified as the "most likely causes," the team should reach consensus on listing those causes in priority order from the "most likely cause."

### 10.2.5   Resources and Skills Required

Performing a cause and effect diagram analysis does not require any specific training. The team members should therefore be able to carry out the analysis after a brief introduction. The number of team members will vary according to the complexity of the system and the criticality of the critical event.

The analysis can be carried out by pen and paper, or with a white-board and Post-It markers. Many of the computerized drawing programs have templates and other aids for drawing cause and effect diagrams that can be useful.

Cause and effect diagrams are described and discussed in textbooks on quality engineering and management, see; for example, Ishikawa (1986) and Bergman and Klefsjö (1994).

### 10.2.6   Standards and Guidelines.

No international standard for cause and effect diagrams has been published, but detailed guidelines may be found in several textbooks on quality engineering.

### 10.2.7   Advantages and Limitations

*Advantages.*   The main advantages are that the cause and effect diagram technique:

- is easy to learn and does not require any extensive training;

- helps determine causes of deviations;

- encourages group participation;

- increases process knowledge;

- helps organize and relate causal factors;

- provides a structure for brainstorming;

- involves all participants.

***Limitations.*** The main limitations are that the cause and effect diagram technique:

- may become very complex;

- requires patience from the participants;

- does not rank the causes in an "if-then" manner;

- cannot be used for quantitative analysis.

## 10.3   Fault Tree Analysis

### 10.3.1   Introduction

A fault tree is a top-down logic diagram that displays the interrelationships between a potential critical event in a system and the causes of this event. The causes at the lowest level are called *basic events* and may be component failures, environmental conditions, human errors, and normal events (i.e., events that are expected to occur during the life span of the system).

Fault tree analysis was introduced in 1962 at Bell Telephone Laboratories, in connection with a safety evaluation of the Minuteman intercontinental ballistic missile launch control system.

### 10.3.2   Objectives and Applications

A fault tree analysis may be qualitative, quantitative, or both, depending on the scope of the analysis. The main objectives of a fault tree analysis are:

(a) To identify all possible combinations of basic events that may result in a critical event in the system.

(b) To find the probability that the critical event will occur during a specified time interval or at a specified time $t$, or the frequency of the critical event.

(c) To identify aspects (e.g., components, barriers, structure) of the system that need to be improved to reduce the probability of the critical event.

Fault tree analysis, one of the most commonly used methods for risk and reliability studies, is especially suitable for analyzing large and complex systems with an ample degree of redundancy. In particular, fault tree analysis has been used successfully in risk analyses within the nuclear (e.g., see NUREG-75/014, 1975), chemical (e.g., see CCPS, 2000), and aerospace industries (e.g., Stamatelatos et al., 2002b). Fault tree analysis has traditionally been applied to mechanical and electromechanical systems, but there is no fundamental reason why the methodology cannot be applied to any type of system.

### 10.3.3 Method Description

*Fault Tree Diagram.* Fault tree analysis is a deductive method, which means that we reason backward in the causal sequence of a specific event. We start with a specified potential critical event in the system, called the TOP *event* of the fault tree. The immediate causal events $E_1, E_2, \ldots$ that, either alone or in combination, will lead to the TOP event are identified and connected to the TOP event through a *logic gate* (see Table 10.2). Next, all the potential causal events $E_{i,1}, E_{i,2}, \ldots$ that may lead to event $E_i$ for $i = 1, 2, \ldots$ are identified and connected to event $E_i$ through a *logic gate*. The procedure is continued deductively until a suitable level of detail is reached. The events at this level make the *basic events* of the fault tree.[2]

Table 10.2 shows the most commonly used fault tree symbols together with a brief description of their interpretation. A number of more advanced fault tree symbols are available but are not covered in this book. A thorough description may be found, for example, in Stamatelatos et al. (2002b).

Fault tree analysis is a *binary* analysis. All events, from the TOP event down to the basic events, are assumed to be binary events that either occur or do not occur. No intermediate states (e.g., the state is 80% good) are therefore allowed in the fault tree.

The fault tree diagram is a *deterministic* model. This means that when the fault tree is constructed and we know the states of all the basic events, the TOP event and the states of all intermediate events are known.

A fault tree is *single event*-oriented, and a separate fault tree must therefore be constructed for each potential TOP event in the system.

**▣ EXAMPLE 10.1   Offshore oil and gas separator**

Consider the oil and gas separator in Figure 10.2. A mixture of high-pressure oil, gas, and water is fed into a separator vessel.

If a blockage occurs in the gas outlet, the pressure in the separator will increase rapidly. To prevent overpressure, two high-pressure switches, $PS_1$ and $PS_2$, are installed in the vessel. Upon high pressure, the pressure switches should send signals to a programmable logic controller, PLC. If a signal from at least one pressure switch is received by the PLC, a closure signal will be sent to the process shutdown valves, $PSD_1$ and $PSD_2$. The shutdown function will fail if both pressure switches fail to send a signal, *or* the PLC fails to handle the signals and send a closure signal to the valves, *or* valves $PSD_1$ and $PSD_2$ both fail to close on demand. The causes of the TOP event "flow into separator fails to be shut down when high pressure occurs" are illustrated in the fault tree in Figure 10.3.

The lowest level in the fault tree in Figure 10.3 is a component failure. In some cases, it may also be relevant to identify the potential causes of a component failure: for example, potential primary failures, secondary failures,

---

[2]The basic events are also called *root nodes* of the tree.

**Table 10.2**   Fault tree symbols.

| | Symbol | Description |
|---|---|---|
| Logic gates | OR-gate | The OR-gate indicates that the output event $A$ occurs if any of the input events $E_i$ occur |
| | AND-gate | The AND-gate indicates that the output event $A$ occurs only when all the input events $E_i$ occur at the same time |
| Input events | Basic event | The basic event represents a basic equipment failure that requires no further development of failure causes |
| | Undeveloped event | The undeveloped event represents an event that is not examined further because information is unavailable or because its consequence is insignificant |
| Description | Comment rectangle | The comment rectangle is for supplementary information |
| Transfer symbols | Transfer-out | The transfer-out symbol indicates that the fault tree is developed further at the occurrence of the corresponding transfer-in symbol |
| | Transfer-in | |

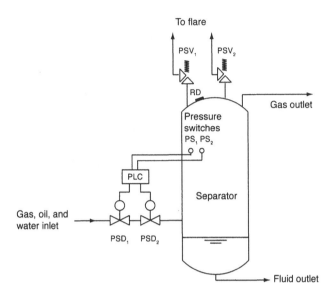

**Figure 10.2**   Oil and gas separator in Example 10.1.

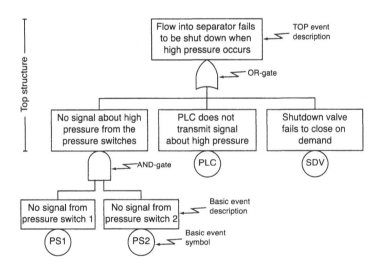

**Figure 10.3**   Fault tree for the shutdown system in Example 10.1.

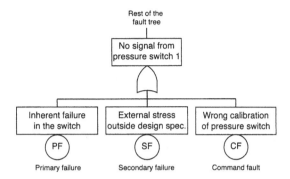

**Figure 10.4**   Primary failure, secondary failure, and command fault for a pressure switch in Example 10.1.

and command faults, as illustrated for a pressure switch failure in Figure 10.4. This level may be pursued further, for example, by identifying potential causes for "wrong calibration of pressure switch." The level at which the analysis is stopped is determined by the objectives of the fault tree analysis.          ⊕

*Common-Cause Failures*   A common-cause failure is a failure of two or more items due to a single specific event or cause and within a specified time interval. In some cases it is possible to identify this common cause explicitly and include it in the fault tree. This is illustrated in the fault tree diagram in Figure 10.5. A parallel system of two pressure switches can fail in two different ways, either as simultaneous individual failures or due to a common cause—in this case that the common tap to the pressure switches is blocked by solids. Common-cause failures and modeling of such failures are treated in detail in Chapter 15.

***Reliability Block Diagrams.***   A fault tree diagram (with only AND- and OR-gates) can always be converted to a reliability block diagram, and vice versa. This is illustrated in Figure 10.6. A reliability block diagram shows the logical connections of functioning items that are needed to fulfill a specified system function. Each function is represented as a functional block and is drawn as a square (see Figure 10.6). If we can proceed through a functional block from one endpoint to the other, we say that the item is functioning. A brief introduction to reliability block diagrams is given in Appendix A. For a more thorough treatment, see, for example, Rausand and Høyland (2004).

The reliability block diagram in Figure 10.6(i) represents a series structure that will fail if item 1 fails, *or* item 2 fails, *or* item 3 fails. A series structure always corresponds to an OR-gate in the fault tree when the basic events represent item failure.

The reliability block diagram in Figure 10.6(ii) is a parallel structure that will fail only when item 1 fails, *and* item 2 *and* item 3 fails. It is therefore clear that the parallel structure corresponds to an AND-gate.

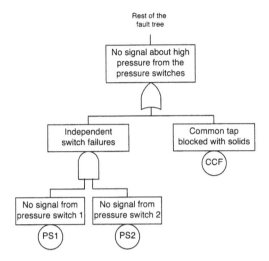

**Figure 10.5**   Explicit modeling of a common-cause failure in a system of two pressure switches.

Note that to save space, we have omitted the rectangles describing the basic events in the fault trees in Figure 10.6. In practical applications, we should always give proper descriptions of the events in the fault tree.

*Minimal Cut Sets.*   A fault tree provides valuable information about possible combinations of basic events that can result in the TOP event. Such a combination of basic events is called a *cut set*, and is defined as:

☞ **Cut set**: A cut set in a fault tree is a set of basic events whose (simultaneous) occurrence ensures that the TOP event occurs.

The most interesting cut sets are those that are *minimal*:

☞ **Minimal cut set**: A cut set is said to be minimal if the set cannot be reduced without losing its status as a cut set.

Let $C_1, C_2, \ldots, C_k$ denote the $k$ minimal cut sets of a fault tree. The number of distinct basic events in a minimal cut set is called the *order* of the cut set. A minimal cut set is said to *fail* when all the basic events of this cut set are occurring at the same time.[3] A minimal cut set can therefore be represented as a fault tree with a single AND-gate, as illustrated in Figure 10.6(ii). In a reliability block diagram, a minimal cut set can be represented as a single parallel structure with $r$ items, where $r$ is the

---

[3] The term *occurring* here may be somewhat misleading. The term does not imply that a basic event occurs exactly at time $t$; it means that the state of the basic event is present at time $t$ (e.g., a component is in a failed state at time $t$).

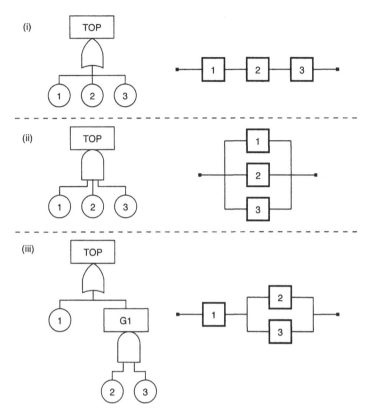

**Figure 10.6**  Relationship between some simple fault tree diagrams and reliability block diagrams.

order of the minimal cut set. All the $r$ items in this parallel structure have to fail for the minimal cut set to fail.

Let $C_j(t)$ be the event where minimal cut set $C_j$ is failed at time $t$, for $j = 1, 2, \ldots, k$. The TOP event occurs at time $t$ when at least one of the minimal cut sets fails at $t$, and can therefore be expressed as

$$\text{TOP}(t) = C_1(t) \cup C_2(t) \cup \cdots \cup C_k(t) \tag{10.1}$$

The fault tree can therefore be represented by an alternative top structure, the minimal cut set fault trees connected through a single OR-gate, as illustrated in Figure 10.7.

To save space, the rectangles describing the basic events are omitted in Figure 10.7. Each minimal cut set is drawn here with three basic events. The basic events in minimal cut set $j$ are illustrated by the symbols $j.1$, $j.2$, and $j.3$, for $j = 1, 2, \ldots, k$. In a real fault tree, the minimal cuts sets will be of different orders and the same basic event may be a member of several minimal cut sets.

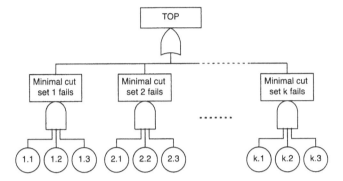

**Figure 10.7**    The TOP event will occur if at least one of the $k$ minimal cut sets fails.

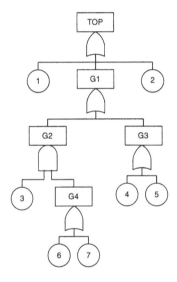

**Figure 10.8**    Example of a fault tree.

For small and simple fault trees, it is feasible to identify the minimal sets by inspection without a formal procedure/algorithm. For large or complex fault trees, an efficient algorithm is needed.

***Identification of Minimal Cut Sets by MOCUS.***    MOCUS (method for obtaining cut sets) is a simple algorithm that can be used to find the minimal cut sets in a fault tree. The algorithm is best explained by an example. Consider the fault tree in Figure 10.8, where the gates are called TOP and G1 to G4. The algorithm starts at the TOP event. If this is an OR-gate, each input to the gate is written in separate rows. Similarly, if the TOP gate is an AND-gate, the inputs to the gate are written in separate columns. In our example the TOP gate is an OR-gate, and we start with

1

G1

2

Since each of the three inputs, 1, G1, and 2, will cause the TOP event to occur, each of them will constitute a cut set.

The idea is to successively replace each gate with its inputs (basic events and new gates) until one has gone through the entire fault tree and is left with only the basic events. When this procedure is completed, the rows in the established matrix represent the cut sets of the fault tree.

Since G1 is an OR-gate:

1

G2

G3

2

Since G2 is an AND-gate:

1

3, G4

G3

2

Since G3 is an OR-gate:

1

3, G4

4

5

2

Since G4 is an OR-gate:

1

3, 6

3, 7

4

5

2

We are then left with the following six cut sets:

$$\{1\}, \{2\}, \{4\}, \{5\}, \{3,6\}, \{3,7\}$$

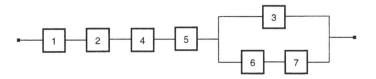

**Figure 10.9**    Reliability block diagram corresponding to the fault tree in Figure 10.8.

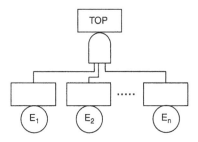

**Figure 10.10**    Fault tree with a single AND-gate.

Note that an OR-gate increases the number of minimal cut sets in the system, while an AND-gate increases the order of the cut sets (i.e., increases the number of basic events in the cut sets).

If the same basic event is represented in two or more places in the fault tree, MOCUS will generally not provide the *minimal* cut sets. It is therefore necessary to check that the cut sets identified are indeed minimal. Such a routine is included when MOCUS is implemented into computer programs for fault tree analysis. In the example above, all the basic events are unique, and the algorithm provides the minimal cut sets.

In Figure 10.9 the fault tree in Figure 10.8 is converted to a reliability block diagram, from which the minimal cut sets can easily be seen. This approach is, however, not feasible for large fault trees and we therefore need an efficient algorithm.

It should be noted that several more efficient algorithms for identification of minimal cut sets have been developed and implemented into computer programs for fault tree analysis.

***Fault Tree with a Single AND-gate.***    Consider a fault tree with a single AND-gate, as illustrated in Figure 10.10.

Let $E_i(t)$ denote that the event $E_i$ is occurring at time $t$, for $i = 1, 2, \ldots, n$. Since the TOP event will occur if and only if all the basic events occur, the Boolean representation of the fault tree is

$$\text{TOP}(t) = E_1(t) \cap E_2(t) \cap \cdots \cap E_n(t) \tag{10.2}$$

The probability that the event is occurring at time $t$ is denoted

$$q_i(t) = \Pr(E_i(t))$$

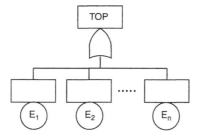

**Figure 10.11**    Fault tree with single OR-gate.

If event $E_i$ is a component failure, then $q_i(t)$ is the *unreliability* or *unavailability* of the component. We assume that the events $E_1(t), E_2(t), \ldots, E_n(t)$ are *independent*. The probability of the TOP event at time $t$, $Q_s(t)$, is then

$$
\begin{aligned}
Q_s(t) &= \Pr(E_1(t) \cap E_2(t) \cap \cdots \cap E_n(t)) \\
&= \Pr(E_1(t)) \cdot \Pr(E_2(t)) \cdots \Pr(E_n(t)) \\
&= q_1(t) \cdot q_2(t) \cdots q_n(t) \\
&= \prod_{i=1}^{n} q_i(t)
\end{aligned}
\tag{10.3}
$$

**Fault Tree With a Single OR-gate.**    Consider a fault tree with a single OR-gate, as illustrated in Figure 10.11.

In this case, any of the basic events will cause the TOP event to occur, and the Boolean representation is

$$
\text{TOP}(t) = E_1(t) \cup E_2(t) \cup \cdots \cup E_n(t)
\tag{10.4}
$$

When all the events $E_1(t), E_2(t), \ldots, E_n(t)$ are independent, the probability of the TOP event at time $t$ is

$$
\begin{aligned}
Q_s(t) &= \Pr(E_1(t) \cup E_2(t) \cup \cdots \cup E_n(t)) \\
&= 1 - \Pr(E_1^*(t) \cap E_2^*(t) \cap \cdots \cap E_n^*(t)) \\
&= 1 - [(1 - q_1(t)) \cdot (1 - q_2(t)) \cdots (1 - q_n(t))] \\
&= 1 - \prod_{i=1}^{n} (1 - q_i(t))
\end{aligned}
\tag{10.5}
$$

**Input Data.**    The basic events in a fault tree can usually be classified into five categories:

1. Failure of a nonrepairable technical item

2. Failure of a repairable technical item (that is repaired when a failure occurs)

3. Failure of a periodically tested technical item (i.e., an item with hidden failures that are only detected through periodic testing)

4. Events that occur with a specific frequency (e.g., natural events such as lightning, storm, and flooding)

5. Events that occur in a specific situation, often called on-demand events (e.g., human error, ignition)

*1. Nonrepairable Item*   Consider the basic event $E_i(t) = $ "The nonrepairable item $i$ is in a failed state at time $t$." The item is assumed to have a constant failure rate $\lambda_i$ and is put into operation at time $t = 0$. The probability of the basic event at time $t$ is then

$$q_i(t) = \Pr(E_i(t)) = 1 - e^{-\lambda_i t} \tag{10.6}$$

When $\lambda_t$ is "small," the following approximation is often used: $q_i(t) \approx \lambda_i t$. More details may be found in Appendix A.

*2. Repairable Item*   Consider the basic event $E_i(t) = $ "The repairable item $i$ is in a failed state at time $t$." Let $\mathrm{MTTF}_i$ be the mean time to failure of the item and $\mathrm{MTTR}_i$ be the mean downtime after a failure. The probability of the basic event at time $t$ is then

$$q_i(t) \approx q_i = \frac{\mathrm{MTTR}_i}{\mathrm{MTTF}_i + \mathrm{MTTR}_i} \tag{10.7}$$

$q_i(t)$ is the unavailability of item $i$ at time $t$. The unavailability approaches the average unavailability $q_i$ when the time $t$ increases, and we therefore often use $q_i$ instead of $q_i(t)$. In (10.7) we assume that failure of item $i$ is detected immediately and that repair action is initiated. After a repair action is completed, the item is "as good as new," and there are therefore no trends in either $\mathrm{MTTF}_i$ or $\mathrm{MTTR}_i$.

Let $\lambda_i$ be the constant failure rate of the item, such that $\mathrm{MTTF}_i = 1/\lambda_i$. Since $\mathrm{MTTR}_i \ll \mathrm{MTTF}_i$, the unavailability may be written as

$$q_i = \frac{\mathrm{MTTR}_i}{\mathrm{MTTF}_i + \mathrm{MTTR}_i} \approx \lambda_i \cdot \mathrm{MTTR}_i \tag{10.8}$$

*3. Periodically Tested Item*   Consider the basic event $E_i(t) = $ "The periodically tested item $i$ is in a failed state at time $t$." In this case, item $i$ may have a hidden failure that is detected only by periodical testing. The time interval between two consecutive tests is denoted $\tau$ and the constant failure rate with respect to the hidden failure mode is $\lambda_i$. After a test, the item is considered to be "as good as new." If we can consider the testing time and the repair time (if required) to be negligible compared to the test interval, the basic event probability is

$$q_i(t) \approx q_i = \frac{\lambda_i \tau}{2} \tag{10.9}$$

Assume now that the function of the item is unavailable during an average repair time, $\text{MTTR}_i$, that is not negligible. The repair time will then need to be included with probability

$$\text{Pr("Item is found in failed state in the test")} = 1 - e^{-\lambda_i \tau} \approx \lambda_i \tau$$

In this case, the basic event probability is

$$q_i(t) \approx \frac{\lambda_i \tau}{2} + \frac{\lambda_i \tau \cdot \text{MTTR}_i}{\tau} = \frac{\lambda_i \tau}{2} + \lambda_i \cdot \text{MTTR}_i \qquad (10.10)$$

**4. Frequency**   This category is used for events that occur from time to time, but with no duration. Although the *probability* of the basic event $i$ at time $t$ is $q_i(t) = 0$, the frequency of the event can be given by $v_i$.

**Remark**:   An event with duration may be treated as a repairable item, where the failure rate is the frequency of the event and the repair time is the duration.   $\oplus$

**5. On-Demand Probability**   Consider the basic event $E_i(t) = $ "Basic event $i$ occurs at time $t$." This category is used to describe events that may occur in a specific context, for example, "operator fails to activate manual shutdown system" and "released gas is ignited." The probability of the basic event is usually assumed to be independent of the time $t$.

$$q_i(t) = q_i \qquad (10.11)$$

**TOP Event Probability.**   As indicated in (10.1) and Figure 10.7, any fault tree diagram can be represented as an alternative fault tree diagram with a single OR-gate with all the minimal cut set failures as input events. From (10.1), the probability, $Q_0(t)$ of the TOP event at time $t$ can be written

$$Q_0(t) = \text{Pr(TOP}(t)) = \text{Pr}\left(C_1(t) \cup C_2(t) \cup \cdots \cup C_k(t)\right) \qquad (10.12)$$

where $C_j(t)$ is the probability that minimal cut set $j$ is failed at time $t$, for $j = 1, 2, \ldots, k$. Minimal cut set $j$ will fail at time $t$ when *all* the basic events $E_{j,i}$ in $C_j$ occur at time $t$. The minimal cut set failure, $C_i(t)$, can therefore be represented as a fault tree with a single AND-gate. The probability that minimal cut set $C_j$ fails at time $t$ is denoted $\breve{Q}_j(t)$. If all the basic events in minimal cut set $C_j$ are independent, we get from (10.3)

$$\breve{Q}_j(t) = \text{Pr}(E_{j,1}(t) \cap E_{j,2}(t) \cap \cdots \cap E_{j,n_j}(t))$$
$$= \prod_{i \in C_j} q_i(t) \qquad (10.13)$$

where $n_j$ is the number of basic events in minimal cut set $C_j$, for $j = 1, 2, \ldots, k$.

If all the minimal cut sets were independent, we could use (10.5) to determine the probability of the TOP event at time $t$ as

$$Q_0(t) = 1 - \prod_{j=1}^{k} \left(1 - \breve{Q}_j(t)\right)$$

A basic event will, however, often be a member of several minimal cut sets, and the minimal cut sets will therefore, generally *not* be independent. This type of dependency will give a positive association[4] between the minimal cut sets, and we can deduce the following approximation:

$$Q_0(t) \lesssim 1 - \prod_{j=1}^{k} \left(1 - \breve{Q}_j(t)\right) \tag{10.14}$$

This formula is called the *upper bound approximation* formula and is used by most of the fault tree analysis programs. Using the right-hand side of equation (10.14) will generally give an adequate approximation. The approximation is *conservative*, meaning that the TOP event probability, $Q_0(t)$, is slightly less than the value calculated.

*Inclusion-Exclusion Method*   The inclusion-exclusion method is an alternative to the upper bound approximation formula and will give a more accurate value for the TOP event probability. It will, at the same time, require more computing resources.

By using the addition rule for probabilities to (10.12), we get

$$\begin{aligned}
Q_0(t) = {}& \sum_{j=1}^{k} \Pr(C_j(t)) - \sum_{i<j} \Pr(C_i(t) \cap C_j(t)) \\
& + \sum_{i<j<\ell} \Pr(C_i(t) \cap C_j(t) \cap C_\ell(t)) \\
& - \cdots + (-1)^{k+1} \Pr(C_1(t) \cap C_2(t) \cap \cdots \cap C_k(t))
\end{aligned} \tag{10.15}$$

Define

$$S_1(t) = \sum_{j=1}^{k} \Pr(C_j(t))$$

$$S_2(t) = \sum_{i<j} \Pr(C_i(t) \cap C_j(t))$$

$$S_3(t) = \sum_{i<j<\ell} \Pr(C_i(t) \cap C_j(t) \cap C_\ell(t))$$

$$\vdots$$

$$S_k(t) = \Pr(C_1(t) \cap C_2(t) \cap \cdots \cap C_k(t))$$

---

[4]Association is discussed further in Chapter 6 of Rausand and Høyland (2004).

Equation (10.15) can now be written

$$Q_0(t) = S_1(t) - S_2(t) + S_3(t) - \cdots + (-1)^{k+1} \cdot S_k(t)$$

$$= \sum_{j=1}^{k} (-1)^{j+1} S_j$$

Approximate values of the TOP event probability can be found by using the inclusion-exclusion principle:

$$Q_0(t) \leq S_1(t)$$
$$S_1(t) - S_2(t) \leq Q_0(t)$$
$$Q_0(t) \leq S_1(t) - S_2(t) + S_3(t) \qquad (10.16)$$
$$\vdots$$

We may, for example, use the first of these inequalities as a conservative approximation of the TOP event probability:

$$Q_0(t) \lesssim \sum_{j=1}^{k} \check{Q}_j(t) \qquad (10.17)$$

since $S_1(t) = \sum_{j=1}^{k} \Pr(C_j(t)) = \sum_{j=1}^{k} \check{Q}_j(t)$. This approximation is called the *rare event approximation*. It is based on the assumption that the probability of simultaneous failure of two or more minimal cut sets is much smaller than the probability of a single minimal cut set failure.

The rare event approximation is seen to be more conservative than the upper bound approximation since

$$Q_0(t) \lesssim 1 - \prod_{j=1}^{k} \left(1 - \check{Q}_j(t)\right) \leq \sum_{j=1}^{k} \check{Q}_j(t) \qquad (10.18)$$

**Sensitivity Analysis.** A sensitivity analysis (see Chapter 16) is carried out to determine how much the TOP event probability changes when one or more input parameters are changed. Questions of interest may, for example, concern the effect on the TOP event probability if:

- All failure rates of a special group of components were 50% higher that the nominal value

- The test interval for a set of detectors were increased from 3 months to 6 months.

In some cases, it may be of interest to see how uncertainties in the input parameters influence the TOP event probability. Such an analysis is referred to as *uncertainty* or *error propagation*, and is usually carried out by Monte Carlo simulation. This is discussed further in Chapter 16. Most of the fault tree programs have a module for sensitivity analysis and/or uncertainty/error propagation.

*Importance of Basic Events.* Several importance measures have been developed to measure the relative importance of a basic event, in comparison to other basic events, with respect to the TOP event probability. The importance of a basic event has two sources: (i) the probability of the basic event, and (ii) where the basic event is placed in the fault tree diagram.

*Birnbaum's Measure* Birnbaum (1969) proposed the following measure of the importance of basic event $i$ in a fault tree:

$$I^B(i \mid t) = \frac{\partial Q_0(t)}{\partial q_i(t)} \tag{10.19}$$

for $i = 1, 2, \ldots, n$.

Birnbaum's measure is thus obtained by partial differentiation of the TOP event probability $Q_0(t)$ with respect to $q_i(t)$, and represents a classical sensitivity measure. If $I^B(i \mid t)$ is large, a small change in $q_i(t)$ will lead to a comparatively large change in the TOP event probability $Q_0(t)$.

Let $Q_0(t \mid E_i)$ and $Q_0(t \mid E_i^*)$ be the conditional probability of the TOP event when it is known that basic event $i$ has occurred $(E_i)$ and not occurred $(E_i^*)$, respectively. We can now show (e.g., see Rausand and Høyland, 2004, Sec. 5.2) that Birnbaum's measure can be expressed as

$$I^B(i \mid t) = Q_0(t \mid E_i) - Q_0(t \mid E_i^*) \tag{10.20}$$

This formula is used by many fault tree programs to calculate Birnbaum's measure. First, the TOP event probability $Q_0(t \mid E_i)$ is calculated by assuming that basic event $i$ has occurred. Then, the TOP event probability $Q_0(t \mid E_i^*)$ is calculated when it is assumed that the basic event has not occurred. Compared to taking the derivative of $Q_0(t)$, the two calculations of the TOP event probability are usually performed much faster by a computer.

*Fussell-Vesely's Measure* J. B. Fussell and W. Vesely suggested the following measure of the importance of basic event $i$ in a fault tree:

$$I^{FV}(i \mid t) \quad = \quad \text{Pr(at least one minimal cut set that contains basic event } i \text{ is failed}$$
$$\text{at time } t \mid \text{TOP event occurs at time } t) \tag{10.21}$$

Let $C_j^i$ denote the minimal cut set $j$ that contains the basic event $i$. The probability that this cut set fails at time $t$ is denoted

$$\breve{Q}_j^i(t) = \Pr(C_j^i(t)) \tag{10.22}$$

Fussell-Vesely's measure can now be expressed as (e.g., see Rausand and Høyland, 2004, Sec. 5.7)

$$I^{FV}(i \mid t) \approx \frac{1 - \prod_{j=1}^{m_i} \left(1 - \breve{Q}_j^i(t)\right)}{Q_0(t)} \tag{10.23}$$

where $m_i$ is the number of minimal cut sets that contain basic event $i$, for $i = 1, 2, \ldots, n$.

The main strength of Fussell-Vesely's measure is that it can be calculated very efficiently.

*Risk Achievement Worth* The risk achievement worth (RAW) of basic event $i$ at time $t$ is defined as

$$I^{\text{RAW}}(i \mid t) = \frac{Q_0(t \mid E_i)}{Q_0(t)} \tag{10.24}$$

RAW is therefore the ratio of the TOP event probability when it is assumed that basic event $E_i$ occurs (e.g., that item $i$ is failed) to the actual TOP event probability.

For coherent systems, the RAW will be larger than 1. The larger $I^{\text{RAW}}(i \mid t)$ is, the more will the TOP even probability increase if basic event $E_i$ should occur. RAW therefore shows where prevention activities should be directed to assure that failures do not occur.

*Risk Reduction Worth* The risk reduction worth (RRW) of basic event $i$ at time $t$ is defined as

$$I^{\text{RRW}}(i \mid t) = \frac{Q_0(t)}{Q_0(t \mid E_i^*)} \tag{10.25}$$

RRW is therefore the ratio of the actual TOP event probability to the TOP event probability if basic event $E_i$ were replaced with a basic event that could never happen (e.g., by an item that was perfectly reliable). RRW is always larger than 1.

For more details about RAW and RRW, see, for example, Stamatelatos et al. (2002b), Rausand and Høyland (2004), and Modarres (2006).

**Application of Importance Measures.** Very often, it is found that relatively few events contribute significantly to the TOP event probability. It is also commonly seen that the events cluster in groups that differ by orders of magnitude from one another. In these cases, their importance are so dramatically different that they are generally not dependent on the preciseness of the data used to calculate the TOP event probability (Stamatelatos et al., 2002b).

The main benefits of the importance measures are that they can:

- Identify basic events with the greatest need to be improved, maintained, or controlled.

- Identify the basic events for which we need to obtain high-quality data. A basic event with low importance will have a very low influence on the TOP event probability. Spending resources to get very accurate data for such events may thus be a waste of money. A relevant approach is therefore first to calculate the TOP event probability and one or more importance measures based on approximate input parameters, and then concentrate the data acquisition resources on the most important basic events.

***Binary Decision Diagrams.*** Fault tree diagrams may alternatively be analyzed by using a binary decision diagram (BDD). A BDD is a network of nodes and arcs, where all arcs are directed and no loops are allowed (e.g., see Andersen, 1999).

Rather than analyzing the fault tree directly, the BDD method first converts the fault tree diagram to a binary decision diagram, which represents the Boolean equation for the TOP event. This approach is not based on minimal cut sets. It will in many cases be more efficient than the traditional approach, and does not need approximation formulas. It does, however, still have some challenges and needs more development.

The BDD approach is presented, for example, in Stamatelatos et al. (2002b) and by Modarres (2006), but is not covered further in this book.

### 10.3.4 Analysis Procedure

A fault tree analysis is normally carried out in five steps (CCPS, 2008):

1. Plan and prepare.

2. Construct the fault tree.

3. Analyze the fault tree qualitatively.

4. Analyze the fault tree quantitatively.

5. Report the analysis.

***Step 1: Plan and Prepare.*** The general tasks of this step are discussed in Chapter 8 and will not be repeated here. Two very important tasks in this step are to:

– Define the TOP event to be analyzed.

– Define the boundary conditions for the analysis.

*Define the TOP Event* It is very important that the TOP event is given a clear and unambiguous definition. If not, the analysis will often be of limited value. As an example, the event description "Fire in the plant" is far too general and vague. The description of the TOP event should always answer the questions:

(a) What is occurring?

(b) Where is it occurring?

(c) When is it occurring?

These three questions are sometimes referred to as the *what, where* and *when* questions. A more precise description of the TOP event above would, for example, be "Fire in the process oxidation reactor during normal production."

*Establish Boundary Conditions*   To get a consistent analysis, it is important that the boundary conditions for the analysis be defined carefully. By boundary conditions, we understand:

- The *physical boundaries* of the system. Which parts of the system are to be included in the analysis, and which are not?

- The *initial conditions*. What is the operational state of the system when the TOP event is occurring? Is the system running on full/reduced capacity? Which valves are open/closed, and which pumps are functioning?

- The boundary conditions with respect to *external stresses*. What type of external stresses should be included in the analysis? By *external stresses* we mean stresses from lightning, storm, earthquake, and so on.

- The *level of resolution*. How far down in detail should we go to identify potential reasons for a failed state? Should we, as an example, be satisfied when we have identified the reason as a "valve failure," or should we break it further down to failures in the valve housing, valve stem, actuator, and so on? When determining the preferred level of resolution, we should remember that the level of detail in the fault tree should be comparable to the level of detail of the available information.

*Computer Programs for Fault Tree Analysis*   Small fault tree diagrams can be drawn by pen and paper or by using a drawing program, but a dedicated fault tree program will be needed for larger fault trees.

Several computer programs for fault tree analysis are available. Most of these programs have a graphical frontend that allows the user to construct and modify fault tree diagrams and have implemented routines for identifying minimal cut sets, calculating the TOP event probability and importance measures, and so on.

**Step 2: Construct the Fault Tree.**   The construction of a fault tree always starts with the TOP event. Thereafter, we carefully identify all fault events that make the immediate, necessary, and sufficient causes that result in the TOP event. These causes are connected to the TOP event via a logic gate. It is important that the first level of causes under the TOP event is put up in a structured way. This first level is often referred to as the *top structure* (see Figure 10.2) of the fault tree. The top structure causes are often taken to be failures in the prime modules of the system, or in the prime functions of the system. We then proceed, level by level, until all fault events have been developed to the prescribed level of resolution. The analysis is, in other words, deductive and is carried out by repeatedly asking "What are the reasons for ...?" The lowest level of events in the fault tree are the basic events.

*Rules for Fault Tree Construction*

1. *Describe the fault events*. Each event must be carefully described (what, where, when) in a rectangle as illustrated in Figure 10.2. Information that does not fit into the limited space in the rectangle should be provided in an associated file.

2. *Evaluate the fault events.* As explained in Section 3.6, component failures may be divided into three groups: *primary failures*, *secondary failures*, and *command faults*. The three groups of failure are illustrated in Figure 10.4.

   When evaluating a component fault event, we ask the question "Can this fault be caused by a primary failure?" If the answer is "yes," the fault event is classified as a *normal* basic event. If the answer is "no," the fault event is classified either as an *intermediate* event that has to be developed further, or as a *secondary* basic event. Secondary basic events are also called *undeveloped events* as they represent fault events that are not examined further. This is either because information is unavailable or because the consequences are considered to be insignificant.

3. *Complete the gates.* All inputs to a specific gate must be defined and described completely before proceeding to the next gate. The fault tree should be completed in levels, and each level should be completed before beginning the next level.

A fault tree for a specified TOP event does not have a unique layout. Several seemingly different fault trees may be logically equivalent and represent the same structure. This is illustrated by the two fault trees in Example 10.2.

**◼ EXAMPLE 10.2   Fire pump failure**

Consider a system of two fire pumps, FP1 and FP2, as illustrated in Figure 10.12. The fire pumps are driven by a common engine, EG. The water flow is opened by a valve, V. A fault tree illustrating the potential causes of the TOP event: "No water from the fire pump system" in the case of a demand is illustrated in Figure 10.13.[5]

The minimal cut sets of the fault tree in Figure 10.13 may be found directly from the fault tree or by converting the fault tree to a reliability block diagram, as illustrated in Figure 10.14. The minimal cut sets are seen to be

$$C_1 = \{V\}, \quad C_2 = \{EG\}, \quad C_3 = \{FP1, FP2\}$$

An alternative version of the fault tree in Figure 10.13 is illustrated in Figure 10.15.

Note that the fault trees in Figures 10.13 and 10.15 are different but logically identical and have the same minimal cut sets. Which of these fault trees we choose to use as a basis for further analysis is not important since they will give the same results.                                                             ⊕

**Step 3: Analyze the Fault Tree Qualitatively.**   A qualitative evaluation of the fault tree may be carried out on the basis of the minimal cut sets. The criticality of a cut

---

[5]This example was suggested by **Ragnar Aarø**, Safetec.

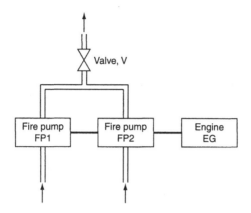

**Figure 10.12**  Fire water system (Example 10.2).

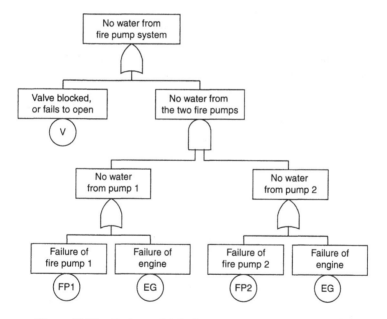

**Figure 10.13**  Fault tree for the fire water system in Example 10.2.

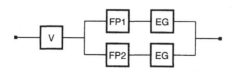

**Figure 10.14**  Reliability block diagram for the fire water system in Example 10.2.

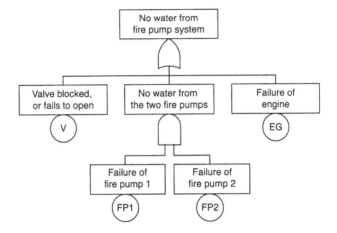

**Figure 10.15**   Alternative fault tree for the fire water system in Example 10.2.

set depends principally on the *order* of the cut set. A cut set of order one is usually more critical than a cut set of order two or more. When we have a cut set of order one, the TOP event will occur as soon as the corresponding basic event occurs. When a cut set has two basic events, both of these have to occur at the same time to cause the TOP event to occur.

Another important factor is the *type* of basic events in a minimal cut set. We may rank the criticality of the various cut sets according to the following ranking of basic events:

1. Human error

2. Active equipment failure

3. Passive equipment failure

This ranking is based on the assumption that human errors occur more frequently than active equipment failures, and that active equipment is more failure-prone than passive equipment (an active or running pump is, for example, more exposed to failures than is a passive standby pump).

Based on this ranking, Table 10.3 shows the criticality of various minimal cut sets of order 2. (Rank 1 is the most critical.)

***Step 4: Analyze the Fault Tree Quantitatively.***   If it is assumed that the basic events are statistically independent and that we have knowledge about the probability of occurrence of each of the basic events in the fault tree, the probability of occurrence of the TOP event, importance measures, and so on, can be calculated by using the formulas in Section 10.3.3. In most cases, this analysis will be done by a fault tree analysis program. Depending on the program, the number of different measures that can be calculated will vary.

**Table 10.3**     Criticality ranking of minimal cut sets of order 2.

| Rank | Basic event 1 (type) | Basic event 2 (type) |
|------|----------------------|----------------------|
| 1 | Human error | Human error |
| 2 | Human error | Active equipment failure |
| 3 | Human error | Passive equipment failure |
| 4 | Active equipment failure | Active equipment failure |
| 5 | Active equipment failure | Passive equipment failure |
| 6 | Passive equipment failure | Passive equipment failure |

### 10.3.5   Resources and Skills Required

Fault tree analysis requires some training and experience. The analysis is time-consuming, but not difficult once the technique has been mastered. Many computer programs are available to assist the analyst in the construction, editing, and quantitative analysis.

To carry out a fault tree analysis, the study team has to have a thorough knowledge about the system and how it is operated. A quantitative fault tree analysis needs a lot of input data, as outlined in Section 10.3.3.

### 10.3.6   Standards and Guidelines

Several standards and guidelines for fault tree analysis have been developed. Some of the most important are:

– *Fault Tree Analysis (FTA)* (IEC 61025, 2006) is the main international standard for fault tree analysis.

– *Fault Tree Handbook*, U.S. Nuclear Regulatory Commission (NUREG-0492, 1981) was one of the first comprehensive treatments of fault tree analysis and is still a valuable reference.

– *Fault tree handbook with aerospace applications* (Stamatelatos et al., 2002b) may be considered a follow-up of NUREG-0492 (1981) and is one of the best and most comprehensive references on fault tree analysis.

– *Guidelines for Hazard Evaluation Procedures* (CCPS, 2008) has a very good chapter on fault tree analysis.

### 10.3.7   Advantages and Limitations

***Advantages.***   The main advantages of fault tree analysis are that the technique

– is easy to use and employs a clear and logical form of presentation;

- is widely used and well accepted;

- can handle complex systems;

- is suitable for many different critical events;

- is suitable for both technical faults and human errors;

- provides the analyst with a better understanding of the potential sources of failure and thereby a means to rethink the design and operation of a system in order to eliminate many potential hazards.

*Limitations.* The main limitations are that the fault tree analysis technique

- loses its clarity when applied to systems that do not fall into simple failed or working states (e.g., human error, adverse weather);

- treats only foreseen events;

- handles sequence-sensitive scenarios poorly;

- does not show the "actors" in the fault tree;

- becomes complicated, time-consuming, and difficult to follow for large systems;

- gives a *static picture* of the combinations of failures and events that can cause the TOP event to occur. Fault tree analysis is therefore not a suitable technique for analyzing dynamic systems, such as switching systems, phased mission systems, and systems subject to complex maintenance strategies.

## 10.4   Bayesian Networks

### 10.4.1   Introduction

A *Bayesian network* is a graphical model that illustrates the causal relationships between key factors (causes) and one or more final outcomes in a system. The network is made up of *nodes* and directed *arcs*. A node describes a state or condition, and an arc indicates a direct influence.

Probabilities can be introduced into the Bayesian network and we can use these to find the probability of the outcome, as we did for fault trees. A Bayesian network is sometimes called a *Bayesian belief network*, *causal network*, or *belief network*.

A Bayesian network analysis may be qualitative, quantitative, or both, depending on the scope of the analysis. An introduction to Bayesian networks is given by Charniak (1991) and by Kjærulff and Madsen (2008).

A Bayesian network analysis is a comprehensive method that can be used for many different purposes and it is outside the scope of this book to cover all these. In this book, we give an elementary introduction to Bayesian networks and focus on how they may be used for causal analysis in a risk analysis, more or less with the same purpose as a fault tree analysis. Readers who want to get a deeper insight are advised to study one of the references cited at the end of the chapter.

### 10.4.2  Objectives and Applications

Objectives of a Bayesian network analysis related to risk analysis include:

(a) Identifying all relevant factors that can significantly influence a critical event (hazardous event or accident).

(b) Illustrating in a network the relationships between the various risk-influencing factors

(c) Calculating the probability of the critical event

(d) Identifying the most important contributors to the probability of the critical event

Bayesian networks are more flexible than fault trees and can replace fault trees in a risk analysis. Bayesian networks are popular in statistics, machine learning, artificial intelligence, and risk and reliability analyses.

### 10.4.3  Method Description

A Bayesian network is a directed acyclic graph, together with a set of probability tables. The graph is represented as a finite set of nodes and a set of directed arcs.[6] An arc may be written $\langle A, B \rangle$, meaning that the arc goes from $A$ to $B$, where $A$ and $B$ are two nodes in the network. That the Bayesian network is acyclic means that cycles are not allowed in the network.

The nodes are drawn as ovals or circles and the arcs as arrows. Each *node* can be represented by a random variable with a discrete distribution. It is possible to use a continuous distribution, but this will make the analysis much more complex. The value of the random variable is called the *state* of the factor that is represented by the node. A variable may have two or more possible states. A good advice is to use as few states as possible, as the complexity of the computation will increase with the number of states. A node can represent any type of variable, be it a measured quantity, a latent variable, or a hypothesis.

Let $A$ and $B$ be the random variables associated with the nodes $A$ and $B$, respectively. For simplicity, the same symbol is used to represent both the node and its associated random variable. We hope that this will not confuse the reader.

An arc from node $A$ to node $B$ represents a statistical dependence between the corresponding variables $A$ and $B$. Thus, the arrow indicates that a value taken by variable $B$ depends on the value taken by variable $A$, or that variable $A$ has a *direct influence* on $B$.

The simplest possible Bayesian network is shown in Figure 10.16, where a node $A$ is linked to a node $B$. In Figure 10.16, node $A$ is called a *parent node* of node $B$, and node $B$ is called a *child node* of node $A$. A node with no parents is called a *root node*. In this figure, $A$ is therefore a root node.

---

[6] Arcs are also called *links*, *arrows*, *vertices*, and *edges*.

**Figure 10.16**    A simple Bayesian network.

The nodes that can be reached on a direct path from $A$ are called the *descendants* of $A$, and the nodes from which $A$ can be reached on a direct path are called the *ancestors* of $A$. Since a Bayesian network is an acyclic graph, a node can never be its own ancestor or its own descendants.

Consider the Bayesian network in Figure 10.16, and let $A$ and $B$ be the random variables that represent the nodes (or factors) $A$ and $B$, respectively. In practical applications, a node is often specified by a name, such as "weather" or "state of component." The random variable then denotes the possible states of the factor: for example, for the factor weather:

$$X_1 = \begin{cases} 1 & \text{raining} \\ 0 & \text{not raining} \end{cases}$$

Node $A$ in Figure 10.16 is a root node, and we call the distribution of $A$ a *marginal distribution*.

The joint probability distribution of $A$ and $B$ is given by

$$\Pr(A = a \cap B = b) = \Pr(A = a) \cdot \Pr(B = b \mid A = a) \tag{10.26}$$

for possible states $a$ and $b$ of $A$ and $B$, respectively. This equation may alternatively be written in the more compact form

$$p_{A,B}(a,b) = p_A(a) \cdot p_{B|A}(b \mid a) \tag{10.27}$$

For simplicity, assume that both $A$ and $B$ have two possible states, 1 and 0, and say that factor $A$ is present when $A = 1$ and that factor $A$ is not present when $A = 0$. The same applies for factor $B$.

**■ EXAMPLE 10.3    Job performance when raining**

Assume that we are going to do a job in a specific time interval tomorrow. The probability of a successful job depends on whether or not it is raining when the job is done. This situation can be illustrated by Figure 10.16, where $A$ denotes the weather and $B$ the job outcome. Let $A = 1$ if it is raining in the specified interval and $A = 0$ if it is not raining. Let $B = 1$ be that the job is successful and $B = 0$ that it is not. Assume that based on the weather forecast, we believe that

$$\Pr(A = 1) = 0.15 \quad \text{and hence that} \quad \Pr(A = 0) = 0.85$$

and that the conditional probabilities are

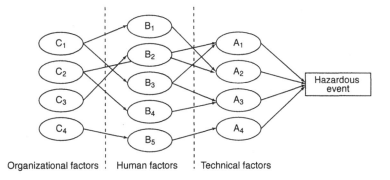

**Figure 10.17**    Example of a Bayesian network showing technical, human, and organizational influencing factors.

| $a$ | $\Pr(B = 1 \mid A = a)$ | $\Pr(B = 0 \mid A = a)$ |
|-----|-------------------------|-------------------------|
| 1   | 0.10                    | 0.90                    |
| 0   | 0.70                    | 0.30                    |

This means that if we know that it will be raining, the probability of a successful job ($B = 1$) is $\Pr(B = 1 \mid A = 1) = 0.10$.

The total probability of a successful job ($B = 1$) is

$$\Pr(B = 1) = \Pr(B = 1 \mid A = 1) \cdot \Pr(A = 1)$$
$$+ \Pr(B = 1 \mid A = 0) \cdot \Pr(A = 0)$$
$$= 0.10 \cdot 0.15 + 0.70 \cdot 0.85 = 0.61 = 61\%$$

$\oplus$

The main purpose of using a Bayesian network in a risk analysis is to model the network of influences on a hazardous event or on an accident. The factors influencing this outcome are the risk-influencing factors (RIFs). The RIFs are identified deductively and are connected by directed arcs.

In some cases, we may distinguish between technical, human, organizational, environmental, and regulatory influencing factors. This is illustrated in Figure 10.17, which for this particular example shows that the hazardous event (e.g., a gas leak in a process plant) is directly influenced by four technical factors. The technical factors are again directly influenced by human factors (e.g., maintenance errors) and the human factors are again directly influenced by various organizational factors (e.g., time pressure, inadequate maintenance procedures). Environmental and regulatory factors are not included in this Bayesian network.

***Assumptions.***    Consider the Bayesian network in Figure 10.18. We will use this network to illustrate the assumptions we need to make to carry out a quantitative analysis of the network:

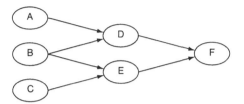

**Figure 10.18**    Bayesian network.

1. First, assume that when the state of node $D$ is known, knowledge about the state of node $A$ will not give any further information about the probability of state $F$. This implies that

$$\Pr(F \mid A \cap D) = \Pr(F \mid D)$$

More generally, this assumption may be written as:

A node is assumed to be independent of its ancestors when we know the states of its parents.

This is consistent with a Markov property (see Section 10.5), since the conditional probability distribution at each node depends only on its parents.

2. In Figure 10.18, nodes $D$ and $E$ are seen to be dependent since they are both influenced by node $B$.

To be able to calculate the probabilities in a Bayesian network, we assume that each node (variable) is *conditionally independent* in the graph when we know the states of all its parents. The concept of conditional independence is defined as:

☞ **Conditional independence**: Consider the three events $K$, $L$, and $M$. If we know that event $M$ has occurred, event $K$ and event $L$ are said to be *conditionally independent*, given $M$, if

$$\Pr(K \cap L \mid M) = \Pr(K \mid M) \cdot \Pr(L \mid M) \qquad (10.28)$$

We now assume that the nodes in Figure 10.18 are conditionally independent given their parents. This means that nodes $D$ and $E$ are independent when we know the status of their parents, that is, the status of nodes $A$, $B$, and $C$. This means that

$$\Pr(D \cap E \mid A \cap B \cap C) = \Pr(D \mid A \cap B) \cdot \Pr(E \mid B \cap C)$$

Let $X$ be a node and let Parent($X$) denote the set of parents to node $X$. In our case Parent($D$) $= A \cap B$ and Parent($E$) $= B \cap C$. When nodes $D$ and $E$ are conditionally independent, then

$$\Pr(D \cap E \mid \text{Parent}(D, E)) = \Pr(D \mid \text{Parent}(D)) \cdot \Pr(E \mid \text{Parent}(E))$$

In a general case, we may then write

$$\Pr(X_1 = x_1 \cap \cdots \cap X_n = x_n) = \prod_{i=1}^{n} \Pr(X_i = x_i \mid \text{Parent}(X_i)) \quad (10.29)$$

where we consider $n$ nodes represented by the variables $X_i$ and $x_i$ is a possible state of $X_i$ for $i = 1, 2, \ldots, n$.

3. When there is no arc between two nodes, this means that they are conditionally independent.

**Conditional Probability Tables.** A conditional probability table (CPT) must be associated with every node. Conditional probabilities represent likelihoods based on prior information or past experience. A CPT gives the distribution of variable for each combination of parent states.

Reconsider the Bayesian network in Figure 10.18 and assume that each variable can have two possible states, 0 and 1. We want to establish probabilities for the random variables representing the nodes. In Figure 10.18, nodes $A$, $B$, and $C$ have no parents, and we therefore have to specify the marginal probability distribution of these variables: for example, as

$$\begin{aligned} \Pr(A = 1) &= 0.85 \\ \Pr(B = 1) &= 0.45 \\ \Pr(C = 1) &= 0.70 \end{aligned} \quad (10.30)$$

Nodes $D$ and $E$ have parents, so the probability distribution of the random variables $D$ and $E$ will therefore depend on the states of their respective parents: for example, as given in Table 10.4. Because of assumption 1 above, a node is dependent only on its parents, not on earlier ancestors. Table 10.4 represents the CPT for node $D$. Several different layouts of the CPT are presented in the literature.

The upper left column header is labeled Parents, and directly below are the names of all nodes having a causal influence over the child node ($D$) in question. In this case, this node has two parents ($A$ and $B$), so there are two columns on that side of the table. On the right-hand side of the table, the upper right column header gives the name of the node with which the CPT is associated. The rest of the table holds the conditional probabilities of the states of $D$ when the specified states of the parents are given. In this case, the child node $D$ has only two states. The conditional probabilities for each state of the parents add up to 1, so one of the last two columns in Table 10.4 is superfluous and could be deleted. In general, if child node $D$ had $r$ different states, we would need $r - 1$ probability columns in Table 10.4. The probabilities in this table are "invented" and included only for illustration. The conditional probability table for node $E$ is set up in a similar way.

The complexity of a CPT increases with the number of states and the number of parents of the node. When the node has no parents (i.e., a root node) the CPT reduces to a listing of the marginal probabilities, as in (10.32).

**Table 10.4** Example of a conditional probability table (CPT) for a node with two parents.

| Parents | | $\Pr(D = d \mid \text{Parents})$ | |
|---|---|---|---|
| $A$ | $B$ | 1 | 0 |
| 0 | 0 | 0.10 | 0.90 |
| 0 | 1 | 0.25 | 0.75 |
| 1 | 0 | 0.50 | 0.50 |
| 1 | 1 | 0.95 | 0.05 |

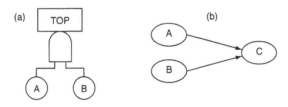

**Figure 10.19** Fault tree with single AND-gate and the corresponding Bayesian network.

**Bayesian Networks and Fault Trees.** A fault tree can easily be converted to a Bayesian network. We illustrate this conversion by looking separately at simple fault trees with (i) one AND-gate and (ii) one OR-gate.

*Fault Tree with Single AND-gate* Figure 10.19(a) illustrates a fault tree with two independent basic events, $A$ and $B$, and a single AND-gate. Part (b) of the figure illustrates a Bayesian network with two root nodes, $A$ and $B$, and an outcome node, $C$.

Let $A$ be a random variable associated with node $A$ and basic event $A$ with the following two states:

$$A = \begin{cases} 1 & \text{if basic event } A \text{ occurs} \\ 0 & \text{if basic event } A \text{ does not occur} \end{cases} \tag{10.31}$$

Let the random variables $B$ and $C$ be defined in the same way.

Since the fault tree has an AND-gate, both of the basic events ($A$ and $B$) have to occur for the TOP event ($C$) to occur, as shown in the truth table for the fault tree in Table 10.5.

Let the (marginal) probabilities of basic event $A$ and $B$ at time $t$ be $q_A(t)$ and $q_B(t)$, respectively. This means that at time $t$,

$$q_A(t) = \Pr(A = 1)$$
$$q_B(t) = \Pr(B = 1) \tag{10.32}$$

**Table 10.5** Truth table for a fault tree with a single AND-gate and two basic events.

| Basic events | | TOP event |
|---|---|---|
| A | B | C |
| 0 | 0 | 0 |
| 0 | 1 | 0 |
| 1 | 0 | 0 |
| 1 | 1 | 1 |

**Table 10.6** Conditional probability table corresponding to a fault tree with a single AND-gate and two basic events.

| Basic events | | TOP event $(C)$ |
|---|---|---|
| A | B | $\Pr(C = 1)$ |
| 0 | 0 | 0.00 |
| 0 | 1 | 0.00 |
| 1 | 0 | 0.00 |
| 1 | 1 | 1.00 |

The TOP event probability can now be calculated as

$$
\begin{aligned}
Q_0(t) &= \Pr(C = 1) = \Pr(A = 1 \cap B = 1) \\
&= \Pr(A = 1) \cdot \Pr(B = 1) = q_A(t) \cdot q_B(t)
\end{aligned}
\tag{10.33}
$$

The corresponding Bayesian network in Figure 10.19 will have the same marginal probabilities (10.32), and the CPT of node $C$ is given in Table 10.6.

*Fault Tree with Single OR-gate*  Figure 10.20(a) illustrates a fault tree with two independent basic events, $A$ and $B$, and a single OR-gate. Part (b) of the figure illustrates a Bayesian network with two root nodes, $A$ and $B$, and an outcome node, $C$. In this case the CPT is given in Table 10.7.

The TOP event probability can now be calculated as

$$
\begin{aligned}
Q_0(t) &= \Pr(C = 1) = 1 - \Pr(C = 0) \\
&= 1 - \Pr(A = 0 \cap B = 0) \\
&= 1 - \Pr(A = 0) \cdot \Pr(B = 0) \\
&= 1 - (1 - q_A(t))(1 - q_B(t))
\end{aligned}
\tag{10.34}
$$

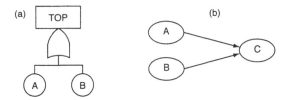

**Figure 10.20**    Fault tree with single OR-gate and the corresponding Bayesian network.

**Table 10.7**    Conditional probability table corresponding to a fault tree with a single OR-gate and two basic events.

| Basic events | | TOP event ($C$) |
|---|---|---|
| $A$ | $B$ | $\Pr(C = 1)$ |
| 0 | 0 | 0.00 |
| 0 | 1 | 1.00 |
| 1 | 0 | 1.00 |
| 1 | 1 | 1.00 |

▣ **EXAMPLE 10.4    Risk-influencing factor**

Let $A$ be a specific hazardous event and let $B$ denote that a specified risk-influencing factor (RIF) is present. Assume that we have estimated that the hazardous event will occur with probability $\Pr(A) = 0.02$. Further, assume that the (marginal) probability of the RIF $B$ being present is 0.20 and that we have estimated, based on accident reports, that the probability of the RIF being present when a hazardous event occurs is $\Pr(B \mid A) = 0.75$. We can now use Bayes formula to find

$$\Pr(A \mid B) = \frac{\Pr(B \mid A) \cdot \Pr(A)}{\Pr(B)} = \frac{0.75 \cdot 0.02}{0.20} = 0.075$$

which is the probability of a hazardous event when we observe that the RIF $B$ is present.    ⊕

Generalizations of Bayesian networks that can represent and solve decision problems under uncertainty are called *influence diagrams*.

### 10.4.4    Analysis Procedure

A Bayesian network analysis includes the following five steps:

1. Plan and prepare.

2. Construct the Bayesian network.

3. Build the conditional probability tables.

4. Analyze the network quantitatively.

5. Report the analysis.

Steps 1 and 5 are discussed in Chapter 8 and are not treated further here.

***Step 2: Construct the Bayesian Network.***   As for fault tree analysis, it is important to specify the end node(s) in a clear and unambiguous way. The next task is then to identify the factors (parents) that may influence the end node(s) and to draw the arcs between the relevant nodes. The process is similar to establishing the top structure of a fault tree. This process is continued to lower-level causal factors until the desired level of resolution is reached.

Many computer programs for Bayesian networks are available. In most practical analyses, an efficient program is needed. Most of these computer programs have a graphical editor that can be used to draw and edit the Bayesian network. The states of each node must next be defined as random variables with a specified discrete value set.

***Step 3: Build the Conditional Probability Tables.***   After defining the node states, the arcs between the nodes need to be described and probabilities assigned.

It is natural to start with the root nodes (i.e., the nodes without parents) and assign probabilities to these. Then the next-level nodes are assigned with the conditional probability distribution of the node given its parents. This is continued until the end node(s) is/are assigned. When this process is completed, all the CPTs have been established.

In this process, the study team must determine the values of the CPT entries. These values could come from expert judgment, some external sources, be estimated from data, or be a combination of the above. It should be noted that for Bayesian networks, the more complex the interactions, the more conditional probabilities there are to specify.

***Step 4: Analyze the Network Quantitatively.***   The various probabilities can now be calculated. In most practical applications it is necessary to use a computer.

Sensitivity analyses provide a ranking of importance of variables relative to the variable of interest (usually the endpoint). These variables indicate where better quantification in the network should be investigated and identify the most influential variables on model endpoints. Subsequently, these are the variables that should be given greater attention. In a management context, it is these variables that may represent key management actions or knowledge gaps. As sensitivity findings can differ for different spatial areas of interest or scenarios tested, key knowledge gaps and priority risks can also differ.

### 10.4.5 Resources and Skills Required

Bayesian networks require some training and experience.

***Standards and Guidelines.*** No international standard has been published for Bayesian networks, but detailed guidelines may be found in several textbooks.

### 10.4.6 Advantages and Limitations

***Advantages.*** The main advantages are that a Bayesian network:

- produces a graph with an intuitive interpretation;
- is based on a mathematically rigorous theory;
- can replace fault tree analysis as part of a risk analysis;
- is more flexible than fault tree analysis (since a binary representation of events is not required);
- can incorporate quantitative and qualitative information;
- can be updated as new information becomes available.

***Limitations.*** The main limitations are that a Bayesian network

- requires a workload that will increase almost exponentially with the number of nodes;
- requires the use of a computer program even for very small systems.

## 10.5 Markov Methods

### 10.5.1 Introduction

In this context, a Markov method is an analytical method that is based on a Markov process with discrete states and continuous time. An excellent introduction to Markov processes and general stochastic processes is given by Ross (1996), and a specific introduction to Markov methods in reliability studies is given by Rausand and Høyland (2004). When we talk about Markov processes in this book, we tacitly assume that the process has a finite number of states and that the time is continuous. A Markov process is a simple stochastic process where the distribution of future states depends only on the present state and not on how the process arrived in the present state.

The application of Markov processes in risk analysis may be illustrated by the following simple example.

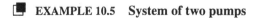 **EXAMPLE 10.5   System of two pumps**

**Table 10.8**   Possible states of a system of two pumps.

| State | Pump 1 | Pump 2 |
|-------|--------|--------|
| 3 | Functioning | Functioning |
| 2 | Functioning | Failed |
| 1 | Failed | Functioning |
| 0 | Failed | Failed |

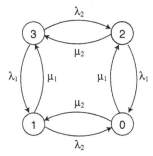

**Figure 10.21**   State transition diagram for the pump system in Example 10.5.

Consider a parallel system of two pumps. Each pump is assumed to have two states, a functioning state and a failed state. Since each of the pumps has two possible states, the parallel structure has $2^2 = 4$ possible states. These states are listed in Table 10.8. The pump system is fully functioning when the state is 3 and failed when the state is 0. In states 1 and 2 the system is operating with only one pump functioning.

The system may start in state 3 at time $t = 0$. If pump 1 fails while in state 3, the system changes to state 1 and we say that it has a transition from state 3 to state 1. The system will change from state 1 to state 3 if pump 1 is repaired. If the system is in state 1, where pump 1 is failed and pump 2 is functioning, and pump 2 fails before pump 1 is repaired, the system will have a transition to state 0. The other transitions can be explained in a similar way.

The states and the transitions may be illustrated by a *state transition diagram* as shown in Figure 10.21. The state transition diagram is also called a *Markov diagram*.

The times until a failure occurs and until a repair is completed are random variables, each with an exponential distribution. The rates of these exponential distributions are shown in the state transition diagram in Figure 10.21, where $\lambda_i$ is the failure rate and $\mu_i$ is the repair rate of pump $i$, for $i = 1, 2$. This means that the mean time to failure (MTTF$_i$) of pump $i$ is $1/\lambda_i$ and its mean repair time (MTTR$_i$) is $1/\mu_i$.

Markov methods can now be used to study the reliability properties of the pump system, and we can, for example, determine

- The average proportion of time that the system will be in each state
- The mean number of times during a specified time interval that the system will visit each state
- The frequency of system failures
- The mean time from startup in state 3 until the system enters state 0 (i.e., the mean time to system failure)    ⊕

### 10.5.2    Objectives and Applications

Markov methods are used to analyze systems with redundancy, interdependency, complex maintenance strategies, and/or sequence-dependent failures. The number of states and the complexity of the state transition diagram increases fast with the number of components of the system. If each component has two states, and the system has $n$ components, the number of states will be $2^n$. In a Markov model, the components may have more than two states: for example, operating, standby, and failed. This option will increase the number of states significantly and the modeling and calculation efforts may become overwhelming.

Markov methods can be used to analyze dynamic systems, for example, standby switching systems and different maintenance strategies, and can therefore be used as an add-on to fault trees, which are not suitable for this purpose. Markov methods can determine a range of reliability measures, some of which are listed in Example 10.5. Markov methods are used in many different application areas: for example, electropower production and distribution, process industry, and computer systems.

### 10.5.3    Method Description

In many applications, we may be able to determine the possible *states* of a system and also to have knowledge about the *transitions* between these states. We number the possible states as $0, 1, \ldots, r$ such that the system can totally have $r + 1$ states. Let $X(t)$ denote the state of the system at time $t$. For a future point of time $t$, the state $X(t)$ is a random variable, and $\{X(t); t \geq 0\}$ is called a *stochastic process* with continuous time.

Let $\mathcal{H}_s$ denote the "history" of the process up to time $s$. This history contains information about which states the system has visited from when it was put into operation at time 0 and until time $s$.

A stochastic process is said to be a *Markov process* if for all $s, t \geq 0$, all nonnegative integers $i, j$, and for all possible histories $\mathcal{H}_s$, we have that

$$\Pr(X(t + s) = j \mid X(s) = i \cap \mathcal{H}_s) = \Pr(X(s + t) = j \mid X(s) = i) \quad (10.35)$$

Equation (10.35) says that if we consider a system that is in state $i$ at time $s$, the probability that this system will be in state $j$ at time $s + t$ is independent of what happened to the system up to time $s$, that is, of the history $\mathcal{H}_s$. This means that the process has *no memory*.

If, in addition, the probability $\Pr(X(s + t) = j \mid X(s) = i)$ is independent of the time $s$, we say that the process has *stationary transition probabilities* and we write

$$P_{ij}(t) = \Pr(X(s + t) = j \mid X(s) = i) \quad \text{for all } s \tag{10.36}$$

This means that if the system is in state $i$ at time $s$, the probability that it will be in state $j$ $t$ time units later is independent of time $s$. From the definition above, we can deduce a range of results (e.g., see Rausand and Høyland, 2004, Chap. 8).

Each time the system enters state $i$, the amount of time it spends in this state before making a transition to a different state is *exponentially* distributed with parameter $\alpha_i$. This means that when the system enters state $i$, it will stay in this state an average time $1/\alpha_i$. When the system leaves state $i$, it enters state $j$ with probability $P_{ij}$, where $P_{ii} = 0$ and $\sum_j P_{ij} = 1$.

If we define $a_{ij} = \alpha_i P_{ij}$, then $\alpha_i = \sum_{j \neq i} a_{ij}$ and we get

$$\lim_{h \to 0} \frac{1 - P_{ii}(h)}{h} = \alpha_i \tag{10.37}$$

and

$$\lim_{h \to h} \frac{P_{ij}(h)}{h} = a_{ij} \tag{10.38}$$

**Kolmogorov Equations.**    In order to get from state $i$ at time 0 to state $j$ at time $t + s$, the process must be in some state $k$ at time $t$. By adding all possible states $k$, we get

$$P_{ij}(t + s) = \sum_{k=0}^{r} P_{ik}(t) P_{kj}(s) \tag{10.39}$$

Equation (10.39) is called the *Chapman-Kolmogorov equation*.

By taking the time derivative of (10.39) we will, after some manipulation, obtain the equations

$$\dot{P}_{ij}(t) = \sum_{\substack{k=0 \\ k \neq j}}^{r} a_{kj} P_{ik}(t) - \alpha_j P_{ij}(t) = \sum_{k=0}^{r} a_{kj} P_{ik}(t) \tag{10.40}$$

Equations (10.40) are known as the *Kolmogorov forward equations*.

**State Equations.**    Let us assume that we know that the Markov process is in state $i$ at time 0, that is, $X(0) = i$. This can be expressed as

$$P_i(0) = \Pr(X(0) - i) = 1$$
$$P_k(0) = \Pr(X(0) = k) = 0 \quad \text{for } k \neq i$$

Since we know the state at time 0, we may simplify the notation by writing $P_{ij}(t)$ as $P_j(t)$. The vector $P(t) = [P_0(t), P_1(t), \ldots, P_r(t)]$ then denotes the state distribution of the Markov process at time $t$, when we *know* that the process started in state $i$ at time 0. Since there are only $r + 1$ possible states, $\sum_{j=0}^{r} P_j(t) = 1$.

The distribution $P(t)$ may be found from the Kolmogorov forward equations

$$\dot{P}_j(t) = \sum_{k=0}^{r} a_{kj} P_k(t) \tag{10.41}$$

where $a_{jj} = -\alpha_j$.

Let us now introduce the *transition rate matrix* $A$:

$$A = \begin{pmatrix} a_{00} & a_{01} & \cdots & a_{0r} \\ a_{10} & a_{11} & \cdots & a_{1r} \\ \vdots & \vdots & \ddots & \vdots \\ a_{r0} & a_{r1} & \cdots & a_{rr} \end{pmatrix} \tag{10.42}$$

where we have introduced the following notation for the diagonal elements:

$$a_{ii} = -\alpha_i = -\sum_{\substack{j=0 \\ j \neq i}}^{r} a_{ij} \tag{10.43}$$

In matrix terms, (10.40) can now be written

$$[P_0(t), \ldots, P_r(t)] \cdot \begin{pmatrix} a_{00} & a_{01} & \cdots & a_{0r} \\ a_{10} & a_{11} & \cdots & a_{1r} \\ \vdots & \vdots & \ddots & \vdots \\ a_{r0} & a_{r1} & \cdots & a_{rr} \end{pmatrix} = [\dot{P}_0(t), \ldots, \dot{P}_r(t)] \tag{10.44}$$

or in a more compact form as

$$P(t) \cdot A = \dot{P}(t) \tag{10.45}$$

Equations (10.45) are called the *state equations* for the Markov process.

### ◼ EXAMPLE 10.6  Single repairable component

Consider a single component. The component has two possible states:

    1  the component is functioning
    0  the component is in a failed state

Transition from state 1 to state 0 means that the component fails, and transition from state 0 to state 1 means that the component is repaired. The transition

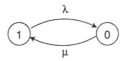

**Figure 10.22**    State transition diagram for a single component (function-repair cycle).

rate $a_{10}$ is thus the failure rate of the component, and the transition rate $a_{01}$ is the repair rate of the component. In this example we use the following notation:

$$a_{10} = \lambda \quad \text{the failure rate of the component}$$
$$a_{01} = \mu \quad \text{the repair rate of the component}$$

The mean sojourn time in state 1 is the mean time to failure, MTTF $= 1/\lambda$, and the mean sojourn time in state 0 is the mean repair time, MTTR $= 1/\mu$. The state transition diagram for the single component is illustrated in Figure 10.22.
The state equations are

$$[P_0(t), P_1(t)] \cdot \begin{pmatrix} -\mu & \mu \\ \lambda & -\lambda \end{pmatrix} = [\dot{P}_0(t), \dot{P}_1(t)] \tag{10.46}$$

The component is assumed to be functioning at time $t = 0$,

$$P_1(0) = 1, \quad P_0(0) = 0$$

Since the two equations in (10.46) are linearly dependent, it is sufficient to use only one of them: for example,

$$-\mu P_0(t) + \lambda P_1(t) = \dot{P}_0(t)$$

and combine this equation with $P_0(t) + P_1(t) = 1$. The solution is

$$P_1(t) = \frac{\mu}{\mu + \lambda} + \frac{\lambda}{\mu + \lambda} e^{-(\lambda + \mu)t} \tag{10.47}$$

$$P_0(t) = \frac{\lambda}{\mu + \lambda} - \frac{\lambda}{\mu + \lambda} e^{-(\lambda + \mu)t} \tag{10.48}$$

For a detailed solution of the differential equation, see Ross (1996, p. 243).
$P_1(t)$ denotes the probability that the component is functioning at time $t$, that is, the *availability* of the component. The limiting availability $P_1 = \lim_{t \to \infty} P_1(t)$ is, from (10.47),

$$P_1 = \lim_{t \to \infty} P_1(t) = \frac{\mu}{\lambda + \mu} \tag{10.49}$$

The limiting availability may therefore be written as the well-known formula

$$P_1 = \frac{\text{MTTF}}{\text{MTTF} + \text{MTTR}} \tag{10.50}$$

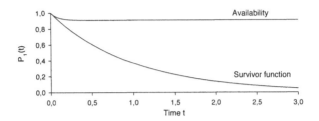

**Figure 10.23**    The availability and the survivor function of a single component ($\lambda = 1$, $\mu = 10$).

When there is no repair ($\mu = 0$), the availability is $P_1(t) = e^{-\lambda t}$, which coincides with the survivor function of the component. The availability $P_1(t)$ is illustrated in Figure 10.23.                                                                                           ⊕

***Steady-State Probabilities.***    In many applications, only the long-run (steady-state) probabilities are of interest, that is, the values of $P_j(t)$ when $t \to \infty$. In Example 10.6 the state probabilities $P_j(t)$ ($j = 0, 1$) approached a steady-state $P_j$ when $t \to \infty$. The same steady state value would have been found irrespective of whether the system started in the operating state or in the failed state.

For the limiting state probabilities to exist, we have to assume that

- All states in a Markov process communicate. This means that if a process starts in state $i$ at some time $t$, it has a positive probability of reaching state $j$ some time in the future. This must apply for any combination $i, j$ of states.

- The Markov process must be *positive recurrent* meaning that if the process starts in a specified state $i$, the expected time to return to this state is finite, for all states $i$.

For a Markov process that fulfills these criteria, the limits

$$\lim_{t \to \infty} P_j(t) = P_j \quad \text{for } j = 0, 1, , \ldots, r \tag{10.51}$$

will always exist and be independent of the initial state of the process (at time $t = 0$). For a proof, see Ross (1996, p. 251). These asymptotic probabilities are often called the *steady-state probabilities* for the Markov process.

If $P_j(t)$ tends to a constant value when $t \to \infty$, then

$$\lim_{t \to \infty} \dot{P}_j(t) = 0 \quad \text{for } j = 0, 1, \ldots, r \tag{10.52}$$

The steady-state probabilities $P = [P_0, P_1, \ldots, P_r]$ must therefore satisfy the matrix equation

**Table 10.9**    Possible states for the pumping system in Example 10.7.

| System state | State of pump 1 | State of pump 2 | System output |
|---|---|---|---|
| 3 | 1 | 1 | 150 L/min |
| 2 | 1 | 0 | 100 L/min |
| 1 | 0 | 1 | 50 L/min |
| 0 | 0 | 0 | 0 L/min |

$$[P_0, P_1, \ldots, P_r] \cdot \begin{pmatrix} a_{00} & a_{01} & \cdots & a_{0r} \\ a_{10} & a_{11} & \cdots & a_{1r} \\ \vdots & \vdots & \ddots & \vdots \\ a_{r0} & a_{r1} & \cdots & a_{rr} \end{pmatrix} = [0, 0, \ldots, 0] \qquad (10.53)$$

which may be abbreviated to

$$\boldsymbol{P} \cdot \boldsymbol{A} = \boldsymbol{0} \qquad (10.54)$$

where, as before,

$$\sum_{j=0}^{r} P_j = 1$$

To calculate the steady-state probabilities, $P_0, P_1, \ldots, P_r$, of such a process, we use $r$ of the $r + 1$ linear algebraic equation from the matrix equation (10.54) and, in addition, the fact that the sum of the state probabilities is always equal to 1. The initial state of the process has no influence on the steady-state probabilities. Note that $P_j$ also may be interpreted as the average, long-run proportion of time that the system spends in state $j$.

### ▣ EXAMPLE 10.7    Pump system reconsidered

Reconsider the pump system in Example 10.5. Each pump can have two states: a functioning state (1) and a failed state (0). A pump is also considered to be in the failed state (0) during repair. Pump 1 is supplying 100 liters per minute (L/min) when it is functioning and nothing when it is not functioning. Pump 2 is supplying 50 L/min when it is functioning and nothing when it is not functioning. The possible states of the system are listed in Table 10.9.

We assume that the pumps fail independent of each other and that they are operated on a continuous basis. The failure rates of the pump are

$\lambda_1$    failure rate of pump 1

$\lambda_2$    failure rate of pump 2

When a pump fails, a repair action is started to bring the pump back into operation. The two pumps are assumed to be repaired independent of each other, by two independent repair crews. The repair rates of the generators are

$$\mu_1 \quad \text{repair rate of pump 1}$$
$$\mu_2 \quad \text{repair rate of pump 2}$$

The corresponding state transition diagram is shown in Figure 10.21. The transition matrix is

$$\mathbf{A} = \begin{pmatrix} -(\mu_1 + \mu_2) & \mu_2 & \mu_1 & 0 \\ \lambda_2 & -(\lambda_2 + \mu_1) & 0 & \mu_1 \\ \lambda_1 & 0 & -(\lambda_1 + \mu_2) & \mu_2 \\ 0 & \lambda_1 & \lambda_2 & -(\lambda_1 + \lambda_2) \end{pmatrix}$$

We can use (10.54) to find the steady-state probabilities $P_j$ for $j = 0, 1, 2, 3$, and we get the following equations:

$$-(\mu_1 + \mu_2)P_0 + \lambda_2 P_1 + \lambda_1 P_2 = 0$$
$$\mu_2 P_0 - (\lambda_2 + \mu_1)P_1 + \lambda_1 P_3 = 0$$
$$\mu_1 P_0 - (\lambda_1 + \mu_2)P_2 + \lambda_2 P_3 = 0$$
$$P_0 + P_1 + P_2 + P_3 = 1$$

Note that we use three of the steady-state equations from (10.54) and, in addition, the fact that $P_0 + P_1 + P_2 + P_3 = 1$. Note also that we may choose any three of the four steady-state equations and get the same solution.

The solution is

$$P_0 = \frac{\lambda_1 \lambda_2}{(\lambda_1 + \mu_1)(\lambda_2 + \mu_2)}$$

$$P_1 = \frac{\lambda_1 \mu_2}{(\lambda_1 + \mu_1)(\lambda_2 + \mu_2)}$$

$$P_2 = \frac{\mu_1 \lambda_2}{(\lambda_1 + \mu_1)(\lambda_2 + \mu_2)}$$

$$P_3 = \frac{\mu_1 \mu_2}{(\lambda_1 + \mu_1)(\lambda_2 + \mu_2)}$$

$$(10.55)$$

Now for $i = 1, 2$ let

$$q_i = \frac{\lambda_i}{\lambda_i + \mu_i} = \frac{\text{MTTR}_i}{\text{MTTF}_i + \text{MTTR}_i}$$

$$p_i = \frac{\mu_i}{\lambda_i + \mu_i} = \frac{\text{MTTF}_i}{\text{MTTF}_i + \text{MTTR}_i}$$

where $\text{MTTR}_i = 1/\mu_i$ is the mean downtime required to repair component $i$, and $\text{MTTF}_i = 1/\lambda_i$ is the mean time to failure of component $i$ ($i = 1, 2$). Thus $q_i$ denotes the average, or limiting, unavailability of component $i$, while $p_i$ denotes the average (limiting) availability of component $i$ ($i = 1, 2$). The steady-state probabilities may thus be written

$$
\begin{aligned}
P_0 &= q_1 q_2 \\
P_1 &= q_1 p_2 \\
P_2 &= p_1 q_2 \\
P_3 &= p_1 p_2
\end{aligned}
\qquad (10.56)
$$

**Remark**: In this simple example, where all failures and repairs are independent events, we do not need to use Markov methods to find the steady-state probabilities. The steady-state probabilities may easily be found by using standard probability rules for independent events. Notice that this applies only for systems with independent failures and repairs.

Assume now that we have the following data:

|  | Pump 1 | Pump 2 |
|---|---|---|
| $\text{MTTF}_i$ | 6 months $\approx$ 4 380 hours | 8 months $\approx$ 5 840 hours |
| Failure rate, $\lambda_i$ | $2.3 \cdot 10^{-4}$ hour$^{-1}$ | $1.7 \cdot 10^{-4}$ hour$^{-1}$ |
| $\text{MTTR}_i$ | 12 hours | 24 hours |
| Repair rate, $\mu_i$ | $8.3 \cdot 10^{-2}$ hour$^{-1}$ | $4.2 \cdot 10^{-2}$ hour$^{-1}$ |

Note that the steady-state probabilities can be interpreted as the mean proportion of time that the system stays in the state concerned. The steady-state probability of state 1 is, for example, equal to

$$
P_1 = \frac{\lambda_1 \mu_2}{(\lambda_1 + \mu_1)(\lambda_2 + \mu_2)} = q_1 p_2 \approx 2.72 \cdot 10^{-3}
$$

Hence

$$
P_1 = 0.002\,72 \left[ \frac{\text{year}}{\text{year}} \right] = 0.002\,72 \cdot 8\,760 \left[ \frac{\text{hours}}{\text{year}} \right] \approx 23.8 \left[ \frac{\text{hours}}{\text{year}} \right]
$$

In the long run the system will stay in state 1 approximately 23.8 hours per year. This does *not* mean that state 1 occurs on average once per year and lasts for 23.8 hours each time.

With the given data, we obtain

| System state | System output | Steady-state probability | Average hours in state per year |
|---|---|---|---|
| 3 | 150 L/min | 0.9932 | 8 700.3 |
| 2 | 100 L/min | $4.08 \cdot 10^{-3}$ | 35.8 |
| 1 | 50 L/min | $2.72 \cdot 10^{-3}$ | 23.8 |
| 0 | 0 L/min | $1.12 \cdot 10^{-5}$ | 0.1 |

### 10.5.4 Analysis Procedure

A Markov analysis as part of a risk analysis is normally carried out in four steps.

1. Plan and prepare.

2. Establish the state transition diagram and the transition rate matrix.

3. Perform quantitative analysis.

4. Report the analysis.

Steps 1 and 4 are described in Chapter 8 and are not treated further here.

***Step 2: Establish State Transition Diagram and Transition Rate Matrix.*** The first task is to identify and describe the relevant system components and to define the states of each component. It is recommended that as few states as possible be used. In most cases, it is sufficient to have two states per component, one functioning state and one failed state.

The second task is to list the components and the defined states in a table similar to Table 10.8. Nonrelevant states should be removed, and identical states should be merged.

The system states can be given any identifier (numbers/letters), but the notation is simplest when we use the numbers $0, 1, 2, \ldots, r$, where $r$ such that $r + 1$ is the total number of states. We recommend that the numbers are allocated such that state 0 is the least wanted state and that $r$ is the most wanted state.

Each state should be described and discussed by the study team to make sure that the state is possible and that the team understands the meaning of the state.

The states can now be drawn as circles on a sheet of paper similar to what is done in Figure 10.21. There are no rules as to where to put the various circles (states), but the final drawing can get rather complex for some layouts. It is generally recommended to use a computer drawing program or, preferably, one of the Markov analysis programs that are available on the market.

The next task is to study each pair of states and determine how the system can come from one state to the other, and vice versa. Each transition is drawn as an arrow. The state transition diagram illustrates the transitions that can take place in a very short interval. This implies that two independent events cannot form a transition. In Figure 10.21, a transition between state 1 and state 2 is not possible because such a transition would imply that the repair of pump 1 is completed at exactly the same time as pump 2 fails. Since these two events are independent, the transition is not permitted.

Associated with each transition (arrow), it is necessary to provide transition rates in the form of constant failure rates ($\lambda_i$) and constant repair rates ($\mu_i$), as done in Figure 10.21.

The transition rate matrix **A** in (10.42) can now be established. The following procedure may be beneficial:

1. Arrange the transition rates $a_{ij}$ for $i \neq j$ as a matrix, similar to the matrix (10.42) (leave the diagonal entries $a_{ii}$ open).

2. Fill in the diagonal elements $a_{ii}$ such that the sum of all entries in each *row* is equal to zero, or by using (10.43).

The state transition diagram and the transition rate matrix **A** should be carefully compared and discussed before starting the quantitative analysis. A lot of useful information can be read directly from the matrix **A**. The diagonal element $a_{ii}$ can tell us directly the rate of departing from state $i$, which is $\alpha_i = -a_{ii}$. This means that if the systems come to state $i$, it will stay there for a random period (sojourn time) that is exponentially distributed with rate $\alpha_i$. The mean sojourn time in state $i$ is hence $1/\alpha_i$. When the sojourn time in $i$ is over, the system will go to state $j \neq i$, with probability $a_{ij}/\alpha_i$.

***Step 3: Perform Quantitative Analysis.*** The state equations can now be readily solved. In most cases, it is sufficient to find the steady-state solutions and we may solve (10.54). For very simple systems, this can be done by hand calculation, but for more realistic cases, a computer program is required. You may use one of the Markov analysis programs on the market, but such programs as MatLab, Scilab, and Octave are also suitable for this purpose.

Several reliability measures may be found: for example:

- $P_i$ for each state. $P_i$ is the probability of finding the system in state $i$ at some specified time in the future, but can also be interpreted as the average proportion of time the system will spend in state $i$.

- The availability $A$ and unavailability $A^*$ of the system.

- The visit frequency $v_i$ to state $i$ [For formulas, e.g., see Rausand and Høyland (2004)]. The expected number of times the system comes to state $i$ during a period of length $t$ is then $v_i t$. This can be used to determine, for example, the repair resources and the required number of spare parts.

- The frequency of system failures. To find this frequency, we first have to determine which states are representing system failures. If, for example, system failure occurs in states 0 and 1, the frequency of system failures is the visit frequency to these states, that is, $\nu_0 + \nu_1$.

- The survivor function $R(t)$ of the system.

- The expected number of failures of the various types.

- The overall mean uptime and downtime of the system.

- The mean time to the first system failure. Formulas for this time are, for example, given in Rausand and Høyland (2004).

*Monte Carlo Simulation*   The Markov state transition diagram can also be treated by Monte Carlo simulation and this will produce the same reliability measures as listed above. By using Monte Carlo simulation, we can also use transition times with nonconstant rates.

### 10.5.5   Resources and Skills Required

To understand all features of a Markov analysis, the user should have a basic course in stochastic processes. The main steps of the Markov method are, however, easy to understand and carry out. For a person who is trained in reliability engineering, 1–2 days of additional training should be sufficient.

Several computer tools for Markov analysis are available, but a good drawing program and a program such as MatLab, Scilab, or Octave should be sufficient.

*Standards and Guidelines.*   An international standard for Markov methods has been published (IEC 61165, 2006), and the theory and application of Markov methods are described in several textbooks (e.g., see Ross, 1996; Pukite and Pukite, 1998; Rausand and Høyland, 2004).

### 10.5.6   Advantages and Limitations

*Advantages.*   The main advantages are that the Markov method:

- is based on a well-documented theory basis and have been applied and verified extensively in many different areas;

- is a suitable tool for analyzing small but complex systems with dynamic properties, which cannot be analyzed adequately using fault trees;

- provides a state transition diagram with important information which is easy for nonspecialists to understand, and which can give a deeper understanding of how the system is operated;

- provides a range of performance measures for the system which are difficult to obtain by other methods.

*Limitations.* The main limitations are that the Markov method:

- is limited to rather small systems with a limited number of states;

- is time-consuming when the number of states increases;

- is limited by the requirements for constant failure rates and constant repair rates;

- is that analysts may have difficulties in translating their problem into a Markov model.

## 10.6  Petri Nets

### 10.6.1  Introduction

A Petri net is a graphical and mathematical tool for modeling and analysis of discrete event systems. The basic concepts of Petri nets were introduced by Carl Adam Petri (Petri, 1962).

This section gives a brief introduction to Petri nets that are applicable in risk analysis. Readers who want a thorough description may consult, for example, David and Alla (2005).[7]

### 10.6.2  Objectives and Applications

Petri nets can be used to solve many different problems in a risk analysis and also add new features to the classical risk analysis models and methods. Petri nets can replace fault trees, event trees, and Markov diagrams and add several new features to the analysis. This makes it possible to include time and dynamic behavior in the fault tree analyses and treat dependencies in the event tree analyses.

Petri nets are used in many different sectors of science and industry: automation (e.g., modeling of production line and design of its control or scheduling of processes), communication (e.g., modeling of communication protocols), chemistry (e.g., modeling of chemical reactions), economy, reliability theory, safety engineering or management (e.g., scheduling of human resources).

### 10.6.3  Method Description

*Graphical Representation.*  A Petri net is a graph. Graphs can generally be considered as an ordered pair $(K, A)$, where $K$ is a set of nodes and $A$ is a set of pairs of distinct nodes describing arcs. When $A$ is a set of ordered nodes, the graph is said to be directed and the arc $a$ in $A$ may be written $a = \langle k_i, k_j \rangle$, meaning that arc $a$ goes from $k_i$ to $k_j$.

---

[7]This section has been coauthored by **Ondřej Nývlt**, Czech Technical University in Prague, Faculty of Electrical Engineering.

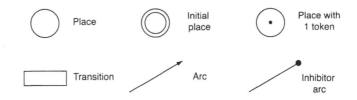

**Figure 10.24**    Elements of the graphics representation of a Petri net.

A Petri net is a *directed graph* with two types of nodes, called places and transitions. The main building blocks of a Petri net are shown in Figure 10.24.

The most basic Petri net is called a *nonmarked* Petri net and consists of:

(a) *Places.* A place gives information about a state or a condition. The (finite) set of all the $n$ distinct places of a Petri net is written $P = \{p_1, p_2, \ldots, p_n\}$. A place is drawn as a circle.

(b) *Transitions.* Transitions represent actions and are active components that are changing the state of the Petri net. The (finite) set of all the $r$ distinct transitions is written $T = \{t_1, t_2, \ldots, t_r\}$. A transition is drawn as a solid bar or a rectangle.

(c) *Directed arcs* are used to connect places and transitions and determine the logical structure of the Petri net. Arcs are drawn as arrows.

An arc can connect a place with a transition or a transition with a place, but cannot directly connect a place with another place or a transition with another transition. This means that the nodes can be divided into two disjoint subsets $P$ (places) and $T$ (transitions) such that any arc always connects nodes from different subsets. A graph with this property is called a *bipartite graph*.

An arc $a$ is represented as an ordered set of two nodes, one place and one transition: for example, $a_1 = \langle p_i, t_j \rangle$. In this case, the arc $a_1$ goes from $p_i$ to $t_j$ and we say that $p_i$ is an *input place* to the transition $t_j$. Alternatively, we may have the arc $a_2 = \langle t_j, p_i \rangle$, where the arc $a_2$ goes from $t_j$ to $p_i$. In this case, we say that the place $p_i$ is an *output place* of the transition $t_j$.

**Marked Petri Nets.**    A *marked* Petri net consists of the same elements as a nonmarked Petri net, but contains, in addition, *tokens* in one or more places. The tokens represent *active* resources and are drawn as solid dots in the places.

A place can contain no tokens, or a number of tokens. The maximum number of tokens a place can hold is called the *capacity* of the place. There may be several input and output arcs between a place and a transition. The number of these arcs is represented as the *weight* of a single arc. The term *capacity* is sometimes used instead of the term *weight*. The weight defines the capacity or multiplicity of the arc. The weight of an arc is marked on the arc, as shown in Figure 10.25. Sometimes, arc weights equal to 1 are not indicated, such that no number means weight 1.

The tokens indicate the absence or presence of, for example, a resource. The *marking* $m(p_i)$ of place $p_i$ is the number of tokens in $p_i$. The marking of a Petri net

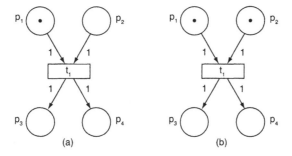

**Figure 10.25**    Nonenabled (a) and enabled (b) transition $t_1$.

is a column vector that has an element for each place that indicates how many tokens are in that place. The marking of $P$ is written $m(P) = (m(p_1), m(p_2), \ldots, m(p_n))^T$.

Change of a state (change of a marking) of a Petri net is caused by the activation of one or more transitions. If an arc is drawn from a place to a transition, it indicates that a token in the place is required to enable the transition.

A transition is *enabled* if and only if:

– Sufficient tokens (resources) are available at all the input places to the transition. *Sufficient* means that each input place must have at least as many tokens as the corresponding input arc weight indicates.

This means that each of the transition's input places must contain at least one token. In addition, the marking $m(p_i)$ must be greater or equal to the weight of the arc from $p_i$ to $t$, for all input places to $t$.

We can distinguish a special type of arc called an *inhibitor arc*, which is blocking a transition if a marking is higher or equal to the weight of the arc. Inhibitor arcs are important in Petri net modeling but are not discussed further in this section.

Activation consists of enabling and firing of transitions. Figure 10.25 shows an example of a nonenabled (a) and an enabled (b) transition $t_1$. A transition can be *fired* if and only if it is enabled.

Firing a transition leads to a change in the markings of the nets, and hence a change in the system state. When an enabled transition is fired, the number of tokens equal to the weights of the associated input arcs are subtracted from the input places and the number of tokens equal to the weights of associated output arcs are added to the output places. The firing process is illustrated in Figure 10.26. Note that the tokens removed and inserted may be different. The structure (places, transitions, and arcs) of a Petri net is static, but dynamic effects are included by the changes of the distribution of tokens.

The network of a Petri net is static, but dynamic effects are included by the firing of transitions.

*Stepwise Simulation*    The "flow" of tokens through the Petri net can be studied by stepwise-firing the transitions. For simple Petri nets, this may be done manually,

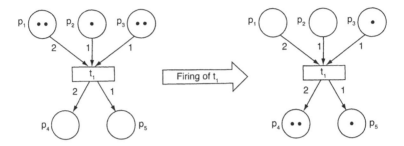

**Figure 10.26**    Example of firing of enabled transition $t_1$ and change of the marking of a Petri net.

but for more complex Petri nets, it may be beneficial to use one of the computer programs for Petri nets. Most of these programs have a module for animation or simulation of a Petri net. The animation can be activated by clicking a transition or it can be set up to run automatically. The animation is a useful tool for testing and debugging the Petri net.

### 10.6.4  Examples of Petri Net Modeling

This subsection provides some examples of how simple systems can be represented by a Petri net.

▉ **EXAMPLE 10.8    Nonrepairable series system**

Consider a nonrepairable series (*noon*) of $n$ components. Since a series system is functioning if and only if all its $n$ components are functioning, the system can be represented by two distinct states (markings).

Let a token in place $p_1$ represent the working state of the system, the firing of transition $t_1$ represent a failure of a component, and a token in place $p_2$ the failed state of the series system.

If we have a system with only one component (1oo1), the Petri net will have only one token, and both arcs, $\langle p_1, t_1 \rangle$ and $\langle t_1, p_2 \rangle$, will have weight 1, as shown in Figure 10.27.

Initially, we assume that the system is in the working state, which means that the token is in place $p_1$. When a failure occurs, the transition $t_1$ is fired and the token in place $p_1$ is absorbed, and then a token is released to place $p_2$, meaning that the system is in a failed state.

A nonrepairable series system of $n$ components can be modeled in the same way. The only difference is that, initially, there are $n$ tokens in $p_1$, one for each component.    ⊕

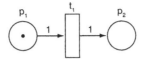

**Figure 10.27**   Petri net representing a nonrepairable 1oo1 system.

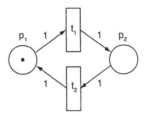

**Figure 10.28**   Petri net representing a repairable 1oo1 system.

### ■ EXAMPLE 10.9   Single repairable component

A repairable single component can be modeled by the Petri net in Figure 10.28. The places $p_1$ and $p_2$ and the transition $t_1$ have the same functions as in Example 10.8, while the firing of transition $t_2$ represents a repair of the component. The repair action absorbs (by $t_2$) the token from place $p_2$ to place $p_1$. This means that firing of this transition changes the state of the component from failed to working. Using a similar model for systems with more than one component, requires the components be repaired one by one.                              ⊕

### ■ EXAMPLE 10.10   Nonrepairable 1oo2 system

A parallel system of two components is a 1oo2 system and can be modeled using Petri nets in more than one way. One option is to use the same approach as in Markov diagrams. Using this approach, there will be only one token in the corresponding Petri net, and and such a distribution of tokens will represent the actual state of the system. For a nonrepairable 1oo2 system of two identical and independent components, this will give a Petri net with three places, as shown in Figure 10.29. Here, a token in $p_1$ represents the system state when both components are functioning, a token in $p_2$ that one component is functioning and the other is in a failed state, and a token in $p_3$ that both components are in a failed state. If the token is in place $p_1$ or $p_2$, the system is functioning. If a token is in place $p_3$, the system is in a failed state. The firing of transition $t_1$ is a failure of the first component and $t_2$ a failure of the second component. Figure 10.30 shows the Petri net for a nonrepairable 1oo2 system with a possible common-cause failure, which is represented by the firing of $t_3$.

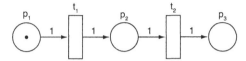

**Figure 10.29**    Petri net representing a nonrepairable 1oo2 system of two identical and independent components.

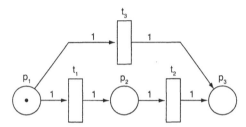

**Figure 10.30**    Petri net representing a nonrepairable 1oo2 system of two identical components with possible common cause failure.

Another approach is to have one token for the state of each component and one token for the system state. In the case of a 1oo2 system, this means three tokens in the corresponding Petri net. The advantage of this approach is that the structure of the Petri net is the same for any parallel system (1oon for any $n$). Only the weights of the arcs and the number of tokens are different. A disadvantage of this approach is that the structure is more complicated and also comprises an inhibitor arc. The graphical representation of this approach is not covered in this book.                                                                     ⊕

■  **EXAMPLE 10.11    Repairable 1oo2 system with common-cause failure**

A repairable 1oo2 system of two identical components and the possibility of common-cause failures may be modeled by the Petri net in Figure 10.31. In this model, we assume that the common-cause does not occur at the same time as independent failures. This Petri net has the same places as the nonrepairable 1oo2 system in Figure 10.30. The firing of transition $t_1$ represents a failure of one of the components, firing of $t_3$ is a failure of the remaining working component. Transition $t_2$ is used to denote a repair of the failed component, transition $t_4$ is for repair of one of the failed components, and transition $t_5$ is introduced to model a common-cause failure. If this transition is fired, the token is moved directly from the working system state $p_1$ to $p_3$, denoting that the system fails.                                                                     ⊕

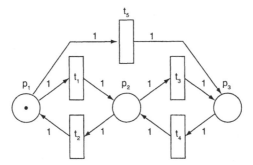

**Figure 10.31**  Petri net representing a repairable 1oo2 system with a common-cause failure.

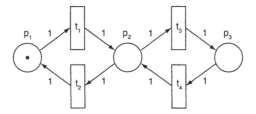

**Figure 10.32**  Representation of a repairable 2oo3 system using a Petri net.

### ■ EXAMPLE 10.12  Repairable 2oo3 system

A 2-out-of-3 (2oo3) system is functioning if at least two of the system's three components are functioning and is a system commonly encountered in risk analyses. To establish a Petri net for a repairable 2oo3 of three identical components, we use the same approach as in previous examples. The Petri net is shown in Figure 10.32. A token in place $p_1$ represents the system state where all three components are in a functioning state. When any of the components fails, the transition $t_1$ is fired and the system changes its state to a degraded, but still functioning state with a token in $p_2$. A failure of any other component will cause firing of transition $t_3$ and change the system state to the failed state (a token in place $p_3$). In this model, all the components will never fail at the same time. Transitions $t_2$ and $t_4$ represent repairs of failed components.                     ⊕

When common-cause failures are possible, we have to add a new place, $p_4$, to model the state where all three components are in a failed state (see the marking shown in Figure 10.33). This state is reachable from all other system states by firing any of the transitions $t_5$, $t_7$, or $t_8$ that represent a common-cause failure. The firing of transition $t_6$ is a repair of one of the failed components.     ⊕

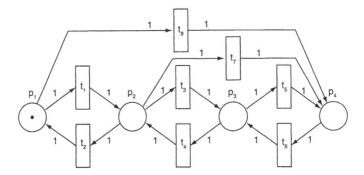

**Figure 10.33**     Petri net for a repairable 2oo3 system with the possibility of a common-cause failure.

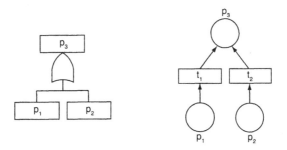

**Figure 10.34**     Petri net for a logical OR-gate.

### ■ EXAMPLE 10.13     Petri nets and fault trees

The logical gates (OR and AND) of a fault tree can be modeled by basic Petri net constructions (Liu and Chiou, 1997; Yang and Liu, 1997). The transformations are easy to use and we can replace each logical gate in a fault tree by the right construction to obtain the corresponding Petri net. All events (TOP, intermediate, and basic) of the fault tree are *places* in the Petri net language. Transitions and directed arcs are used to construct a logical function of the transformed gate. The transformations of the basic gates OR and AND are shown in Figures 10.34 and 10.35.

If there is a token in place $p_1$ in the Petri net construction for the OR-gate shown in Figure 10.34, transition $t_1$ is enabled and will immediately be fired. This gives a token in place $p_3$ independently on the presence of a token in place $p_2$. The same is true if a token is present in place $p_2$. It is seen that this Petri net construction corresponds to the logical OR function.

In the Petri net construction for the AND gate in Figure 10.35, the transition $t_1$ is enabled if and only if there is a token in place $p_1$ and place $p_2$ at the same time. Then this transition will be fired and a token appears in the place $p_3$.     ⊕

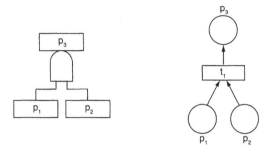

**Figure 10.35**   Petri net for a logical AND-gate.

### 10.6.5   Mathematical Representation

***Incidence Matrix.***   A Petri net can be represented by various types of matrices.

Consider a Petri net with places $P = \{p_1, p_2, \ldots, p_n\}$ and transitions $T = \{t_1, t_2, \ldots, t_r\}$. We can define an $r \times n$ matrix $W^-$ as follows: For the position $(i, j)$, place the weight of the arc connecting place $j$ with transition $i$, in the position if transition $i$ has input from place $j$. If transition $i$ does not have input from place $j$, place a 0 in place $(i, j)$.

We will illustrate the various matrices by the example of a repairable 2oo3 system with common-cause failures shown in Figure 10.33. This Petri net has four places $\{p_1, p_2, p_3, p_4\}$ and eight transitions $\{t_1, t_2, t_3, t_4, t_5, t_6, t_7, t_8\}$.

The $W^-$ matrix for the Petri net in Figure 10.33 is given by

$$W^- = \begin{array}{c} \\ p_1 \\ p_2 \\ p_3 \\ p_4 \end{array} \begin{array}{cccccccc} t_1 & t_2 & t_3 & t_4 & t_5 & t_6 & t_7 & t_8 \\ \left(\begin{array}{cccccccc} 1 & 0 & 0 & 0 & 0 & 0 & 0 & 1 \\ 0 & 1 & 1 & 0 & 0 & 0 & 1 & 0 \\ 0 & 0 & 0 & 1 & 1 & 0 & 0 & 0 \\ 0 & 0 & 0 & 0 & 0 & 1 & 0 & 0 \end{array}\right) \end{array} \tag{10.57}$$

We note that $W^-$ represents arcs going from places to transitions.

In the same way, we can define an $r \times n$ matrix $W^+$ as follows: For position $(i, j)$, place the weight of the arc connecting transition $i$ with place $j$ in the position if transition $i$ has an output to place $j$. If transition $i$ does not have an output to place $j$, place a 0 in place $(i, j)$.

The $W^+$ matrix for the Petri net in Figure 10.33 is given by

$$W^+ = \begin{array}{c} \\ p_1 \\ p_2 \\ p_3 \\ p_4 \end{array} \begin{array}{cccccccc} t_1 & t_2 & t_3 & t_4 & t_5 & t_6 & t_7 & t_8 \\ \left(\begin{array}{cccccccc} 0 & 1 & 0 & 0 & 0 & 0 & 0 & 0 \\ 1 & 0 & 0 & 1 & 0 & 0 & 0 & 0 \\ 0 & 0 & 1 & 0 & 0 & 1 & 0 & 0 \\ 0 & 0 & 0 & 0 & 1 & 0 & 1 & 1 \end{array}\right) \end{array} \tag{10.58}$$

and $W^+$ is seen to represent arcs going from transition to places. We now define the matrix $W = W^+ - W^-$. For the Petri net in Figure 10.33, this becomes

$$
W = \begin{array}{c}
\phantom{p_1} \\
p_1 \\
p_2 \\
p_3 \\
p_4
\end{array}
\begin{array}{cccccccc}
t_1 & t_2 & t_3 & t_4 & t_5 & t_6 & t_7 & t_8 \\
\left( \begin{array}{rrrrrrrr}
-1 & 1 & 0 & 0 & 0 & 0 & 0 & -1 \\
1 & -1 & -1 & 1 & 0 & 0 & -1 & 0 \\
0 & 0 & 1 & -1 & -1 & 1 & 0 & 0 \\
0 & 0 & 0 & 0 & 1 & -1 & 1 & 1
\end{array} \right)
\end{array}
\tag{10.59}
$$

This matrix $(W)$ is called the *incidence matrix* for the Petri net and represents the *structure* of the Petri net. When we know the incidence matrix, we can draw the Petri net. The incidence matrix may be interpreted in the following way: Consider a transition $j$, for example $t_4$. From (10.59), we see that transition $t_4$ has no input or output (0) from/to places $p_1$ and $p_4$, an output (1) to place $p_2$, and an input $(-1)$ from place $p_3$.

The incidence matrix only describes the structure of the Petri net and is independent of the marking and firing of transition. A nonmarked Petri net can therefore be uniquely specified by the triple $\langle P, T, W \rangle$.

**Initial Marking.** The initial marking is the marking $m_0$ of the Petri net when the analysis is started. Remember that $m_0$ is a column vector.

**Firing Sequence.** A firing sequence $s$ is the sequence of transitions that were enabled and fired: for example, $s = \langle t_1, t_2, t_3 \rangle$. If the initial marking is $m_0$, the marking after $t_1$ has been fired, is $m_1$. Then transition $t_2$ is fired, giving the new marking $m_2$, and finally $t_3$ is fired, giving marking $m_3$. This can be written as

$$
m_0 \xrightarrow{t_1} m_1 \xrightarrow{t_2} m_2 \xrightarrow{t_3} m_3
$$

When the firing sequence $s$ is given, the sequence may also be summarized as

$$
m_0 \xrightarrow{s} m_3
$$

Let $S$ denote the set of all possible firing sequences.

**Reachable Marking.** Assume that a Petri net has initial marking $m_0$. A marking $m$ is said to be reachable from $m_0$ if there exists a firing sequence $s \in S$ such that

$$
m_0 \xrightarrow{s} m
$$

The *reachability set* $R(m_0)$ is the set of all markings $m$ that can be reached from the initial marking $m_0$ with a finite set of transitions.

**Reachability Tree and Graph.** From the initial marking $m_0$, we can generate "new" markings for the enabled transitions. Following the same principle, from each new marking, more markings can be generated until repeated nodes are encountered along a path from $m_0$ or no transitions are enabled. A node in a reachability tree represents a marking that can be generated from $m_0$. Each arc represents the firing of a transition, which transforms one marking to another.

A *reachability graph* of a Petri net is a directed graph where the reachable markings are the nodes and the directed arcs go from a class of markings to another class of markings. An example is shown in Figure 10.39. For more information about reachability trees and graphs, see Ye et al. (2003), who also present an algorithm for constructing the reachability graph. Several of the computer programs for Petri net analysis can draw the reachability graph.

*Characteristic Vector.* A characteristic vector is a column vector $u$ giving the number of times that each transition $t \in T$, in the firing sequence $s$ is fired. The vector $u$ is said to be a *possible* characteristic vector if at least one firing sequence $s \in S$ starting from the initial marking $m_0$ gives this characteristic vector. Several firing sequences $s \in S$ may correspond to the same possible characteristic vector $u$ (e.g., see David and Alla, 2005).

For the repairable 2oo3 system with common-cause failures in Example 10.12, there are eight transitions and we may, for example, have the firing sequence $s = \langle t_1, t_3, t_5 \rangle$. The characteristic vector of this sequence is $u = (1, 0, 1, 0, 1, 0, 0, 0)^T$. This means that transitions $t_1, t_3$, and $t_5$ each were fired once and that the transitions $t_2, t_4, t_6, t_7$, and $t_8$ were not fired.

In this example, each transition appears at most once. For a general characteristic vector $u = (u_1, u_2, \ldots, u_r)^T$, the element $u_j$ is the number of times the transition $t_j$ appears in the firing sequence $s$.

*Fundamental Equation.* The development of a Petri net from an initial marking $m_0$ to a marking $m$ is described by the fundamental (or state) equation of a Petri net:

$$m = m_0 + W \cdot u \tag{10.60}$$

where $W$ is the incidence matrix for the Petri net and $u$ is a characteristic vector. For the 2oo3 system with common-cause failures in Example 10.12 with incidence matrix (10.59), initial marking $m_0 = (1, 0, 0, 0)^T$, and characteristic vector $u = (1, 0, 1, 0, 1, 0, 0, 0)^T$, we get the new marking

$$m = m_0 + W \cdot u = (0, 0, 0, 1)^T$$

According to the fundamental equation, two firing sequences, $s_1$ and $s_2$, with the same characteristic vector $u$ result in the same marking. Hence, the (possible) order of transitions in a firing sequence has no influence on the marking that will be reached. The reverse is not true, because two sequences resulting in the same marking $m$ from an initial marking $m_0$ do not necessarily have the same characteristic vector.

*Invariants.* The structural properties of a Petri net can be studied by the *invariants* of the Petri net. These properties depend only on the topological structure of the net and not on the initial marking $m_0$. There are two main types of invariants, the place invariants (*P-invariants*) and the transition invariants (*T-invariants*). Here, we are interested mainly in the P-invariants.

*P-invariants*  A P-invariant is a column vector $f$ of integer, nonnegative elements that has dimension $n$, where $n$ is the number of places of the Petri net, and where the nonzero elements correspond to the places that belong to the P-invariant, and the zero elements correspond to something else.

A P-invariant is defined by

$$f^T \cdot W = 0 \qquad (10.61)$$

The P-invariant $f$ is said to be a *proper* P-invariant if $f \neq 0$.

If the fundamental equation (10.60) is multiplied by the transposed P-invariant $f^T$, we get $f^T \cdot m = f^T \cdot m_0 + f^T \cdot W \cdot u$. Since $f^T \cdot W = 0$, this reduces to

$$f^T \cdot m = f^T \cdot m_0 \qquad (10.62)$$

for all reachable markings $m$. Equation (10.62) implies that a P-invariant is a set of places for which a specified (positive integer) linear combination of its tokens always remains constant for all reachable markings. The process is stable with regard to the involved resources. A P-invariant will therefore neither lose nor gain resources (tokens) (e.g., see David and Alla, 2005).

It follows from (10.61) that:

- When $f$ is a P-invariant, $k \cdot f$ is also a P-invariant when $k$ is an integer, non-negative constant.

- When $f_1$ and $f_2$ are P-invariants, $f_1 + f_2$ is also a P-invariant.

This means that an integer, nonnegative linear combination of P-invariants is also a P-invariant. A P-invariant is said to be *minimal* when it cannot be written as a linear combination of other P-invariants.

Equation (10.61) also implies that for each transition $t_i$, then $f^T \cdot c_{t_i}(W) = 0$, where $c_{t_i}(W)$ is the column of the incidence matrix for transition $t_i$ for $i = 1, 2, \ldots, r$.

P-invariants are important means for analyzing Petri nets, since they allow the structure of the Petri net to be investigated independent of any dynamic process. An important task of the analysis is to identify the set of minimal P-invariants, which are also called *generators*. For this purpose, an algorithm has been developed by Martinez and Silva (1982) and is used in many software tools for Petri net analysis.

*T-invariants*  From the fundamental equation (10.60), it is seen that all firing sequences with a characteristic vector $u$ with the property $W \cdot u = 0$ will not change the initial marking. An integer nonnegative characteristic vector with this property is said to be a *transition invariant*, or *T-invariant*. A T-invariant is a vector of dimension $r$ (i.e., the number of transitions) and is said to be a *proper* T-invariant when $u \neq 0$.

**Stochastic Petri Nets.**  A Petri net is said to be a *stochastic Petri net* when random waiting times are associated with places or transitions. When a waiting time is associated with a place, a token arriving at the place will enable a transition only after the waiting time has elapsed. Similarly, when a waiting time is associated with a transition, the transition is enabled as soon as its input place contains a token, but can only be fired after the waiting time is elapsed. Here, we only consider waiting times associated with transitions and say that the transition has a stochastic or *random firing time*.

In its basic form, a stochastic Petri net is assumed to have exponentially distributed firing times, but more advanced approaches have been developed allowing both deterministic firing times and general firing time distributions. For a more rigorous treatment of stochastic Petri nets, see, for example, Kartson et al. (1994) and Haas (2002).

A stochastic Petri net can be transformed into a Markov model and be analyzed by the methods described in Section 10.5. The *graph of reachable markings* of the stochastic Petri net will be a Markov diagram. This is illustrated in Figures 10.36 and 10.37. Any fault tree can be transformed into a stochastic Petri net and analyzed as either a Petri net or a fault tree, as illustrated in Example 10.16.

***Stochastic Petri Nets Analyzed by Monte Carlo Simulation.***    Quantitative analysis of a stochastic Petri net can be accomplished by analytical methods, but is most done readily using Monte Carlo simulation. Several of the integrated computer programs for Petri net analysis have modules for Monte Carlo simulation, and there are also available Monte Carlo simulators that can be used as add-ons to other programs. Case studies illustrating how Petri nets are analyzed by Monte Carlo simulation are presented, for example, by Briš and Kochaníčková (2006) and Schoenig (2004).

## 10.6.6    Examples of Mathematical Representation

Some example of how simple Petri nets can be given a mathematical representation are presented in the following.

### ▣ EXAMPLE 10.14    Repairable single component

Reconsider the repairable single component in Example 10.9, and add two parameters (a constant failure rate $\lambda$ to the transition $t_1$ and a constant repair rate $\mu$ to the transition $t_2$). The result is a stochastic Petri net, and from the graph of reachable marking in Figure 10.37, it is obvious that this Petri net is another formulation of the Markov diagram shown in Figure 10.36. The marking $m_0$ corresponds to the state 1 in the Markov diagram and the marking $m_1$ to state 2. Using this fact, we can calculate steady-state probabilities for both states of the component in the same way as in the corresponding Markov diagram: the probability of being in the working state (i.e., the probability that the token is in the place $p_1$) is $\mu/(\mu + \lambda)$, and the probability of being in the failed state (i.e., the probability that the token is in the place $p_2$) is $\lambda/(\mu + \lambda)$.    $\oplus$

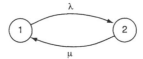

**Figure 10.36**    Markov diagram of a repairable single component.

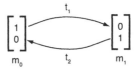

**Figure 10.37**    Graph of reachable markings of a repairable single component.

## ◼ EXAMPLE 10.15    Repairable 1oo2 system with common-cause failure

Reconsider Example 10.11, where a repairable 1oo2 system with common-cause failures was studied. This system can be extended with firing rates for each transition:

- We add a firing rate $2\lambda_i$ to the transition $t_1$, where the parameter $\lambda_i$ is an independent failure rate for a component. This rate is multiplied by 2, because there are two components that can fail.

- We add a firing rate $\mu$ to the transition $t_2$, which represents the repair rate of a component.

- We add a firing rate $\lambda_i + \lambda_c$ to the transition $t_3$, which represents the possibility that the remaining working component will fail because of a common cause ($\lambda_c$) or an independent cause ($\lambda_i$).

- We add a firing rate $2\mu$ to the transition $t_4$, which means that we choose one from two identical failed components to repair.

- We add a firing rate $\lambda_c$ to the transition $t_5$, which is a rate of occurrence of an external event which causes the failure of both components at the same time (also called the common-cause failure rate).

This Petri net with its graph of reachable markings (shown in Figure 10.39) corresponds to the Markov diagram in Figure 10.38. Probabilities of all the system states can be calculated using the standard Markov approach with the transition rate matrix $A$ (10.63):

$$A = \begin{pmatrix} -2\mu & 2\mu & 0 \\ \lambda_i + \lambda_c & -(\lambda_i + \lambda_c + \mu) & \mu \\ \lambda_c & 2\lambda_i & -(2\lambda_i + \lambda_c) \end{pmatrix} \quad (10.63)$$

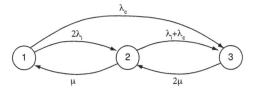

**Figure 10.38**    Markov diagram of a repairable 1oo2 system with common-cause failures.

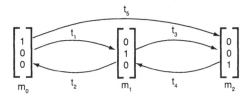

**Figure 10.39**    Graph of reachable markings of a repairable 1oo2 system with common-cause failures.

$\oplus$

■ **EXAMPLE 10.16    Fault tree**

In fault trees modeled by Petri nets, we use an approach that differs from those used in earlier examples. Transitions represent only logical functions (correspond to gates of a fault tree), so they have no probability parameters. We add probabilities/failure rates only to places that represent basic events in the fault tree. In the case of modeling a fault tree, we do not need any tokens in the corresponding Petri net and can hence use a nonmarked Petri net. To obtain the probability of a TOP event of a fault tree, we have to follow logical operations specified by transitions starting with the places representing basic events.

The fault tree in Figure 10.40 can be represented by the Petri net in Figure 10.41. The TOP event is represented by place $p_1$, and the places $\{p_4, p_5, p_6, p_7\}$ represent basic events with the probabilities $\{0.1, 0.05, 0.2, 0.3\}$. The probability of the intermediate event represented by place $p_2$ is an outcome of a logical OR operation of the probabilities associated with the places $p_4$ and $p_5$ and is equal to $p_4 + p_5 - p_4 p_5 = 0.145$. The probability of the intermediate event represented by place $p_3$ is equal to 0.06 since it is the outcome of a logical AND operation of the probabilities of the places $p_6$ and $p_7$. The probability of the TOP event represented by place $p_1$ is again the product of the logical AND (of the places $p_2$ and $p_3$) and is equal to 0.0087.    $\oplus$

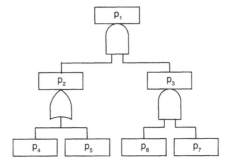

**Figure 10.40**    A simple fault tree.

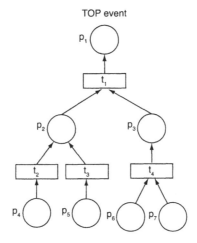

**Figure 10.41**    A Petri net representing the fault tree in Figure 10.40.

## 10.6.7  Extensions of Petri Nets

A variety of extensions to the standard Petri nets have been developed. Among these are colored and timed Petri nets.

***Colored Petri Nets.***    A colored Petri net is used for large Petri nets with repeated parts. The aim of a colored Petri net is to compact these large nets using tokens with colors and functions connected with arcs (e.g., see Jensen and Kristensen, 2009).

***Stochastic Activity Networks.***    A Stochastic activity network (SAN) is an extension of a stochastic Petri net. Gates are introduced to add more flexibility in defining enabling and completion rules, and they are helpful to reduce the size of the models. In addition, and rewards are used to take costs into account. More details about SANs can be found in Sanders and Meyer (2001).

### 10.6.8 Analysis Procedure

As explained earlier in the section, a Petri net is a very flexible tool that can be used to model a wide range of systems. In this chapter we are interested mainly in modeling that can shed light on the causes of a specified critical event.

A Petri net analysis as part of a risk analysis is normally carried out in five steps.

1. Plan and prepare.

2. Construct the Petri net and allocate the initial tokens and weights of arcs.

3. Analyze the Petri net qualitatively to verify the flow of tokens and the adequacy of the Petri net.

4. Perform quantitative analysis of the Petri net.

5. Report the analysis.

Steps 1 and 5 are described in Chapter 8 and are not treated further here.

***Step 2: Construct the Petri Net.*** A critical event often occurs as a change of the system state. The possible changes in the system state can be modeled by a Petri net in several different ways:

(a) The places represent the possible states of the system, and a single token is used to indicate the actual system state. All arcs have weight 1. In this case, the Petri net is similar to a Markov diagram.

(b) The places are in this case representing the possible states of the components, and tokens are used to indicate the actual state of each component. Additional places can be added to represent the states of the entire system. In this case, the arcs can have different weights. The tokens can also represent other features, such as the actual state of the system, one item in a $k$oo$n$ system, an available item in a storage, an available repair team, and so on.

As we mentioned earlier in this section, a Petri net can fully replace a fault tree. Everything we can do with a fault tree, we can also do with Petri nets.

When establishing the Petri net structure, it may be beneficial to use one of the computer programs for Petri net analysis. Most of these programs have a graphical editor for drawing and editing Petri nets. As for Markov methods, there are no strict rules for where to locate the various places on the paper (or screen), but some layouts may lead to a very complex diagram. Examples of Petri nets may be found in textbooks and on the Internet. It may be beneficial to study some of these examples before you start drawing your own Petri net.

A complex Petri net should, preferably, be drawn and tested as modules before these are connected into the main net.

***Step 3: Perform Qualitative Analysis of the Petri Net.***   When the Petri net has been constructed, we can read a lot of interesting properties from the net. If the Petri net is used as a replacement for a fault tree, we get mainly the same information as we get from the fault tree. The P-invariants can be used to find the minimal path sets and the T-invariants can be used to find the minimal cut sets. If a Petri net is replacing a Markov diagram, we can read the same information from the Petri net as we would read from the Markov diagram.

The dynamic effects of a Petri nets can be studied by animating the Petri net and observing how the tokens are moved when the transitions are fired. For very simple Petri nets, this can be studied by pen and paper, but for more complex Petri nets, we need a suitable computer program. Several Petri net programs have modules that can show the flow of tokens. These modules are often denoted Petri net animators or simulators.

***Step 4: Perform Quantitative Analysis of the Petri Net***

*Input Data*   The required input data to a quantitative analysis depends on the specific application of the Petri net. If the Petri net is used as a replacement for a fault tree, we need the same input data as the fault tree, and if the Petri net replaces a Markov diagram, we need the same input data as for a Markov analysis.

*Calculation*   For very small systems, we can construct a Petri net model and do the calculations by pen and paper and hand calculation. For more complex systems, we will need a computer, at least for the matrix calculations. Many of the Petri net computer programs have (i) a graphical input module for constructing the Petri net, (ii) a simulator where we can study the flow of tokens, and (iii) a calculation module that can find the incidence matrix and determine the P- and T-invariants. Some programs also have a module for Monte Carlo simulation of stochastic Petri nets. Some tools (e.g., TimeNET[8]) are more advanced and can, for example, handle stochastic Petri nets with both exponentially and nonexponentially distributed firing times.

## 10.6.9   Resources and Skills Required

The study team must have a good knowledge about the process or system being modeled using Petri nets. For the graphical representation no special skills are required, only sufficient understanding of the notation/terminology of Petri nets and the principles of moving tokens. The mathematical representation of the Petri net requires some basic understanding of matrix algebra. For more complex, nonbasic types of Petri nets and for analysis of special properties, it is necessary to understand the basics of the graph theory with its algorithms, theory of probability, and some reliability theory.

---

[8]For information about TimeNET, see `http://www.tu-ilmenau.de/fakia/TimeNET.timenet.0.html`.

A wide range of software tools have been developed for Petri net analysis. Several of these have a good user interface and are easy to use. An overview of the most relevant software tools is given at `http://www.informatik.uni-hamburg.de/TGI/PetriNets/`.

Another approach is to use a general mathematical program, such as Matlab, Scilab, or Octave. In this case, basic knowledge of using this software is needed. A toolbox for Petri net analysis in Matlab has been developed by Svádová and Hanzálek (2001).

***Standards and Guidelines.***    An international standard for so-called high-level Petri net analysis has been developed (ISO/IEC 15909-1, 2004). Most recently, an IEC-standard for basic Petri nets has been released (IEC 62551, 2012). A large number of guidelines and textbooks on Petri nets are, also available.

## 10.6.10    Advantages and Limitations

***Advantages.***    The main advantages are that a Petri net:

- is based on a universal technical modeling language;

- is able to model almost any hardware, software, and also human (e.g., operator) function and interactions with the environment;

- can be used to model complex processes;

- can be simulated (executed) in order to illustrate and test system behavior;

- has wide and universal use in many different sectors of science;

- has substantial modeling possibilities: static/dynamic time-dependent behavior; stochastic processes, and so on;

- gives a graphical representation that is easy to understand with strong descriptive ability;

- has a mathematical representation that is very powerful for analysis of properties of Petri nets and for solving problems;

- has the ability to model and improve any fault tree analysis, event tree analysis, Markov process, and other constructs from reliability and safety engineering and to modify/extend them with additional properties and information;

- has no limitation on the level of modeling detail;

- is very useful for analysis of sequences and timing of operations and events.

***Limitations.*** The main limitations of Petri net analysis are related to:

- the terminology, since the analysts have to understand the "language" of Petri nets;

- the universality—sometimes the universality itself is a disadvantage;

- the lack of documented application in risk and reliability engineering (the application is growing, but is still limited);

- Petri nets can become very large, complex, and confusing.


## 10.7  Additional Reading

The following titles are recommended for further study related to Chapter 10.

- *Fault tree handbook with aerospace applications* (Stamatelatos et al., 2002b) is an authoritative text on fault tree construction and analysis. It is written for aerospace applications, but is a valuable source also for other application areas.

- *Bayesian networks without tears* (Charniak, 1991) gives a simple introduction to Bayesian networks and is a good starting point for learning about Bayesian networks.

- *Bayesian Networks and Influence Diagrams: A Guide to Construction and Analysis* (Kjærulff and Madsen, 2008) gives a thorough introduction to Bayesian networks.

- *System Reliability Theory: Models, Statistical Methods, and Applications* (Rausand and Høyland, 2004) gives a more detailed introduction to fault tree and Markov analysis than that in this book, but with the same notation.

- *Discrete, Continuous, and Hybrid Petri Nets* (David and Alla, 2005) gives a good and thorough description of Petri net construction and analysis and is recommended as an introduction to Petri net theory.

# CHAPTER 11

# DEVELOPMENT OF ACCIDENT SCENARIOS

## 11.1 Introduction

This chapter deals with the third question in the triplet definition of risk: How can the possible consequences of a hazardous event be determined? An accident scenario was defined in Chapter 2 as a sequence of events from a hazardous (or initiating) event to an end event with undesired consequences. This may also be regarded as a pathway from a hazardous event to an asset. Development of accident scenarios means to identify and describe the possible pathways from a hazardous event to one or more assets. Identification of relevant hazards and hazardous (or initiating) events was discussed in Chapter 9.

A hazardous event may in practice lead to a wide range of consequences to assets (see Chapter 2). Which assets should be considered depends on the objectives of the analysis. The analysis may focus on a single asset or several assets at the same time. Some authors prefer to use the term *target* instead of *asset*. The development of accident scenarios is also called *accident sequence analysis*.

*Risk Assessment: Theory, Methods, and Applications,* First Edition.
By Marvin Rausand. Copyright © 2011 John Wiley & Sons, Inc.

### 11.1.1 Objectives of the Development of Accident Scenarios

The objectives of developing accident scenarios are to:

(a) Determine the possible accident scenarios (event sequences) that can possibly take place after a specified hazardous event has occurred.

(b) Identify existing and possible reactive barriers that can stop or mitigate the various accident scenarios.

(c) Identify external events or conditions that can influence each accident scenario.

(d) Determine and describe the possible end events of each accident scenario.

(e) Determine the consequences of each end event (and accident scenario).

(f) Determine the probability of each end event and the frequency of each accident scenario.

### 11.1.2 Methods for Development of Accident Scenarios

The following methods are commonly used for development of accident scenarios:

*Event tree analysis*
Event tree analysis is by far the most commonly used method for the development of accident scenarios. The method has been used with success since the early 1970s and within many different application areas. Fault trees can be nicely integrated into the event tree to analyze barrier failures. The event tree structure is suitable for quantitative analysis.

*Event sequence diagrams*
An event sequence diagram is mainly the same as an event tree but uses a different graphical layout.

*Cause-consequence analysis*
A cause-consequence analysis diagram is also similar to an event tree, but includes logic gates that can be used to combine event sequences to get a more compact diagram.

*Consequence analysis methods*
To determine the consequences of end events, a wide range of consequence models and methods is required. Among these are models/methods to determine fire loads, explosion loads, distribution of toxic gases, and so on.

The development of accident scenarios depends strongly on the type of hazards and system characteristics, and it is not possible to cover all issues in this book. Since event tree analysis is the most commonly used method, the main focus is on this method. Event sequence diagrams and cause-consequence analysis are presented briefly. At the end of the chapter, some issues related to quantification of consequences are mentioned.

## 11.2   Event Tree Analysis

### 11.2.1   Introduction

Event tree analysis is a graphical and probabilistic method for modeling and analysis of accident scenarios. The method is inductive and follows a forward logic. The resulting diagram displays the possible accident scenarios (i.e., event sequences) that may follow a specified hazardous event. The responses of the system/plant to the hazardous event are illustrated in the event tree. External events that influence the accident scenario may also be incorporated into the event tree. The origin of event tree analysis is not clear, but an early application was in the comprehensive *Reactor Safety Study* (NUREG-75/014, 1975).

### 11.2.2   Objectives and Applications

The main objectives of an event tree analysis are to:

(a) Identify the accident scenarios that may follow the hazardous event.

(b) Identify the barriers that are (or are planned to be) provided to prevent or mitigate the harmful effects of the accident scenarios.

(c) Assess the applicability and reliability of these barriers in relevant accident scenarios.

(d) Identify internal and external events that may influence the event sequences of the scenario—or its consequences.

(e) Determine the probability of each accident scenario.

(f) Determine and assess the consequences of each accident scenario.

Development of potential accident scenarios is an essential element in a risk analysis, and event tree analysis is usually the preferred method for this purpose. Event tree analysis can be used to analyze all types of technical systems, with or without operators.

Event trees may be developed independently or follow from fault tree analysis, where fault tree analysis is used to study the causes of a hazardous event, while event tree analysis is used to study the possible accident scenarios following the same event. As such, the two methods fit nicely into the bow-tie structure.

The event tree analysis may be qualitative, quantitative, or both, depending on the objectives of the analysis and the availability of relevant data. Event tree analysis has been used successfully in the nuclear industry, the chemical process industry, and in several other application areas. Event tree analysis is also commonly used for human reliability assessment (see Chapter 13).

### 11.2.3 Method Description

The starting point of an event tree analysis is a hazardous event that has been identified, for example, by one of the hazard identification methods in Chapter 9. The occurrences of the hazardous event are often modeled by a homogeneous Poisson process with frequency $\lambda$, which is the expected number of occurrences per year (or some other time unit).

***Barriers.***   In most well-designed systems, the possible hazardous events have been identified during the design process and a number of *barriers* have been provided to stop, or mitigate the consequences of such events. Barriers are also called *defenses*, *safeguards*, *safety functions*, and *layers of protection* (or *protection layers*). The barrier concept was introduced in Chapter 2 and is discussed further in Chapter 12.

The barriers may comprise technical equipment, human interventions, emergency procedures, and combinations of these, and may range from simple devices to complex safety systems. Whenever possible, the barriers are designed to be independent such that a failure of one barrier does not influence the performance of other barriers. This may not be easy to obtain, and the principle of independency may also reduce the efficiency and flexibility of the system. In some application areas, it is therefore a trend to integrate several barriers: for example, with shared computers and networks. This is claimed to increase the flexibility of the system and indirectly to improve safety.

***Pivotal Events.***   A simple event tree is illustrated in Figure 11.1. The tree starts with the hazardous event and *splits* at certain stages in the structure. The splitting takes place when specified *pivotal events* occur. The pivotal events are listed above the tree structure in Figure 11.1. The pivotal events may be functions or failures of barriers, but may also be events or states such as:

- Human error.

- Gas is ignited.

- The wind is blowing toward a residential area.

- It is not possible to evacuate the affected area.

- The outside temperature is below 0°C (freezing temperature).

- The hazardous event occurs during the night when people are sleeping.

These events or states are sometimes called *hazard-promoting events* or *hazard-promoting factors*. The event tree will have at least one split at each pivotal event.

***Graphical Representation.***   The event tree diagram is usually drawn from left to right, starting from the hazardous event. The pivotal events are listed as headings above the tree diagram. It is recommended that each pivotal event be formulated as a "negative" statement: for example, "Barrier $A$ fails on demand" or "Gas is ignited."

For each pivotal event, at least one branch splits into two new branches: The upper branch signifies that the event description in the box above the node (illustrated by •) is "true," and a lower branch signifies that it is "false." By this approach, the most serious accident scenarios will come highest up in the event tree diagram, as shown in Figure 11.1. Most event trees have binary splitting into "true" or "false," but it is also possible to construct event trees with more than two branches. An example of such an event tree is shown later in this chapter. The events that start from the same node are mutually exclusive and the sum of the respective probabilities of occurrence must be equal to 1.

It is crucial that the pivotal events be modeled to correspond to the timing and occurrence of events in the accident scenario. If the ordering of the pivotal events is not correct, the results from the analysis will, in most cases, be wrong. If required, a pivotal event may be subdivided into several subevents with their own ordering of subevents. It is also important to remember that each event is conditional on the occurrence of its precursor events.

## ▣ EXAMPLE 11.1   Fire in a production hall

A sprinkler system that can extinguish a potential fire in an early phase is installed in a production hall. If a fire starts, the consequences will depend on whether or not the sprinkler system is functioning and if the workers in the hall can be evacuated rapidly and efficiently. A simplified event tree for this system is shown in Figure 11.1. Four accident scenarios are identified. Scenario 1 may be described verbally by the following events:

$A$. A fire starts in the production hall.

$B$. The fire spreads quickly.

$C$. The sprinkler system fails to function.

$D$. The $n$ workers cannot be evacuated fast enough.

The accident scenarios (i.e., the pathways through the event tree) can now be described by these four events using Boolean expressions.

Scenario 1: Multiple fatalities  $(A \cap B \cap C \cap D)$

Scenario 2: Significant material loss  $(A \cap B \cap C \cap D^*)$

Scenario 3: Fire controlled  $(A \cap B \cap C^*)$

Scenario 4: Fire contained  $(A \cap B^*)$

where $A^*$ denotes the nonoccurrence of event $A$, and similarly for $B$, $C$, and $D$.

$\oplus$

There is no accepted standard on how to draw an event tree, and several layouts may be found in the literature. Figure 11.2 shows a slightly different layout that

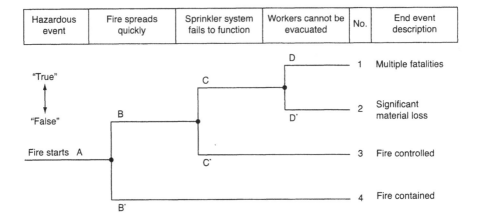

**Figure 11.1**   Event tree for Example 11.1.

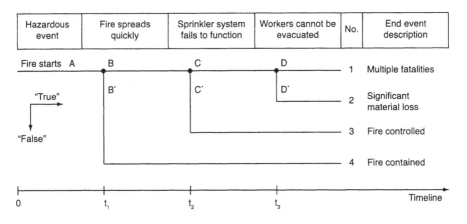

**Figure 11.2**   Alternative layout of the event tree for Example 11.1, including a timeline.

is often used. In Figure 11.2 we have also included a *timeline* illustrating the time span between the activation of the various pivotal events. In most cases it may be impossible to give an accurate estimate of the time spans, but it may sometimes be possible to give rough estimates that can be helpful in the further analysis.

*Multiple Branching*   In Figure 11.1 each pivotal event splits at least one branch into *two* new branches. In some cases, it may be relevant to split a branch into more than two new branches. Consider, for example, a major leakage in a gas storage vessel. The area around the storage vessel may be divided in three nonoverlapping sectors; in the first sector, there is a primary school; in the second sector, there is a residential area; the third sector is not inhabited. In this case it may be relevant to use

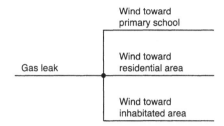

**Figure 11.3**   Event tree that splits into three branches.

| Hazardous event | Wind toward populated area | Wind toward primary school | End event description |
|---|---|---|---|

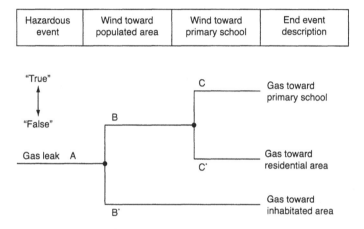

**Figure 11.4**   The event tree in Figure 11.3 drawn with binary splitting.

the three branches illustrated in Figure 11.3. The event tree in Figure 11.3 can also be drawn with binary splitting as shown in Figure 11.4. The approach in Figure 11.3 is, however, seen to give a more compact tree.[1]

***Pivotal Events Analyzed by Fault Trees.***   Fault trees are often used to model the branching from a node in the event tree. Usually, a fault tree is constructed for the "true" output of a split, as illustrated in Figure 11.5.

If the required input data are available, the TOP event probability of each fault tree can now be calculated by the formulas presented in Chapter 10. The TOP event probability for a pivotal event will hence be the probability that the split goes in the upper ("worst case") direction.

***End Events.***   The accident scenarios are developed until we reach the *end event*.[2] What should be defined as an end event is sometimes a problematic question. Should we, for example, stop the development of the event tree when a person is harmed, or

---

[1]Figures 11.3 and 11.4 were suggested by professor **Stein Haugen**, NTNU.
[2]Some authors use the term *end state* instead of *end event*.

| Hazardous event | Fire spreads quickly | Sprinkler system fails to function | Workers cannot be evacuated | No. | End event description |
|---|---|---|---|---|---|

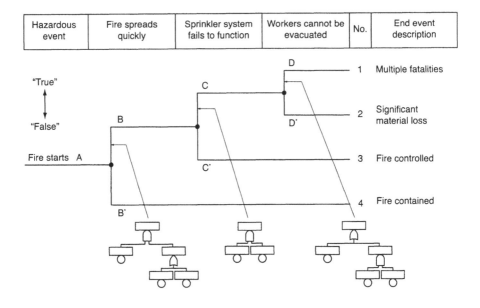

**Figure 11.5**    Pivotal events of an event tree analyzed by fault trees.

should we consider whether the injured person gets first aid, is brought to a hospital, and so on? Similarly, should we stop the development of the event tree when a major explosion occurs, or should we also study the following consequences? These questions should be decided as part of the objectives and the scope of the risk analysis.

The delimitation may lead to the fact that some sequences are stopped at an early stage. If, for example, the objective of the risk analysis is to study the effects of a gas leak *within* a process plant, we may stop the event sequences that only lead to off-side consequences.

The end events are sometimes analyzed further by various computerized consequence models, as outlined briefly in Section 11.6. Due to the binary splitting, the end events will be mutually exclusive and cannot occur at the same time.

***Quantitative Analysis.***    For each pivotal event, the probability that the event is "true" (on demand) is a *conditional probability* given the hazardous event and the specific event sequence leading up to the pivotal event.

To determine the frequency (or probability) of the various accident scenarios is rather straightforward and is best illustrated by an example. Reconsider the event tree in Figure 11.1 for Example 11.1.

Let $\lambda_A$ denote the frequency of the hazardous event $A$: "Fire starts." In this example, $\lambda_A$ is assumed to be equal to $10^{-2}$ per year, which means that on the average, an explosion will occur once every 100 years. The first node represents the pivotal event (hazard promoting events/factors) $B$: "Fire spreads quickly." Assume that we have found that $\Pr(B \mid A) = 0.8$. The conditional probability $\Pr(B \mid A)$ is used to make it clear that event $B$ is considered when event $A$ has already occurred.

For the second node, $C$ denotes the barrier failure "Sprinkler system fails to function." The conditional probability of this event is assumed to be

$$\Pr(C \mid A \cap B) = 0.01$$

The third node is related to the evacuation of the workers, and event $D$ is "Workers cannot be evacuated" (sufficiently fast). The probability of this event must be determined given that a fire has started and spreads quickly and that the sprinkler system is not functioning. We may assume that the workers are panicking and are rushing to the exits—and also that some exits may be blocked by the fire. Assume that we have found that

$$\Pr(D \mid A \cap B \cap C) = 0.30$$

As before, let $B^*$, $C^*$ and $D^*$ denote the negation (nonoccurrence) of the events $B, C$, and $D$, respectively. We know that $\Pr(B^*)$ is equal to $1 - \Pr(B)$, and so on.

The frequencies (per year) of the four end events or accident scenarios in Figure 11.1 may now be calculated as follows:

Scenario 1: Multiple fatalities

$$
\begin{aligned}
\lambda_1 &= \lambda_A \cdot \Pr(B \cap C \cap D) \\
&= \lambda_A \cdot \Pr(B \mid A) \cdot \Pr(C \mid A \cap B) \cdot \Pr(D \mid A \cap B \cap C) \\
&= 10^{-2} \cdot 0.8 \cdot 0.01 \cdot 0.30 \approx 2.4 \cdot 10^{-5} \quad \text{per year}
\end{aligned}
$$

Scenario 2: Significant material loss

$$
\begin{aligned}
\lambda_2 &= \lambda_A \cdot \Pr(B \cap C \cap D^*) \\
&= \lambda_A \cdot \Pr(B \mid A) \cdot \Pr(C \mid A \cap B) \cdot \Pr(D^* \mid A \cap B \cap C) \\
&= 10^{-2} \cdot 0.8 \cdot 0.99 \approx 5.6 \cdot 10^{-5} \quad \text{per year}
\end{aligned}
$$

Scenario 3: Fire controlled

$$
\begin{aligned}
\lambda_3 &= \lambda_A \cdot \Pr(B \cap C^* \cap A) \\
&= \lambda_A \cdot \Pr(B \mid A) \cdot \Pr(C^* \mid A \cap B) \\
&= 10^{-2} \cdot 0.8 \cdot 0.01 \approx 8.0 \cdot 10^{-3} \quad \text{per year}
\end{aligned}
$$

Scenario 4: Fire contained

$$
\begin{aligned}
\lambda_4 &= \lambda_A \cdot \Pr(B^*) \\
&= 10^{-2} \cdot 0.20 \approx 2.0 \cdot 10^{-3} \quad \text{per year}
\end{aligned}
$$

It is seen that the frequency of a specific accident scenario is obtained by multiplying the frequency of the hazardous event by the conditional probability for each pivotal

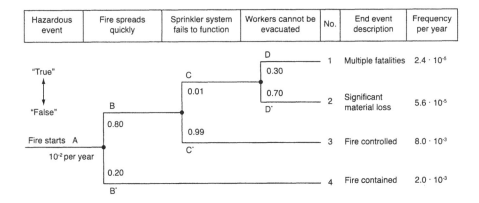

**Figure 11.6** Event tree with frequency calculation.

event along the pathway leading to the end event (of the accident scenario) in question. The result of the quantitative analysis may be presented by adding an extra column to the event tree, as illustrated in Figure 11.6.

If we assume that occurrences of the hazardous event may be described by a homogeneous Poisson process and that all the probabilities of the pivotal events are constant and independent of time, the occurrences of each accident scenario will also follow a homogeneous Poisson process (e.g., see Rausand and Høyland, 2004).

*Remark*: In a more complex event tree, the same barrier may be activated in several (previous) pathways. This means that when the barriers are activated, they may have experienced different previous loads, and this means that we should use different barrier failure probabilities in different event sequences. An example is a sprinkler system where an explosion may, or may not, have taken place before the sprinkler system is activated. Without an explosion, the failure probability may, for example, be less than 1%, while after the explosion, the entire sprinkler system may have been blown away and the failure probability of the system may be close to 100%. ⊕

**Dependencies.** All the probabilities in an event tree are, in principle, conditional probabilities, indicating that there are various dependencies between the pivotal events, and even between the pivotal events and the hazardous event.

Dependencies and modeling of dependencies are discussed in Chapter 15. Some categories of dependencies are:

– The *same components* may be present in two or more barriers. This problem was mentioned in the paragraph above on barriers. If we use fault trees to analyze the barriers, this means that the same basic event will enter into two or more "independent" fault trees.

- *Environmental dependencies* may cause several "independent" barriers to fail. These failures may often be modeled as common-cause failures.

- *Common-cause failures* between basic events in the same fault tree—and also between different fault trees. If we use the beta-factor model (see Chapter 15), this will be similar to having the same (virtual) basic event in two or more fault trees.

- *Functional dependencies* on other systems, utilities, components, or operator actions.

- Dependencies between the *hazardous event* and the pivotal events.

- Dependencies between pivotal events, not per se, but due to the *physical consequences* of a previous pivotal event. The pivotal event "gas is ignited" is not connected directly to the pivotal event "fire pumps do not start," but the fire/explosion following the first pivotal event may, for example, destroy the control lines to the fire pumps.

Some of these dependencies are difficult to handle. In classical fault tree analysis, there are no straightforward ways to account for shared and/or dependent basic events in two or more fault trees, but Andrews and Dunnett (2002) have proposed an approach based on binary decision diagrams that can solve part of the problem.

When analyzing dependencies, it is also important to remember that human operators may initiate recovery actions and in this way compensate for dependencies. This is discussed further in Chapter13.

**Event Trees Analyzed by Petri Nets.** Petri nets, introduced in Section 10.6, are a suitable tool to analyze event trees with dependent pivotal events.[3] To illustrate the use of Petri nets in this context, consider an event tree that has been established with fault trees for each of the pivotal events, as illustrated in Figure 11.7. This event tree has a single explicit dependency in the form of a shared basic event in the two fault trees.

*Graphical Representation* The first step is to convert each of the fault trees for the pivotal events into a nonmarked Petri net, as described in Section 10.6. The TOP event of the fault trees and the hazardous event are next defined as places and connected into a single Petri net, using the construction for a logical AND gate. This process is called *synchronization* in the Petri net language. If dependencies between the fault trees are disregarded, the Petri net for the event tree in Figure 11.7 would be as shown in Figure 11.8.

*Including Dependencies* The dependencies must be carefully transformed into the Petri net. Each *explicit* dependency has to be modeled as a combination of a single

[3]This subsection has been coauthored by **Ondřej Nývlt**, Czech Technical University in Prague, Faculty of Electrical Engineering.

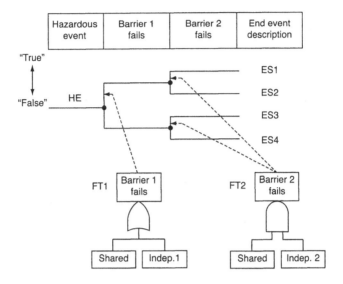

**Figure 11.7**    Simple model situation with one explicit dependency.

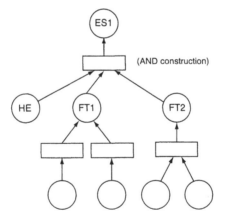

**Figure 11.8**    Petri net representing the event tree in Figure 11.7, when dependencies between the fault trees are disregarded.

*place* and a single *transition* and added to the Petri net for the independent case, as shown in Figure 11.9. The *transition* of this dependency must be connected to all the places that are representing the dependent events in the relevant fault trees, such that it "feeds" the places.

An explicit dependency (e.g., shared basic event) that is input to an OR-gate can be represented directly in the Petri net, while the same dependency, that is input to an AND-gate is slightly more difficult to represent. Since a transition can never be linked directly to a transition; "dummy" places have to be inserted into this Petri net.

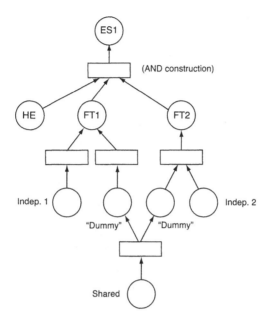

**Figure 11.9**    Petri net representing the event tree in Figure 11.8, including the explicit dependency from the shared basic event.

*Remark*: The reader may wonder why the shared basic events in the two fault trees are not simply merged into one place and why arcs are not drawn directly into the two relevant transitions. The reason for this is a property called *conflict* in the Petri net (e.g., see David and Alla, 2005). When a token is in such a merged ("shared") place, we would have to choose which transition will be fired. To fire both transitions, it is necessary to have two tokens in the merged place "shared." Such a model will not represent our event tree.                                                                                          ⊕

Note that dependent basic events that are included more than once in the same fault tree have to be modeled in the same way. To have the same basic event several places in the same fault tree does not create any problems in this approach.

*Quantitative Analysis*    The quantitative analysis of the resulting Petri net can be done by the methods described in Section 10.6. In most cases, it will be relevant to use a computer program, and we can often chose between an analytical solution and Monte Carlo simulation.

***Fault Tree-to-Event Tree Transformation.***    System functions/failures that are modeled by fault trees or reliability block diagrams can also be modeled by event trees. We will not go deeply into this transformation, just illustrate the approach by a simple example. Consider a system of three independent components that is functioning if component 1 *and* component 2 or 3 are functioning. This function may be illus-

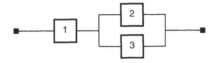

**Figure 11.10**     Reliability block diagram.

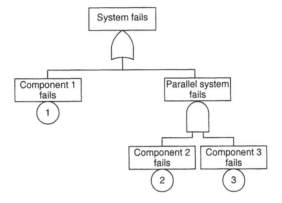

**Figure 11.11**     Fault tree corresponding to the reliability block diagram in Figure 11.10.

trated by the reliability block diagram in Figure 11.10. The corresponding fault tree
in Figure 11.11 shows that the system fails if component 1 fails *or* components 2 and
3 fail.

The probability of system failure when all the three components are independent
is

$$
\begin{aligned}
\Pr(\text{system failure}) &= \Pr(E_1 \cup (E_2 \cap E_3)) \\
&= \Pr(E_1) + \Pr(E_2 \cap E_3) - \Pr(E_1 \cap E_2 \cap E_3) \\
&= \Pr(E_1) + \Pr(E_2) \cdot \Pr(E_3) \qquad (11.1) \\
&\quad - \Pr(E_1) \cdot \Pr(E_2) \cdot \Pr(E_3) \\
&= \Pr(E_1) + (1 - \Pr(E_1)) \cdot \Pr(E_2) \cdot \Pr(E_3)
\end{aligned}
$$

where $E_i$ denotes the event that component $i$ is failed and $E_i^*$ denotes that it is
functioning, for $i = 1, 2, 3$.

An event tree illustrating the various system events is shown in Figure 11.12. We
note that the system has four *disjoint* end events, where two end events represent
system function and two end events represent system failure. The disjoint end events
have the following Boolean expressions:

Scenario 1: $E_1$ (i.e., system failure)

Scenario 2: $E_1^* \cap E_2 \cap E_3$ (i.e., system failure)

Scenario 3: $E_1^* \cap E_2 \cap E_3^*$ (i.e., system is functioning)

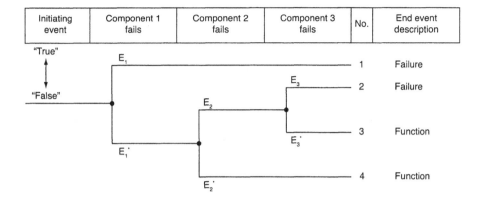

| Initiating event | Component 1 fails | Component 2 fails | Component 3 fails | No. | End event description |
|---|---|---|---|---|---|

**Figure 11.12** Event tree corresponding to the reliability block diagram in Figure 11.10 and the fault tree in Figure 11.11.

Scenario 4: $E_1^* \cap E_2^*$ (i.e., system is functioning)

If we arrange the three components in another sequence, the event tree will get another shape, but we still get four end events.

The probability of system failure from the event tree is:

$$
\begin{aligned}
\Pr(\text{system failure}) &= \Pr(\text{end event 1}) + \Pr(\text{end event 2}) \\
&= \Pr(E_1) + \Pr(E_1^* \cap E_2 \cap E_3) \\
&= \Pr(E_1) + (1 - \Pr(E_1)) \cdot \Pr(E_2) \cdot \Pr(E_3)
\end{aligned}
\tag{11.2}
$$

which is the same answer as we got from the fault tree in (11.1).

**Consequences.** In this context, consequences represent harm to one or more assets. An end event of an event tree is usually a description of the results of the accident scenario, and it is sometimes a complicated task to transform this description into quantitative consequences.

A possible approach is to split the end events of the event tree analysis into various consequence categories, as illustrated in Figure 11.13. In this example the following categories are used:

– Loss of lives

– Material damage

– Environmental damage

The consequences may be ranked within each category. In Figure 11.13, the category "loss of lives," is split into the subcategories 0, 1–2, 3–5, 6–20, and $\geq$ 21 fatalities. For the categories "material damage" and "environmental damage" the subcategories are: negligible (N), low (L), medium (M), and high (H). What is meant

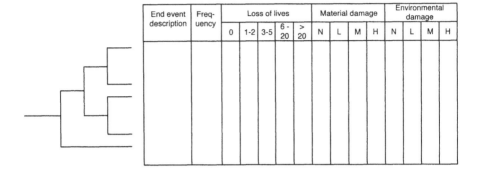

| End event description | Freq-uency | Loss of lives | | | | | Material damage | | | | Environmental damage | | | |
|---|---|---|---|---|---|---|---|---|---|---|---|---|---|---|
| | | 0 | 1-2 | 3-5 | 6 - 20 | > 20 | N | L | M | H | N | L | M | H |
| | | | | | | | | | | | | | | |

**Figure 11.13**    Presentation of results from an event tree analysis.

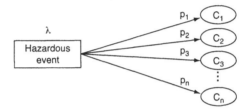

**Figure 11.14**    Consequence spectrum related to hazardous event.

by these categories has to be defined in each particular case (see Chapter 4). If we are unable to put the consequences into a single group, we may give a probability distribution over the subcategories. The outcome may, for example, be that nobody will be killed with probability 50%, 1–2 persons will be killed with probability 40%, and 3–5 persons will be killed with probability 10%.

When we have estimated the end event frequency, it is possible to estimate the fatal accident rate (FAR) and other risk metrics associated with the hazardous event specified.

Summing up the results, we obtain the *risk picture* or *consequence spectrum* related to the hazardous event, as illustrated in Figure 11.14, where $\lambda$ is the frequency of the hazardous event, $C_i$ is the (vector of) consequences of end event $i$, and $p_i$ is the conditional probability of $C_i$ when the hazardous event has occurred, for $i = 1, 2, \ldots, n$. The consequence spectrum was introduced and discussed briefly in Chapter 2.

### 11.2.4 Analysis Procedure

An event tree analysis is usually carried out in seven steps (see also CCPS, 2008):

1. Plan and prepare.

2. Define the hazardous event.

3. Identify barriers and pivotal events.

4. Construct the event tree.

5. Describe the resulting accident scenarios.

6. Determine probabilities/frequencies for the accident scenarios.

7. Report the analysis.

The analysis workflow is illustrated in Figure 11.15. Steps 1 and 7 are described in Chapter 8 and therefore are not covered here.

***Step 2: Define the Hazardous Event.*** The hazardous events are usually identified, described, and evaluated in earlier steps of the risk assessment process. To be of interest for a further event tree analysis, the hazardous event must give rise to several potential accident scenarios. If the hazardous event can lead to only one specific accident scenario, fault tree analysis is a more suitable method of analyzing the problem.

***Remark***: Various analysts may define slightly different hazardous events. For a safety analysis of, for example, an oxidation reactor, one analyst may choose "Loss of cooling water to the reactor" as a relevant hazardous event. Another analyst may choose "Rupture of cooling water pipeline" as a hazardous event. Both of these may be equally correct, but as a general rule, we should define the hazardous event as the first significant deviation from a normal situation that will, inevitably, lead to harm if the development of the following event sequences is not stopped. ⊕

After having chosen a relevant hazardous event, it must be described carefully:

– What type of event is it?

– Where does the event take place?

– When does the event take place?

It is recommended that the hazardous events that require similar treatment be grouped, to facilitate reuse of event trees and make the analysis more efficient.

***Step 3: Identify Barriers and Pivotal Events.*** In most cases, the hazardous event has been identified and anticipated as a possible critical event in the design phase. In such cases, barriers have usually been provided to deal with the event. The purpose of a barrier is to stop a specified event sequence or to mitigate the consequences.

The barriers (e.g., physical barriers, safety systems, procedures, operator actions) that respond to the hazardous event are discussed and classified in Chapter 12. The analyst must identify all barriers that have an impact on the consequences of an hazardous event, in the sequence in which they are assumed to be activated.

The possible accident scenarios, and sometimes also the barriers, will be affected by various hazard-promoting events/factors. All the pivotal events identified must be arranged in the sequence in which they are "activated."

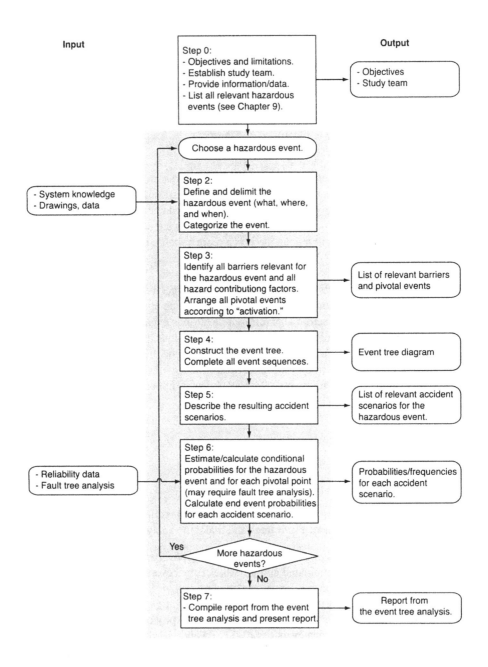

**Figure 11.15** Analysis workflow for event tree analysis.

***Step 4: Construct the Event Tree.*** The event tree displays the chronological development of event sequences, starting with the hazardous event. For each node (pivotal event), the study team has to decide whether or not the associated barrier or factor will have any influence on the specific event pathway. If the node has influence, the tree is split and the two resulting branches are drawn. If not, the branch continues without any split.

If the diagram is too big to be drawn on a single page, it is possible to isolate branches and draw them on different pages. The different pages may be linked together by transfer symbols. To avoid too many branches of the tree, the study team should try to reduce the tree by eliminating impossible branches and branches with negligible consequences.

To assure the adequacy of the tree structure, the study team should repeatedly ask such questions as:

- Does the system operate in this event tree branch or at this point in the event sequence with the conditions specified?

- Does the success or failure of the system influence the end event?

- Could the operation of a given system in this point of the accident scenario lead to success of a safety function?

- Does the operation of this system influence the operation of other systems?

***Step 5: Describe the Resulting Event Sequences.*** The last step in the qualitative part of the analysis is to describe the various event sequences (accident scenarios) arising from the hazardous event. One or more of the sequences may represent a safe recovery and a return to normal operation or an orderly shutdown. The sequences of importance, from a safety point of view, are those that result in harm to assets.

The analyst must strive to describe the resulting consequences in a clear and unambiguous way. When the consequences are described, the analyst may rank them according to their criticality. The structure of the diagram, clearly showing the progression of the accident, helps the analyst in specifying where additional procedures or safety systems will be most effective in protecting against these accidents.

***Step 6: Analyze the Event Tree Quantitatively.*** If data are available, a quantitative analysis of the event tree may be carried out to provide frequencies or probabilities of the resulting consequences. The following data are required:

- The frequency (or probability) of the hazardous event.

- The (conditional) probability of failure on demand (PFD) for each barrier.

- The probability of each accident-promoting event/factor.

The calculations are carried out according to the procedure described in Section 11.2.3.

■  **EXAMPLE 11.2    Offshore oil and gas separator**

Reconsider Example 10.1, which is a part of the processing section on an off-shore oil and gas production installation. A mixture of oil, gas, and water coming from the various wells is collected in a wellhead manifold and led into two identical process trains. The gas, oil, and water are separated in several separators. The gas from the process trains is then collected in a compressor manifold and led to the gas export pipeline via compressors. The oil is loaded onto tankers and the water is cleaned and reinjected into the reservoir.[4]

Figure 10.2 shows a simplified sketch of a section of one of the process trains. The mixture of oil, gas, and water from the wellhead manifold is led into the separator, where the gas is (partly) separated from the fluids. The process is controlled by a *process control system* which is not illustrated in the figure. If the process control system fails, a separate *process safety system* should prevent a major accident. This example is limited to this process safety system. The process safety system has three barriers:

1. On the inlet pipeline, two process shutdown (PSD) valves, $PSD_1$ and $PSD_2$, are installed in series. The valves are fail-safe closed and are held open by hydraulic (or pneumatic) pressure. When the hydraulic (pneumatic) pressure is bled off, the valves will close by the force of a precharged actuator. The system supplying hydraulic (pneumatic) pressure to the valve actuators is not illustrated in Figure 10.2.

   Two pressure switches, $PS_1$ and $PS_2$, are installed in the separator. If the pressure in the separator increases above a set value, the pressure switches should send a signal to a logic unit (PLC). If the PLC receives at least one signal from the pressure switches, it will send a signal to the PSD valves to close.

2. Two pressure safety valves (PSV) are installed to relieve the pressure in the separator in case the pressure increases beyond a specified high pressure. The PSV valves, $PSV_1$ and $PSV_2$, are equipped with a spring-loaded actuator that may be adjusted to a preset pressure.

3. A rupture disc (RD) is installed on top of the separator as a last safety barrier. If the other safety systems fail, the rupture disc will open and prevent the separator from rupturing or exploding. If the rupture disc opens, the gas will blow out from the top of the separator and maybe into a blowdown system.

The activation pressures for the three barriers of the process safety system are illustrated in Figure 11.16. We will get different consequences depending on whether or not the three protection systems are functioning and the system is therefore suitable for an event tree analysis. The hazardous event is "blockage

---

[4]A similar example is also discussed in Rausand and Høyland (2004).

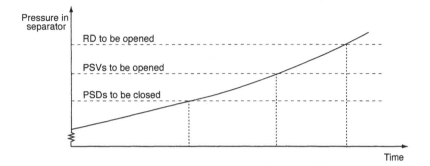

**Figure 11.16**    Activation pressures for the three barriers of the process safety system.

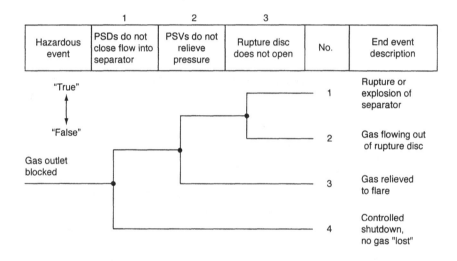

**Figure 11.17**    An event tree for the hazardous event "blockage of the gas outlet line."

of the gas outlet line." A possible event tree for this hazardous event is shown in Figure 11.17. The four accident scenarios are seen to give very different consequences. The most critical scenario, "rupture or explosion of separator," may lead to total loss of the installation if the gas is ignited. The probability of this scenario is, however, very low since the rupture disc is a very simple and reliable item. The second most critical scenario is "gas flowing out of rupture disc." The criticality of this scenario depends on the design of the system, but may for some installations be very critical if the gas is ignited. The next scenario, "gas relieved to flare," is usually a noncritical event but will lead to an economic loss ($CO_2$ tax) and production downtime. The last scenario is a controlled shutdown that will only lead to production downtime.

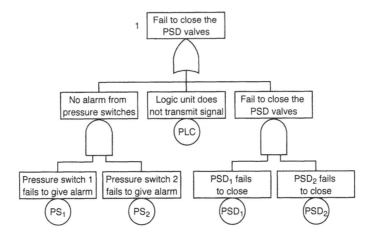

**Figure 11.18** Fault tree for barrier 1, the automatic shutdown system.

Each barrier in the event tree may be analyzed by a fault tree that is linked to the event tree. Such a fault tree is illustrated for barrier 1, the automatic shutdown system, in Figure 11.18. ⊕

### 11.2.5 Resources and Skills Required

An event tree analysis may in some cases be carried out by a single analyst, but it will usually be beneficial to engage a study team of 2–4 persons. The team may use brainstorming techniques in the analysis. At least one of the team members should have experience with event tree analysis. The other team members may be technical personnel who are familiar with the system and its operational procedures. The analysis workload depends on the complexity of the system and how well the team members understand the system. An event tree analysis of a medium/small process plant can, in most cases, be completed within 3–6 days.

A quantitative event tree analysis will require access to data sources (see Chapter 7). Several computer programs for event tree analysis are available, but many analysts find it sufficient to use a spreadsheet program.

***Standards and Guidelines.*** No international standards have, so far, been developed for event tree analysis. A guideline for event tree analysis may, for example, be found in CCPS (2008).

### 11.2.6 Advantages and Limitations

***Advantages.*** The main advantages are that event tree analysis:

– is widely used and well accepted;

- is well documented and simple to use;

- clearly presents the event sequences following a hazardous event—and the consequence spectrum;

- provides a good basis for evaluating the need for new or improved barriers;

- can be used to justify allocation of resources for improvements;

- can identify system weaknesses and single-point failures;

- does not require that end events need to be foreseen.

*Limitations.* The main limitations are that event tree analysis:

- has no accepted standard for the graphical layout of the event tree;

- requires that the sequence of pivotal events has to be foreseen;

- requires that hazardous events must be analyzed one by one;

- does not facilitate incorporation of partial successes or failures;

- is not well suited for handling dependencies in the quantitative analysis;

- does not show acts of omission.

In practice, many event trees are ended before the "final" consequences are reached. This is, however, not a weakness of the method, but of its practice.

## 11.3  Event Sequence Diagrams

An *event sequence diagram* is similar to an event tree, but uses different symbols and a slightly different layout. According to Stamatelatos et al. (2002a), the event sequence diagram is easier to understand by practitioners, but may be more confusing as a basis for quantitative analysis. Every event sequence diagram may be converted into an event tree. A simple illustration of an event sequence diagram is given in Figure 11.19.

## 11.4  Cause-Consequence Analysis

The cause-consequence analysis was introduced by Nielsen (1971) for application in nuclear power plants. Cause-consequence analysis is similar to event tree analysis, but has another graphical layout. It integrates fault tree analysis with the event sequence analysis, and can also combine event sequences to give a more compact tree structure.

   A simple illustration of a cause-consequence analysis diagram is given in Figure 11.20. Cause-consequence is discussed further by Andrews and Ridley (2002), who use a slightly different graphical representation.

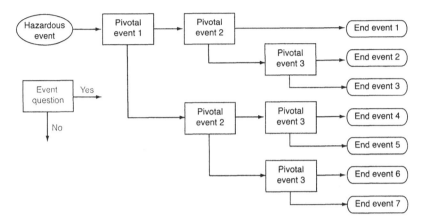

**Figure 11.19**    Event sequence diagram.

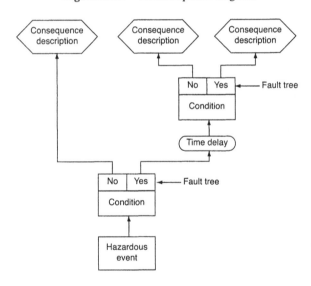

**Figure 11.20**    Cause-consequence analysis diagram.

Cause-consequence analysis has mainly the same advantages and limitations as an event tree analysis. The main difference is that the cause-consequence diagrams are more compact.

## 11.5  Escalation Problems

Some accident scenarios show a very rapid increase in the seriousness of the event sequences—called an *escalation*. In principle, this escalation can be modeled by event trees, but may in practice be very problematic since it is often very difficult to foresee what events may take place. Examples of pivotal events that often result in escalation are:

– Explosions

– Fireballs

– Jet fires

– Pool fires

## 11.6   Consequence Models

A risk analysis may be applied to many different systems, and the end events may therefore have many different characteristics. It is therefore not possible to cover all these consequences in this book.

Consequence modeling involves the use of analytical models to quantify the possible harm to assets caused by the various end events of an event tree. Consequence analysis of accident scenarios in a chemical process plant may, for example, require models related to:

– Fire loads

– Explosion loads

– Distribution of fires (e.g., in buildings)

– Discharge of toxic material

– Dispersion of gas clouds

– Dispersion of toxic fluids in rivers and in the sea

– Toxicity of fluids

– Dose-response models for various toxic materials—for people and animals

– Evacuation of personnel

– and a long range of other issues.

Most consequence modeling today makes use of computer codes—and in many cases, computer simulations. The models are typically employed for the following purposes (e.g., see Borysiewicz et al., 2007):

– To categorize the hazardous event
  – release of flammable material, release of toxic material, falling object

– To determine the mode of transmission to the assets
  – airborne or waterborne dispersion, high thermal radiation

- To calculate effects on the assets
  - thermal radiation effects, exposure to toxic substances, effects of blast over-pressure

- To take allowance of mitigating effects
  - shelter, evacuation, medical treatment

- To assess consequences
  - assess probability of death, injury, environmental harm, economic loss


## 11.7 Additional Reading

The following titles are recommended for further study related to Chapter 11.

- *Guidelines for Hazard Evaluation Procedures* (CCPS, 2008) gives a thorough description of event tree analysis and several other methods.

- *Offshore Risk Assessment: Principles, Modeling and Application of QRA Studies* (Vinnem, 2007). Chapter 6 includes a thorough discussion of event tree analysis.

- *Probabilistic risk assessment procedures guide for NASA managers and practitioners* (Stamatelatos et al., 2002a). Chapter 6 provides a good introduction to event tree analysis. Examples of event trees may be found in several chapters. Chapter 6 also gives an introduction to event sequence diagrams. Examples of event sequence diagrams may be found in several chapters.

- *Risk Analysis in Engineering* (Modarres, 2006). Chapter 3 gives a description of qualitative and quantitative aspects of event tree analysis.

- *Hazard Analysis Techniques for System Safety* (Ericson, 2005). Chapter 12 is a readable outline of event tree analysis with a focus on qualitative aspects.

- *Guidelines for Chemical Process Quantitative Risk Analysis* (CCPS, 2000). This book gives a thorough presentation of many models and methods for consequence analysis in chemical process plants.

- *A guide to quantitative risk assessment for offshore installations* (Spouge, 1999). Chapter 10 of this technical report gives a thorough description of consequence models for hydrocarbon events, and Chapters 14–21 cover other consequences such as blowouts, riser accidents, process leaks, transport accidents, and so on.

- *Quantitative risk assessment (QRA)* (Borysiewicz et al., 2007). This highly readable report has several appendices describing various types of consequence models that are relevant for the chemical process industry.

- *Guidelines for Quantitative Risk Assessment (The Purple Book)* (VROM, 2005). Several consequence models for the process industry are described.

# CHAPTER 12

# BARRIERS AND BARRIER ANALYSIS

## 12.1 Introduction

Most well-designed systems have protection equipment or other features to protect people, the environment, and other assets against harm should failures or dangerous deviations occur in the system. The equipment and features that are installed for this purpose are called *safety barriers*, or simply *barriers*. Several other names are used in the literature, for example: *countermeasures, safety functions/systems, safety critical functions/systems, defense measures, defenses, lines of defense, layers of protection* (or *protection layers*), and *safeguards*. In this book, we use mainly the term *barrier*, but other terms will also be used in relation to methods that center on an alternative term: for example, the layer of protection analysis (LOPA) method.

Barriers have been mentioned in several previous chapters without a proper definition. The aim of this chapter is to define and discuss the barrier concept and to show how barriers can be classified into special categories. A special type of barrier, called *safety instrumented systems*, is described in more detail, and some methods for barrier analysis are introduced. These methods are:

– *Hazard-Barrier Matrices* enter into a simple qualitative method that identifies all hazards in a system and all the barriers that have already been, or are planned to be, introduced to protect against these hazards. The hazards and the barriers are displayed in a matrix diagram that can be used to evaluate the adequacy of the barriers.

– *Safety Barrier Diagrams* illustrate the possible event sequences (i.e., accident scenarios) from one or more initiating events to end events where assets can be harmed. Existing and/or planned barriers are included in the diagram. The barrier diagram is similar to and can, in most cases, be converted to an event tree. In this way the barrier diagram can be analyzed by the quantitative methods described for event trees in Chapter 11.

– *Energy Flow/Barrier Analysis* (EFBA) is another name for energy trace/barrier analysis (ETBA) which was developed as part of the MORT framework (see Chapter 6). The aim of EFBA is to identify all possible paths from energy sources to vulnerable assets and to assess whether these paths have adequate barriers.

– *Layer of Protection Analysis* (LOPA) is a semiquantitative risk assessment method for process risk. LOPA should preferably be integrated with a HAZOP study. The process deviations that are identified in the HAZOP study are developed further in LOPA, with a focus on both traditional barriers and safety instrumented systems. The method will produce a rough estimate of the risk related to the various process deviations. LOPA can also be used to determine whether safety instrumented systems are required as barriers, and if so, to determine the required safety integrity level (SIL) of these systems.

– *Barrier and Operational Risk Analysis* (BORA) is a quantitative method that has been developed in Norway for analyzing the risk of release scenarios on offshore oil and gas installations. BORA uses Bayesian networks to illustrate the effect of a set of risk-influencing factors (RIFs) on barrier failures and other critical events. A scoring and weighing procedure is used to quantitatively determine the effect of the various RIFs for a specific installation. BORA has been developed for a rather narrow application, but the main ideas may also be relevant in a more general context.

## 12.2   Barriers and Barrier Classification

### 12.2.1   Barriers

The barrier concept may be defined as:

☞ **Safety barrier**: A physical and/or nonphysical means planned to prevent, control, or mitigate undesired events or accidents (Sklet, 2006b).

When focusing on the purpose or the function of a barrier, we often use the term *barrier function*. The barrier function of a safety shutdown valve in a pipeline is, for example, to stop the flow in the pipeline.

☞ **Barrier function**: A function planned to prevent, control, or mitigate undesired events or accidents (Sklet, 2006b).

To highlight the system, measure, person, or procedure that carries out the barrier function, we use the term *barrier element*. The driver's front airbag in an automobile is, for example, the barrier element that carries out the barrier function "Prevent the driver's head from crashing into the steering wheel." The protection system comprising one or more barrier elements is called a *barrier system*.

☞ **Barrier system**: A system that has been designed and implemented to perform one or more barrier functions (Sklet, 2006b).

The airbag system in a modern automobile comprises several airbags and hence is a barrier system. Some barrier systems in a process plant are listed in Example 12.1.

**▉ EXAMPLE 12.1   Barrier systems in a process plant**

A process plant will usually have the following barriers related to fire and explosion:

- Fire and gas detection and emergency shutdown systems

- Systems to isolate ignition sources and ventilation

- Fire and explosion walls

- Passive fire protection

- Fire extinguishing systems

- Deluge systems for fire or fume release

- Pressure relief systems

- Evacuation systems

- Fire and evacuation training                                                    ⊕


## 12.2.2  Barrier Classification

Barriers can be classified in many different ways, some of which are introduced briefly in the following.

***Proactive and Reactive Barriers.***    In many applications it may be beneficial to distinguish between proactive and reactive barriers:

☞ **Proactive barrier**: A barrier that is installed to prevent or reduce the probability of a hazardous event. A proactive barrier is also called a *frequency-reducing* barrier.

☞ **Reactive barrier**: A barrier that is installed to avoid, or reduce the consequences of a hazardous event. A reactive barrier is also called a *consequence-reducing* barrier or *mitigating* barrier.

Some proactive and reactive barriers related to driving an automobile are listed in Example 12.2.

■ **EXAMPLE 12.2    Barriers related to driving an automobile**

When driving an automobile, we are protected by a range of barriers. Among these are:

*Proactive barriers:*

1. Electronic stability program (ESP) system
2. Antilock braking system (ABS)
3. Driver training
4. Speed limits and speed control
5. Traffic signals
6. Clearing, salting, and sanding of roads
7. Midroad barriers


*Reactive barriers:*

8. Seat belts
9. Headrests
10. Airbag system
11. Shockabsorbing body
12. Fireresistant upholstery
13. Door locks that can be opened after a collision                                ⊕

***Active and Passive Barriers.*** Barriers may be classified further as active or passive:

☞ **Active barrier**: A barrier that is dependent on the actions of an operator, a control system, and/or some energy sources to perform its function.

Examples of active barriers are: fire alarm systems, fire extinguishing systems, emergency shutdown systems in process plants, and airbag systems in automobiles.

☞ **Passive barrier**: A barrier that is integrated into the design of the workplace and does not require any human actions, energy sources, or information sources to perform its function.                                                          ⊕

Examples of passive barriers are: fire and explosion walls, passive fire protection, and shields in process plants and midroad barriers.

***Related to the Energy Source.*** In the classical energy-barrier model discussed in Section 6.4, a barrier is set between an energy source and a vulnerable asset. According to this model, an accident will take place if dangerous energy gets out of control and there are no effective barriers between the energy source and the asset. In Figure 6.1, the barrier is illustrated as an entity between the energy source (i.e., hazard) and the target, which can have various functions:

(a) Prevent energy from being released from the energy source—or minimize the amount of energy released

(b) Separate the vulnerable asset from the energy source in time and space

(c) Protect the asset, for example, by personal protective equipment

***Snorre Sklet's Classification.*** Sklet (2006b) classifies barriers as active or passive and as physical/technical or human/operational, as illustrated in Figure 12.1. Active technical barriers are further divided into three groups:

(a) *Safety instrumented systems*: safety systems comprising one or more sensors, one or more logic solvers, and one or more actuating units, such as valves, circuit breakers, and motors. Safety instrumented systems are discussed further in Section 12.4.

(b) *Other technology safety-related systems*: active safety systems that do not have any integrated logic: for example, pressure relief valves.

(c) *External risk reduction facilities*, i.e., safety systems that are not part of the study object: for example, fire engines, ambulances, and search and rescue helicopters. For more limited study objects, for example, a reactor in a chemical process plant, facilities outside the boundaries of the study object, such as flood walls and blast walls, are considered external risk reduction facilities.

The classification of active technical barriers is the same as in the standard IEC 61508 (2010).

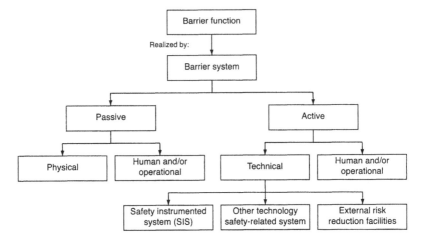

**Figure 12.1**   Classification of barriers (based on Sklet, 2005).

***James Reason's Classification.***   Reason (1997) classifies barriers according to their objectives:

(a) Create *understanding* and *awareness* of local hazards.

(b) Give clear *guidance* on how to operate safely.

(c) Provide *alarms* and *warnings* when danger is imminent.

(d) *Restore* the system to a safe state in an off-normal situation.

(e) *Interpose* safety barriers between the hazards and the potential losses.

(f) *Contain* and *eliminate* the hazards should they escape this barrier.

(g) Provide the means of *escape* and *rescue* should hazard containment fail.

***The ARAMIS Classification.***   ARAMIS (accidental risk assessment methodology for industries in the framework of the Seveso II directive) is a European project that was carried out to support the EU major accident hazard directive (EU, 1996). As part of ARAMIS (e.g., see Salvi and Debray, 2006), four categories of barriers are defined, related to:

(a) *Avoidance.* Removing all potential causes of accidents by changing the design.

(b) *Prevention.* Accomplished by reducing the probability of a hazardous event or by reducing its consequences.

(c) *Control.* Limiting deviations from the normal and also delimiting emergency situations.

(d) *Protection.* Protecting assets from the consequences of a hazardous event.

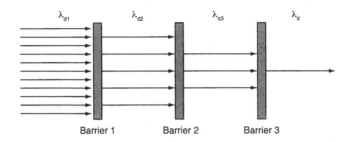

**Figure 12.2**   Sequence of safety barriers.

*Erik Hollnagel's Classification.*   A number of barrier classifications are presented and discussed by Hollnagel (2004). One of these distinguishes between types of barriers:

(a) *Material barriers.* These are physical barriers, such as fences, guardrails, containers, protective clothing, and fire walls.

(b) *Functional barriers.* Functional barriers are active and include locks, physical interlocking, passwords, entry codes, and so on.

(c) *Symbolic barriers.* These barriers require interpretation, such as road signaling systems, signs, markers, instructions, and work permits.

(d) *Immaterial barriers.* Barriers that are not physically present, including operator competence, laws, guidelines, safety principles, monitoring, and supervision.

*Full and Partial Barriers.*   Barriers may be classified as either full or partial. A full barrier can, when it is functioning, completely prevent a cause from developing into a consequence. A partial barrier cannot fully prevent a cause from generating a consequence, even when it is functioning perfectly. An alarm is an example of such a barrier.

*Sequence of Barrier Activation.*   Multiple safety barriers are usually installed to be activated in a predefined sequence. Barriers can therefore be classified according to their sequence and frequency of activation. This is illustrated in Figure 12.2, where barrier 1 is demanded rather frequently (with frequency $\lambda_{d1}$).[1] Some of these demands are stopped by barrier 1 such that barrier 2 is demanded less frequently (with frequency $\lambda_{d2}$). Some of these demands are again stopped by barrier 2, which leaves rather few demands on barrier 3 (with frequency $\lambda_{d3}$). Even fewer, if any, demands will pass barrier 3, and so on. Similarly, the first barrier may reduce the *force* of the demand, such that barrier 2 is demanded with a lower force, and so on.

[1]The figure was suggested by **Jin Hui**, NTNU.

◼ **EXAMPLE 12.3   Barriers in oil/gas wells**

In the oil and gas industry, well barriers are often classified as *primary barriers*, *secondary barriers*, and so on, according to their proximity to the pressurized reservoir. The primary barriers are closest to the reservoir and include the downhole safety valve, the tubing string below the downhole safety valve, and the production packer. If there is leakage through the primary barrier, it should be stopped by the secondary barrier, which comprises the production casing, the tubing hanger, the tubing above the downhole safety valve, the X-mas tree, and so on. If the secondary barrier is not able to stop the leakage, the tertiary barrier will be exposed; and so on. The barrier elements mentioned above will vary depending on how the well is completed and on the current operational status. In Norway, operation is allowed only when at least two tested barriers are in place.
⊕

The main categories of barriers (protection layers) for a process plant are illustrated in Figure 12.3. The figure indicates that if one protection layer fails, there are more layers that can take over, compensate for the failure, and mitigate the consequences. The various protection layers in Figure 12.3 are explained and discussed in detail in Annex B of CCPS (2007).

## 12.3   Barrier Properties

The level of confidence we can have in a barrier should be evaluated based on the following criteria:

(a) *Specificity*. The barrier should be capable of detecting and preventing or mitigating the consequences of a *specified* hazardous event(s). In addition, it should be verified that the effects of activating the barrier must not lead to other accidents.

(b) *Adequacy*. The adequacy of a barrier can, according to Hollnagel (2004), be judged by its:

- Ability to prevent accidents within the design basis
- Ability to meet the requirements that are set by relevant standards and norms
- Capacity, which must not be exceeded by changes to the primary system

If a barrier is inadequate, additional barriers must be established.

(c) *Independence*. A barrier should preferably be independent of all the other barriers associated with the specified hazardous event. Independence requires that the performance is not affected by the failure of another barrier or the conditions that caused another barrier to fail. Most important, the barrier must be independent of the initiating event. Some challenges related to independent barriers are discussed by Stack (2009).

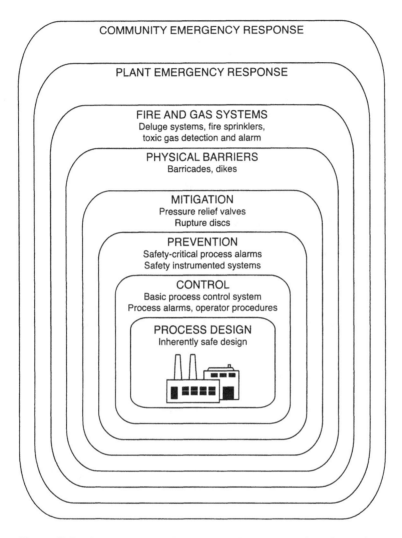

**Figure 12.3** Protection layers for a process plant (adapted from CCPS, 2007).

(d) *Dependability*. The protection provided by the barrier should reduce the identified risk by a known and specified amount. The barrier must thus be dependable, in the sense that it can be counted on to do what it was intended to do. A barrier's lack of dependability is assessed based on its probability of failure in a demand situation, as calculated by using proven models and available data. In addition, the following criteria should be met (Hollnagel, 2004):

- All necessary signals must be detectable when barrier activation is required.

  Active barriers must be fail-safe and tested, by either self-testing or regular proof testing.

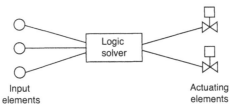

**Figure 12.4** The main elements of a safety instrumented system.

- Passive barriers must be inspected routinely.

(e) *Robustness.* The barrier should be sufficiently robust:

- To be able to withstand extreme events, such as fire and flooding.

- Not to be disabled by the activation of another barrier.

(f) *Auditability.* The barrier should be designed to permit regular periodic validation of the protective function, including proof testing and maintenance of the barrier function.

The criteria above are adapted from CCPS (1993), Hollnagel (2004), and HSE (2008).

## 12.4 Safety Instrumented Systems

A safety instrumented system (SIS) is a special type of barrier system that consists of one or more input elements (e.g., sensors), one or more logic solvers, and one or more actuating elements,[2] such as valves, circuit breakers, and motors. The main elements of a simple safety instrumented system are illustrated in Figure 12.4.

Safety instrumented systems are used in many sectors of our society: for example, as emergency shutdown systems in hazardous chemical plants, fire and gas detection and alarm systems, pressure protection systems, and dynamic positioning systems for ships and offshore platforms. Other applications are automatic train stop (ATS) systems, aircraft flight control system, antilock brake (ABS) and airbag systems in automobiles, and systems for interlocking and controlling the exposure dose of medical radiotherapy machines.

A safety instrumented system may be installed as either a *proactive* or *reactive* *barrier* in a specified hazardous system, which is referred to as the *equipment under control* (EUC). The EUC may be equipment, such as machinery, apparatus, or a plant used for manufacturing, processing, transportation, or other activities.

---

[2]Actuating elements are called *final elements* in some standards.

■ **EXAMPLE 12.4    SIS in automobiles**

An automobile may be considered as an EUC where the ESP system and the ABS brakes are proactive SISs, while the airbag system is a reactive SIS.    ⊕

### 12.4.1  Safety Instrumented Function

A safety instrumented function is defined as:

☞ **Safety instrumented function (SIF):** A barrier function that is implemented by a SIS and that is intended to achieve or maintain a safe state for the EUC with respect to a specific deviation (process demand). A SIS may consist of one or more SIFs.

A SIF is always related to a specific deviation in the EUC. In process systems, this deviation is often called a *process demand.*

*Main Failure Modes.*    There are two main failure modes related to a SIF:

(a) When the specified deviation occurs in the EUC, the SIS is not able to perform the required SIF. This is called a *fail-to-function* failure mode.

(b) The SIF is performed without the presence of a predefined deviation (process demand) in the EUC. This failure mode is called a *spurious activation*, *spurious trip*, or *false alarm.*

■ **EXAMPLE 12.5    Airbags in automobiles**

Consider the airbag system in an automobile. The airbag system is installed to protect the driver and other people in the car if the deviation "collision" should occur. The fail-to-function failure mode occurs if the airbag is not blown up in a collision, and a spurious activation takes place if the airbag is blown up without any prior collision—and may also be a dangerous failure mode.    ⊕

### 12.4.2  High- and Low-Demand Mode of Operation

Deviations may be classified according to their frequency of occurrence. Some deviations occur so frequently that the safety system is operated almost continuously. An example of such a safety system are the brakes of an automobile. Deviations in brake operations will occur several times each time we drive the automobile, and brake failures and malfunctions may therefore be detected almost immediately. The brakes are said to be a safety system with a *high-demand mode of operation.*

Other deviations occur very infrequently and the safety system is therefore in a passive state for long periods of time, as is true for the airbag system in an automobile. The airbag system remains passive until a specified deviation occurs, and is said to be a safety system with a *low-demand mode of operation.*

The boundary point between high and low demand is not always clear, and is often taken to be once per year. If deviations occur more often than once per year, the SIS is operating in high-demand mode, and when the deviations are less often than once a year, the SIS is operating in low-demand mode. The mode of operation will strongly influence how the reliability of the SIS is analyzed, and the selection of a boundary point has therefore been discussed (e.g., see Liu and Rausand, 2011; Jin et al., 2011).

### 12.4.3  Testing of SIS Functions

Many SIS elements are off-line elements that are activated only when a specified deviation occurs in the EUC. A gas detector should, for example, be activated only when gas is present. Such an element may fail in the passive position and the failure may remain undetected (hidden) until the element is activated or tested.

***Diagnostic Testing.***  In a modern SIS the logic solver is programmable and may carry out *diagnostic testing* during online operation. This is accomplished by sending frequent signals to the input elements, and partly also to the actuating elements, and comparing the responses with predefined values. In many cases, the logic solver consists of two or more redundant units that can carry out diagnostic testing of each other. The fraction of failures that can be revealed by diagnostic testing is called the *diagnostic coverage*. The diagnostic testing may be carried out so often that failures are detected almost immediately.

***Proof Testing.***  Diagnostic testing cannot reveal all failure modes and failure causes, and many low-demand SISs are therefore proof tested at regular intervals of length $\tau$. The objective of a proof test is to reveal hidden failures and to verify that the system is (still) able to perform the required functions should a deviation occur. It is sometimes not feasible to carry out fully realistic proof tests, because it may be technically impractical or very time-consuming. Another reason may be that the test itself leads to high risk. It is, for example, not realistic to fill a room with toxic gases to test a gas detector. Rather, the gas detector is tested with a nontoxic test gas that is input directly to the gas detector through a test pipe.

Some actuating items employ an actuating principle that it is not possible to proof test without destroying the item. This is, for example, the case for the pyrotechnic seat belt tensioners in automobiles.

### 12.4.4  Failures and Failure Classification

A general introduction to failures and failure classification was given in Chapter 3. For SIS and SIS elements, the following failure mode classification is often used (IEC 61508, 2010):

(a) *Dangerous (D).* The SIS does not fulfill its required safety-related functions upon demand. These failures may be split further into:

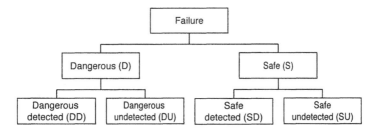

**Figure 12.5** SIS failure mode classification.

- *Dangerous undetected (DU)* are dangerous failures that prevent activation on demand and are revealed only by testing or when a demand occurs.
- *Dangerous detected (DD)* are dangerous failures that are detected immediately when they occur, for example, by a diagnostic test.

(b) *Safe failure (S)*. The SIS has a nondangerous failure. These failures may be split further into:

- *Safe undetected (SU)* are nondangerous failures that are not detected by automatic self-testing.
- *Safe detected (SD)* are nondangerous failures that are detected by automatic self-testing.

This failure mode classification is illustrated in Figure 12.5. The failure modes may also be classified according to the cause of the failure (e.g., see Hokstad and Corneliussen, 2004):

(a) *Random hardware failures.* These are physical failures where the supplied service deviates from the specified service due to physical degradation of the item. Random hardware failures can be split further into:

- *Aging failures*: occur under conditions within the design envelope of the item. Aging failures are also called *primary failures*.
- *Stress failures*: occur due to excessive stresses on the item. The excessive stresses may be caused by external causes or by human errors during operation and maintenance. Stress failures are also called *secondary failures*.

(b) *Systematic failures*. These failures are nonphysical failures where the service supplied deviates from the service specified without any physical degradation of the item. The failures can only be eliminated by modification of the design or of the manufacturing process, operational procedures, or documentation. The systematic failures can be split further into two categories:

- *Design failures* are initiated during engineering, manufacturing, or installation and may be latent from the first day of operation. Examples include

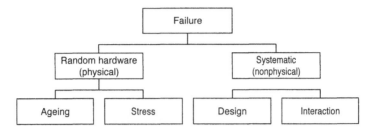

**Figure 12.6** Failure classification by cause of failure (Reproduced from Hokstad and Corneliussen (2004) with permission from Elsevier).

software failures, sensors that do not discriminate between true and false demands, and fire/gas detectors that are installed in the wrong place, such that they are prohibited from detecting the demand.

– *Interaction failures* are initiated by human errors during operation or maintenance/testing. Examples include miscalibration of sensors during testing and loops that are left in the override position after completion of maintenance. Another example is scaffolding that covers up a sensor and thus makes it impossible to detect an actual demand.

The failure mode classification based on the cause of failure is shown in Figure 12.6. SIS failures related to human and organizational factors are discussed by Schönbeck et al. (2010).

**■ EXAMPLE 12.6   Safety shutdown valve**

A safety shutdown valve is installed in a gas pipeline feeding a production system. If an emergency occurs in the production system, the valve should close and stop the gas flow. The valve is a hydraulically operated gate valve. The gate valve has a *fail-safe* actuator and is opened and kept open by hydraulic control pressure on the piston. The fail-safe function is achieved by a steel spring that is compressed by the hydraulic pressure. When the hydraulic pressure is bled off, the valve is closed automatically by the spring force.

The valve is connected to an ESD system. When an emergency situation is detected in the production system, an electric signal is sent to the valve control system and the pressure in the actuator is bled off.

The main failure modes of the valve are:

– *Fail to close on command* (FTC). This failure mode may be caused by a broken spring, a blocked return line for the hydraulic fluid, too high friction between the stem and the stem seal, too high friction between the gate and the seats, or by sand, debris, or hydrates in the valve cavity.

– *Leakage (through the valve) in closed position* (LCP). This failure mode is caused mainly by corrosion and/or erosion on the gate or the seat. It may also be caused by misalignment between the gate and the seat.

– *Spurious trip* (ST). This failure mode occurs when the valve closes without a signal from the ESD system. It is caused by a failure in the hydraulic system or leakage in the supply line from the control system to the valve.

– *Fail to open on command* (FTO). When the valve is closed, it may fail to reopen. Possible causes may be leakage in the control line, too-high friction between the stem seals and the stem, too-high friction between the gate and the seats, or by sand, debris, or hydrates in the valve cavity.

The valve has been installed to close the flow (and maintain closure) following a demand. Failure modes FTC and LCP prevent this function and are therefore *dangerous* failure modes with respect to safety. ST and FTO failures are normally not dangerous with respect to safety but will cause production shutdown and lost income.

Since the valve is normally in the open position, we are not able to detect dangerous failure modes unless we try to close the valve. FTC and LCP failures are hence *hidden* during normal operation and are therefore DU failure modes. To reveal and repair DU failures, the valve is proof tested periodically with test interval $\tau$. This means that the valve is tested at times $0, \tau, 2\tau, \ldots$. A typical test interval may be 3 to 12 months. During a standard test, the valve is closed and tested for leakage. The cause of a DU failure may occur at a random point in time within a test interval, but will not be manifested (revealed) until the valve is tested or an attempt is made to close the valve for operational reasons.

The ST failure will stop the flow and will usually be detected immediately. An ST failure is therefore an SD failure. In some systems, the ST failure may also have significant safety implications.

The FTO failure may occur after a test and is thus an evident failure. It will cause a repair intervention but will have no extra safety implications since the gas flow is shut down when the failure occurs. The FTO failure is therefore an SD failure.                                                      ⊕

### 12.4.5  Voting Logic

To enhance the overall reliability of the SIS, the logic solver is often set up with a voting logic, especially related to the input elements. If there are $n$ input elements, a certain number of them, say $k$, may be required to signal the logic solver to transmit the signal to the actuating elements. This is called $k$-out-of-$n$ voting and is sometimes written $k$oo$n$. Consider, for example, a gas detection system with four gas detectors in a process plant. A 2oo4 voting means that at least two of the four detectors must detect gas and transmit the required signal to the logic solver for this to activate shutdown of the process.

As mentioned above, SIS elements will usually have two main failure modes: fail-to-function and spurious activation. Many input elements are designed to react fast with respect to their essential function (e.g., to detect gas) and may consequently also have spurious activations (i.e., a false alarm). Very often, the rate of spurious activations is of the same order of magnitude as the rate of fail-to-function failures. A SIS with input elements that are configured with 1oo$n$ voting will activate the actuating elements when a single signal is received by the logic solver. For the gas detection system above, this would mean that the process is shut down each time a gas detector has a spurious activation. To reduce this problem, the input elements are often set up with a $k$oo$n$ voting, where $k \geq 2$, meaning that at least two input elements have to be activated spuriously at "nearly" the same time to activate the actuating elements.

A $k$oo$n$ voting configuration is functioning if at least $k$ of its $n$ elements are functioning, and will fail when more than $n - k$ elements are failing at the same time. A 2oo4 configuration is hence functioning when at least two elements are functioning and will fail when at least three elements are failing. It is important to be careful at this point, since it is easy to misinterpret the situation in, for example, a fault tree analysis. A fault tree is used to model how a system can fail, and the fault tree for the input elements with a 2oo4 voting must therefore be drawn such that at least three simultaneous failures are required to produce the TOP event. To reduce the chance of making errors, some authors use the notation 2oo4:G ("good") and 3oo4:F ("failed").

### 12.4.6   IEC 61508

Several standards have been issued for setting requirements to SISs. The most important of these standards is IEC 61508, *Functional Safety of Electrical/Electronic/-Programmable Electronic Safety-Related Systems*. IEC 61508 is a comprehensive standard with seven parts that outline how the functional safety of a SIS should be managed:

Part 1: General requirements

Part 2: Requirements for E/E/PE safety-related systems

Part 3: Software requirements

Part 4: Definitions and abbreviations

Part 5: Examples of methods for the determination of safety integrity levels

Part 6: Guidelines on the application of IEC 61508-2 and IEC 61508-3

Part 7: Overview of techniques and measures

The first three parts are normative, while the remaining four parts provide informative annexes to the standard. In IEC 61508 a SIS is referred to as an "electrical/electronic/-programmable electronic (E/E/PE) safety-related system."

The standard is generic and can be applied to any safety-related application in any industry sector.

*Application-Specific Standards.* A main objective of IEC 61508 is to facilitate the development of application-specific standards, such as:

- IEC 61511, *Functional safety: Safety Instrumented Systems for the Process Industry Sector* (three parts)

- IEC 61513, *Nuclear Power Plants: Instrumentation and Control for Systems Important to Safety—General Requirements for Systems*

- IEC 62278, *Railway Applications: Specification and Demonstration of Reliability, Availability, Maintainability, and Safety (RAMS)*

- ISO 26262, *Road Vehicles: Functional Safety*

- IEC 62061, *Safety of Machinery: Functional Safety of Safety-Related Electrical, Electronic, and Programmable Electronic Control Systems*

- IEC 60601, *Medical Electrical Equipment* (several parts)

IEC 61508 is a performance-based standard. This means that the standard intends to describe the required behavior of systems and processes rather than giving prescriptive requirements on how the systems should be implemented. However, taking into account the extensiveness of the standard, some users may still find it rather prescriptive.

*Safety Life-Cycle.* Central to IEC 61508 is the *safety life-cycle* concept (from concept design, through hazard and risk analysis, specification, implementation, operation, and maintenance, to decommissioning), which addresses the steps necessary to achieve functional safety in a systematic and auditable manner.

The implementation of the standard involves identifying the hazards associated with the EUC and the EUC control system. In the process industry EUC control is the basic process control system (BPCS). Protection relying on other technology and external risk reduction facilities is considered to the extent that they contribute to the overall risk reduction in relation to a particular deviation.

A risk analysis is then carried out to determine the risk associated with the EUC and the EUC control system. If this risk is above the upper level of tolerability, the standard requires that a *safety function* be put into place to reduce the risk to a tolerable level. The safety function will have an associated safety integrity requirement (e.g., a probability of failure on demand), which is a measure of the risk reduction associated with the safety function.

Two concepts are used to describe the desired safety and reliability performance; the functional safety requirements, stating what the SIS is required to do, and the safety integrity requirements, stating how well the SIS is required to perform.

## 12.4.7 Safety Integrity Levels

IEC 61508 requires that the risk reduction achieved is quantified and expressed as a *safety integrity level* (SIL). Safety integrity is a fundamental concept in IEC 61508 and is defined as

**Table 12.1** Intervals of the average probability of failure on demand ($\text{PFD}_{\text{avg}}$) and the probability of a dangerous failure per hour (PFH) corresponding to the safety integrity levels.

| SIL | $\text{PFD}_{\text{avg}}$ | PFH |
|-----|---------------------------|-----|
| 4 | $\geq 10^{-5}$ to $< 10^{-4}$ | $\geq 10^{-9}$ to $< 10^{-8}$ |
| 3 | $\geq 10^{-4}$ to $< 10^{-3}$ | $\geq 10^{-8}$ to $< 10^{-7}$ |
| 2 | $\geq 10^{-3}$ to $< 10^{-2}$ | $\geq 10^{-7}$ to $< 10^{-6}$ |
| 1 | $\geq 10^{-2}$ to $< 10^{-1}$ | $\geq 10^{-6}$ to $< 10^{-5}$ |

*Source*: IEC 61508 (2010).

☞ **Safety integrity**: The probability of a safety-related system satisfactorily performing the required safety functions under all the stated conditions within a specified period of time.

IEC 61508 defines four discrete safety integrity levels, with SIL 4 the highest level and SIL 1 the lowest. Each level corresponds to an interval in average probability of failure on demand ($\text{PFD}_{\text{avg}}$) and the probability of a dangerous failure per hour (PFH), as shown in Table 12.1.

Apart from the quantitative measures, the standard sets out different qualitative requirements for the system design and several other life-cycle phases, depending on the SIL required. Together, these quantitative and qualitative requirements determine which SIL a safety instrumented system can claim upon system startup, that is, the SIL *achieved*.

### 12.4.8 Probability of Failure on Demand

The quantitative measure for a SIS operating in low-demand mode is the probability of failure on demand (PFD), which is related only to DU failures. Consider a SIS element with constant failure rate $\lambda_{\text{DU}}$ with respect to DU failures. If the element is put into function at time $t = 0$, the probability of failure on demand at time $t$ of this element is given by

$$\text{PFD}(t) = \text{Pr}(T_{\text{DU}} \leq t) = 1 - e^{-\lambda_{\text{DU}} t}$$

This probability increases with the time $t$, and the element is therefore proof tested at time $\tau$ to check whether or not it is still functioning. Assume that the proof test is *perfect*, such that all failures are revealed, that the element is repaired to an "as good as new" state if a failure is revealed during the test, and that the time required for testing and possible repair can be considered negligible. In this case the element can be considered as new at time $\tau$, and the next test interval will have the same stochastic properties as the first test interval (of length $\tau$).

The PFD as a function of time can therefore be illustrated as shown in Figure 12.7.

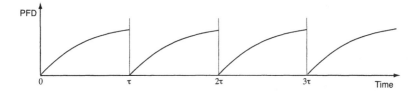

**Figure 12.7** PFD of a periodically tested element.

In IEC 61508 it is recommended that the integrity of the SIS element be assessed based on the *average* value of the PFD. Since all the test intervals have the same stochastic properties, we may determine the $\text{PFD}_{\text{avg}}$ from the first interval as

$$\text{PFD}_{\text{avg}} = \frac{1}{\tau} \int_0^\tau \left( 1 - e^{-\lambda_{\text{DU}} t} \right) dt = 1 - \frac{1}{\lambda_{\text{DU}} \tau} \left( 1 - e^{-\lambda_{\text{DU}} \tau} \right) \qquad (12.1)$$

When $\lambda_{\text{DU}} \tau$ is a "small" number, this result can be approximated adequately by

$$\text{PFD}_{\text{avg}} \approx \frac{\lambda_{\text{DU}} \tau}{2} \qquad (12.2)$$

The approximation is discussed in detail in Chapter 10 of Rausand and Høyland (2004), where several other associated formulas are also derived.

Formula (12.2) is applicable for a single SIS element that is tested periodically and where the assumptions presented above are fulfilled. Most programs for fault tree analysis, for example, use this formula.

When considering a SIS with several elements, it is first necessary to establish the system structure and then assess each element before combining these into an assessment of the entire system. Several methods can be used for this purpose: for example:

– Approximation formulas (e.g., as presented in Chapter 10 of Rausand and Høyland, 2004)

– Fault tree analysis

– Markov methods

– Monte Carlo simulation

Which method is most appropriate will depend on the complexity of the SIS. An important issue related to the PFD of a complex SIS is the possibility of common-cause failures. Such failures are treated in detail in Chapter 15.

### 12.4.9 Probability of Dangerous Failure per Hour

According to IEC 61508 (2010), the safety integrity of high-demand systems should be assessed based on the system's probability of dangerous failure per hour (PFH).

A high-demand SIS is used mainly as a proactive barrier to reduce the probability of hazardous events. Examples of high-demand systems include machinery control systems, ABS brakes in automobiles, and dynamic positioning systems for ships and offshore oil and gas platforms. The PFH of such systems may be calculated as the frequency (per hour) of dangerous system failures. This calculation may be more or less complex, depending on the system configuration (e.g., see Liu and Rausand, 2011).

Assessment of the safety integrity becomes more complex for systems with a "medium"-demand mode of operation, where deviations are occurring more often than once per year, but so infrequently that the operating personnel may be able to intervene and correct failures before a demand occurs. This problem is discussed by Jin et al. (2011).

## 12.5 Hazard-Barrier Matrices

A *hazard-barrier matrix* is a useful tool for identifying and evaluating barriers after the hazards have been identified. The main objectives of a hazard-barrier matrix are to:

(a) Identify barriers that are (or should be) implemented as protection against a specified hazard.

(b) Identify barriers that are able to protect against more than one hazard.

(c) Identify hazards for which protection is inadequate.

(d) Verify the adequacy of the existing barriers and indicate where improvements are needed.

An example of a hazard-barrier matrix is shown in Figure 12.8. In this matrix, the hazards identified are listed in the first (left) column and the barriers available or proposed are listed in the first row. The hazards should preferably be grouped into categories, such as mechanical hazards, electrical hazards, and so on. In the same way, the barriers should also be grouped into categories, such as physical barriers, administrative barriers, and so on. The efficiency of each barrier should then be evaluated with respect to the various hazards. If the barrier is relevant for the hazard, this is marked in the matrix by a sign (e.g., ×) and its perceived effectiveness may, for example, be indicated by a color code.

A completed hazard-barrier matrix shows the barriers that are in place to protect against a given hazard and may hence indicate where improvements are needed. The hazard-barrier matrix makes a good starting point for a barrier analysis and it can be followed up by considering the reliability of the barriers and the risk implications of their failure (US DOE, 1996a).

| Hazard category | Hazard description | Barrier 1 | Barrier 2 | Barrier 3 | Barrier 4 | Barrier 5 | | | | Barrier n |
|---|---|---|---|---|---|---|---|---|---|---|
| Mechanical | Descript. M1 | | X | | | | | | | |
| | Descript. M2 | X | | | | | | | | |
| | | | | | | | | | | |
| | | | | | | | | | | |
| Electrical | Descript. E1 | | X | | X | | | | | X |
| | Descript. E2 | | | X | | | | | | |
| | | | | | | | | | | |

**Figure 12.8**    Hazard-barrier matrix.

## 12.6  Safety Barrier Diagrams

A *safety barrier diagram* is a graphical tool for analysis of safety barriers. Duijm and Markert (2009) define a safety barrier diagram as:

☞ **Safety barrier diagram**: A graphical presentation of the evolution of unwanted events (initiating events or conditions) through different system states depending on the functioning of the safety barriers intended to abort this evolution.

The main objectives of a safety barrier diagram are to:

(a) Identify barriers that are (or should be) present in a specified accident scenario (i.e., an event sequence from an initiating event or cause to a final consequence)

(b) Illustrate the sequence in which the various barriers are to be activated.

(c) Identify safety barriers that are common for several accident scenarios.

(d) Identify hazards for which protection is inadequate.

(e) Verify the adequacy of the existing barriers and indicate where improvements are needed.

The basic elements of a safety barrier diagram are illustrated in Figure 12.9. A safety barrier diagram has similarities to both a fault tree and an event tree. Each barrier is drawn as a rectangle and has one or more inputs, representing the demands for the barrier, and one or more outputs, representing the situation after the barrier has acted on the demands. The outputs can represent successful barrier activation, but also failure or partial failure of the barrier function. AND-gates and OR-gates may be used to connect the branches of the safety barrier diagram.

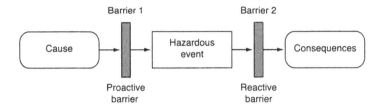

**Figure 12.9** The main elements of a safety barrier diagram.

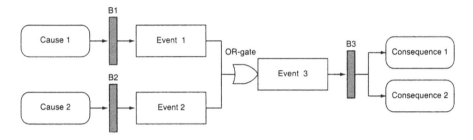

**Figure 12.10** Safety barrier diagram (simple example).

A slightly more comprehensive safety barrier diagram is shown in Figure 12.10. In this example, barrier B1 is installed to prevent cause 1 from leading to the unwanted event 1. In the same way, barrier B2 is installed to prevent cause 2 from leading to the unwanted event 2. If event 1 or event 2 occurs, this will lead to event 3. Barrier B3 is installed to prevent event 3 from leading to unwanted consequences. If B3 does not function properly, this will lead to consequence 1 and consequence 2 with certain probabilities. Many more examples and details on how to construct safety barrier diagrams are given by Duijm (2009) and Duijm and Markert (2009).

***Barrier Diagrams for Oil Well Integrity Assessment.*** Barrier diagrams have been used in the oil and gas industry for more than thirty years for assessing oil well integrity. These diagrams, also called *well barrier diagrams*, illustrate possible flowpaths from the oil reservoir to the surroundings. The barriers in the various flowpaths are illustrated in the diagram in a similar way as in Figure 12.10. The barrier diagram is used for both qualitative and quantitative analysis, and the diagram can easily be converted to a fault tree for further analysis.

## 12.7 Bow-tie Diagrams

The bow-tie diagram, discussed several times in this book, is also a useful model for safety barrier analysis. A bow-tie diagram has many of the same objectives and features as those of a safety barrier diagram, but is more structured in its division between proactive and reactive barriers.

## 12.8  Energy Flow/Barrier Analysis

### 12.8.1  Introduction

*Energy flow/barrier analysis* (EFBA) is a qualitative method that can be used to identify hazards and determine the effectiveness of barriers that are employed or suggested to mitigate the risk from these hazards. The method traces the pathways from energy sources in a system to the assets that may be affected adversely by the energy.

The method, also known as *energy trace/barrier analysis* (ETBA), was developed as an integral part of the management oversight and risk tree (MORT) framework (Johnson, 1980). A brief introduction to MORT is given in Chapter 6. ETBA was developed originally as a tool for accident investigation, but can also be used in risk analyses.

### 12.8.2  Objectives and Applications

The main objectives of EFBA are to:

(a)  Identify all sources of (dangerous) energy in a system.

(b)  Identify the barriers that are relevant to each energy source.

(c)  Assess the ability of each barrier to prevent a dangerous energy flow to the (vulnerable) assets (humans, equipment, or the environment).

An EFBA can be used whenever it is needed to assure that a specific asset is safeguarded against a potential energy source that can impose harm. The EFBA can also be integrated successfully with a preliminary hazard analysis (see Chapter 9) and can be used for several purposes (Clemens, 2002):

– In system design

– When developing procedures

– When planning/judging operational readiness

– During accident investigation

– When making "safe to enter" decisions at accident sites

### 12.8.3  Analysis Procedure

An EFBA can be carried out in seven steps:

1. Plan and prepare.

2. Identify the energy sources in the system.

3. Identify assets affected.

4. Describe the energy pathways.

5. Identify and evaluate barriers.

6. Propose improvements.

7. Report the analysis.

Steps 1 and 7 are described in Chapter 8 and are not treated further here.

***EFBA Worksheet.***    An EFBA worksheet is used to guide and document the analysis process. Several different worksheets have been proposed in the literature. Some of these worksheets are very simple, having only three or four columns. A slightly more complex EFBA worksheet is shown in Figure 12.11.

***Step 2:  Identify the Energy Sources in the System.***    The study team examines the system and tries to identify all energy sources in the system. The checklists mentioned in Chapters 3 and 9 may be useful to avoid overlooking relevant hazards. The results are entered into column 2 in the EFBA worksheet in Figure 12.11, where the type and amount of energy are also recorded.

***Step 3:  Identify Assets Affected.***    For each energy source identified in step 2, the study team must identify the assets that may be affected by that particular energy source. Which assets to include will depend on the objective of the study, but humans and the environment will always be among the relevant assets. The results are entered into column 4 in the EFBA worksheet in Figure 12.11.

***Step 4:  Describe the Energy Pathways.***    The energy pathways from the energy source to the asset must be identified for each energy source/asset pair. The pathways are described briefly in column 3 of the worksheet. It is important to remember that every energy source may have multiple pathways and affect different assets.

***Step 5:  Identify and Evaluate Barriers.***    Existing or proposed barriers must be identified and described briefly for each energy pathway found in step 4. The adequacy of the barriers for each energy pathway is assessed and the result is entered into column 6 of the worksheet. A brief assessment of the risk related to each particular pathway is made and entered into column 7, for example, by using a scale from 1 to 10.

***Step 6: Propose Improvements.***    Based on steps 2–5, the study team recommends improvements to the barriers. These may be related to adding new barriers, improving existing barriers, and even removing barriers. As part of this step, it may be beneficial to consider Haddon's ten countermeasure strategies for controlling harmful energy flow (see Chapter 6).

Study object:

Reference:

Date: 2010-12-20

Name: Marvin Rausand

| No. | Energy source (type, amount) | Energy hazard (energy pathway) | Affected asset | Barriers (controls) | Barrier effectiveness | Risk | Recommended action | Comments |
|-----|------|------|------|------|------|------|------|------|
| (1) | (2) | (3) | (4) | (5) | (6) | (7) | (8) | (9) |
| | | | | | | | | |

**Figure 12.11**  EFBA worksheet.

### 12.8.4   Advantages and Limitations

*Advantages.*   The EFBA provides a systematic process to identify hazards associated with energy sources and determines if current or planned barriers are adequate countermeasures to protect exposed assets. Other main advantages are that EFBA is:

- simple to understand and simple to use and does not require extensive resources;

- systematic, in the sense that most energy sources are easily recognized;

- suitable in combination with other methods: for example, preliminary hazard analysis;

- suitable for corrective action recommendations since the results from the EFBA are naturally translated into actions.

*Limitations.*   The main limitations are that EFBA is:

- limited by the ability of the analyst to identify all the energy sources;

- poor at identifying all system hazards—only the hazards associated with energy sources are revealed, and not all sources of harm to targets are readily recognized as energy sources;

- sometimes confusing as to causes and countermeasures;

- poor on reproducibility for cases that are not obvious or simple.

### 12.9   Layer of Protection Analysis

### 12.9.1   Introduction

*Layer of protection analysis* (LOPA) is a semiquantitative process risk analysis method that was introduced in CCPS (1993). LOPA is principally intended for deciding whether existing safety barriers are adequate, or if additional barriers are needed. Another application is allocation of SIL requirements to safety instrumented functions (see Section 12.4). Note that in the LOPA terminology, safety barriers are called *layers of protection* or *protection layers*.

*Independent Protection Layer.*   The concept of an independent protection layer was introduced in CCPS (1993) and is defined as:

☞ **Independent protection layer (IPL)**: A device, system, or action which is capable of preventing a scenario from proceeding to its undesired consequence independent of the initiating event or the action of any other layer of protection associated with the scenario. The effectiveness and independence of an IPL must be auditable.

More specifically, a protection layer (barrier) is said to be an IPL if:

1. The protection provided by the IPL reduces the identified risk by at least a factor of 10. This means that the probability of failure on demand (PFD) of the IPL must be less than $10^{-1}$.

2. The protection layer fulfills the requirements in Section 12.3 with respect to *specificity*, *independence*, *dependability*, and *auditability*.

All IPLs are therefore protection layers, but not all protection layers are IPLs.

### 12.9.2 Objectives and Applications

A LOPA may provide answers to the following questions related to a specified accident scenario:

(a) Which protection layers are involved in the accident scenario?

(b) Which of these protection layers fulfill the requirements of an IPL?

(c) How much risk reduction can/should each IPL provide?

(d) How much risk reduction can/should all the IPLs provide?

(e) Is it necessary to implement an extra IPL?

(f) Is it necessary to implement a safety instrumented function (SIF)?

(g) If the answer to question (f) is *yes*, what is the target safety integrity level (SIL) of this SIF?

LOPA was developed initially for the chemical process industry but is also used in the oil and gas industry. LOPA is typically carried out during or immediately after a HAZOP study or a HAZOP revalidation. Integrating LOPA with the HAZOP study is advantageous, as the study team will be more familiar with the plant.

LOPA can be used at any point in the life cycle of a project or process, but is most cost-effective when process flow diagrams are complete and the P&IDs are under development during the front-end phase. For existing processes, LOPA should be used during or after a HAZOP review or revalidation.

### 12.9.3 Method Description

The starting point of LOPA is a set of initiating events or deviations that are identified by a HAZOP study. In LOPA, an *initiating event* is usually one of the possible causes of a *hazardous event* as defined in Chapter 2, but may also be a later event in the causal sequence. An initiating event may give rise to one or more accident scenarios. Usually, one or more protection layers are implemented to control or mitigate the effects of the initiating event as illustrated in the bow-tie diagram in Figure 12.12.

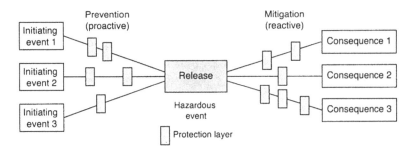

**Figure 12.12**   Bow-tie diagram illustrating the initiating events and protection layers in a LOPA.

The hazardous event in Figure 12.12 represents a release event in a plant. A number of initiating events may lead to this release: for example, "insufficient tightening of the bolts of a flange after maintenance" and "misplacement of gasket in valve housing after maintenance." In Figure 12.12 there are three initiating events, but in a real case, there may be many more. Protection layers are installed to identify and control the initiating event and prevent them from leading to a release. Protection layers related to the two examples mentioned above may be "third-party inspection by a supervisor or area engineer" and "pressure testing before production startup after maintenance." The same protection layer may be common to more than one initiating event. A release may give rise to several consequences, depending on the success or failure of the mitigating protection layers.

In Chapter 2, an *accident scenario* was defined as a sequence of events from a specified initiating event until a specified end event, which can be illustrated in a bow-tie diagram as a path from an initiating event to a specific consequence. In LOPA, accident scenarios are analyzed one by one. It is important that each accident scenario is well defined prior to proceeding with the remaining steps of the analysis. Some of the scenarios in the event tree will have end events with no significant consequence. These scenarios can hence be disregarded in the rest of the analysis.

The development of the various accident scenarios that follow from a specific initiating event may be illustrated by an event tree, as illustrated in Figure 12.13. Only the IPLs are considered when establishing the LOPA event tree. In Figure 12.13, a path from the initiating event to the end event constitutes one accident scenario. Four different accident scenarios are shown in the figure.

Quantitative event tree analysis, as outlined in Chapter 11, can now be used to determine the frequencies of the various accident scenarios if sufficient input data are available. Since LOPA is a semiquantitative analysis, it is not an objective to find exact values for the PFD of the various IPLs. Usually, only the order of magnitude of the PFDs is given, such as $10^{-1}$, $10^{-2}$, and so on.

If the risk related to an accident scenario is deemed to be unacceptable with the current protection layers, it will be necessary to improve the protection layers and/or introduce additional protection layers. By LOPA, the user can determine the total amount of risk reduction that is required and analyze the risk reduction that can be

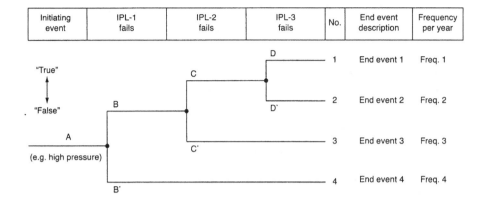

**Figure 12.13**    LOPA event tree illustrating the protection layers.

achieved by various IPLs. If additional risk reduction is required beyond what is provided by standard protection layers, a SIF may be needed. The SIL of this SIF can then be determined directly from the additional risk reduction required. LOPA is therefore a commonly preferred method for SIL allocation to the various SIFs (e.g., see IEC 61511, 2003).

Note that LOPA does not suggest which barriers to add or which design changes to choose, but it will assist in deciding between alternatives.

***LOPA Worksheet.***    A LOPA worksheet is used to guide and document the analysis process. Most LOPA worksheets are similar to Figure 12.14, but minor variations may be found in the literature. The various columns in the worksheet are discussed as we describe the analysis procedure in Section 12.9.4.

### 12.9.4  Analysis Procedure

A LOPA can be carried out in eight steps:

1. Plan and prepare.

2. Develop accident scenarios.

3. Identify initiating events and determine their frequencies.

4. Identify IPLs and determine their PFD.

5. Estimate the risk related to each accident scenario.

6. Evaluate the risk.

7. Consider options to reduce the risk.

8. Report the analysis.

The following description of the LOPA procedure was inspired by Frederickson (2002), BP (2006), and Summers (2003).

***Step 1: Plan and Prepare.***   This step is explained in detail in Chapter 8. Here, we just make some comments on the composition of the study team and to the data required.

The study team should consist of:

- An operator who is familiar with operating the process under consideration

- An engineer with expertise on the process

- A representative from the manufacturer (when LOPA is used in the design phase of the plant)

- A process control engineer

- An instrument/electrical maintenance person with experience from the process under consideration

- A risk analysis specialist

At least one person in the study team should be trained in the LOPA methodology.

The data that should be available for the analysis include:

- HAZOP worksheets or a report from preliminary hazard analysis (if any of these analyses have been used to identify initiating events, causes, protection layers, and consequences to assets).

- Cause and effect charts (if such charts have been used to determine the role of SIFs to protect the process facility against hazards).

- P&IDs.

- Possible safety requirement specification (SRS) for existing SIFs.

***Step 2: Develop Accident Scenarios.***   This step is accomplished most efficiently by event tree analysis. An event tree is established for each initiating event (revealed by the HAZOP study) and only protection layers that are IPLs are included as pivotal points in the event tree diagram. Since the IPLs are independent, the frequency of an accident scenario is found by multiplying the frequency of the initiating event with the PFD or the probability of ineffectiveness of the IPLs. Possible non-barrier pivotal events should be considered when determining the frequency of the scenarios.

The consequences of the relevant end events cause harm to assets (e.g., personnel, the environment, and material assets). If an end event cannot give any significant harm to any asset, the corresponding scenario is disregarded from further analysis.

Several accident scenarios may give the same end event. Each different and unique end event is described, given a reference number, and entered into columns 1 and 2 of the LOPA worksheet in Figure 12.14. The severity of each end event is evaluated and classified, for example, as high (H), medium (M), or low (L) and entered into column 3 of the LOPA worksheet.

Analysis object: Process system A

Reference: Process diagram 14.3-2010

Date: 2010-12-15

Name: M. Rausand (LOPA leader)

| End event | | | Initiating event | | Protection layers | | | | Intermediate event frequency (per year) | Required SIF PFD | Mitigated event frequency (per year) | Note |
|---|---|---|---|---|---|---|---|---|---|---|---|---|
| Ref. no. | Description | Severity level | Description | Frequency (per year) | Process design | BPCS | Response to alarms | Engineered mitigation | | | | |
| (1) | (2) | (3) | (4) | (5) | (6) | (7) | (8) | (9) | (10) | (11) | (12) | (13) |
| 1 | Overpressure in separator not controlled; potentially 10 fatalities | H | Blocked gas outlet from separator | 0.07 | 1.0 | 1.0 | 0.5 | PSV 0.01 | $3.5 \cdot 10^{-4}$ | $2 \cdot 10^{-3}$ (SIL 2) | $7.0 \cdot 10^{-7}$ | |

**Figure 12.14** LOPA worksheet.

***Step 3: Identify Initiating Events and Determine Frequencies.*** For each unique end event identified in step 2, the associated initiating events are listed in column 4 of the LOPA worksheet. The LOPA team should study each initiating event carefully and focus on related questions that start with "what," "when," and "where."

If LOPA is not done as part of the HAZOP study, the team must estimate the frequency (per year) of each initiating event. The frequencies are entered into column 5 of the LOPA worksheet. The LOPA team should then decide whether the initiating event can be eliminated or adequately controlled by *inherently safe design*. If this is the case, a LOPA will not be necessary for this initiating event.

***Step 4: Identify IPLs and Determine Their PFD.*** Next, the LOPA team identifies and lists all the existing protection layers related to each specific initiating event. This is usually done as part of the HAZOP analysis, but the LOPA team should go through every protection layer and check that they understand the layers' functions and limitations. The LOPA team should be careful not to place too much confidence in the capacity and the integrity of the various protection layers (e.g., see Summers, 2003).

The LOPA team then compares each protection layer with the IPL requirements to decide which protection layers comply with these requirements. The protection layers that do not meet the IPL requirements are not considered further in the analysis. The IPLs should be listed and given a unique reference number.

Step 4 should be carried out in parallel with step 2, since the results from step 4 are required when establishing the event tree diagrams in step 2.

The IPLs must be classified into the main groups of:

1. Process design

2. Basic process control system (BPCS)

3. Operator response to alarms

4. Engineered mitigation such as dikes, pressure relief, and existing safety instrumented systems

5. Additional mitigation in the form of restricted access, and so on (this group is sometimes omitted and is not included in the LOPA worksheet in Figure 12.14)

The IPLs listed must next be arranged in the sequence in which they will be activated in relation to each initiating event.

The LOPA team must next estimate the PFD for each IPL (e.g., see Section 12.4 and Appendix A). The total PFD for each main group (1–4) above is then calculated and entered into columns 6–9 in the LOPA worksheet, respectively.

***Step 5: Estimate the Risk Related to Each End Event.*** The frequency of each accident scenario (i.e., for each initiating event) is now determined by multiplying the entries in columns 5–9. The result is entered into column 10, which represents an intermediate estimate of the frequency of the accident scenario.

A rough and intermediate estimate of the frequency of an end event can be found by adding the intermediate frequencies in column 10 for the accident scenarios that lead to the same end event. Adding these frequencies will give a conservative approximation since the initiating events are not necessarily neither disjoint nor independent events, but can occur at the same time, due to a common root cause.

***Step 6: Evaluate the Risk.*** If the intermediate event probability in step 5 is less than the acceptance criterion for this severity level, additional protection layers are not required. A risk matrix may be used to determine whether the risk is tolerable or whether additional IPLs are required for further risk reduction.

If, on the other hand, the intermediate event frequency is higher than the acceptance criterion, additional protection is required. Inherently safe design methods and solutions should be considered before additional protection layers and safety instrumented systems are applied. If inherently safe design changes can be made, column 6 is updated and a new intermediate event frequency is calculated. If no further changes to IPLs in groups 1–5 above are successful, a safety instrumented function (SIF) is required.

***Step 7: Consider Options to Reduce the Risk.*** If the evaluation in step 6 implies that a SIF is needed, the requirement for the associated PFD is found by dividing the tolerable mitigated event frequency in column 12 by the intermediate event frequency in column 10. The associated SIL is then determined from the PFD required.

If a higher or lower value of the PFD is chosen, the mitigated event frequency is recalculated by multiplying columns 10 and 11. The result is entered into column 12. This procedure is continued until the LOPA team has calculated a mitigated event frequency for all the relevant end events.

***Step 8: Report the Analysis.*** This step was discussed in Chapter 8 and is not treated further here.

### 🖳 EXAMPLE 12.7   Oil and gas separator

Reconsider the oil and gas separator in Examples 10.1 and 11.2 with the end event "overpressure in separator not controlled." This is a very serious state that may lead to up to ten fatalities. The severity is classified as high (H) and entered into column 3 in the LOPA worksheet in Figure 12.14. A possible initiating event is "blocked gas outlet from separator." Note that in a more detailed LOPA, several (root) causes of this event may be defined as separate initiating events, but these are not covered in this example. The frequency of the initiating event is estimated to be 0.07 event per year, or on the average one event every 14.3 years in operation. The frequency is entered into column 5 in the LOPA worksheet.

Next, the possible protection layers and the IPLs are considered. Since it is considered impossible to improve the process design or the basic process control system (BPCS), the PFD improvement to these is set to be 1.0. We next assume that an operatoᵣ may intervene and stop the process before the end event occurs. This may be questionable in practice, but in this example, we have assumed that this has a probability of 0.50 to be successful. This means that the PFD of this intervention is also 0.50 (column 8) and that every other demand will be handled successfully by the operator. (Note: The operator does not fulfill the criteria of being an IPL.) A pressure safety valve (PSV) is entered as an engineering mitigation measure in column 9. Based on experience data, the PFD of this valve is estimated to be 0.01, which means that in 99 out of 100 cases, the PSV will be able to relieve the pressure in the separator before a critical overpressure occurs.

By multiplying the numbers in columns 5–9, we get the intermediate end event frequency in column 10 to be $3.5 \cdot 10^{-4}$ per year. This means that the end event will occur on a specific separator approximately once every 2 850 years. This may sound like a rather safe system, but taking into account the high consequence (up to ten fatalities and huge material consequences) and also the high number of similar systems, it will be an unacceptable risk.

Based on a careful analysis, an end event frequency of $7.0 \cdot 10^{-7}$ or less per year is considered tolerable (column 12) in relation to the benefit we get from this system. This means that we need an extra risk reduction equal to $7.0 \cdot 10^{-7}/3.5 \cdot 10^{-4} = 2.0 \cdot 10^{-3}$ to meet the tolerability requirement. This can be achieved by implementing a SIF with a PFD $\leq 2.0 \cdot 10^{-3}$. This means that we have to specify a SIL 3 SIF to be on the safe side. A SIL 2 SIF has a PFD in the interval $10^{-3} < \text{PFD} \leq 10^{-2}$. A SIF with a PFD $= 2.0 \cdot 10^{-3}$ is therefore SIL 2, but so is also a SIF with PFD $= 10^{-2}$. The latter will give a mitigated frequency of $3.5 \cdot 10^{-6}$, which is not acceptable!                    ⊕

### 12.9.5  Standards and Guidelines

No international standard has been developed specifically for LOPA, but LOPA is described thoroughly in

- *Functional Safety: Safety Instrumented Systems for the Process Industry Sector* (IEC 61511, 2003).

LOPA is described and discussed in several books and scientific articles. The most detailed description may be found in

- *Layer of Protection Analysis: Simplified Process Risk Assessment* (CCPS, 2001).

### 12.9.6  Advantages and Limitations

*Advantages.*   The main advantages are that LOPA:

- helps focus the resources on the most critical protection layers;

- provides a common base for discussing the risk related to an accident scenario;

- often reveals process safety issues that were not identified in previous qualitative hazards analyses;

- requires less time and fewer resources than a QRA, but is more rigorous than a HAZOP;

- complies with IEC 61511;

- determines whether a SIS or alternative means of protection is required, and establishes the associated SIL if a SIS is chosen.

*Limitations.* The main limitations are that LOPA:

- may be excessive for simple or low-risk decisions;

- may be overly simplistic for very complex systems;

- is not suitable when it results in the need for a SIF with SIL 3 or higher;

- requires that risk tolerance criteria be established for the LOPA study before the process starts;

- does not decide the specific IPLs that should be used. This decision depends on the experience and expertise of the LOPA team.

## 12.10   Barrier and Operational Risk Analysis

### 12.10.1   Introduction

The *barrier and operational risk analysis* (BORA) method was developed in Norway to analyze both proactive and reactive barriers in the *operational phase* of oil and gas installations. BORA can be used both for qualitative and quantitative analyses of barriers and can take into account operational, human, and organizational factors.

Risk-influencing factors (RIFs) are central elements in BORA and are classified as technical, human, and organizational. Examples of RIFs are given in Table 12.2. It is worth noting that a RIF is neither an event nor a state that fluctuates over time. This section gives a brief introduction to the BORA method and is based mainly on Sklet (2006a)[3] and Haugen et al. (2007).

### 12.10.2   Objectives and Applications

The objectives of BORA are:

(a) To identify barriers on an offshore production installation, including both physical and nonphysical barrier elements.

(b) To identify and describe the role of each barrier in an accident scenario.

---

[3] A main part of the BORA development was done as part of Snorre Sklet's Ph.D. project. The author of this book had the pleasure of being his Ph.D. supervisor.

(c) To identify factors (RIFs) that influence the performance and integrity of each barrier.

(d) To determine the effect of each RIF on the barrier integrity.

BORA is tailormade for offshore oil and gas installations, but the main ideas can also be used in other applications.

### 12.10.3  Method Description

Based on an extensive literature study and a large number of reports of accidents and near misses, Sklet (2006a) grouped the most likely hydrocarbon releases on an oil and gas installation (offshore platform) into seven main groups. In turn, these are divided into 20 representative scenarios.

***Hydrocarbon Release Scenarios.***    The 20 scenarios are listed below and are explained further by (Sklet, 2006a).

1. Release due to operational errors during normal production

    (a) Release due to mal-operation of valve(s) during manual operations

    (b) Release due to mal-operation of temporary hoses

    (c) Release due to lack of water in water locks in the drainage system

2. Release due to latent failure introduced during maintenance

    (a) Release due to incorrect fitting of flanges or bolts during maintenance

    (b) Release due to valve(s) in incorrect position after maintenance

    (c) Release due to erroneous choice or installation of sealing device

3. Release during maintenance of hydrocarbon system (requiring disassembling)

    (a) Release due to error prior to or during disassembling of the hydrocarbon system

    (b) Release due to breakdown of the isolation system during maintenance

4. Release due to technical/physical failures

    (a) Release due to degradation of valve seals

    (b) Release due to degradation of flange gasket

    (c) Release due to loss of bolt tensioning

    (d) Release due to degradation of welded pipes

    (e) Release due to internal corrosion

    (f) Release due to external corrosion

    (g) Release due to erosion

5. Release due to process upsets

   (a) Release due to overpressure

   (b) Release due to overflow/overfilling

6. Release due to external events
   Release caused by structural failure of the containment due to external loads that exceed the strength of the material. Two types of external impact are identified as most common: (a) falling objects and (b) bumping/collision, but these may be analyzed as one common scenario.

7. Release due to design-related failures
   Design-related failures are latent failures introduced during the design phase that cause release during normal production.

*Generic Barrier Block Diagrams.* A hydrocarbon release scenario is defined as the event sequence from an initiating event or a deviation (e.g., wrong position of the valve after maintenance) up to a possible hydrocarbon release. To prevent such releases, various barriers are applied. Sklet (2006a) identifies the most relevant barriers for each scenario and describes each scenario by a generic *barrier block diagram*, as illustrated in Figure 12.15.

The barrier block diagram starts with an initiating event or a deviation that will lead to a hydrocarbon leak if the development is not stopped by one or more barriers. In the barrier block diagram, the barriers are listed in the order in which they are activated. A horizontal arrow leading out of a barrier box indicates that the barrier is functioning as intended, whereas a vertical arrow below a barrier box indicates that the barrier has failed. The possible paths from the initiating event to the end events are obtained by following the arrows in the diagram, as shown in Figure 12.15. Paths that provide the same, or nearly the same, end event are linked to keep the barrier block diagram as compact as possible. In some cases this procedure gives end events that cover several slightly different (sub) end events.

### ▣ EXAMPLE 12.8 Flange maintenance errors

Assume that the production is shut down for maintenance and that a flange is opened for inspection and replacement of seals. After the seals are replaced, the maintenance personnel put the flange in place and tighten the bolts. Possible errors may be that the seal is skewed, the flange is not aligned, or that the bolts have not been tightened sufficiently. If any of these deviations is present, an initiating event may occur. To prevent this incident from leading to hydrocarbon release, the maintenance personnel should perform a thorough check of their own work (barrier 1a), and an area technician should perform a third-party control of the work (barrier 1b). As part of the startup procedure, a leak test (barrier 2) should be performed on the flange before production is started. The possible event sequences that follow the initiating event are shown in the barrier block diagram in Figure 12.15. If at least one of the three barriers is functioning

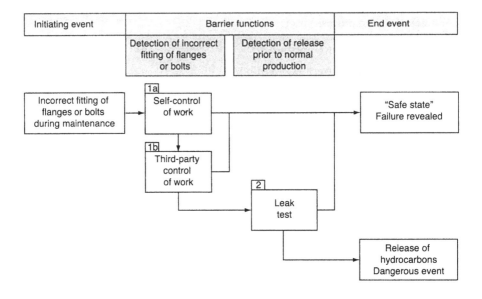

**Figure 12.15**   Barrier block diagram for release from a flange (adapted from Sklet, 2005).

satisfactorily, the end event will be " safe condition." Note that the three paths to this end event do not give exactly the same effect. If the first two barriers (1a and 1b) fail while barrier 2 is functioning, the startup procedure has to be stopped and the flange repaired. This therefore gives an additional loss of production. ⊕

The barrier block diagram is a compact version of an event tree, and the methods for quantitative event tree analysis can therefore also be applied to barrier block diagrams.

### 12.10.4   Analysis Procedure

A BORA analysis is carried out in nine steps:

1. Plan and prepare.

2. Establish barrier block diagrams.

3. Evaluate the safety barriers.

4. Provide initial data.

5. Establish Bayesian networks.

6. Determine installation-specific state of RIFs.

7. Rank the importance of the RIFs.

8. Determine installation-specific probabilities.

9. Calculate installation-specific risk.

10. Report the analysis.

Steps 1 and 10 are discussed in detail in Chapter 8 and are not commented on further here.

Each step must be thoroughly prepared before the next step is begun. In the following, a description of each step is given. A more detailed description is given by Haugen et al. (2007). See also Vinnem (2007).

**Step 2: Establish Barrier Block Diagrams.**  A barrier block diagram has to be established for each of the 20 representative release scenarios (see above). If the physical system on the platform matches the representative scenario, the generic barrier block diagram in Haugen et al. (2007) can be used. If not, the scenario and the generic barrier block diagram must be modified. This will, for example, be the case if the platform has other types of barriers or more/fewer barriers than those in the generic barrier block diagram.

It is important to make sure that all members of the study team understand the scenario described in the (possibly modified) barrier block diagrams.

**Step 3: Evaluate the Safety Barriers.**  In this step, the barriers in each barrier block diagram are considered in relation to the following factors:

– The initiating event (i.e., the event that activates the barrier function).

– The barrier's effect on the accident scenario (if it is functioning as intended).

– The barrier response time (i.e., the period from when a deviation occurs until the barrier performs its function).

– The reliability and availability of the barrier, which describe the ability of the barrier to perform its intended functions with a given effect and response.

– The robustness of the barrier (i.e., the ability to resist certain accidental loads and function as intended in the accident scenario).

In many cases it is necessary to analyze the reliability or availability of the barrier using fault tree analysis (see Chapter 10). The generic TOP event in the fault tree is "the failure of a barrier system's ability to perform a specified barrier function" and must thus be adapted to each barrier in the scenarios. The results of the qualitative fault tree analysis are represented by a record of basic events and a list of minimal cut sets.

**Step 4: Provide Initial Data.**  The purpose of this step is to provide input data for the barrier failure frequencies and the basic events in the fault trees that were constructed in step 3. Such data may come from the platform's maintenance system and incident reports, but in most cases, we must suffice with generic data from sources such as OREDA (2009). The data used in the analysis should, as far as possible, be documented in a data dossier (see Chapter 7).

**Table 12.2**   Survey of relevant risk-influencing factors (RIFs).

| | |
|---|---|
| *Human factors* | *Administrative factors* |
|   &minus; Competence and skills |   &minus; Procedures |
|   &minus; Workload and stress |   &minus; Work permit |
|   &minus; Working environment |   &minus; Available task descriptions |
|   &minus; Fatigue |   &minus; Documentation |
| *Task-related factors* | *Organizational factors* |
|   &minus; Methodology |   &minus; Programs |
|   &minus; Task supervision |   &minus; Work practice |
|   &minus; Task complexity |   &minus; Supervision |
|   &minus; Time pressure |   &minus; Communication |
|   &minus; Tools |   &minus; Tidiness and cleaning |
|   &minus; Spare parts |   &minus; Support systems |
| *Technical factors* |   &minus; Acceptance criteria |
|   &minus; Equipment design |   &minus; Simultaneous activities |
|   &minus; Material properties |   &minus; Management of changes |
|   &minus; Process complexity | |
|   &minus; Man-machine interface | |
|   &minus; Maintainability/accessibility | |
|   &minus; System feedback | |
|   &minus; Technical condition | |

A detailed description of each RIF is given by Haugen et al. (2007).

***Step 5: Establish Bayesian Networks.***   In this step, Bayesian networks (see Chapter 10) are used to illustrate the influence of the various RIFs on each barrier function. A list of relevant RIFs is given in Table 12.2 and discussed further by Haugen et al. (2007).

For simple barriers, the Bayesian network may show the RIFs that influence barrier failure directly. For other, more complex barriers, it will first be necessary to construct a fault tree and then identify the RIFs that influence the basic events in the fault tree. To avoid too extensive analysis, the number of RIFs applied in each Bayesian network should be relatively small (e.g., $\leq 6$).

A Bayesian network for the barrier failure "Area technician does not detect flange failure" in Example 12.8 is shown in Figure 12.16. To determine which RIFs have

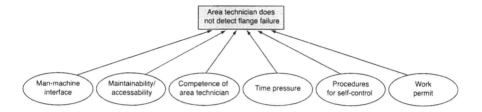

**Figure 12.16** Bayesian network for the event "Area technician does not detect flange failure" (adapted from Aven et al., 2006).

**Table 12.3** State scores for RIFs.

| Score | Explanation |
|-------|-------------|
| A | Status corresponds to the best standard in the industry |
| B | Status corresponds to a level better than the industry average |
| C | Status corresponds to the industry average |
| D | Status corresponds to a level slightly worse than the industry average |
| E | Status corresponds to a level considerably worse than the industry average |
| F | Status corresponds to the worst practice in the industry |

*Source*: Data from Haugen et al. (2007).

an impact on a specific event, it is recommended to start with the RIFs in Table 12.2 and choose those that are regarded as most relevant to the event considered.

***Step 6: Determine the Installation-Specific State of the RIFs.*** In this step, the state of each RIF found in step 5 is evaluated for the actual installation and given a score from A to F, based on Table 12.3.

The assessment of the state of the RIFs can be done in several ways: for example, by structured interviews of key personnel, observations of the work, surveys, and the use of checklists. Different performance standards can be used further to measure the condition of the barriers in relation to the minimum requirements and best practice. Accident/incident investigation reports can also provide useful information.

***Step 7: Rank the Importance of the RIFs.*** When the installation-specific state of RIFs is mapped, the study team must determine the *importance* of the RIFs, that is, their effect on the probabilities or frequencies of the barrier failures or the basic events in the fault tree. The importance ranking is done by means of expert judgments, and will usually involve a general discussion between staff and analysts. The following procedure may be used:

– Identify the most important RIF based on general discussions.

- Give this RIF a relative weight of 10.

- Compare the importance of the other RIFs with the most important and give them weights according to the scale 10–8–6–4–2.

- Discuss and assess whether the results are realistic.

Afterward, the importance weights are normalized such that their sum is 1, or 100%, as illustrated in Example 12.9, where $\omega_i$ is the normalized importance weight of RIF$_i$, for $i = 1, 2, \ldots, n$.

**▣ EXAMPLE 12.9   The importance of RIFs**

Consider the Bayesian network in Figure 12.3 and assume that we have found the following importance weights:

| $i$ | RIF$_i$ | Weight$_i$ | Adjusted weight, $\omega_i$ |
|---|---|---|---|
| 1 | Man-machine interface | 2 | 5.56% |
| 2 | Maintainability/accessibility | 6 | 16.67% |
| 3 | Competence of area technician | 6 | 16.67% |
| 4 | Time pressure | 10 | 27.78% |
| 5 | Control procedure | 8 | 22.22% |
| 6 | Work permit | 4 | 11.11% |
| | Sum | 36 | 100% |

The adjusted weights $\omega_i$, adding up to 100%, are given in the last column. Note that the importance weights in this example are only an illustration and are not based on a thorough analysis.                                                                    $\oplus$

**Step 8: Determine Installation-Specific Probabilities.**   The data found in step 4 are mainly generic data reflecting industry averages. The purpose of step 8 is to adapt these data to make them more relevant to the installation being analyzed. This adaptation is done using the results from steps 5–7. The data we arrive at by this approach are called *installation-specific data.*

Consider an event $H$, which can be either a barrier failure or a basic event of a fault tree that describes the causes of a barrier failure. Let $\Pr(H)_{\mathrm{gen}}$ denote the probability of the event $H$ as obtained by using the generic data from step 4.

The installation-specific probability of $H$ is denoted $\Pr(H)_{\mathrm{inst}}$ and is expressed in BORA as

$$\Pr(H)_{\mathrm{inst}} = \Pr(H)_{\mathrm{gen}} \cdot \sum_{i=1}^{n} \omega_i \cdot Q_i \qquad (12.3)$$

where $n$ is the number of RIFs used in the Bayesian network in step 5, $\omega_i$ is the normalized importance weight of $RIF_i$ from step 7, and $Q_i$ is a value expressing the installation-specific state of $RIF_i$. The value of $Q_i$ is obtained using the following procedure (Sklet et al., 2006):

1. Determine the lowest relevant probability of $H$, $\Pr(H)_{\text{low}}$, by expert judgment.

2. Determine the highest relevant probability of $H$, $\Pr(H)_{\text{high}}$, by expert judgment.

3. For each $RIF_i$, where $i = 1, 2, \ldots, n$, let

$$Q_i(s) = \begin{cases} \Pr(H)_{\text{low}}/\Pr(H)_{\text{gen}} & \text{if } s = A \\ 1 & \text{if } s = C \\ \Pr(H)_{\text{high}}/\Pr(H)_{\text{gen}} & \text{if } s = F \end{cases}$$

where $s$ denotes the score the RIF was given in step 6. This means that $s$ can take the values A, B, ..., F.

### ⬛ EXAMPLE 12.10    Flange maintenance reconsidered

Reconsider Example 12.9 and assume that based on generic data sources, the probability of the event $H$: "Area technician does not detect flange failure" is found to be $\Pr(H)_{\text{gen}} = 0.40$. This means that the area technician detects only 60% of the flange failures, or 3 out of 5 failures.

Consider, for example, $RIF_3$: "Competence of area technician", and assume that a group of experts has found that if this RIF had the best state that can be found in the industry (A), the probability would be $\Pr(H)_{\text{low}} = 0.30$. If this RIF had the worst state found in the industry (F), the probability would be $\Pr(H)_{\text{high}} = 0.55$. In this evaluation, it is assumed that all the other RIFs are kept constant.

If $RIF_3$ is given score A, then $Q_3 = \Pr_{\text{low}} / \Pr_{\text{gen}} = 0.35/0.40 = 0.875$. If $RIF_3$ is given score C, then $Q_3 = 1$, and if $RIF_3$ is given score F, then $Q_3 = \Pr_{\text{high}} / \Pr_{\text{gen}} = 0.55/0.40 = 1.375$. To calculate the $Q$-factors for the scores B, D, and E, Aven et al. (2006) recommend a linear "interpolation." This means that the $Q$-factor for score B is the average value of the $Q$-factors for the scores A and C, which in this example is $(0.875 + 1)/2 \approx 0.938$. To calculate the $Q$-factors for the scores D and E, we divide the difference between the $Q$-factor for score F and the $Q$-factor for score C by 3 and get $\Delta = (1.375 - 1)/3 = 0.125$. The $Q$-factor for score D is found as the $Q$-factor of score C plus $\Delta$, that is, $1 + \Delta = 1.125$, while the $Q$-factor for score E is found as the $Q$-factor for score C plus twice the value of $\Delta$, that is, $1 + 2\Delta = 1.250$.

The $Q$-factors for $RIF_3$: "Area technician does not detect flange failure" for the various state scores are therefore found to be:

| State score | $Q$-factor |
|:---:|:---:|
| A | 0.875 |
| B | 0.938 |
| C | 1.000 |
| D | 1.125 |
| E | 1.250 |
| F | 1.375 |

⊕

*Remark*: Haugen et al. (2007) do not provide adequate justification for selecting the weighing factors as shown in Example 12.10. It is, however, argued that this procedure gives sufficiently accurate results to give great practical benefit.

Another problem is related to how we determine $Pr(H)_{low}$ and $Pr(H)_{high}$ for a RIF. As explained above, the other RIFs are kept unchanged when a specific RIF is changed to the best and then the worst condition in the industry. In practice this will be problematic because the RIFs can have a mutual dependency. Such dependence will also cause problems in other parts of the analysis.                                ⊕

*Step 9:   Calculate the Installation-Specific Risk.*   The final step in the analysis is to calculate the installation-specific risk of hydrocarbon release, by using the installation-specific probabilities from step 8 in the risk model. The revised risk takes into account the technical, human, operational, and organizational aspects of the RIFs.

### 12.10.5   Resources and Skills Required

The BORA method is costly because it requires extensive knowledge of the complex issues at oil and gas installations, which requires personnel with system knowledge to cooperate with risk analysts.

### 12.10.6   Advantages and Limitations

*Advantages.*   The main advantages are that BORA:

- can be used to determine the installation-specific risk;

- contributes to a better understanding of the safety barriers;

- gives a better insight about the RIFs and their influence on the barrier dependability and integrity.

***Limitations.***   The main limitations are that BORA:

- requires access to extensive data, which may not exist in current databases;

- determines the importance of the RIFs based on the weights 10–8–6–4–2 without any proper justification;

- determines the weighing factors $Q_i$ without any proper justification. The procedure may seem arbitrary, but it is claimed that this does not reduce the applicability and value of the method.

## 12.11   Additional Reading

The following titles are recommended for further study related to Chapter 12.

- *Safety barriers: Definition, classification, and performance* (Sklet, 2006b) provides a good survey of the theory related to safety barriers.

- *Barriers and Accident Prevention* (Hollnagel, 2004) is an important source on barrier theory and analysis.

- *Safety Instrumented Systems in the Oil and Gas Industry: Concepts and Methods for Safety and Reliability Assessments in Design and Operation* (Lundteigen, 2009). This Ph.D. thesis gives a thorough description of the main issues related to safety integrity assessment of low-demand SISs.

- *System Reliability Theory: Models, Statistical Methods, and Applications* (Rausand and Høyland, 2004). Chapter 10 of this book gives a thorough introduction to quantitative analysis of low-demand SISs.

- *Basic Guide to System Safety* (Vincoli, 2006). Chapter 9 of this book gives an introduction to energy trace and barrier analysis (ETBA) in the format of the MORT approach.

- *Hazard Analysis Techniques for System Safety* (Ericson, 2005). Chapter 19 of the book gives an introduction to ETBA and refers to the technique as Barrier analysis.

- *Lines of defence/layers of protection analysis in the COMAH context* (Franks, 2003) is an important source of information about LOPA.

- *Operational risk analysis: Total analysis of physical and non-physical barriers* (Haugen et al., 2007). This technical report gives a thorough description of the BORA approach.

- *Offshore Risk Assessment: Principles, Modeling and Application of QRA Studies* (Vinnem, 2007) discusses several approaches to barrier analysis.

# CHAPTER 13

# HUMAN RELIABILITY ANALYSIS

> The nice thing about being a psychologist is that you can sit in your ivory tower and not be forced to quantify human errors. Unfortunately, that is ultimately what HRA is all about.
> —E. M. Dougherty, Jr. (1990)

## 13.1 Introduction

Humans are involved in all life phases of most technical systems, from design through construction, operation, management, maintenance, and system upgrade, to decommissioning/disposal. Humans tend to make errors and it is often said that *"to err is human."* As humans, we are generally more complex than technical systems and it is therefore difficult to predict the types of errors that we may commit.

A feature that makes us very different from technological systems is our ability to detect and recover our own errors as well as errors committed by other persons or by

**Knut Øien**, SINTEF/NTNU, has made important contributions to this chapter.

technical systems. Bearing this in mind, we may claim that human actions contribute significantly to risk—but also to *safety*.

*Human errors* are often claimed to account for somewhere between 60% and 90% of all accidents in industry and transport. Such a statement may be counterproductive. Since humans are involved in all phases of a system's life cycle, almost all accidents can be traced back to some kind of human error or inadequate decisions in an earlier phase. This view is supported by the following quotation:

> Since no system has ever built itself, since very few systems operate themselves, and since furthermore no systems maintain themselves, the search for a human in the path of events leading to failure is bound to succeed. [...] The assumption that a human has failed will therefore always be vindicated (Hollnagel, 2005).

Another statement explaining the high percentage of human errors as *attributed* causes of accidents is:

> Formal accident investigations usually start with an assumption that the operator must have failed, and if this attribution can be made, that is the end of serious inquiry (Perrow, 1984).

In this book, we are interested mainly in errors that can be committed by users or operators of technical systems, to identify potential *human error modes* and *human error probabilities* (HEPs). We tacitly assume that in the same way that technical equipment can fail in a system, so can a human operator commit errors. We realize that this is a simplistic view and that humans are much more complex than technical components. It is, however, beyond the scope of this book to go deeper into all aspects of human behavior, and the reader is advised to consult the more specialized literature (e.g., see Reason, 1990, 2008; Hollnagel, 1998; Spurgin, 2009; Pesme and Le Bot, 2010).

The terms *human error* and *human reliability* may be defined as:

☞ **Human error**: An out-of-tolerance action, or deviation from the norm, where the limits of acceptable performance are defined by the system. These situations can arise from problems in sequencing, timing, knowledge, interfaces, procedures, and other sources (NUREG/CR-6883, 2005).

☞ **Human reliability**: The probability that a person: (i) correctly performs some system-required activity in a required time period (if time is a limiting factor) and (ii) performs no extraneous activity that can degrade the system. *Human unreliability* is the opposite of this definition (IMO, 2002).

There is a vast literature on human errors and human reliability. Some sources recommended for further study are listed at the end of the chapter. The objective of this chapter is not to give a full account of the literature on human errors and human reliability, but rather, to outline some approaches that can be an adequate part of a quantitative risk assessment.

### 13.1.1 Human Reliability Analysis

A human reliability analysis (HRA) is a systematic identification and evaluation of the possible errors that may be made by operators, maintenance personnel, and other personnel in the system. The main objectives of an HRA are (NEA, 2004a):

(a) To ensure that the key human interactions are systematically identified, analyzed, and incorporated into the risk analysis in a traceable manner.

(b) To quantify the probabilities of their success and failure.

(c) To provide insights that may improve human performance. Examples include improvements in the man-machine interface, procedures and training, better match between task demands and human capabilities, increasing prospects for successful recovery, minimizing the impact of dependencies between human errors, and so on.

The HRA may be qualitative or quantitative. When the HRA is quantitative, the main quantity of interest is the HEP. There are two main reasons for quantifying HEPs: (i) to compare the probabilities of different errors, and (ii) to use the HEPs as input in quantitative risk assessments.

*Main Steps of an HRA.*   The main steps of a typical quantitative HRA are to:

1. Identify critical operations where human errors could lead to accidents and/or operational problems.

2. Analyze the relevant tasks and break them down into subtasks and task steps.

3. Identify potential human error modes and, if possible, error causes and performance-influencing factors.

4. Determine the human error probabilities (HEPs) for each error mode and for the complete task.

Each step can be split into several substeps.

*HRA Methods.*   Many methods have been developed for HRA, and it is not possible to describe all of them in this book. We have chosen to focus on a few of the most frequently used methods and divide these into three categories:

– Task analysis methods (steps 1 and 2)

– Human error identification methods (step 3)

– Human error quantification methods (step 4)

Methods covering all four steps of an HRA are sometimes referred to as *total HRA frameworks*.

*Main Benefits.*   The main benefits of an HRA are that it:

- Provides quantitative estimates of potential and credible human errors.

- Identifies weaknesses in operator interfaces with the system.

- Identifies causes of human errors to support development of preventive or miti-gating measures.

- Demonstrates quantitative improvements in human interfaces.

- Improves the value of the risk assessment by including human elements.

### 13.1.2   Human Errors

The term *human error* is often used very loosely. When using this term, we assume that everybody understands what it means, but their understanding may sometimes be far from what we meant. It is therefore important to have a clear definition of a human error (see above).

A human error may be related to a single individual or to a group of individuals. Some authors and organizations avoid using the term *human error* and use more neutral terms, such as *action error* or *erroneous action*.

A human error is usually related to a specified task, which is defined as:

☞ **Task**: Collection of actions carried out by operators in order to achieve an objec-tive or a goal state.

Tasks may be broken down into subtasks, subtasks may sometimes be broken down into sub-subtasks, and so on. At the lowest and most detailed level are *actions*.

An underlying premise is that significant human errors occur as a result of a com-bination of plant conditions and certain personal factors that trigger error mecha-nisms in personnel.

Seen in relation to a bow-tie model (see Figure 5.2), human errors may:

1. Contribute as causes of a hazardous event, as maintenance errors, calibration errors, testing errors, and so on.

2. Be directly related to the hazardous event. The human error may be the sole reason for the hazardous event or its direct triggering event.

3. Be related to the consequences of the hazardous event: for example, failure to activate a manual safety system and maintenance errors related to (reactive) barriers.

For most well-designed systems, the significant hazardous events have been iden-tified and barriers have been implemented. The required human actions are therefore understood and described in procedures. Our task is therefore to analyze the reliabil-ity of these actions. Some typical human errors are listed in Table 13.1.

Table 13.1   Typical human errors.

| Physical errors | Mental errors |
|---|---|
| – Action omitted | – Lack of knowledge of system/situation |
| – Action incomplete | – Lack of attention |
| – Too much action | – Failure to remember procedures |
| – Too little action | – Communication breakdowns |
| – Action in wrong direction | – Miscalculation |
| – Wrong action executed | |
| – Action mistimed | |
| – Action on wrong object | |
| – Action repeated | |

### 13.1.3   Human Error Probability

The term *human error probability* may be defined as:

☞ **Human error probability (HEP)**: The probability that an error will occur when a given task is performed.

It is often assumed that tasks are carried out as independent Bernoulli trials with constant error probability HEP. The number of human errors $z$ during $n$ tasks is then binomially distributed $(n, \text{HEP})$. In such a case the HEP can be estimated as

$$\text{HEP}^* = \frac{z}{n} = \frac{\text{number of errors}}{\text{number of opportunities for error}} \qquad (13.1)$$

This estimate is problematic since it is not always straightforward to count the number $n$ of opportunities for making errors. A subjective or Bayesian interpretation of HEP may therefore be more appropriate in this case (see Chapter 2).

The HEP is usually assumed to be independent of time, such that we have the same HEP for each task, irrespective of when the task is carried out. This is in contrast to the probability of failures of technical equipment, which usually will increase with time/deterioration of the equipment. A human operator is hence assumed to be "as good as new" when any task is performed.

### 13.1.4   Human Error Modes

The term *human error mode* is analogous to the term *failure mode* for technical items, and may be defined as:

☞ **Human error mode**: The effect by which a human error can be observed.

As a failure mode of a technical item may be interpreted as a deviation from a functional requirement, a human error mode may be interpreted as a deviation from a procedure or from an intended way to carry out a task or an action.

■ **EXAMPLE 13.1    Error related to turning a switch**

Consider an operator who should turn a switch one step in the clockwise direction when a specified signal is given. Possible human error modes comprise:

- Does not turn the switch

- Turns the switch two or more steps clockwise

- Turns the switch counterclockwise

- Turns the wrong switch (if more than one switch)                              ⊕

## 13.1.5  Classification of Human Errors

There are various ways of classifying human errors, but no universally accepted taxonomy has been developed. Three classification systems or taxonomies are, however, used more often than the others:

- The skill-, rule-, and knowledge-based behavior models proposed by Rasmussen (1983).

- The slip, lapse, mistake, and violation classification proposed by Reason (1990).

- The errors of omission and commission proposed by Swain and Guttmann (1983).

***Skill-, Rule-, and Knowledge-Based Behavior.***    One of the most influential models for human behavior is the skill-, rule-, and knowledge-based behavior (SRK) model of Rasmussen (1983).  Basically, the three levels represent the following types of behavior:

S: *Skill-based.* Subconscious, automated actions such as bicycling—requiring little or no cognitive effort. Skill-based behavior depends on the operator's practice in performing the task. Skill-based errors tend to relate to routine activities in familiar circumstances.

R: *Rule-based.* Actions according to an explicit rule or procedure. Rule-based behavior is when the operator does not have the same level of practice as for skill-based behavior when performing a task. There may be some hesitation in recalling the procedure, the procedure may not be carried out in the proper sequence, or some steps may not be performed precisely. Rule-based errors are often concerned with the misapplication or inappropriate use of problem-solving rules.

K: *Knowledge-based.* Coping with unfamiliar situations without a procedure (e.g., diagnosis) requires conscious problem solving and decision-making. Knowledge-based behavior includes situations where the operator needs to contemplate the situation, interpret information, or make a difficult decision.

***Slips, Lapses, Mistakes, and Violations.*** According to Reason (1990), there are four types of human error (unsafe acts) that may lead to major accidents:

(a) *Slip.* An action that is carried out with a correct intention but a faulty execution. A slip is an action that is not planned and usually is not a very dangerous event (e.g., inadvertently pushing the wrong button, reading error, slip of the tongue[1]).

(b) *Lapse.* A failure to execute an action due to a lapse of memory or because of a distraction. A lapse may not necessarily be evident to anyone other than the person who experienced the lapse. Lapses may be dangerous and are difficult to contain (e.g., omitting a step in a sequence of actions, "jumping" from one sequence to another, more familiar, sequence of actions). Slips and lapses will usually not be eliminated by training and need to be designed out (HSE, 2005a).

(c) *Mistake.* A correct execution of an incorrect intention. An operator may believe an action to be correct when it is, in fact, wrong. She may, for example, press the wrong button or switch off the wrong engine. Mistakes often appear in situations where the behavior is based on remembered rules or familiar procedures and are generally more dangerous than slips and lapses. Training is important to avoid mistakes.

(d) *Violation.* A person deliberately applies a rule or procedure that is different from what she knows is required, even though she may often do it with good intent. A familiar rule violation is when someone knowingly drives her car above the speed limit. Violations differ from slips, lapses, and mistakes because they are deliberate, or illegal actions (e.g., deliberately failing to follow procedures).

Slips and lapses may happen to even the most experienced or highly motivated people, while mistakes are often caused by lack of experience or inadequate training. Violations may range from simple "corner-cutting" to dangerous macho behavior, and may be classified as (HSE, 2005a):

1. *Routine violations.* Behavior in opposition to a rule, procedure, or instruction that has become the normal way of behaving within the current context.

---

[1]Note that such errors may be noncritical slips in some contexts and critical errors in other contexts.

2. *Exceptional violations.* These are rare and happen only in unusual and particular circumstances, when something goes wrong in unpredicted circumstances: for example, during an emergency situation.

3. *Situational violations.* These violations occur as a result of factors dictated by the worker's immediate workspace or environment (physical or organizational).

4. *Acts of sabotage.* These are self-explanatory, although the causes are complex, ranging from vandalism by a demotivated employee to terrorism.

Since violations are forbidden, the violators usually do not tell anyone what they are doing. Violations may therefore remain hidden failures.

Slips, lapses, and mistakes are very different from violations, even though all four categories of errors can result in a hazardous situation. The difference lies in the intent. A violation is a deliberate act, whereas the others are unintentional.

**Errors of Omission and Commission.**   The classification of human errors as errors of omission and errors of commission was proposed by Swain and Guttmann (1983) and is illustrated in Table 13.2.

An *error of omission* occurs when a task or an action is omitted: for example, when leaving out a step in a procedure. In Reason's classification, an error of omission is usually a lapse.

An *error of commission* is done when the operator does something that is incorrect and not required. An example is when a valve should be locked in closed position, but is locked open. Errors of commission are important for three reasons:

– They are rather rare, but do occur from time to time.

– They can have a large impact on the safety of a system.

– They are difficult to identify and therefore difficult to prevent.

Human errors can be categorized in several other ways, and a survey is given by Miguel (2006).

### 13.1.6   Performance-Influencing Factors

Human performance in complex systems is influenced by many different factors. These factors, called *performance influencing factors* (PIFs), can affect human performance in a positive or a negative manner. Many human reliability analysis methods use PIFs in the estimation of human error probabilities.

☞ **Performance-influencing factor (PIF)**: A factor that influences human performance and human error probabilities. Performance-influencing factors may be external to humans or may be a part of their internal characteristics.

**Table 13.2** Errors of omission and errors of commission.

| Error categories | | Subcategories |
|---|---|---|
| 1. Error of omission | . | 1.1.1.1 Required actions are not carried out |
| | | (a) Entire task omitted |
| | | (b) Step in task omitted |
| 2. Error of commission | 2.1 Incomplete failure | 2.1.1.1 Task is not done completely |
| | 2.2 Complete failure | |
| | 2.2.1 Execution error | 2.2.1.1 Wrong action is committed |
| | | 2.2.1.2 Right action is committed on wrong object |
| | | 2.2.1.3 Redundant action is committed |
| | 2.2.2 Time-related error | 2.2.2.1 Action is too early |
| | | 2.2.2.2 Action is too late |
| | | 2.2.2.3 Duration of action too short |
| | | 2.2.2.4 Duration of action too long |
| | 2.2.3 Sequence error | 2.2.3.1 Actions carried out in wrong sequence |

Common PIFs include procedures, training, and aspects of the displays and control facilities of the plant. Performance-influencing factors are also called *performance-shaping factors* (PSFs), *error-producing conditions* (EPC), and several other names.

There are three main types of PIFs (e.g., see Stamatelatos et al., 2002a):

(a) *External PIFs.* Factors that are external to the operators, such as task complexity, human-machine interface, written procedures, work environment, and management and organizational factors.

(b) *Internal PIFs.* Factors that are part of operators' internal characteristics, such as operator training, experience, and familiarity with task, health, and motivation.

(c) *Stressors.* Factors producing mental and physical stress: for example, task speed and load, fatigue, vibration.

A list of PIFs is presented in Table 13.3. Such a list may be a useful extension to the generic hazard list presented in Table 3.1.

A comprehensive taxonomy of performance-influencing factors (PIFs) has been developed by Kim and Jung (2003), based on four main groups: human, system, task, and environment.

### 13.1.7  Causes of Human Error

The causes of a human error may be related to the individual or the organization.

*Individual.*    People have attitudes, skills, habits, and personalities that can be weaknesses or strengths related to the tasks they are performing. The individual characteristics influence their behavior in many different ways. Some of these characteristics are fixed and cannot be changed, whereas others, such as skills and attitudes, may be changed and enhanced.

*Organization.*    A range of organizational factors influence both individual and group behavior but are often overlooked during the design of work and during accident investigations. The organizational causes are often attributed to the organization's safety culture, which may be defined as:

☞ **Safety culture**: The product of the individual and group values, attitudes, competencies, and patterns of behavior that determine the commitment to, and the style and proficiency of, an organization's health and safety management. Organizations with a positive safety culture are characterized by communications founded on mutual trust, by shared perceptions of the importance of safety, and by confidence in the efficacy of preventive measures (HSE, 2005b).

An organization with a good safety culture is one that gives priority to safety and realizes that safety has to be managed like other areas of the business. All organizations should strive to establish their own positive safety culture. Safety culture is affected by such factors as (e.g., see ICAO, 2009):

**Table 13.3**    Performance-influencing factors (not exhaustive).

| Situational characteristics | Psychological stresses |
|---|---|
| – Climate (e.g., temperature) | – Task speed and load |
| – Noise and vibration | – Fear of failure, job loss |
| – Lighting | – Monotony |
| – Cleanliness/tidiness | – Sustained attention |
| – Workhours and breaks | – Motivational conflicts |
| – Staffing | – Psychological stresses |
| – Actions by supervisors, peers, union representatives | – Fatigue, pain, discomfort |
| | – Hunger, thirst |
| – Rewards, recognition, benefits | – Temperature extremes |
| – Organizational structure | – Constricted movement |
| – Job instructions | – Lack of physical exercise |
| **Task and equipment characteristics** | **Individual factors** |
| – Job requirements | – Previous training and/or experience |
| – Task complexity | – Present skill |
| – Task frequency and repetitiveness | – Personality and intelligence |
| – Feedback (knowledge of results) | – Motivation and attitudes |
| – Task criticality and narrowness | – Physical condition |
| – Team structure | – Social factors (family and friends) |
| – Man-machine interface factors (e.g., tool design, layout of computer screens) | |

- Management's actions and priorities

- Policies and procedures

- Involvement of all employees

- Commonly agreed and understood goals

- Supervisory practices

- Safety planning and goals

- Actions in response to unsafe behaviors

- Employee training and motivation

- Maintenance of competence

Safety culture is discussed further, for example, by Peters and Peters (2006).

## 13.2 Task Analysis

In order to identify human error modes, we must first understand the tasks that are being carried out. If we do not fully understand the tasks that people will perform, and the manner in which they are to be carried out, we cannot comprehensively identify where errors may originate. The tasks are studied most effectively by a task analysis.

☞ **Task analysis**: Detailed examination of the observable activities associated with the execution of a required task or piece of work.

A task analysis will normally comprise (Rosness, 1994):

– A breakdown of the task into subtasks and simple task steps.

– A description of the allocation of task steps between different persons. This description gives an indication of communication needs.

– A description of the temporal dependencies between subtasks or task steps.

– Classification of task types (and task step types).

– Identification of cues and feedback supporting each task step.

A high number of task analysis methods have been developed, all of which seek to decompose a task into steps and substeps that describe human activities in terms of physical actions and/or cognitive processes (e.g., diagnosis, decision-making) in interacting with the system; see, for example, Kirwan and Ainsworth (1992), who list more than 20 different task analysis techniques. In this section, we describe two such methods: hierarchical task analysis and tabular task analysis.

### 13.2.1 Hierarchical Task Analysis

*Hierarchical task analysis* (HTA) is a systematic method for describing how work is (or should be) organized in order to meet the goal of a specified task. This is done by identifying in a top-down fashion the overall goal of a task, the various subtasks and sub-subtasks, and the conditions under which they should be carried out in order to meet the goal. In this way, the task may be represented as a hierarchy of subtasks and operations or actions that people must do to meet the goal of the task (e.g., see Kirwan and Ainsworth, 1992).

HTA is widely used in human reliability analysis and often forms the first step in more detailed analyses. HTA involves breaking down the task into a hierarchy of goals, operations, and plans (Salmon et al., 2003):

– *Goals.* The goal(s) associated with the task in question. (What should be accomplished?)

- *Operations.* The observable behaviors or actions that the operator has to perform in order to accomplish the goal of the task in question. Operations are also referred to as subtasks or actions.

- *Plans.* Statements (decisions or planning) of the conditions that are necessary to carry out the operations. These are important since they describe the conditions that the operators have to attend to.

The term *action* is often used for the most elementary subtasks, such as closing a valve, operating a switch, or checking a meter.

***Objectives and Applications.***   The objectives of an HTA are to:

(a) Determine how the work should be organized to meet a specific goal.

(b) Determine how an overall goal can be broken down in subgoals, sub-subgoals, and so on.

(c) Determine the actions that operators have to perform to meet the goals at different levels.

(d) Identify the plans (conditions) that are necessary for each subtask and action.

(e) Determine the necessary subtasks in new work processes.

HTA is a generic method and can be used in all types of application areas. HTA has been applied successfully in process control, military applications, aviation, power generation, and so on. The task in question may range from a simple to a rather complex task and may involve both human tasks and tasks performed by the technical system.

***Analysis Procedure.***   The analysis process is similar to that of the *functional analysis system technique* (FAST), which is often used for the functional breakdown of technical equipment (Rausand and Høyland, 2004, pp. 80-81). Through HTA, the analyst explores tasks by establishing a hierarchical task description. The main steps of the analysis are:

1. Plan and prepare.

2. Determine the overall goal of the task.

3. Determine the task subgoals.

4. Decompose each subgoal.

5. Analyze plans.

6. Report the analysis.

Steps 1 and 6 are discussed in Chapter 8 and are not treated further here.

*Step 2: Determine the Overall Goal of the Task*   The overall goal and the performance requirements of the task are clearly described.

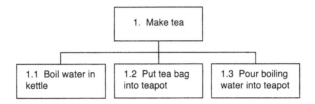

**Figure 13.1** HTA diagram for the task "make tea" in Example 13.2 (first level).

*Step 3: Determine the Task Subgoals* The overall goal of the task is broken down into 3–5 subgoals.

*Step 4: Decompose Each Subgoal* The subgoals identified in step 3 are broken down into further subgoals and operations. The decomposition continues as far as required. The lowest level of any branch is always an action. While everything above an action specifies goals, actions actually say what needs to be done.

An HTA diagram is established as a tree-like structure. An example of the first level of a HTA diagram is shown in Figure 13.1. The analyst can stop the analysis (decomposition of operations) when she considers it justified. Sometimes operations need to be described in considerable detail; sometimes they can be described very briefly.

*Step 5: Analyze Plans* Plans are included in the HTA diagram at the point where each task is split into subtasks to provide details about how the tasks are actually carried out, such as sequence information. A simple plan would say: "Do 1, then 2, and then 3." Once the plan is completed, the operator returns to the superordinate level.

A simple example of an HTA is described in Example 13.2.

### ◼ EXAMPLE 13.2 Making tea

A very simple task is to make tea in a teapot. The goal of this task is to *make tea*. This goal can be accomplished by three subtasks:

1. Make tea

   1.1 Boil water in kettle.

   1.2 Put tea bag into teapot.

   1.3 Pour boiling water into teapot.

The task may be illustrated by the hierarchical diagram in Figure 13.1.

Each subtask may be broken down into sub-subtasks. Subtask 1.2 may, for example, be broken down as follows, where we have introduced a *plan* or condition for the operation:

1.2  Put tea bag into teapot

*Plan*: Do 1.2.1, if teapot is not empty or is not clean, do 1.2.2, then do 1.2.3 and 1.2.4 in order.

1.2.1  Find and check teapot.

1.2.2  Empty and/or clean teapot.

1.2.3  Find/select tea bag.

1.2.4  Put the tea bag into teapot.                                    ⊕

**Resources and Skills Required.**    No specific skills are required, and a few hours training in HTA will usually be sufficient. The time required to complete an HTA depends on the complexity of the task and the level of detail required for the analysis. For very complex tasks, the time required may be substantial. HTA can be carried out using only pencil and paper, but a simple drawing program may be helpful.

### Advantages and Limitations

*Advantages*    The main advantages are that a HTA is (see also CCPS, 1994; DEF-STAN 00-250, 2008):

– well documented and the most commonly used task analysis method;

– easy to learn, easy to implement, and requires minimal training;

– generic and can be applied to a variety of tasks;

– informative and gives the user good insight into the task being analyzed;

– flexible such that tasks can be analyzed to any required level of detail.

*Limitations*    The main limitations are that an HTA:

– is descriptive rather than analytical;

– can be time-consuming for complex and large tasks;

– does not easily provide any scenario description;

– provides little information regarding collaboration;

– does not identify the participants involved in the task and the roles they play.

## 13.2.2   Tabular Task Analysis

*Tabular task analysis* (TTA) can be used on a particular task or scenario to examine the individual (bottom level) actions that are identified by an HTA or a similar method. Two main concepts of a TTA are:

(a) *Cues.* The cues indicate to the operator that an action can/should be initiated.

(b) *Feedback.* The feedback informs the operator about the effects of carrying out the action.

A cue may come from the system, for example, when a computer program presents a box with a question to be answered or a menu to select from. In some actions, cues are given as messages, orders, requests, or confirmation from other persons. Cues may also come from a checklist. In many cases, the only cue is that the previous action has been performed. Actions that are only cued by sequence are often easy to forget, in particular if they are functionally isolated. An action is functionally isolated if its goal (function) is very different from the goals of the preceding or following actions. This is, for example, the case for actions needed to bring a system back to the normal operating state after a maintenance task.

An action may be repeated erroneously if feedback is absent, weak, or delayed. Ideally, the operator should receive feedback that shows both her own actions and their effect on the system. If the operator pushes a button to close a valve, she needs to know (i) whether she has pushed the right button (*action feedback*) and (ii) whether the valve has in fact closed (*effect feedback*). Action feedbacks are sometimes called *traces*.

TTA is a simple method that helps the analyst detect and understand human-machine interface problems related to inadequate cues and feedback. Furthermore, the analyst is forced to get familiar with the details of the human-machine interface, which places her in a good position to perform an HRA.

***Objectives and Applications.***   The objectives of a TTA are to:

(a) Examine the individual actions of a more complex task.

(b) Identify and evaluate the adequacy of the cues for each action.

(c) Identify and evaluate the adequacy of the feedback from each action (both action and effect feedback).

(d) Identify possible errors related to each action (optional).

TTA is a generic method and can be used in all types of application areas and has been shown to be useful in the following contexts:

- Design or evaluation of human-machine interfaces.

- Preparation for, or as part of a detailed HRA.

- Preparation of operational procedures.

Study object: Process section P1

Date: 2010-12-20

Reference:

Name: Marvin Rausand

| No. | Action (description) | Cues | Feedback | Possible errors | Comments |
|-----|---------------------|------|----------|-----------------|----------|
| 1 | Close manual valve PV1 | - Signal from control room<br>- Checklist | - Downstream manometer<br>- Visual observation | - Close wrong valve<br>- Does not close the valve properly | |

**Figure 13.2**    Example of a simple TTA table.

**Analysis Procedure.**    The steps needed to perform a TTA are:

1. Plan and prepare.

2. List all actions in a TTA table.

3. Identify cues.

4. Identify feedback.

5. Identify possible errors.

6. Report the analysis.

Steps 1 and 6 are discussed in Chapter 8 and are not treated further here.

*Step 2: List All Actions in a TTA Table*    The main element of a tabular task analysis is the TTA table. The TTA table has columns for number and description of actions, cues, feedback, possible errors, and comments. An example of a simple TTA table is shown in Figure 13.2. A more thorough example may be found in Stanton et al. (2005). In this step the format of the TTA table is agreed upon and the relevant actions are recorded in sequence in the first two columns of the table (number and description). The TTA table in Figure 13.2 can be extended in various ways: for example, by including classification of each task step and/or timing requirements.

*Step 3: Identify Cues*    The cues for each action are identified and recorded in the third column. Pictures or sketches of the situation may be attached to the analysis if a cuing is difficult to describe.

*Step 4: Identify Feedback*   The feedback for each action is identified and recorded in column 4. For simple actions, such as movement, installation, and manipulation of objects, the feedback is visual and direct, and in some cases tactile. Otherwise, the feedback is expressed in terms of the indicators and annunciators which the operator can see, and the audible acknowledgments.

For some actions, the feedback is so obvious that it is of little use to specify it in detail. If the action is to fill in a form, the feedback is usually that the form has been completed. It is then admissible to record the feedback for such actions as "trivial" if it is clear that the quality of feedback is of no significance for the action performance. This allows the analyst to spend more time on critical and difficult actions. Pictures or sketches of the situation may be attached to the analysis if the feedback is difficult to describe.

*Step 5: Identify Possible Errors*   In this step, the possible errors related to the action are identified and recorded. The errors should, whenever possible, be recorded as human error modes. This step will not be part of the analysis when the TTA is used only as a task analysis.

*Comments*   For each action, comments may be recorded in the last column. Comments may include:

- Assumptions made during the analysis

- Additional information needed to complete the analysis

- Notes on possible man-machine interface problems (e.g., poor feedback or lack of cuing)

- Proposed improvements of the man-machine interface

### Advantages and Limitations

*Advantages*   The main advantages are that a TTA (see also Stanton et al., 2005):

- is a flexible technique that allows any factor associated with the task to be analyzed;

- has the potential to provide a very comprehensive analysis of a particular task;

- is entirely generic and can be used in any domain;

- provides a much more detailed description of tasks than the HTA;

- is potentially very exhaustive if the correct categories are used.

*Limitations*   The main limitations are that a TTA:

- may be a very time-consuming technique to apply;

- requires information that is often not available to the study team.

## 13.3   Human Error Identification

*Human error* (mode) *identification* (HEI) refers to identification, description, and analysis of possible erroneous actions in performing a task. To identify all possible errors is usually impossible, and Swain and Guttmann (1983) state that:

> Even the best analyst cannot identify all possible modes of human response. No one can predict unlikely extraneous acts by plant personnel. Still, given sufficient time, a skilled analyst can identify most of the important tasks to be performed in a system and most of the ways in which errors are likely to be committed.

To be able to identify as many of the critical human error modes as possible, we need to use one or more structured approaches. A very high number of methods for human error identification have been proposed, under many different names. Several authors present structured lists of the various methods (e.g., see Stanton et al., 2005).

As part of human error identification, it is also important to consider the various tasks that are, or should be, performed when the system is in an abnormal state.

In this section, we present three methods for human error identification:

1. Action error mode analysis (AEMA), which is similar to an FMECA (see Chapter 9)

2. Human HAZOP, which is a variant of the HAZOP used in the process industry (see Chapter 9)

3. The systematic human error reduction and prediction approach (SHERPA)

### 13.3.1   Action Error Mode Analysis

Several approaches for HEI that are more or less similar to failure modes, effects, and criticality analysis (FMECA) have been proposed. In this book we refer to these methods as *action error mode analysis* (AEMA).

The analysis starts with a listing of individual (bottom level) actions: for example, coming from an HTA or a TTA. Possible errors in the execution of each action are identified by using experience, checklists, guidewords, or brainstorming, mainly in the same way as for hardware FMECA and HAZOP. The consequences of the errors may be analyzed, for example, by event tree analysis.

***Objectives and Applications.***   The objectives of an AEMA are to:

(a) Identify how each action can conceivably fail (i.e., what are the human error modes?)

(b) Determine the causes of these human error modes.

(c) Identify the effects each human error mode can have on the rest of the task that is analyzed.

(d) Describe how the human error modes can be detected.

Study object: Process section P1

Date: 2010-12-20

Reference:

Name: Marvin Rausand

| No. | Action (description) | Action error mode | Action error cause | Action error consequences | Risk | Risk-reducing measure | Comments |
|-----|---------------------|-------------------|-------------------|--------------------------|------|----------------------|----------|
| 1 | Close manual valve PV1 | Close wrong valve | - Procedure error<br><br>- Communication error<br><br>- Valve marking inadequate<br><br>- Lapse | May lead to explosion | H | | |

**Figure 13.3**   Example of an AEMA worksheet.

(e)  Determine how critical the various human error modes are.

(f)  Identify risk-reducing actions/features that may be relevant.

AEMA is a generic method that can be applied to most types of actions. The AEMA output provides a basis for identifying critical error modes that may lead to unacceptable consequences. Furthermore, possible barriers and recovery opportunities can be identified based on the event sequence. The AEMA can be carried out for all actions or only for some selected actions.

***Analysis Procedure.***    An AEMA procedure is similar to the FMECA procedure described in Chapter 9 and is therefore not described in detail here. The AEMA will usually have less focus on quantifying the frequency and the severity of the various human error modes, and the AEMA worksheet is therefore often more simple than an FMECA worksheet. A typical AEMA worksheet is shown in Figure 13.3.

***Resources and Skills Required.***    The AEMA can be carried out by a single analyst or by a study team. The analysis principles are easy to grasp for persons with experience with FMECA and HAZOP. No specialist knowledge of psychology or human factors is required. The analyst/team should have access to relevant checklists.

***Advantages and Limitations.***    The advantages and limitations of AEMA are similar to those for the hardware FMECA.

### 13.3.2  Human HAZOP

Human HAZOP is derived from the traditional hazard and operability (HAZOP) method used in the process industry (see Chapter 9) and uses guidewords (e.g., see Table 13.4) to identify credible human errors (e.g., see Kirwan and Ainsworth, 1992).

***Objectives and Applications.***   The objectives of a human HAZOP are to:

(a) Identify all deviations from the intended performance of the various actions, their causes, and all the hazards associated with these deviations.

(b) Decide whether actions are required to control the hazards, and if so, to identify the ways in which the problems can be solved.

(c) Ensure that actions decided are followed up.

(d) Make operators aware of hazards related to the various actions.

***Analysis Procedure.***   The human HAZOP procedure is similar to the process HA-ZOP procedure described in Chapter 9. The human HAZOP is carried out by a HAZOP team of 3–10 team members. For a chemical plant, it is recommended that the HAZOP team comprises:

- HAZOP team leader

- Human factors specialist

- Project engineer

- Process engineer

- Operating team leader

- Control room operator

- HAZOP secretary

The human HAZOP is based on a listing and description of actions. A stepwise operating procedure may be used if it is known to be complete and correct. The output from a job safety analysis (see Chapter 14) may also be used as input to the HAZOP study. In some cases, it may be necessary to carry out a task analysis (an HTA, or preferably a TTA) before the HAZOP study is initiated.

For a detailed human HAZOP, the task description should specify who performs each action and what controls (e.g., pushbutton, switches) and displays (e.g., control lamps, indicators) are used.

Each action is next analyzed in the same way as the *nodes* in a traditional process HAZOP study. A set of guidewords are combined with considerations about omissions and commissions, and potential and credible errors within the system are highlighted (Stanton et al., 2005).

There is no standard for human HAZOP, and several authors have developed their own set of guidewords (or error types). Two examples are given in Tables 13.4 and 13.5.

A human HAZOP should answer the following questions:

(a) What human error modes can possibly occur when performing the task?

Table 13.4   Human HAZOP guidewords.

| Process HAZOP guidewords | Human HAZOP guidewords |
| --- | --- |
| No | Not done |
| Less | Less than |
| More | More than |
| As well as | As well as |
| Other than | Other than |
| | Repeated |
| | Sooner than |
| Reverse | Later than |
| | Misordered |
| Part of | Part of |

*Source*: Data from Whalley (1992).

(b)  What are the main causes of these errors?

(c)  How likely is each of these errors?

(d)  Is it possible to recover/correct the error mode (when it has occurred)?

(e)  How can such a recovery be accomplished, and what is the probability of success?

(f)  What are the consequences of each error mode?

(g)  How serious are the consequences of each error mode?

(h)  Which risk-reducing measures can/should be implemented?

The results from the analysis are usually recorded in a human HAZOP worksheet. An example of a human HAZOP worksheet is shown in Figure 13.4.

### Advantages and Limitations

*Advantages*   The main advantages are that a human HAZOP is:

– attractive to engineers;

– structured and thorough;

– supported by checklists for each step;

– simple and does not require in-depth knowledge of human reliability or cognitive psychology;

**Table 13.5**   Human Hazop guide-words.

| Basic guidewords | Additional guidewords |
|---|---|
| – No action | – Purpose |
| – More action | – Clarity |
| – Less action | – Training |
| – Wrong action | – Abnormal conditions |
| – Part of action | – Maintenance |
| – Extra action | – Safety |
| – Other action | |
| – More time | |
| – Less time | |
| – Out of sequence | |
| – More information | |
| – Less information | |
| – No information | |
| – Wrong information | |

*Source*: Data from Shorrock et al. (2003).

Study object:  Process section P1

Reference:

Date: 2010-12-20

Name: Marvin Rausand

| No. | Action (description) | Guideword | Action error (description) | Causes | Consequences | Prob. | Severity | Recovery path | Design improvements |
|---|---|---|---|---|---|---|---|---|---|
| 1 | Close manual valve PV1 | Other than | Close wrong valve | - Procedure error<br><br>- Communication error<br><br>- Valve marking inadequate<br><br>- Lapse | May lead to explosion | L | H | | |

**Figure 13.4**   Example of a human HAZOP worksheet.

– flexible and can be narrowed down after consequence identification, to reduce the analysis effort;

– applicable to actions that are specified in different degrees of detail. This makes the method useful at an early stage when the task can be described only in outline, as well as when a detailed task description is available.

*Limitations*    The main limitations are that a human HAZOP:

– relies on a group of experts to be able to assess the possible reasons behind the errors identified by using the guidewords;

– can be time-consuming;

– requires significant effort.

### 13.3.3  SHERPA

The *systematic human error reduction and prediction approach* (SHERPA) was developed for the nuclear industry, but has also been applied in several other areas, including aviation and the process industry (Embrey, 1986).

***Objectives and Applications.***    The objectives of SHERPA are to:

(a) Identify all human action errors related to the study object, their causes, and consequences.

(b) Assess the probability and the severity of the action error mode.

(c) Identify possible recovery actions that may prevent the error from leading to significant consequences.

(d) Decide whether actions are required to control the hazards, and if so, to identify ways in which the problems can be solved.

(e) Make operators aware of hazards related to the various actions.

SHERPA is a generic technique that can be applied to almost all types of actions. It has been used in a wide range of studies and has been proved to be effective and to have good validity.

***Analysis Procedure.***    SHERPA uses an HTA together with an *error taxonomy* to identify potential and credible human errors for a specified action. The potential error modes are classified into five groups, as shown in Table 13.6. The analyst uses subjective judgment and the SHERPA error mode taxonomy in Table 13.6 to determine the credible error modes for each action, as identified by the task analysis. A credible error is one the analyst judges to be possible.

For each credible error mode, the analyst describes the form the error would take, such as "operator turns the switch in wrong direction." Next, the analyst determines

**Table 13.6** SHERPA error mode taxonomy.

| | |
|---|---|
| *Action errors* | *Information retrieval errors* |
| – Operation too long/short | – Information not obtained |
| – Operation mistimed | – Wrong information obtained |
| – Operation in wrong direction | – Information retrieval incomplete |
| – Operation too little/much | *Communication errors* |
| – Misalignment error | – Information not obtained or communicated |
| – Right operation on wrong object | |
| – Wrong operation on right object | – Wrong information obtained or communicated |
| – Operation omitted | |
| – Operation incomplete | *Selection errors* |
| – Wrong operation on wrong object | – Selection omitted |
| *Checking errors* | – Wrong selection |
| – Check omitted | |
| – Check incomplete | |
| – Right check on wrong object | |
| – Wrong check on right object | |
| – Check mistimed | |
| – Wrong check on wrong object | |

any consequences of the error and any error recovery steps that would need to be taken if the error mode occurs. Then the analyst ranks the probability (low, medium, or high) and the criticality (low, medium, or high) of the error and describes any potential design remedies (i.e., how the interface design could be modified to prevent the error).

A detailed procedure for performing a SHERPA analysis is given by Stanton et al. (2005), and a case study using SHERPA to predict design-induced errors on the flight deck of a civil aircraft is presented by Harris et al. (2005). The steps required to carry out a SHERPA analysis are similar to those described for AEMA and are therefore not described further here.

The results of the analysis are recorded in a SHERPA worksheet as shown in Figure 13.5. Several variants of this worksheet have been proposed (see also Salmon et al., 2005).

### Advantages and Limitations

*Advantages* The main advantages are that a SHERPA is:

- structured and comprehensive;

Study object: Process section P1                                    Date: 2010-12-20
Reference:                                                          Name: Marvin Rausand

| No. | Action (description) | Action error mode | Action error causes | Action error consequences | Recovery | Prob. | Severity | Remedial actions | Comments |
|---|---|---|---|---|---|---|---|---|---|
| 1 | Close manual valve PV1 | Close wrong valve | - Procedure error<br><br>- Communication error<br><br>- Valve marking inadequate<br><br>- Lapse | May lead to explosion | Error captured by supervisor | L | H | - Improved supervision<br>- Improved procedure | |

**Figure 13.5**   Example of a SHERPA worksheet.

- well documented and supported by checklists for each step;

- applicable to actions that are specified in different degrees of detail;

- simple and does not require in-depth knowledge of human reliability or cognitive psychology;

- well tested and that a number of studies have shown good validity for the technique.

*Limitations*   The main limitations are that SHERPA:

- does not consider cognitive components of the error mechanisms;

- can be tedious and time-consuming;

- requires significant effort;

- is strongly dependent on the skill of the analyst(s). The consistency of the method when used by different analysts has been questioned.

## 13.4   HRA Methods

In 2009, the UK Health and Safety Executive made a survey of available HRA methods and identified 72 different methods (HSE, 2009). These were evaluated and compared and the report concluded that 17 of the methods were suitable for human reliability assessment in high-hazard industries.

The HRA methods may be classified into two different groups:

1. *First-generation HRA methods.* The HRA methods of the first generation were developed to provide input to a quantitative risk analysis (QRA/PRA) and tried to integrate human actions and human errors into this risk analysis. The most

commonly used method of this generation is the *Technique for Human Error Rate Prediction*, which is known as THERP (Swain and Guttmann, 1983). THERP is described by Miller and Swain (1987) as:

> The THERP approach uses conventional reliability technology modified to account for greater variability and interdependence of human performance as compared with that of equipment performance [...] The procedures of THERP are similar to those employed in conventional reliability analysis, except that human task activities are substituted for equipment outputs.

Since the first-generation HRA methods are straightforward add-ons to the risk analysis, they are easy for risk analysts to understand and have therefore been used in many practical analyses.

The methods encourage the analyst to break the task into single actions and consider the potential impact of performance-influencing factors (PIFs). By combining these influences, the analyst can determine a nominal human error probability (HEP). The methods are often criticized for failing to consider such things as the cognitive issues, impact of context, organizational factors, and errors of commission (e.g., see Miguel, 2006; HSE, 2009).

Three of the first-generation methods are described in this section:

(a) *THERP*: technique for human error rate prediction

(b) *HEART*: human error assessment and reduction technique

(c) *SLIM-MAUD*: success likelihood index methodology, multiattribute utility decomposition

2. *Second-generation HRA methods.* Development of second-generation HRA methods began in the early 1990s and is ongoing. These methods attempt to consider the context and errors of commission in human error prediction (HSE, 2009).

These methods may be distinguished from first-generation methods by the fact that they should (i) be able to describe the underlying causes of specific erroneous human actions, or the context in which human errors occur, (ii) be able to identify various kinds of human error modes that might deteriorate the safety condition of a plant, and (iii) be able to quantify the HEP on the basis of error-producing conditions or context.

The second-generation HRA methods are much more complex than the first generation methods. They do not fit as easily into the standard risk analysis methods and are sometimes presented in a language that is difficult to understand for analysts who do not have training in psychology.

These methods incorporate guidelines or strategies for quantifying human performance, although in a less prescriptive and reductive way than the first-generation methods, and putting more emphasis on complex and cognitive (nonobservable) aspects of human reliability as opposed to the more behavioristic approach of the earlier techniques (HSE, 2009).

The second-generation methods use a theory-based error taxonomy that often coincides with a cognitive model of human behavior. Among the best known second-generation methods are:

(a) *CREAM*: cognitive reliability and error analysis method

(b) *ATHEANA*: a technique for human error analysis

(c) *MERMOS*: method d'évaluation de la realisation des mission operateur pour la sûreté[2]

A description of CREAM is given later in this section, while ATHEANA and MERMOS are described only briefly. All the methods mentioned are publicly available, except for MERMOS, which is the property of Electricité de France (EDF).

## 13.4.1 THERP

The *technique for human error rate prediction* (THERP) was developed as early as 1961 for the U.S. Nuclear Regulatory Commission (Swain and Guttmann, 1983) and has become the most widely used method for quantitative human reliability analysis. THERP is a total method for human reliability assessment and deals with (i) task analysis, (ii) human error identification and representation, and (iii) quantification of human error probabilities.

The THERP handbook (Swain and Guttmann, 1983) is indispensable when performing a THERP analysis. The handbook gives a detailed explanation of the various steps of the analysis and also contains tables with nominal error probabilities.

THERP is still regarded as one of the main methods for HRA, although it has been subject to considerable criticism.

THERP models human errors using event trees (see Section 11.2) and models of dependence, but also considers performance influencing factors, which in THERP are called *performance-shaping* factors (PSFs).

***Objectives and Applications.*** According to Swain and Guttmann (1983) the objective of THERP is

> [...] to predict the human error probabilities and to evaluate the degradation of a man-machine system likely to be caused by human errors alone or in connection with equipment functioning, operational procedures and practices, or other system and human characteristics that influence system behavior.

Originally, THERP was developed for military application and was developed further within the nuclear industry. Subsequently, THERP has been used in many different sectors, such as offshore oil and gas production.

THERP is considered to be particularly effective in quantifying errors in highly proceduralized activities.

---

[2]English: Method for assessing the performance of operator actions with respect to safety.

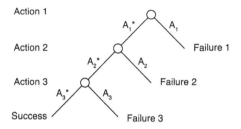

**Figure 13.6**    Example of a THERP event tree.

***Method Description.***    The main elements of THERP are:

(a) A database of generic or *nominal* HEPs for a number of basic actions that may be modified by the analyst to reflect the effect of the actual PSFs on the scenario.

Twenty-seven HEP tables are included in part IV of the handbook. The generic HEP values are based on expert judgment supplemented by recorded data.

(b) A dependency model that is used to assess the degree of dependency between two actions (e.g., if an operator fails to detect an alarm, the failure to carry out appropriate corrective actions reliably cannot be treated independent of the first error).

(c) An event tree modeling approach that combines HEPs calculated for individual steps in the task into an overall HEP for the task as a whole.

(d) A method for assessing error recovery options.

THERP is a comprehensive technique and only the rudiments can be covered in this section. For more information, the reader is referred to the THERP handbook (Swain and Guttmann, 1983) or to Kirwan (1994).

*THERP Event Trees*    Event trees are used to map actions in a time sequence together with other pivotal events and to assign probabilities to each event. This approach enables THERP results to be easily integrated into the quantitative risk analysis. THERP uses a graphical layout of the event tree that is slightly different from the event trees we presented in Chapter 11, but the logical structure is the same. An example of a THERP event tree is shown in Figure 13.6.

The task illustrated in Figure 13.6 consists of three actions. Each action can result in two possible outcomes, $A_i$ (error) or $A_i^*$ (no error), for $i = 1, 2, 3$. The total outcome of the task may be "success" (all actions performed without error) or failures 1, 2 or 3. These three failures will sometimes give the same effect, and we may then combine them into the same category.

The probabilities of the various outcomes can be calculated by the standard rules for conditional probabilities:

$$\Pr(\text{failure 1}) = \Pr(A_1)$$
$$\Pr(\text{failure 2}) = \Pr(A_1^* \cap A_2) = \Pr(A_2 \mid A_1^*) \cdot \Pr(A_1^*)$$
$$\Pr(\text{failure 3}) = \Pr(A_1^* \cap A_2^* \cap A_3) = \Pr(A_3 \mid A_1^* \cap A_2^*) \cdot \Pr(A_1^* \cap A_2^*)$$
$$= \Pr(A_3 \mid A_1^* \cap A_2^*) \cdot \Pr(A_2^* \mid A_1^*) \cdot \Pr(A_1^*)$$

To find these probabilities, we need to determine the HEP $= \Pr(A_i)$ of each action $i$, for $i = 1, 2, 3$, and also the dependencies between the various actions.

*Nominal Human Error Probability (HEP$_n$)*    In the THERP data tables, each nominal HEP, hereafter called HEP$_n$, is presented together with 90% uncertainty bounds or an error factor $k$. It is tacitly assumed that the uncertainty of a HEP can be modeled by a lognormal distribution. Let HEP$_n$ be the nominal HEP presented in the handbook, and let HEP$_{0.05}$ and HEP$_{0.95}$ be the 0.05 and the 0.95 percentiles of the lognormal distribution, respectively. The uncertainty in HEP can then be expressed as

$$\Pr(\text{HEP}_{0.05} \leq \text{HEP} \leq \text{HEP}_{0.95}) = 0.90 \tag{13.2}$$

Let the error factor $k$ be expressed by

$$k = \sqrt{\frac{\text{HEP}_{0.95}}{\text{HEP}_{0.05}}} \tag{13.3}$$

If we assume that the nominal HEP$_n$ is the *median* of the lognormal distribution (Rausand and Høyland, 2004, Sec. 2.14), the 90% uncertainty bounds may be written as

$$\Pr(\text{HEP}_n / k \leq \text{HEP} \leq \text{HEP}_n \cdot k) = 0.90 \tag{13.4}$$

Most of the nominal HEPs in the THERP handbook are expert estimates and only a small fraction are based on empirical data. Several studies have later shown the THERP data to be reasonably satisfactory (NEA, 1998).

**Remark**: To model the uncertainty in HEP by a lognormal distribution may seem a strange choice, since HEP is a probability and hence bounded to the interval $[0, 1]$, while the lognormal distribution takes all values in $[0, \infty)$ with positive probability. The beta distribution on $[0, 1]$ would seem to be a more natural choice.     $\oplus$

*Performance Shaping Factors (PSFs)*    In THERP, the operator is treated in much the same way as components in a technical system. The aim of THERP is to predict the HEPs and to evaluate the impact that these errors will have on the safety and reliability of the overall system. THERP acknowledges that human performance can be influenced by a range of PSFs. These PSFs are used to alter the nominal HEPs according to the analyst's judgment (Miguel, 2006).

The PSFs are divided into three main classes:

1. External PSFs

   - Situational characteristics
   - Task characteristics
   - Job and task instructions

2. Internal PSFs

   - Organismic factors

3. Stressors

   - Psychological stressors
   - Physiological stressors

A number of specific PSFs under each class are listed and discussed in the THERP handbook. The analyst must identify the PSFs that seem likely to influence the HEP. The discussions in the THERP handbook about the various PSFs are highly readable, and it is recommended that you read these sections carefully before you start selecting specific PSFs.

*Basic Human Error Probability (HEP$_b$)*    Consider a specified action and let HEP$_n$ be the nominal HEP for this action as found in the THERP handbook. If only one PSF is found to influence the HEP, the *basic* HEP for the action is determined by

$$HEP_b = HEP_n \cdot PSF \tag{13.5}$$

This means that THERP uses a multiplicative model in the same way as failure rates are adjusted by covariates in MIL-HDBK 217F (see Chapter 7). PSF is a number that modifies the HEP$_n$. If PSF $> 1$, the basic HEP is greater than the nominal HEP, and if PSF $< 1$, the basic HEP is less than the nominal HEP. PSF $= 1$ means that the basic HEP is equal to the nominal HEP.

HEP is a probability and can therefore only take values in the interval $[0, 1]$. We must therefore be careful when choosing values for PSF such that our HEP$_b$ does not fall outside this interval. If, for example, we have HEP$_n = 0.4$ and PSF $= 3$, then HEP$_b = 1.2$, which does not make any sense, but might be interpreted as HEP$_b = 1.0$.

When several PSFs, say PSF$_1$, PSF$_2$, ..., PSF$_k$, are found to influence the HEP, the basic HEP is found by

$$HEP_b = HEP_n \cdot \prod_{i=1}^{k} PSF_i \tag{13.6}$$

In practice, more than 2 or 3 PSFs are rarely used for an individual action.

*Time Reliability Correlation (TRC)* The HEP of an action in an accident scenario may in some cases be time dependent. This time dependency comes from the THERP diagnosis model where the diagnosis failure probability is described as a function of the time $t$ that is available for diagnosis. The total HEP is then

$$\text{HEP}(t) = \Pr(T > t) + \Pr(A) \tag{13.7}$$

where $\Pr(A)$ is the HEP of postdiagnosis actions and $T$ is the (random) time required to complete the diagnosis. The THERP analyst can choose among three different curves for $\Pr(T > t)$ in the handbook, depending on the knowledge and experience of the operator (e.g., see NEA, 1998).

The premise for the TRC model is that time is the prime factor that affects the performance of the task (e.g., diagnosis). The time $t$ entered in the model is the estimated allowable time for correct diagnosis, which equals the maximum allowable time established by the system analysts minus the estimated time needed to get to a proper location and to perform required postdiagnosis action after a correct diagnosis.

*Dependencies Between Errors* Assume that an operator has committed an error $A$. The next action may end up in an error $B$. The errors $A$ and $B$ may be dependent such that the conditional probability $\Pr(B \mid A)$ is higher than if the event $A$ had not occurred. The causes of error $B$ may be split in two categories:

1. The error $B$ is a direct consequence of error $A$ [i.e., $\Pr(B \mid A) = 1$]. This will be the case with probability $\beta$.

2. The error $B$ is independent of whether error $A$ has occurred or not [i.e., $\Pr(B \mid A) = \Pr(B)$]. This case will occur with probability $1 - \beta$.

The dependency between the two consecutive human errors $A$ and $B$ is therefore modeled in THERP as

$$\Pr(B \mid A) = \beta + (1 - \beta) \Pr(B) \tag{13.8}$$

The parameter $\beta$, called the *dependency factor*, is the probability that the error $A$ will lead directly to error $B$. We note that when $\beta = 0$, then $\Pr(B \mid A) = \Pr(B)$, which means that $A$ and $B$ are independent and error $A$ will not influence the probability of committing error $B$. When $\beta = 1$, then $\Pr(B \mid A) = 1$ and we have "complete dependency," meaning that error $A$ will always lead to error $B$. Some typical values for $\beta$ are recommended in the THERP handbook:

$\beta = 0.05$—for low dependency

$\beta = 0.15$—for moderate dependency

$\beta = 0.50$—for high dependency

The THERP handbook gives detailed guidelines for how to determine the dependency factor $\beta$ for two tasks and for two persons. Check Chapters 10 and 18 of the handbook for details.

*Remark*: Note that the THERP dependency model (13.8) is very similar to the $\beta$-factor model for technical components (see Chapter 15). $\oplus$

*Error Recovery*  THERP may be used to quantify a number of error recovery options (Swain and Guttmann, 1983, Fig. 20-1):

- Personnel redundancy: The acting operator is checked by another operator or supervisor.

- Subsequent procedure step or task.

- Annunciating display (audible alarm).

- Periodical scanning inside control room or walk-around inspection outside the control room.

Probabilities for the various recovery options are provided in the THERP handbook.

***Analysis Procedure.***  The procedures of THERP are similar to those employed in conventional reliability analysis, except that human task activities are substituted for equipment functions. A THERP analysis can be carried out as a sequence of the following steps:

1. Plan and prepare.

2. Analyze task.

3. Develop event trees.

4. Assign nominal HEPs.

5. Assess the effect of PSFs and dependencies.

6. Determine the effects of recovery factors.

7. Determine success and failure probabilities.

8. Analyze sensitivity.

9. Recommend changes.

10. Report the analysis.

Steps 3 through 5 may have to be repeated to evaluate the changes. A slightly different procedure is described by Seong (2009).

*Step 1: Plan and Prepare*   This step is described in Chapter 8. Before starting the THERP analysis we assume that a quantitative risk analysis is being performed and that event trees have been established describing the relevant accident scenarios. Tasks performed by humans/operators may enter into one or more pivotal events (e.g., barriers) of the event trees. Human errors related to each of these tasks must be identified and analyzed. This is the objective of THERP.

*Step 2: Analyze Task*   The scenarios of interest are defined as part of the development of accident scenarios (see Chapter 11). As part of this activity, the study team specifies the critical tasks in the scenarios. The THERP analysis is, as such, driven by the needs of the hardware risk assessment.

Each of the critical tasks are then subject to a detailed task analysis. THERP does not give strict requirements to the task analysis method, and an HTA is in most cases sufficient.

THERP is usually applied at the level of specific tasks and the steps within these tasks. The starting point of the analysis is the lowest level in the HTA—the actions. The main error types of these actions are:

(a) Errors of omission (omit step or entire task)

(b) Errors of commission

(c) Selection error

   – Selects wrong control

   – Mispositions control

   – Issues wrong command

(d) Sequence error (action carried out in wrong order)

(e) Time error (too early/too late)

(f) Quantitative error (too little/too much)

From a system point of view, a human error is considered to be an error only when it reduces or has the potential for reducing system reliability, system safety, or the probability that some other system success criterion will be met.

For each task step in the task analysis, the analyst attempts to identify *error-likely situations*, in which the operator demand is likely to exceed her capacity.

*Step 3: Develop Event Trees*   An event tree is next used to map the possible operator performances. This process is also called *representation*. The THERP handbook uses a graphical layout of the event tree that is different from the one that is presented in Chapter 11. Each pivotal point in the event tree has two branches, one representing a correctly performed action and the other an erroneous action, that is a human error. An example of a THERP event tree is given in Figure 13.6. There is no logical difference between these two ways of drawing the event tree and we may therefore use the same layout as in Chapter 11 if we find this more convenient. The event tree maps the sequence of the various actions and errors. Each branch in the event tree ends up in an *end event* or *end state*. If we know the HEPs for each pivotal point, we may calculate the probabilities of the end events.

As part of this step, the study team should also consider potential *recovery actions*. In many cases, the operator will be able to correct errors that have been made. For example, if an operator forgets to press a pushbutton, she may become aware of this error when performing the next step in her procedure and rapidly correct the mistake. If the error recovery opportunities are not taken into account, the task error probabilities may be overestimated (e.g., see Kirwan, 1994).

*Step 4: Assign Nominal HEPs*   Chapter 20 of the THERP handbook consists of 27 data tables from which the nominal HEPs to be included in the THERP event tree are derived. It also includes a search scheme to help the analyst (i) to find the most appropriate table for a given type of human error, (ii) to adjust the nominal values in the tables when required, and (iii) to establish uncertainty bounds of the point estimates, if required.

When a task is evaluated for which there are no tabled HEPs in the handbook, it is recommended to assign a nominal HEP of 0.003 as a general error of omission or commission if it is judged to be some probability of either type of error. When evaluating abnormal events, a nominal HEP of 0.001 is assigned to those tasks for which the tables or text indicate that the HEP is "negligible" under normal conditions. This allows for the effects of stress that are associated with abnormal events.

*Step 5: Assess the Effect of PSFs and Dependencies*   The nominal HEP values have to be adjusted for plant-specific PSFs in order to arrive at *basic HEPs*. The nominal HEPs are based on "average" industrial conditions and they may be modified upward or downward. The basic HEPs do not take the previous tasks into account, which means that they are unconditional values, whereas the HEPs entered into the limbs of the HRA event tree must be conditional HEPs (except for the first task). This is obtained using the dependency tables in Chapter 20 of the handbook.

*Step 6: Determine the Effects of Recovery Factors*   The effect of recovery factors is quantified according to

$$\text{HEP}_r = \text{HEP}_n \cdot \prod_{j=1}^{m} w_j \cdot \prod_{k=1}^{n} \text{RF}_k \qquad (13.9)$$

where $w_j$ is a correction factor for PSF $j$, for $j = 1, 2, \ldots, m$, and $\text{RF}_k$ is recovery factor $k$ related to the error we are considering for $k = 1, 2, \ldots, n$. The factors can be found in the handbook.

*Step 7: Determine Success and Failure Probabilities*   When the estimates of the conditional probabilities of success or failure of each limb in the tree have been determined, the probability of each path through the tree is calculated by multiplying the probabilities of all limbs in the path. The probabilities must take into account the interdependency between the limbs in the tree.

When recovery is included and more than one person may correct an error, the level of dependency is also assessed and entered into the analysis. The analyst should keep in mind that the effect of dependence on human-error probabilities is always highly situation-specific. The concepts presented in the THERP handbook should be followed precisely.

*Step 8: Analyze Sensitivity*   If required, a sensitivity analysis may be carried out. See Chapter 16 for details about sensitivity analysis.

*Step 9: Recommend Changes*   Recommend changes to the system to reduce the system failure rate to an acceptable level.

*Step 10: Report the Analysis*   This step is described in Chapter 8.

**Resources and Skills Required.**   To carry out a THERP analysis, the THERP handbook (Swain and Guttmann, 1983) is essential since THERP is critically dependent on its database of nominal human error probabilities (HEPs) and a variety of other parameters.

THERP is a comprehensive and complex method and will require substantial training. Swain and Guttmann (1983) state clearly that the method is intended to assist trained risk analysts in quantifying human reliability. James Reason claims:

> THERP remains an art form—exceedingly powerful when employed by people as experienced as Alan Swain and his immediate collaborators, but of more doubtful validity in the hands of others (Reason, 1990, p. 224).

A reviewer of the THERP handbook, a human factors specialist, once said:

> The handbook is like an instrument, a "violin." It looks simple, but it requires skills and arts to use it.

**Advantages and Limitations.**   Assignment of nominal HEPs is often considered to be the most important role of THERP, yet the real importance is the methodological structure of the technique.

*Advantages*   The main advantages are that THERP is (see also Kirwan, 1994):

- well documented with an extensive history of successful usage;

- based on a powerful methodology that can be audited;

- founded on a database of information that is included in the THERP handbook.

*Limitations*   The main limitations are that THERP:

- can be resource intensive and time-consuming;

- requires a level of detail that can be excessive for many assessments.

A main criticism of THERP is its focus on the behavioral level of human performance. The human is treated in almost the same way as a machine component, apart from PSFs. Therefore, errors concerned with issues such as decision-making are not tackled.

## 13.4.2  HEART

The *human error assessment and reduction technique* (HEART) was developed by Williams (1986) and is intended to be used as a quick and efficient method for HRA. It is a general method that is intended to be applicable to any situation or industry where human reliability is important.

HEART was developed based on a review of the literature on human factors and, in particular, of experimental evidence showing the effects of various parameters on human performance. The HEPs are determined from a set of nominal HEPs and a selection and assessment of a set of performance-influencing factors, which in HEART are called *error-producing conditions* (EPCs). The HEPs are determined on the *task level* as opposed to THERP, where the tasks are broken down to basic actions and HEPs are determined for each action.

***Objectives and Applications.***    The objective of HEART is to provide realistic HEPs in a fast and efficient way, with focus on errors that may have a significant effect on the system in question.

The generic data are mainly derived from the nuclear industry, but HEART may also be used in several other industries.

***Method Description.***    The main elements of HEART are:

1. *Generic task types.* HEART defines eight generic task types. All tasks to be analyzed have to be classified into one of these eight generic types (a ninth task type is used for tasks that do not fit into the eight types).

2. *A table of nominal HEPs.* Nominal HEPs are listed for each generic task type, with 90% uncertainty bounds.

3. *Error-producing conditions* (EPCs). Thirty-eight different EPCs are used to modify the nominal HEPs for each generic task type. Quantitative values are provided for the influence of the EPCs.

4. *Calculation method.* A method for calculating the context-specific HEP is provided.

*Generic Task Types*    In HEART, all tasks are classified into one out of nine generic task types:

1. Totally familiar, performed at speed with no idea of likely consequences

2. Shift or restore system to new or original state on a single attempt without supervision or procedures

3. Complex task requiring a high level of comprehension and skill

4. Fairly routine task performed rapidly or given scant attention

5. Routine highly practised, rapid task involving a relatively low level of skill

6. Restore or shift a system to the original or new state following procedures with some checking

7. Completely familiar, well-designed, highly practised routine task occurring several times per hour

8. Respond correctly to system command even when there is an augmented or automated supervisory system

9. None of the above

*Nominal Human Error Probability (HEP$_n$)*  For each of the generic task types, a nominal human error probability, HEP$_n$, is given, together with a 90% uncertainty interval in the same way as for THERP. For generic task type 1, the nominal HEP is, for example, 0.55, and the uncertainty interval is 0.35 to 0.97.

In HEART, the nominal HEP is called *nominal human unreliability*. We will, however, use the term *nominal HEP*.

*Error-Producing Conditions (EPC)*  The nominal HEP is modified according to the presence and strength of a set of EPCs. An EPC is another name for a performance-influencing (or shaping) factor.

The EPCs used in HEART are related to:

– Unfamiliarity

– Shortage of time

– Low signal-to-noise ratio

– Ease of information suppression

– Ease of information assimilation

– Model mismatch (operator/designer)

– Reversing unintended actions

– Channel capacity overload

– Technique unlearning

– Transfer of knowledge

– Performance standard ambiguity

– Mismatch between perceived/real risk

A total of 38 specific EPCs are supplied together with multiplication factors $w_i$ ($i = 1, 2, \ldots, 38$) as part of the technique. The multiplication factors range between 1.02 and 17.

*Assessed Human Error Probability (HEP$_a$)*   To assess the HEP for a specified task, the analyst has to:

1. Select the generic task type to which the task should belong (one out of nine)

2. Select which of the 38 EPCs are expected to influence the HEP

3. Record the multiplication factors $w_i$ for the EPCs selected

4. Evaluate the EPCs and select a factor $p_i$ for each EPC. In HEART, the factor $p_i$ is called the *assessed proportion of effect* (POA) and has to be determined by the analyst. The POA factor must fulfill $0 \leq p_i \leq 1$ for all $i$ and should be determined as the degree of presence of EPC $i$.

In the same way as for THERP, HEART also uses a multiplicative model, where the the effect of EPC $i$ is taken into account by multiplying HEP$_n$ by

$$[(w_i - 1) \cdot p_i] + 1 \quad \text{for } i = 1, 2, \ldots, 38$$

Since all the multiplication factors $w_i$ are greater than 1, inclusion of an EPC will always increase the HEP$_a$. Considering all the 38 EPCs, the assessed HEP becomes

$$\text{HEP}_a = \text{HEP}_n \cdot \prod_{i=1}^{38} ([(w_i - 1) \cdot p_i] + 1) \tag{13.10}$$

It is not always clear whether a selected EPC is already covered in the nominal HEP. If the EPC is already covered, we give it double weight when modifying HEP$_n$ by this EPC.

*Remedial Measures*   HEART provides detailed suggestions for remedial measures related to each of the 38 EPCs and also to five generic error-producing tasks. For more details, see Williams (1986).

**Analysis Procedure.**   A HEART analysis can be divided in the following eight steps (see also Salmon et al., 2003):

1. Plan and prepare.

2. Perform a hierarchical task analysis.

3. Assign generic task type and nominal HEP.

4. Determine EPCs and assign multiplication factors .

5. Assess the POA of the EPCs.

6. Calculate the context-specific HEP.

7. Consider remedial measures.

8. Report the analysis.

HEART is documented in Williams (1986) and Kirwan (1994). Since the HEART data tables are required to perform the analysis, you should have one of these references available.

Steps 1 and 8 are discussed in Chapter 8 and are not treated further here.

*Step 2: Perform HTA*  The study team performs an HTA according to the procedure described in Section 13.4.

*Step 3: Assign Generic Task Type and Nominal HEP*  The study team considers the tasks one by one. Each task is assigned to one of the nine generic task types and a corresponding nominal HEP is found from tables in Williams (1986) or Kirwan (1994).

*Step 4: Determine EPCs and Assign Multiplication Factors*  In this step a set of relevant EPCs are selected from the 38 possible EPCs, and the multiplication factors $w_i$ of each EPC are determined. It is recommended that the user delimit the number ($\leq 4$) and select only significant EPCs.

*Step 5: Assess the POA of the EPCs*  The study team determines the assessed proportion of the effect (POA) for each of the EPCs selected. This is a rating between 0 and 1 (0 = low, 1 = high) and is based on the team's subjective judgment.

*Step 6: Calculate the Context-Specific HEP*  The context-specific HEP is next calculated as

$$\text{HEP}_r = \text{HEP}_n \cdot \prod_{i=1}^{38} \left( [(w_i - 1) \cdot p_i] + 1 \right) \tag{13.11}$$

*Step 7: Consider Remedial Measures*  The study team determines whether there are any possible remedial measures that can be taken to reduce or stop the incidence of the error identified. HEART provides some generic remedial measures, but the study team may be required to provide additional measures, depending on the nature of the error and the system being analyzed.

**Resources and Skills Required.**  The HEART technique is simple to use, requires little training, and does not require tools apart from a pen and paper. The associated HEART documentation is, however, required (HEART generic categories, HEART error-producing conditions, etc.).

### *Advantages and Limitations*

*Advantages*   The main advantages are that HEART:

- is appreciated by engineers and does not require extensive skills and resources;

- is reasonably well documented;

- provides remedial action for each error-producing condition;

- is relatively quick and straightforward to use;

- is highly flexible and has been used extensively in many sectors of industry (e.g., chemical, aviation, railway);

- has a significant error-reducing potential;

- gives the analyst a quantitative output;

- is one of the few HRA techniques that have been validated empirically (HSE, 2009).

*Limitations*   The main limitations are that HEART (see also Kirwan, 1994):

- can only assess single tasks;

- does not provide enough guidance for the analyst on a number of key aspects, such as task classification and also in determining the assessed proportion of effect;

- needs further validation;

- data for nominal HEPs are of questionable origin;

- is open to subjective variability between analysts;

- does not model dependencies.

A main criticism of HEART is that the EPC data have never been fully released, and it is therefore not possible to fully review the validity of the EPC database. There is a lack of justification for the simple multiplicative model that sees human error as a function of EPCs (some EPCs, or PSFs, will interact with each other).

### 13.4.3  CREAM

The *cognitive reliability and error analysis method* (CREAM), developed by Holl-nagel (1998), is a second-generation HRA method. In CREAM, human errors are assumed to have multiple causes and consequently, there is no single solution to prevent a future human error. All human actions occur within a *context* that will influence the person's actions. An important part of CREAM is therefore to analyze and understand this context. It is assumed that the control an operator has over his actions determines the reliability of his performance. A cognition model called the *contextual control model* (COCOM) has therefore been developed to assess this degree of control.

***Objectives and Applications.*** The objectives of CREAM are to:

(a) Identify those parts of the work, tasks or actions that require or depend on human cognition, and which therefore may be affected by variations in cognitive reliability.

(b) Determine the conditions under which the reliability of cognition may be reduced, and where therefore the actions may constitute a source of risk.

(c) Provide an appraisal of the consequences of human performance on system safety, which can be used in PRA/PSA.

(d) Develop and specify modifications that improve these conditions, hence serve to increase the reliability of cognition and reduce the risk.

CREAM was developed for the nuclear power industry but is a generic technique that can be applied in many application areas involving the operation of complex, dynamic systems. The method has, for example, been used in NASA projects and applied to a rail crash scenario. CREAM can be used both predictively, to predict potential human errors, and retrospectively, to analyze and quantify errors.

***Method Description.*** CREAM uses its own terminology for describing how errors happen. The main error causes are called *genotypes*, and the error modes, or manifestations of the errors, are called *phenotypes*. These concepts are used to describe how errors could potentially occur and to define the links between the causes and consequences of the error being analyzed. The genotypes are classified into three categories: individual, technical, and organizational causes, and the phenotypes are classified according to:

(a) Timing: too early, too late, omission

(b) Duration: too long, too short

(c) Sequence: reversal, repetition, commission, intrusion

(d) Object: wrong action, wrong object

(e) Force: too much, too little

(f) Direction: wrong direction

(g) Distance: too short, too far

(h) Speed: too fast, too slow

CREAM uses a nonhierarchical organization of categories linked by subcategories called *antecedents* and *consequents*. These are also classified into the categories individual, technical, and organizational. The individual category lists consequents related to the physical and cognitive limitations of a person. The technical category lists consequents related to technical failures. The organizational category lists consequents related to shortcomings in the organization in which a person operates. Several tables of antecedents and consequents have been developed to support the analysis.

**Analysis Procedure.**    The starting point of a CREAM analysis is a scenario that has been identified by a fault tree or event tree analysis. The analysis can be divided in the following eight steps (e.g., see Stanton et al., 2005):

1. Plan and prepare.

2. Perform task analysis (e.g., HTA).

3. Describe the context.

4. Specify the hazardous events.

5. Determine error propagation.

6. Select task steps for quantification.

7. Predict performance quantitatively.

8. Report the analysis.

Steps 1 and 8 are discussed in Chapter 8 and are not treated further here.

*Step 2: Perform a Task Analysis*    In this step the task or scenario in question is analyzed. It is recommended that a hierarchical task analysis (HTA) be used and that the analyst include considerations of both the organization and the technical system as well as looking at the operator and control tasks. The task analysis will produce a list of human actions to be analyzed further.

*Step 3: Describe the Context*    When the HTA in step 2 is completed, the analyst describes the context in which the task or scenario takes place. This involves considering several aspects of the context, called *common performance conditions* (CPCs), which are similar to the performance-influencing/shaping factors. CREAM distinguishes between nine CPCs:

1. Adequacy of organization

2. Working conditions

3. Adequacy of the man-machine interface and operational support

4. Availability of procedures/plans

5. Number of simultaneous goals

6. Available time

7. Time of day

8. Adequacy of training and experience

9. Quality of crew collaboration

The analyst must use subjective judgment to rate each CPC that is relevant for the task/scenario.

*Step 4: Specify the Hazardous Events*   In this step the analyst specifies the hazardous events that will be subject to human error predictions. Hollnagel (1998) suggests that event trees are used for this step, but since a task analysis has already been conducted in step 2, the results from this analysis may also be used. The analyst(s) should specify the tasks or task steps that are to be subject to further analysis (e.g., see Stanton et al., 2005).

*Step 5: Determine Error Propagation*   In step 5 the analyst describes how a hazardous event potentially can lead to an error occurrence. To predict errors, the analyst constructs a consequent/antecedent (error mode/error cause) matrix. The rows on the matrix show the possible consequents and the columns show the possible antecedents. The analyst starts by finding the classification group in the column headings that correspond to the initiating event (e.g., for missing information, it would be communication). The next step is to find all the rows that have been marked for this column. Each row should point to a possible consequent, which in turn may be found among the possible antecedents. The author suggests that in this way, the prediction can continue in a straightforward way until there are no paths left (Hollnagel, 1998). Each error should be recorded along with the associated causes (antecedents) and consequences (consequents).

*Step 6: Select Task Steps for Quantification*   Depending on the analysis requirements, a quantitative analysis may be required. If so, the analyst selects the error cases that require quantification. It is recommended that if quantification is required, all of the errors identified should be selected for quantification.

*Step 7: Predict Performance Quantitatively*   CREAM produces an overall assessment of the performance reliability expected for a task. The probability of error depends on the control mode the operator is in. By calculating the effects of the combined CPCs, a control mode is allocated. The analyst then focuses on performing further analysis on the situation of concern. Tables showing how CPCs affect one another are included in CREAM. For details about the quantitative analysis, see Hollnagel (1998).

**Resources and Skills Required.**   CREAM is a comprehensive and complicated method that requires substantial training. For very simple cases, CREAM can be applied using pen and paper, but a computer program will be required for most realistic cases. A software package has been developed to aid the analysts (Hollnagel, 1998).

*Standards and Guidelines*   There are no standards describing CREAM, but the method is described thoroughly in Hollnagel (1998) and it is strongly recommended that you study this book carefully before using CREAM and have the book available when performing the analysis.

### Advantages and Limitations

*Advantages*   The main advantages are that CREAM:

- is well documented in Hollnagel (1998);

- has the potential to be very exhaustive;

- considers the context;

- is a clear, structured, and systematic approach to error identification/quantification;

- can be used for both retrospective and predictive analyses;

- can be used both qualitatively and quantitatively.

*Limitations*   The main limitations are that CREAM:

- appears complicated and daunting to the novice user;

- is more comprehensive and more resource intensive than most other methods;

- has not been used extensively;

- does not offer remedial measures (i.e., ways to recover human errors are not given/considered);

- requires analysts with knowledge of human factors and cognitive psychology.

### 13.4.4   Other HRA Methods

A wide range of HRA methods have been developed, as already mentioned. In addition to THERP, HEART, and CREAM, we describe SLIM, ATHEANA, and MER-MOS briefly below. For a survey of many different methods, see, for example, HSE (2009).

***SLIM.*** The *success likelihood index methodology* (SLIM), developed for applications in U.S. nuclear power plants (NUREG/CR-3518, 1984), is an expert judgment method that can be used to analyze tasks that require problem solving. Experts in the task identify, assess, and weigh factors that influence task performance. The expert judgments are used to generate application-specific HEP estimates which are calibrated by observed HEP data.

A basis for SLIM is the observation that only a small set of PSFs will influence the HEP significantly and the assumption that experts will be able to assess the relative importance of these PSFs. It is further assumed that the experts are able to make a numerical rating as to how good or bad the PSFs are related to the task being analyzed, where "good" or "bad" mean that the PSFs will either reduce or increase the HEP.

When the weights and ratings are obtained, these are multiplied for each PSF and the resulting products are then summed to give the *success likelihood index* (SLI), which represents the overall belief of the experts regarding the effects of the PSFs on the HEP. The SLIs are then transformed into HEPs using the logarithmic relationship

$$\log \Pr(\text{success}) = a \cdot (\text{SLI}) + b$$

where $a$ and $b$ are empirically derived constants. The HEP for the task being analyzed is then found as

$$\text{HEP} = 1 - \exp(\log \Pr(\text{success}))$$

A computer-based version of SLIM has been developed based on multiattribute utility decomposition (MAUD). Kirwan (1994) claims that this method is a sophisticated approach which helps to ensure that the experts prevent biases that could affect their judgment.

A SLIM-MAUD analysis may be accomplished through the following steps:

1. Plan and prepare.

2. Determine the relevant PSFs.

3. Rate the tasks using the PSF scale.

4. Check for independency.

5. Weigh the PSFs.

6. Calculate the SLIs and convert them to HEPs.

7. Assess the uncertainty of the HEPs.

8. Identify proposals for error reduction and assess the effect of these.

9. Report the analysis.

SLIM may be used for a wide range of tasks at various levels of detail. The results produced by SLIM are, however, very sensitive to the quality of the expert judgments, and the calibration step has proved vulnerable to inaccuracies. Considerable resources are required, due to the number of experts needed.

***ATHEANA.***  *A technique for human error analysis* (ATHEANA) is a second-generation HRA approach that was developed for application in U.S. nuclear power plants (NUREG-1624, 2000; NUREG-1880, 2007). A central element of ATHEANA is the concept of *error-forcing context*, defined as:

☞ **Error-forcing context (EFC):** The situation that arises when particular combinations of *performance-shaping factors* and *plant conditions* create an environment in which unsafe actions are more likely to occur.

ATHEANA can be used both for a retrospective analysis of a serious event that has occurred and for a prospective analysis of potential future human errors, and can be used to obtain both qualitative and quantitative results.

An ATHEANA analysis can be carried out in eight steps (NUREG-1880, 2007):

1. Plan and prepare.

2. Describe the PRA accident scenario and its nominal context, including the norm of operations within the environment, considering actions and procedures.

3. Define the human failure events and/or unsafe actions that may affect the task in question.

4. Assess the relevant human performance information and characterizing factors that could lead to potential vulnerabilities.

5. Search for plausible deviations from the PRA scenario in terms of any probable divergence in the normal environmental operating behavior in the context of the situational scenario.

6. Evaluate the potential for recovery.

7. Estimate the HEPs for the human failure events and the unsafe acts.

8. Report the analysis.

ATHEANA is well documented and described thoroughly in NUREG-1624 (2000) and NUREG-1880 (2007). The most significant advantage of ATHEANA is that it provides a richer and more holistic understanding of the context of the human factors than do the first-generation methods. ATHEANA relies on a multidisciplinary team and seeks out inputs from a wide variety of sources in order to identify the error-forcing contexts.

***MERMOS.***  Méthode d'évaluation de la réalisations des missions opérateur pour la sûreté (MERMOS)[3] is a second-generation HRA approach developed by Electricité de France (EDF) for use in French nuclear power plants. A basis for MERMOS is the observation that an individual human error by itself is insufficient to explain why

---

[3]English: Method for assessing the performance of operator actions with respect to safety.

a team of operators fails to control a reactor during an accident. To overcome this limitation, MERMOS defines human error in a collective context.

An important concept in MERMOS is the *human factor mission*, which refers to the safety critical actions that the operating system has to initiate and carry out to handle an emergency. The performance of the human factor mission is the responsibility of the *emergency operations system* (EOS), comprising the operating crew, operating procedures, the man-machine interface, the formal organization, and the workplace. Instead of assuming that human error is a decisive element of failure, it is embedded within the EOS as one of its elements. For each potential emergency, a *functional analysis* is carried out to determine the human factor missions that have to be performed to recover or mitigate the accident.

MERMOS has two modules:

*Module 1.* Identify and define the human factor missions by a functional analysis, and describe the characteristics of each human factor mission and its context in a standard form. To aid the analysis, a database of human factor missions and potential failure scenarios has been established.

*Module 2.* Carry out a qualitative and quantitative analysis of the human factor missions.

MERMOS is a proprietary tool owned by EDF and the documentation available is limited. EDF has reported good results from using MERMOS, but its validity and reliability have yet to be established.

## 13.5 Additional Reading

The following titles are recommended for further study related to Chapter 13.

- *A Guide to Practical Human Reliability Assessment* (Kirwan, 1994) gives a straightforward and practical introduction to many aspects of human reliability and is a good starting point for learning how to integrate human reliability into quantitative risk analyses.

- *Human Factors Methods: A Practical Guide for Engineering and Design* (Stanton et al., 2005) gives a thorough survey of human factor methods and provides a good introduction to task analysis.

- *Review of human reliability assessment methods* (HSE, 2009) gives a survey of and compares a high number of HRA methods.

- *Managing the Risks of Organizational Accidents* (Reason, 1997) is a must for all people working with human and organizational factors related to risk assessment.

# CHAPTER 14

# JOB SAFETY ANALYSIS

## 14.1 Introduction

A *job safety analysis* (JSA) is a simple risk assessment method that is applied to review job procedures and practices in order to identify potential hazards and determine risk-reducing measures. Each job is broken down into specific tasks, for which observation, experience, and checklists are used to identify hazards and associated controls and safeguards. The JSA is carried out by a team, and most of the work is done in a *JSA meeting*. The results from the analysis are documented in JSA worksheets, as illustrated in Figure 14.2. Alternative names for JSA are *safe job analysis* (SJA), *job hazard analysis* (JHA), and *task hazard analysis* (THA).

## 14.2 Objectives and Applications

A JSA is used for three main purposes.

*1. Nonroutine jobs* A JSA is carried out for new and nonroutine jobs that are considered to have a high risk in order to:

*Risk Assessment: Theory, Methods, and Applications,* First Edition.
By Marvin Rausand. Copyright © 2011 John Wiley & Sons, Inc.

(a) Make the operators aware of inherent or potential hazards that may be encountered when executing the job;

(b) Provide pre-job safety instructions;

(c) Give operators guidance on how to deal with hazards events if such events should happen;

(d) Teach operators and supervisors how to perform the job correctly and in the safest possible way.

*2. Dangerous routine jobs*    A JSA is performed to scrutinize and make improvements to jobs that have led to several incidents or accidents. More detailed objectives are to:

(a) Reveal hazardous motions, postures, activities, or work practices of individual employees;

(b) Help determine how hazards should be managed in the work environment;

(c) Teach supervisors and employees how to perform operations correctly;

(d) Enhance communication between management and employees regarding safety concerns;

(e) Increase employee involvement in the safety process;

(f) Provide new personnel with "on-the job" safety awareness training;

(g) Create a basis for training and orienting new employees into the work environment.

*3. New work procedures*    A JSA may be used as a basis for establishing work instructions for new routine jobs.

In a JSA, the job is broken down into individual tasks or actions, and each of these is analyzed to reveal any actual or potential hazards that may be associated with these tasks/actions. Because of its in-depth and detailed nature, the JSA can identify potential hazards that may go undetected during routine management observations or audits. JSA has been used for many years and in many branches of industry and has been shown to be an effective tool for identifying hazardous conditions and unsafe acts.

## 14.3  Analysis Procedure

The analysis procedure will be slightly different for the three categories of applications (see Section 14.2). For all categories, a JSA will typically include the following seven steps:

1. Plan and prepare.

2. Become familiar with the job.

3. Break down the job.

4. Identify the hazards.

5. Categorize frequencies and consequences.

6. Develop solutions.

7. Report the analysis.

Each step must be completed before starting the next step. The various steps are explained in more detail below, and the analysis workflow for JSA is shown in Figure 14.1.

**Step 1: Plan and Prepare.**   This task was discussed in Chapter 8. To decide which jobs are in need for a JSA, the following criteria may be used:

1. Nonroutine jobs

   – System hazard analyses have indicated that the job is critical or dangerous.

   – The job has in the past produced a fatality or disabling injury in the same or a similar system.

   – The job involves hazardous materials or hazardous energy sources.

   – The job is new.

2. Dangerous routine jobs

   – The job has produced a high frequency of incidents or accidents.

   – The job has lead to one or more severe accidents or to incidents with potentially high severity.

   – The job involves hazardous materials.

   – The job involves hazardous energy sources.

   – The job is complex.

3. New work procedures.

   – All jobs that can potentially cause harm.

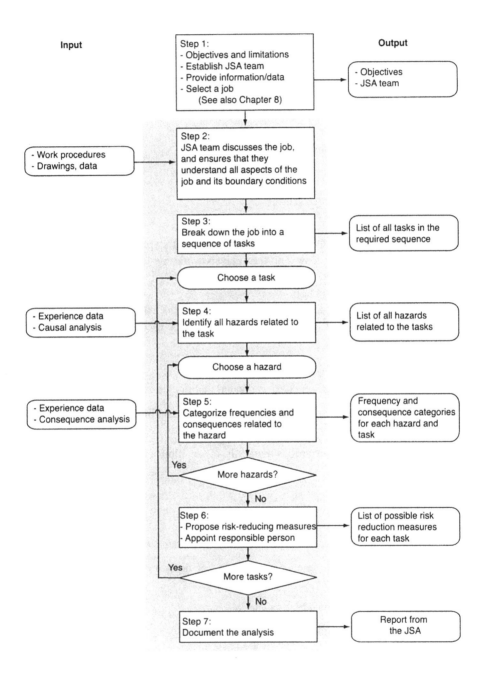

**Figure 14.1**  Analysis workflow for JSA.

*JSA Team*   The analysis is performed by a team comprising:

- A JSA leader (preferably the supervisor of the job to be analyzed).

- The line manager who is responsible for the job.

- An HSE representative.

- The workers who are going to do the job. The number of workers who should be involved depends on the type of job. If only a few workers are going to carry out the job, all of them should be involved in the analysis. If, however, the objective of the JSA is to establish safe work procedures that will apply for a large number of workers, it may be relevant to involve 2 or 3 workers who are familiar with the job.

If the job is complex, it may be beneficial to appoint a secretary, who can record the results into the JSA worksheets.

It is important that at least one of the team members have knowledge and experience with JSA. If none of the team members fulfill this requirement, an extra person with such knowledge should be invited to the team.

*JSA Meeting*   Most of the analysis is done in a JSA meeting where all team members must be present. The JSA meeting for nonroutine jobs should take place as close in time to the job execution as possible.

*Background Information*   Before the JSA meeting, the JSA leader should, when relevant:

- Provide written work procedures, manuals, drawings and other information relevant to the job. It is important that the information be up-to-date and reflect the current situation.

- Develop a preliminary breakdown of the job sequence into distinct tasks and list the tasks in the order in which they are to be performed.

*JSA Worksheet*   The JSA leader must prepare a suitable JSA worksheet that can be used to record the findings during the JSA meeting. Two alternative worksheets are shown in Figures 14.2 and 14.3.

**Step 2: Become Familiar with the Job.**   The JSA leader presents the job and its boundary conditions to the team members. The team discusses various aspects of the job and ensures that all team members understand the job and the various aspects related to it. If in doubt, more information has to be provided and it may also be necessary to visit the workplace and make observations. A JSA is not suitable for jobs that are defined too broadly: for example, "repairing an engine," or too narrowly: for example, "opening the valve."

***Step 3: Break Down the Job.*** Most jobs can be broken down into a sequence of tasks. The starting point of this step is the preliminary job breakdown that has been made by the JSA leader prior to the meeting. It is important that the tasks be described briefly and be action-oriented. For each task, *what* is to be done should be described, for example, by using words such as *lift, place, remove, position, install,* and *open*—not *how* this is done. The level of detail required is determined by the level of hazard. Tasks that do not have the potential to cause significant hazards do not need to be broken down into lower levels. When the job breakdown is done, the sequence of the tasks should, if relevant, be verified by the worker(s) to ensure completeness and accuracy. A rule of thumb is that most jobs can be described in fewer than ten tasks.

The following aspects should be considered:

(a) The task as it is planned to be done

(b) The preparation before the task, and the closing of the task

(c) Special activities such as tool provision, cleaning, and so on

(d) Correction of deviations that may occur

It may also be relevant to consider:

(e) Maintenance and inspection/testing of equipment and tools

(f) Corrective maintenance tasks

This step of the analysis will often be more time-consuming than the subsequent hazard identification in step 4. It is important that the task descriptions be short and that all tasks be covered. Before starting to identify hazards in step 4, the JSA team should ensure that the list of tasks is as complete as possible.

***Step 4: Identify the Hazards.*** Once the job has been broken down into tasks, each task is reviewed to identify any actual or potential hazards. To accomplish this, the team may wish to observe a similar job being carried out, and consult accident reports, employees, management/supervisors, industrial or manufacturing organizations, or other companies with similar operations. Hazard checklists, similar to those used in relation to a preliminary hazard analysis (see Chapter 9), are useful at this stage. One such checklist is, for example, included in ISO 12100 (2010). A brief checklist is also supplied in Appendix 2 of OSHA (2002). Questions such as those listed in Table 14.1 may also be useful when identifying hazards.

***Step 5: Categorize Frequencies and Consequences.*** To be able to prioritize between different risk reduction actions, each hazard needs to be evaluated with respect to frequency and potential consequences. The frequency and consequences may be classified according to the categories in Tables 4.8 and 4.9, but other and more simple categories may also be used: for example "high," "medium," and "low."

In many JSAs, the frequency and consequence categorization is skipped and not documented in the JSA worksheet. An alternative JSA worksheet without risk evaluation is shown in Figure 14.3.

Job: Lift containers from ship to quay   Date: 2011-01-20

Reference: Job 14/C   JSA team members: Names

| No. | Task | Hazard/cause | Potential consequences | Risk Freq. | Risk Cons. | RPN | Risk reducing measure | Responsible |
|---|---|---|---|---|---|---|---|---|
| 1 | Attach four hooks to the container | Heavy hooks | Back problems | 3 | 1 | 4 | Better design of hook or hook fasteners | |
| | | Crushing between the hook and the container | Crushing harm to fingers and/or arms | 3 | 1 | 4 | Mandatory use of protective gloves | |
| | | Fall on same level | Fall injury | 4 | 1 | 5 | More tidy work area | |
| | | Fall to lower level | Severe fall injury | 2 | 3 | 5 | Better design of ladder | |
| 2 | Lift the container | Container swings toward worker | Serious crushing harms, possible fatality | 2 | 4 | 6 | The worker must stand behind a barrier when the lifting is started. The container must always be lifted vertically. | |
| | | Container crashes into an other object which falls toward worker | Serious crushing harms, possible fatality | 3 | 4 | 7 | Remove objects that may come in contact with the lifting. The worker must be standing behind a barrier when the lifting is started. | |
| | | Container falls down, ruptured wires | Serious crushing harms, possible fatality | 2 | 4 | 6 | Labor must withdraw to a location x when the container has left the ground | |

**Figure 14.2**  JSA worksheet (example).

**Table 14.1**   Questions used to identify hazards.

---

- Is there danger for striking against, being struck by, or otherwise making harmful contact with an object?
- Can any body part get caught in, by, or between objects?
- Do tools, machines, or equipment present any hazards?
- Can the worker make harmful contact with moving objects?
- Can the worker slip or trip?
- Can the worker fall from one level to another or even fall on the same level?
- Can the worker suffer strain from lifting, pushing, bending, or pulling?
- Is the worker exposed to extreme heat or cold?
- Is excessive noise or vibration a problem?
- Is there a danger from falling objects?
- Is lighting a problem?
- Can weather conditions affect safety?'
- Are there flammable, explosive, or electrical hazards?
- Is harmful radiation a possibility?
- Can contact be made with hot, toxic, or caustic substances?
- Are there dust, fumes, mists, or vapors in the air?

---

*Source*: The questions are based partly on CCOHS (2009). The list is not complete.

***Step 6: Develop Solutions.***   Once the hazards have been identified and assessed, the JSA team proposes one or more of the following measures to manage or eliminate the associated risk.

- Engineering controls

  - Eliminate or minimize the hazard through design changes. Change the physical conditions that create the hazards. Substitute a less hazardous substance. Modify or change equipment and tools.
  - Enclose the hazard or the personnel.
  - Isolate the hazard with guards, interlocks, or barriers.

- Administrative controls

  - Use written procedures, work permits, safe practices.
  - Introduce exposure limitations.
  - Improve training.
  - Increase monitoring and supervision during the job.
  - Reduce the frequency of the job or of a task.

| Job Safety Analysis (JSA) | No. |
|---|---|
| Job sequence: | |
| Task: | No. |
| JSA team members: | |
| Task description: | |
| Hazards: | |
| Potential consequences: | |
| Risk-reducing measures: | |
| Required safety equipment: | |
| Required personal protection equipment: | |
| Date and signature: | |

**Figure 14.3** Alternative JSA worksheet.

- Find a safer way to do the job.

– Personal protective equipment

- Hard hats
- Safety glasses

- Protective clothing
- Gloves
- Hearing protection
  ...and so on.

For further details, see, for example, OSHA (2002) and CCOHS (2009).

***Step 7: Report the Analysis.***   The results from the JSA are usually documented in a worksheet, for example as shown in Figures 14.2 and 14.3. More details may also be found in Chapter 8.

### ▣ EXAMPLE 14.1   Lifting heavy containers

A number of heavy containers are to be lifted from a ship to a quay. The containers are lifted by a large crane. A worker attaches four hooks to each container. To attach the hooks, he has to climb a portable ladder, fetch a hook and attach it to the container. The hook is rather heavy and the work position is awkward. It is therefore easy to get back problems. It is further possible to crush fingers and hands between the hook and the container. When the hooks are attached, the worker signals the crane operator to start lifting the container. During this operation, the container may swing and hit the worker. Other hazards are related to falls on the same level and from the ladder.

Figure 14.2 shows some few hazards related to this job. The figure is meant as an illustration and is not based on a thorough analysis.   ⊕

## 14.4   Resources and Skills Required

JSA is a simple analysis and does not require any formal education or deep analytical skills. The analysis must, however, be carried out by personnel who are familiar with the particular job and who know the system in which it is executed.

The number of team members that are required depends on the complexity of the job, and may vary from 2 to 12. At least one of the team members should be familiar with the analysis method and have some experience from earlier JSAs.

The time needed to carry out a JSA depends on the complexity of the job and the experience of the team members. A single task may not need more than 5-10 minutes. A job with 10 tasks may then be completed in 2–3 hours.

A JSA requires a fairly extensive collection of information. This includes information that is necessary both to understand the tasks and to identify hazards. For systems that have been in operation for some time, a lot of experience is often available. First and foremost, this is found among those who do the work and with supervisor(s). The information is collected through:

- Interviews

- Written job instructions (may be inaccurate and often incomplete)

- Manuals for machinery

- Work studies, if they exist

- Direct observation of tasks

- Audiovisual aids (photography or video recording)

- Reports of accidents and near misses

Observations and interviews are necessary for the analysis to be done correctly. It is also important to establish a good and trustful contact with the persons who carry out the work to be analyzed.

## 14.5   Advantages and Limitations

*Advantages.*   The main advantages are that a JSA:

- gives the workers training in safe and efficient work procedures;

- increases the workers' awareness of safety problems;

- introduces new employees to the job and safe work procedures;

- provides pre-job instructions for irregular jobs;

- identifies safeguards that need to be in place;

- enhances employee participation in workplace safety;

- promotes positive attitudes about safety.

*Limitations.*   The main limitation of a JSA is that it may be too time-consuming and confusing for complex jobs.

## 14.6   Additional Reading

The following titles are recommended for further study related to Chapter 14.

- *Job hazard analysis* is a guideline issued by the U.S. Occupational Health and Safety Authority (OSHA, 2002).

- *Common Model for Safe Job Analysis (SJA)* is a guideline published by the Norwegian Oil Industry Association (OLF-090, 2006).

- *Job safety analysis made simple* is a guideline by the Canadian Centre for Occupational Health and Safety (CCOHS, 2009).

- *Task risk assessment* is a guideline published by Step Change in Safety (Step Change, 2007).

- *Basic Guide to System Safety* (Vincoli, 2006). Section 4.4 gives an introduction to JSA.

# CHAPTER 15

# COMMON-CAUSE FAILURES

CCF analysis is an integral part of any PSA, from the unavailability of systems to the dominant accident scenarios.

—Apostolakis and Moieni (1987)

## 15.1 Introduction

Common-cause failures (CCFs) have been considered in probabilistic risk analyses of nuclear power plants since the early 1970s (e.g., see NUREG-75/014, 1975). This industry has since then had a continuous focus on CCFs, and has been a driving force for the development of CCF models and with respect to collection and analysis of data related to CCFs. The aviation industry has also given these failures close attention, and the Norwegian offshore oil and gas industry has since the mid-1980s

*Risk Assessment: Theory, Methods, and Applications,* First Edition.
By Marvin Rausand. Copyright © 2011 John Wiley & Sons, Inc.

focused on CCFs related to reliability assessment of safety instrumented systems (e.g., see Hauge et al., 2010).

More recently, the IEC 61508 (2010) standard focuses on the need to control CCFs in order to maintain the safety integrity level (SIL) of safety instrumented functions (see Section 12.4). The standard suggests a method of calculating the probability of failure on demand where the contribution of CCF is modeled by the well-known beta-factor model.

## 15.2  Basic Concepts

### 15.2.1  Dependent Failures

When components of a system fail, the failures cannot always be considered as independent events. Two main types of dependency can be distinguished: *positive* and *negative*. If the failure of one component leads to an increased tendency for another component to fail, the dependency is said to be positive. If, on the other hand, the failure of one component leads to a reduced tendency for another component to fail, the dependency is called negative.

■ **EXAMPLE 15.1   System with two components**

Consider a system of two components, 1 and 2. Let $E_i$ denote the event that component $i$ is in a failed state, for $i = 1, 2$. The probability that both components are failed is

$$\Pr(E_1 \cap E_2) = \Pr(E_1 \mid E_2) \cdot \Pr(E_2) = \Pr(E_2 \mid E_1) \cdot \Pr(E_1)$$

The two components are *independent* when $\Pr(E_1 \mid E_2) = \Pr(E_1)$ and $\Pr(E_2 \mid E_1) = \Pr(E_2)$, such that

$$\Pr(E_1 \cap E_2) = \Pr(E_1) \cdot \Pr(E_2)$$

The components have a *positive dependency* when $\Pr(E_1 \mid E_2) > \Pr(E_1)$ and $\Pr(E_2 \mid E_1) > \Pr(E_2)$, such that

$$\Pr(E_1 \cap E_2) > \Pr(E_1) \cdot \Pr(E_2)$$

and the components have a *negative dependency* when $\Pr(E_1 \mid E_2) < \Pr(E_1)$ and $\Pr(E_2 \mid E_1) < \Pr(E_2)$, such that

$$\Pr(E_1 \cap E_2) < \Pr(E_1) \cdot \Pr(E_2)$$

⊕

This chapter is based on joint work with **Per Hokstad**, SINTEF. Section 15.6 is reproduced from Hokstad and Rausand (2008) with permission from Springer.

Positive dependency is usually the most relevant type of dependency in risk analyses, but negative dependency may also occur in practice. Consider, for example, two components that influence each other by producing vibrations or heat. When one component is "down" for repair, the other component will have an improved operating environment, and its probability of failure is reduced.

### 15.2.2  Intrinsic and Extrinsic Dependencies

Dependencies may be classified as intrinsic or extrinsic. An *intrinsic dependency* is a dependency where the status and performance of a component are affected by the status of another component in a system. This type of dependency is often deliberately designed into the system, for example, when a component is needed only when another component is failed.

An *extrinsic dependency* is due to external sources such as harsh environment or human intervention. For more about intrinsic and extrinsic dependencies, see NUREG/CR-6268 (2007).

### 15.2.3  Cascading Failures

A special type of intrinsic dependency occurs when the failure of one component leads to increased loads on one or more other components in the system and causes these to fail. This dependency is sometimes called *intercomponent dependency* or *cascading failures*.

☞ **Cascading failures**: A sequence of component failures where the first failure shifts its load to one or more nearby components such that these fail and again shift their load to other components, and so on.

Cascading failures may be modeled explicitly: for example, by Markov diagrams or Petri nets. Cascading failures have been experienced especially in power grids and computer networks, but can also occur in mechanical and electromechanical systems.

### 15.2.4  Common-Cause Failures

Consider a system of two components, 1 and 2. Let $E_i$ denote the event that component $i$ is in a failed state, for $i = 1, 2$. One way of formulating dependency stems from the idea that the components are susceptible to some common stress that causes simultaneous failures. When this common stress occurs, the event "$E_1$ and $E_2$" (i.e., $E_1 \cap E_2$) is referred to as a *CCF event*. The CCF event may be due to several types of intrinsic and extrinsic dependencies. The following categories are sometimes distinguished:

- Physical dependencies

- Functional dependencies

– Location/environmental dependencies

– Plant configuration-related dependencies

– Human dependencies

There is no generally accepted definition of CCF. This implies that people in different industry sectors may have different opinions of what a CCF event is. Smith and Watson (1980) review nine different definitions of CCF and suggest that a definition of CCF must encompass the following six attributes:

1. The components affected are unable to perform as required.

2. Multiple failures exist within (but not limited to) redundant configurations.

3. The failures are a "first in line" type of failure, not the result of cascading failures.

4. The failures occur within a defined critical time period (e.g., the time that a plane is in the air during a flight).

5. The failures are due to a single underlying defect or physical phenomenon (the common cause of the failures).

6. The effect of failures must lead to some major disabling of the system's ability to perform as required.

In the nuclear power industry, a CCF event is defined as

☞ **Common-cause failure (CCF)**: A dependent failure in which two or more component fault states exist simultaneously, or within a short time interval, and are a direct result of a shared cause (NEA, 2004b).

In the space industry, a CCF event is defined as "the failure (or unavailable state) of more than one component due to a shared cause during the system mission" (Stamatelatos et al., 2002a). The term *CCF* implies the existence of a cause-effect relationship that links the CCF event to some cause. Such a relationship is not, however, reflected in most of the CCF models that are presented later in this chapter (e.g., see Littlewood, 1996).

A crucial question related to the definition of CCF is how to interpret the term *simultaneous*. It is obvious that there can be a strong dependency even if the failures do not occur at the same time. In the Stamatelatos et al. (2002a) definition, a multiple failure is classified as a CCF event if the failures occur during the same mission. Such a mission may last a long time. In the aviation industry the term *CCF* is used for multiple failures during the same flight. For safety instrumented systems, the main functional failures are often *hidden* and can only be detected during periodic function tests. In this case, it seems natural to classify a multiple failure as a CCF if failures of redundant components occur within the same test interval (e.g., see Lundteigen and Rausand, 2007). The test interval may extend over several months and even years.

Since the failures are hidden and not detected until the test is carried out, it is not easy to decide whether the failures that are detected in a test have occurred due to the same cause or whether they have occurred at the same time.

### ▣ EXAMPLE 15.2   Fire detectors

Consider a set of fire detectors that are installed in the same room. The detectors are sensitive to humidity and will tend to fail if the humidity in the room increases above a certain level. If the humidity becomes too high, the detectors will deteriorate and fail, but not necessarily at the same time. The failures may be spread out over a rather long period of time. When the detectors are checked in the periodic test, the problem is likely be detected, and both the failed and deteriorated detectors will be repaired or replaced.           ⊕

Whether or not the multiple failures that are detected in the test represent a true CCF event must be decided on the basis of a thorough investigation of the causes of the component failures. The common cause may, for example, be erroneous maintenance or environmental stresses (e.g., vibration, high temperature, or high humidity). These causes may lead to failures of different multiplicities. Following this argument, a common cause may lead to just one component failing; thus a CCF of multiplicity 1 is also possible.

Analysts are sometimes tempted to treat all multiple failures that occur close in time as CCFs. We should try to avoid this. The classification of multiple failures as CCFs should be based on the cause of the failures.

Dependent failures have particularly been studied in systems where there is a high risk for fatal accidents. Methods for controlling and preventing such failures have been developed during safety analyses within the aviation and nuclear power industries.

### ▣ EXAMPLE 15.3   Offshore drilling rig

A CCF event occurred in 1982 in Canadian waters when the entire 84-man crew on the Ocean Ranger semi-submersible drilling rig was lost when the rig sank due to a total loss of ballast control and of stability. The U.S. National Transportation Safety Board inquiry into the disaster found that the loss of control was due to ingress of seawater into the ballast control panel when a portlight glass broke in severe storm conditions. Despite four hours of frenetic effort, the crew failed to rectify the situation.

A similar accident occurred in the North Sea in 1986 when a semi-submersible rig lost ballast control and was almost lost. On this occasion, the fault was lack of a filter and ingress of foreign particles into the hydraulic systems, which prevented several control valves from closing correctly.           ⊕

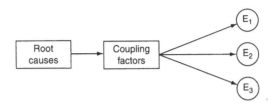

**Figure 15.1** Root causes in combination with coupling factors lead to CCFs ($E_i$ denotes that item $i$ is failed, for $i = 1, 2, 3$).

IEC 61508 (2010) defines a CCF as a "failure which is the result of one or more events, causing coincident failures of two or more separate channels in a multiple channel system, leading to system failure." The last part of this definition, "...leading to system failure," is controversial. This statement implies that if two channels fail simultaneously in a three-channel system, it is a CCF if the voting is 2-out-of-3 (2oo3), but not if the voting is 1oo3. This is because a 1oo3 system is still functioning when two channels are in a failed state.

## 15.3 Causes of CCFs

It is often found to be useful to split CCF causes into *root causes* and *coupling factors* (e.g., see Parry, 1991; Paula et al., 1991). A root cause is a basic cause of a component failure (e.g., a corrosive environment), while a coupling factor explains why several components are affected by the same root cause (e.g., inadequate material selection for several valves). Root causes and coupling factors leading to CCFs are illustrated in Figure 15.1.

### 15.3.1 Root Causes

A *root cause* of a failure is defined as:

☞ **Root cause**: The root cause of a specified failure is the most basic cause that, if corrected, would prevent recurrence of this and similar failures.

A series of causes of an accident (or TOP event) can often be identified, one leading to another. This series of causes should be pursued until the fundamental, correctable cause has been identified (US DOE, 1992). The concept of root cause is tied to that of defense, because there are, in many cases, several possible corrective actions (i.e., defenses) that can be taken to prevent recurrence. Knowledge of root causes allows system designers to incorporate barriers for reducing the susceptibility to both single failures and CCFs.

Root causes of CCF events have been investigated in a number of studies, and several classification schemes have been proposed and used to categorize these events (e.g., see Paula et al., 1991; NEA, 2004b; US DOE, 1992; Rasmuson, 1991). Several of these studies have shown that the majority of the root causes in complex systems are related to human actions and procedural deficiencies. A study of centrifugal pumps in nuclear power plants indicates that the root causes of about 70% of all CCFs are of this category (Miller et al., 2000).

In practice, root causes of component failures can seldom be determined from failure reports. CCF root causes have to be identified through root cause analyses, supported by checklists of generic root causes (US DOE, 1992). The description of a CCF in terms of a single root cause is in many cases too simplistic (Parry, 1991), and Cooper et al. (1993) therefore advocate using the concept of *common failure mechanism* instead of root cause to cater to multiple root causes.

## 15.3.2 Coupling Factors

A *coupling factor* may be defined as:

☞ **Coupling factor**: A property that makes multiple components susceptible to failure from a single shared cause.

Examples of coupling factors include[1]:

– Same design

– Same hardware

– Same software

– Same installation staff

– Same maintenance or operation staff

– Same procedures

– Same environment

– Same location

Studies of CCFs in nuclear power plants indicate that the majority of coupling factors contributing to CCFs are related to operational aspects (Miller et al., 2000).

To save money and ease operation and maintenance, the technical solutions in many industries become more and more standardized. This applies both to hardware and software and increases the presence of coupling factors. SINTEF, the Norwegian research organization, has carried out several studies of the impacts of this type of standardization on Norwegian offshore oil and gas installations, where new operational concepts and reduced manning levels are feeding this trend (Hauge et al., 2006).

---

[1]A more detailed survey of coupling factors is given in NEA (2004b), NUREG/CR-5485 (1998), and Childs and Mosleh (1999).

## 15.4 Modeling of CCFs

### 15.4.1 Explicit vs. Implicit Modeling

CCFs can be modeled *explicitly* or *implicitly*. If a specific cause of a CCF can be identified and defined, this cause may be included explicitly in the system logic models: for example, as a basic event in the fault tree model as illustrated in Figure 15.2, or as a functional block in a reliability block diagram (e.g., see Stamatelatos et al., 2002b; Rausand and Høyland, 2004). Explicit causes may also be included in event trees. Examples of causes that may be modeled explicitly are:

– Human errors

– Utility failures (e.g., electricity, cooling, heating)

– Environmental events (e.g., earthquake, lightning)

📖 **EXAMPLE 15.4    Explicit modeling of common-cause failures**

Two pressure sensors are installed on a pressurized vessel. The pressure sensor system fails when both sensors fail at the same time. This can happen as two independent failures or as a CCF where both sensors fail, as illustrated in the fault tree in Figure 15.2. The pressure sensors are installed on a common tap (thin pipe) on the vessel. If the tap is plugged with solids, the sensors will not be able to detect high pressure in the vessel. The sensors are calibrated regularly by the same test team. If they miscalibrate one sensor, they are likely to make the same error regarding the other sensor. These explicit causes of common-cause failures are illustrated in the fault tree in Figure 15.2.                        ⊕

Some causes of dependencies are difficult or even impossible to identify and model explicitly. These are called *residual causes* and are catered to by implicit modeling. Residual causes cover many different root causes and coupling factors, such as common manufacturer, common environment, and maintenance errors. There are so many causes that an explicit representation of all of them in a fault tree or an event tree would not be manageable.

When establishing the implicit model, it is important to remember which causes were covered in the explicit model, so that they will not be counted twice. For small system modules, it may be possible to use Markov techniques and/or Petri nets to model both explicit and implicit causes, as illustrated in Chapter 10 (see also Lundteigen and Rausand, 2009).

### 15.4.2 Modeling Approach

Modeling and analysis of CCF as part of a risk or reliability study should, in general, comprise at least the following steps (see also Rasmuson, 1991; Johnston, 1987):

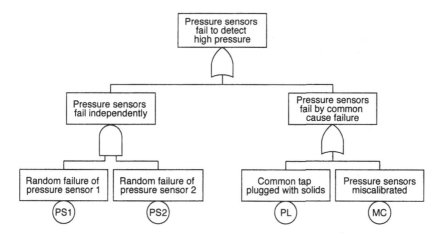

**Figure 15.2**    Explicit modeling of common-cause failure of a system with two pressure sensors (adapted from Summers and Raney, 1999).

1. *Develop system logic models.* This activity comprises system familiarization, system functional failure analysis, and establishment of system logic models (e.g., fault trees, reliability block diagrams, and event trees).

2. *Identify common-cause component groups.* This involves identifying the groups of components for which the assumption about independency is suspected not to be correct.

3. *Identify root causes and coupling factors.* The root causes and coupling factors are identified and described for each common-cause component group. Suitable tools are checklists and root cause analysis.

4. *Assess component defenses.* The common-cause component groups are evaluated with respect to their defenses against the root causes that were identified in the previous step.

5. *Establish explicit models.* Explicit CCFs are identified for each common-cause component group and included in the system logic model.

6. *Include implicit models.* Residual CCFs not covered in step 5 are included in an implicit model, as discussed later in this section. The parameters of this model have to be estimated based on checklists (e.g., see IEC 61508, 2010) or available data.

7. *Quantify and interpret the results.* The results from the previous steps are merged into an overall assessment of the system. The step will also cover importance, uncertainty, and sensitivity analyses—and reporting of results. In most cases we will not be able to find high-quality input data for the explicitly

modeled CCF causes. However, even with low-quality input data, or "guessti-mates," the result will usually be more accurate than those that will be obtained by including the explicit causes in a general (implicit) CCF model.

The CCF models that are discussed in the rest of this section are limited to implicit causes of CCF.

### 15.4.3 Multiplicity of Failures

A failure of a component can be a single failure or one failure in a set of multiple failures. The number of simultaneously failed components is called the *multiplicity* of the failure. In the following, the components are referred to as *channels*. We are interested in studying this multiplicity and its distribution.

Consider a system with $n$ channels. In many CCF models, the following assumptions are made:

– There is complete symmetry in the $n$ channels, and the components of each channel have the same constant failure rate.

– All combinations where $k$ channels fail and $n - k$ channels do not fail have the same probability of occurrence.

– Removing $j$ of the $n$ channels will have no effect on the probabilities of failure of the remaining $n - j$ channels.

Several distributions of the multiplicity of failures can be defined and we will come back to some of these later in the chapter. Here, we will simply illustrate the situation for a system with three identical channels.

**System with Three Channels.** Let $E_i^*$ denote that channel $i$ is functioning and $E_i$ that it has failed, for $i = 1, 2, 3$. The failure of a specific channel, say channel 1, can be involved in four disjoint failure scenarios:

– The failure of channel 1 is involved in a single failure; that is, $E_1 \cap E_2^* \cap E_3^*$.

– The failure of channel 1 is, together with the failure of channel 2, involved in a double failure; that is, $E_1 \cap E_2 \cap E_3^*$.

– The failure of channel 1 is, together with the failure of channel 3, involved in a double failure; that is, $E_1 \cap E_2^* \cap E_3$.

– Channel 1 has, together with channels 2 and 3, a triple failure; that is, $E_1 \cap E_2 \cap E_3$.

Similar expressions can be derived for channels 2 and 3.

Let $g_{k,n}$ denote the probability of a specific combination of functioning and failed channels, such that (exactly) $k$ channels are in a failed state and $n - k$ channels are functioning. The probability of a *specific* single (individual) failure is then

$$\begin{aligned} g_{1,3} &= \Pr(E_1 \cap E_2^* \cap E_3^*) \\ &= \Pr(E_1^* \cap E_2 \cap E_3^*) = \Pr(E_1^* \cap E_2^* \cap E_3) \end{aligned} \tag{15.1}$$

The probability of a *specific* double failure is

$$
\begin{aligned}
g_{2,3} &= \Pr(E_1 \cap E_2 \cap E_3^*) \\
&= \Pr(E_1 \cap E_2^* \cap E_3) = \Pr(E_1^* \cap E_2 \cap E_3)
\end{aligned}
\tag{15.2}
$$

and the probability of a triple failure is

$$
g_{3,3} = \Pr(E_1 \cap E_2 \cap E_3)
\tag{15.3}
$$

Let $Q_{k:3}$ be the probability that a system with three identical channels has a (unspecified) failure with multiplicity $k$, for $k = 1, 2, 3$. Failures of multiplicity 1 and 2 can occur in three different ways, and therefore

$$
Q_{1:3} = \binom{3}{1} \cdot g_{1,3} = 3 \cdot g_{1,3}
$$

$$
Q_{2:3} = \binom{3}{2} \cdot g_{2,3} = 3 \cdot g_{2,3}
\tag{15.4}
$$

$$
Q_{3:3} = \binom{3}{3} \cdot g_{3,3} = g_{3,3}
$$

*Conditional Probability of a Specific Multiplicity*   Assume that we observe (test) a channel and find the channel in a failed state. Without loss of generality, we can assume that this is channel 1. Let $Q$ denote the probability of this event. When such a failure is observed, we know that the multiplicity of failures is either 1, 2, or 3. Let $f_{k,3}$ be the conditional probability that the failure has multiplicity $k$ when we know that a specific channel has failed, for $k = 1, 2, 3$. For a triple failure, the failure of channel 1 is included in the triple failure event, and we have

$$
f_{3,3} = \Pr(E_1 \cap E_2 \cap E_3 \mid E_1) = \frac{\Pr(E_1 \cap E_2 \cap E_3)}{\Pr(E_1)} = \frac{g_{3,3}}{Q}
\tag{15.5}
$$

For a double failure, the failure of channel 1 is included in two out of the three possible failure combinations in (15.2). By using the same argument as above, we get the conditional probability of having a double failure involving channels 1 and 2 as

$$
\frac{g_{2,3}}{Q}
$$

and the conditional probability of a double failure involving channels 1 and 3 is

$$
\frac{g_{2,3}}{Q}
$$

The conditional probability of a double failure involving channel 1 and one of the other channels is

$$
f_{2,3} = \frac{g_{2,3}}{Q} + \frac{g_{2,3}}{Q} = \frac{2g_{2,3}}{Q}
\tag{15.6}
$$

For a single failure, the failure of channel 1 is included in only one failure combination in (15.1). The conditional probability that the failure of channel 1 is a single failure is

$$f_{1,3} = \frac{g_{1,3}}{Q} \tag{15.7}$$

and we note that $f_{1,3} + f_{2,3} + f_{3,3} = 1$ since there are only three disjoint possibilities.

Similar formulas can be established for systems with a general number $n$ of identical channels.

## 15.5 The Beta-factor Model

The *beta-factor model* introduced by Fleming (1975) is still the most commonly used CCF model. The beta-factor model may be explained by the following simple situation: Consider a system of $n$ identical channels each with constant failure rate $\lambda$. Given that a specific channel has failed, this failure will, with probability $\beta$, have caused all the $n$ channels to fail, and with probability $1 - \beta$, involve only the given channel. The system will then have a CCF rate $\lambda_C = \beta\lambda$, where all $n$ channels fail. In addition, each channel has a rate of independent failures, $\lambda_I = (1-\beta)\lambda$. The total failure rate of a channel may be written as

$$\lambda = \lambda_I + \lambda_C \tag{15.8}$$

The parameter $\beta$ may be expressed as

$$\beta = \frac{\lambda_C}{\lambda_I + \lambda_C} = \frac{\lambda_C}{\lambda} \tag{15.9}$$

and can therefore be interpreted as the relative proportion of CCFs among all failures of a channel. The $\beta$-factor can further be considered as the conditional probability that a failure of a channel is a CCF, that is,

$$\Pr(\text{CCF} \mid \text{channel failure}) = \beta$$

The beta-factor model may also be regarded as a *shock model* where shocks occur randomly according to a homogeneous Poisson process with rate $\lambda_C$. Each time a shock occurs, all the channels of the system fail, irrespective of the status of the channels. Each channel may hence fail due to two independent causes: shocks and channel-specific (individual) causes. The rate $\lambda_I$ is sometimes called the rate of *individual* failures.

### 15.5.1 Parallel System of Identical Channels

Consider a parallel system of $n$ identical channels with failure rate $\lambda$. An external event may occur that causes failure in each and every channel of the system. This

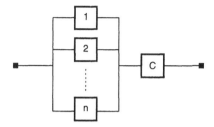

**Figure 15.3**    Parallel system with common-cause "component".

external event can be represented as a "hypothetical" component ($C$) that is in series with the rest of the system. The system is illustrated by the reliability block diagram in Figure 15.3. When using the beta-factor model, the failure rate of component $C$ is $\lambda_C = \beta\lambda$, while the $n$ channels in the parallel structure in Figure 15.3 may be considered as independent with individual failure rate $\lambda_I = (1 - \beta)\lambda$.

The survivor function of the system is now (see Appendix A)

$$R(t) = (1 - (1 - R_I(t))^n)$$
$$= \left(1 - \left(1 - e^{-(1-\beta)\lambda t}\right)^n\right) \cdot e^{-\beta\lambda t} \qquad (15.10)$$

***Remark***: For a fixed $\beta$, the rate of CCFs, $\lambda_C = \beta\lambda$, in the beta-factor model is seen to increase with the total failure rate $\lambda$. Systems with many failures will hence also have many CCFs. Since repair and maintenance is often claimed to be a prime cause of CCFs, it is relevant to assume that systems requiring a lot of repair will also have many CCFs. $\qquad\qquad\qquad\qquad\qquad\qquad\qquad\qquad\qquad\qquad\oplus$

When a failure occurs, the *multiplicity* of the failure event is either one or $n$. Intermediate values of the multiplicity are not possible when using the beta-factor model. The conditional probabilities of the possible multiplicities of failures are (see Section 15.4.3):

$$f_{1,n} = 1 - \beta$$
$$f_{k,n} = 0$$
$$f_{n,n} = \beta$$

for $k = 2, 3, \ldots, n - 1$.

This is illustrated in Figure 15.4 for a system of three identical channels, where, as before, $E_i$ denotes the failure of channel $i$, for $i = 1, 2, 3$. Assume that we have observed (tested) one of the channels, say channel 1, and found this channel to be in a failed state. We are hence within the circle $E_1$, and the numbers 0, $\beta$, and $1 - \beta$ in the circle indicate the conditional probabilities of involvement of the three channels in the failure. $1 - \beta$ is the probability that the observed failure is a single (individual) failure, $\beta$ is the probability that the observed failure is a complete failure with multiplicity 3, and the zeros indicate that failures with multiplicity 2 are not possible.

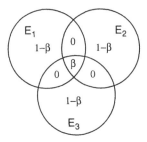

**Figure 15.4**    Fractions of different multiplicities of failures for a system with three identical channels when using the beta-factor model.

### ■ EXAMPLE 15.5    Probability of failure on demand

Consider a system of three identical smoke detectors that are configured as a 1oo3 system. This means that the system is functioning when at least one of its three channels is functioning. The critical failure rate of the detectors has been estimated to be $\lambda = 5.0 \cdot 10^{-6}$ failure per hour. The detectors are exposed to CCF, and we assume that these failures can be modeled by a beta-factor model with $\beta = 0.07$.

Critical failures are hidden failures and the system is therefore tested at regular intervals of length $\tau = 2\,190$ hours (i.e., three months). If we assume that the testing is perfect and that the detectors are "as good as new" after each test, the probability of failure on demand (PFD) is given by[2]

$$PFD = 1 - \frac{1}{\tau} \int_0^\tau R(t)\, dt$$

where $R(t)$ is the survivor function of the 1oo3 configuration as given in (15.10). We get

$$PFD = 1 - \frac{1}{\tau} \int_0^\tau \left( 1 - \left( 1 - e^{-(1-\beta)\lambda t} \right)^3 \right) \cdot e^{-\beta \lambda t}$$

$$\approx \frac{((1-\beta)\lambda \tau)^3}{4} + \frac{\beta \lambda \tau}{2} \approx 2.64 \cdot 10^{-7} + 3.83 \cdot 10^{-4}$$

The total PFD for this system is seen to be approximately $3.83 \cdot 10^{-4}$. If the system is supposed to operate on a continuous basis, this means that the system function is unavailable (i.e., we are unprotected) 0.0383% of the time, that is, approximately 3.36 hours per year (1 year $\approx 8\,760$ hours).

The approximation above is made by series expansion and is considered to be adequate in this case. The first term in the answer is the contribution from the independent failures, while the last term is from CCFs. The contribution

---

[2] Basic theory and formulas for PFD calculation may be found in Rausand and Høyland (2004, Chap. 10).

from CCFs is seen to dominate the result totally, and we would get an adequate approximation to the PFD by considering only the CCF failures.

We also note the special feature of the beta-factor model that the dominating contribution to the PFD from the CCFs is unchanged for all $k$oo$n$ configurations. We will therefore get approximately the same PFD for all configurations: for example, for 1oo2, 1oo3, and 2oo3 voting. $\oplus$

Due to its simplicity, the beta-factor model is often preferred in practical applications of (implicit) CCF modeling. IEC 61508 recommends using the beta-factor model to quantify the PFD of safety instrumented systems (see Chapter 12).

The parameter $\beta$ is easy to interpret and also rather easy to estimate when data are available. Note that several data sources, such as OREDA, present estimates for the total failure rate, $\lambda$. In many analyses, this failure rate is accepted and taken as being constant. This approach implies that the rate $\lambda_I$ of individual (single) failures will be reduced when we increase the value of $\beta$. Other data sources, such as MIL-HDBK-217F, present only the individual failure rate, $\lambda_I$, and the rate of CCFs must therefore be added to give the total failure rate.

### 15.5.2 Systems with Nonidentical Channels

The original beta-factor was defined for identical channels with the same constant failure rate $\lambda$. Many systems are, however, diversified with channels that are not identical. In this case it is more difficult to define and interpret the beta-factor. An approach sometimes used is to define the rate of CCFs as a fraction $\beta$ of the geometric average of the failure rates of the components, such that

$$\lambda_C = \beta \cdot \left( \prod_{i=1}^{n} \lambda_i \right)^{1/n} \tag{15.11}$$

### 15.5.3 C-Factor Model

The C-factor model introduced by Evans et al. (1984) is essentially the same model as the beta-factor model, but defines the fraction of CCFs in another way. In the C-factor model, the CCF rate is defined as $\lambda_C = C \cdot \lambda_I$, that is, as a fraction of the individual failure rate $\lambda_I$. The total failure rate may then be written as $\lambda = \lambda_I + C \cdot \lambda_I$. In this model, the individual failure rate $\lambda_I$ is kept constant and the CCF rate is added to this rate to give the total failure rate.

### 15.5.4 Plant-Specific Beta-Factors

The defenses against CCF events that are implemented in a plant will affect the fraction of CCF events. Estimates of $\beta$ based on generic data are therefore of limited value. The defenses can, according to NUREG/CR-6268 (2007), be classified as:

– Functional barriers

- Physical barriers

- Monitoring and awareness

- Maintenance staffing and scheduling

- Component identification

- Diversity

There are several suggestions as to how to choose a "correct" $\beta$, based on the defenses implemented and the actual system's vulnerability to possible causes of CCF events. Three of the methods that are designed to determine application-specific $\beta$'s are reviewed briefly in this section.

***Humphreys' Method.***    One of the first methods used to determine a plant-specific $\beta$ was suggested by Humphreys (1987). He identifies eight factors that are considered to be important for the actual value of $\beta$ (grouped as *design*, *operation*, and *environment*). The various factors are weighed as shown in Table 15.1, based on expert judgment and discussions among reliability engineers. Some other potential factors are not included because they were found to be too difficult to quantify. The eight factors are described in the appendix of Humphreys (1987), where a classification system is defined with five levels, from a (= worst) to e (= best). For a specific application, the eight factors are classified into levels a–e, and given weights (score) according to Table 15.1. A simple procedure is used next to produce an application-specific $\beta$ estimate:

1. The sum of column "a," representing the worst possible case should correspond to $\beta = 0.3$, a value that is considered to be a realistic worst-case scenario.

2. The sum of column "e," representing the best possible case should correspond to $\beta = 0.001$ (i.e., it is not realistic to attain any lower value of $\beta$).

3. To allow the convenience of whole numbers, a divisor of 50 000 was chosen, in which case the sum of column "a" should be 15 000, and the sum of column "e" should be 50.

The application-specific $\beta$ is determined by adding the weights for the categories chosen and dividing by 50 000.

### ◼ EXAMPLE 15.6    Identical channels

Consider a system of identical channels. This system will be a worst case (i.e., category "a") with respect to the subfactor "similarity," and will receive the weight 1 750 for this factor. If all the other factors are of the best category "e," the total weight will be 1 795, and the estimated value of $\beta$ is hence 0.036. This means that the lowest possible value of $\beta$ for a system of identical channels is 3.6% when we use the method of Humphreys (1987).                              ⊕

**Table 15.1**  Factors and weights in Humphreys (1987) method

| Factor | Subfactor | Weights | | | | |
|---|---|---|---|---|---|---|
| | | a | b | c | d | e |
| Design | Separation | 2 400 | 580 | 140 | 35 | 8 |
| | Similarity | 1 750 | 425 | 100 | 25 | 6 |
| | Complexity | 1 750 | 425 | 100 | 25 | 6 |
| | Analysis | 1 750 | 425 | 100 | 25 | 6 |
| Operation | Procedures | 3 000 | 720 | 175 | 40 | 10 |
| | Training | 1 500 | 360 | 90 | 20 | 5 |
| Environment | Control | 1 750 | 425 | 100 | 25 | 6 |
| | Tests | 1 200 | 290 | 70 | 15 | 4 |

*IEC 61508 Method.*   IEC 61508, part 6, Annex D, suggests an approach that is based on an idea similar to the one suggested by Humphreys (1987). The IEC approach is adapted to safety instrumented systems (see Chapter 12). Application-specific $\beta$-values are calculated separately for input elements, logic solvers, and final elements. To estimate $\beta$, about 40 specific questions have to be evaluated/answered concerning the following factors for each type of element of the safety system (IEC 61508, 2010; Smith and Simpson, 2005):

1. Degree of physical separation/segregation

2. Diversity/redundancy (e.g., different technology, design; different maintenance personnel)

3. Complexity/maturity of design/experience

4. Use of assessments/analyses and feedback data

5. Procedures/human interface (e.g., maintenance/testing)

6. Competence/training/safety culture

7. Environmental control (e.g., temperature, humidity; personnel access)

8. Environmental testing

The system elements are then assigned scores $X_i$ and $Y_i$ related to question $i$, where $X_i$ is selected if diagnostic testing will lead to improvement and $Y_i$ is selected if not. The ratio $X_i / Y_i$ presents the benefit of diagnostic testing as a defense against CCF related to question $i$. Next, total scores are calculated using simple formulas and compared with predefined values in Table D.4 in part 6 of IEC 61508 to give the estimate of $\beta$. The result of this procedure is one out of five possible $\beta$-values;

0.5% (applies to logic only); 1%, 2%, 5%, and 10% (input and final elements only). The highest possible $\beta$-value for input and final elements is therefore 10%, which is a low value compared to Humphreys's method. The main reason for this is that most SIS channels are subject to frequent diagnostic testing and that failures can thereby be removed and CCFs can be avoided.

There are two scores $X$ and $Y$, since the IEC standard gives different $\beta$'s for detected failures and undetected failures, and hence also incorporates the diagnostic coverage (DC) into the calculation of $\beta$.

**Unified Partial Method.**   The unified partial method (UPM) was developed for the British nuclear power industry (e.g., see Zitrou and Bedford, 2003) and is based on the beta-factor model. In the UPM framework, there are eight categories of defenses against CCFs:

1. Environmental control

2. Environmental testing

3. Analysis

4. Safety culture

5. Separation

6. Redundancy and diversity

7. Understanding

8. Operator interaction

The actual system is assigned one of five possible levels $x_{i,j}$ for $i = 1, 2, \ldots, 5$, across each defense, $j = 1, 2, \ldots, 8$, and scores $s_j(x_{i,j})$ are given accordingly from generic tables that have been deduced from past research. The overall beta-factor is obtained as a scaled sum of these scores.

The UPM model has been discussed by Zitrou et al. (2004, 2007, 2010), where a novel approach based on Bayesian networks or influence diagrams (see Chapter 10) is suggested for assessment of the plant-specific beta-factor.

## 15.6   More Complex CCF Models

### 15.6.1   Model Assumption

The same assumptions as made in Section 15.4.3 apply. These assumptions imply that we do not have to specify completely new parameters for each $n$. The parameters defined to handle CCF for $n = 2$ are retained for $n = 3$, and so on.

*Remark*: Beckman (1995) is very critical to these assumptions and claims that the susceptibility to CCF is architecture sensitive and postulates that triply redundant architectures are three times more sensitive to CCF than are dual architectures. He does not, however, give any formal justification for his assertions.                    ⊕

Let $Z$ denote the number of failed channels when a CCF occurs in a system with $n$ channels. We have seen that when using the beta-factor model, $Z$ can take on only the values 1 and $n$. Various generalizations are suggested. Either we could assume some parametric distribution of $Z$, say a binomial distribution, or we could allow $Z$ to have a completely general distribution, but could introduce various ways to parameterize the distribution.

In the remaining part of this section we first consider $Z$ to have a parametric distribution. Next, we look at the general cases, in particular the multiple Greek letter model. Finally, we present the multiple beta-factor (MBF) model and a special case of this model.

### 15.6.2   The Binomial Failure Rate Model and Its Extensions

The binomial failure rate (BFR) model was introduced by Vesely (1977). The situation under study is as follows: A system is composed of $n$ identical channels. Each channel can fail at a random time, independent of every other channel, and they are all supposed to have the same individual (independent) failure rate $\lambda_I$.

The BFR model is based on the premise that CCFs result from shocks to the system (Evans et al., 1984). The shocks occur randomly according to a homogeneous Poisson process with rate $v$. Whenever a shock occurs, each of the individual channels is assumed to fail with probability $p$, independent of the states of the other channels. The number $Z$ of channels failing as a consequence of the shock is thus binomially distributed $(n, p)$. The probability that the multiplicity, $Z$, of failures due to a shock is equal to $z$ is

$$\Pr(Z = z) = \binom{n}{z} p^z (1 - p)^{n-z} \qquad (15.12)$$

for $z = 0, 1, \ldots, n$.

The mean number of channels that fail in one shock is therefore $E(Z) = np$. It is now assumed that (i) the shocks and the independent failures occur independent of each other, and that (ii) all failures are discovered and repaired immediately, and the repair time is negligible. These assumptions imply that the time between independent failures of a channel, in the absence of shocks, is exponentially distributed with failure rate $\lambda_I$, and the time between shocks is exponentially distributed with rate $v$. The number of independent failures of a specific channel in any time period of length $t_0$ is therefore Poisson distributed with parameter $\lambda_I t_0$, and the number of shocks in the same time period is Poisson distributed with parameter $v t_0$.

The channel failure rate caused by shocks thus equals $pv$, and the total failure rate of one specific channel equals

$$\lambda = \lambda_I + pv \qquad (15.13)$$

By using this model, we have to estimate the independent failure rate $\lambda_I$ and the two parameters $\nu$ and $p$. The parameter $\nu$ relates to the degree of "stress" on the system, while $p$ is a function of the built-in channel protection against external shocks. Note that the BFR model is identical to the beta-factor model when the system has only two channels.

The assumption that the channels will fail independent of each other, given that a shock has occurred, represents a rather serious limitation, and this assumption is often not satisfied in practice. The problem can, to some extent, be remedied by defining one fraction of the shocks as being "lethal" shocks, that is, shocks that automatically cause all the channels to fail; that is, $p = 1$. If all the shocks are "lethal," one is back to the beta-factor model. Observe that in this case, $p = 1$ corresponds to the situation in which there is no built-in protection against these shocks.

Situations where independent failures occur together with nonlethal as well as lethal shocks are often realistic. Such models are, however, rather complicated, even if the nonlethal and lethal shocks occur independent of each other.

### 15.6.3 The Multiple Greek Letter Model

Several extensions of the beta-factor model have been suggested, three of the best known being:

- The basic parameter (BP) model (Mosleh, 1991)

- The alpha-factor model (Mosleh and Siu, 1987; NUREG/CR-4780, 1989)

- The multiple Greek letter (MGL) model (Fleming et al., 1986)

The MGL model introduced by Fleming et al. (1986) is discussed briefly below. A more recent model, the multiple beta-factor (MBF) model, is presented in the next subsection. The alpha-factor model is a CCF model recommended for use in aerospace applications (Stamatelatos et al., 2002a).

In the MGL model, various conditional probabilities are introduced as Greek letters:

$\beta =$ the conditional probability that the cause of a failure of a specific channel will be shared by at least one additional channel

$\gamma =$ the conditional probability that a channel failure known to be shared by at least one additional channel will be shared by at least two additional channels

$\delta =$ the conditional probability that a channel failure known to be shared by at least two additional channels will be shared by at least three additional channels

Additional Greek letters are introduced for higher multiplicities of failures. We note that the beta-factor model is a special case of the MGL model when $n = 2$, and also when all the parameters of the MGL model, except for $\beta$, are equal to 1.

***System with Three Identical Channels.*** We illustrate the MGL model by a system with $n = 3$ channels. As before, let $E_i$ denote failure of channel $i$, for $i = 1, 2, 3$, and let $Z$ denote the multiplicity of failures. Assume that it has been observed that channel 1 has failed, and let $\Pr(E_1) = Q$ denote the (unconditional) probability of this event. From the definition of $\beta$ it follows that

$$\Pr(E_1 \cap Z > 1) = \Pr(Z > 1 \mid E_1) \cdot \Pr(E_1) = \beta Q$$

This means that the probability that channel 1 experiences a single failure is

$$\Pr(E_1 \cap Z = 1) = 1 - \Pr(E_1 \cap Z > 1) = 1 - \beta Q$$

The probability that channel 1 experiences a failure with multiplicity 2 or more is

$$
\begin{aligned}
\Pr(E_1 \cap Z > 2) &= \Pr(Z > 2 \mid E_1) \cdot \Pr(E_1) \\
&= \Pr(Z > 2 \mid Z > 1 \cap E_1) \cdot \Pr(Z > 1 \mid E_1) \cdot \Pr(E_1) \\
&= \beta \gamma Q
\end{aligned}
$$

Since the system has only three channels, $Z > 2$ is the same as $Z = 3$. This means that the probability that channel 1 experiences a triple failure is

$$\Pr(E_1 \cap Z = 3) = \beta \gamma Q$$

The probability that channel 1 experiences a double failure can now be found from the fact that the multiplicity must be either 1, 2, or 3:

$$
\begin{aligned}
\Pr(E_1 \cap Z = 2) &= 1 - \Pr(E_1 \cap Z = 1) - \Pr(E_1 \cap E_3) \\
&= 1 - (1 - \beta Q) - \beta \gamma Q \\
&= \beta (1 - \gamma) Q
\end{aligned}
$$

In the same way, for any $n$ we can state the probability of failure of any multiplicity expressed by conditional probabilities (i.e., Greek letters).

### 15.6.4   The Multiple Beta-Factor Model

The multiple beta-factor (MBF) model was developed as part of the PDS[3] approach (Hokstad and Corneliussen, 2004) and is similar to the MGL model. In the MBF model, the probability $Q_{koon}$ that a $koon$ system fails is given by

$$Q_{koon} = C_{koon} \cdot \beta Q \tag{15.14}$$

where $Q$ is the probability that a channel is in a failed state, $C_{koon}$ is a factor that depends on the configuration of the system, and $\beta$ is the conditional probability of

---

[3] PDS is the abbreviation of the Norwegian translation of "reliability of computer-based safety systems." The PDS approach has been developed by SINTEF, the Norwegian research organization.

exactly one extra failure when we know that one channel has failed. The parameter $\beta$ depends neither on the number $n$ of channels nor on the system configuration. When $n = 2$, the parameter $\beta$ has the same interpretation as in the beta-factor model. Note that the parameter $\beta$ in this model is slightly different from the $\beta$ in the MGL model.

We start by illustrating the MBF model for a system with three channels of the same type.

**System with Three Identical Channels.**  Consider a system with three identical channels, and as in Section 15.4.3, let $E_i^*$ denote that channel $i$ is functioning and $E_i$ that channel $i$ has failed. Assume that we observe (test) one of the channels, chosen at random, and find that this channel is in a failed state. Let $Q$ denote the unconditional probability of this event, that is, with no regard to the state of the other channels. Without loss of generality, we can assume that the failed channel is channel 1. Let $\beta$ be the probability that a second channel (channel 2 or 3) has also failed. Further, let $\beta_2$ denote the conditional probability that the third channel fails when we know that two channels have failed.

The probability of a triple failure is, from equation (15.1)

$$
\begin{aligned}
g_{3,3} &= \Pr(E_1 \cap E_2 \cap E_3) \\
&= \Pr(E_3 \mid E_1 \cap E_2) \cdot \Pr(E_2 \mid E_1) \cdot \Pr(E_1) \\
&= \beta_2 \beta \cdot Q
\end{aligned}
$$

When we observe a channel (channel 1) and find it in a failed state, the conditional probability that the failure is a triple failure is

$$
f_{3,3} = \frac{g_{3,3}}{Q} = \beta_2 \beta \tag{15.15}
$$

The probability of a specific double failure (e.g., failure of components 1 and 2) is, from equation(15.2)

$$
\begin{aligned}
g_{2,3} &= \Pr(E_1 \cap E_2 \cap E_3^*) \\
&= \Pr(E_3^* \mid E_1 \cap E_2) \cdot \Pr(E_2 \mid E_1) \cdot \Pr(E_1) \\
&= (1 - \beta_2)\beta Q
\end{aligned}
$$

Since the channels are of the same type, we get the same answer for all three combinations of double failures.

When a channel (channel 1) has failed, the conditional probability that the failure is a double failure involving channels 1 and 2 is

$$
f_{2,3}^{(2)} = \frac{g_{2,3}^{(2)}}{Q} = (1 - \beta_2)\beta
$$

and similarly, the conditional probability that the failure is a double failure involving channels 1 and 3 is

$$
f_{2,3}^{(3)} = \frac{g_{2,3}^{(3)}}{Q} = (1 - \beta_2)\beta
$$

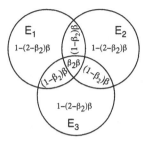

**Figure 15.5** Fractions of different multiplicities of failures when using the multiple beta-factor (MBF) model for a system of three identical channels.

The conditional probability that the failure of channel 1 is a double failure involving one of the other channels is

$$f_{2,3} = f_{2,3}^{(2)} + f_{2,3}^{(3)} = 2(1 - \beta_2)\beta$$

When a channel is found to be in a failed state, the multiplicity of failures must be either 1, 2, or 3 and we have $f_{1,3} + f_{2,3} + f_{3,3} = 1$. The conditional probability that the failure of channel 1 is a single (individual) failure is thus

$$f_{1,3} = 1 - f_{2,3} - f_{3,3} = 1 - (2 - \beta_2)\beta$$

When a channel failure is observed, the fractions of the possible multiplicity of failures are

$$\begin{align}
f_{1,3} &= 1 - (2 - \beta_2)\beta \\
f_{2,3} &= 3(1 - \beta_2)\beta \\
f_{3,3} &= \beta_2\beta
\end{align} \tag{15.16}$$

These fractions are illustrated in Figure 15.5.

As in Section 15.4.3, let $Q_{k:3}$ be the probability that a system with three identical channels has a (unspecified) failure with multiplicity $k$, for $k = 1, 2, 3$. Since failures of multiplicity 1 and 2 can occur with three different combinations of channels, we get

$$\begin{align}
Q_{1:3} &= 3\,(1 - (2 - \beta_2)\beta) \cdot Q \\
Q_{2:3} &= 3(1 - \beta_2)\beta \cdot Q \\
Q_{3:3} &= \beta_2\beta \cdot Q
\end{align} \tag{15.17}$$

**_Possible Configurations of Three Channels._** A system with three channels can be configured in three different ways; as a 1oo3 (parallel) structure, as a 2oo3 structure, or as a 3oo3 (series) structure.

A 1oo3 structure is functioning as long as at least one channel is functioning and will fail only when all the channels fail. The probability of system failure of a 1oo3 structure is therefore

$$Q_{1oo3} = Q_{3:3} = \beta_2\beta \cdot Q \tag{15.18}$$

A 2oo3 structure is functioning as long as at least two of its three channels are functioning. The system will fail when at least two of its three channels fail. The probability of system failure is

$$Q_{2oo3} = Q_{2:3} + Q_{3:3} = (3 - 2\beta_2)\beta \cdot Q \qquad (15.19)$$

A 3oo3 (series) structure will fail as soon as one of its three channels fails, and the probability of system failure is

$$Q_{3oo3} = Q_{1:3} + Q_{2:3} + Q_{3:3} = (3 - (3 - \beta_2)\beta) \cdot Q \qquad (15.20)$$

The MBF model was given by $Q_{koon} = C_{koon} \cdot \beta Q$. By comparing with the results above, we get the configuration factors

$$\begin{aligned} C_{1oo3} &= \beta_2 \\ C_{2oo3} &= 3 - 2\beta_2 \end{aligned} \qquad (15.21)$$

**System with n Identical Channels.**    The approach presented above for a system of three channels can be extended to a system with $n$ identical channels. By increasing the number of channels from $m$ to $m + 1$, we have, each time, to introduce a new parameter $\beta_m$, where $\beta_m$ is the conditional probability of $m + 1$ failures when $m$ channels have failed. With the same notation as in Section 15.4.3, we can write

$$\beta_m = \Pr(E_1 \cap E_2 \cap \cdots \cap E_{m+1} \mid E_1 \cap E_2 \cap \cdots \cap E_m) \qquad (15.22)$$

The probability that exactly $m$ *specified* channels have failed out of $n$ channels is

$$g_{m,n} = \Pr(E_1 \cap E_2 \cap \cdots E_m \cap E_{m+1}^* \cap \cdots \cap E_n^*) \qquad (15.23)$$

Due to the symmetry assumption in Section 15.4.3, we can interchange subscripts as long as there are $m$ events $E_i$ and $n - m$ events $E_i^*$. The probability of exactly $m$ of the $n$ channels being in a failed state is

$$Q_{m:n} = \binom{n}{m} g_{m,n} \qquad (15.24)$$

By determining $g_{m,n}$ we also get an expression for

$$Q_{koon} = \Pr(\text{at least } n - k + 1 \text{ failed}) = \sum_{m=n-k+1}^{n} Q_{m:n} \qquad (15.25)$$

We have defined $Q_{koon} = C_{koon} \cdot \beta Q$ and can therefore use (15.25) to find a general expression for the configuration factor $C_{koon}$.

To determine $g_{m,n}$, observe that by direct argument

$$g_{n,n} = \left( \prod_{j=1}^{n-1} \beta_j \right) \cdot Q \qquad (15.26)$$

From the symmetry assumption and the law of total probability, we have that $g_{m,n-1} = g_{m,n} + g_{m+1,n}$, and we may hence find $g_{m,n}$ recursively from

$$g_{m,n} = g_{m,n-1} - g_{m+1,n} \quad \text{for } m = 1, 2, \ldots, n \tag{15.27}$$

Starting with $g_{2,2} = \beta_1 Q$ (where $\beta_1 = \beta$) and $g_{1,2} = (1-\beta_1)Q$, and then using the expression above for $g_{n,n}$, we recursively find $g_{n-1,n}, g_{n-2,n}, \ldots$ for $n = 3, 4, 5, \ldots$. Thus, we find the explicit expression

$$g_{m,n} = Q \cdot \sum_{i=0}^{n-m} (-1)^i \binom{n-m}{i} \prod_{j=1}^{m-1+i} \beta_j \tag{15.28}$$

In equation (15.28) the term $Q \cdot \prod_{j=1}^{m-1} \beta_j$ is a common factor. So for $m \geq 2$ we have $\beta Q$ as a common factor, and introduce $G_{m,n} = g_{m,n}/\beta Q$. Thus

$$G_{m,n} = \frac{g_{m,n}}{\beta Q} = \sum_{i=0}^{n-m} (-1)^i \binom{n-m}{i} \prod_{j=2}^{m-1+i} \beta_j \quad \text{for } m = 2, 3, \ldots, n \tag{15.29}$$

and by (15.24), (15.25), and (15.29) it follows that

$$C_{koon} = \sum_{m=n-k+1}^{n} \binom{n}{m} G_{m,n} \quad \text{for } k = 1, 2, \ldots, n-1 \tag{15.30}$$

All configuration factors may now be expressed explicitly by the $\beta_i$'s.

**Special Cases and Numerical Values for Configuration Factors.**    The explicit expressions for the configuration factors $C_{koon}$ are seen to be rather complex for large $n$. In most cases we do not have sufficient information to estimate all the relevant $\beta_i$'s, and we therefore have to make do with a simpler approach. We consider two special cases:

*Case 1: $\beta_j = \beta_2$, for $j \geq 2$*    In this case we get $G_{m,n} = \beta_2^{m-2}(1 - \beta_2)^{n-m}$ for $m = 2, 3, \ldots, n$. By inserting this value in (15.30), we get

$$C_{koon} = \sum_{m=n-k+1}^{n} \binom{n}{m} \beta_2^{m-2}(1 - \beta_2)^{n-m} \quad \text{for } k = 1, 2, \ldots, n-1$$

*Case 2: $\beta_j = \beta_3$ for $j \geq 3$*    In this case,

$$C_{koon} = \beta_2 \sum_{m=n-k+1}^{n} \binom{n}{m} \beta_3^{m-3}(1 - \beta_3)^{n-m} \quad \text{for } k = 1, 2, \ldots, n-2$$

$$C_{(n-1)oon} = 1 - \frac{\beta_2}{\beta_3} + \beta_2 \sum_{m=2}^{n} \binom{n}{m} \beta_3^{m-3}(1 - \beta_3)^{n-m}$$

**Table 15.2** Values of configuration factors, $C_{koon}$, for the MBF model.

| Parameter | Configuration | | | | | | | | |
|---|---|---|---|---|---|---|---|---|---|
| choice | 1oo3 | 2oo3 | 1oo4 | 2oo4 | 3oo4 | 1oo5 | 2oo5 | 3oo5 | 4oo5 |
| Gamma | 0.0 | 3.0 | 0.0 | 0.0 | 6.0 | 0.0 | 0.0 | 0.0 | 15.0 |
| Base case | 0.3 | 2.4 | 0.15 | 0.75 | 4.0 | 0.08 | 0.45 | 1.2 | 6.0 |
| Sensitivity | 0.5 | 2.0 | 0.25 | 1.25 | 2.8 | 0.12 | 0.75 | 2.0 | 3.3 |
| Beta | 1.0 | 1.0 | 1.0 | 1.0 | 1.0 | 1.0 | 1.0 | 1.0 | 1.0 |

*Note*: $C_{1oo2} = 1$ for all parameter choices.

The parameter $\beta_2$ is a probability and can take any value in the interval $[0, 1]$. The choice of $\beta_2$ has a dominating effect on the configuration factor. The knowledge about the "true" value of $\beta_2$ is in most cases very limited. It may therefore be useful to define a generic value as a *base case*, which is applicable when little information is available. For a well-designed system, we have reason to believe that the $\beta_2$ value is usually closer to 0 than to 1. Based on expert judgment for failure multiplicity distributions, we suggest the value $\beta_2 = 0.3$ as a base case.

For a system with $n = 3$ identical channels, the base case configuration factors become

$$C_{1oo3} = \beta_2 = 0.30$$
$$C_{2oo3} = 3 - 2\beta_2 = 2.40$$

For $k \geq 3$ the value $\beta_k = 0.5$ is suggested as a base case unless more information is available.

By choosing the value $\beta_2 = 1$, we get the ordinary beta-factor model. The other extreme, $\beta_2 = 0$, is here referred to as the *gamma factor model* (see Figure 15.6).

Table 15.2 presents some numerical values of $C_{koon}$ for some selected configurations and for the four model alternatives:

- Gamma: $\beta_2 = 0$, $\beta_j = 0.5$ for all $j \geq 3$

- Base case: $\beta_2 = 0.3$, $\beta_j = 0.5$ for all $j \geq 3$

- Sensitivity: $\beta_j = 0.3$ for all $j \geq 2$

- Beta: $\beta_j = 1$ for all $j \geq 2$

The fractions of failures for a system of three identical channels are illustrated in Figure 15.6 for the gamma factor, base case, and the beta-factor models.

The MBF model has a complexity intermediate between the very simple beta-factor model and the rather detailed modeling (e.g., the MGL model) used by some analysts (e.g., in the nuclear industry). If some consensus can be reached on generic $C_{koon}$ values, then more realistic input and better decision support is obtained than simply by applying $C_{koon} = 1$ for all configurations, as suggested by the beta-factor model.

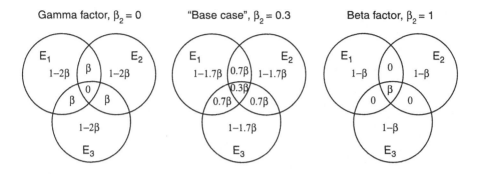

**Figure 15.6**    Multiple beta-factor (MBF) model for a triplicated system ($n = 3$). Three different choices of the parameter $\beta_2$.

## 15.7    Additional Reading

The following titles are recommended for further study related to Chapter 15.

- *Guidelines on Modeling Common-Cause Failures in Probabilistic Risk Assessment* (NUREG/CR-5485, 1998).

- *Probabilistic risk assessment procedures guide for NASA managers and practitioners* (Stamatelatos et al., 2002a). Chapter 10 of this guideline gives a good survey of available CCF models.

- *Procedures for Treating Common-Cause Failures in Safety and Reliability Studies, volume 2: Analytical Background and Techniques.* (NUREG/CR-4780, 1989).

- *Common-Cause Failure Database and Analysis System: Event Data Collection, Classification, and Coding* (NUREG/CR-6268, 2007).

- *Risk Analysis in Engineering: Techniques, Tools, and Trends* (Modarres, 2006). Section 3.5 of this book gives a survey of models for CCFs.

- *Common-cause failure modeling: Status and trends* (Hokstad and Rausand, 2008) gives a survey of CCF models, similar to this chapter, but also presents ideas on how to estimate the parameters of the models.

# CHAPTER 16

# UNCERTAINTY AND SENSITIVITY ANALYSIS

> ...in this world, nothing can be said to be certain, except death and taxes.
>
> —Benjamin Franklin

## 16.1 Introduction

All results from a quantitative risk analysis are uncertain to some degree. In some cases, the uncertainty may be large and the conclusions based on the risk analysis may therefore be questionable. Several guidelines for risk analysis require that uncertainty analyses be conducted as part of the risk analysis, such that it can be demonstrated that the conclusions reached using quantitative risk analysis have taken uncertainty into account (e.g., see HSE, 1989, 2003a).

The uncertainty may be due to many different causes, ranging from use of inadequate models and data to misinterpretation of system functions and failure to identify potential accident scenarios.

To *take uncertainty into account* does not necessarily require a complex and formal uncertainty analysis. In many cases, a conservative approach to risk analysis

*Risk Assessment: Theory, Methods, and Applications,* First Edition.
By Marvin Rausand. Copyright © 2011 John Wiley & Sons, Inc.

using conservative model approximations and conservative values of input parameters may be sufficient for the decision-maker to have confidence in the results from the analysis. The requirement for a careful uncertainty analysis is obviously also dependent on the importance of the decision to be made. In any case, the study team should be aware of problems related to uncertainty and do their best to avoid or reduce the uncertainty in all steps of the risk analysis process.

In most risk analyses, it will not be feasible to quantify the total uncertainty of the results from the risk analysis. Such a quantification will, in our opinion, be more uncertain than the risk estimates themselves. What we can do, however, is to consider systematically the uncertainty of all steps in the risk analysis process, quantify what it is possible to quantify, and then document our efforts. This must be done in such a way that the decision-maker and other stakeholders are confident that we have done a high-quality job and that we have used the best knowledge available.

The main result of the risk analysis is, as described in Chapter 4, a *risk picture* that is to be used as input to some decision. The risk picture is a listing of all the potential hazardous events related to the study object, together with the associated probabilities and descriptions and/or analysis of the consequences. In some cases, we may extract various risk metrics from the risk picture, such as FAR, PLL, F-N curves, and risk contours, as described in Chapter 4, and use these as decision support.

The main elements of the risk analysis process related to decision-making are illustrated in Figure 16.1. To use analytical methods, we have to use models of the study object. Since a model will always be a simplification of the real system, *model uncertainty* is inevitably introduced. This also applies for the models of accident scenarios and consequences. Moreover, to use the models, we need input data of various types. Some of these data may come from the actual study object, but most of the data will usually be expert judgments or come from generic data sources, which may be more or less relevant for the study object. This will introduce *data-* or *parameter uncertainty*. Very often the scope of the analysis is limited, and we may also fail to identify hazardous events and failure mechanisms because we have limited knowledge or too few resources for the analysis. This will lead to *completeness uncertainty*. Too often, accident investigations find that the actual accident course had not been identified in the risk analyses that have been performed.

Uncertainty analysis is a complex and controversial undertaking and we will not go into all aspects of this issue in this chapter. The objective is, rather, to shed some light on the concept of uncertainty, describe the most common categories of uncertainty related to risk analysis, discuss the main causes of uncertainty, and present some methods that can be used to analyze the uncertainty.

A sensitivity analysis is different from an uncertainty analysis. The objective of a sensitivity analysis is to determine the change in the output of a mathematical model with respect to changes in the model or its input values. The results from the sensitivity analysis can be used to (i) evaluate the applicability of the model, (ii) determine parameters for which it is important to obtain more accurate values, (iii) determine the effects of minor changes of the model, and (iv) understand the behavior of the system being modeled.

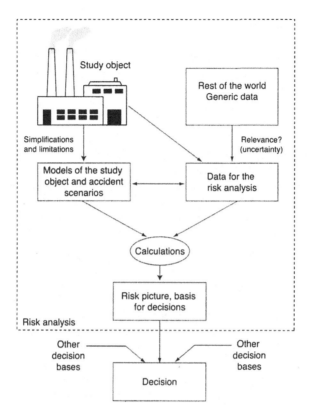

**Figure 16.1**   Risk analysis in decision-making.

## 16.2   Uncertainty

The term *uncertainty* is used with many different meanings in the literature on risk analysis. Some authors state that risk is uncertainty about the future and that consequently, risk is equal to uncertainty. Others claim that risk and uncertainty are two different concepts that do not, necessarily, have anything to do with each other. Since all interpretations between these two extremes may be found in the literature, it may be relevant to claim that there is a great uncertainty about uncertainty.

The term *uncertainty* conveys doubt ("It is uncertain that she will be able to complete the job on schedule") or lack of knowledge ("I am uncertain whether or not this fluid is toxic"). In this book, we consider risk and uncertainty as two different terms. The risk related to a study object is expressed by the risk picture that is the result of a risk analysis. This risk picture will generally be used as a basis for decision-making, as illustrated in Figure 16.1, together with many other bases, such as production assessment, cost and profit assessments, and so on. To be able to make a good decision, the decision-maker has to trust that her decision basis is as correct as possible. The decision-maker is therefore interested in knowing to which degree she can trust the results of the risk analysis—that is, to know the uncertainty of the results from the risk analysis.

We therefore use the term *uncertainty* as a "measure" of the confidence we have in the results of the risk analysis. We have put the word *measure* in quotes to indicate that the uncertainty does not always need to be quantified.

The term *uncertainty* is well defined in the important book *Science and Decisions: Advancing Risk Assessment* issued by the U.S. National Research Council in 2009:

☞ **Uncertainty**: Lack or incompleteness of information. Quantitative uncertainty assessment attempts to analyze and describe the degree to which a calculated value may differ from the true value; it sometimes uses probability distributions. Uncertainty depends on the quality, quantity, and relevance of data and on the reliability and relevance of models and assumptions (US National Research Council, 2009).

### 16.2.1 Studies of Uncertainty

A number of studies have been carried out to determine the uncertainty of the results of quantitative risk analyses. A benchmark study of risk analyses of chemical plants was managed by the EU Joint Research Centre (JRC) in the period 1988–1990. Eleven organizations specializing in risk analysis from different European countries were asked to perform a risk analysis of a reference study object, an ammonia storage facility (Amendola et al., 1992), to evaluate the state of the art on risk analysis and to obtain estimates of the uncertainty in quantitative risk analyses. The results of this study showed a significant variability in risk estimates between the different study teams.

A follow-up benchmark exercise, called ASSURANCE (Assessment of uncertainties in risk analysis of chemical establishments), was completed in 2001. In this study, seven risk analysis teams from different European countries performed a risk analysis of another ammonia storage facility. Applying the lessons from the first benchmark, the project was separated in discrete steps, to better center the work of the experts, allowing comparison of the intermediate results that enter in the final evaluation of risks.

The results showed a similar considerable spread in both the frequencies and the consequence analyses, suggesting that consensus on methodologies, models, and basic assumptions had not been reached in Europe (e.g., see Abrahamsson, 2002).

### 16.3 Categories of Uncertainty

It is sometimes useful to distinguish between two main categories of uncertainty:

1. *Aleatory uncertainty.* The word *aleatory* derives from the Latin *alea*, which means the rolling of dice.

2. *Epistemic uncertainty.* The word *epistemic* derives from the Greek *episteme*, which means knowledge.

These categories are described below.

## 16.3.1 Aleatory Uncertainty

☞ **Aleatory uncertainty**: This uncertainty is caused by natural variation and randomness. Examples of aleatory uncertainty are variations in wind speed, wind direction, precipitation, product quality, and so on.

Aleatory uncertainty is also called *variability, random uncertainty, inherent uncertainty*, and *irreducible uncertainty*. Aleatory uncertainty is observed when an experiment is repeated several times under equivalent conditions, yet the results obtained differ from each other. Increasing the number of experiments does not reduce the variability but will give us more accurate information about the probability distribution describing the variability of the result.

▣ **EXAMPLE 16.1   Toxic gas cloud**

Consider an accident scenario involving a toxic gas cloud. The consequences of the gas cloud will depend on the wind direction at the actual time. By observing the wind direction on this location over a certain time period, we may fit a probability distribution $F(d)$ for the various directions $d$. We are not able to say with certainty that the gas cloud will blow toward a vulnerable asset when the accident scenario occurs, but we can use the distribution $F(d)$ to find the probability of this event.                                                                          ⊕

## 16.3.2 Epistemic Uncertainty

☞ **Epistemic uncertainty**: This uncertainty is caused by lack of knowledge, and can, in principle, be eliminated if we can acquire sufficient knowledge about the study object.

Epistemic uncertainty is also called *ignorance, subjective uncertainty, knowledge-based uncertainty, phenomenological uncertainty*, and *reducible uncertainty*.

Ignorance can be classified in two types: recognized and unrecognized ignorance. *Recognized ignorance* means that we are aware that we are ignorant and that, hopefully, we take precautions when performing a risk analysis. *Unrecognized ignorance* is a more dangerous category since we do not know that we do not know.

**▣ EXAMPLE 16.2   Nanotechnology**

A large number of new products based on nanotechnology are currently being introduced. Many people are worried about the consequences the nanoparticles may have on their health and on the environment. At present (2011), these effects are not known and the epistemic uncertainty related to the use of nanotechnology is therefore high. As more experience with nanotechnology is gained, the epistemic uncertainty will be reduced.                                                    ⊕

*Remark*: The Danish physicist Niels Bohr (1885–1962) made significant contributions to our understanding of atomic structures and quantum mechanics. He asserted that atomic states and related phenomena could be described adequately by probability theory *combined* with the laws of physics. In this respect, he entered into a discussion with Albert Einstein, another famous physicist, who claimed that all physical phenomena could be explained and described by the laws of physics only. He claimed that if we know all the input variables, we should be able to predict the output by using the laws of physics. If we, for example, toss a coin on the floor, and know the vertical distance to the floor, the output direction and velocity, the weight and dimensions of the coin, and so on, we should be able to predict whether the trial will give a head or a tail. Consequently, there would be no need for any probability theory, according to Einstein. The discussion between Bohr and Einstein got rather lively, and at some stage Einstein stated: "God does not play dice". With the terminology we have just introduced, Einstein claimed that all uncertainty is epistemic. In hindsight, Bohr's way of treating the problem has been far more successful than Einstein's.                                                    ⊕

At a fundamental level, uncertainty is simply lack of certainty, and it should not be necessary to classify the uncertainty into different categories. Most analysts, however, find it useful to use the categories mentioned above (e.g., see Winkler, 1996; Anderson and Hattis, 1999; Der Kiureghian and Ditlevsen, 2009). It should, however, be observed that the borderline between aleatory and epistemic uncertainty is not fixed. As new knowledge becomes available, we are able to explain new features of a situation such that the aleatory uncertainty is reduced. At the end, perhaps all uncertainty is epistemic.

The terms *confidence* and *accuracy* are sometimes used to mean the opposite of uncertainty. When the uncertainty is large, our confidence is low.

## 16.4   Contributors to Uncertainty

Several aspects can contribute to uncertainty of the results from a risk analysis. As indicated in Section 16.1, uncertainty is often classified into the three main categories:

(a) Model uncertainty

(b) Parameter uncertainty

(c) Completeness uncertainty

As discussed in Chapter 2, several concepts in risk analysis are often used with different meanings. This may cause confusion when communicating the results from the risk analysis. In addition, most people are not trained in probability theory and may not fully understand the meaning of small probabilities, for example, $10^{-6}$. This may create additional uncertainty in the decision-making process.

### 16.4.1 Model Uncertainty

Risk analyses are based on a large number of models, ranging from structural models of the system, stochastic models for input values, models of human behavior, accident models, dispersion models, evacuation models, and so on. The models are always a simplification of the real situation, and are set up such that we can use mathematical and other analytical tools to deduce properties of interest.

In most cases, we may choose between several models and methods, all of which have their own strengths and weaknesses and will be more or less suitable for the problem at hand. To be able to choose the most adequate models and methods, the analysts need to know their properties and at the same time have a thorough knowledge of the technical and operational aspects of the study object.

The model uncertainty may stem from:

1. *Choice of model*: Does the model reflect the main properties of the study object?

2. *Understanding of the model*: Does the analysts fully understand the model with respect to:

   (a) The objectives of the model?
   (b) The assumptions that need to be fulfilled?
   (c) The limitations of the model?
   (d) The computational capacities and requirements?
   (e) The input data requirements?

The choice of models and methods will also be determined by the data available. It is not useful to select a detailed model if we cannot find the input data that are required. This is illustrated in Figure 16.1.

There are two main types of models: *deterministic* and *probabilistic* (i.e. stochastic). Both types are used in risk analysis. Deterministic models are used mainly to describe physical phenomena, such as pressure buildup and physical impact. Examples of probabilistic models are life distributions, wind direction probabilities, and so on.

Some aspects that are very difficult to model are:

- Human behavior in critical situations

- Human reliability and human recovery of faulty situations

- Organizational factors: for example, the organization's safety culture

- Violations of rules and procedures

- Software functions and software reliability

- Effects of maintenance and aging

- Hazards caused by modifications of the system

- Causes and factors that are not measurable

In many cases we will have incomplete knowledge regarding the consequences of a hazardous event. This is, for example, the case for many dangerous substances. We do not always know whether or not a cocktail of various substances is carcinogenic. New knowledge is made available regularly, but since new substances and new applications are steadily introduced, there is still a long way to go. In this regard, it may be relevant to remember the long discussions as to on whether or not the use of mobile phones may cause brain tumors, or whether living near a high-voltage power line may cause health problems.

Another problem is linked to the escalation of damage. Our knowledge of the event sequences after a hazardous event is often limited. How will a gas leak spread? What will happen if an explosion comes before a fire? What effects will the explosion have on the sprinkler systems, fire pumps, and so on? Although research has been carried out for some application areas (e.g., nuclear power plants, offshore oil and gas installations), knowledge is still limited in most fields.

### 16.4.2 Parameter Uncertainty

A risk analysis requires a wide range of data. In this chapter, these data are called *parameters*. Data sources for the various parameters are treated in Chapter 7. Examples of parameters are:

- Failure rates for the various components and for the various failure modes

- Repair times and downtimes for the various components

- Intervals between proof tests

- Common-cause failure rates—or $\beta$-factors

- Human error probabilities and effects of performance-influencing factors

- Wear parameters for deteriorating components

- Ignition probabilities for gas releases

- Frequencies for natural events (e.g., flooding, avalanche, lightning, earthquake)

- Exposure data (who, where, for how long)

- Activity data (e.g., production rate/volume, staffing)

- Process data

- Weather data (e.g., dominating wind direction, wind speed, precipitation)

For most of these categories, the data available will be uncertain with respect to:

- The quality of the data and the data collection

- The amount of data (e.g., the time in service)

- The estimation procedures (approximations, conservative)

- The use of expert judgments

As illustrated in Figure 16.1, the data may come directly from the study object or from generic data sources. For new systems, the data related to component reliability will all come from generic sources and expert judgments. The question is then how relevant they are for the study object. A special challenge is related to technology under rapid development. Field data will inevitably be "old" since we need a certain experience base to estimate parameters. These data may therefore be irrelevant for the current technology.

When deciding on whether a set of parameter estimates is adequate, it may be relevant to ask: Would the decision be different if the data were different? Would additional data collection and research probably lead to a different decision? How long will it take to collect the information, how much would it cost, and would the resulting decision be significantly different?

### 16.4.3 Completeness Uncertainty

Completeness uncertainty is related to the general quality of the risk analysis process, its objectives and scope, the competence of the study team, the way the analyses are performed, and so on. Two main factors that influence the uncertainty are:

(a) Is the background material for the risk analysis correct and up to date?

(b) Have all the potential hazardous events been identified?

As indicated in Chapter 8, a large number of drawings and documents are used in a risk analysis. If these are not correct and up to date, the risk analysis may be performed on a system that is different from the actual system.

The objective of the hazard identification is to produce a comprehensive list of possible hazardous events, and possibly also to identify priorities between them and make decisions on which of them require further analysis. The dominant question regarding uncertainty at this stage is that of completeness.

– Have all the hazardous events that can possibly lead to accidents been identified?

– Have any important cases been omitted when selecting hazardous events for further analysis?

– Have any hazardous events been excluded from the scope of the risk analysis?

The methods for hazard identification in Chapter 9 are effective but require the analysts to have adequate knowledge of the technical, phenomenal, and operational aspects of the study object. Special challenges are related to:

– Complex systems

– Tightly coupled systems (i.e., systems where a failure in one item rapidly spreads to other items)

– New technology, or known technology used for new applications

– Systems with open boundaries to the environment, where events outside the system may lead to hazardous events within the system boundaries

In addition, there is a set of issues on which we lack sufficient knowledge. For these and other reasons, it is often far from straightforward to identify all the potential hazardous events.

> The largest contributor to uncertainty appeared to be the variety in the scenario definition, where analyst judgment and selection of release modes lead to large differences in effects (Pasman et al., 2009).

A hazardous event that is not identified will not be analyzed and will not be present in the risk picture. An unidentified hazardous event will inevitably lead to a nonconservative computed risk.

The competence of the study team will always be decisive for the quality of the risk analysis process. If the study team has a lack of competence in risk analysis and/or lack of knowledge about the study object, this will usually lead to great uncertainty in the results from the risk analysis. In many cases, the study team has to make assumptions to be able to use the available models and methods. Linkov and Burmistrov (2003) have compared the results from several teams using the same models and found significant differences.

Risk analyses sometimes have strict time and cost limits. This means that the study team will have to choose simple and fast methods and that there is limited room for making in-depth analyses. This may lead to significant uncertainties in the results from the risk analysis.

Many of the methods in risk analysis are based on approximation formulas. Most of these formulas provide conservative results, but there are still several methods that give nonconservative approximations. Sources of calculation uncertainty include that (i) the analyst enters wrong values (printing/punching errors, mixing values), and (ii) the analyst misinterprets input or output values due to inexperience.

The uncertainty related to completeness of the analysis is very difficult to quantify and may be the most significant contributor to uncertainty.

### 16.4.4 When Uncertainty Analysis is Required

A quantitative uncertainty analysis is considered to be required when:

- The initial screening calculations, using conservatively biased point estimates, indicate the need for further investigation before making a decision.

- The consequences of an erroneous risk estimate are high.

On the other hand, a uncertainty analysis may *not* be required when:

- The risk analysis indicates that the risk acceptance criteria for the system are met with a good margin and that the risk analysis sufficiently support robust decision-making (e.g., see Hammonds et al., 1994; Dezfuli et al., 2010)

In most cases, it will be appropriate to explore alternative assumptions involved in the risk analysis. Through a process of sensitivity analysis, the study team can explore which uncertainties are more important in a risk management context and allocate their efforts accordingly. Important uncertainties may be represented by probability distributions based on the judgment and reasoning of experts.

### 16.5 Uncertainty Propagation

By uncertainty propagation we study the effect of varying all the input variables to a model at the same time. This can be done by:

1. Analytical methods

2. Monte Carlo simulation

Both approaches are described briefly in this section. In both cases we assume that we have a specific mathematical model. Examples of such models are:

- The survivor function of technical system [e.g., $R(t) = e^{-\lambda_1 t} + e^{-\lambda_2 t} - e^{-(\lambda_1 + \lambda_2)t}$ for a parallel system of two independent components with constant failure rates $\lambda_1$ and $\lambda_2$, respectively]

- The TOP event probability of a fault tree [e.g., as given by the upper bound approximation formula $Q_0(t) = 1 - \prod_{i=1}^{k}(1 - \check{Q}_i(t))$, where the minimal cut set failure probabilities $\check{Q}_i(t)$ for $i = 1, 2, \ldots, k$ may be functions of failure rates, testing intervals, and repair times for the various components]

- Models describing the dispersion of toxic clouds

Uncertainty propagation is used to analyze the uncertainty of the output variable caused by *parameter uncertainty* of the input variables. The method cannot be used to analyze the model uncertainty.

### 16.5.1   Analytical Methods

A wide range of mathematical models are used in risk analyses. These may range from simple additive or multiplicative models to very complex models. In this section, we consider simple models described by an output variable $Y$ and a set of input variables $X = (X_1, X_2, \ldots, X_n)$: for example,

$$Y = g(X_1, X_2, \ldots, X_n) = g(X) \tag{16.1}$$

We assume that the input variables are independent random variables with mean $E(X_i) = \mu_i$ and the variance $\mathrm{Var}(X_i) = \sigma_i^2$, for $i = 1, 2, \ldots, n$. Our goal is to determine the mean $E(Y) = \mu_Y$ and variance $\mathrm{Var}(Y) = \sigma_Y^2$ of the output variable $Y$.

For the simple additive model $Y_1 = g(X) = \sum_{i=1}^{n} X_i$, the mean of $Y_1$ is

$$E(Y_1) = \mu_{Y_1} = \sum_{i=1}^{n} \mu_i \tag{16.2}$$

and the variance of $Y$ is

$$\mathrm{Var}(Y_1) = \sigma_{Y_1}^2 = \sum_{i=1}^{n} \sigma_i^2 \tag{16.3}$$

From the central limit theorem (see Appendix A), we know that $Y_1$ is approximately normally (Gaussian) distributed when $n$ is "large," and we can use this distribution to determine the probabilistic characteristics of $Y_1$: for example, to find the probability $\Pr(Y_1 > y_0)$ for some specific value $y_0$.

A simple multiplicative model, $Y_2 = g(X) = \prod_{i=1}^{n} X_i$ of the same $n$ variables, may be reduced to an additive model by taking the logarithms,

$$\ln Y_2 = \ln \left( \prod_{i=1}^{n} X_i \right) = \sum_{i=1}^{n} \ln X_i \tag{16.4}$$

Again, we may use the central limit theorem to claim that the variable $\ln Y_2$ is approximately normally distributed, which means that $Y_2$ is approximately lognormally distributed.

For a general form of $g(X)$, we may use Taylor series expansion around $\mu = (\mu_1, \mu_2, \ldots, \mu_n)$ to write

$$Y = g(\mu) + \sum_{i=1}^{n} \left[ \frac{\partial g(X)}{\partial X_i} \right]_{X=\mu} (X_i - \mu_i)$$

$$+ \frac{1}{2!} \sum_{j=1}^{n} \sum_{i=1}^{n} \left[ \frac{\partial^2 g(X)}{\partial X_i \partial X_j} \right]_{X=\mu} \left[ (X_i - \mu_i)(X_j - \mu_j) \right] + \Delta \tag{16.5}$$

where $\Delta$ is a residual term containing terms of order 3 and higher. It should be noted that all derivatives are evaluated for the mean or nominal value $\mu$. If the deviations $X_i - \mu_i$ are relatively small, the higher powers will be very small, and if the function is relatively smooth in the region of interest, the higher derivatives will be very small. Under these conditions, the residual term $\Delta$ will be very small (e.g., see Abrahamsson, 2002).

The mean value of (16.5) is

$$E(Y) = g(\mu) + \sum_{i=1}^{n} \left[\frac{\partial g(X)}{\partial X_i}\right]_{X=\mu} E(X_i - \mu_i)$$

$$+ \frac{1}{2!} \sum_{j=1}^{n} \sum_{i=1}^{n} \left[\frac{\partial^2 g(X)}{\partial X_i \partial X_j}\right]_{X=\mu} E\left[(X_i - \mu_i)(X_j - \mu_j)\right] + E(\Delta) \quad (16.6)$$

For many functions $g(X)$, the residual term is so small that it can be neglected. Since the mean value of $X_i$ is $\mu_i$, the second term in (16.6) vanishes. Further, since we have assumed that $X_1, X_2, \ldots, X_n$ are independent variables, the covariances $\text{Cov}(X_i, X_j) = E\left[(X_i - \mu_i)(X_j - \mu_j)\right] = 0$ for all $i \neq j$. All elements of the double summation for which $i \neq j$ will therefore vanish. The variance of $X_i$ is $\text{Var}(X_i) = E\left[(X_i - \mu_i)(X_i - \mu_i)\right] = E(X_i - \mu_i)^2 = \sigma_i^2$, and (16.6) can therefore be written

$$E(Y) \approx g(\mu) + \frac{1}{2} \sum_{i=1}^{n} \left[\frac{\partial^2 g(X)}{\partial X_i^2}\right]_{X=\mu} \sigma_i^2 \quad (16.7)$$

The variance of $Y$ may be determined by taking the variance of (16.5). Since $g(\mu)$ is constant, we skip this term. If we also skip the third term in (16.5) and use the assumption about independence, we get

$$\text{Var}(Y) \approx \text{Var} \sum_{i=1}^{n} \left[\frac{\partial g(X)}{\partial X_i}\right]_{X=\mu} (X_i - \mu_i)$$

$$= \sum_{i=1}^{n} \left[\frac{\partial g(X)}{\partial X_i}\right]_{X=\mu}^2 \sigma_i^2 \quad (16.8)$$

■ **EXAMPLE 16.3  Parallel system of two components**

Consider a parallel system of two independent components 1 and 2. Let $p_i$ be the availability of component $i$, for $i = 1, 2$. The availability of the series system is $Y = g(p_1, p_2) = p_1 + p_2 - p_1 \cdot p_2$ (see Appendix A). Assume that we consider the availabilities uncertain and that we believe that the mean values are $E(p_1) = \mu_1 = 0.92$ and $E(p_2) = \mu_2 = 0.94$, and that the standard deviations are $\text{SD}(p_1) = \sigma_1 = 0.03$ and $\text{SD}(p_2) = \sigma_2 = 0.04$, respectively.

If we calculate the system availability by using the mean values, we get $g(\mu_1, \mu_2) = \mu_1 + \mu_2 - \mu_1 \cdot \mu_2 = 0.9952$. The mean value of $Y$ may be found from (16.6), where

$$\frac{\partial^2 g(p_1, p_2)}{\partial p_1^2} = \frac{\partial^2 g(p_1, p_2)}{\partial p_2^2} = 0$$

such that in this case we have that

$$E(Y) = g(\mu_1, \mu_2) \approx 0.9952$$

The variance of $Y$ may be found from (16.8), where

$$\frac{\partial g(p_1, p_2)}{\partial p_1} \Big|_{p=\mu} = 1 - p_2 \Big|_{p=\mu} = 1 - \mu_2 = 1 - 0.94 = 0.06$$

Similarly, we get

$$\frac{\partial g(p_1, p_2)}{\partial p_2} \Big|_{p=\mu} = 1 - \mu_1 = 1 - 0.92 = 0.08$$

and the variance of $Y$ is therefore found from (16.8) to be

$$\mathrm{Var}(Y) \approx 0.06 \cdot (0.03)^2 + 0.08 \cdot (0.04)^2 = 1.82 \cdot 10^{-4}$$

which means that the standard deviation of $Y$ is $\mathrm{SD}(Y) = \sqrt{\mathrm{Var}(Y)} \approx 0.0135$. Note that we need to use this result with caution since $Y$ is a probability and can never be greater than 1.0. ⊕

## 16.5.2 Monte Carlo Simulation

Most risk analysts use Monte Carlo simulation to study the uncertainty propagation in mathematical models like (16.1). To use this approach, we have to choose a probability distribution that best reflects our knowledge about the uncertainty, for each of the input variables in (16.1). The Monte Carlo simulation is performed by repeated sampling from the probability distributions of each variable. By using a pseudorandom generator on a computer, we can obtain one value ($X_i = x_i$) from each distribution. The simulated value $x = (x_1, x_2, \ldots, x_n)$ is used to calculate the output value $y = g(x)$. This is repeated a high number of times and we obtain a large sample of $y$-values. This sample may be plotted as a histogram and we can determine the sample mean and the sample variance, which will be estimates of $E(Y)$ and $\mathrm{Var}(Y)$, respectively. The simulation process is illustrated in Figure 16.2.

*Generation of Random Variables with a Specified Distribution.* Let $X$ be a random variable with distribution function $F_X(x)$ which is strictly increasing for all $x$, such that $F_X^{-1}(z)$ is uniquely determined for all $z \in (0, 1)$. Further, let $Z = F_X(X)$. Then the distribution function $F_Z(z)$ is

$$\begin{aligned} F_Z(z) &= \Pr(Z \leq z) = \Pr(F_X(X) \leq z) \\ &= \Pr(X \leq F_X^{-1}(z)) = F_X\left(F_X^{-1}(z)\right) = z \quad \text{for } 0 < z < 1 \end{aligned} \tag{16.9}$$

Hence $Z = F_X(X)$ has a uniform distribution over $(0, 1)$. This implies that if a random variable $Z$ has a uniform distribution over $(0, 1)$, then $X = F_X^{-1}(Z)$ has the distribution $F_X(x)$.

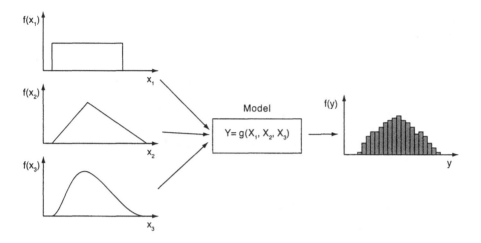

**Figure 16.2**    Uncertainty propagation by Monte Carlo simulation.

This result is used to generate random variables $X_1, X_2, \ldots$ with a specified distribution function $F_X(x)$. The variables $Z_1, Z_2, \ldots$, which are uniformly distributed over $(0, 1)$ may be generated by a pseudorandom generator on a computer. The variables $X_i = F_X^{-1}(Z_i)$ for $i = 1, 2, \ldots$ will then have the distribution function $F_X(x)$.

Because of the reliance on random number generation and repeated computation, we need to use a computer to perform Monte Carlo simulation. A wide range of simulation programs are available. Some of these are generic programs which are linked to a spreadsheet program such as Excel, while others are programs dedicated for a special purpose. Many fault tree analysis programs, for example, have a special module for uncertainty propagation based on Monte Carlo simulation.

Advantages of Monte Carlo simulation include:

- It is easy to use.

- Can be applied directly to the model. We do not need to develop surrogate models, for example by Taylor expansion.

- We may choose among many different distributions for the input variables and also test various alternatives.

- Many tailor-made programs are available.

A major drawback is the extensive computation time for complex models. Several approaches have been developed to make the simulation more efficient (e.g., see Abrahamsson, 2002; Stamatelatos et al., 2002b; Modarres, 2006).

📱 **EXAMPLE 16.4    Constant failure rate**

Consider a component with constant failure rate $\lambda$. The probability that this component will survive the time interval $(0, t)$ is $R(t) = \exp(-\lambda t)$. By studying various data sources, we find that our uncertainty about the value of $\lambda$ may be modeled by a lognormal distribution with median $\lambda_m = 5 \cdot 10^{-5}$ (hours)$^{-1}$ and an error factor $k = 3$, such that we believe that the "true" value of $\lambda$ lies in the interval $(\lambda_m / k, \lambda_m \cdot k)$ with probability 90%.

This case can be easily simulated in Excel and after, for example, $t = 1\,000$ hours and 500 simulations, the estimated mean and standard deviation of $R(t)$ is found to be:

– Estimated mean of $R(1000) \approx 0.9397$

– Estimated standard deviation of $R(t) \approx 0.0395$                                    ⊕

## 16.6  Sensitivity Analysis

Sensitivity analysis in the context of risk analysis may be defined as:

☞ **Sensitivity analysis**: Analysis that examines how the results of a calculation or model vary as individual assumptions are changed (AS/NZS 4360, 1995).

A sensitivity analysis is a quantitative examination of how the outputs from the analysis varies with the changing of:

– The input parameters (e.g., failure rates, probabilities, repair times)

– The assumptions of the analysis (e.g., related to operation, maintenance, independence)

– The structure of the model (e.g., structure of a fault tree)

In some cases, this variation can be very large, and the output can be strongly dependent on the input values.

Traditional sensitivity analysis is conducted by changing one uncertain input at a time and showing how the results of a model change over the range of possible values of that one input. Two-way sensitivity analysis is also common (varying two inputs at the time and plotting the results in a two-dimensional space).

Sensitivity analysis is most commonly used to study the effects of variations in the input parameters. As above, assume that we are using the mathematical model $g(X) = g(X_1, X_2, \ldots, X_n)$, where $X_1, X_2, \ldots, X_n$ are $n$ independent input variables/parameters. Further assume that the mean or nominal value for $X_i$ is $\mu_i$ for $i = 1, 2, \ldots, n$. The sensitivity of this model with respect to the variable $X_i$ is defined as

$$I(i) = \frac{\partial g(X)}{\partial X_i}\bigg|_{X=\mu} \tag{16.10}$$

For a fault tree analysis, we may want to study the variation in the TOP event probability $Q_0(t)$ when we change the probability $q_j(t)$ of input event $j$. We may study the TOP event variation $\Delta Q_0(t)$ as a function of a specified variation $\Delta q_j(t)$ of the input event probability. In this case, we study the variation $\Delta Q_0(t)$ by varying only one input parameter. It is also relevant to study $\Delta Q_0(t)$ by, for example, increasing all the input event probabilities by, say, 20%.

Sensitivity analysis is aimed at identifying the most important variables in a model, that is, the variables that have the greatest impact on the model output. The sensitivity analysis will also identify components for which the quality of data are or are not sensitive for the analysis.

When it is possible to establish a mathematical expression of an output value as a function of the input values, we may determine the sensitivity of the input parameters by taking the partial derivatives of this function. This is common practice in fault tree analysis where we determine the sensitivity by Birnbaum's measure of importance:

$$I^B(j \mid t) = \frac{\partial Q_0(t)}{\partial q_j(t)} \tag{16.11}$$

An importance measure is used to calculate the relative contribution of the uncertainty in each input parameter to the uncertainty in the model output. Several importance measures have been proposed, and the most important of these are discussed by Rausand and Høyland (2004). A thorough discussion of uncertainty importance measures is given by Aven and Nøkland (2010). Most computer programs for fault tree analysis can determine several measures of importance.

Sensitivity analysis is often performed using what-if questions. By changing the value of a certain parameter at a time while maintaining all others at their nominal value, we can study the relative impact each change has on the model output. The model (e.g., a fault tree) is then kept constant as we tacitly assume that it is an adequate representation of the system. A sensitivity analysis can be used further to reveal model weaknesses, to study the effects of specific assumptions and simplifications, and also in some cases be used to study the effect of proposed risk-reducing actions.

It may also be relevant to study the sensitivity with respect to variations of the model. In a fault tree analysis, we may, for example, study the change in the TOP event probability by configuring four gas detectors as a 2-out-of-4 system instead of a 3-out-of-4 system.

Sensitivity analysis can help the analyst understand the dynamics of the system. Experimenting with a wide range of values can give insights into the behavior of the system in extreme situations. Sensitivity analysis can be used to direct attention to those subsystems and elements that have the highest impact on the risk of a system.

## 16.7  Additional Reading

The following titles are recommended for further study related to Chapter 16.

– *Guidance on the Treatment of Uncertainties Associated with PRAs in Risk-Informed Decision Making* (NUREG-1855, 2009) is concerned mainly with risk analyses of nuclear power plants, but is also a valuable source of information for other application areas.

– *Uncertainty in Industrial Practice: A Guide to Quantitative Uncertainty Management* (de Rocquigny et al., 2008) gives a thorough treatment of many aspects of uncertainty and sensitivity analysis.

– *Risk Analysis in Engineering: Techniques, Tools, and Trends* (Modarres, 2006). Chapter 5 of this book provides a thorough discussion of uncertainty and also presents several methods for uncertainty analysis.

– *Uncertainty in Quantitative Risk Analysis: Characterisation and Methods of Treatment* (Abrahamsson, 2002). This Ph.D. thesis gives a good introduction to many different areas of uncertainty analysis.

– *Science and Decisions: Advancing Risk Assessment* (US National Research Council, 2009). Chapter 4 of this book defines and discusses all the main concepts and terms used in uncertainty analysis. The main focus of this book is environmental risk assessment and dose-response analysis, but is also a valuable source for other applications of risk analysis.

– *Uncertainties in risk analysis: Six levels of treatment* (Paté-Cornell, 1996) discusses several ways of treating uncertainty in a risk analysis.

# CHAPTER 17

# DEVELOPMENT AND APPLICATIONS OF RISK ASSESSMENT

...what we learn from history is that people don't learn from history.

—George Bernard Shaw

## 17.1 Introduction

This chapter gives a brief survey of the development and status of the application of risk assessment in some selected areas. The survey does not cover all application areas and is far from complete. The survey is from Norway, Europe, and the United States, with a few comments about Australia and Canada. This does not mean that risk assessment is not relevant in other parts of the world; it only indicates that the author is not familiar with development in these areas.

The sequence in which the various application areas are presented does not indicate any order of importance, but the first two or three areas are presented according to the timing of the development of methods and tools for risk assessment.

**Knut Øien**, SINTEF/NTNU, has made important contributions to this chapter.

*Risk Assessment: Theory, Methods, and Applications,* First Edition.
By Marvin Rausand. Copyright © 2011 John Wiley & Sons, Inc.

A goal of this chapter is also to provide some help to learn more about how and to what extent risk assessments are used in the various application areas. For this reason, some important organizations are listed for each application area. A main criterion for selecting these organizations has been the amount of information that can be found on their Internet pages. A starting point for acquiring more information is therefore to visit their Internet pages. More information and links to these and other organizations may be found on the book's homepage, `http://www.ntnu.edu/ross/books/risk`.

Another starting point for getting more information is to identify laws, regulation, standards, and guidelines related to risk assessment within the various application areas. A brief list of some of these is therefore provided for each area. More information may be found by checking the book's reference list or by searching the Internet.

The following application areas are described according to a similar structure:

- Defense and defense industry

- Nuclear power industry

- Process industry

- Offshore oil and gas industry

- Space industry

- Aviation

- Railway transport

- Marine transport

- Machinery systems

A few other areas are mentioned briefly:

- Environmental risk

- Critical infrastructures

- Risk and vulnerability assessments

Several standards are mentioned in this chapter. Standards tend to be updated rather frequently such that the versions referred to in this chapter will soon be outdated. When you search for standards, please check that you get the most recent version.

Readers who are not familiar with risk assessments may find that there are too many references to standards and organizations in this chapter, while readers who are risk specialists in the specific areas may find that important references and organizations are lacking. I have tried to find an adequate balance, but may have missed both targets.

## 17.2    Defense and Defense Industry

### 17.2.1    Introduction

Risk assessment was developed as a scientific discipline after World War II. The first standard for a reliability/risk analysis method, the MIL-STD-1629 for failure mode and effects analysis (FMEA), was issued in 1949. The aim of this standard was to integrate risk and reliability considerations into the development of new products, to avoid failures and failure effects in the practical use of the products. The fault tree analysis method was developed by Bell laboratories in 1962 for safety analysis of the launching system of the intercontinental ballistic missile LGM-30 Minuteman. Fault tree analysis was then used by the Boeing Company to study the Minuteman missile system and also in the design of commercial aircraft. The system safety standard MIL-STD-882, *System Safety Program Requirements*, was issued in 1969 and was based partly on the requirements to the Minuteman missile system.

### 17.2.2    Important Organizations

Organizations that influence how risk assessments are performed and/or provide standards and guidelines for risk assessment of defense systems include:

- The Reliability Information Analysis Center (RIAC) is a U.S. Department of Defense information analysis center in the fields of reliability, maintainability, quality, supportability, and interoperability.

- The U.S. Department of Defense (DoD) has made available a number of reports within the area of reliability and risk analysis.

- The UK Defence Standardization maintains a web site of UK defense standards and a lot of related information.

### 17.2.3    Legislation, Standards, and Guidelines

The defense industry has to follow the same laws and regulations as civil activities, with a few exceptions. A large number of military standards and guidelines have been developed and among these are:

- MIL-S-38130 (US Air Force 1964) *Military Specification for Safety* (This was one of the first standards setting requirements for safety and was a forerunner for MIL-STD-882).

- MIL-STD-882, *System Safety Program Requirements*.

- DEF STAN 00-56 (2007), *Safety Management Requirements for Defence Systems*, Parts 1 and 2 (includes requirements for a safety management system and safety cases).

- ANSI-GEIA-STD-0010, *Standard best practices for system safety program development and execution*.

– *Risk management guide for DoD acquisition*, (6th ed.) (US DOD, 2006).

## 17.2.4  Risk Assessment

The defense industry has traditionally had much more focus on reliability than on risk. This is also clearly reflected in the number of military standards that have been developed.

Today, the defense industry applies risk assessment for many different purposes. As all employers, the defense industry has a duty of care to its employees, the general public, and the wider environment. They therefore have to establish a safety/risk management system and carry out risk assessments as does any other industry (e.g., see DEF STAN 00-56, 2007).

The defense industry sometimes distinguishes between tactical risk and safety risk and defines these terms as follows:

☞ **Tactical risk** is risk concerned with hazards that exist because of the presence of either the enemy or an adversary. It applies to all levels of war and across the spectrum of operations.

Tactical risk is not a topic of this book and no further comments are therefore given to this type of risk.

☞ **Safety risk** includes all operational risk considerations other than tactical risk. It includes risks to friendly forces and risks posed to civilians by an operation as well as its impact on the environment. It can include activities associated with hazards concerning friendly personnel, civilians, equipment readiness, and environmental conditions.

The defense industry today has a strong focus on risk related to acquisitions, and the U.S. Department of Defense has therefore developed a special risk management guide for this purpose (US DOD, 2006).

## 17.3  Nuclear Power Industry

### 17.3.1  Introduction

The first nuclear plants were used for weapon production and were therefore located away from densely populated areas. Isolation was then the main safety strategy. Commercial power production, begun in 1956, necessitated that the plants be located close to densely populated areas. The safety strategy then became *defense-in-depth.*

*Defense-in-Depth.*  The main idea of the defense-in-depth strategy is to have a number of barriers between the radioactive materials and the surroundings, such that the probability of simultaneous failure of all the barriers is very small. The defense-in-depth strategy was implemented in the regulations, and nuclear power plants were considered to be "safe enough" when the regulatory requirements were met.

☞ **Defense-in-depth**: A design and operational philosophy with regard to nuclear facilities that calls for multiple layers of protection to prevent and mitigate accidents. It includes the use of controls, multiple physical barriers to prevent release of radiation, redundant and diverse key safety functions, and emergency response measures (U.S. NRC).

The probabilistic approach to risk assessment appeared in the nuclear industry in the 1970s in the United States, but also in the United Kingdom and France.

*U.S. Nuclear Regulatory Commission.* The U.S. Atomic Energy Commission (AEC) was established in 1946. After having been strongly criticized, AEC was reorganized and became the U.S. Nuclear Regulatory Commission (NRC) in 1975. One of the main responsibilities of the NRC is to ensure that the operations of nuclear power plants present no undue risk to public health and safety. NRC has published a wide range of high-quality reports/guidelines related to risk assessment of nuclear installations. These reports, called NUREG reports, can be downloaded from the NRC web site.

*U.S. Reactor Safety Study.* The *Reactor Safety Study* (NUREG-75/014, 1975) was carried out in the period 1972–1975. The study is also known as the WASH 1400 and the Rasmussen report, after Norman C. Rasmussen (1928–2003) of MIT, who managed the study. The study covered the risk of 100 U.S. nuclear power plants and was a milestone in the development of risk assessment. WASH 1400 was based mainly on fault tree analysis, but it was soon realized that fault tree analysis could not solve all the safety problems. This led to the development of a framework based on a combination of fault tree and event tree analysis. Common mode/cause failures and parameter uncertainties were also introduced as part of the risk assessment framework. The WASH 1400 report is now considered obsolete, but its analysis framework is still used in most quantitative risk analyses in the nuclear sector and many other industry sectors.

The WASH 1400 study was updated and improved in 1990 by the NUREG-1150, *Severe Accident Risks: An Assessment for Five U.S. Nuclear Power Plants.* The risk analyses of U.S. nuclear power plants have been available to the public and widely discussed, and the methods have been developed further within the nuclear industry. WASH 1400 was discussed fiercely, and several NUREG reports have been published describing and discussing the various risk assessment methods. Some of the issues are: component reliability data, common-cause failures, human reliability, uncertainty, consistency, and comparison of risk analyses (US NRC, 2007).

*Common-Cause Failure Analysis.* As a follow-up to WASH 1400, a number of new approaches to common-cause failure (CCF) analysis were proposed, some of which are described in Chapter 15. The development of the multiple greek letter (MLG) and alpha-factor models led to release of the important NUREG/CR-4780

(1989), a joint Nuclear Regulatory Commission (NRC) and Electric Power Research Institute (EPRI) report. This report was later replaced by or updated in NUREG/CR-5485 (1998).

### 17.3.2 Important Organizations

Some main organizations relevant for risk assessment in the nuclear power industry are:

- The International Atomic Energy Authority (IAEA) was established in 1957 and is located in Vienna, Austria.

- The Nuclear Energy Agency (NEA) was established in 1958 (under OECD) and is located in Paris, France.

- The International Nuclear Safety Advisory Group (INSAG) is linked to IAEA.

- The U.S. Nuclear Regulatory Commission (NRC) (see above).

- The World Association of Nuclear Operators (WANO) was established in 1989, partly as a reaction to the *Chernobyl* accident in 1986.

### 17.3.3 Legislation, Standards, and Guidelines

International safety requirements for nuclear power plants are issued by the IAEA, of which two are listed below. A large number of NUREG reports that are relevant for PRAs are available at NRC's web site. Some early NUREG reports are mentioned here together with a couple of IAEA reports:

- IAEA NS-R-1 (2000): *Safety of Nuclear Power Plants: Design, Safety Requirements.*

- IAEA NS-R-2 (2000): *Safety of Nuclear Power Plants: Operation.*

- NUREG/CR-2300 (1983): *PRA Procedures Guide: A Guide to the Performance of Probabilistic Risk Assessments for Nuclear Power Plants.*

- NUREG/CR-2815 (1984): *Probabilistic Safety Analysis Procedures Guide.*

- IAEA-TECHDOC-1200 (2001): *Applications of probabilistic safety assessment for nuclear power plants* (IAEA, 2001).

- IAEA-TECHDOC-1267 (2002): *Procedures for conducting probabilistic safety assessment for non-reactor nuclear facilities.*

### 17.3.4  Risk Assessment

The use of quantitative risk assessment has become commonplace for all phases of the life of a nuclear power plant, including siting, design, construction, operation, and decommissioning. Quantitative risk assessments in the nuclear power industry are called *probabilistic risk assessments* (PRAs) in the United States and *probabilistic safety assessments* (PSAs) in most other countries. For simplicity, we use the term PRA in the rest of this section. The PRAs are carried out mainly as described in Part II of this book and are classified into three "levels":

*Level 1 PRA* is the first part of the PRA and is carried out to identify all the event sequences that may lead to core damage and to estimate their probabilities. It starts with conditions that are well known, usually with a reactor operating at full power. All of the systems that work to protect the reactor are modeled, usually by detailed fault tree analyses. Since the workings of these systems are well understood, the uncertainty of the result is relatively small. A level 1 PRA will normally include at least:

- Event tree analysis of all initiating events and descriptions of all associated accident scenarios
- Human reliability assessment
- Common-cause failure analysis
- Fault tree analysis of all relevant TOP events
- Importance measures for basic events
- Uncertainty analysis (completeness, models, parameters)

The risk related to such external events as earthquake, flooding, and aircraft crashes is also normally part of the level 1 PRA.

*Level 2 PRA* is carried out to determine the amount, probability, and timing of radioactive substances that may be released from the containment (i.e., assuming that the core is damaged, how much radioactivity might be released to the environment?). The analysis assesses the physical progress and timing of a reactor accident in various accident sequences. The analysis is based mainly on event trees combined with simulation.

*Level 3 PRA* may be carried out to assess the risk to people and the environment if radioactivity should escape from containment. Highly variable factors such as wind speed and direction will affect the results.

The U.S. NRC has made a clear commitment to move toward risk-informed and performance-based regulation and to use the insights from PRAs to complement traditional engineering methods when making regulatory decisions about power plants and the handling of nuclear waste. This is a "risk-informed" approach or risk-informed decision-making (RIDM), as discussed briefly in Chapter 1. European regulators have followed this development, but have so far not given similar outspoken commitments, in spite of the fact that risk-informed and performance-based considerations have already been used in many regulatory decisions (Wahlström, 2003).

***Living PRAs.*** Both the IAEA and the U.S. NRC focus on *living PRAs*. A living PRA is a PRA that is kept updated and reflects the current design and operational features of the plant, and is documented in such a way that each aspect of the model can be related directly to existing plant information, plant documentation or the analysts' assumptions. The living PRA is used for design verification, assessment of potential changes to the plant design or operation, design of training programs, and assessment of changes to the plant licensing basis (IAEA, 2001).

## 17.4  Process Industry

### 17.4.1  Introduction

The development of risk assessment in the process industry has been driven mainly by many accidents. The *Flixborough* accident in England in 1974 and the *Seveso* accident in Italy in 1976 led to a strong focus on process safety in Europe and also to the development of an EU directive on major accident hazards—the *Seveso directive*, approved in 1981. This directive was later amended after the Bhopal tragedy in India in 1984 and the *Sandoz* fire in Switzerland in 1986. In 1996 a major revision of the directive was approved as an answer to the *Piper Alpha* accident in the North Sea in 1988. The new directive is called the *Seveso II directive* (EU, 1996). All enterprises within the EU that produce or store large quantities of dangerous chemicals are obliged to follow the requirements in the Seveso II directive. Similar requirements have been implemented in several other countries, including Australia and the United States.

Because of the inherent potential for major accidents associated with large-scale chemical processes, this industry has itself actively pursued operational safety.

In the United States the fire and explosion in 2005 at BP's *Texas City* refinery, killing 15 workers and injuring more than 170 others, significantly increased the focus on process safety for both the authorities and the industry.

### 17.4.2  Important Organizations

- The U.S. Occupational Safety and Health Administration (U.S. OSHA)

- The European Agency for Safety and Health at Work (EU OSHA)

- The U.S. Environmental Protection Agency (EPA)

- The Center for Chemical Process Safety (CCPS) is a corporate membership organization operated by the American Institute of Chemical Engineers (AIChE). CCPS was established in 1985, and its first publication, *Guidelines for Hazard Evaluation Procedures*, came in 1990. A long line of process safety guidelines have since then been produced. A historical account of CCPS' process safety activities is given by Hendershot (2009).

- The Major Accident Hazards Bureau (MAHB) is part of the EU Joint Research Centre and supports the EU on issues related to the Seveso II directive. MAHB operates the Seveso II accident databases.

- The European Process Safety Centre (EPSC), established in 1992, is an industry-funded organization promoting process safety in Europe.

- The oil companies' European association for environment, health, and safety in refining and distribution (CONCAWE).

### 17.4.3   Legislation, Standards, and Guidelines

The main regulations related to major process accidents are:

- *Council Directive 96/82/EC of 9 December 1996 on the Control of Major Accident Hazards Involving Dangerous Substances (Seveso II Directive)* (EU, 1996).

- The U.S. OSHA standard 29 CFR 1910.119, *Process safety management of highly hazardous chemicals* (1992) is the U.S. counterpart of the Seveso II directive.

- The U.S. EPA standard 40 CFR Part 68, *Chemical accidents prevention provisions* (1999).

- API RP 750, *Recommended practice for the management of process hazards*, American Petroleum Institute.

- NOHSC 1014 (2002), *National Standard for the Control of Major Hazard Facilities'* is the Australian counterpart to the Seveso II directive.

Several other directives and standards have been developed for special process risks.

*Europe.*   The objective of the Seveso II directive (EU, 1996) is to prevent major accidents and delimit their consequences to people and the environment.

The application of the Seveso II directive depends on the quantities of dangerous substances present (or likely to be present) at an establishment. Two levels ("tiers") of duty are specified in the directive, corresponding to two different quantities (or thresholds) of dangerous substances. Sites exceeding the higher, "upper tier," threshold are subject to more onerous requirements than those that only qualify as "lower tier."

Several important reports related to risk assessment and the Seveso II directive have been developed. Among these are:

- *Accidental risk assessment methodology for industries in the context of the Seveso II directive* (ARAMIS, 2004).

- *Guidelines for Quantitative Risk Assessment (The Purple Book)* (VROM, 2005).

- *Quantitative Risk Assessment (QRA)* (Borysiewicz et al., 2007).

*United States.* The U.S. OSHA process safety management (PSM) standard and the EPA chemical accident prevention provisions were the first U.S. federal regulations designed specifically to prevent major chemical accidents that could harm workers, the public, and the environment.

The implementation of 29 CFR 1910.119 is based on 14 interrelated core elements that define the process system:

1. Employee participation

2. Process safety information

3. *Process hazard analysis* (PrHA)

4. Operating procedures

5. Training requirements

6. Contractors

7. Pre-startup safety review

8. Mechanical integrity

9. Hot work permits

10. Management of change

11. Incident investigation

12. Emergency planning and response

13. Compliance audits

14. Availability of trade secret information

Detailed comments on each item may be found in Appendix C to 29 CFR 1910.119 (see U.S. OSHA's homepage, http://www.osha.gov).

*Australia.* The *National Standard for the Control of Major Hazard Facilities'* [NOHSC 1014 (2002)] is consistent with the Seveso II directive.

### 17.4.4 Risk Assessment

*HAZOP.* The hazard and operability (HAZOP) technique (see Chapter 9) was developed in the1960s and became a standard technique for most companies involved in the design of chemical processes and operations, first in the UK and later in other European countries. The history of HAZOP has been described by Kletz (1999), who was safety advisor at ICI and involved in the development of the HAZOP technique.

The popularity of the HAZOP method was boosted after the *Flixborough* accident in 1974. Several guidelines and books on the HAZOP method have been published (e.g., Kletz, 1999; Crawley et al., 2000), and HAZOP is today a standard module in chemical engineering degree courses in many countries.

The HAZOP method has been extended to be applicable to more than design and operation of technical process plants. Today, modified HAZOP techniques are also used to analyze complex work procedures, human errors, and software.

**Canvey Island.** One of the first comprehensive quantitative risk assessments was the analysis in 1978 of the health and safety risks associated with the petrochemical installations on Canvey Island, a highly industrial area on the north bank of the Thames River.

After 1975, the process industry began to adopt the risk analysis procedures that were developed in the *Reactor Safety Study* (NUREG-75/014, 1975).

**Process Hazard Analysis.** In the United States a process hazard analysis (PrHA) is required by 29 CFR 1910.119. As part of this analysis, the operator has to:

– Determine locations of potential safety problems.

– Identify corrective measures to improve safety.

– Preplan emergency actions to be taken if safety controls fail.

The following analytical methods for PrHA are suggested in the standard:

– What-if

– Checklist

– What-if/checklist (i.e., SWIFT)

– Hazard and operability study (HAZOP)

– Failure mode and effect analysis (FMEA)

– Fault tree analysis, or

– An appropriate equivalent methodology

To facilitate the implementation of the PSM standard, the DOE handbook *Chemical process hazards analysis* was published in 1996 with an update in 2004 (US DOE, 2004). The handbook provides a detailed step-by-step procedure on how to carry out the process hazard analysis (PrHA).

**ARAMIS.** The EU research project *Accidental risk assessment methodology for industries in the framework of the Seveso II directive* (ARAMIS) was carried out in the period 2001–2004 with joint efforts from several European universities and research institutions. The project developed an integrated methodology for risk assessment related to the Seveso II directive. The methodology is described thoroughly in the ARAMIS user guide and in a large number of publications (e.g., see Salvi and Debray, 2006).

## 17.5   Offshore Oil and Gas Industry

### 17.5.1   Introduction

Risk assessments in the offshore oil and gas industry were first used in the Norwegian sector of the North Sea and were accentuated after the *Bravo* blowout in the Ekofisk field in 1977 and the capsizing of the semisubmersible living-quarters platform *Alexander Kielland* in 1980. As a consequence of the Bravo blowout, the comprehensive research program *Safety Offshore* was initiated by the Norwegian Research Council, with the objective of developing risk assessment approaches for offshore activities and generally improving the safety of offshore activities. Beginning in 1981, the Norwegian Petroleum Directorate (NPD) required a detailed risk assessment of all new platform concepts.

In 1988, a series of explosions that followed an initial release of gas from a compressor module on the *Piper Alpha* North Sea platform east of Aberdeen killed 167 persons. The investigation of the *Piper Alpha* accident, by Lord Cullen, recommended a set of new requirements for risk assessments.

In 2010, the *Deepwater Horizon* accident in the Gulf of Mexico again put a strong focus on safety in the offshore oil and gas industry. A blowout killed 11 workers, produced a huge fire, and caused the entire platform to sink and the largest offshore oil spill in the U.S. history.

The offshore oil and gas industry is exposed to a number of additional hazards compared to onshore plants. There is the transport from the shore to the installation, the compact design, the risk associated with shipping impact, the risk from structural collapse, the effects of weather and even seismic loading on the support structure and finally, the risk from production and well operations while personnel are asleep in their quarters.

### 17.5.2   Important Organizations

Some main organizations relevant for risk assessment in the offshore oil and gas industry are:

– The Petroleum Safety Authority Norway

– The UK Health and Safety Executive, Offshore Division

– The U.S. Bureau of Ocean Energy Management, Regulation and Enforcement (BOEMRE)[1]

– The National Offshore Petroleum Safety Authority (NOPSA), Australia

– The American Petroleum Institute (API)

– The International Association of Oil & Gas Producers (OGP)

---

[1] Former U.S. Minerals Management Service.

– The International Association of Drilling Contractors (IADC)

– Standard Norge—NORSOK

### 17.5.3 Legislation, Standards, and Guidelines

– ISO 17776: *Petroleum and Natural Gas Industries—Offshore Production Installations: Guidelines on Tools and Techniques for Hazard Identification and Risk Assessment* (ISO 17776, 2002).

– API 14C (2007): *Recommended practice for analysis, design, installation, and testing of basic surface systems for offshore production platforms.*

*Norway.* Current regulations concerning the implementation and use of risk analyses in petroleum activities, issued by the Norwegian Petroleum Safety Authority (PSA) and the Norwegian Ministry of the Environment, are split into five parts:

1. "Regulations relating to health, safety and the environment in the petroleum activities and at certain offshore facilities" (the framework regulations).

2. "Regulations relating to management and the duty to provide information on the petroleum activities and at certain offshore facilities" (the management regulations).

3. "Regulations relating to design and outfitting of facilities, etc. in the petroleum activities" (the facilities regulations).

4. "Regulations relating to conducting petroleum activities" (the activities regulations).

5. "Regulations relating to technical and operational matters at onshore facilities in the petroleum activities, etc." (The technical and operational regulations).

A specific risk analysis standard has been developed to support the Norwegian offshore safety legislation:

– NORSOK Z-013: *Risk and emergency preparedness analysis* (NORSOK Z-013, 2010)

*United Kingdom.* The main set of regulations related to risk assessment in the UK offshore oil and gas activities is:

– The Offshore Installations (Safety Case) Regulations, 2005.

An associated "Explanatory Memorandum" describes and explains the various clauses of the regulations. The role of quantitative risk assessment in the safety case is outlined in detail in HSE's Offshore Information Sheet No. 2/2006. Several of the risk measures that were discussed in Chapter 4 of this book (e.g., IRPA and PLL) are also recommended measures in this information sheet.

***Australia.***  The main set of regulations related to risk assessment in Australian off-shore oil and gas activities is:

– Offshore Petroleum and Greenhouse Gas Storage Act, 2006.

The regulations requires a safety case approach, which is explained in detail in the Internet pages for NOPSA. The required risk assessment, called *formal safety assessment* (FSA), focuses mainly on *major accident events* (MAEs).

☞ **Major accident event (MAE):** An event connected with a facility, including a natural event, having the potential to cause multiple fatalities of persons at or near the facility (http://www.nopsa.gov.au).

### 17.5.4  Risk Assessment

In Norway, quantitative risk analyses are carried out according to the NORSOK Z-013 (2010) standard, which is very much in line with the procedures described in this book.

In the UK, the safety requirement must be demonstrated through a *safety case*. The safety case must demonstrate that:

– The installation has an adequate safety management system.

– All major hazards have been identified and the associated risks are controlled.

– Risks have been evaluated and reduced to a level that is as low as reasonably practicable (ALARP).

Quantitative risk assessment is the most important technique used to identify major accident hazards and to show that the risks have been made ALARP, and is explicitly required as part of the safety case regulations.

A survey of approaches and methods may also be found on the web site for the International Association of Oil & Gas Producers (OGP); http://info.ogp.org.uk.

### 17.6  Space Industry

### 17.6.1  Introduction

The U.S. National Aeronautic and Space Administration (NASA) has had a restrained view on probabilistic risk analyses. Until the launch-pad fire during testing of the *Apollo* spacecraft in 1967, NASA relied mainly on worst-case failure modes and effects analysis (FMEA), even if an FMEA is mainly qualitative and has several weaknesses, such as focusing on single items and not being able to aggregate risk at the system level. Quality assurance and quality control was taken care of through "good engineering practice." After this accident, in which three astronauts died, NASA initiated a systematic effort with risk analysis. They first contracted Boeing to perform a risk assessment, and a fault tree analysis was performed for the entire *Apollo* system. This activity was greatly hampered when General Electric performed a "full probabilistic risk analysis" of a potential landing on the moon. The analysis showed that the probability of a successful operation was less than 5%. The history proved that this result was far too pessimistic, and NASA lost confidence in probabilistic risk analysis, and it took several years before NASA continued its risk analysis efforts.

The reliance on FMEA for safety assessment lasted until the *Challenger* accident in 1986. The investigation report of the *Challenger* accident criticized NASA for not estimating the probability of failure of the various space shuttle elements. In 1988, the report "Post-Challenger Evaluation of Space Shuttle Risk Assessment and Management" recommended that "probabilistic risk assessment approaches be applied to the Shuttle risk management program at the earliest possible date."

The first PRA was conducted on the space shuttle in 1988 (for the Galileo mission) and the study was updated in 1993. The first major PRA of the space shuttle was done by assistance from an external consultant in 1995 and was based on recent developments within the nuclear industry. A Bayesian update of this PRA was done in 1996, and PRA continued to be used on the space shuttle, the International Space Station, and as part of the Constellation program.

In 1998, the NPG 7120.5A, *NASA Program and Project Management Processes and Requirements* was issued, stating that:

- The program or project manager must apply risk management principles as a decision-making tool which enables programmatic and technical success.

- Program and project decisions must be made in an orderly risk management effort.

- Risk management includes identification, assessment, mitigation, and disposition of risk throughout the PAPAC (provide aerospace products and capabilities) process.

The PRA guideline *Probabilistic risk assessment procedures guide for NASA managers and practitioners* (Stamatelatos et al., 2002a) was issued in 2002 and comprehensive PRAs have been used regularly since 2003.

## 17.6.2 Important Organizations

Some main organizations relevant for risk assessment in the space industry are:

- The U.S. National Aeronautic and Space Administration (NASA)

- The European Space Agency (ESA)

- European Cooperation for Space Standardisation (ECSS)

### 17.6.3 Legislation, Standards, and Guidelines

Several standards have been developed (e.g., ECSS), but the most comprehensive and authoritative texts are:

- *Probabilistic risk assessment procedures guide for NASA managers and practitioners* (Stamatelatos et al., 2002a)

- *Fault tree handbook with aerospace applications* (Stamatelatos et al., 2002b)

- *NASA risk-informed decision making handbook* (Dezfuli et al., 2010)

### 17.6.4 Risk Assessment

Following the *Challenger* accident in 1986, NASA introduced a probabilistic risk analysis program to support the safety management activities in both the design and operational phase of its manned space shuttles. This work lead to the publication of the probabilistic risk assessment (PRA) guidelines for the space shuttle program and later to the more general PRA guideline.

Currently, NASA is using PRA in a wide range of situations. The most extensive PRA conducted is the full-scope PRA, which models all the potential scenarios that may lead to undesired end events, such as loss of crew and potential injury to the public. The basic causes that are modeled include hardware failures, human errors, process errors, and phenomenological events.

## 17.7 Aviation

### 17.7.1 Introduction

In the 1930s, the aviation industry was perhaps the most advanced branch of industry and safety was maintained basically by trial and error. The term *fly-fix-fly* was associated with an aircraft making a circuit, and if it failed, they would fix it and fly again. This process was repeated until an acceptable solution was obtained. This approach was not acceptable in the defense industry, and especially not for developing nuclear weapons.

The aviation industry has traditionally used FMEA and fault tree analysis and established detailed fault trees for each possible system failure (e.g., total failure of an engine), but has not combined these fault trees with event tree analysis to develop accident scenarios.

The FAA carried out a risk assessment of operations at airports in 1999. The analysis was based on quantitative fault tree and event tree analyses.

Other techniques were adopted to calculate the public risk in the vicinity of Schiphol airport. In this study, the risk in the region surrounding the airport was based on parameters representing population distribution, flight operations data, aircraft fleet data, and aircraft accident rates. The effects of different risk reduction strategies were also included: for example, adding an additional runway or changing the aircraft fleet mix.

### 17.7.2 Important Organizations

Some main organizations relevant for risk assessment in the aviation industry are:

- The International Civil Aviation Organization (ICAO) is a UN specialized agency with the objective of improving safety, security, environmental protection, and efficiency in civil aviation.

- The European Aviation Safety Agency (EASA) was established in 2003 as the rule-making and standard-setting organization for all aviation safety regulation on behalf of the EU member states. The agency is responsible for certification of aircraft and related products, and is further responsible for the rules related to the design and maintenance of aircraft products and parts.

- The U.S. Federal Aviation Administration (FAA).

- The UK Civil Aviation Authority (CAA). A lot of useful information may be found on the CAA web site.

- EUROCONTROL (European Organization for the Safety of Air Navigation) was established to harmonize and integrate air navigation services in Europe, aiming at the creation of a uniform air traffic management (ATM) system for civil and military users.

- The International Air Transport Association (IATA).

- The Flight Safety Foundation (FSF) was formed in 1947 to contribute to the improvement of global aviation safety. FSF is an independent membership organization with members from around 150 countries.

### 17.7.3 Legislation, Standards, and Guidelines

Some main guidelines that are relevant for risk assessment in the aviation industry are:

- *Safety management manual (SMM)* (ICAO, 2009)

- *System safety handbook* (US FAA, 2000).

- *Risk management handbook* (US FAA, 2009).

### 17.7.4 Risk Assessment

The risk assessments that are performed in the aviation industry are mainly in line with the procédures described in this book. The risk is often quantified relative to flight hours or to the number of takeoffs. A risk measure that is commonly used is the fatal accident rate (FAR), which for aviation is defined as:

FAR = number of fatal accidents per 100 000 flight hours

### 17.7.5 Helicopter Transport

SINTEF, the Norwegian research organization, has carried out a detailed risk assessment of helicopter transportation from land to, and between, offshore oil and gas installations (Herrera et al., 2010). The work focused on North Sea helicopter accidents and incidents in order to calculate the risk in terms of fatalities per million person flight hours. This was achievable due to the recording of flight hours and personnel carried by the North Sea operators.

The work also studies the factors that influence risk in terms of frequency and consequence, termed risk-influencing factors (RIFs). Estimated values for the respective importance of each RIF were elicited by means of a series of expert panels, which then allowed the RIFs with the largest impact on overall risk to be identified.

## 17.8 Railway Transport

### 17.8.1 Introduction

Railway safety has traditionally been rule-based, where rules and regulations have been changed and improved after each accident. Detailed technical specifications have been used as a basis for new system acquisitions. These specifications have been based on the experiences gained by railway operators and on common international rules. Risk analyses in railway operations are of relatively recent date (beginning of the 1990s), motivated by some major organizational changes (privatization/outsourcing), increased technical complexity, accidents, and general knowledge of modern safety management. In the UK, a *safety case* regime was introduced in 1994, but this was terminated when the EU Railway safety directive (EU, 2004) was implemented in 2006.

As for most other application areas, the development of safety legislation and requirements for risk assessments have been driven by several major accidents. Some of the most influential railway accidents in Europe are:

– Three trains crashed at *Clapham Junction* in southwest London, UK in 1988 (35 dead and approximately 500 injured).

– A high-speed train derailed near *Eschede* in Germany in 1998 due to a wheel fracture (101 dead and 88 injured).

– Two trains crashed at *Ladbroke Grove* in London, UK in 1999 (31 dead and more than 520 injured); also known as the Paddington train crash.

### 17.8.2 Important Organizations

Some main organizations relevant for risk assessment in railway transport are:

– The European Railway Agency (ERA).

– The U.S. Federal Railroad Administration

– The UK Office of Rail Regulation (ORR)

– The UK Rail Safety and Standards Board (RSSB)

### 17.8.3 Legislation, Standards, and Guidelines

The Safety Appliance Act is a U.S. federal law that made air brakes and automatic couplers mandatory on all trains in the United States. This was perhaps the first law related to railway safety. It was enacted on March 2, 1893.

More recent laws and standards comprise:

– The EU Railway Safety Directive (EU, 2004)

– The EU regulations on the adoption of a common safety method on risk evaluation and assessment (Regulation 352/2009) related to the Railway Safety Directive

– The UK railways and other guided transport systems (safety) regulations, 2006

– IEC 62278: *Railway Applications: Specification and Demonstration of Reliability, Availability, Maintainability, and Safety (RAMS)* (IEC 62278, 2002)[2]

The railway industry has adopted most of the risk assessment approaches used in, for example, the nuclear industry, and has actively discussed the application of risk assessment and published a wide range of useful reports. Among these are:

– The *Engineering Safety Management (The Yellow Book)* (RSSB, 2007) is published by the UK Rail Safety and Standards Board and gives a good introduction to risk assessment and risk control of railway systems.

– The report *Risk tolerability in rail safety regulation* (NTC, 2004) by the National Transport Commission in Australia gives a thorough discussion of risk and risk acceptance in railway operations.

### 17.8.4 Risk Assessment

The EU Railway safety directive (EU, 2004) requires the railway operators to implement a safety management system and to carry out risk assessments using *common safety methods*. A special EU regulation (352/2009) on "the adoption of a common safety method on risk evaluation and assessment as referred to in Article 6(3)(a) of Directive 2004/49/EC of the European Parliament and of the Council" entered into force in July 2010. The risk management process and the common safety methods described in this EU regulations are very much in line with the corresponding methods described in this book.

---

[2] Based on the European norm EN 50126.

## 17.9  Marine Transport

### 17.9.1  Introduction

A high number of ship accidents have lead to many fatalities (*Herald of Free Enterprise, Estonia*) and extensive pollution (*Amoco Cadiz, Exxon Valdez, Erika, Prestige*). Maritime operations are international by nature, and safety is therefore regulated primarily by the International Maritime Organization (IMO). Until recently, the safety regulation has been rule-based, and new rules have emerged based on the frequent accidents. Major accidents have often caused new rules with the aim of preventing a recurrence of the same type of accident. This approach has lead to many rules and hence complicated management. IMO has therefore initiated a risk-based approach and developed a risk analysis approach that is known as *formal safety assessment* (FSA).

### 17.9.2  Important Organizations

Some main organizations relevant for risk assessment of marine transport are:

- The International Maritime Organization (IMO), a specialized agency of the United Nations that develops international conventions and codes for the promotion of safety at sea and the prevention of pollution

- The European Maritime Safety Agency (EMSA), established in 2002, provides technical and scientific assistance to the European Commission and Member States in the proper development and implementation of EU legislation on maritime safety, pollution by ships, and security onboard ships

### 17.9.3  Legislation, Standards, and Guidelines

In order to establish common international standards, IMO works by consensus, and its regulations do not go into effect until they have been ratified by a sufficient number of maritime states. Each ratifying state must enact the regulations in its own domestic legislation, and its own inspectors then enforce them. In the interim, IMO issues codes that are widely used on a voluntary basis, although they are not legally enforceable.

Some specific regulations are:

- International convention for safety of life at sea (SOLAS) 1974

- International maritime dangerous goods code

- U.S. 33 CFR 96, "Rules for the safe operation of vessels and safety management systems"

– The U.S. Maritime Transportation Security Act (2004), designed to protect U.S. ports and waterways from a terrorist attack, requiring vessels and port facilities to conduct risk/vulnerability assessments

***Classification Society Rules.*** Classification societies are independent organizations that issue rules for the safety of ships and offshore installations, performing ongoing surveys and inspections to ensure that these rules are being followed. Their main purpose is to protect the ship and its cargo, and the rules apply primarily to the strength of the hull and the reliability of its essential machinery and equipment. Important classification societies include Lloyd's Register, Det Norske Veritas, Bureau Veritas, and the American Bureau of Shipping. Some rules made by the classification societies require risk assessments addressing specific hazards (HSE, 2001a).

### 17.9.4 Risk Assessment

A good introduction to marine/maritime risk assessment is given in HSE (2001a).

***Formal Safety Assessment.*** Formal safety assessment (FSA) is a systematic risk assessment approach (IMO, 2002) developed by IMO partly as a response to the Piper Alpha disaster. In 1997, IMO agreed on guidelines for the use of risk assessment as a basis for developing maritime safety and environmental regulations, and FSA is now being applied to the IMO rule-making process.

FSA can be used as a tool to help evaluate new regulations or to compare proposed changes with existing standards. The FSA approach is somewhat similar to the risk assessment approach described in this book and consists of five steps:

1. Identify hazards (i.e., list all relevant accident scenarios with potential causes and outcomes).

2. Assess the risk (i.e., analyze and evaluate each important accident scenario).

3. Propose risk control options (i.e., devise regulatory measures to control and reduce the identified risks).

4. Assess the cost-benefit of each risk control option.

5. Make recommendations for decision-making (i.e., provide information about the hazards, their associated risks and the cost-effectiveness of alternative risk control options).

Application of FSA may be particularly relevant to proposals for regulatory measures that have far-reaching implications in terms of costs to the maritime industry or the administrative or legislative burdens that may result.

***SAFEDOR.*** SAFEDOR (Design, Operation, and Regulation for Safety) is an EU research program that was carried out in the period 2005–2009. Some of the main results from SAFEDOR integrating the new IMO approach are documented in the book *Risk-Based Ship Design: Methods, Tools, and Applications* (Papanikolaou, 2009).

**Figure 17.1**   The CE logo.

## 17.10   Machinery Systems

### 17.10.1   Introduction

The first version of the EU machinery directive (89/392/EEC) was approved in 1989. The directive was one of the first "new method" directives, in which only the essential health and safety requirements are given in the directive and where detailed requirements are left to harmonized standards. The directive has been revised and a large number of harmonized standards have been developed. These standards were first published as European norms, EN standards, but later transformed into international standards, mainly ISO standards.

To be able to sell and use machinery equipment in Europe, the equipment has to fulfill the requirements of the machinery directive. This compliance is shown by a CE logo (see Figure 17.1) affixed on the equipment and an accompanying "declaration of conformity." In many cases, a risk assessment is required as part of the system documentation.

Similar requirements have been implemented in many countries that export machinery equipment to Europe.

### 17.10.2   Legislation, Standards, and Guidelines

Relevant regulation and standards:

- The EU Machinery Directive 2006/42/EC

- Guide to application of the Machinery Directive 2006/42/EC

- EN 1050: *Safety of Machinery: Principles for Risk Assessment* (i.e., the initial risk assessment standard)

- *Safety of Machinery—General Principles for Design: Risk Assessment and Risk Reduction* (ISO 12100, 2010)

- ANSI B11.TR3 (2000): *Risk Assessment and Risk Reduction: A Guide to Estimate, Evaluate, and Reduce Risks Associated with Machine Tools.*

### 17.10.3   Risk Assessment

If a risk assessment of the machinery equipment is required, the assessment must be carried out according to ISO 12100 (2010). The terminology and the approach described in this standard is rather similar to the risk assessment approach described in this book. The main difference is ISO 12100's extra focus on the operators' ability to escape an accident scenario under development.

The risk has to be analyzed for all the relevant life phases of the equipment:

1. Construction (including assembly and testing)

2. Transport (packing, lifting, loading, unloading, and unpacking)

3. Assembly, installation, and commissioning (preparation for the installation, adjustments, and assembly)

4. Setting, teaching/programming, and/or process changeover

5. Operation (fastening, loading, starting, etc.)

6. Cleaning and maintenance (dismounting, mounting, stop, restart)

7. Fault finding/troubleshooting

8. Decommissioning/dismantling

Supplementary information related to machinery safety may be found in Macdonald (2004).

## 17.11    Other Application Areas

Risk assessment are used in many more application areas that those listed above. Some of these areas are listed and discussed briefly in the current section.

### 17.11.1    Environmental Risk

Potential harm to the environment should be dealt with in all risk assessments and is covered in the risk assessment approach described in this book. In some cases, it may be required to put extra focus on the environmental aspects and also to cover the harmful effects from continuous and planned releases, and we then talk about *environmental risk assessments*. Harmful effects on human health are sometimes included, and we may refer to the analysis as a risk assessment for human health and the environment.

Several EU directives require environmental risk assessments. Among these are 93/67/EEC, "laying down the principles for assessment of risks to man and the environment of substances . . . ." This book is limited to the risk of discrete hazardous events, so environmental risk assessments for continuous releases and planned releases are therefore outside its scope.

## 17.11.2  Critical Infrastructures

The term *critical infrastructure* is used to describe assets that are essential for the functioning of a society and its economy. Critical infrastructures comprise:

- Energy and utilities (e.g., electrical power, natural gas, oil production, and transmission systems)

- Communications and information technology (e.g., telecommunications, broadcasting systems, software, hardware, and networks, including the Internet)

- Finance (e.g., banking, securities, and investment)

- Health care (e.g., hospitals, health care and blood supply facilities, laboratories and pharmaceuticals)

- Food (e.g., safety, distribution, agriculture, and food industry)

- Water (e.g., drinking water and wastewater management)

- Transportation (e.g., air, rail, marine, and surface)

- Safety (e.g., chemical, biological, radiological and nuclear safety, hazardous materials, search and rescue, emergency services, and dams)

- Government (e.g., services, facilities, information networks, assets, and key national sites and monuments)

- Manufacturing (i.e., provision of products and services)

An early initiative was the report *Critical foundations: Protecting America's infrastructures* (President's Commission on Critical Infrastructure Protection, 1997). In the United States, the protection of critical infrastructures is part of the broader concept of *homeland security*. The U.S. Department of Homeland Security has developed a risk assessment approach called the *Risk Assessment and Management Program* (RAMP).

An alternative risk assessment approach called RAMCAP Plus has been developed by the ASME. The main steps of this approach are:

1. Asset characterization

2. Threat characterization

3. Consequence analysis (based on engineering judgment)

4. Vulnerability analysis

5. Threat assessment (consider deterrents and estimate attractiveness)

6. Risk assessment

7. Risk management

### 17.11.3 Municipal Risk and Vulnerability Assessments

All the municipalities in Norway have to carry out risk and vulnerability assessments related to their main duties and services as a basis for emergency planning and dimensioning of resources. A guideline for these assessments has been developed by the Norwegian Directorate for Civil Protection and Emergency Planning (DSB).

Most municipalities in Norway have conducted risk and vulnerability assessments based on this guideline. The same type of analysis is also used by various infrastructure operators/owners. The main steps in the risk and vulnerability analysis follow.

***Step 1: Identify and Select Relevant Accident Scenarios.*** Most municipal risk and vulnerability analysis can be based on preliminary hazard analysis (PHA; see Chapter 9).

The possible accident scenarios (adverse events) can be identified in several different ways:

(a) Divide the municipality into functions, activities, and/or physical areas and identify which hazards and accident scenarios may be relevant for each part.

(b) Consider the various hazards (e.g., as listed above), and identify where in the municipality these hazards might lead to accidents.

(c) Identify the most important assets within the municipality and identify what could possibly happen to them.

Any combination of these approaches may also be relevant.

The accident scenarios that may occur will depend on the specific municipality. A generic categorization may sometimes be used as a checklist, for example:

- Natural events (floods, landslides, storms, unusually large snowfall, etc.)

- Damage to or loss of infrastructure (electricity, water, sewerage, data networks, etc.)

- Major traffic accidents (road, rail, aircraft, ships)

- Fire (forests, buildings, hospitals, nursing homes, cultural heritage objects, industry)

- Explosions (fuel storage, chemical industry, etc.)

- Major industrial accidents

- Dam ruptures

- Acute pollution (drinking water, rivers, lakes, etc.)

- Events related to special events with large crowds (football matches, pop concerts, etc.)

- Sabotage or vandalism

- Radioactive fallout

The municipality will normally have a set of assets that are important to protect. Among these might be:

- Hospital

- Nursing homes

- Schools

- Cultural heritage objects

   ... and many others.

The hazard identification process will normally produce a wide range of possible accident scenarios. Most often, it will not be possible to analyze all the events in detail, and it is therefore important to select a few representative scenarios within each category.

As a complement to the preliminary hazard analysis, it is sometimes appropriate to use a simple SWIFT analysis (Chapter 9), where the following types of questions are asked: " What can happen if (for example) ... "

... a tank truck collides with a car in tunnel B?

... foot and mouth disease breaks out and spreads to several farms?

... a major fire breaks out in a nursing home?

... a large rockslide that destroys a main road and a railway line simultaneously?

... the municipal drinking-water source gets contaminated?

***Step 2: Evaluate the Relevant Accident Scenarios.***   The next main step is to evaluate the selected accident scenarios with respect to frequencies and consequences. This can be done in the same way as for a standard PHA, with three to five categories for each.

Hazardous events in a municipality may affect infrastructures individually or simultaneously. For a municipality, it is important for preparedness planning to know, for example, if the loss of electricity has consequences for the water supply, which residents are affected, and whether it can lead to life-threatening situations.

***Step 3: Evaluate Emergency Preparedness.***   During this step, the following questions are asked for each of the relevant accident scenarios:

- What plans do we have to handle such an accident?

- Are these plans adequate?

– Do we have sufficient equipment, personnel, and resources to execute the plans?

– Is the equipment maintained and available?

– Are the equipment and resources located in adequate places?

– Are the personnel adequately trained for this mission?

– What help can we get from external resources (private, other municipalities, the state)?

– How should we inform inhabitants and the media about the accident?

***Step 4: Revise and Allocate Resources.*** The objective of this step is to decide if parts of the municipality's emergency preparedness have to be changed or improved. What new personnel and new equipment are required? What new contingency plans must be established?

***Other Countries.*** Similar risk and vulnerability analyses are also mandatory in other countries, including Sweden and Denmark. The U.S. Federal Emergency Management Agency (FEMA), which is part of the U.S. Department of Homeland Security, has developed guidelines for emergency preparedness, but these are focused mainly on single persons and families.

## 17.12  Closure

The objective of this book was to give an introduction to risk assessment, to the methods for risk assessment, and to some important problem areas related to risk assessment. This final chapter has given a survey of the development of risk assessment and of how risk assessment is used in some main application areas.

Several methods, problem areas, and applications have, however, barely been mentioned or are not treated at all. Among these are:

(a) *Organizational factors in risk assessment.* Risk researchers have long realized that organizational factors have a strong influence on the risk. This influence is especially important to human errors and human reliability. Important organizational factors in this respect include safety culture, training, work planning, job safety analyses, and so on. Organizational factors may also influence the technical reliability directly through maintenance planning, provision of tools, supervision, and so on. Mohaghegh et al. (2009) proposes a new approach and gives many references to relevant literature.

(b) *Risk assessment of dynamic systems.* Most of the methods presented in this book are relevant mainly for static systems and systems where the mode of operation is changed rather slowly or infrequently. Several approaches have been proposed for dynamic systems, but none of them has, so far, been generally accepted. An early, and very good, account of this problem area is given by Siu (1994).

(c) *Maintenance in risk assessment.* Several studies have shown that a rather high percentage of fatal accidents in industry can be attributed to maintenance. The accidents occur either during the maintenance actions, because of inadequately performed maintenance, or because of lacking maintenance. Hale et al. (1998) outline an approach and provide references to studies showing that maintenance accounted for 30–40% of all fatal accidents in the process and construction industries studied.

(d) *Software in risk assessment.* Software is integrated in most complex systems today. This problem area was mentioned in Chapter 12 when safety instrumented systems were discussed, but without a thorough treatment. Some of the methods described in Part II may also be used on systems containing software, but cannot handle all problems. Leveson (1995) is an early reference on this problem area.

(e) *Environmental risk assessment.* There are two main categories of environmental risk assessments: (i) where the environment is an asset that needs to be protected, and (ii) where the environment is the hazard. Both categories are mentioned several times in the book, but are not treated adequately. The environment is different from most other assets since it can accommodate some harm and clean up by itself (e.g., oil spill in the sea). Such effects are studied within the research area *industrial ecology.* The second category is becoming more important as the climate is changing, and takes an increasing number of lives each year. Risk assessment and emergency planning within this area are therefore very important issues.

(f) *Project risk assessment.* Too many projects are not completed with correct quality and/or within the time and cost limits that were agreed upon. Projects are different from most other application areas since buffers and redundancies are usually more readily available. Risk assessment and risk management of projects is today a very important area that requires more research, especially for large projects.

(g) *Homeland security.* Harm to systems and functions caused by deliberate hostile actions has been mentioned a few times in this book, but are not treated in any detail. Some of the methods in Part II may be applied to this problem area but will often need to be adapted. Garrick (2008) gives an introduction to parts of this problem area.

**PART III**

# APPENDICES

# APPENDIX A

# ELEMENTS OF PROBABILITY THEORY

Probability theory is nothing but common sense reduced to calculation ....
—Pierre-Simon Laplace, 1812

## A.1 Introduction

This appendix gives an introduction to some of the main results from probability theory and statistics. It is not intended to be comprehensive, but rather a brief repetition that may be useful when reading the rest of the book. Some elementary concepts from reliability theory are also introduced. Readers who are familiar with probability theory and statistics may skip this appendix. More extensive introductions to probability theory may, for example, be found in Ross (2004, 2007) and Dudewicz and Mishra (1988).

*Risk Assessment: Theory, Methods, and Applications,* First Edition.
By Marvin Rausand. Copyright © 2011 John Wiley & Sons, Inc.

## A.2    Outcomes and Events

### A.2.1    Events and Boolean Operations

*Random Experiment.*    A random experiment is an experiment that may be repeated over and over again under "essentially the same conditions." Examples of random experiments include simple experiments such as flipping a coin, counting failures over time, and observing whether or not an airplane crashes during landing.

In many cases it may be impossible to repeat the same experiment under exactly the same conditions. We will, however, refer to the trial as a random experiment whenever we can *imagine* that it can be repeated under approximately the same conditions.

*Single Outcome.*    The result of a specific random experiment is called a single outcome, or just an *outcome*. The letter $e$ is often used to denote a single outcome.

*Sample Space.*    The set of all possible single outcomes of a random experiment is called the *sample space* and is represented by the symbol $S$. The sample space may have a finite, countable, or noncountable number of single outcomes. A sample space with a finite number $n$ of single outcomes may be written as $S = \{e_1, e_2, \ldots, e_n\}$.

*Event.*    An event $E$ is a specified set of possible single outcomes in the sample space $S$. We write $E \subset S$ where $\subset$ denotes subset. Most events are compound events comprising several single outcomes, but a single outcome $e$ is also an event and is sometimes called a *simple event*.

### ▉ EXAMPLE A.1

A random experiment consists of flipping a coin. The sample space for this experiment is

$$S = \{e_1, e_2\} = \{H, T\}$$

where $e_1 = H$ means that the outcome of the toss is a head, and $e_2 = T$ that it is a tail.    $\oplus$

### ▉ EXAMPLE A.2

Consider a football match between two teams, $A$ and $B$. We are interested in observing the result of the match measured as a number of goals to each team. In this case the sample space is

$$S = \{(0,0), (0,1), (1,0), (1,1), (0,2), (2,0), (1,2), (2,1), \ldots\}$$

In this case, an outcome may, for example, be $(2,0)$, which means that team $A$ wins the match with two goals against nil. Team $A$ can win the match in many

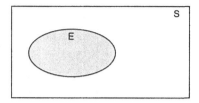

**Figure A.1**    Venn diagram with one event $E$.

different ways. If the outcome $e$ is part of the set $E_1 = \{(1,0),(2,0),(2,1),\ldots\}$, then team $A$ has won. This set, $E_1$, is an event in $S$. The events we consider in this book can usually be stated in verbal terms, such as

$$\text{"Team } A \text{ wins"} \iff e \in E_1$$

Another event, $E_2$, is "no more than 2 goals in the match," and is represented by the set $E_2 = \{(0,0),(0,1),(1,0),(1,1),(2,0),(0,2)\}$.    $\oplus$

**Complementary Event.**    The *complementary event* of an event $E$ with respect to $S$ is the subset of all outcomes of $S$ that are *not* in $E$. The complementary event of $E$ is denoted by the symbol $E^*$.

The complementary event of the sample space $S$ must, per definition, be empty, and is therefore called the *null set* or *empty set* and is denoted by $\emptyset$.

**Venn Diagram.**    To illustrate the sample space and the various events, it is common to use a *Venn diagram*, illustrated in Figure A.1. In this diagram the outer rectangle represents the sample space $S$. All the possible outcomes of the experiment are represented as single points in the rectangle. The ellipse $E$ comprises all the outcomes that are part of the event $E$. The complementary event $E^*$ contains all outcomes in $S$ that are not in $E$.

**Intersection of Events.**    The *intersection* of two events, $E_1$ and $E_2$, is denoted by the symbol $E_1 \cap E_2$, and is the event containing all outcomes that are common to $E_1$ and $E_2$.

■ **EXAMPLE A.3**

In Example A.2, the intersection is

$$E_1 \cap E_2 = \{(1,0),(2,0)\}$$

Team $A$ wins the match *and* there are no more than two goals.    $\oplus$

**Union of Events.**    The *union* of two events, $E_1$ and $E_2$, is denoted by the symbol $E_1 \cup E_2$, and is the event containing all outcomes that belong to $E_1$ or $E_2$ or both [see Figure A.2(a)].

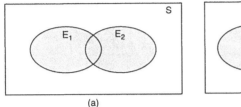
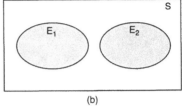

(a)          (b)

**Figure A.2**    Venn diagram of two events, $E_1$ and $E_2$. In (a) the two events are overlapping and in (b) their intersection is empty.

**Mutually Exclusive Events.**    Two events, $E_1$ and $E_2$, are *mutually exclusive*, or *disjoint* if $E_1 \cap E_2 = \emptyset$, that is, if $E_1$ and $E_2$ have no outcomes in common. This is illustrated in Figure A.2(b) and means that events $E_1$ and $E_2$ cannot occur at the same time.

## A.2.2  Simple Systems

We will now consider a system comprising several components. Each component has two possible states; *functioning* or *failed*. Let the system have $n$ distinct components, and let the state of component $i$ be denoted by $X_i$, for $i = 1, 2, \ldots, n$. The state of component $i$ is represented by the *state variable*

$$X_i = \begin{cases} 1 & \text{if component } i \text{ is functioning} \\ 0 & \text{otherwise} \end{cases} \tag{A.1}$$

$X = (X_1, X_2, \ldots, X_n)$ is called the *state vector* of the system.

The state of the system can be described by the binary function

$$\phi(X) = \phi(X_1, X_2, \ldots, X_n) \tag{A.2}$$

where

$$\phi(X) = \begin{cases} 1 & \text{if the system is functioning} \\ 0 & \text{otherwise} \end{cases} \tag{A.3}$$

The function $\phi(X)$ is called the *structure function* of the system.

**Series Systems.**    A system that is functioning if and only if *all* of its $n$ components are functioning is called a *series system* (e.g., see Rausand and Høyland, 2004). The structure function is

$$\phi(X) = X_1 \cdot X_2 \cdots X_n = \prod_{i=1}^{n} X_i \tag{A.4}$$

and we observe that $\phi(X) = 1$ if and only if $X_i = 1$ for all $i = 1, 2, \ldots, n$.

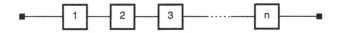

**Figure A.3**    Reliability block diagram of a series system.

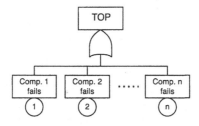

**Figure A.4**    Fault tree representing a series system.

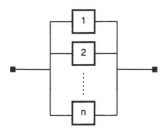

**Figure A.5**    Reliability block diagram of a parallel system.

The series system is illustrated by the *reliability block diagram* in Figure A.3.

Let the event $E_i$ denote that component $i$ is in a failed state, for $i = 1, 2, \ldots, n$, and let $E_S$ denote system failure. Since the system fails when at least one of the components fails, we have that

$$E_S = E_1 \cup E_2 \cup \cdots \cup E_n$$

System failure can also be represented by a fault tree, illustrated in Figure A.4. The "gate" in the top of the tree is called an OR-*gate* and the TOP event "system failure" will occur if event $E_1$ *or* event $E_2$ *or* ... occurs. Fault trees are discussed in Section 10.3.

**Parallel System.**    A system that is functioning if at least one of its $n$ components is functioning is called a *parallel system* (e.g., see Rausand and Høyland, 2004). A parallel system with $n$ components may be illustrated by the reliability block diagram in Figure A.5.

The structure function of the parallel system can be written

$$\phi(X) = 1 - (1 - X_1)(1 - X_2) \cdots (1 - X_n) = 1 - \prod_{i=1}^{n}(1 - X_i) \qquad (A.5)$$

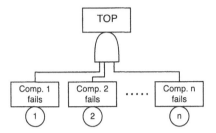

**Figure A.6** Fault tree representing a parallel system.

and we observe that $\phi(X) = 0$ if and only if $X_i = 0$ for all $i = 1, 2, \ldots, n$.

A parallel system will fail when all the components fail at the same time. With the same notation as above, we have

$$E_S = E_1 \cap E_2 \cap \cdots \cap E_n$$

System failure can also be represented by a fault tree, illustrated in Figure A.6. The "gate" in the top of the tree is called an AND-*gate*, and the TOP event "system failure" will occur if event $E_1$ *and* event $E_2$ *and* ... occur at the same time.

## A.3 Probability

The probability concept was introduced in Section 2.3, where we distinguished between (i) the classical interpretation of probability, (ii) the frequentist interpretation, and (iii) the subjective or Bayesian interpretation. Irrespective of the interpretation used, the rules and mathematical expressions of probability remain the same.

In the following, we define the main terminology for probability calculation and present the main rules and formulas.

### A.3.1 Definition of Probability

Let $S$ be the sample space of a random experiment. For each event $E$ of the sample space, we assume that a number $\Pr(E)$ is defined and satisfies the following three conditions:

1. $0 \leq \Pr(E) \leq 1$

2. $\Pr(S) = 1$

3. For any sequence of events $E_1, E_2, \ldots$ that are mutually exclusive, such that $E_i \cap E_j = \emptyset$ for all $i \neq j$, then

$$\Pr\left(\bigcup_{i=1}^{\infty} E_i\right) = \sum_{i=1}^{\infty} \Pr(E_i) \tag{A.6}$$

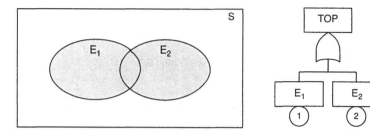

**Figure A.7**   Event $E_1$ or event $E_2$ occurs.

The quantity $\Pr(E)$ is called the *probability* of the event $E$.

The conditions imply that the probability of an event $E$ must always be between zero and 1. A probability of 1 means that the event is certain to occur. An event with probability zero means the event is impossible or certain not to occur. If the events have no single outcomes in common, the probability of either of them happening is the sum of their probabilities.

## A.3.2   Basic Rules for Probability Calculations

***Probability of Complementary Events.***   Let $E^*$ be the complementary event of the event $E$. The probability of $E^*$ is given by

$$\Pr(E^*) = 1 - \Pr(E) \tag{A.7}$$

The probability of an event $E$ happening is therefore equal to 1 minus the probability of the event $E$ not happening.

***Addition Rule of Probability.***   If $E_1$ and $E_2$ are any two events, then

$$\Pr(E_1 \cup E_2) = \Pr(E_1) + \Pr(E_2) - \Pr(E_1 \cap E_2) \tag{A.8}$$

Equation (A.8) is called the *addition rule* of probability. The addition rule is illustrated by the Venn diagram and the fault tree in Figure A.7. Note that when $E_1$ and $E_2$ are mutually exclusive (disjoint), then

$$\Pr(E_1 \cup E_2) = \Pr(E_1) + \Pr(E_2)$$

This is illustrated in Figure A.2(b).

The addition rule can be easily extended such that for a sequence $E_1, E_2, \ldots, E_n$ of events that are *mutually exclusive*, then

$$\Pr(E_1 \cup E_2 \cup \cdots \cup E_n) = \Pr(E_1) + \Pr(E_2) + \cdots + \Pr(E_n)$$

$$= \sum_{i=1}^{n} \Pr(E_i) \tag{A.9}$$

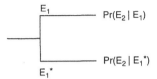

**Figure A.8**   Probability tree.

*Conditional Probability.*   Assume that we are interested in finding the probability of event $E_2$ when we know that event $E_1$ has already occurred. If event $E_1$ has occurred, then we are interested in the relative proportion of $E_2$, which is a subset of $E_1$, namely $E_1 \cap E_2$. For this reason, the conditional probability of $E_2$ given $E_1$ is defined by

$$\Pr(E_2 \mid E_1) = \frac{\Pr(E_1 \cap E_2)}{\Pr(E_1)} \tag{A.10}$$

if $\Pr(E_1) > 0$.

**▉  EXAMPLE A.4**

Let event $E_2$ be a process upset of a certain type in a process plant. We want to study how the probability of the process upset, $\Pr(E_2)$, depends on whether or not a critical level controller is functioning. Let $E_1$ be the event that the level controller is failed. This situation can be illustrated by the tree structure in Figure A.8.

We note that the probabilities of the end nodes of the tree are:

- $\Pr(E_2 \mid E_1)$ (i.e., the probability of a process upset when the level controller is failed)

- $\Pr(E_2 \mid E_1^*)$ (i.e., the probability of a process upset when the level controller is functioning)

The tree in Figure A.8 is called a *probability tree* or an *event tree*.          ⊕

*Product Rule of Probability.*   From (A.10), we note that

$$\Pr(E_1 \cap E_2) = \Pr(E_2 \mid E_1) \cdot \Pr(E_1) = \Pr(E_1 \mid E_2) \cdot \Pr(E_2) \tag{A.11}$$

The intersection of $E_1$ and $E_2$ is illustrated by the Venn diagram and the fault tree in Figure A.9. This can be generalized, by induction, to the following result

$$\Pr(E_1 \cap E_2 \cap \cdots \cap E_k)$$
$$= \Pr(E_1) \cdot \Pr(E_2 \mid E_1) \cdot \Pr(E_3 \mid E_1 \cap E_2) \cdots \Pr(E_k \mid E_1 \cap \cdots \cap E_{k-1})$$

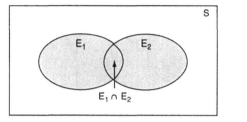 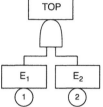

**Figure A.9**   Event $E_1$ and event $E_2$ occur.

***Independent Events.***   Two events $E_1$ and $E_2$ are said to be *independent* if the occurrence of one of the events gives us no information about whether or not the other event will occur; that is, the events have no influence on each other. This means that the two events $E_1$ and $E_2$ are independent if and only if

$$\Pr(E_2 \mid E_1) = \Pr(E_2) \quad \text{or} \quad \Pr(E_1 \mid E_2) = \Pr(E_1)$$

in which case we may write

$$\Pr(E_1 \cap E_2) = \Pr(E_1) \cdot \Pr(E_2) \tag{A.12}$$

If a sequence $E_1, E_2, \ldots, E_n$ of events are *independent*, then

$$\Pr(E_1 \cap E_2 \cap \cdots \cap E_n) = \Pr(E_1) \cdot \Pr(E_2) \cdots \Pr(E_n) = \prod_{i=1}^{n} \Pr(E_i) \tag{A.13}$$

***Remark***: When $\Pr(E_1 \cap E_2) \neq \Pr(E_1) \cdot \Pr(E_2)$ the events $E_1$ and $E_2$ are said to be *dependent*. The "link" between $E_1$ and $E_2$ is logical, not necessarily causal.   ⊕

***Partition of the Sample Space.***   A collection of events $E_1, E_2, \ldots, E_n$ in a sample space $S$ is said to be a *partition* of $S$ if $E_1, E_2, \ldots, E_n$ are mutually exclusive and

$$S = E_1 \cup E_2 \cup \cdots \cup E_n$$

A partition of the sample space $S$ is illustrated in Figure A.10.

***Total Probability.***   Let $F$ be an event in the sample space $S$, and let $E_1, E_2, \ldots, E_n$ be a partition of $S$. The probability of $F$ can then be written

$$\Pr(F) = \sum_{i=1}^{n} \Pr(F \cap E_i) = \sum_{i=1}^{n} \Pr(F \mid E_i) \cdot \Pr(E_i) \tag{A.14}$$

***Bayes Formula.***   If the events $E_1, E_2, \ldots, E_n$ constitute a partition of the sample space $S$, where $\Pr(E_i) > 0$ for all $i = 1, 2, \ldots, n$, then for any event $F$ in $S$ such that $\Pr(F) > 0$,

$$\Pr(E_j \mid F) = \frac{\Pr(F \cap E_j)}{\sum_{i=1}^{n} \Pr(F \cap E_i)} = \frac{\Pr(F \mid E_j) \cdot \Pr(E_j)}{\sum_{i=1}^{n} \Pr(F \mid E_i) \cdot \Pr(E_i)} \tag{A.15}$$

for all $j = 1, 2, \ldots, n$.

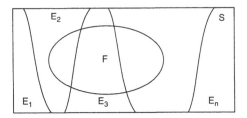

**Figure A.10** Partition of the sample space.

### A.3.3 Uniform Probability Models

The simplest probability model we can make is the model known as the *uniform probability model*. Let $S$ be a finite, nonempty, sample space with $n$ outcomes. The uniform probability model on $S$ is defined by

$$\Pr(e) = \frac{1}{n} \quad \text{for all } e \in S \tag{A.16}$$

Consider an event $E$ in $S$ comprising $n_E$ distinct outcomes. When having a uniform probability model, the probability of the event $E$ is

$$\Pr(E) = \frac{n_E}{n} \tag{A.17}$$

**▪ EXAMPLE A.5**

Consider the random experiment of tossing a (fair) six-sided dice. The sample space is $S = \{1, 2, 3, 4, 5, 6\}$, and the number of outcomes is $n = 6$. The probability of getting the outcome $e = 2$ is

$$\Pr(2) = \frac{1}{6}$$

The event $E =$ "even number" consists of the outcomes $\{2, 4, 6\}$. The probability of $E$ is therefore

$$\Pr(E) = \frac{n_E}{n} = \frac{3}{6} = 0.50$$

⊕

### A.4 Random Variables

A random variable is a function that associates a real number with each outcome in the sample space. In the frequentist approach (see Chapter 2), a random variable is a quantity that can be measured.

In this book a capital letter, say $X$, is used to denote a random variable, and a corresponding lowercase letter, $x$ in this case, for one of its values.

## A.4.1  Discrete Random Variables

A random variable is said to be *discrete* if the variable can take on at most a countable number of values.

### ▉ EXAMPLE A.6

Consider a group of persons, and select a person at random from this group. The group is then the sample space $S$ and the person is an outcome $e$ from the sample space. We want to measure a property of the outcome, say the total number of brothers and sisters this person has. Let $X$ denote this number. We note that $X$ is a function of the outcome, and that $X$ is a discrete variable. When we have selected the person and observed the variable, we know the value. This value is denoted $x$, and we may, for example, get the result $x = 2$. The randomness in this experiment is connected to the outcome. We do not know the value of $X$ because we do not know which person will be selected. Once we have selected the outcome, we can, in many cases, "measure" the number of brothers/sisters without any uncertainty. ⊕

*Probability Mass Function.* Let $X$ be a discrete random variable that can take values in the set $\{x_1, x_2, \ldots\}$, and let $\Pr(X = x_i)$ denote the probability that the variable $X$ takes the value $x_i$ for some $i$. This probability can be interpreted as the probability of obtaining an outcome that is measured (by $X$) to be $x_i$. We then have that:

1. $\Pr(X = x_i) \geq 0$ for all $i = 1, 2, \ldots$

2. $\sum_{i=1}^{\infty} \Pr(X = x_i) = 1$

*Distribution Function.* The distribution function of the discrete random variable $X$ is

$$F(x) = \Pr(X \leq x) = \sum_{x_i \leq x} \Pr(X = x_i) \tag{A.18}$$

The distribution function is sometimes called the *cumulative distribution function.* The probability that the random variable $X$ has a value in the interval $(x_i, x_j]$ is

$$\Pr(x_i < X \leq x_j) = \Pr(X \leq x_j) - \Pr(X \leq x_i) = F(x_j) - F(x_i) \tag{A.19}$$

for $x_i < x_j$.

*Mean Value, Variance, and Standard Deviation.* The *mean value* of a discrete random variable $X$ with value set $\{x_1, x_2, \ldots\}$ is

$$E(X) = \mu = \sum_{i=1}^{\infty} x_i \cdot \Pr(X = x_i) \tag{A.20}$$

Let $g(X)$ be a function of $X$. The mean value of the random variable $g(X)$ is

$$E[g(X)] = \sum_{i=1}^{\infty} g(x_i) \cdot \Pr(X = x_i) \qquad \text{(A.21)}$$

The *variance* of $X$ is

$$\text{Var}(X) = E\left[(X - \mu)^2\right] = \sum_{i=1}^{\infty} (x_i - \mu)^2 \Pr(X = x_i) \qquad \text{(A.22)}$$

The *standard deviation* of $X$ is

$$\text{SD}(X) = \sqrt{\text{Var}(X)} \qquad \text{(A.23)}$$

**Marginal and Conditional Distributions.**   Let $X_1$ and $X_2$ be two discrete random variables. The *joint* probability mass function of $X_1$ and $X_2$ is

$$\Pr(X_1 = x_1 \cap X_2 = x_2)$$

which is also written as $\Pr(X_1 = x_1, X_2 = x_2)$.

The *conditional* probability that $X_2 = x_2$, given that $X_1 = x_1$ is

$$\Pr(X_2 = x_2 \mid X_1 = x_1) = \frac{\Pr(X_1 = x_1 \cap X_2 = x_2)}{\Pr(X_1 = x_1)} \qquad \text{(A.24)}$$

The *marginal* probability mass function of $X_2$ is

$$\Pr(X_2 = x_2) = \sum_{\text{All } x_1} \Pr(X_1 = x_1 \cap X_2 = x_2) \qquad \text{(A.25)}$$

**Covariance and Correlation Coefficient.**   Let $X_1$ and $X_2$ be two random variables for which the means and variances exist. Consider the mathematical expectation

$$E[(X_1 - E(X_1)) \cdot (X_2 - E(X_2))] = E(X_1 \cdot X_2) - E(X_1) \cdot E(X_2)$$

This number is called the *covariance* of $X_1$ and $X_2$ and is denoted by $\text{Cov}(X_1, X_2)$. The *correlation coefficient* of $X_1$ and $X_2$ is defined by

$$\rho(X_1, X_2) = \frac{E[(X_1 - E(X_1)) \cdot (X_2 - E(X_2))]}{\sqrt{\text{Var}(X_1) \cdot \text{Var}(X_2)}} \qquad \text{(A.26)}$$

The correlation coefficient measures the degree of association between the random variables $X_1$ and $X_2$, that is, the strength of a linear relationship between the two variables. The correlation coefficient is always between $-1$ and $1$. Positive correlation means that $X_1$ and $X_2$ tend to be large together. Negative correlation means that $X_1$ tends to be large when $X_2$ is small, and vice versa. If $X_1$ and $X_2$ are independent, then the correlation is zero.

## A.4.2   Continuous Random Variables

Let $T$ be a random variable with a value set that is not countable. We say that $T$ is a continuous random variable if there exists a nonnegative function $f(t)$, defined for all values of $t$, having the property that for any set $A$ of real numbers

$$\Pr(T \in A) = \int_A f(t)\, dt$$

The function $f(t)$ is called the *probability density function* of the random variable $T$.

In this appendix we use $T$ to denote a continuous random variable. The reason for this is that for many applications in this book, the random variable will be a *time* to a failure or an event. It therefore feels natural to denote this time by $T$. This is only for convenience, and we could as well have replaced $T$ with any other capital letter. A time $T$ will generally take on only positive, real values. Other types of continuous random variables may take values on the whole axis, from $-\infty$ to $+\infty$, or be limited to some interval(s) on this axis. In the main part of this appendix we assume that $T$ is positive, but we deviate from this assumption for some specific distributions. We hope that this will not confuse the reader.

The probability density function $f(t)$ fulfills:

1. $f(t) \geq 0$   for all $t$

2. $\int_0^\infty f(t)\, dt = 1$

3. $\Pr(a < T \leq b) = \int_a^b f(t)\, dt$

In the next sections, we assume that the random variable $T$ is the time to failure of an item, and introduce the main probabilistic measures for such a variable.

**Time to Failure.**   By the *time to failure* of an item we mean the time elapsing from when the item is put into operation until it fails for the first time. We set $t = 0$ as the starting point. The time to failure is, at least to some extent, subject to chance variations. It is therefore natural to interpret the time to failure as a random variable, $T$.

The state of the item at time $t$ may be described by the state variable $X(t)$, which is also a random variable.

$$X(t) = \begin{cases} 1 & \text{if the item is functioning at time } t \\ 0 & \text{if the item is in a failed state at time } t \end{cases}$$

The connection between the discrete state variable $X(t)$ and the time to failure $T$ is illustrated in Figure A.11.

Note that the time to failure $T$ is not always measured in calendar time. It may also be measured by more indirect time concepts, such as

- the number of times a switch is operated

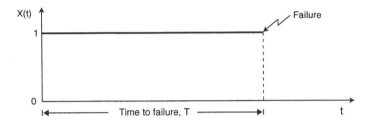

**Figure A.11**   The state variable and the time to failure of an item.

- the number of kilometers driven by a car

- the number of rotations of a bearing

- the number of cycles for a periodically working item

From these examples, we notice that time to failure may sometimes be a discrete variable. A discrete variable can, however, be approximated by a continuous variable. Here, unless stated otherwise, we will always assume that the time to failure $T$ is a continuous variable.

**Distribution Function.**   The distribution function of $T$ is defined by

$$F(t) = \Pr(T \leq t) \quad \text{for } t > 0 \tag{A.27}$$

We note that $F(t)$ is the probability that the item will fail in the time interval $(0, t]$.

**Probability Density Function.**   The probability density function $f(t)$ is

$$
\begin{aligned}
f(t) = \frac{d}{dt} F(t) &= \lim_{\Delta t \to 0} \frac{F(t + \Delta t) - F(t)}{\Delta t} \\
&= \lim_{\Delta t \to 0} \frac{\Pr(t < T \leq t + \Delta t)}{\Delta t}
\end{aligned}
\tag{A.28}
$$

This implies that when $\Delta t$ is small,

$$\Pr(t < T \leq t + \Delta t) \approx f(t) \cdot \Delta t \tag{A.29}$$

The distribution function $F(t)$ and the probability density function $f(t)$ are illustrated is Figure A.12.

**Survivor Function.**   The survivor function of an item is defined by

$$R(t) = 1 - F(t) = \Pr(T > t) \quad \text{for } t > 0 \tag{A.30}$$

Hence $R(t)$ is the probability that the item does not fail in the time interval $(0, t]$, or, in other words, the probability that the item survives the time interval $(0, t]$ and is still functioning at time $t$. The survivor function is illustrated in Figure A.13.

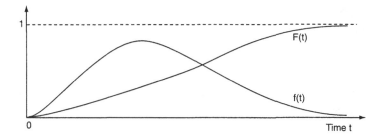

**Figure A.12**   Distribution function $F(t)$ and probability density function $f(t)$.

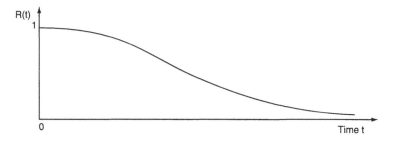

**Figure A.13**   The survivor function $R(t)$.

**Failure Rate Function.**   The probability that an item will fail in the time interval $(t, t + \Delta t]$ when we know that the item is functioning at time $t$ is given by the conditional probability

$$\Pr(t < T \le t + \Delta t \mid T > t) = \frac{\Pr(t < T \le t + \Delta t)}{\Pr(T > t)} = \frac{F(t + \Delta t) - F(t)}{R(t)}$$

By dividing this probability by the length of the time interval, $\Delta t$, and letting $\Delta t \to 0$, we get the failure rate function $z(t)$ of the item

$$
\begin{aligned}
z(t) &= \lim_{\Delta t \to 0} \frac{\Pr(t < T \le t + \Delta t \mid T > t)}{\Delta t} \\
&= \lim_{\Delta t \to 0} \frac{F(t + \Delta t) - F(t)}{\Delta t} \frac{1}{R(t)} = \frac{f(t)}{R(t)}
\end{aligned}
\tag{A.31}
$$

This implies that when $\Delta t$ is small,

$$\Pr(t < T \le t + \Delta t \mid T > t) \approx z(t) \cdot \Delta t \tag{A.32}$$

Note the difference between the probability density function $f(t)$ and the failure rate function $z(t)$. Assume that we start out with a new item at time $t = 0$ and at time $t = 0$ ask "What is the probability that this item will fail in the interval $(t, t + \Delta t]$?" According to (A.29), this probability is approximately equal to the probability density function $f(t)$ at time $t$ multiplied by the length of the interval,

$\Delta t$. Next consider an item that has survived until time $t$, and that we at time $t$ ask "What is the probability that this item will fail in the next interval $(t, t + \Delta t]$?" This (conditional) probability is according to (A.32) approximately equal to the failure rate function $z(t)$ at time $t$ multiplied by the length of the interval, $\Delta t$.

**Mean Value.** Let $T$ be the time to failure of an item. The *mean time to failure* (MTTF) or *expected value* of $T$ is

$$\text{MTTF} = E(T) = \int_0^\infty t f(t) \, dt \tag{A.33}$$

Since $f(t) = -R'(t)$,

$$\text{MTTF} = -\int_0^\infty t R'(t) \, dt$$

By partial integration

$$\text{MTTF} = -[t R(t)]_0^\infty + \int_0^\infty R(t) \, dt$$

If MTTF $< \infty$, it can be shown that $[t R(t)]_0^\infty = 0$. In that case

$$\text{MTTF} = \int_0^\infty R(t) \, dt \tag{A.34}$$

It is often easier to determine MTTF by (A.34) than by (A.33).

**Median Life.** The median life $t_m$ is defined by

$$R(t_m) = 0.50 \tag{A.35}$$

The median divides the distribution in two halves. The item will fail before time $t_m$ with 50% probability, and will fail after $t_m$ with 50% probability.

**Variance.** The variance of $T$ is

$$\text{Var}(T) = \sigma^2 = E\left[(T - \mu)^2\right] = \int_0^\infty (t - \mu)^2 f(t) \, dt \tag{A.36}$$

**Marginal and Conditional Distributions.** Let $T_1$ and $T_2$ be two continuous random variables with probability density functions $f_1(t)$ and $f_2(t)$, respectively. The *joint* probability density function of $T_1$ and $T_2$ is written as $f(t_1, t_2)$. The *marginal* probability density function of $T_1$ is

$$f_1(t_1) = \int_0^\infty f(t_1, t_2) \, dt_2 \tag{A.37}$$

The conditional probability density function of $T_2$ when we have observed that $T_1 = t_1$ is

$$f(t_2 \mid t_1) = \frac{f(t_1, t_2)}{f_1(t_1)} \quad \text{for } f_1(t_1) > 0 \tag{A.38}$$

This result may, for example, be used to find

$$\Pr(a < T_2 < b \mid T_1 = t_1) = \int_a^b f(t_2 \mid t_1)\, dt_2 \tag{A.39}$$

and the conditional mean value as

$$E(T_2 \mid t_1) = \int_0^\infty t_2\, f(t_2 \mid t_1)\, dt_2 \tag{A.40}$$

***Independent Variables.***  The two continuous random variables $T_1$ and $T_2$ are independent if $f(t_2 \mid t_1) = f_2(t_2)$ and $f(t_1 \mid t_2) = f_1(t_1)$, which is the same as saying that $T_1$ and $T_2$ are independent if

$$f(t_1, t_2) = f_1(t_1) \cdot f_2(t_2) \quad \text{for all } t_1 \text{ and } t_2$$

The definition is easily extended to more than two variables.

***Convolution.***  Let $T_1$ and $T_2$ be two independent variables with probability density functions $f_1$ and $f_2$, respectively. It is sometimes important to be able to find the distribution of $T_1 + T_2$

$$
\begin{aligned}
F_{1,2}(t) &= \Pr(T_1 + T_2 \leq t) \\
&= \iint_{x+y \leq t} f_1(x) f_2(y)\, dx\, dy \\
&= \int_0^\infty \int_0^{t-y} f_1(x) f_2(y)\, dx\, dy \\
&= \int_0^\infty \left( \int_0^{t-y} f_1(x)\, dx \right) f_2(y)\, dy \\
&= \int_0^\infty F_1(t-y) f_2(y)\, dy
\end{aligned}
\tag{A.41}
$$

The distribution function $F_{1,2}$ is called the *convolution* of the distributions $F_1$ and $F_2$ (the distribution functions of $T_1$ and $T_2$, respectively).

By differentiating $F_{1,2}(t)$ with respect to $t$, the probability density function $f_{1,2}(t)$ of $T_1 + T_2$ is obtained as

$$f_{1,2}(t) = \int_0^\infty f_1(t-y) f_2(y)\, dy \tag{A.42}$$

## A.5    Some Specific Distributions

### A.5.1    Discrete Distributions

**The Binomial Distribution.**    The binomial distribution is used in the following situation:

1. We have $n$ independent trials.

2. Each trial has two possible outcomes $E$ and $E^*$.

3. The probability $\Pr(E) = p$ is the same in all trials.

This situation is called a *binomial situation*, and the trials are sometimes referred to as *Bernoulli trials*. The "bi" in binomial indicates *two* possible outcomes.

Let $X$ denote the number of the $n$ trials that have outcome $E$. Then $X$ is a discrete random variable with probability mass function

$$\Pr(X = x) = \binom{n}{x} p^x (1 - x)^{n-x} \quad \text{for } x = 0, 1, \ldots, n \qquad \text{(A.43)}$$

where $\binom{n}{x}$ is the *binomial coefficient*

$$\binom{n}{x} = \frac{n!}{x!(n - x)!} \qquad \text{(A.44)}$$

The distribution (A.43) is called the *binomial distribution* $(n, p)$, and we sometimes write $X \sim \text{bin}(n, p)$. Here, $n$, the number of trials, is usually a known constant, while $p$ is a *parameter* of the distribution. The parameter $p$ is usually an unknown constant and is not directly observable. It is not possible to "measure" a parameter. The parameter can only be *estimated* as a relative frequency based on observations of a high number of trials.

The mean value and the variance of $X$ are

$$E(X) = np \qquad \text{(A.45)}$$
$$\text{Var}(X) = np(1 - p) \qquad \text{(A.46)}$$

### ▉ EXAMPLE A.7

A fire pump is tested regularly. During the tests we attempt to start the pump and let it run for a short while. We observe a "fail to start" (event $E$) if the fire pump cannot be started within a specified interval. Assume that we have performed $n = 150$ tests and that we can consider these tests to be independent. In total, $X = 2$ events $E$ have been recorded. From (A.45) we know that $p = E(X)/n$ and it is therefore natural to estimate the fail-to-start probability by

$$\hat{p} = \frac{x}{n} = \frac{2}{150} \approx 0.0133 = 1.33\%$$

⊕

## ▣ EXAMPLE A.8

A 2-out-of-3 system is a system that is functioning when at least 2 of its 3 components are functioning. We assume that the components are independent, and let $X$ be the number of components that are functioning. Let $p$ be the probability that a specific component is functioning. This situation may be considered as a binomial situation with $n = 3$ trials, and $X$ therefore has a binomial distribution. The probability $p_S$ that the 2-out-of-3 system is functioning is

$$p_S = \Pr(X \geq 2) = \Pr(X = 2) + \Pr(X = 3)$$

$$= \binom{3}{2} p^2 (1 - p)^{3-2} + \binom{3}{3} p^3 (1 - 3)^{3-3}$$

$$= 3p^2 (1 - p) + p^3 = 3p^2 - 2p^3$$

⊕

**The Geometric Distribution.**    Assume again that we have a binomial situation, and let $Z$ be the number of trials until the first trial with outcome $E$. If $Z = z$, this means that the first $(z - 1)$ trials will result in $E^*$, and that the first $E$ will occur in trial $z$. The probability mass function for $Z$ is then

$$\Pr(Z = z) = (1 - p)^{z-1} p \quad \text{for } z = 1, 2, \ldots \tag{A.47}$$

The distribution (A.47) is called the *geometric distribution*. We have that

$$\Pr(Z > z) = (1 - p)^z$$

The mean value and the variance of $Z$ are

$$E(Z) = \frac{1}{p} \tag{A.48}$$

$$\text{Var}(Z) = \frac{1 - p}{p^2} \tag{A.49}$$

**The Poisson Distribution and the Poisson Process.**    In risk analysis it is often assumed that events occur according to a *homogeneous Poisson process* (HPP). An HPP is a stochastic process where we count the number of occurrences of an event $E$.

To be an HPP, the following conditions must be fulfilled:

1. The number of occurrences of $E$ in one time interval is independent of the number that occurs in any other disjoint time interval. This implies that the HPP has no memory.

2. The probability that event $E$ will occur during a very short time interval is proportional to the length of the time interval and does not depend on the number of events occurring outside this time interval.

3. The probability that more than one event will occur in a very short time interval is negligible.

Without loss of generality we let $t = 0$ be the starting point of the process.

Let $N_E(t)$ be the number of times event $E$ occur during the time interval $(0, t]$. The discrete random variable $N_E(t)$ is called a *Poisson random variable*, and its probability distribution is called a *Poisson distribution*. The probability mass function of $N_E(t)$ is

$$\Pr(N_E(t) = n) = \frac{(\lambda_E t)^n}{n!} e^{-\lambda_E t} \quad \text{for } n = 0, 1, \ldots \tag{A.50}$$

where $\lambda_E > 0$ is a parameter and $e = 2.71828\ldots$.

The mean number of occurrences of $E$ in the time interval $(0, t)$ is

$$E(N_E(t)) = \sum_{n=0}^{\infty} n \cdot \Pr(N_E(t) = n) = \lambda_E t \tag{A.51}$$

and

$$\lambda_E = \frac{E(N(t))}{t}$$

The parameter $\lambda_E$ is therefore the mean number of occurrences of $E$ per time unit, and is called the *rate* of the Poisson process or the rate of occurrence of events $E$.

The variance of $N_E(t)$ is

$$\text{Var}(N_E(t)) = \lambda_E t \tag{A.52}$$

### A.5.2  Continuous Distributions

***The Exponential Distribution.***   Let us assume that the time to failure $T$ of an item is exponentially distributed with parameter $\lambda$. The probability density function of $T$ is then given by

$$f(t) = \begin{cases} \lambda e^{-\lambda t} & \text{for } t > 0, \lambda > 0 \\ 0 & \text{otherwise} \end{cases} \tag{A.53}$$

The distribution function is

$$F(t) = \Pr(T \leq t) = 1 - e^{-\lambda t} \quad \text{for } t > 0 \tag{A.54}$$

The probability density function and the distribution function of the exponential distribution are illustrated in Figure A.14.

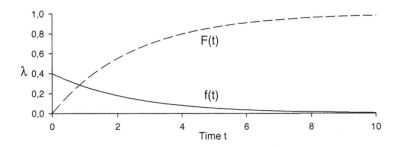

**Figure A.14** Exponential distribution ($\lambda = 0.4$).

The reliability (survivor) function becomes

$$R(t) = \Pr(T > t) = \int_t^\infty f(u)\,du = e^{-\lambda t} \quad \text{for } t > 0 \tag{A.55}$$

The mean time to failure is

$$\text{MTTF} = \int_0^\infty R(t)\,dt = \int_0^\infty e^{-\lambda t}\,dt = \frac{1}{\lambda} \tag{A.56}$$

The variance of $T$ is

$$\text{Var}(T) = \frac{1}{\lambda^2} \tag{A.57}$$

and the failure rate function is

$$z(t) = \frac{f(t)}{R(t)} = \frac{\lambda e^{-\lambda t}}{e^{-\lambda t}} = \lambda \tag{A.58}$$

Accordingly, the failure rate function of an item with exponential life distribution is constant (i.e., independent of time).

The results (A.56) and (A.58) compare well with the use of the concepts in everyday language. If an item has on the average $\lambda = 4$ failures/year, the mean time to failure MTTF of the item is 1/4 year.

Now suppose that an item has exponential time to failure $T$. For such an item

$$\Pr(T > t + x \mid T > t) = \frac{\Pr(T > t + x)}{\Pr(T > t)} = \frac{e^{-\lambda(t+x)}}{e^{-\lambda t}} = e^{-\lambda x} = \Pr(T > x)$$

This implies that the probability that an item will be functioning at time $t + x$, given that it is functioning at time $t$, is equal to the probability that a new item has a time to failure longer than $x$. Hence, the remaining lifetime of an item that is functioning at time $t$, is independent of $t$. This means that the exponential distribution has no "memory."

An assumption of exponentially distributed lifetime therefore implies that:

- A used item is stochastically *as good as new*. Thus, there is no reason to replace a functioning item.

- For the estimation of the survivor function, the mean time to failure, and so on, it is sufficient to collect data on the number of hours of observed time in operation and the number of failures. The age of the items is of no interest in this connection.

The exponential distribution is the most commonly used life distribution in applied risk and reliability analyses. The reason for this is its mathematical simplicity and that it leads to realistic lifetime models for certain types of items.

***The Exponential Distribution and the Poisson Process.***   Assume that failures occur according to a Poisson process with rate $\lambda$, and let $N(t)$ be the number of failures in the time interval $(0, t]$. The probability mass function of $N(t)$ is

$$\Pr(N(t) = n) = \frac{(\lambda t)^n}{n!} e^{-\lambda t} \quad \text{for } n = 0, 1, \ldots$$

Let $T_1$ be the time from $t = 0$ until the first failure, $T_2$ be the time between the first and second failures, and so on. The variables $T_1, T_2, \ldots$ can now be shown to be independent and exponentially distributed with parameter $\lambda$ (e.g., see Rausand and Høyland, 2004).

***The Weibull Distribution.***   The Weibull distribution is one of the most widely used life distributions in reliability analysis. The distribution is named after the Swedish professor Waloddi Weibull (1887-1979), who developed the distribution for modeling the strength of materials. The Weibull distribution is very flexible and can, through an appropriate choice of parameters, model many types of failure rate behaviors.

The time to failure $T$ of an item is said to be Weibull distributed with parameters $\alpha$ and $\lambda$ if the distribution function is given by

$$F(t) = \begin{cases} 1 - e^{-(\lambda t)^\alpha} & \text{for } t > 0, \ \lambda > 0, \ \alpha > 0 \\ 0 & \text{otherwise} \end{cases} \tag{A.59}$$

The corresponding probability density function is

$$f(t) = \frac{d}{dt} F(t) = \begin{cases} \alpha \lambda^\alpha t^{\alpha-1} e^{-(\lambda t)^\alpha} & \text{for } t > 0 \\ 0 & \text{otherwise} \end{cases} \tag{A.60}$$

where $\lambda$ is a *scale* parameter and $\alpha$ is referred to as a *shape* parameter. Note that when $\alpha = 1$, the Weibull distribution is equal to the exponential distribution. The probability density function $f(t)$ is illustrated in Figure A.15 for selected values of $\alpha$. The survivor function is

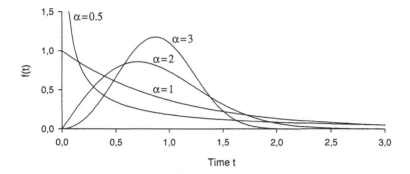

**Figure A.15**   The probability density function of the Weibull distribution for selected values of the shape parameter $\alpha$ ($\lambda = 1$).

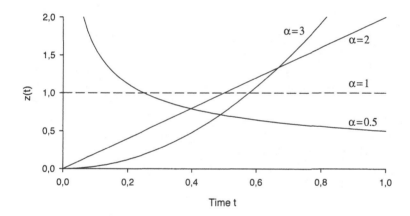

**Figure A.16**   The failure rate function of the Weibull distribution for selected values of the shape parameter $\alpha$ ($\lambda = 1$).

$$R(t) = \Pr(T > t) = e^{-(\lambda t)^{\alpha}} \quad \text{for } t > 0 \qquad (A.61)$$

and the failure rate function is

$$z(t) = \frac{f(t)}{R(t)} = \alpha \lambda^{\alpha} t^{\alpha-1} \quad \text{for } t > 0 \qquad (A.62)$$

The failure rate function $z(t)$ of the Weibull distribution is illustrated in Figure A.16 for selected values of $\alpha$. Because of its flexibility, the Weibull distribution may be used to model life distributions where the failure rate function is decreasing, constant, and increasing.

The mean time to failure, MTTF, of the Weibull distribution is

$$\text{MTTF} = \int_0^\infty R(t)\, dt = \frac{1}{\lambda} \Gamma \left( \frac{1}{\alpha} - 1 \right) \tag{A.63}$$

where $\Gamma(\cdot)$ is the gamma function defined by:[1]

$$\Gamma(x) = \int_0^\infty t^{x-1} e^{-t}\, dt \quad \text{for } t > 0$$

In particular, we have

$$\Gamma(n+1) = n! \quad \text{for } n = 0, 1, 2, \ldots$$

The variance of $T$ is

$$\text{Var}(T) = \frac{1}{\lambda^2} \left[ \Gamma \left( \frac{2}{\alpha} + 1 \right) - \Gamma^2 \left( \frac{1}{\alpha} + 1 \right) \right]$$

**The Normal (Gaussian) Distribution.**   The most commonly used distribution in statistics is the normal (Gaussian) distribution. A random variable $T$ is said to be normally distributed with mean $\nu$ and variance $\tau^2$ when the probability density function of $T$ is

$$f(t) = \frac{1}{\sqrt{2\pi} \cdot \tau} e^{-(t-\nu)^2 / 2\tau^2} \quad \text{for } -\infty < t < \infty \tag{A.64}$$

To simplify the notation we sometimes write $T \sim \mathcal{N}(\nu, \tau^2)$. The probability density function $f(t)$ is symmetric about a vertical axis through $t = \nu$, and has the $t$-axis as a horizontal asymptote. The curve has its points of inflection at $t = \nu \pm \tau$. The total area under the curve and above the horizontal axis is equal to 1.

In the special case when $\nu = 0$ and $\tau^2 = 1$ the distribution is called the *standard normal distribution* and we denote it by $\mathcal{N}(0, 1)$.

If the random variable $X \sim \mathcal{N}(\nu, \tau^2)$ and $\tau^2 > 0$, then $U = (X - \nu)/\tau \sim \mathcal{N}(0, 1)$. The random variable $U$ is said to be standardized.

The distribution function of a random variable $U$ with standard normal distribution is usually denoted by $\Phi(u) = \Pr(U \leq u)$. The corresponding probability density function is

$$\phi(u) = \frac{1}{\sqrt{2\pi}} e^{-u^2/2} \tag{A.65}$$

The distribution function of the general normal distribution $T \sim \mathcal{N}(\nu, \tau^2)$ may be written as

$$F(t) = \Pr(T \leq t) = \Pr \left( \frac{T - \nu}{\tau} \leq \frac{t - \nu}{\tau} \right)$$
$$= \Pr \left( U \leq \frac{t - \nu}{\tau} \right) = \Phi \left( \frac{t - \nu}{\tau} \right) \tag{A.66}$$

---

[1] The gamma function is a standard function in computer programs such as MATLAB, Scilab, and GNU Octave.

### EXAMPLE A.9

Let $T$ denote the time to failure of a technical item and assume that $T$ has a normal distribution with mean $\nu = 20\,000$ hours and variance $\tau^2$ where $\tau = 5\,000$ hours. The probability that the item will fail in the time interval from $t_1 = 17\,000$ hours to $t_2 = 21\,000$ hours is

$$\Pr(t_1 < T \le t_2) = \Pr\left(\frac{t_1 - \nu}{\tau} < \frac{T - \nu}{\tau} \le \frac{t_2 - \nu}{\tau}\right)$$

$$= \Phi\left(\frac{t_2 - \nu}{\tau}\right) - \Phi\left(\frac{t_1 - \nu}{\tau}\right)$$

$$= \Phi(0.200) - \Phi(-0.600) \approx 0.305$$

$\oplus$

Let $T_1, T_2, \ldots, T_n$ be independent and identically distributed $\mathcal{N}(\nu, \tau^2)$. It can be shown that

$$\sum_{i=1}^{n} T_i \sim \mathcal{N}\left(n\nu, n\tau^2\right)$$

The sum of independent normally distributed random variables is hence also normally distributed, and

$$\frac{\sum_{i=1}^{n} T_i - n\nu}{\sqrt{n}\,\tau} = \frac{\frac{1}{n}\sum_{i=1}^{n} T_i - \nu}{\tau}\sqrt{n} \sim \mathcal{N}(0, 1)$$

By using the notation $\bar{T} = \frac{1}{n}\sum_{i=1}^{n} T_i$, the last expression can be written as

$$\frac{\bar{T} - E(\bar{T})}{\sqrt{\mathrm{Var}(\bar{T})}} \sim \mathcal{N}(0, 1) \tag{A.67}$$

**The Gamma Distribution.**  Let $T_1, T_2, \ldots, T_n$ be independent and exponentially distributed with parameter $\lambda$. The sum $V = T_1 + T_2 + \cdots + T_n$ is then gamma distributed with parameters $\lambda$ and $n$. The probability density function of the random variable $V$ is

$$f(v) = \frac{\lambda}{\Gamma(n)}(\lambda v)^{n-1}e^{-\lambda v} \quad \text{for } v > 0 \tag{A.68}$$

The parameter $n$ in (A.68) is not restricted to positive integers, but can take any positive value.

The mean and variance of $V$ are

$$E(V) = \frac{n}{\lambda} \tag{A.69}$$

$$\mathrm{Var}(V) = \frac{n}{\lambda^2} \tag{A.70}$$

▣ **EXAMPLE A.10**

Consider a component that is exposed to a series of shocks that occur according to a Poisson process with rate $\lambda$. The time intervals $T_1, T_2, \ldots$ between consecutive shocks are then independent and exponentially distributed with parameter $\lambda$. Assume that the component fails exactly at shock $n$, and not earlier. The time to failure $\sum_{i=1}^{n} T_i$ is then gamma distributed with parameters $\lambda$ and $n$.    ⊕

**The Beta Distribution.**    A random variable $T$ is said to have a beta distribution with parameters $r$ and $s$ if the probability density function of $T$ is given by

$$f(t) = \frac{\Gamma(r+s)}{\Gamma(r)\Gamma(s)} t^{r-1}(1-t)^{s-1} \quad \text{for } 0 \leq t \leq 1 \qquad (A.71)$$

The mean and variance of $T$ are

$$E(T) = \frac{r}{r+s} \qquad (A.72)$$

$$\mathrm{Var}(T) = \frac{rs}{(r+s)^2(r+s+1)} \qquad (A.73)$$

**The Uniform Distribution.**    Let $T$ have a beta distribution with parameters $r = 1$ and $s = 1$. The probability density function is then

$$f(t) = \begin{cases} 1 & \text{for } 0 \leq t \leq 1 \\ 0 & \text{otherwise} \end{cases}$$

This distribution is called the *uniform* or *rectangular distribution*. The uniform distribution is considered a special case of the beta distribution when $r = 1$ and $s = 1$.

In general, we say that a random variable $T$ has a uniform distribution over the interval $[a, b]$ when the probability density function is

$$f(t) = \begin{cases} \frac{1}{b-a} & \text{for } a \leq t \leq b \\ 0 & \text{otherwise} \end{cases} \qquad (A.74)$$

The mean and variance of $T$ are

$$E(T) = \frac{a+b}{2} \qquad (A.75)$$

$$\mathrm{Var}(T) = \frac{(b-a)^2}{12} \qquad (A.76)$$

**The Strong Law of Large Numbers.**    Let $X_1, X_2, \ldots$ be a sequence of independent random variables with a common distribution (discrete or continuous) with mean value $E(X_i) = \mu$. Then, with probability 1,

$$\lim_{n \to \infty} \frac{1}{n} \sum_{i=1}^{n} X_i = \mu \qquad (A.77)$$

This important result is called the *strong law of large numbers*, stating that the average of a sequence of independent random variables having the same distribution will, with probability 1, converge to the mean of that distribution.

**The Central Limit Theorem.**   Let $X_1, X_2, \ldots$ be a sequence of independent, identically distributed random variables, each with mean $\nu$ and variance $\tau^2$. Let $\bar{X}$ be the empirical mean of the $n$ first variable in this sequence such that

$$\bar{X} = \frac{1}{n} \sum_{i=1}^{n} X_i$$

Then the distribution of

$$\frac{\bar{X} - E(\bar{X})}{\sqrt{\mathrm{Var}(\bar{X})}} = \frac{\bar{X} - \nu}{\tau} \sqrt{n}$$

tends to the standard normal distribution as $n \to \infty$. That is,

$$\mathrm{Pr}\left( \frac{\bar{X} - \nu}{\tau} \sqrt{n} \leq y \right) \to \frac{1}{\sqrt{2\pi}} \int_{-\infty}^{y} e^{-t^2/2} \, dt \tag{A.78}$$

as $n \to \infty$. This result is called the *central limit theorem* and is valid for *any* distribution of the $X_i$'s.

### ◼ EXAMPLE A.11

Let $X$ have a binomial distribution with parameters $n$ and $p$. The $X$ can be considered as a sum of $n$ independent random variable that are $\mathrm{bin}(1, p)$. We can therefore use the central limit theorem to conclude that the distribution of

$$\frac{X - E(X)}{\sqrt{\mathrm{Var}(X)}} = \frac{X - np}{\sqrt{np(1 - p)}}$$

approaches the standard normal distribution as $n \to \infty$. The normal approximation is considered to be good for values of $n$ and $p$ such that $np(1 - p) \geq 10$.

$\oplus$

## A.6    Point and Interval Estimation

A random variable is described by its probability distribution. This distribution is usually dependent on one or more parameters. A variable with an exponential life distribution has, for example, one parameter—the failure rate $\lambda$. Since the parameters characterize the distribution, we are usually interested in estimating the values of the parameters.

A parameter is an unknown quantity that is part of a probability distribution. We can observe numerical values for random variables, but never for parameters. Parameters are, per definition, not observable. In the pure classical approach we assume that parameters are real quantities, but unknown to us. A gas detector is, for example, assumed to have a failure rate $\lambda$, which is a *property* of the gas detector.

An *estimator* of an unknown parameter is simply a statistic (i.e., a function of one or more random variables) that "corresponds" to that parameter. A particular numerical value of an estimator that is computed from observed data is called an *estimate*. We may distinguish between a point estimator and an interval estimator. A *point estimator* is a procedure leading to a single numerical value for the estimate of the unknown parameter. An *interval estimator* is a random interval in which the true value of the parameter lies with some probability. Such a random interval is usually called a *confidence interval*.

### A.6.1   Point Estimation

Let $X$ be a random variable with distribution function that depends on a parameter $\theta$. The distribution may be denoted by $F(x \mid \theta)$ and can be continuous or discrete. Let $X_1, X_2, \ldots, X_n$ be a random sample of $n$ observations of the variable $X$. Our problem is to find a statistic $Y = g(X_1, X_2, \ldots, X_n)$ such that if $x_1, x_2, \ldots, x_n$ are the observed numerical values of $X_1, X_2, \ldots, X_n$, then the number $y = g(x_1, x_2, \ldots, x_n)$ will be a good point estimate of $\theta$.

There are a number of properties required of a good point estimator. Among these are:

- The point estimator should be *unbiased*. That is, the long-run average, or mean value of the point estimator, should be equal to the parameter that is estimated, $E(Y) = \theta$.

- The point estimator should have *minimum variance*. Since the point estimator is a statistic, it is a random variable. This property states that the minimum variance point estimator has a variance that is smaller than any other estimator of the same parameter.

The estimator of $\theta$ is often denoted $\hat{\theta}$. This symbol is sometimes used for both the estimator and the estimate, which may be confusing.

■ **EXAMPLE A.12**

Consider a binomial situation where we have $n$ independent trials. Each trial can result in either the event $E$ or not. The probability $p = \Pr(E)$ is the same in all trials. Let $X$ be the number of occurrences of the event $E$. A natural estimator for the parameter $p$ is then

$$\hat{p} = \frac{X}{n} \tag{A.79}$$

The estimator $\hat{p}$ is seen to be unbiased since

$$E(\hat{p}) = E\left(\frac{X}{n}\right) = \frac{E(X)}{n} = \frac{np}{n} = p$$

The variance of $\hat{p}$ is

$$\text{Var}(\hat{p}) = \frac{p(1-p)}{n}$$

It can be shown that $\hat{p}$ is the minimum variance estimator for $p$.    ⊕

**Maximum Likelihood Estimation.**    Maximum likelihood estimation (MLE) is a general approach to point estimation of parameters. Let $X_1, X_2, \ldots, X_n$ be $n$ independent and identically distributed random variables with probability density function $F(x \mid \theta)$. The parameter $\theta$ may be a single parameter or a vector of parameters. Here, we assume that $\theta$ is a single parameter. Assume that we have observed the data set $x = x_1, x_2, \ldots, x_n$. The MLE approach says that we should find the parameter value $\hat{\theta}$ (if it exists) with the highest chance of giving this particular data set, that is, such that

$$f(x_1, x_2, \ldots, x_n \mid \hat{\theta}) \geq f(x_1, x_2, \ldots, x_n \mid \theta)$$

for any other value of $\theta$.

We introduced and discussed the likelihood function $L(\theta \mid x)$ in Chapter 2. In this case, the likelihood function is given by

$$L(\theta \mid x) = \prod_{i=1}^{n} f(x_i \mid \theta) \tag{A.80}$$

where $x$ is a vector of known values and $L(\theta \mid x)$ is a function of $\theta$. Note that $L(\theta \mid x)$ is not a probability distribution.

The maximum likelihood estimate $\hat{\theta}$ is found by maximizing $L(\theta \mid x)$ with respect to $\theta$. In practice, it is often easier to maximize the log likelihood function $\ln[L(\theta \mid x)]$, which is valid since the logarithmic function is monotonic.

The log likelihood function is given by

$$\ln[L(\theta \mid x)] = \sum_{i=1}^{n} \ln f(x_i \mid \theta) \tag{A.81}$$

The maximum likelihood estimate may now be found by solving

$$\frac{\partial}{\partial \theta} \ln[L(\theta \mid x)] = 0 \tag{A.82}$$

and by showing that the solution in fact gives a maximum.

## A.6.2 Interval Estimation

An interval estimator of the parameter $\theta$ is the distance between two statistics that includes the true value of $\theta$ with some probability. To obtain an interval estimator of $\theta$, we need to find two statistics $\theta_L$ and $\theta_U$ such that the probability is

$$\Pr(\theta_L \leq \theta \leq \theta_U) = 1 - \varepsilon \tag{A.83}$$

The interval

$$\theta_L \leq \theta \leq \theta_U$$

is called a $100(1-\varepsilon)$ percent *confidence interval* for the parameter $\theta$. The interpretation of the interval is that if we carry out repeated experiments and construct intervals as above, then $100(1-\varepsilon)$ percent of them will contain the true value of $\theta$. The statistics $\theta_L$ and $\theta_U$ are called the lower and upper *confidence limits*, respectively, and $(1-\varepsilon)$ is called the *confidence coefficient*.

### ◼ EXAMPLE A.13

Let $X$ be a normally distributed random variable with unknown mean $v$ and *known* variance $\tau^2$. Let $X_1, X_2, \ldots, X_n$ be a random sample of $n$ independent observations of $X$. For the normal distribution, the average value

$$\frac{1}{n} \sum_{i=1}^{n} X_i = \bar{X} \sim \mathcal{N}(v, \tau^2/n)$$

such that

$$\frac{\bar{X} - v}{\tau} \sqrt{n} \sim \mathcal{N}(0, 1) \tag{A.84}$$

A natural estimator for the unknown mean $v$ is

$$\hat{v} = \bar{X} = \frac{1}{n} \sum_{i=1}^{n} X_i \tag{A.85}$$

This estimator is unbiased since $E(\hat{v}) = v$, and the variance is $\text{Var}(\hat{v}) = \tau^2/n$. From (A.84) we get

$$\Pr\left(-z_{\varepsilon/2} \leq \frac{\bar{X} - v}{\tau} \sqrt{n} \leq z_{\varepsilon/2}\right) = 1 - \varepsilon \tag{A.86}$$

where $z_{\varepsilon/2}$ is the upper-tail percentile point of the standard normal distribution such that the probability to the right of $z_{\varepsilon/2}$ is $\varepsilon/2$. Equation (A.86) can be rewritten as

$$\Pr\left(\bar{X} - z_{\varepsilon/2}\tau/\sqrt{n} \leq v \leq \bar{X} - z_{\varepsilon/2}\tau/\sqrt{n}\right) = 1 - \varepsilon \tag{A.87}$$

We have thus found a $100(1 - \varepsilon)$ percent confidence interval for the mean $\nu$ with

Lower confidence limit: $\nu_L = \bar{X} - z_{\varepsilon/2}\tau/\sqrt{n}$

Upper confidence limit: $\nu_U = \bar{X} + z_{\varepsilon/2}\tau/\sqrt{n}$

The lower and upper confidence limits are random variables (statistics). When we have observed the numerical values of $X_1, X_2, \ldots, X_n$, we can calculate the *estimates* of the confidence limits. $\oplus$

**Remark**: When an interval is calculated, it will either include the true value of the parameter $\theta$, or it will not. If the experiment were repeated many times, the interval would cover the true value of $\theta$ in $100(1 - \varepsilon)$ percent of the cases. Thus we would have a strong confidence that $\theta$ is covered by the interval, but it is wrong to say that there is a $100(1 - \varepsilon)$ percent probability that $\theta$ is included in the interval. The parameter $\theta$ is not stochastic. It has a true but unknown value (e.g., see Aven, 2003). $\oplus$

## A.7 Bayesian Approach

By degree of probability we really mean, or ought to mean, degree of belief . . . .
—Augustus De Morgan (1847)

Bayesian or subjective probability was introduced and discussed briefly in Chapter 2. We will now assume that unwanted events $E$ occur according to a homogeneous Poisson process (HPP) with rate $\lambda_E$. In the Bayesian approach, the analyst is assumed to have a prior belief about the value of $\lambda_E$. This prior belief is formulated as a probability density function $\pi(\lambda_E)$ of a random variable $\Lambda_E$. If the analyst has a clear and strong opinion about the value of $\Lambda_E$, she will choose a peaked or "narrow" distribution. If she has only a vague opinion, she will choose a "spread-out" distribution. Which distribution to choose is not very important as such, but it might lead to very complicated mathematical formulas. It is therefore strongly recommended to choose a distribution class for the prior that is *conjugate* to the distribution of the evidence.

 **Conjugate distributions**: Two distributions (a) and (b) are conjugate if they have the following property: If the prior distribution is (a) and the evidence distribution is (b), then the posterior distribution (given the evidence) is also (a) (although with different parameter values from the prior distribution).

In this case, the evidence is the number $N_E = n$ of occurrences of event $E$ that is observed during an accumulated time period of length $t$. The evidence has a Poisson distribution given by

$$\Pr(N_E = n \mid \lambda_E) = \frac{(\lambda_E \cdot t)^n}{n!} e^{-\lambda_E t} \quad \text{for } n = 0, 1, 2, \ldots \tag{A.88}$$

It can be shown that the conjugate to this evidence distribution is the *gamma distribution*. The analyst should therefore choose her prior as a gamma distribution

$$\pi(\lambda_E) = \frac{\beta}{\Gamma(\alpha)} (\beta \lambda_E)^{\alpha-1} e^{-\beta \lambda_E} \tag{A.89}$$

This is the probability density function of the gamma distribution with parameters $\alpha, \beta$. The symbol $\Gamma(\alpha)$ is the gamma function of $\alpha$ (e.g., see Rausand and Høyland, 2004, App. A).

The gamma distribution is very flexible, and most relevant prior beliefs can be modeled by choosing the values of the parameters $\alpha$ and $\beta$ appropriately. The (prior) mean value of $\Lambda_E$ is

$$E(\Lambda_E) = \int_0^\infty \lambda_E \pi(\lambda_E) \, d\lambda_E = \frac{\alpha}{\beta} \tag{A.90}$$

and the standard deviation is

$$\text{SD}(\Lambda_E) = \frac{\sqrt{\alpha}}{\beta} \tag{A.91}$$

These two formulas can be used to determine the parameters $\alpha$ and $\beta$ that best fit the analyst's belief about the value of $\lambda_E$. The prior mean value is sometimes used as a *prior estimate* $\hat{\lambda}_E$ for $\lambda_E$.

The analyst's posterior probability density function when the evidence $(n, t)$ is given can now be found by using Bayes formula (see Chapter 2):

$$\pi(\lambda_E \mid n, t) \propto \pi(\lambda_E) \cdot L(\lambda_E \mid N_E(t) = n) \tag{A.92}$$

The "proportionality" constant $k$ is given by

$$\pi(\lambda_E \mid n, t) = \frac{1}{k} \pi(\lambda_E) \cdot L(\lambda_E \mid N_E(t) = n) \tag{A.93}$$

For $\pi(\lambda_E \mid n, t)$ to be a true probability density function, its integral must be equal to 1.

$$\int_0^\infty \pi(\lambda_E \mid n, t) \, d\lambda_E = \frac{1}{k} \int_0^\infty \pi(\lambda_E) \cdot L(\lambda_E \mid N_E(t) = n) \, d\lambda_E = 1$$

The constant $k$ is therefore

$$
\begin{aligned}
k &= \int_0^\infty \pi(\lambda_E) \cdot L(\lambda_E \mid N_E(t) = n) \, d\lambda_E \\
&= \int_0^\infty \frac{\beta}{\Gamma(\alpha)} (\beta\lambda_E)^{\alpha-1} e^{-\beta\lambda_E} \cdot \frac{(\lambda_E t)^n}{n!} e^{-\lambda_E t} \, d\lambda_E \\
&= \frac{\beta^\alpha t^n}{\Gamma(\alpha) n!} \int_0^\infty \lambda_E^{\alpha+n-1} e^{-(\beta+n)\lambda_E} \, d\lambda_E \\
&= \frac{\beta^\alpha t^n}{\Gamma(\alpha) n!} \frac{\Gamma(n+\alpha)}{(\beta+t)^{n+\alpha}}
\end{aligned}
\tag{A.94}
$$

By combining (A.88), (A.89), (A.93) and (A.94), we obtain the posterior density

$$
\pi(\lambda_E \mid n, t) = \frac{(\beta+t)^{\alpha+n}}{\Gamma(\alpha+n)} \lambda_E^{\alpha+n-1} e^{-(\beta+t)\lambda_E}
\tag{A.95}
$$

which is recognized as the gamma distribution with parameters $(\alpha + n)$ and $(\beta + t)$.

We have thus shown that the gamma distribution and the Poisson distribution are conjugate. A thorough discussion of Bayesian probability theory is given, for example, in Lindley (2007) and Dezfuli et al. (2009).

## A.8 Probability of Frequency Approach

The approach outlined below is called the *probability of frequency* approach by some authors (e.g., see Kaplan and Garrick, 1981; Garrick, 2008). Note that the approach reconciles two interpretations of probability: (i) The occurrence of events is modeled as a classical stochastic process where the rate of the process $\lambda$ is an unknown parameter, and (ii) the analyst's uncertainty about the value of $\lambda$ is modeled by a subjective probability distribution.

### A.8.1 Prior Distribution

Assume that we study the reliability of a new type of gas detector, and that we believe that the time to failure $T$ of the gas detector is distributed exponentially with failure rate $\lambda$. The parameter $\lambda$ is unknown, but the new gas detector is similar to previous types of detectors of which we have some experience.

From this experience combined with careful examination of the new gas detector, we feel that we have some *prior* information about the "unknown" failure rate $\lambda$. By using subjective probabilities, this prior information can be expressed as a prior distribution of $\Lambda$, where $\Lambda$ is the failure rate considered as a random variable. The prior distribution can be expressed, for example, by the prior density $\pi(\lambda)$ as illustrated in Figure A.17.

This approach is very flexible and can express both very detailed prior information (as a narrow, peaked density) and vague information (as a spread-out density).

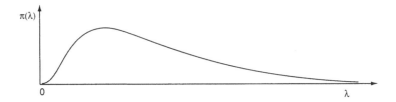

**Figure A.17**    Prior density for the failure rate.

We may choose the form of the prior distribution such that it describes our prior knowledge. A commonly used distribution is the gamma distribution

$$\pi(\lambda) = \frac{\beta}{\Gamma(\alpha)}(\beta\lambda)^{\alpha-1}e^{-\beta\lambda} \quad \text{for } \lambda > 0 \tag{A.96}$$

Note that here we use a parameterization of the gamma distribution other than the one we used in Equation (A.68). The parameter $\lambda$ has been replaced by $\beta$, and $n$ by $\alpha$. The reason for choosing the gamma distribution is that it is easy to use and at the same time very flexible. We may describe a wide variety of our prior knowledge by selecting the values of the parameters $\alpha$ and $\beta$ appropriately.

**Prior Estimate.**    The prior distribution, as illustrated in Figure A.17, expresses our total knowledge about the unknown parameter $\lambda$. In some cases, it is necessary to present a single value (an estimate of $\lambda$), and this estimate is most often chosen to be the mean value of the prior distribution. When the gamma distribution (A.96) is used as prior distribution, we get

$$\hat{\lambda} = \int_0^\infty \pi(\lambda)\, d\lambda = \frac{\alpha}{\beta} \tag{A.97}$$

The median of the prior distribution is sometimes used as an alternative to the mean.

## A.8.2    Likelihood

The likelihood of $E$ given the evidence $D_1$ is written as $L(E \mid D_1)$. Mathematically, $L(E \mid D_1)$ is equal to $\Pr(D_1 \mid E)$, but the interpretation of the two concepts is truly different. While the first expresses the likelihood that the state of nature is $E$ when the evidence $D_1$ is given, the second expresses the probability that the evidence is equal to $D_1$ when the state of nature is $E$, and hence is given. A better way of expressing Bayes formula in (2.4) is therefore

$$\Pr(E \mid D_1) = \frac{1}{\Pr(D_1)} \cdot \Pr(E) \cdot L(E \mid D_1) \tag{A.98}$$

Since $\Pr(D_1)$ denotes the marginal probability of the evidence $D_1$, it is independent of $E$ and can therefore be considered as a "normalizing constant" in (A.98). We can therefore write

$$\Pr(E \mid D_1) = \begin{pmatrix} \text{normalizing} \\ \text{constant} \end{pmatrix} \cdot \Pr(E) \cdot L(E \mid D_1)$$

which can be written as

$$\Pr(E \mid D_1) \propto \Pr(E) \cdot L(E \mid D_1) \tag{A.99}$$

where the symbol $\propto$ means "proportional to." In the following we will use $k$ to denote $\Pr(D_1)$ in the "normalizing constant."

In some cases, the analyst's prior belief about the state of nature can be expressed by a continuous random variable $\Theta$ with some probability density function $\pi(\theta)$ for $\theta \geq 0$. When the analyst has a strong belief about the value of $\Theta$, she may choose a "narrow" or "peaked" probability density function, and when she has a vague belief, she may choose a "spread-out" density to express her belief.

Her posterior belief, after having studied the evidence $D_1$, can now be expressed by her posterior probability density function:

$$\pi(\theta \mid D_1) \propto \pi(\theta) \cdot L(\theta \mid D_1) \tag{A.100}$$

where $L(\theta \mid D_1)$ is the likelihood of $\theta$ when the evidence $D_1$ is given. By introducing a constant $k$, (A.100) can be written as

$$\pi(\theta \mid D_1) = \frac{1}{k} \cdot \pi(\theta) \cdot L(\theta \mid D_1)$$

For $\pi(\theta \mid D_1)$ to be a probability density function, its integral must be equal to 1, such that

$$\int_0^\infty \pi(\theta \mid D_1)\, d\theta = \frac{1}{k} \int_0^\infty \pi(\theta) \cdot L(\theta \mid D_1)\, d\theta = 1$$

The constant $k$ must therefore be

$$k = \int_0^\infty \pi(\theta) \cdot L(\theta \mid D_1)\, d\theta \tag{A.101}$$

The posterior density can therefore be written as (Bayes formula)

$$\pi(\theta \mid D_1) = \frac{\pi(\theta) \cdot L(\theta \mid D_1)}{\int_0^\infty \pi(\theta) \cdot L(\theta \mid D_1)\, d\theta} \tag{A.102}$$

### ▉ EXAMPLE A.14

Consider a binomial situation where:

1. We carry out $n$ independent trials.

2. Each trial has two possible outcomes $A$ and $A^*$.

3. The probability of outcome $A$ is $\Pr(A) = \theta$ in all the $n$ trials.

Let $X$ be the number of trials that result in $A$. The probability distribution of $X$ is then given by the binomial distribution:

$$\Pr(X = x \mid \theta) = \binom{n}{x} \theta^x (1 - \theta)^{n-x} \quad \text{for } x = 0, 1, \ldots, n$$

Assume now that we know that the trials can be performed in two different ways (1) and (2), but that which of these options is used is unknown. If option (1) is chosen, the probability of $A$ is $\Pr(A) = \theta_1$, and if option (2) is chosen, then $\Pr(A) = \theta_2$. We do not know which option was used, but we know that all the $n$ trials were performed in the same way. We may formulate this by saying that the state of nature is expressed by the random variable $\Theta$, which has two possible values $\theta_1$ and $\theta_2$.

An analyst is interested in finding the probability that option (1) was used, such that $\Theta = \theta_1$. Based on previous experience, she believes that on the average, a fraction $\alpha$ of the trials are performed according to option (1). Her initial or *prior* belief about the event $\Theta = \theta_1$ is therefore given by her prior probability

$$\Pr(\Theta = \theta_1) = \alpha$$

The analyst carries out $n$ trials and get the evidence $D_1 = \{X = x\}$. The probability of getting this result is obviously dependent on the unknown state of nature $\Theta$, that is, whether option (1) or option (2) was used. The likelihood of $\Theta = \theta_1$ when the evidence $D_1$ is given is

$$L(\Theta = \theta_1 \mid D_1) = \binom{n}{x} \theta_1^x (1 - \theta_1)^{n-x}$$

Her posterior probability of $\Theta = \theta_1$ is given by

$$\Pr(\Theta = \theta_1 \mid D_1) \propto \Pr(\Theta = \theta_1) \cdot L(\Theta = \theta_1 \mid D_1)$$

$$\propto \alpha \cdot \binom{n}{x} \theta_1^x (1 - \theta_1)^{n-x} \tag{A.103}$$

To be a probability distribution, we must have that

$$\Pr(\Theta = \theta_1 \mid D_1) + \Pr(\Theta = \theta_2 \mid D_1) = 1$$

When we introduce the proportionality constant $k$, it must fulfill

$$\frac{1}{k} \left[ \alpha \cdot \binom{n}{x} \theta_1^x (1 - \theta_1)^{n-x} + (1 - \alpha) \cdot \binom{n}{x} \theta_2^x (1 - \theta_2)^{n-x} \right] = 1$$

The analyst's posterior belief about $\Theta = \theta_1$ when the evidence $D_1$ is given is then

$$\Pr(\Theta = \theta_1 \mid D_1) = \frac{\alpha \cdot \binom{n}{x}\theta_1^x(1 - \theta_1)^{n-x}}{\alpha \cdot \binom{n}{x}\theta_1^x(1 - \theta_1)^{n-x} + (1 - \alpha) \cdot \binom{n}{x}\theta_2^x(1 - \theta_2)^{n-x}} \tag{A.104}$$

The proportionality constant $k$ or the denominator of (A.104) is seen to be the *marginal* probability of $D_1$ (see Appendix A).

The analyst can now make a new set of $n_2$ in the same way, observe the evidence $D_2$, and use formula (2.5) and get a further updated degree of her belief about $\Theta = \theta_1$. $\qquad \oplus$

The importance of realizing that a likelihood is not a probability is illustrated by Example A.15.

### ▣ EXAMPLE A.15

Consider a component with time to failure $T$ that is assumed to be exponentially distributed with constant failure rate $\lambda$. The failure rate is not observable, but $\lambda$ describes the "state of the nature." The probability density function of $T$ when $\lambda$ is given is

$$f(t \mid \lambda) = \lambda \cdot e^{-\lambda t}$$

The likelihood function of $\lambda$ when the time to failure is observed to be $t$ is

$$L(\lambda \mid t) = \lambda \cdot e^{-\lambda t}$$

If $L(\lambda \mid t)$ were a probability density, its integral should be equal to 1, but here

$$\int_0^\infty L(\lambda \mid t)\, d\lambda = \int_0^\infty \lambda \cdot e^{-\lambda t}\, d\lambda = \frac{\lambda}{t}$$

Since the integral is not always equal to 1, we conclude that $L(\lambda \mid t)$ is *not* a probability density function. $\qquad \oplus$

## A.8.3 Posterior Analysis

We again consider the gas detectors introduced above.

***Life Model.*** The probability density function of the time to failure, $T$, of a gas detector when we know the failure rate $\lambda$, may be written as

$$f(t \mid \lambda) = \lambda e^{-\lambda t} \tag{A.105}$$

Note that we now include the parameter $\lambda$ in $f(t \mid \lambda)$ to make it clear that the probability density function is also a function of $\lambda$.

To obtain information about $\lambda$, we carry out a number of experiments and observe the times $t_1, t_2, \ldots, t_{n_1}$ to failure of $n_1$ gas detectors. We assume that the corresponding $n_1$ times to failure are independent variables. The joint probability density function of these variables is then

$$f(t_1, t_2, \ldots, t_{n_1} \mid \lambda) = \prod_{i=1}^{n_1} \lambda \, e^{-\lambda t_i} = \lambda^{n_1} e^{-\lambda \sum_{i=1}^{n_1} t_i} \tag{A.106}$$

The random variables $T_1, T_2, \ldots, T_{n_1}$ are all observable, meaning that we assign numerical values to each of them when the experiment is carried out. The parameter $\lambda$ is not observable.

**Posterior Distribution.**    We can now update our prior knowledge by using the information gained from the data $d_1 = \{t_1, t_2, \ldots, t_{n_1}\}$. The prior distribution (A.96) and the distribution of the data $d_1$ (A.106) can be combined by using Bayes formula (A.102) to give the *posterior distribution*

$$\pi(\lambda \mid d_1) = \frac{f(d_1 \mid \lambda) \cdot \pi(\lambda)}{f(d_1)} \tag{A.107}$$

By using the prior distribution (A.96) and the distribution for the data (A.106), we get, after some calculation,

$$\pi(\lambda \mid d_1) = \frac{\beta + \sum_{i=1}^{n_1} t_i}{\Gamma(\alpha + n_1)} \left( \left( \beta + \sum_{i=1}^{n_1} t_i \right) \lambda \right)^{\alpha + n_1} e^{-\left( \beta + \sum_{i=1}^{n_1} t_i \right) \lambda} \tag{A.108}$$

This distribution is seen to be a gamma distribution with parameters

$$\alpha_1 = \alpha + n_1$$

$$\beta_1 = \beta + \sum_{i=1}^{n_1} t_i$$

The posterior distribution $\pi(\lambda \mid d_1)$ expresses all our current knowledge about the parameter $\lambda$, based on our prior knowledge and the knowledge gained through observing the data $d_1$.

By choosing the exponential distribution for the data and the gamma distribution for the parameter $\lambda$, we observe that the posterior distribution belongs to the same class of distributions as the prior. Exponential and gamma distributions, are therefore said to be *conjugate* distributions, as introduced in Chapter 2.

**Posterior Estimate.**    In the same way as for the prior situation, we can now find a posterior estimate for $\lambda$:

$$\hat{\lambda}_1 = \frac{\alpha_1}{\beta_1} = \frac{\alpha + n_1}{\beta + \sum_{i=1}^{n_1} t_i} \tag{A.109}$$

If we are content with this estimate, we may terminate the analysis and use this estimate. If not, we may observe a new set of $n_2$ items and get the data $d_2$. We use the posterior distribution based on the first data set, $(n_1, d_1)$ as our new prior distribution and update this prior with the new data set $(n_2, d_2)$ to get a new posterior distribution. The new posterior distribution will again be the gamma distribution, and we can find a new posterior estimate by the same procedure as above. This approach is often referred to as *Bayesian updating*.

Note that this estimate can be used even if no events $E$ (i.e., $n = 0$) have been observed in the time interval of length $t$. Also note that as the amount of evidence increases (i.e., $n$ and $t$ increase), the importance of the values of $\alpha$ and $\beta$ is reduced. As a limit, the estimate (A.109) will be equal to the estimate obtained by the frequentist approach in Section A.6.

***Credibility Intervals.***    A credibility interval is the Bayesian analogue to a confidence interval. A credibility interval for $\lambda$ at level $(1 - \varepsilon)$ is an interval $(a(d), b(d))$ such that the conditional probability, given the data $d$, satisfies

$$\Pr(a(d) < \lambda < b(d) \mid d) = \int_{a(d)}^{b(d)} f_{\lambda|d}\,(\theta \mid d)\,d\lambda = 1 - \varepsilon \qquad \text{(A.110)}$$

Then the interval $(a(d), b(d))$ is an interval estimate of $\lambda$, in the sense that the conditional probability of $\lambda$ belonging to the interval, given the data $d$, is equal to $1 - \varepsilon$.

## A.9  Additional Reading

The following titles are recommended for further study related to Appendix A.

- *Introduction to Probability Models* (Ross, 2007) is a very good introduction to classical probability theory.

- *Introduction to Probability and Statistics for Engineers and Scientists* (Ross, 2004) is another very good introductory text by Sheldon Ross, which also covers estimation and testing of hypotheses.

- *Probability Theory: The Logic of Science* (Jaynes, 2003) gives a survey of probability theory, but is more philosophical than the first two titles.

- *Understanding Uncertainty* (Lindley, 2007) is a good introduction to Bayesian probability theory. The book is written in a simple language with few formulas and is easy to read for people with little training in mathematics.

# APPENDIX B

# ACRONYMS

| | |
|---|---|
| AEMA | Action error mode analysis |
| AFR | Annual fatality rate |
| AIChE | American Institute of Chemical Engineers |
| ALARA | As low as reasonably achievable |
| ALARP | As low as reasonably practicable |
| API | American Petroleum Institute |
| ARAMIS | Accidental risk assessment methodology for industries in the framework of the Seveso II directive |
| ASME | American Society of Mechanical Engineers |
| ATHEANA | A technique for human error analysis |
| BDD | Binary decision diagram |
| BFR | Binomial failure rate |
| BOEMRE | Bureau of Ocean Energy Management, Regulation and Enforcement |
| BORA | Barrier and operational risk analysis |

| | |
|---|---|
| BPCS | Basic Process Control System |
| CAF | Cost of averting a fatality |
| CBA | Cost-benefit analysis |
| CCF | Common-cause failure |
| CCPS | Center for Chemical Process Safety |
| CDF | Core damage frequency |
| CM | Corrective maintenance |
| COCOM | Contextual control model |
| CPC | Common performance condition |
| CPT | Conditional probability table |
| CREAM | Cognitive reliability and error analysis method |
| DD | Dangerous detected (failure) |
| DoD | U.S. Department of Defense |
| DoE | U.S. Department of Energy |
| DPM | (Number of) deaths per million |
| DU | Dangerous undetected (failure) |
| EDF | Electricité de France |
| EFBA | Energy flow/barrier analysis |
| EFC | Error-forcing context |
| EMSA | European Maritime Safety Agency |
| EN | European norm (standard) |
| EOS | Emergency operations system |
| EPA | U.S. Environmental Protection Agency |
| EPC | Error-producing condition |
| EPRI | Electric Power Research Institute |
| EPSC | European Process Safety Centre |
| ERA | European Railway Agency |
| ESD | Emergency shutdown |
| ESDV | Emergency shutdown valve |
| ESA | European Space Agency |
| ESP | Electronic stability program (in cars) |
| ETA | Event tree analysis |
| ETBA | Energy trace/barrier analysis |
| EU | European Union |
| EUC | Equipment under control |
| FAR | Fatal accident rate |

| | |
|---|---|
| FEMA | U.S. Federal Emergency Management Agency |
| FMEA | Failure modes and effects analysis |
| FMECA | Failure modes, effects, and criticality analysis |
| F-N | Frequency–number of fatalities |
| FRACAS | Failure reporting analysis and corrective action system |
| FSA | Formal safety assessment |
| FTA | Fault tree analysis |
| FTF | Fail to function |
| GAMAB | Globalement au moins aussi bon |
| GAME | Globalement au moins équivalent |
| GCAF | Gross cost of averting a fatality |
| GIDEP | Government Industry Data Exchange Program |
| HAZID | Hazard identification |
| HAZOP | Hazard and operability study |
| HEART | Human error analysis and reduction technique |
| HEI | Human error identification |
| HEMP | Hazard and effects management process |
| HEP | Human error probability |
| HFI | Human factors integration |
| HMSO | Her Majesty's Stationary Office |
| HPP | Homogeneous Poisson process |
| HRA | Human reliability analysis |
| HRO | High-reliability organization |
| HSE | Health, safety, and environment |
| HSE | Health and Safety Executive (UK) |
| HSWA | Health and Safety at Work Act (UK) |
| HTA | Hierarchical task analysis |
| IAEA | International Atomic Energy Agency |
| ICAF | Implied cost of averting a fatality |
| ICAO | International Civil Aviation Organization |
| IEC | International Electrotechnical Commission |
| IEEE | Institute of Electrical and Electronic Engineers |
| IMO | International Maritime Organization |
| INSAG | International Nuclear Safety Advisory Group |
| IPL | Independent protection layer |
| IR | Individual risk |

| | |
|---|---|
| IRPA | Individual risk per annum |
| ISO | International Organization for Standardization |
| JHA | Job hazard analysis |
| JRC | Joint Research Centre |
| JSA | Job safety analysis |
| LIRA | Localized individual risk (average) |
| LNG | Liquefied natural gas |
| LOC | Loss of containment |
| LOPA | Layer of protection analysis |
| LRF | Large release frequency |
| LSIR | Location-specific individual risk |
| LTA | Less than adequate |
| LTI | Lost time injury |
| LTIF | Lost time injury frequency |
| LWF | Lost workdays frequency |
| MAE | Major accident event |
| MAHB | Major Accident Hazards Bureau |
| MARS | Major Accident Reporting System |
| MAUD | Multiattribute utility decomposition |
| MBF | Multiple beta factor |
| MDT | Mean downtime |
| MEM | Minimum endogenous mortality |
| MERMOS | Method d'évaluation de la realisation des mission operateur pour la sûreté |
| MGL | Multiple Greek letter |
| MLD | Master logic diagram |
| MLE | Maximum likelihood estimator |
| MMS | Mineral Management Service |
| MOCUS | Method for obtaining cut sets |
| MORT | Management Oversight and Risk Tree |
| MTBF | Mean time between failures |
| MTO | Man-technology-organization |
| MTTF | Mean time to failure |
| MTTR | Mean time to repair |
| NASA | National Aeronautics and Space Administration |
| NEA | Nuclear Energy Agency |
| NOAEL | No observed adverse effect level |

| | |
|---|---|
| NOPSA | National Offshore Petroleum Safety Authority, Australia |
| NRC | Nuclear Regulatory Commission |
| NS | Norwegian standard |
| NTNU | Norwegian University of Science and Technology |
| NUREG | Title of reports from U.S. NRC (Nuclear Regulatory Commission) |
| OGP | International Association of Oil & Gas Producers |
| OREDA | Offshore reliability data |
| OSHA | Occupational Safety and Health Administration |
| PDS | Reliability of computer-based safety systems (in Norwegian) |
| PEF | Potential equivalent fatality |
| PFD | Probability of failure on demand |
| PHA | Preliminary hazard analysis |
| P&ID | Piping and instrumentation diagram |
| PIF | Performance influencing factor |
| PLC | Programmable logic controller |
| PLL | Potential loss of life |
| PM | Preventive maintenance |
| POA | Assessed proportion of effect |
| POB | People on board |
| PRA | Probabilistic risk assessment |
| PrHA | Process hazard assessment |
| PSA | Probabilistic safety assessment |
| PSD | Process shutdown |
| PSF | Performance-shaping factor |
| QRA | Quantitative risk analysis (or assessment) |
| RAM | Reliability, availability, and maintainability |
| RAMP | Risk Assessment and Management Program |
| RAMS | Reliability, availability, maintainability, and safety |
| RAW | Risk achievement worth |
| RBD | Reliability block diagram |
| RBDM | Risk-based decision-making |
| RCM | Reliability-centered maintenance |
| RIAC | Reliability Information Analysis Center, U.S. Department of Defense |
| RIDM | Risk-informed decision-making |
| RIF | Risk-influencing factor |
| RLE | Reduction in life expectancy |

| | |
|---|---|
| ROCOF | Rate of occurrence of failures |
| RPN | Risk priority number |
| RRR | Rapid risk ranking |
| RRW | Risk reduction worth |
| RSSB | Railway Standards and Safety Board (UK) |
| SAE | Engineering Society for Advancing Mobility in Land Sea Air and Space |
| SFAIRP | So far as is reasonably practicable |
| SHE | Safety, health, and environment |
| SHERPA | Systematic error reduction and prediction approach |
| SIF | Safety instrumented function |
| SIL | Safety integrity level |
| SIS | Safety instrumented system |
| SJA | Safe job analysis |
| SLI | Success likelihood index |
| SLIM | Success likelihood index method |
| SMS | Safety management system |
| SRF | Small release frequency |
| SRK | Skill-, rule-, and knowledge-based (behavior) |
| STAMP | System-theoretic accident model and processes |
| STEP | Sequentially timed event plotting |
| SWIFT | Structured what-if technique |
| THA | Task hazard analysis |
| THERP | Technique for human error rate prediction |
| TOR | Tolerability of risk |
| TRA | Total risk analysis |
| TRC | Time reliability correlation |
| TTA | Tabular task analysis |
| UK | United Kingdom |
| UPM | Unified partial method |
| USCG | U.S. Coast Guard |
| VAF | Value of averting a fatality |
| VROM | Ministry of Housing, Spatial Planning and the Environment, The Netherlar |
| VSL | Value of a statistical life |
| WOAD | World Offshore Accident Data |

# APPENDIX C

# GLOSSARY

*Acceptable risk.* Risks considered insignificant and not justifying further effort to reduce them (HSE, 2001a).

The risk that is understood and agreed to by the program/project, governing authority, mission directorate, and other customer(s) such that no further specific mitigating action is required (NASA, 2007).

Risk which is accepted in a given context based on the current values of society and in the enterprise (NS 5814, 2008).

The residual risk remaining after controls have been applied to associated hazards that have been identified, quantified to the maximum extent practicable, analyzed, communicated to the proper level of management, and accepted after proper evaluation [SSDVC-28 (DOE)].

*Accident.* A sudden, unwanted, and unplanned event or event sequence that leads to harm to people, the environment, or other assets.

An unintended event or sequence of events that causes death, injury, or environmental or material damage (DEF-STAN 00-56, 2007).

An unwanted transfer of energy, because of lack of barriers and/or controls, producing injury to persons, property, or process, preceded by sequences of planning and operational errors, which failed to adjust to changes in physical or human factors and produced unsafe conditions and/or unsafe acts, arising out of the risk in an activity, and interrupting or degrading the activity (Johnson, 1980).

Alternative term: Mishap.

*Accident scenario.* A specific sequence of events from an initiating event to an undesired consequence (or harm) (adapted from IMO, 2002).

*Active barrier.* A barrier that is dependent on the actions of an operator, a control system, and/or some energy sources to perform its function.

*ALARP (As low as reasonably practicable).* A level of risk that is not intolerable, and cannot be reduced further without the expenditure of costs that are grossly disproportionate to the benefit gained.

A risk is ALARP when it has been demonstrated that the cost of any further risk reduction, where the cost includes the loss of defense capability as well as financial or other resource costs, is grossly disproportionate to the benefit obtained from that risk reduction (DEF-STAN 00-56, 2007).

*Aleatory.* Pertaining to stochastic (nondeterministic) events, the outcome of which is described by a probability. From the Latin *alea* (game of chance, die) (Dezfuli et al., 2009).

*Analysis.* Examination of anything complex to understand its nature or to determine its essential features.

*AND-gate.* A Boolean logic element used to develop fault trees. The output event related to this gate exists only if all the input events exist at the same time.

*Asset.* Something we value and want to preserve.

*Availability.* The ability of an item (under combined aspects of its reliability, maintainability, and maintenance support) to perform its required function at a stated instant of time or over a stated period of time (IEC 60050-191, 1990).

*Barrier.* Physical or engineered system or human action (based on specific procedures or administrative controls) that is implemented to prevent, control, or impede released energy from reaching the assets and causing harm.

Measure that reduces the probability of realizing a hazard's potential for harm and reduces its consequence.

*Note*: Barriers may be physical (materials, protective devices, shields, segregation, etc.) or nonphysical (procedures, inspection, training, drills, etc.) (ISO 17776, 2002).

*Basic event.* The bottom or "leaf" events of a fault tree. The limit of resolution of the fault tree. Examples of basic events are component failures and human errors

(Stamatelatos et al., 2002b).

An event in a fault tree that represents the lowest level of resolution in the model such that no further development is necessary (e.g., equipment item failure, human failure, or external event) (CCPS, 2008).

*Basic risk factors (BRF).* Those features of an operation that are wrong and have been so for a long time, but remain hidden because their influences do not surface without a local trigger (Wagenaar et al., 1990).

*Bayesian probability.* An approach to probability, representing a personal degree of belief, given some state of knowledge, that something will occur.

*Bow-tie diagram.* An illustration of a hazardous event that links the hazards and causes that potentially lead to an event to the consequences of that event. It is so called because of its shape, with the hazardous event being in the center of the bow-tie.

*Brainstorming.* Brainstorming is used to identify possible solutions to problems and potential opportunities for improvement. Brainstorming is a technique for tapping the creative thinking of a team to generate and clarify a list of ideas, problems, and issues.

*Broadly acceptable risk.* Risk considered acceptable by consensus among people in society, in particular those who find such concepts helpful in decision-making (HSE, 2001a).

A level of risk deemed to be negligible and requiring no further action.

*Cascading failure.* A sequence of component failures where the first failure shifts its load to one or more nearby components such that these fail and again shift their load to other components, and so on.

*Common-cause component group.* A group of usually similar components (in mission, manufacturer, maintenance, environment, etc.) that are considered to have a high potential for failure because of the same cause or causes (NUREG/CR-6268, 2007).

*Common-cause failure.* A dependent failure in which two or more component fault states exist simultaneously, or within a short time interval, and are a direct result of a shared cause (NEA, 2004b).

Multiple component faults that occur at the same time or that occur in a relatively small time window and that are due to a common cause (Stamatelatos et al., 2002a).

Failure, which is the result of one or more events, causing coincident failures of two or more separate channels in a multiple-channel system, leading to system failure (IEC 61508, 2010).

Failure of two or more structures, systems, and components due to a single specific event or cause (IAEA, 2007).

*Conditional independence.* Consider the three events $A$, $B$, and $C$. If we know that event $C$ has occurred, event $A$ and event $B$ are said to be *conditionally independent*, given $C$, if

$$\Pr(A \cap B \mid C) = \Pr(A \mid C) \cdot \Pr(B \mid C)$$

*Consequence.* The outcome of an event expressed qualitatively or quantitatively, being a loss, injury, disadvantage, or gain. There may be a range of possible outcomes associated with an event.

The outcome of an accident (IMO, 2002).

*Corrective maintenance.* The actions performed, as a result of failure, to restore an item to a specified condition.

The maintenance carried out after a failure has occurred and intended to restore an item to a state in which it can perform its required function.

*Coupling factor.* A property that makes multiple components susceptible to failure from a single shared cause.

The condition or mechanism through which failures of multiple components are coupled (NUREG/CR-6268, 2007).

*Critical items list.* A listing comprised of all critical items identified as a result of performing an FMECA.

*Cut set.* A cut set in a fault tree is a set of basic events whose (simultaneous) occurrence ensures that the TOP event occurs.

*Defense-in-depth.* A design and operational philosophy with regard to nuclear facilities that calls for multiple layers of protection to prevent and mitigate accidents. It includes the use of controls, multiple physical barriers to prevent release of radiation, redundant and diverse key safety functions, and emergency response measures (U.S. NRC)

*Demand.* Condition or event that requires a protective system or device to take appropriate action to prevent or mitigate consequences.

*Desired risk.* Risk that is sought, not avoided, because of the thrill and intrinsic enjoyment is brings.

*Distribution function.* Consider a random variable $X$. The distribution function of $X$ is

$$F_X(x) = \Pr(X \le x)$$

*Downtime.* The period of time during which an item is not in a condition to perform its required function.

*Energy path.* Path of energy flow from source to target.

*Energy source.* Any material, mechanism, or process that contains potential energy that can be released. The concern is that the released energy may cause harm to a potential target (Ericson, 2005).

*Epistemic.* Pertaining to the degree of knowledge of models and parameters. From the Greek *episteme* (knowledge) (Dezfuli et al., 2009).

*Equipment under control (EUC).* Equipment, machinery, apparatus, or plant used for manufacturing, process, transportation, medical, or other activities (IEC 61508, 2010).

*Error.* A departure from acceptable or desirable operation (e.g., of a component or system) that can result in unacceptable or undesirable consequence.

*Escalation.* Spread of the impact of a hazardous event to equipment or other areas, thereby causing an increase in the consequences of the event (ISO 17776, 2002)

An indirect outcome of an accident. Escalations can be considered as separate accidents that are initiated by the consequences of other accidents (NSW, 2003).

*Event.* Incident or situation that occurs in a particular place during a particular interval of time (AS/NZS 4360, 1995).

*Fail safe.* A design property of an item that prevents its failures from being critical.

A design feature which ensures that a system remains safe, or in the event of a failure, causes the system to revert to a state that will not cause a mishap (MIL-STD-882D, 2000)

*Failure.* The termination of the ability to perform a required function.

An unacceptable deviation from the design tolerance or in the anticipated delivered service, an incorrect output, or the incapacity to perform the desired function (Stamatelatos et al., 2002a).

A cessation of proper function or performance; inability to meet a standard; nonperformance of what is requested or expected (Stamatelatos et al.).

Inability of a structure, system, or component to function within acceptance criteria (IAEA, 2007).

*Failure cause.* The physical or chemical processes, design defects, quality defects, part misapplication, or other processes which are the basic reason for failure or which initiate the physical process by which deterioration proceeds to failure (MIL-STD-1629A, 1980).

Circumstances during design, manufacture, or use that have led to a failure (IEC 60050-191, 1990).

*Failure effect.* The consequence(s) a failure mode has on the operation, function, or status of an item (MIL-STD-1629A, 1980).

*Failure mode.* The effect by which a failure is observed on the failed item.

*Failure mode and effect analysis (FMEA).* A procedure by which each potential failure mode in a system is analyzed to determine the results or effects thereof on the system and to classify each potential failure mode according to its severity (MIL-STD-1629A).

*Failure rate.* The rate at which failures occur as a function of time. If $T$ denotes the time to failure of an item, the failure rate $z(t)$ is defined as

$$z(t) = \lim_{\Delta t \to 0} \frac{\Pr(t < T \le t + \Delta t \mid T > t)}{\Delta t}$$

The failure rate is sometimes called *force of mortality* (FOM).

*Failure symptom.* An identifiable physical condition by which a potential failure can be recognized.

*Fatal accident rate (FAR).* The expected number of fatalities per 100 million exposure hours of a activity.

*Fault.* A defect, imperfection, mistake, or flaw of varying severity that occurs within some hardware or software component or system. *Fault* is a general term and can range from a minor defect to a failure (Stamatelatos et al., 2002a).

Abnormal condition that may cause a reduction in, or loss of, the capability of a functional unit to perform a required function (IEC 61508, 2010).

*Fault tolerance.* Ability of a functional unit to continue to perform a required function in the presence of faults or errors (IEC 61508, 2010).

*Formal safety assessment (FSA).* A formal investigation of the nature, likelihood and impact of potential major accident events and the means to prevent or minimize their occurrence or consequences to as low as is reasonably practicable. Within the context of the safety case the term *formal safety assessment* may also refer to the reporting of facility-specific studies conducted by the operator that provide reasoned arguments and judgments about the findings of the formal investigation.

*Frequency.* The number of occurrences per unit time (e.g., per year).

*Frequentist probability.* An approach to probability that concerns itself with the frequency of events in a long series of trials, or is based on a data set.

*Functioning state.* The state when an item is performing a required function (see also "Operating state").

*Gradual failure.* Failure that could be anticipated by prior examination or monitoring.

*Grossly disproportionate.* The bias in favor of safety when assessing what is reasonably practicable (HSE, 2001a).

*Group risk.* The risk experienced by an entire group of people exposed to a hazard. It is often expressed as the relationship between the frequency and the number of people affected by an event (HSE, 2001a).

Alternative term: Societal risk.

*Harm.* Physical injury or damage to the health of people, or damage to property or the environment (IEC 60300-3-9, 1995).

*Hazard.* A source of danger that may cause harm to an asset.

A source of potential harm or a situation with a potential to cause loss, an uncontrolled exchange of energy

Any real or potential condition that can cause injury, illness, or death to personnel; damage to or loss of a system, equipment or property; or damage to the environment (MIL-STD-882D, 2000).

The potential in an activity (or condition or situation) for sequence(s) of errors, oversights, changes, and stresses to result in an accident; a source of risk or peril (Johnson, 1980).

A potential to threaten human life, health, property, or the environment (IMO, 2002).

*Hazard analysis.* The process of describing in detail the hazards and accidents associated with a system, and defining accident sequences (DEF-STAN 00-56, 2007).

*Hazard identification.* The process of identifying and listing the hazards and accidents associated with a system (DEF-STAN 00-56, 2007).

*Hazard log.* A document that records details of hazards and potential accidents identified during safety analyses of a system, product, or other change and logs the safety documentation produced (RSSB, 2007).

*Hazard rate.* Same as "Failure rate."

*Hazardous event.* The first event in a sequence of events that, if not controlled, will lead to undesired consequences (harm) to some assets.

*Hazardous situation.* Circumstance in which people, property, or the environment are exposed to one or more hazard(s).

*HAZOP (Hazard and operability study.* A systematic functional hazard identification process that uses an expert group to conduct a structured analysis of a system using a series of guide words to explore potential hazards.

*Hidden failure.* A failure not evident to a crew or operator during the performance of normal duties.

*Human error.* A departure from acceptable or desirable practice on the part of the individual or group of individuals that can result in unacceptable or undesirable risks.

An out-of-tolerance action, or deviation from the norm, where the limits of acceptable performance are defined by the system. These situations can arise from problems in sequencing, timing, knowledge, interfaces, procedures, and other sources (NUREG/CR-6883, 2005).

*Human error mode.* The effect by which a human error can be observed.

*Human error probability (HEP).* The probability that an error will occur when a given task is performed.

*Human reliability.* The probability that a person: (i) correctly performs some system-required activity in a required time period (if time is a limiting factor) and (ii) performs no extraneous activity that can degrade the system. *Human unreliability* is the opposite of this definition (IMO, 2002).

*Incident.* Unplanned, uncontrolled event, which under different circumstances could have resulted in an accident (RSSB, 2007).

An unplanned and unforeseen event that may or may not result in harm to one or more assets.

*Independent events.* Two events, $E_1$ and $E_2$, that fulfill the relationship $\Pr(E_1 \cap E_2) = \Pr(E_1) \cdot \Pr(E_2)$.

*Independent protection layer (IPL).* A device, system, or action that is capable of preventing a scenario from proceeding to its undesired consequence independent of the initiating event or the action of any other layer of protection associated with the scenario. The effectiveness and independence of an IPL must be auditable.

*Individual risk.* The frequency with which an individual may be expected to sustain a given level of harm from the realization of specified hazards (IChemE, 1992).

*Initiating event.* The initiator, unsafe act, and/or unsafe condition that initiated the adverse event flow, which resulted in an accident scenario.

An initiating event is the beginning of an accident scenario. It is an event that triggers subsequent chains of events.

A single event that requires the starting of the plant safety functions. The initiating event can be an internal or external event (e.g., a component failure, a natural phenomenon or a human-caused hazard) (STUK, 2003).

An identified event that upsets the normal operations of the system and may require a response to avoid undesirable outcomes (adapted from IAEA, 2002).

*Inspection.* Activities such as measuring, examining, testing, gauging one or more characteristics of a product or service, and comparing these with specified requirements to determine conformity.

*Localized individual risk (LIRA).* The probability that an average unprotected person, permanently present at a specified location, is killed in a period of one year due to an accident at a hazardous installation (e.g., see Jonkman et al., 2003).

*Maintenance.* The combinations of all technical and corresponding administrative actions, including supervision actions, intended to retain an entity in, or restore it to, a state in which it can perform its required function (IEC 60050-191, 1990).

*Major accident event (MAE).* An event connected with a facility, including a natural event, having the potential to cause multiple fatalities of persons at or near the facility (http://www.nopsa.gov.au).

*Major hazards.* These are hazardous activities with a potential for causing major accidents (i.e., ones involving several fatalities at once, severe damage to material assets, or major pollution).

*Mean time to failure (MTTF).* Let $T$ denote the time to failure of an item, with probability density $f(t)$ and survivor function $R(t)$. The mean time to failure is the mean (expected) value of $T$, which is given by

$$\text{MTTF} = \int_0^\infty t \cdot f(t) \, dt = \int_0^\infty R(t) \, dt$$

*Mean time to repair (MTTR).* Let $D$ denote the downtime (or repair time) after a failure of an item. Let $f_D(d)$ denote the probability density of $D$, and let $F_D(d)$ denote the distribution function of $D$. The mean time to repair is the mean (expected) value of $D$, which is given by

$$\text{MTTR} = \int_0^\infty t \cdot f_D(t) \, dt = \int_0^\infty (1 - F_D(t)) \, dt$$

MTTR is sometimes called the *mean downtime (MDT)* of the item. In some situations MTTR is used to denote the mean *active* repair time instead of the mean downtime of the item.

*Mechanical integrity.* The process of ensuring that process equipment is fabricated from the proper materials of construction and is installed, maintained, and replaced properly to prevent failures and accidental releases (EPA 40 CFR Part 68).

*Method.* A technique or tool. A regular, disciplined, systematic set of procedures used according to an underlying, detailed, logically ordered plan.

*Minimal cut set.* A cut set is said to be minimal if the set cannot be reduced without losing its status as a cut set.

*Mitigation.* Action to reduce the severity, seriousness, or painfulness of something.

Limitation of the undesirable effects of a particular event (ISO 17776, 2002).

Measures of minimizing the consequences of an accident after it has started. It is sometimes used loosely to refer to all types of risk reduction (HSE, 2001a).

Specific activities, technologies, or equipment designed or deployed to capture or control substances upon loss of containment to minimize exposure of the public or the environment. Passive mitigation means equipment, devices, or technologies that function without human, mechanical, or other energy input. Active mitigation means equipment, devices, or technologies that need human, mechanical, or other energy input to function (EPA 40 CFR Part 68).

*Monte Carlo analysis.* A computer-based method that uses statistical sampling techniques to obtain a probabilistic approximation to the solution of a mathematical equation or model.

*Monte Carlo simulation.* The process of approximating the output of a model by repetitive random application of a model's algorithm.

*Near accident.* An unplanned and unforeseen event that could reasonably have been expected to result in harm to one or more assets, but actually did not.

*Negligible risk.* This is risk that are so small that there is no cause for concern about them, and no reason to take action to reduce them (HSE, 2001a).

*Operating state.* The state when an entity is performing a required function (IEC 60050-191, 1990).

*Organizational accident.* A comparatively rare, but often catastrophic, event that occurs within complex modern technologies (e.g., nuclear power plants, commercial aviation, the petrochemical industry, chemical process plants, marine and rail transport, banks, and stadiums), and have multiple causes involving many people operating at different levels of their respective companies. Organizational accidents will often have devastating effects on uninvolved populations, assets, and the environment (Reason, 1997).

*OR-gate.* A Boolean logic element used to develop fault trees. The output event related to this gate exists if at least one of the input events exists.

*Parameter.* A constant characterizing a probability density function or a cumulative distribution function of a random variable.

*Passive barrier.* A barrier that is integrated into the design of the workplace and does not require any human actions, energy sources, or information sources to perform its function.

*Percentile.* Let $X$ be a random variable with distribution function $F(x)$. The upper $100\epsilon\%$ percentile $x_\epsilon$ of the distribution $F(x)$ is defined such that

$$\Pr(X > x_\epsilon) = \epsilon$$

*Performance-shaping factors (PSF).* A set of influences on the performance of an operating crew resulting from the human-related characteristics of the plant, the crew, and the individual operators. Example characteristics include procedures, training, and human-factors aspects of the displays and control facilities of the plant (NUREG-1880, 2007).

*Posterior probability.* An individual's belief in the occurrence of the event $E$ based on her prior belief *and* some additional evidence $D_1$.

*Potential equivalent fatality (PEF).* A convention for aggregating harm to people by regarding major and minor injuries as being equivalent to a certain fraction of a fatality (RSSB, 2007).

*Potential loss of life (PLL).* PLL is the predicted long-term average number of fatalities in a system or an activity (usually per year).

PLL is the expected number of fatalities within a specified population (or, within a specified area $A$) per annum.

Alternative term: Expected number of fatalities per year.

*Precautionary principle.* Where there are threats of serious or irreversible damage, lack of full scientific certainty should not be used as a reason for postponing cost-effective measures to prevent environmental degradation (UN, 1992).

*Preventive maintenance.* The maintenance carried out at predetermined intervals or corresponding to prescribed criteria and intended to reduce the probability of failure or the performance degradation of an item.

*Prior probability.* An individual's belief in the occurrence of an event $E$ prior to any additional collection of evidence related to $E$.

*Probability.* Probability is a real number in the scale 0 to 1 attached to a random event. It can be related to a long-run relative frequency of occurrence or to a degree of belief that an event will occur. For a high degree of belief, the probability is near 1.

*Probability density.* Consider a random variable $X$. The probability density function $f_X(x)$ of $X$ is

$$f_X(x) = \frac{dF_X(x)}{dx} = \lim_{\Delta x \to \infty} \frac{\Pr(x < X \le x + \Delta x)}{\Delta x}$$

where $F_X(x)$ denotes the distribution function of $X$.

*Qualitative risk analysis.* A risk analysis in which probabilities and consequences are determined purely qualitatively.

*Quality.* The totality of features and characteristics of a product or service that bear on its ability to satisfy stated or implied needs.

*Quanitative risk analysis.* A risk analysis that provides numerical estimates for probabilities and/or consequences—sometimes along with associated uncertainties.

*Reasonably practicable.* This means that the cost (in terms of money, time, or trouble) involved in implementing a measure in not grossly disproportionate to the benefit gained (HSE, 2001a).

*Redundancy.* In an entity, the existence of more than one means for performing a required function (IEC 60050-191, 1990).

Existence of means, in addition to the means that would be sufficient for a functional unit to perform a required function or for data to represent information (IEC 61508, 2010).

*Reference accident scenario.* An accident scenario that is considered to be representative for a set of accident scenarios that are identified in a risk analysis, where the scenarios in the set are considered to be likely to occur.

*Reliability.* The ability of an item to perform a required function, under given environmental and operational conditions and for a stated period of time.

*Repair.* The part of corrective maintenance in which manual actions are performed on the entity (IEC 60050-191, 1990).

*Required function.* A function, or a combination of functions, of an entity, which is considered necessary to provide a given service (IEC 60050-191, 1990).

*Residual risk.* The risk that remains after engineering, administrative, and work practice controls have been implemented (SEMATECH, 1999).

*Resilience.* The ability to accommodate change without catastrophic failure, or the capacity to absorb shocks gracefully.

*Risk.* The combined answer to three questions: (1) What can go wrong? (2) What is the likelihood of that happening? and (3) What are the consequences?

The chance of something happening that will have an impact upon objectives. It is measured in terms of consequences and likelihood (AS/NZS 4360, 1995).

*Risk acceptance.* An informed decision to accept the consequences and the likelihood of a particular risk (AS/NZS 4360).

The systematic process by which relevant stakeholders agree that risk may be accepted (DEF-STAN 00-56, 2007).

*Risk analysis.* Systematic use of available information to identify hazards and to estimate the risk to individuals, property, and the environment (IEC 60300-3-9, 1995).

*Risk assessment.* Overall process of risk analysis and risk evaluation (IEC 60300-3-9, 1995).

*Risk avoidance.* An informed decision not to become involved in a risk situation (AS/NZS 4360, 1995).

*Risk-based decision-making.* A process that uses quantification of risks, costs, and benefits to evaluate and compare decision options competing for limited resources (adapted from US DOE, 1998).

*Risk estimation.* The systematic use of available information to estimate risk (DEF-STAN 00-56, 2007).

*Risk evaluation.* Process in which judgments are made on the tolerability of the risk on the basis of a risk analysis and taking into account factors such as socio-economic and environmental aspects (IEC 60300-3-9, 1995).

Process used to determine risk management priorities by comparing the level of risk against predetermined standards, target risk levels, or other criteria (AS/NZS 4360, 1995).

*Risk indicator.* A parameter that is estimated based on risk analysis models and by using generic and other available data. A risk indicator presents our knowledge about a specific aspect of the risk of a *future* activity or a *future* system operation.

*Risk-influencing factor.* A relatively stable condition that influences the risk.

*Risk-informed decision-making.* An approach to decision-making in which insights from quantitative risk analyses are considered together with other insights and factors.

An approach to decision-making representing a philosophy whereby risk insights are considered together with other factors to establish requirements that better focus the attention on design and operational issues commensurate with their importance to health and safety (adapted from NUREG-1855, 2009).

*Risk management.* A continuous management process with the objective to identify, analyze, and assess potential hazards in a system or related to an activity, and to identify and introduce risk control measures to eliminate or reduce potential harms to people, the environment, or other assets.

*Risk perception.* The subjective judgment about the characteristics and severity of risk.

*Risk reduction.* A selective application of appropriate techniques and management principles to reduce either the likelihood of an occurrence or its consequences, or both (AS/NZS 4360, 1995).

*Root cause.* The root cause of a specified failure is the most basic cause that, if corrected, would prevent recurrence of this and similar failures.

*Safety.* A state where the risk has been reduced to a level that is as low as reasonably practicable (ALARP) and where the remaining risk is generally accepted.

Freedom from those conditions that can cause death, injury, occupational illness, or damage to or loss of equipment or property (MIL-STD-882D, 2000).

The expectation that a system does not, under defined conditions, lead to a state in which human life is endangered (DEF-STAN 00-56, 2007).

Absence of unacceptable levels of risk to life, limb, and health (from unwillful acts).

State in which the possibility of harm to persons or of property damage is reduced to, and maintained at or below, an acceptable level through a continuing process of hazard identification and safety risk management (ICAO, 2009).

*Safety case.*   A document demonstrating the adequacy of safety management arrangements for a system or an installation.

A documented body of evidence that provides a demonstrable and valid argument that a system is adequately safe for a given application and environment over its lifetime (UK CAA, 2006).

A formal presentation of evidence, arguments, and assumptions aimed at providing assurance that a system, product, or other change to a railway has met its safety requirements and that the safety requirements are adequate (RSSB, 2007).

*Safety critical.*   A term applied to any condition, event, operation, process, or item whose proper recognition, control, performance, or tolerance is essential to safe system operation and support (e.g., safety critical function, safety critical path, or safety critical component) (MIL-STD-882D, 2000).

*Safety culture.*   The product of individual and group values, attitudes, competencies, and patterns of behavior that determine commitment to, and the style and proficiency of, an organization's health and safety management. Organizations with a positive safety culture are characterized by communications founded on mutual trust, by shared perceptions of the importance of safety, and by confidence in the efficacy of preventive measures (HSE, 2005b).

*Safety instrumented function (SIF).*   A barrier function that is implemented by a SIS and that is intended to achieve or maintain a safe state for the EUC with respect to a specific deviation (process demand). A SIS may consist of one or more SIFs.

*Safety integrity.*   Probability of a safety-related system performing the required safety functions satisfactorily under all the stated conditions within a specified period of time (IEC 61508, 2010).

*Safety integrity level (SIL).*   Discrete level (one out of a possible four) for specifying the safety integrity requirement of the safety functions to be allocated to the E/E/PE safety-related systems, where safety integrity level 4 has the highest level of safety integrity and safety integrity level 1 has the lowest (IEC 61508, 2010, Part 4).

*Safety performance.* An account of all accidents that occurred in a specified (past) time period, together with observed frequencies and consequences for each type of accident.

*Safety performance indicator.* A parameter that is estimated based on experience data from a specific installation or an activity. A safety performance indicator therefore tells us what has happened.

*Scenario.* A sequence of events, such as an account or synopsis of a projected course of action or events (NASA, 2008).

An outline or model of an expected or assumed future sequence of events.

*Security.* Dependability with respect to the prevention of unauthorized access and/or handling of information.

Absence of risk to life, health, property, and environment from willful acts of individual(s).

*Sensitivity.* The variation in the output of a mathematical model with respect to changes in the values of the inputs to the model.

*Severity.* Seriousness of the consequences of an event expressed either as a financial value or as a category.

The consequences of a failure mode. Severity considers the worst potential consequence of a failure, determined by the degree of injury, property damage, or system damage that could ultimately occur.

*Single failure point.* The failure of an item that would result in failure of the system and is not compensated for by redundancy or alternative operational procedure.

*Societal risk.* The relationship between frequency and the number of people suffering from a specified level of harm in a given population from the realization of specific hazards (IChemE, 1992).

This is another term for group risk.

*Stakeholder.* People and organizations who may affect, be affected by, or perceive themselves to be affected by, a decision or an activity ISO 31000.

*State variable.* A variable $X(t)$ associated with an item such that:

$$X(t) = \begin{cases} 1 & \text{if the item is functioning at time } t \\ 0 & \text{if the item is in a failed state at time } t \end{cases}$$

*State vector.* A vector $X(t) = (X_1(t), X_2(t), \ldots, X_n(t))$ of the state variables of the $n$ components comprising the system.

*Structure function.* A variable $\phi(X(t))$ associated with a system (with state vector $X(t)$) such that:

$$\phi(X(t)) = \begin{cases} 1 & \text{if the system is functioning at time } t \\ 0 & \text{if the system is in a failed state at time } t \end{cases}$$

*Subjective probability.* A numerical value in the interval $[0, 1]$ representing an individual's *degree of belief* about whether or not an event will occur.

*Survivor function.* Let $T$ denote the time to failure of an item. The survivor function $R(t)$ of the item is

$$R(t) = \Pr(T > t) \quad \text{for } t \geq 0$$

$R(t)$ is sometimes called the *reliability function* or the *survival probability at time t* of the item.

*System.* Composite entity, at any level of complexity, of personnel, procedures, materials, tools, equipment, facilities, and software. The elements of this composite entity are used together in the intended operational or support environment to perform a given task to achieve a specific objective (IEC 60300-3-9, 1995).

Set of elements that interact according to a design, where an element of a system can be another system, called a *subsystem*, which may be a controlling system or a controlled system and may include hardware, software, and human interaction (IEC 61508, 2010).

The combination of elements that function together to produce the capability to meet a need. The elements include all hardware, software, equipment, facilities, personnel, processes, and procedures needed for this purpose (NASA, 2007).

*Systematic failure.* Failure related in a deterministic way to a certain cause, which can only be eliminated by a modification of the design or of the manufacturing process, operational procedures, documentation, or other factors (IEC 61508, 2010).

*System safety.* The effort to make things as safe as possible by systematic use of engineering and management tools to identify, analyze, and control hazards.

*Task.* Collection of actions carried out by operators to achieve an objective or a goal state.

*Task analysis.* Detailed examination of the observable activities associated with the execution of a required task or piece of work.

*Test interval.* The elapsed time between the initiation of identical tests on the same sensor, channel, etc.

*Threat.* Anything that might exploit a vulnerability.

A hazard that is linked to a *deliberate* and *evil* action.

*Threat agent.* A person or a thing, which acts, or has the power to act, to cause, carry, transmit, or support a threat.

A person who exploits a threat and commits an action that may lead to a hazardous event. The threat agent does not need to be a single person, but can be a group of people, an organization, and even a nation. Threat agents may be internal (e.g., own employees) or external people.

*Tolerable risk.* Risk that is accepted in a given context based on the current values of society (ISO 17776, 2002).

*Trigger.* A condition or event that is required for a hazard to give rise to an accident (RSSB, 2007).

An event or condition that is required for a hazard to give rise to an accident.

*Uncertainty.* An imperfect state of knowledge or a variability resulting from a variety of factors, including, but not limited to, lack of knowledge, applicability of information, physical variation, randomness or stochastic behavior, indeterminacy, judgment, and approximation (NASA, 2008).

*Vulnerability.* The lacking ability of an object to resist the impacts of an unwanted event and to restore to its original state or function following the event.

A *weakness* of an asset or group of assets that can be exploited by one or more threat agents: for example, to gain access to the asset and subsequent destruction, modification, theft, and so on, of the asset or parts of the asset.

*Worst-case accident scenario.* The accident scenario with the highest consequence that is physically possible regardless of likelihood (Kim et al., 2006).

*Worst credible accident scenario.* The highest-consequence accident scenario identified that is considered plausible or reasonably believable (Kim et al., 2006).

# Bibliography

Abrahamsson, M. (2002). *Uncertainty in Quantitative Risk Analysis: Characterisation and Methods of Treatment*. PhD thesis, Department of Fire Safety Engineering, Lund University, Lund, Sweden.

Ale, B. J. M. (2005). Tolerable or acceptable: A comparison of risk regulation in the United Kingdom and in the Netherlands. *Risk Analysis*, 25:231–241.

Amendola, A., Contini, S., and Ziomas, I. (1992). Uncertainties in chemical risk assessment: Results of a European benchmark exercise. *Journal of Hazardous Materials*, 29:347–363.

Andersen, H. R. (1999). An introduction to binary decision diagrams. Lecture notes, IT University of Copenhagen, Copenhagen, Denmark.

Anderson, E. L. and Hattis, D. (1999). Uncertainty and variability. *Risk Analysis*, 19:47–49.

Andrews, J. D. and Dunnett, S. J. (2002). Event-tree analysis using binary decision diagrams. *IEEE Transactions on Reliability*, 49(2):230–238.

Andrews, J. D. and Moss, T. (2002). *Reliability and Risk Assessment*. Professional Engineering Publ., London.

Andrews, J. D. and Ridley, L. M. (2002). Application of the cause-consequence diagram method to static systems. *Reliability Engineering and System Safety*, 75:47–58.

Apostolakis, G. and Moieni, P. (1987). The foundations of models of dependence in probabilistic safety assessment. *Reliability Engineering*, 18(3):177–195.

ARAMIS (2004). Accidental risk assessment methodology for industries in the context of the Seveso II directive. Technical report EVSG1-CT-2001-00036, Fifth Framework Programme of the European Community, Energy, Environment and Sustainable Development, http://aramis.jrc.it.

Arendt, J. S. (1990). Using quantitative risk assessment in the chemical process industry. *Reliability Engineering and System Safety*, 29:133–149.

Ashenfelter, O. (2005). Measuring value of a statistical life: Problems and prospects. Working paper 505, Princeton University, Princeton, NJ.

AS/NZS 4360 (1995). *Risk Management*. Standards Association of Australia, Sydney, Australia.

ATSB (2006). International fatality rates: A comparison of Australian civil aviation fatality rates with international data. B2006/0002, Australian Transport Safety Bureau, Canberra, Australia.

Attwood, D., Khan, F., and Veitch, B. (2006). Occupational accident models: Where have we been and where are we going? *Journal of Loss Prevention in the Process Industries*, 19(6):664–682.

AusAID (2005). Managing risk. AUSGuideline 6.3, Australian Agency for International Development, Canberra, Australia.

Aven, T. (2003). *Foundations of Risk Analysis*. Wiley, Chichester, UK.

Aven, T. (2007). On the ethical justification for the use of risk acceptance criteria. *Risk Analysis*, 27:303–312.

Aven, T. (2008). *Risk Analysis: Assessing Uncertainties Beyond Expected Values and Probabilities*. Wiley, Chichester, UK.

Aven, T. and Nøkland, T. E. (2010). On the use of uncertainty importance measures in reliability and risk analysis. *Reliability Engineering and System Safety*, 95:127–133.

Aven, T. and Renn, O. (2009a). On risk defined as an event where the outcome is uncertain. *Journal of Risk Research*, 12(1):1–11.

Aven, T. and Renn, O. (2009b). The role of quantitative risk assessments for characterizing risk and uncertainty and delineating appropriate risk management options, with special emphasis on terrorism risk. *Risk Analysis*, 29(4):587–600.

Aven, T., Sklet, S., and Vinnem, J. E. (2006). Barrier and operational risk analysis of hydrocarbon releases (BORA-Release). Part I. Method description. *Journal of Hazardous Materials*, 137:681–691.

Aven, T. and Vinnem, J. E. (2005). On the use of risk acceptance criteria in the offshore oil and gas industry. *Reliability Engineering and System Safety*, 90:15–24.

Ayyub, B. M. (2001). *Elicitation of Expert Opinions for Uncertainty and Risks*. CRC Press, Boca Raton, FL.

Ball, D. J. and Floyd, P. J. (1998). Societal risks. Technical report, Health and Safety Executive, London.

Basra, G. and Kirwan, B. (1998). Collection of offshore human error probability data. *Reliability Engineering and System Safety*, 61:77–93.

Bayes, T. (1763). An essay towards solving a problem in the doctrine of chances. *Philosophical Transactions of the Royal Society*, 53:370–418.

Beckman, L. V. (1995). Match redundant system architectures with safety requirements. *Chemical Engineering Progress*, pages 54–61.

Bedford, T. and Cooke, R. M. (2001). *Probabilistic Risk Analysis: Foundations and Methods*. Cambridge University Press, Cambridge, UK.

Bergman, B. and Klefsjö, B. (1994). *Quality: From Customer Needs to Customer Satisfaction*. McGraw-Hill, London.

Bernstein, P. L. (1996). *Against the Gods: The Remarkable Story of Risk*. Wiley, New York.

Bier, V. M. (1999). Challenges to the acceptance of probabilistic risk analysis. *Risk Analysis*, 19:703–710.

Bird, F. E. and Germain, G. L. (1986). *Practical Loss Control Leadership*. International Loss Control Institute, Loganville, GA.

Birnbaum, Z. W. (1969). On the importance of different components in a multicomponentsystem. In Krishnaiah, P. R., editor, *Multivariate Analysis*, pages 581–592. Academic Press, San Diego.

Blanchard, B. S. and Fabrycky, W. J. (1998). *Systems Engineering and Analysis*. Prentice Hall, Upper Saddle River, NJ, 3rd edition.

Borysiewicz, M. J., Borysiewicz, M. A., Garanty, I., and Kozubal, A. (2007). Quantitative risk assessment (QRA). Technical report, CoE MANHAZ, Institute of Atomic Energy, Otwock-Swierk, Poland.

Bottelberghs, P. H. (2000). Risk analysis and safety policy developments in the Netherlands. *Journal of Hazardous Materials*, 71:59–84.

BP (2006). Guidance on practice for layer of protection analysis (LOPA). Technical report GP 48-03, BP Group, London.

Brissaud, F., Barros, A., Bérenguer, C., and Charpentier, D. (2011). Reliability analysis for new technology-based transmitters. *Reliability Engineering and System Safety*, 96(2):299–313.

Brissaud, F., Charpentier, D., Fouladirad, M., Barros, A., and Bérenguer, C. (2010). Failure rate evaluation with influencing factors. *Journal of Loss Prevention in the Process Industries*, 23(2):187–193.

Briš, R. and Kochaníčková (2006). Stochastic Petri net approach to production availability evaluation of special test case. In *ESREL Proceedings*.

Cameron, R. F. and Willers, A. (2001). Use of risk assessment in the nuclear industry with specific reference to the Australian situation. *Reliability Engineering and System Safety*, 74:275–282.

Cardwell, G. (2008). The application of the four essentials bow tie diagram to enhance business success. *Total Quality Management*, 19:37–45.

CASU (2002). Making it happen: A guide to risk managers on how to populate a risk register. Technical report, The Controls Assurance Support Unit, University of Keele, Staffordshire, UK.

CCOHS (2009). Job safety analysis made simple. Technical report, Canadian Centre for Occupational Health and Safety, http://www.ccohs.ca/oshanswers.

CCPS (1993). *Guidelines for Safety Automation of Chemical Processes*. Center for Chemical Process Safety, American Institute of Chemical Engineers, New York.

CCPS (1994). *Guidelines for Preventing Human Error in Process Safety*. Center for Chemical Process Safety, American Institute of Chemical Engineers, New York.

CCPS (1998). *Guidelines for Improving Plant Reliability Through Data Collection and Analysis*. Center for Chemical Process Safety, American Institute of Chemical Engineers, New York.

CCPS (2000). *Guidelines for Chemical Process Quantitative Risk Analysis*. Center for Chemical Process Safety, American Institute for Chemical Engineers, New York, 2nd edition.

CCPS (2001). *Layer of Protection Analysis: Simplified Process Risk Assessment*. Center for Chemical Process Safety, American Institute of Chemical Engineers, New York.

CCPS (2007). *Guidelines for Safe and Reliable Instrumented Protective Systems*. Wiley and Center for Chemical Process Safety, American Institute of Chemical Engineers, Hoboken, NJ.

CCPS (2008). *Guidelines for Hazard Evaluation Procedures.* Wiley and Center for Chemical Process Safety, American Institute of Chemical Engineers, Hoboken, NJ, 3rd edition.

Charniak, E. (1991). Bayesian networks without tears. *AI Magazine*, 12(4):51–63.

Childs, J. A. and Mosleh, A. (1999). A modified FMEA tool for use in identifying and assessing common cause failure risk in industry. In *Proceedings Annual Reliability and Maintainability Symposium.*

Clemens, P. L. (2002). Energy flow/barrier analysis. Slide presentation.

CNCS (2009). Guidance on the use of deterministic and probabilistic criteria in decision-making for class I nuclear facilities. Draft RD-152, Canadian Nuclear Safety Commission, Ottawa, Canada.

Cockshott, J. E. (2005). Probability bow-ties: A transparent risk management tool. *Trans IChemE. Part B: Process Safety and Environmental Protection*, 83(B4):307–316.

Comer, P. J., Fitt, J. S., and Østebø, R. (1986). A driller's HAZOP method. SPE paper 15876, Society of Petroleum Engineers, European Petroleum Conference, London.

Cooke, R. M. (1991). *Experts in Uncertainty: Opinion and Subjective Probability in Science.* Oxford University Press, New York.

Cooper, S. E., Lofgren, E. V., Samanta, P. K., and Wong, S.-M. (1993). Dependent failure analysis of NPP data bases. *Nuclear Engineering and Design*, 142:137–153.

Crawley, F., Preston, M., and Tyler, B. (2000). *HAZOP: Guide to Best Practice.* Institution of Chemical Engineers, Rugby, UK.

David, R. and Alla, H. (2005). *Discrete, Continuous, and Hybrid Petri Nets.* Springer, Berlin.

de Finetti, B. (1974). *Theory of Probability*, volume 1 and 2. Wiley, New York.

de Jong, H. H. (2007). Guidelines for the identification of hazards. How to make unimaginable hazards imaginable? NLR-CR-2004-094, EUROCONTROL, Brussels.

de Rocquigny, E., Devictor, N., and Tarantola, S. (2008). *Uncertainty in Industrial Practice: A Guide to Quantitative Uncertainty Management.* Wiley, Chichester, UK.

DEF-STAN 00-250 (2008). Human factors for designers of systems. Part 4: HFI methods, tools and techniques. Standard, UK Ministry of Defence, London.

DEF-STAN 00-56 (2007). Safety management requirements for defence systems. Standard, UK Ministry of Defence, London.

Der Kiureghian, A. and Ditlevsen, O. (2009). Aleatory or epistemic? Does it matter? *Structural Safety*, 31(2):105–112.

Dezfuli, H., Kelly, D., Smith, C., Vedros, K., and Galyean, W. (2009). Bayesian inference for NASA probabilistic risk and reliability analysis. NASA/SP-2009-569, U.S. National Aeronautics and Space Administration, Washington, DC.

Dezfuli, H., Stamatelatos, M., Maggio, G., Everett, C., and Youngblood, R. (2010). NASA risk-informed decision making handbook. Handbook NASA/SP-2010-576, U.S. National Aeronautics and Space Administration, Washington, DC.

Douglas, M. and Wildavsky, A. A. (1983). *Risk and Culture: An Essay on the Selection of Technological and Environmental Dangers*. University of California Press, London.

Dudewicz, E. J. and Mishra, S. A. (1988). *Modern Mathematical Statistics*. Wiley, New York.

Duijm, N. J. (2009). Safety-barrier diagrams as a safety management tool. *Reliability Engineering and System Safety*, 94:332–341.

Duijm, N. J. and Markert, F. (2009). Safety-barrier diagrams as a tool for modelling safety of hydrogen applications. *International Journal of Hydrogen Energy*, 34:5862–5868.

Elms, D. G. (1992). Risk assessment. In Blockley, D., editor, *Engineering Safety*, chapter 2, pages 28–46. McGraw-Hill, London.

Embrey, D. E. (1986). SHERPA: A systematic human error reduction and prediction approach. In *International Meeting on Advances in Nuclear Power Systems*, Knoxville, TN.

EN 50126 (1999). *Railway Applications: The Specification and Demonstration of Reliability, Availability, Maintainability and Safety (RAMS)*. European Norm, Brussels.

Ericson, C. A. (2005). *Hazard Analysis Techniques for System Safety*. Wiley, Hoboken, NJ.

ESReDA (1999). Handbook on quality of reliability data. Working group report , European Reliability Data Association, Det Norske Veritas, Høvik, Norway.

EU (1996). *Council Directive 96/82/EC of 9 December 1996 on the Control of Major Accident Hazards Involving Dangerous substances (Seveso II Directive)*. Official Journal of the European Communities, L 10 (1997).

EU (2003). *Council Directive 2003/42/EC of 13 June 2003 on Occurrence Reporting in Civil Aviation.* Official Journal of the European Communities L167/23 (2003).

EU (2004). *Council Directive 2004/49/EC of 29 April 2004 on the Licencing of Railway Undertakings (Railway Safety Directive).* Official Journal of the European Union, L 220/16 (2004).

EU-JRC (2006). Land use planning guidelines in the context of article 12 of the Seveso II directive 96/82/EC as amended by directive 105/2003/EC. Technical report, European Commission, Joint Research Centre, Ispra, Italy.

Evans, A. W. and Verlander, N. Q. (1997). What is wrong with criterion FN-lines for judging the tolerability of risk? *Risk Analysis*, 17:157–168.

Evans, M. G. K., Parry, G. W., and Wreathall, J. (1984). On the treatment of common-cause failures in system analysis. *Reliability Engineering*, 9:107–115.

Farmer, F. (1967). Siting criteria: A new approach. *Atom*, 128:152–170.

Fischhoff, B., Lichtenstein, S., and Keeney, R. L. (1981). *Acceptable Risk.* Cambridge University Press, Cambridge, UK.

Fleming, K. N. (1975). A reliability model for common mode failures in redundant safety systems. Technical Report GA-A13284, General Atomic Company, San Diego, CA.

Fleming, K. N., Mosleh, A., and Deremer, R. K. (1986). A systematic procedure for the incorporation of common cause events into risk and reliability models. *Nuclear Engineering and Design*, 93:245–279.

Foster, H. D. (1993). Resilience theory and system evaluation. In Wise, J. A., Hopkin, V. D., and Stager, P., editors, *Verification and Validation of Complex Systems: Human Factors Issues*, pages 35–60. Springer, Berlin.

Franks, A. (2003). Lines of defence/layers of protection analysis in the COMAH context. HSE-report , Amey VECTRA, Warrington, UK.

Frederickson, A. A. (2002). The layer of protection analysis (LOPA) method. Technical report, Safety User Group, http://www.safetyusergroup.com.

Garrick, B. J. (2008). *Quantifying and Controlling Catastrophic Risks.* Academic Press, San Diego, CA.

Gertman, D. I. and Blackman, H. S. (1994). *Human Reliability & Safety Analysis Data Handbook.* Wiley, New York.

Gibson, J. J. (1961). The contribution of experimental psychology to the formulation of the problem of safety. In *Behavioral Approaches to Accident Research.* Association for the Aid of Crippled Children, New York.

Groeneweg, J. (2002). *Controlling the Controllable: Preventing Business Upsets.* Global Safety Group Publications, Leiden, The Netherlands, 5th edition.

Grøtan, T. O., Størseth, F., and Albrechtsen, E. (2011). Scientific foundations of addressing risk in complex and dynamic environments. *Reliability Engineering and System Safety*, 96:706–712.

Haas, P. J. (2002). *Stochastic Petri Nets.* Springer, New York.

Haddon, W. (1970). On the escape of tigers: An ecologic note. *American Journal of Public Health and the Nation's Health*, 8(12):2229–2234.

Haddon, W. (1980). Advances in the epidemiology of injuries as a basis for public policy. *Landmarks in American Epidemiology*, 95(5):411–421.

Hale, A. R., Heming, B. H. J., Smit, K., Rodenburg, F. G. T., and van Leeuwen, N. D. (1998). Evaluating safety in the management of maintenance activities in the chemical process industry. *Safety Science*, 28:21–44.

Hambly, E. C. (1992). Preventing disasters. Royal Institution Discourse, London.

Hammer, W. (1993). *Product Safety Management and Engineering.* American Society for Safety Engineers, Des Plaines, IL, 2nd edition.

Hammonds, J. S., Hoffman, F. O., and Bartell, S. M. (1994). An introductory guide to uncertainty analysis in environmental and health risk assessment. Technical Report ES/ER/TM-35/R1, Oak Ridge National Laboratory, Oak Ridge, TN.

Hansson, S. O. (1996). Decision-making under great uncertainty. *Philosophy of the Social Sciences*, 26:369–386.

Hansson, S. O. (2010). Risk: Objective or subjective, facts or values. *Journal of Risk Research*, 13(2):231–238.

Harris, D., Stanton, N. A., Marshall, A., Young, M. S., Demagalski, J., and Salmon, P. (2005). Using SHERPA to predict designed-induced error on the flight deck. *Aerospace Science and Technology*, 9(6):525–532.

Hauge, S., Lundteigen, M. A., Hokstad, P., and Håbrekke, S. (2010). *Reliability Prediction Method for Safety Instrumented Systems.* SINTEF, Trondheim, Norway.

Hauge, S., Onshus, T., Øien, K., Grøtan, T. O., Holmstrøm, S., and Lundteigen, M. A. (2006). Independence of safety systems on offshore oil and gas installations – status and challenges (in Norwegian). STF50 A06011, SINTEF, Trondheim, Norway.

Haugen, S., Seljelid, J., Sklet, S., Vinnem, J. E., and Aven, T. (2007). Operational risk analysis: Total analysis of physical and non-physical barriers. Research report 200254-07, Preventor, Bryne, Norway.

Heinrich, H. W. (1931). *Industrial Accident Prevention: A Scientific Approach.* McGraw-Hill, New York.

Hendershot, D. C. (2009). A history of process safety and loss prevention in the American Institute of Chemical Engineers. *Process Safety Progress*, 28(2):105–113.

Hendrick, K. and Benner, L. (1987). *Investigating Accidents with STEP.* Marcel Dekker, New York.

Herrera, I. A., Håbrekke, S., Kråkenes, T., Hokstad, P., and Forseth, U. (2010). Helicopter safety study (hss-3). Research report SINTEF A15753, SINTEF, Trondheim, Norway.

Hirst, I. L. (1998). Risk assessment: A note on F-n curves, expected numbers of fatlities, and weighted indicators of risk. *Journal of Hazardous Materials*, 57:169–175.

Hokstad, P. and Corneliussen, K. (2004). Loss of safey assessment and the IEC 61508 standard. *Reliability Engineering and System Safety*, 83:111–120.

Hokstad, P., Jersin, E., and Sten, T. (2001). A risk influence model applied to north sea helicopter transport. *Reliability Engineering and System Safety*, 74:311–322.

Hokstad, P. and Rausand, M. (2008). Common cause failure modeling: Status and trends. In Misra, K. B., editor, *Handbook of Performability Engineering*, chapter 39, pages 621–640. Springer, London.

Holand, P. (1996). *Offshore Blowouts: Causes and Trends.* PhD thesis, Department of Production and Quality Engineering, Norwegian Institute of Technology, Trondheim, Norway.

Hollnagel, E. (1998). *Cognitive Reliability and Error Analysis Method: CREAM.* Elsevier, Oxford.

Hollnagel, E. (2004). *Barriers and Accident Prevention.* Aldershot, Ashgate, UK.

Hollnagel, E. (2005). Human reliability assessment in context. *Nuclear Engineering and Technology*, 37(2):159–166.

Hollnagel, E., Woods, D. D., and Leveson, N. (2006). *Resilience Engineering: Concepts and Precepts.* Ashgate, Aldershot, UK.

Holmgren, Å. and Thedén, T. (2009). Risk analysis. In Grimvall, G., Holmgren, Å., Jacobsson, P., and Thedén, T., editors, *Risks in Technological Systems*, chapter 13. Springer, London.

HSE (1989). *Quantified Risk Assessment: Its Input to Decision Making.* HMSO, London.

HSE (1992). *The Tolerability of Risk from Nuclear Power Stations.* HMSO, London.

HSE (1999). The implementation of CORE-DATA, a computerized human error probability database. Research report 245/1999, Health and Safety Executive, London.

HSE (2001a). *Marine Risk Assessment.* HMSO, London.

HSE (2001b). *Reducing risks, protecting people; HSE's decision-making process.* HMSO, Norwich.

HSE (2003a). Good practice and pitfalls in risk assessment. Research report RR151, Health and Safety Executive, London.

HSE (2003b). *Transport Fatal Accidents and FN-Curves (1967–2001).* HMSO, London.

HSE (2005a). Human factors in the management of major accident hazards. Inspector toolkit , Health and Safety Executive, London.

HSE (2005b). A review of safety culture and safety climate literature for the development of the safety culture inspection toolkit. Research report 367, Health and Safety Executive, London.

HSE (2006). Five steps to risk assessment. Booklet INDG163, Health and Safety Executive, London.

HSE (2008). Optimising hazard management by workforce engagement and supervision. Research report RR637, Health and Safety Executive, London.

HSE (2009). Review of human reliability assessment methods. Research report RR679, Health and Safety Executive, London.

Huang, Y.-H. (2007). *Having a New Pair of Glasses: Applying Systematic Accident Models on Road Safety.* PhD thesis, Linköping University, Linköping, Sweden.

Humphreys, R. A. (1987). Assigning a numerical value to the beta factor common cause evaluation. In *Proceedings: Reliability'87,* volume 2C.

IAEA (1994a). Convention on nuclear safety. INFCIRC/449, International Atomic Energy Agency, Vienna, Austria.

IAEA (1994b). Safety assessment of research reactors and preparation of the safety analysis report. Safety Series 35-G1, International Atomic Energy Agency, Vienna, Austria.

IAEA (2001). Applications of probabilistic safety assessment (PSA) for nuclear power plants. Technical Report IAEA-TECDOC-1200, International Atomic Energy Agency, Vienna, Austria.

IAEA (2002). Procedures for conducting probabilistic safety assessment for non-reactor nuclear facilities. Technical report IAEA-TECDOC-1267, International Atomic Energy Agency, Vienna, Austria.

IAEA (2007). IAEA safety glossary: Terminology used in nuclear safety and radiation protection. Technical report, International Atomic Energy Agency, Vienna, Austria.

ICAO (2009). Safety management manual (SMM). Technical report 9859 AN/474, International Civil Aviation Organization, Montreal, Canada.

IChemE (1992). Nomenclature for hazard and risk assessment in the process industries. Technical report, Institution of Chemical Engineers, Rugby, UK.

IEC 60050-191 (1990). *International Electrotechnical Vocabulary, chapter 191, Dependability and Quality of Service*. International Electrotechnical Commission, Geneva.

IEC 60300-3-4 (2007). *Dependability Management. Part 3-4: Application Guide— Guide to the Specification of Dependability Requirements*. International Electrotechnical Commission, Geneva.

IEC 60300-3-9 (1995). *Dependability Management—Application Guide: Risk Analysis of Technological Systems*. International Electrotechnical Commission, Geneva.

IEC 60812 (2006). *Procedure for Failure Mode and Effects Analysis*. International Electrotechnical Commission, Geneva.

IEC 61508 (2010). *Functional Safety of Electrical/Electronic/Programmable Electronic Safety-Related Systems, Parts 1-7*. International Electrotechnical Commission, Geneva.

IEC 61511 (2003). *Functional Safety: Safety Instrumented Systems for the Process Industry Sector, Part 1-3*. International Electrotechnical Commission, Geneva.

IEC 62278 (2002). *Railway applications: Specification and Demonstration of Reliability, Availability, Maintainability, and Safety (RAMS)*. International Electrotechnical Commission, Geneva.

IEC 62551 (2012). *Analysis Techniques for Dependability: Petri Net Techniques*. International Electrotechnical Commission, Geneva.

IEC 61025 (2006). *Fault Tree Analysis (FTA)*. International Electrotechnical Commission, Geneva, 2nd edition.

IEC 61165 (2006). *Application of Markov Techniques*. International Electrotechnical Commission, Geneva, 2nd edition.

IEEE Std. 500 (1984). *IEEE Guide for the Collection and Presentation of Electrical, Electronic, Sensing Component, and Mechanical Equipment Reliability Data for Nuclear Power Generating Stations.* IEEE and Wiley, New York.

IFE (2009). Assessing organizational factors and measures in accident investigation (in Norwegian). Technical report IFE/HR/F-2009/1406, Institutt for Energiforskning (IFE), Kjeller, Norway.

IMO (2002). Guide for formal safety assessment (FSA) for use in the IMO rule-making process. Technical report MSC/1023, International Maritime Organization, London.

Ishikawa, K. (1986). *Guide to Quality Control.* Productivity Press, Cambridge, MA.

ISO 12100 (2010). *Safety of Machinery— General Principles for Design: Risk Assessment and Risk Reduction.* International Organization for Standardization, Geneva.

ISO 14224 (2006). *Petroleum, Petrochemical, and Natural Gas Industries: Collection and Exchange of Reliability and Maintenance Data for Equipment.* International Organization for Standardization, Geneva.

ISO 17776 (2002). *Petroleum and Natural Gas Industries—Offshore Production Installations: Guidelines on Tools and Techniques for Hazard Identification and Risk Assessment.* International Organization for Standardization, Geneva.

ISO 31000 (2009). *Risk Management: Principles and Guidelines.* International Organization for Standardization, Geneva.

ISO 9000 (2005). *Quality Management Systems: Fundamentals and Vocabulary.* International Organization for Standardization, Geneva.

ISO/IEC 15909-1 (2004). *Systems and Software Engineering—High-Level Petri Nets. Part 1: Concepts, Definitions, and Graphical Notation.* International Organization for Standardization, Geneva.

Jaynes, E. T. (2003). *Probability Theory: The Logic of Science.* Cambridge University Press, Cambridge.

Jensen, K. and Kristensen, L. M. (2009). *Coloured Petri Nets: Modelling and Validation of Concurrent Systems.* Springer, Berlin.

Jin, H., Lundteigen, M. A., and Rausand, M. (2011). Reliability performance of safety instrumented systems: A common approach for both low- and high-demand mode of operation. *Reliability Engineering and System Safety*, 96:365–373.

Johansen, I. L. (2010a). Foundations and fallacies of risk acceptance criteria. ROSS report 201001, Norwegian University of Science and Technology, Trondheim, Norway.

Johansen, I. L. (2010b). Foundations of risk assessment. ROSS report 201002, Norwegian University of Science and Technology, Trondheim, Norway.

Johnson, W. G. (1980). *MORT Safety Assurance System*. Marcel Dekker, New York.

Johnston, B. D. (1987). A structured procedure for dependent failure analysis (dfa). *Reliability Engineering*, 19:125–136.

Jonkman, S. N., van Gelder, P. H. A. J. M., and Vrijling, J. K. (2003). An overview of quantitative risk measures for loss of life and economic damage. *Journal of Hazardous Materials*, A99:1–30.

Kaplan, S. (1997). The words of risk analysis. *Risk Analysis*, 17:407–417.

Kaplan, S. and Garrick, B. J. (1981). On the quantitative definition of risk. *Risk Analysis*, 1:11–27.

Kartson, D., Balbo, G., Donatelli, S., Franceschinis, G., and Conte, G. (1994). *Modeling with Generalized Stochastic Petri Nets*. Wiley, New York.

Kasperson, R. E., Renn, O., Slovic, P., Brown, H. S., Emel, J., Goble, R., Kasperson, J. X., and Ratick, S. (1988). The social amplification of risk: A conceptual framework. *Risk Analysis*, 8:177–187.

Khan, F. and Abbasi, S. (2002). A criterion for developing credible accident scenarios for risk assessment. *Journal of Loss Prevention in the Process Industries*, 15(6):467–475.

Khan, F. I. and Abbasi, S. A. (1999). Major accidents in process industries and an analysis of causes and consequences. *Journal of Loss Prevention in the Process Industries*, 12:361–378.

Kim, D., Kim, J., and Moon, I. (2006). Integration of accident scenario generation and multiobjective optimization for safety-cost decision making in chemical processes. *Journal of Loss Prevention in the Process Industries*, 19(6):705–713.

Kim, J. W. and Jung, W. (2003). A taxonomy of performance influencing factors for human reliability analysis of emergency tasks. *Journal of Loss Prevention in the Process Industries*, 16(6):479 – 495.

Kirwan, B. (1994). *A Guide to Practical Human Reliability Assessment*. Taylor & Francis, London.

Kirwan, B. and Ainsworth, L. K. (1992). *A Guide to Task Analysis*. Taylor & Francis, London.

Kjærulff, U. B. and Madsen, A. L. (2008). *Bayesian Networks and Influence Diagrams: A Guide to Construction and Analysis*. Springer, Berlin.

Kjellén, U. (2000). *Prevention of Accidents Through Experience Feedback*. Taylor & Francis, London.

Kletz, T. (1998). *What Went Wrong? Case Histories of Process Plant Disasters.* Gulf Publishing Company, Houston, TX.

Kletz, T. (1999). *Hazop and Hazan.* Taylor & Francis, London, 4th edition.

Klinke, A. and Renn, O. (2002). A new approach to risk evaluation and management: Risk-based, precaution-based, and discourse-based strategies. *Risk Analysis,* 22(6):1071–1094.

Kontogiannis, T., Leopoulos, V., and Marmaras, N. (2000). A comparison of accident anaysis techniques for safety-critical man-machine systems. *Industrial Ergonomics,* 25:327–347.

Kvaløy, J. T. and Aven, T. (2005). An alternative approach to trend analysis in accident data. *Reliability Engineering and System Safety,* 90:75–82.

La Porte, T. R. and Consolini, P. M. (1991). Working in practice but not in theory: Theoretical challenges of "high-reliability organizations". *Journal of Public Administration Research and Theory,* 1:19–47.

Laheij, G. M. H., Post, J. G., and Ale, B. J. M. (2000). Standard methods for land-use planning to determine the effects on societal risk. *Journal of Hazardous Materials,* 71:269–282.

Leveson, N. (1995). *Safeware. System Safety and Computers: A Guide to Preventing Accidents and Losses Caused by Technology.* Addison-Wesley, Reading, MA.

Leveson, N. (2004). A new accident model for engineering safer systems. *Safety Science,* 42(4):237–270.

Lindley, D. V. (2007). *Understanding Uncertainty.* Wiley, Hoboken, NJ.

Linkov, I. and Burmistrov, D. (2003). Model uncertainty and choices made by modelers: Lessons learned from the International Atomic Energy Agency model intercomparisons. *Risk Analysis,* 23:1297–1308.

Littlewood, B. (1996). The impact of diversity upon common mode failures. *Reliability Engineering and System Safety,* 51:101–113.

Liu, T. S. and Chiou, S. B. (1997). The application of Petri nets to failure analysis. *Reliability Engineering and System Safety,* 57:129–142.

Liu, Y. and Rausand, M. (2011). Reliability assessment of safety instrumented systems subject to different demand modes. *Journal of Loss Prevention in the Process Industries,* 24:49 – 56.

Lundberg, J., Rollenhagen, C., and Hollnagel, E. (2009). What-you-look-for-is-what-you-find: The consequences of underlying accident models in eight accident investigation manuals. *Safety Science,* 47(10):1297–1311.

Lundteigen, M. A. (2009). *Safety Instrumented Systems in the Oil and Gas Industry: Concepts and Methods for Safety and Reliability Assessments in Design and Operation.* PhD thesis, Norwegian University of Science and Technology, Trondheim, Norway.

Lundteigen, M. A. and Rausand, M. (2007). Common cause failures in safety instrumented systems on oil and gas installations: Implementing defense measures through function testing. *Journal of Loss Prevention in the Process Industries*, 20(3):218–229.

Lundteigen, M. A. and Rausand, M. (2009). Reliability assessment of safety instrumented systems in the oil and gas industry: A practical approach and a case study. *International Journal of Reliability, Quality and Safety Engineering*, 16:187–212.

Lupton, D. (1999). *Risk*. Routledge, London.

Macdonald, D. (2004). *Practical Machinery Safety*. Newnes/Elsevier, Oxford.

Machilis, G. E. and Rosa, E. A. (1990). Desired risk: Broadening the social amplification of risk framwork. *Risk Analysis*, 10:161–168.

Macza, M. (2008). A Canadian perspective of the history of process safety management legislation. In *8th International Symposium on Programmable Electronic Systems in Safety-Related Applications*, Cologne, Germany.

Martinez, J. and Silva, M. (1982). A simple and fast algorithm to obtain all invariants of a generalized petri net. In Girauld, C. and Reisig, W., editors, *Informatik-Fachberichte 52: Application and Theory of Petri Nets: Selected Papers from the First and Second European Workshop on Application and Theory of Petri Nets, Strasbourg, Sept. 23–26, 1980, Bad Honnef, Sept. 28–30, 1981*, pages 301–310, London. Springer.

Miguel, A. R. (2006). *Human Error Analysis for Collaborative Work*. PhD thesis, Department of Computer Science, University of York, York, UK.

MIL-HDBK-217F (1991). *Reliability Prediction of Electronic Equipment*. U.S. Department of Defense, Washington, DC.

MIL-STD-1629A (1980). *Procedures for Performing a Failure Mode, Effects, and Criticality Analysis*. U.S. Department of Defense, Washington, DC.

MIL-STD-2155 (1985). *Failure Reporting, Analysis and Corrective Action System*. U.S. Department of Defense, Washington, DC.

MIL-STD-882D (2000). *Standard Practice for System Safety*. U.S. Department of Defense, Washington, DC.

Miller, A. G., Kaufer, B., and Carlson, L. (2000). Activities on component reliability under the OECD Nuclear Energy Agency. *Nuclear Engineering and Design*, 198:325–334.

Miller, D. P. and Swain, A. D. (1987). Human error and human reliability. In Salvendy, G., editor, *Handbook of Human Factors*. Wiley, New York.

Modarres, M. (2006). *Risk Analysis in Engineering: Techniques, Tools, and Trends*. Taylor & Francis, Boca Raton, FL.

Mohaghegh, Z., Kazemi, R., and Mosleh, A. (2009). Incorporating organizational factors into probabilistic risk assessment (pra) of complex socio-technical systems: A hybrid technique formalization. *Reliability Engineering and System Safety*, 94:1000–1018.

Mosleh, A. (1991). Common cause failures: An analysis methodology and example. *Reliability Engineering and System Safety*, 34:249–292.

Mosleh, A. and Siu, N. O. (1987). A multi-parameter common cause failure model. In *9th International Conference on Structural Mechanics in Reactor Technology*, pages 147–152, Lausanne, Switzerland.

Moss, T. R. (2005). *The Reliability Data Handbook*. ASME Press, New York.

NASA (2007). NASA systems engineering handbook. Technical Report NASA/SP-2007-6105, U.S. National Aeronautics and Space Administration, Washington, DC.

NASA (2008). Agency risk management procedural requirements. NASA Procedural Requirements NPR:8000.4A, U.S. National Aeronautics and Space Administration, Washington, DC.

NASA (2010). Technical probabilistic risk assessment (PRA) procedures for safety and mission success for NASA programs and projects. NASA Procedural Requirements NPR 8705.5A, U.S. National Aeronautics and Space Administration, Washington, DC.

NEA (1998). Critical operator actions: Human reliability modeling and data issues. Technical report NEA/CSNI/R(98)1, Nuclear Energy Agency, Paris.

NEA (2004a). Human reliability analysis in probabilistic safety assessment for nuclear power plants. CSNI technical opinion papers 4, Nuclear Energy Agency, Paris.

NEA (2004b). International common-cause failure data exchange. ICDE general coding guidelines. Technical report R(2004)4, Nuclear Energy Agency, Paris.

Nielsen, D. S. (1971). The cause/consequence diagram method as a basis for quantitative accident analysis. Technical report RISO-M-1374, Danish Atomic Energy Commission, Risö, Roskilde, Denmark.

Niwa, Y. (2009). A proposal for a new accident analysis method and its application to a catastrophic railway accident in Japan. *Cognition, Technology & Work*, 11:187–204.

Nordland, O. (2001). When is risk acceptable? In *Presentations at 19th International System Safety Conference*, page , Huntsville, AL.

NORSOK Z-013 (2010). Risk and emergency preparedness analysis. Norsok standard, Standard Norge, Oslo, Norway.

NRI (2009). NRI MORT user's manual. Technical report NRI-1, The Noordwijk Risk Initiative Foundation, http://www.nri.eu.com/NRI1.pdf.

NS 5814 (2008). *Requirements for Risk Assessment*. Standard Norge, Oslo, Norway, Norwegian edition.

NSW (2003). Hazard identification, risk assessment, and risk control no. 3. Technical report, New South Wales, Department of Urban and Transport Planning, Sydney, Australia.

NSW (2008a). HAZOP guidelines: Hazardous industry planning advisory paper no. 8. Technical report, New South Wales, Department of Planning, Sydney, Australia.

NSW (2008b). Risk criteria for land use safety planning: Hazardous industry planning advisory paper no. 4. Technical report, New South Wales, Department of Planning, Sydney, Australia.

NTC (2004). Risk tolerability in rail safety regulation. Issues paper, National Transport Commission, Melbourne, Australia.

NUREG-0492 (1981). *Fault Tree Handbook*. U.S. Nuclear Regulatory Commission, Office of Nuclear Regulatory Research, Washington, DC.

NUREG-1624 (2000). *Technical Basis and Implementation Guidelines for a Technique for Human Error Analysis (ATHEANA)*. U.S. Nuclear Regulatory Commission, Washington, DC, revised edition.

NUREG-1855 (2009). *Guidance on the Treatment of Uncertainties Associated with PRAs in Risk-Informed Decision Making*. U.S. Nuclear Regulatory Commission, Office of Nuclear Regulatory Research, Washington, DC.

NUREG-1880 (2007). *ATHEANA User's Guide*. U.S. Nuclear Regulatory Commission, Office of Nuclear Regulatory Research, Washington, DC.

NUREG-75/014 (1975). *Reactor Safety: An Assessment of Accident Risk in U.S. Commercial Nuclear Power Plants*. U.S. Nuclear Regulatory Commission, Washington, DC.

NUREG/CR-3518 (1984). *SLIM-MAUD: An Approach to Assessing Human Error Probabilities Using Structured Expert Judgment*. U.S. Nuclear Regulatory Commission, Washington, DC.

NUREG/CR-4780 (1989). *Procedures for Treating Common-Cause Failures in Safety and Reliability Studies, volume 2, Analytical Background and Techniques*. U.S. Nuclear Regulatory Commission, Washington, DC.

NUREG/CR-5485 (1998). *Guidelines on Modeling Common-Cause Failures in Probabilistic Risk Assessment.* U.S. Nuclear Regulatory Commission, Washington, DC.

NUREG/CR-6268 (2007). *Common-Cause Failure Database and Analysis System: Event Data Collection, Classification, and Coding.* U.S. Nuclear Regulatory Commission, Office of Nuclear Regulatory Research, Washington, DC.

NUREG/CR-6823 (2003). *Handbook of Parameter Estimation for Probabilistic Risk Assessment.* U.S. Nuclear Regulatory Commission, Office of Nuclear Regulatory Research, Washington, DC.

NUREG/CR-6883 (2005). *The SPAR-H Human Reliability Analysis Method.* U.S. Nuclear Regulatory Commission, Washington, DC.

OLF-090 (2006). *Common Model for Safe Job Analysis (SJA).* The Norwegian Oil Industry Association, Stavanger, Norway, 2nd edition.

OREDA (2009). *OREDA Reliability Data.* OREDA Participants, Available from: Det Norske Veritas, NO 1322 Høvik, Norway, 4th edition.

OSHA (2002). Job hazard analysis. Technical report OSHA 3071, Occupational Safety and Health Administration, Washington, DC.

Ouyang, M., Hong, L., Yu, M.-H., and Fei, Q. (2010). Stamp-based analysis on the railway accident and accident spreading: Taking the china-jiaoji railway accident for example. *Safety Science*, 48:544–555.

Pandey, M. D. and Nathwani, J. S. (2004). Life quality index for the estimation of societal willingness-to-pay for safety. *Structural Safety*, 26:181–199.

Papanikolaou, A., editor (2009). *Risk-Based Ship Design: Methods, Tools and Applications.* Springer, Berlin.

Papazoglou, I. A. and Aneziris, O. N. (2003). Master logig diagram: Method for hazard and initiating event identification in process plants. *Journal of Hazardous Materials*, A97:11–30.

Parry, G. W. (1991). Common cause failure analysis: A critique and some suggestions. *Reliability Engineering and System Safety*, 34:309–320.

Pasman, H. J., Jung, S., Prem, K., Rogers, W. J., and Yang, X. (2009). Is risk analysis a useful tool for improving safety? *Journal of Loss Prevention in the Process Industries*, 22:769–777.

Paté-Cornell, M. E. (1996). Uncertainties in risk analysis: Six levels of treatment. *Reliability Engineering and System Safety*, 54:95–111.

Paula, H. M., Campbell, D. J., and Rasmuson, D. M. (1991). Qualitative cause-defense matrices: Engineering tools to support the analysis and prevention of common cause failures. *Reliability Engineering and System Safety*, 34:389–415.

Perrow, C. (1984). *Normal Accidents: Living with High-Risk Technologies*. Basic Books, New York.

Pesme, H. and Le Bot, P. (2010). Lessons learned on HRA benchmarking: the EDF point of view with MERMOS. In *PSAM 10.* , Seattle, WA.

Peters, G. A. and Peters, B. J. (2006). *Human Error: Causes and Control*. Taylor & Francis, Boca Raton, FL.

Petri, C. A. (1962). *Kommunikation mit Automaten*. PhD thesis, University of Bonn, Bonn, Germany.

President's Commission on Critical Infrastructure Protection (1997). Critical foundations: Protecting America's infrastructures. http://www.fas.org/sgp/library/pccip.pdf.

Pukite, J. and Pukite, P. (1998). *Modeling for Reliability Analysis: Markov Modeling for Reliability, Maintainability, Safety and Supportability Analyses of Complex Computer Systems*. IEEE Press, Piscataway, NJ.

Qureshi, Z. H. (2008). A review of accident modelling approaches for complex critical sociotechnical systems. Technical report DSTO-TR-2094, Defence Science and Technology Organization, Edinburgh, Australia.

Rasmuson, D. M. (1991). Some practical considerations in treating dependencies in pras. *Reliability Engineering and System Safety*, 34:327–343.

Rasmussen, J. (1983). Skills, rules, knowledge: Signals, signs and symbols and other distinctions in human performance models. *IEEE Transactions on Systems, Man and Cybernetics*, 13:257–267.

Rasmussen, J. (1997). Risk management in a dynamic society: A modelling problem. *Safety Science*, 27:183–213.

Rasmussen, J. and Svedung, I. (2000). *Proactive Risk Management in a Dynamic Society*. Swedish Rescue Services Agency (Currently: The Swedish Civil Contingencies Agency), Karlstad, Sweden.

Rausand, M. (1991). *Risikoanalyse; Veiledning til NS 5814*. Tapir Akademisk Forlag, Trondheim, Norway.

Rausand, M. and Høyland, A. (2004). *System Reliability Theory: Models, Statistical Methods, and Applications*. Wiley, Hoboken, NJ, 2nd edition.

Rausand, M. and Øien, K. (1996). Basic concepts of failure analysis. *Reliability Engineering and System Safety*, 53 (1):73–83.

Rausand, M. and Utne, I. B. (2009a). Product safety—principles and practices in a life cycle perspective. *Safety Science*, 47:939–947.

Rausand, M. and Utne, I. B. (2009b). *Risikoanalyse: Teori og metoder.* Tapir Akademisk Forlag, Trondheim, Norway.

Reason, J. (1990). *Human Error.* Cambridge University Press, Cambridge, UK.

Reason, J. (1997). *Managing the Risks of Organizational Accidents.* Ashgate, Aldershot, UK.

Reason, J. (2008). *The Human Contribution: Unsafe Acts, Accidents and Heroic Recoveries.* Ashgate, Farnham, UK.

Rosa, E. A. (1998). Metatheoretical foundations for post-normal risk. *Journal of Risk Research*, 1(1):15–44.

Rosness, R. (1994). Human dependability methods for control and safety systems. STF75 A93060, SINTEF, Trondheim, Norway.

Rosness, R., Guttormsen, G., Steiro, T., Tinmannsvik, R. K., and Herrera, I. A. (2004). Organizational accidents and resilient organizations: Five perspectives. STF38 A04403, SINTEF, Trondheim, Norway.

Ross, S. M. (1996). *Stochastic Processes.* Wiley, New York.

Ross, S. M. (2004). *Introduction to Probability and Statistics for Engineers and Scientists.* Elsevier, Amsterdam.

Ross, S. M. (2007). *Introduction to Probability Models.* Elsevier, Amsterdam.

Royal Society (1992). Risk: analysis, perception and management. Report of a Royal Society study group. Royal Society, London.

RSC (2007). Note on: Hazard and operability studies (HAZOP). Technical report, Royal Society of Chemistry, Environmental Health and Safety Committee, London.

RSSB (2007). *Engineering Safety Management (The Yellow Book)*, volume 1 and 2. Rail Safety and Standards Board, London.

SAE ARP 5580 (2001). *Recommended Failure Modes and Effects Analysis (FMEA) Practices for Non-automobile Applications.* The Engineering Society for Advancing Mobility in Land, Sea, Air, and Space, Warrendale, PA.

Salmon, P., Regan, M., and Johnston, I. (2005). Human error and road transportation: Phase one—literature review. Technical report 256, Accident Research Centre, Monash University, Victoria, Australia.

Salmon, P., Stanton, N. A., and Walker, G. (2003). Human factors design methods review. Technical Report HFIDT/WP1.3.2/1, Brunel University, Uxbridge, UK.

Salvi, O. and Debray, B. (2006). A global view on ARAMIS, a risk assessment methodology for industries in the framework of the SEVESO II directive. *Journal of Hazardous Materials*, 130:187–199.

Sammarco, J. J. (2003). *A Normal Accident Theory-Based Complexity Assessment Methodology for Safety-Related Embedded Computer Systems*. PhD thesis, College of Engineering and Mineral Resources, West Virginia University, Morgantown, WV.

Sammarco, J. J. (2005). Operationalizing normal accident theory for safety-related computer systems. *Safety Science*, 43:697–714.

San 821-2 (1973). MORT – The management oversight and risk tree. Technical Report AT(04-3)-821, U.S. Atomic Energy Commission, Division of Operational Safety, Washington, DC.

Sanders, W. H. and Meyer, J. F. (2001). Stochastic activity networks: Formal definitions and concepts. In *Lecture Notes in Computer Science*, volume 2090, pages 315–343. Springer.

Schäbe, H. (2001). Different approaches for determination of tolerable hazard rates. In Zio, E., Demichela, M., and Piccinini, N., editors, *Towards a Safer World (ESREL'01)*. Politechico di Torino, Turin, Italy.

Schoenig, R. (2004). *Definition d'une methodologie de conception des systèmes mechatroniques surs de fonctionnement*. PhD thesis, Institut National Polytechnique de Lorraine, Nancy, France.

Schönbeck, M., Rausand, M., and Rouvroye, J. (2010). Human and organisational factors in the operational phase of safety instrumented systems: A new approach. *Safety Science*, 48:310–318.

SEMATECH (1992). *Failure Mode and Effect Analysis (FMEA): A Guide for Continuous Improvement for the Semiconductor Equipment Industry*. SEMATECH, Austin, TX.

SEMATECH (1999). Hazard analysis guide: A reference manual for analyzing safety hazards on semiconductor manufacturing equipment. Technical report 99113846A-ENG, International SEMATECH, Austin, TX.

Seong, P. H. (2009). *Reliability and Risk Issues in Large Scale Safety-Critical Digital Control Systems*. Springer, London.

Shorrock, S., Kirwan, B., and Smith, E. (2003). Individual and group approaches to human error prediction: A tale of three systems. In *IBC Conference on Preventing Human Errors and Violations*, London.

Shrader-Frechette, K. (1991). *Risk and Rationality: Philosophical Foundations for Populist Reforms*. University of California Press, Berkeley, CA.

Siu, N. (1994). Risk assessment for dynamic systems: An overview. *Reliability Engineering and System Safety*, 43:43–73.

Skjong, R., Vanem, E., and Endresen, Ø. (2007). Risk evaluation criteria. Technical report, SAFEDOR-D-4.5.2 DNV.

Sklet, S. (2002). Methods for accident investigation. ROSS report 200208, Norwegian University of Science and Technology, Trondheim, Norway.

Sklet, S. (2004). Comparison of some selected methods for accident investigation. *Journal of Hazardous Materials*, 111:29–37.

Sklet, S. (2005). *Safety Barriers on Oil and Gas Platforms; Means to Prevent Hydrocarbon Releases*. PhD thesis, Norwegian University of Science and Technology (NTNU), Trondheim, Norway.

Sklet, S. (2006a). Hydrocarbon releases on oil and gas production platforms: Release scenarios and safety barriers. *Journal of Loss Prevention in the Process Industries*, 19:481–493.

Sklet, S. (2006b). Safety barriers: Definition, classification, and performance. *Journal of Loss Prevention in the Process Industries*, 19:494–506.

Sklet, S., Vinnem, J. E., and Aven, T. (2006). Barrier and operational risk analysis of hydrocarbon releases (BORA-Release). Part II: Results from a case study. *Journal of Hazardous Materials*, 137:692–708.

Slovic, P. (1987). Perception of risk. *Science*, 236:280–285.

Slovic, P. (1992). Perception of risk: Reflections on the psychometric paradigm. In Golding, D. and Krimsky, S., editors, *Theories of Risk*, pages 117–152. Praeger, London.

Smith, A. M. and Watson, I. A. (1980). Common cause failures: A dilemma in perspective. *Reliability Engineering*, 1(2):127–142.

Smith, D. J. and Simpson, K. G. L. (2005). *Functional Safety: A Straightforward Guide to Applying the IEC 61508 and Related Standards*. Elsevier, Burlington, UK.

Spouge, J. (1999). A guide to quantitative risk assessment for offshore installations. Technical report, DNV Technica, London.

Spurgin, A. J. (2009). *Human Reliability Assessment: Theory and Practice*. CRC Press, Boca Raton, FL.

Stack, R. J. (2009). Evaluating non-independent protection layers. *Process Safety Progress*, 28(4):317–324.

Stamatelatos, M., Apostolakis, G., Dezfuli, H., Everline, C., Guarro, S., Moieni, P., Mosleh, A., Paulos, T., and Youngblood, R. (2002a). Probabilistic risk assessment procedures guide for NASA managers and practitioners. Technical report, U.S. National Aeronautics and Space Administration, Washington, DC.

Stamatelatos, M., Vesely, W., Dugan, J., Fragola, J., Minarick, J., and Railsback, J. (2002b). Fault tree handbook with aerospace applications. Technical report, U.S. National Aeronautics and Space Administration, Washington, DC.

Stanton, N. A., Salmon, P. M., Walker, G. H., Baber, C., and Jenkins, D. P. (2005). *Human Factors Methods: A Practical Guide for Engineering and Design.* Ashgate, Aldershot, UK.

Step Change (2007). Task risk assessment. Guide, Step Change in Safety, Aberdeen, Scotland.

Stewart, M. G. and Melchers, R. E. (1997). *Probabilistic Risk Assessment of Engineering Systems.* Chapman & Hall, London.

Størseth, F., Rosness, R., and Guttormsen, G. (2010). Exploring safety critical decision-making. In Briš, R., Soares, C. G., and Martorell, S., editors, *Reliability, Risk, and Safety: Theory and Applications,* pages 1311–1317. Taylor & Francis, London.

Strategy Unit (2002). Risk: Improving government's capability to handle risk and uncertainty. Technical report, U.K. Cabinet Office, Strategy Unit, London.

STUK (2003). Probabilistic safety analysis in safety management of nuclear power plants. Guide YVL2.8, Radiation and Nuclear Safety Authority, Helsinki, Finland.

Suchman, E. A. (1961). A conceptual analysis of the accident problem. *Social Problems,* 8(3):241–246.

Summers, A. E. (2003). Introduction to layers of protection analysis. *Journal of Hazardous Materials,* 104:163–168.

Summers, A. E. and Raney, G. (1999). Common cause and common sense, designing failure out of your safety instrumented system (SIS). *ISA Transactions,* 38:291–299.

Svádová, M. and Hanzálek, Z. (2001). Matlab toolbox for petri nets. In *22nd International Conference ICATPN 2001,* pages 32–36.

Svedung, I. and Rasmussen, J. (2002). Graphic representation of accident scenarios: mapping system structure and the causation of accidents. *Safety Science,* 40:397–417.

Swain, A. D. and Guttmann, H. (1983). Handbook of human reliability analysis with emphasis on nuclear power plant applications. Technical report NUREG/CR-1278, Nuclear Regulatory Commission, Washington, DC.

Timmerman, P. (1986). The risk puzzle: some thoughts. *Ethics and Energy,* 6:1–2.

Treasury Board (2001). Integrated risk management framework. Technical report, Treasury Board of Canada, Ottawa, Canada.

Tripod Solutions (2007). Tripod beta. User guide, Tripod Solutions, Den Helder, The Netherlands, http://www.advisafe.com.

UK CAA (2006). Guidance on the conduct of hazard identification, risk assessment and the production of safety cases—for aerodrome operators and air traffic service providers. Technical report CAP 760, Civil Aviation Authority, Gatwick Airport, UK.

UK CAA (2008). Safety management systems: Guidance to organisations. Technical report, Civil Aviation Authority, Safety Regulation Group, Gatwick Airport, UK.

UN (1992). Report of the United Nations conference on environment and devleopment, Rio Declaration on environment and development. Technical report, United Nations, New York.

US DOD (2006). Risk management guide for DoD acquisition. Technical report, U.S. Department of Defense, Washington, DC.

US DOE (1992). Root cause analysis guidance document. Technical Report DOE-NE-STD-1004-92, U.S. Department of Energy, Office of Nuclear Energy, Washington, DC.

US DOE (1996a). Hazard and barrier analysis guidance document. Technical Report EH-33, U.S. Department of Energy, Office of Operating Experience Analysis and Feedback, Washington, DC.

US DOE (1996b). Process safety management for highly hazardous chemicals. DOE-HDBK-1101-86, U. S. Department of Energy, Washington, DC.

US DOE (1998). Guidelines for risk-based prioritization of DOE activities. Technical report DOE-DP-STD-3023-98, U.S. Department of Energy, Washington, DC.

US DOE (1999). Conducting accident investigations. Technical report, U.S. Department of Energy, Washington, DC.

US DOE (2004). Chemical process hazard analysis. Technical Report DOE-HDBK-1100-2004, U.S. Department of Energy, Washington, DC.

US FAA (2000). System safety handbook. Technical report, Federal Aviation Administration, Washington, DC.

US FAA (2009). Risk management handbook. Technical Report FAA-H-8083-2, Federal Aviation Administration, Washington, DC.

US National Research Council (2009). *Science and Decisions: Advancing Risk Assessment*. National Research Council, National Academies Press, Washington, DC.

US NRC (2007). Probabilistic risk assessment. Fact sheet, U.S. Nuclear regulatory Commission, Washington, DC.

USCG (2008). Risk based decision making. RBDM guidelines, U.S. Coast Guard, http://www.uscg.mil/hq/cg5/cg5211/E-Guidelines.asp.

Vesely, W. E. (1977). Estimating common cause failure probabilities in reliability and risk analyses: Marshall-Olkin specializations. In Fussell, J. B. and Burdick, G. R., editors, *Nuclear Systems Reliability Engineering and Risk Assessment*, pages 314–341. SIAM, Philadelphia.

Vincoli, J. W. (2006). *Basic Guide to System Safety*. Wiley, Hoboken, NJ, 2nd edition.

Vinnem, J. E. (2007). *Offshore Risk Assessment: Principles, Modeling and Application of QRA Studies*. Springer, London, 2nd edition.

VROM (2005). Guidelines for quantitative risk assessment (the purple book). Technical Report PGS 3, The Netherlands Ministry of Housing, Spatial Planning and the Environment.

Wagenaar, W. A., Hudson, P. T. W., and Reason, J. T. (1990). Cognitive failures and accidents. *Applied Cognitive Psychology*, 4:273–294.

Wahlström, B. (2003). Risk informed approaches for plant life management: Regulatory and industry perspectives. In *Presentation at FISA 2003, EU Research in Reactor Safety*, page , Luxembourgh.

Weick, K. E. and Sutcliffe, K. M. (2007). *Managing the Unexpected: Resilient Performance in an Age of Uncertainty*. Jossey-Bass, Sa Francisco, CA, 2nd edition.

Whalley, S. (1992). Minimising the cause of human error. In Kirwan, B. and Ainsworth, L. K., editors, *A Guide to Task Analysis*. Taylor & Francis, London.

Wilde, G. J. S. (1982). The theory of risk homeostasis: Implications for safety and health. *Risk Analysis*, 2:209–225.

Williams, J. C. (1986). HEART – a proposed method for assessing and reducing human errors. In *Ninth Advances in Reliability Technology Symposium*, Birmingham, UK.

Winkler, R. L. (1996). Uncertainty in probabilistic risk assessment. *Reliability Engineering and System Safety*, 54:127–132.

Yang, S. K. and Liu, T. S. (1997). Failure analysis for an airbag inflator by Petri nets. *Quality and Reliability Engineering International*, 13(3):139–151.

Ye, X., Zhou, J., and Song, X. (2003). On reachability graphs of (p)etri nets. *Computers and Electrical Engineering*, 29:263–272.

Yosie, T. F. and Herbst, T. D. (1998). Using stakeholder processes in environmental decisionmaking. Technical report, The Global Development Research Center. Available at http://www.gdrc.org/decision/nr98ab01.pdf.

Zitrou, A. and Bedford, T. (2003). Foundation of the UPM common cause model. In *Proceedings ESREL 2003*, pages 1769–1775, Lisse, The Netherlands. Balkema.

Zitrou, A., Bedford, T., and Walls, L. (2004). Developing soft factors inputs to common cause failure models. In Spitzer, C., Schmocker, U., and Dang, V. N., editors, *Probabilistic Safety Assessment and Management (PSAM 7 – ESREL'04)*, pages 825–830. Springer, Berlin.

Zitrou, A., Bedford, T., and Walls, L. (2007). An influence diagram extension of the unified partial method for common cause failures. *Quality Technology & Quantitative Management*, 4(1):111–128.

Zitrou, A., Bedford, T., and Walls, L. (2010). Bayes geometric scaling model for common cause failure rates. *Reliability Engineering and System Safety*, 95:70–76.

Øien, K. (2001). *Risk Control of Offshore Installations. A Framework for the Establishment of Risk Indicators*. PhD thesis, Department of Production and Quality Engineering, Norwegian University of Science and Technology, Trondheim, Norway.

# Index

*Risk Assessment: Theory, Methods, and Applications,* First Edition.
By Marvin Rausand. Copyright © 2011 John Wiley & Sons, Inc.

**635**

# STATISTICS IN PRACTICE

*Human and Biological Sciences*

Brown and Prescott · Applied Mixed Models in Medicine
Ellenberg, Fleming and DeMets · Data Monitoring Committees in Clinical Trials:
  A Practical Perspective
Lawson, Browne and Vidal Rodeiro · Disease Mapping With WinBUGS and MLwiN
Lui · Statistical Estimation of Epidemiological Risk
*Marubini and Valsecchi · Analysing Survival Data from Clinical Trials and
  Observation Studies
Parmigiani · Modeling in Medical Decision Making: A Bayesian Approach
Senn · Cross-over Trials in Clinical Research, *Second Edition*
Senn · Statistical Issues in Drug Development
Spiegelhalter, Abrams and Myles · Bayesian Approaches to Clinical Trials and Health-
  Care Evaluation
Turner · New Drug Development: Design, Methodology, and Analysis
Whitehead · Design and Analysis of Sequential Clinical Trials, *Revised Second Edition*
Whitehead · Meta-Analysis of Controlled Clinical Trials

*Earth and Environmental Sciences*

Buck, Cavanagh and Litton · Bayesian Approach to Interpreting Archaeological Data
Cooke · Uncertainty Modeling in Dose Response: Bench Testing Environmental Toxicity
Gibbons, Bhaumik, and Aryal · Statistical Methods for Groundwater Monitoring,
  *Second Edition*
Glasbey and Horgan · Image Analysis in the Biological Sciences
Helsel · Nondetects and Data Analysis: Statistics for Censored Environmental Data
Helsel · Statistics for Censored Environmental Data Using Minitab® and R,
  *Second Edition*
McBride · Using Statistical Methods for Water Quality Management: Issues, Problems
  and Solutions
Webster and Oliver · Geostatistics for Environmental Scientists

*Industry, Commerce and Finance*

Aitken and Taroni · Statistics and the Evaluation of Evidence for Forensic Scientists,
  *Second Edition*
Brandimarte · Numerical Methods in Finance and Economics: A MATLAB-Based
  Introduction, *Second Edition*
Brandimarte and Zotteri · Introduction to Distribution Logistics
Chan and Wong · Simulation Techniques in Financial Risk Management
Jank · Statistical Methods in eCommerce Research
Jank and Shmueli · Modeling Online Auctions
Lehtonen and Pahkinen · Practical Methods for Design and Analysis of Complex
  Surveys, *Second Edition*
Lloyd · Data Driven Business Decisions
Ohser and Mücklich · Statistical Analysis of Microstructures in Materials Science
Rausand · Risk Assessment: Theory, Methods, and Applications

*Now available in paperback.

Printed in the United States
By Bookmasters